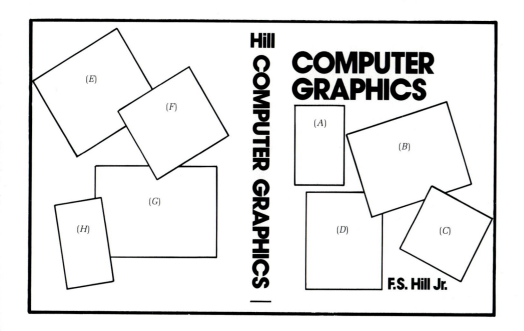

FRONT COVER (Clockwise from upper left):
(A) Wireframe urn, created in the graphics class at the University of Massachusetts.   (B) Faceted chess pieces on chessboard tesselation. (Courtesy of Pansophic Systems, Inc.)   (C) Tesselation based on "Amorous Bugs" (see Section 5.2).   (D) A ray-traced scene by Russell Turner (see Chapter 18).

BACK COVER (Clockwise from upper left):
(E) The Mandelbrot Set (see Chapter 5), by Brett Diamond.   (F) Mathematical function with hidden surfaces eliminated.   (G) Ray-traced scene: "Martini Glass and Dice," by Al Barr. (Courtesy of Raster Technologies.)   (H) Ray-traced sphere and stellation on mirrored surface, by Brett Diamond.

About the Author:

F. S. Hill, Jr., is Professor of Electrical and Computer Engineering at the University of Massachusetts—Amherst. He received a Ph.D. degree from Yale University in 1968, worked for three years in digital data transmission at Bell Telephone Laboratories, and joined the university in 1970. He is the author of numerous articles in the field of signal processing, communications, and computer graphics. He has been editor and associate editor of the *IEEE Communications Society Magazine.* He is coauthor of *Introduction to Engineering* and has won several awards for outstanding teaching.

Computer Graphics

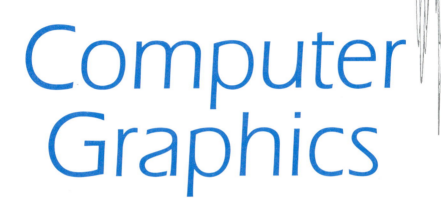

Computer
Graphics

Francis S. Hill, Jr.

Department of Electrical and Computer Engineering
University of Massachusetts

Macmillan Publishing Company

New York

Collier Macmillan Publishers

London

Editor: John Griffin
Production Supervisor: Ron Harris
Production Manager: Pam Kennedy Oborski
Text Designer: Jack Ehn
Cover Designer: Sheree L. Goodman

This book was set in 10/12 Melior by T.S.I. Graphics and printed and bound by Von Hoffmann Press. The cover was printed by Von Hoffmann Press.

Macmillan Publishing Company
866 Third Avenue, New York, New York 10022

Collier Macmillan Canada, Inc.

        Library of Congress Cataloging-in-Publication Data
Hill, Francis S.
   Computer graphics / Francis S. Hill, Jr.
      p. cm.
   Bibliography: p.
   Includes index.
   ISBN 0-02-354860-6
   1. Computer graphics.   I. Title.
T385.H549   1990   89-31610
006.6—dc20   CIP

Printing: 1 2 3 4 5 6 7 8   Year: 0 1 2 3 4 5 6 7 8 9

TO
Merilee
and to
Greta, Jessie, and Rosy

Preface

Computer graphics is a fascinating area of computer science. It is widely used as a tool for visualizing information in a broad variety of fields, including science and engineering, medicine, architecture, and entertainment. Interactive graphics programs let people work with computers in a natural manner: a user can supply information to the program through simple hand movements and receive information back through pictures. Computer graphics is helping to change the way people perceive and use computers, and it is available on even the lowest-cost computers today, making it readily accessible to everyone.

This book teaches the concepts and techniques of computer graphics. It teaches people how to write programs that produce graphical pictures and images of many kinds of information. It is designed as a text for either a one- or two-semester course in computer graphics at the junior, senior, or graduate level. It can also be used for self-study. It is aimed principally for students majoring in computer science or engineering but will also suit students in other fields, such as physics, mathematics, business, and art.

Prerequisites

In general, the reader should have at least one semester of experience writing computer programs in a modern language such as Pascal, C, or FORTRAN. Some experience with elementary data structures such as linked lists is desirable but not essential, since alternative approaches based on arrays are described.

The reader should have the equivalent of one year of college mathematics; knowledge of elementary algebra, geometry, and trigonometry is assumed. Some exposure to calculus and matrices is useful but not necessary, as an appendix introduces those parts of matrix theory that are used in the book.

Philosophy

The basic philosophy of this book is that graphics programming is learned by doing it: One must write and test real programs that drive real graphics devices to comprehend fully what is going on. One of the principal goals of the book is to show readers how to translate geometric concepts first into a clear mathematical expression and then into program code that works on a computer. Readers first learn how to develop simple routines to produce pictures on whatever graphics display devices they have available. Then methods for producing drawings of ever more complex objects and data are presented in a step-by-step fashion.

Code Fragments

Over 140 examples of tested code fragments, written in Pascal, serve as examples to show one way to implement an algorithm. These fragments appear throughout the text and illustrate real-life applications of the theory.

Exercises and Problems

More than 440 drill exercises appear throughout the book. These are of the "stop-and-think" variety that don't require programming and allow readers to self-test their grasp of the material. Over 180 programming problems appear at the end of chapters. These are suitable for homework assignments and range from the simple to the challenging.

Illustrations

Numerous two- and four-color drawings, photographs, and stereo drawings are used throughout the text to illustrate technique and theory. Computer graphics is of course a very visual discipline, and the figures help to fine-tune the reader's ability to visualize geometric relationships. This is particularly true for three-dimensional graphics, where the stereo pictures help enormously to reveal the geometric concepts being discussed. For suggestions on how to view the stereo pictures, please see the note that precedes the table of contents.

Device Independence

A college graphics laboratory may contain a sizable number of graphics devices, but only a few of each type or model. It can be frustrating for the instructor and student alike to write different programs for so many idiosyncratic devices. To reduce such frustration levels this book takes a device-independent approach. All the graphics in the first part of the book are built out of applications of a single short routine called *lineNDC*() that draws a line between two points. All programming of applications accesses the graphics capability of a device through this routine. A different version of this routine—called a device driver—is fashioned for each type of device. The student can write programs without having to know beforehand which devices will be available. To test a program the student finds the nearest available graphics device, activates the appropriate driver, and is ready to run the application.

Appendix 1 gives examples of actual simple device drivers for several classes of graphics output devices. (Additional ones are provided in the accompanying instructor's manual.) This information is useful in helping the reader or instructor over the first hurdle of producing simple pictures on whatever devices are available.

Complete, Up-to-Date Organization

Computer graphics equipment changes rapidly: Each year we see ever more dazzling displays and ever faster computations. But while pictures of equipment and the images they produce slip quickly out of date, the underlying theory and mathematics of computer graphics has become very stable. The body of knowledge required to produce effective graphics programs rests on a small set of key mathematical topics, including vectors, parametric representations, affine transformations, homogeneous coordinates, and projections. Great care has been given in this book to both clarifying and exposing the beauty of these topics.

Flexible Organization

There is much more in this book than can be covered in a one-semester course. The book has been arranged so the instructor can select different groups of chapters for close study, depending on the interests and backgrounds of a class.

Several such paths through the book are suggested here.

- For a one-semester undergraduate course: Chapters 1, 2, 3, and 4 and parts of 7, 10, 11, and 12.

- For a two-semester undergraduate course add the rest of Chapters 7, 9, 15, 16, 17, and 18.

- For a one-semester graduate course: Chapters 1, 2, 3, 4, 6, 7, 9, 10, 11, and 12.

- For a two-semester graduate course add Chapters 8, 13, 15, 16, 17, and 18.

- For those interested in emphasizing modeling and 3D graphics, this material is concentrated in Chapters 10, 12, 15, 17, and 18.

- For emphasis on raster graphics, Chapters 13, 15, 16, 17, and 18 are of particular interest.

All suggested paths include Chapters 1, 2, and 3 as fundamental. Chapter 1 can be read quickly, with the instructor focusing early on notions of NDC, device drivers, windows and viewports, and producing simple line drawings. The crucial parts of Chapter 4 are dealing with polygons and the important technique of representing a curve parametrically. The material of Chapter 5 is not essential to the development of later ideas, although many students—particularly those with an interest in the arts—vastly enjoy producing such pictures. Chapter 6 is important for gaining an understanding of interactive graphics, but if an instructor prefers to focus only on the production of pictures this chapter can be omitted.

Chapter 7 contains essential information on the use of vectors in graphics. Even students already versed in vectors should peruse it to see how valuable ordinary vector tools are in graphics algorithms. Chapter 8 makes a good project for students interested primarily in two-dimensional graphics. Chapter 9 is important for an understanding of smoothly varying surfaces but may be omitted if interest is greatest in viewing faceted models. Chapter 10 introduces the fascinating world of three-dimensional (3D) graphics based on wireframe models.

Chapter 11 discusses in detail another pivotal tool in graphics, the affine transformation, and shows how it is applied in graphics applications. And Chapter 12 moves deeper into 3D graphics, introducing the important "synthetic camera," and developing the various types of projections used in graphics.

In Chapter 13 we change gears and discuss a variety of topics peculiar to raster graphics, including scan conversion, region filling, antialiasing, and the powerful BitBlt operation. Chapter 14 discusses curve and surface design based on Bezier and B-spline methods.

Chapter 15 shows how solid objects that are modeled as "polygon meshes" can be drawn with smooth shading to achieve greater realism. The classical lighting models, which involve diffuse and specular components of light, are introduced, and Gouraud and Phong shading are described.

Methods for defining and classifying colors numerically are discussed in Chapter 16, leading to the CIE standard chromaticity diagram and its various uses. Chapter 17 attacks the surface elimination problem and presents several specific algorithms in detail.

In Chapter 18 we develop a complete working ray tracer, for achieving stunning visual realism. The development is incremental, so the reader can build it in small working pieces. The chapter also shows how to include the effects of mirrorlike and transparent objects.

Supplements

An accompanying instructor's manual provides solutions to most exercises and suggests additional projects. Complete demonstration programs of techniques developed in the text are explained and listed. Reprints of several articles on interesting geometric ideas provide the instructor with engaging background material for the student. Also included in the manual are guides to additional device drivers, to help the instructor in developing drivers for a wider variety of graphics device.

A diskette containing many of the code fragments and demonstration programs accompanies the instructor's manual. The demonstration programs are suitable for use in the classroom, and students can work with them and enhance them as well.

Acknowledgments

This book has grown out of notes used in a course I have been teaching at the University of Massachusetts for the last nine years. During this time a large number of students have helped to develop demonstrations and make suggestions for improving the courses. They have also produced many exquisite graphical samples, some of which appear here. Some students who have been particularly helpful are Tarik Abou-Raya, Earl Billingsley, Dennis Chen, Scott Davidson, Daniel Dee, Brett Diamond, Bruce Filgate, Jay Greco, Marc Infield, Tom Kopec, Adam Lavine, Tuan Le, Andreas Meyer, John Michael, David Mount, Bruce Nichol, Mike Purpura, Chris Russell, Russell Turner, Bill Verts, Shel Walker, Ken Ward, and Clay Yost.

I apologize for any inadvertent omissions.

Several colleagues have provided inspiration and guidance during the germination of the book. I am particularly grateful to Charles Hutchinson for his support in starting the graphics effort at the university, to Michael Wozny for his enthusiasm and encouragement in its development, and to Charlé Rupp for the many creative ideas in graphics he passed on to me. I would especially like to thank Daniel Bergeron, Robert Wilke, Tim Clement, and Brian Barsky, who made substantial contributions to the coherence and readability of the book. I would like to thank the following individuals, and many others who are not mentioned by name, for their advice and help: Marc P. Armstrong, University of Iowa; J. Eugene Ball, University of Delaware; Brian A. Barsky, University of California–Berkeley; Marc Berger, University of Colorado, R. Daniel Bergeron, University of New Hampshire; Tim Clement, University of Manchester; John T. Demel, The Ohio State University; Edward N. Ferguson, University of Maine; Georges Grinstein, University of Lowell; Mark W. Koch, Clarkson University; Leo J. LaFrance, New Mexico State University; Peichung F. Lai, University of Alabama; Ralph E. Lee, University of Missouri–Rolla; Joel Neisen, University of Minnesota; Chuck Nelson, University of Idaho; Spencer W. Thomas, University of Michigan; Deborah Walters, State University of New York–Buffalo; Frank G. Walters, University of Missouri–Rolla; Robert Wilke, The Ohio State University.

Special thanks to my editor, John Griffin, for his continuing guidance and encouragement during the preparation of the book, and to Ron Harris, whose expertise and care during production have markedly improved it. Anne Dolan-Niles helped enormously organizing the voluminous correspondence connected with the book, and Andy Casiello produced many of the photographs.

Finally, thanks to my parents, to my wife Merilee, and to our children Greta, Jessie, and Rosy, for all their patience and support while this book slowly took shape.

F. S. H., Jr.

Note to the reader
How to View the Stereo Pictures

It can be challenging to visualize things in three-dimensional (3D) space, and figures in a book are limited to showing projections of objects on a flat page. One way to counter this limitation dramatically is to view images stereoscopically. The eye–brain system is remarkable: If slightly different views of a scene are shown to the left and right eyes, a scene can appear to "jump out of the page" with a convincing sense of depth.

Many stereoscopic figures appear throughout the book to clarify discussions of 3D situations. They look like a pair of almost identical figures placed side by side. To gain the full value of these stereo pictures allow (coerce) your left eye to look at the left-hand one and your right eye to look at the right-hand one. This may take some practice, since we go about our lives focusing both eyes on the same points. Some people catch on quickly; others, after many bleary-eyed attempts; some people, never. Of course the figures still help to clarify the discussion even without the stereo effect.

One way to practice is to hold the index fingers of each hand upright in front of you, about 2 inches apart, and to stare "through them" at a blank wall in the distance. Each eye sees two fingers, of course, but two of the fingers seem to overlap in the middle. This overlap is precisely what is desired when looking at stereo figures: Each eye sees two figures, but the middle ones are brought into perfect overlap. When the middle ones fuse together like this, the brain constructs out of them a single 3D image. Some people find it helpful to place a piece of white cardboard between the two figures and to rest their nose on it. The cardboard barrier prevents each eye from seeing the image intended for the other eye.

An inexpensive cardboard viewer is available from the Taylor–Merchant Corporation; 212 West 35 Street; New York, NY 10001. The instructor can request that the college bookstore stock these viewers.

Brief Contents

Appendixes

Contents

Appendixes

Introduction to Computer Graphics

"Begin at the beginning," the King said gravely,
"and go on till you come to the end; then stop."

Lewis Carroll, *Alice in Wonderland*

Goals of the Chapter

- To provide an overview of the computer graphics field.
- To introduce important terminology.
- To give examples showing how computer graphics is used.
- To outline the development process of a graphics application program.
- To discuss the issue of device independence and program portability.
- To discuss graphics standards.

1.1   What Is Computer Graphics?

Computer graphics provides a set of tools to create pictures and to interact with them in natural ways. The tools consist of both hardware and software, and together they permit programmers to fashion programs with a strong graphics capability. Data are presented visually through shapes, colors, and texture rather than by tables of numbers. Words and numbers are replaced whenever possible by pictures, because the eye–brain system is better at recognizing and interpreting visual representations. With interactive graphics a person instructs the computer using natural hand movements, such as pointing and drawing.

Computer graphics has become an important technical discipline within computer science and engineering, with its own set of fascinating ideas, techniques, and sometimes astonishing graphics devices. This book presents the principal mathematical and algorithmic techniques used in graphics today, as well as the programming methods to build the tools needed to implement them.

1.1.1 The Major Ingredients

We first shall establish a framework for discussing computer graphics, by defining various terms used throughout the text. Some of them may be familiar to programmers, but within a graphics framework they acquire new meanings. Some terms are first defined informally, just to set the stage; then those requiring a more formal definition are reintroduced when appropriate.

Application/Application Programmer

An **application** is a computer program that applies the resources of a computer to a specific task. For example, a word processor is an application, as is a simulation program, an arcade game, an accounting package, or a typesetting program. **Application programmers** are the people who write applications, using all available hardware and software tools to construct an application that works properly.

A **graphics application** is designed to produce graphics—visual representations in the form of pictures, slides, and so forth. This book explains how to create effective graphics applications, such as a program that plots graphs based on tables of scientific data, a "paint" application that allows freehand drawing on a computer, and an interactive program to design logic circuits. Several examples of such applications are described in the next section.

The User

The user runs the application, directs its sequence of actions, and observes the fruits of its labors. Sometimes the user is also the application programmer and therefore understands all of its inner workings. But serious applications are so expensive to develop that to be cost effective they must be used by many people over a long period of time. So users often know little about the internal logic of the application or about programming. They "know" the application only through the user's manual, the "interface" presented while the program is running, and the experience they gain from trying it out. Users often become experts—talented designers of structures such as turbine blades and airplane wings, or valued inventors of digital logic circuits—without ever knowing how the program operates, the language in which it was written, or who wrote it. Thus it is essential to provide an understandable and visually accessible interface to the users, and graphics offers the tools to do this.

Display Device

A **display device** presents text and pictures to the user. There are several ways to categorize display devices, such as hard-copy versus soft-copy, monochrome versus color, or character versus graphics displays.

When text or pictures are created on a **hard-copy** device, a permanent record of the image is created. The most familiar example is a printer. Some printers can print only individual text characters, and so they aren't particularly useful for graphics. Others can produce both text and graphics by printing patterns of closely spaced dots. Figure 1.1 (left) shows text and graphics produced on the kind of dot matrix printer frequently used with personal computers, and Figure 1.1 (right) shows output from a laser printer. Laser printers can place dots very closely—at densities of 300 or more dots per inch—and so can produce very high-quality graphics.

Another common hard-copy device is the **pen plotter**, such as those shown in Figure 1.2. A pen travels over the paper, leaving a trail of colored ink. Some plotters have a carousel that holds several pens which the program can exchange automatically in order to draw in different colors. When the picture is complete, the user removes the paper and thus has a permanent copy of the picture. There are also **drum plotters**, as shown in Figure 1.3, on which the paper rolls back and forth on a drum to provide one direction of motion, while the pen moves back and forth at the top of the drum to provide the other direction.

Another kind of hard-copy device is a **film recorder**, in which the picture is drawn directly onto photographic film for later development. Images can also be directly "drawn" on videotape with a video tape recorder, again providing a hard copy.

There are also various types of **soft-copy** displays whose pictures are not permanent but last only until the display is overwritten with a new picture or is

Figure 1.1.
Text and graphics on a dot matrix printer (left) and on a laser printer (right).

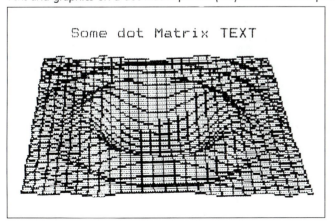

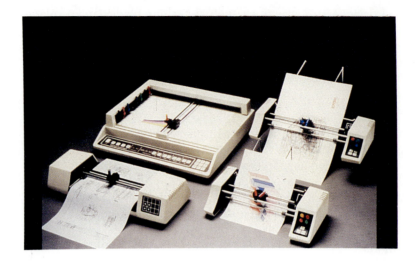

Figure 1.2.
Example of pen plotters (Courtesy of Houston Instrument Division, Ametek, Inc.)

turned off. The user doesn't have to change paper or film between successive pictures, and so soft-copy displays are convenient for generating and "previewing" many pictures during a session. By far the most common display surface is the **screen** of a TV-like "video monitor," an example of which is shown in Figure 1.4. It's so common that we often use screen as a generic name for a display device, even though the actual device may not be a video monitor at all.

A video monitor is frequently called a **CRT display**, or **cathode ray tube**, because of the technology on which it is based. Figure 1.5 shows the inner workings of such a display. The picture is drawn on the inside of the screen by means of an electron beam that strikes a phosphor coating. The phosphor material glows in some characteristic color wherever the beam strikes it. The beam

Figure 1.3.
A drum plotter. (Courtesy of Houston Instrument Division, Ametek, Inc.)

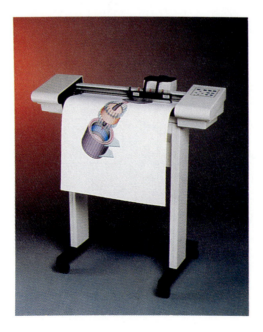

Figure 1.4.
A video monitor. (Photo
courtesy of Hewlett-Packard
Company.)

emerges from an **electron gun**, and it must be controlled at each instant in two
ways:

- *Intensity.* The intensity control determines the number of electrons
  striking the spot of phosphor and therefore how brightly the spot will
  glow. (A color monitor uses several beams—see the following.)

- *Position.* The deflection controls alter the direction of the beam from
  straight ahead to the desired position horizontally and vertically on the
  screen. This determines where the spot of light will appear.

Another important distinction in displays is between monochrome and col-
or video displays. A **monochrome** display uses a single electron gun and a
single type of phosphor, and so it can draw in only one color, although different
parts of the picture can have different brightnesses. A color display has three
guns and three types of phosphor, as seen in Figure 1.6. One type of phosphor
glows with a green color when struck by electrons, a second type glows red, and
a third glows blue. During the CRT's manufacture, the three types of phosphor
are coated in a "triad" pattern on the inside surface of the screen, as shown
in Figure 1.6. The deflection circuitry is much the same as in a monochrome
display; all three beams are deflected together and strike the screen at approx-

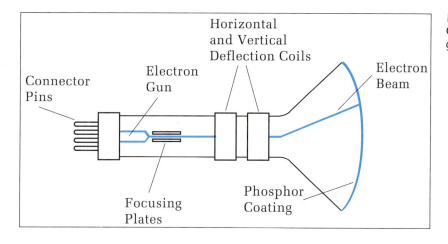

Figure 1.5.
Operation of a monochromatic
graphics monitor.

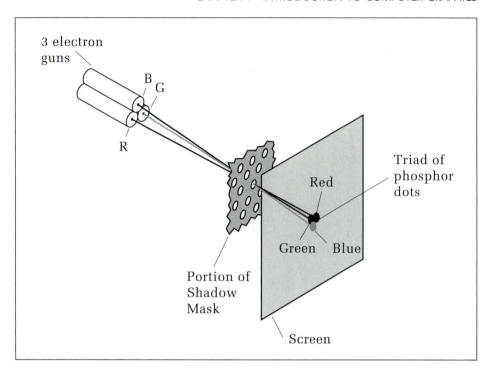

Figure 1.6.
Operation of a color graphics monitor with mask.

imately the same place. However, a mask having tiny holes is carefully positioned inside the tube so that each of the beams can hit only one type of phosphor. For convenience, we often call the electron gun whose beam strikes the red-glowing phosphor the "red gun"; likewise for the "green gun" and "blue gun."

By manipulating these three guns, many colors can be formed. For example, to make a dot on the screen glow in some color such as yellow—which consists of the superposition of the colors red and blue (see Chapter 16)—both the red and blue beams are turned on in nearly equal intensities. The adjacent red and blue dots of phosphor glow; the eye blends together the two colors; and a dot of yellow appears. To make the yellow more pinkish, the intensity of the red beam is increased. If the green beam is also turned on, the spot will appear white, as white is the superposition of red, blue, and green. In this fashion a huge number of colors can be displayed by carefully controlling the intensities of the three beams.

All programmers are familiar with **character displays** (also called alphanumeric displays), which show only alphabetic characters, numbers, and a few punctuation marks. Character displays are the most common and least expensive computer terminals available. They are connected to a keyboard so that a user can enter characters for such tasks as word processing, program editing, electronic mail, and data entry. They typically display characters in one of 24 rows, each row having 80 columns. Some character displays can also draw simple horizontal and vertical lines and so can draw simple boxes.

Graphics displays, on the other hand, can draw a rich variety of lines and other shapes. As discussed fully in Chapter 2 the two main types of graphics displays are line drawing and raster. **Line-drawing** displays can draw only lines. Figure 1.7 shows an example. A line-drawing device receives simple end-

Figure 1.7.
Image on a line-drawing graphics display (Courtesy of Evans and Sutherland.)

point coordinate information, (x_1, y_1) and (x_2, y_2), and produces the corresponding line. **Raster displays**, on the other hand, define pictures by a rectangular array of dots called **pixels**, for "picture elements." Figure 1.4 shows an example. When sent the proper patterns of pixels, raster displays not only can draw lines, they also can fill in regions of the screen with some color. Each type of graphics device has advantages and disadvantages, as we shall point out in several places in the text.

To increase their flexibility, graphics displays usually have a text mode and a graphics mode. In a **text mode** they act as ordinary character terminals for program entry and the like. In a **graphics mode** they interpret the data they receive as commands to draw graphics. They can be switched from one mode to the other by keystrokes or under program control.

Host Computer

The **host computer** is the processor on which the application runs. It may or may not be tightly coupled with the graphics display. In some cases the host computer is a **self-contained** system such as a personal computer, containing an interactive computer terminal with built-in microprocessor, memory, and mass storage. Figure 1.8 shows an example, an Apple Macintosh II computer. The self-contained system gives the user total control over all of the system's resources and can rapidly respond to the user's requests. The processor running the application is closely tied to the graphics display. But the basic speed of the processor and the memory available can be limiting. Furthermore, the most powerful software packages for a particular job may not be available on a given personal computer system or may not be affordable for only a single user.

At the other extreme, the host is a large, remotely located computer that communicates with the user's terminal over some sort of communication line. The **remote host** system usually consists of a much faster computer with vast amounts of storage and many peripheral devices such as printers and plotters. Often, powerful and expensive software packages are immediately available after being installed. Editors, compilers, debuggers, and linkers assist the programmer in the development of the application, whereas other tools (statistical routines, database management packages, graphics packages, and so forth) can be made part of the application itself and in that way become available to the user.

Figure 1.8.
A personal computer. (Courtesy
of Apple Computer, Inc.)

The graphics display in such a system is loosely connected to the host. Graphics data must pass over the communications link that connects the terminal to the system. Some links, such as two modems connected by a telephone line, transmit data very slowly, causing graphics to be drawn at a frustratingly slow pace.

Another limitation is that a remote host system often simultaneously serves many users and runs different applications and so may respond slowly to each user.

The **networked** configuration provides the best of both worlds. The user or programmer works at an interactive terminal such as a personal computer with its local processing power and so enjoys the control and responsiveness of that system, and also has access to various **servers** over high-speed communications links. Compute servers can carry out some of the intense computational processing at high speeds; file servers can supply huge amounts of data quickly; and print or plot servers can provide hard-copy output for graphics. This tends to be an expensive environment to acquire, but for demanding jobs it may be worth it, for both users and programmers.

1.1.2 The Graphics Workstation

The place where the user works with an interactive graphics application is known as the **graphics workstation**. It may be just a personal computer or a graphics terminal connected to a remote host, but the word has taken on the connotation of power and speed. A "high-end" graphics workstation has a local processor, mass storage, a high-resolution graphics display, and various specialized input devices. Figure 1.9 shows an example of an advanced workstation with various input devices. In addition to a graphics display some workstations also have a **dialogue display**. A workstation that contains both types of terminals can separate the pure drawing of pictures from any dialogue between the user and the application, which leaves the entire graphics display surface free for drawing. Furthermore, because the dialogue display is large, the user can be given more complete "prompts" for the next choice of action (e.g., "Point to the part to be rotated") and "echoes" reporting the effects of the previous action (e.g., "That circle does not fit in the space provided") (see Chapter 6). A menu of

Figure 1.9.
Advanced Workstation.
(Courtesy of Hewlett-Packard
Company.)

options can remain fixed on the dialogue display at all times, without interfering with the graphics. In later chapters we shall describe programming techniques that take advantage of a dialogue display when it is available. When a dialogue display isn't available, much the same effect can be obtained using "windowing" facilities. Among other handy features, windows permit portions of the display surface to be covered momentarily with message areas or menus, as shown in Figure 1.10. Although these dialogue areas obscure parts of the display while they are being used, the obscured underlying parts are restored when the window is no longer needed.

1.2 Examples of Graphics Applications

This section looks briefly at a variety of applications that use computer graphics, demonstrating the range of situations that can benefit from graphics. We shall also describe in detail several of these applications as design case studies.

- *Presentation graphics—slide production.* A particularly important area within computer graphics has come to be known as "presentation graphics" or "business graphics." This area deals with the production of professional-looking pictures, often in the form of slides to be shown to a group of customers, colleagues, or management. Such slides often contain bar charts or pie charts that summarize complex information in a readily digestible form. As shown in Figure 1.11, the emphasis is often on quality and visual appeal in order to make a particular point, with careful consideration of the color and positioning of the information on the slide.

  In order to produce such slides, one needs a **graphics editor** application that accepts data in list or table form and automatically formats them into the user's choice of a bar chart, line plot, or whatever. The user

Figure 1.10.
Message areas appearing in windows. (Courtesy of Versacad Corp.)

then moves around the charts on the display, adds annotations in some pleasing font, changes colors, and so on until the picture has the desired look and appeal. At this point the picture is usually sent to a film recorder to obtain a high-quality slide. Writing a graphics editor application is discussed in Chapter 6.

- *Paint system.* Another kind of graphics editor is a **paint** system, an application that allows a user to act as an artist with the help of a computer. The user fashions the image by sketching—often using a tablet or light pen—and by selecting colors and patterns to create the desired effects. Figure 1.12 shows a picture created on such a system. The application provides many tools for the artist. For example, previously wrought images can be called up from mass storage and merged with new images; "palettes" of different colors can be accessed and displayed; and many different textures can be created instantly by means of simple commands.

Figure 1.11.
High-quality slide-presentation graphics. (Courtesy of Management Graphics.)

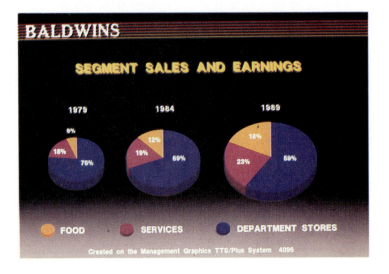

Figure 1.12.
Image created with *IMAGES II+* paint system. (Courtesy of Audrey Fleisher, Computer Graphics Laboratories, Inc.)

● *Scientific data presentation*. Scientific data are often complex, and relationships among the ingredients of an experiment can be difficult to visualize. Graphics provides a superb tool for presenting scientific information in a way that can be easily grasped. When data are displayed in the right way, scientists often have new insights and better comprehend the underlying process they are investigating. A revealing display of scientific data also enhances the communication of ideas to colleagues. Figure 1.13 shows an example. A surface is seen to undulate up and down in a fashion the eye can grasp immediately. The surface height represents one quantity (such as temperature or the concentration of a chemical), which is displayed against two other quantities to produce a three-dimensional plot. Conversely, if these data were presented as just a table of numbers, one would have to study the table laboriously in order to obtain the same information.

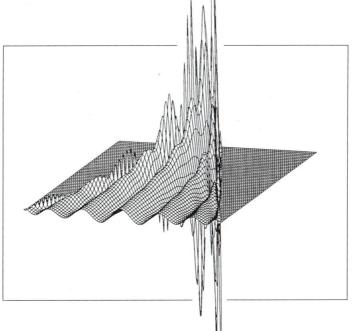

Figure 1.13.
Display of complex scientific data. (Courtesy of Ping Dong.)

- *Interactive logic circuit design.* One of the most important uses of computer graphics today is in **computer-aided design (CAD)**, in which a computer assists in the design process. Figure 1.14 shows a CAD application to design an electronic logic circuit that might form part of a new computer. The designer adds new logic elements (gates) to the circuit by pointing with a light pen to a certain gate **icon** (a small picture of the type of gate required) in an icon menu and "dragging" it to the desired position within the circuit. By means of simple pointing actions, the designer can add, delete, and connect gates to achieve the desired circuit. At this point, **simulation** software can be invoked to test how a real version of the circuit would perform. Based on the results of the simulation, the designer can adjust the circuit and test it once again.

  A CAD application such as this consists of several parts. A **graphics front-end** routine allows the user to interact with a picture of the circuit and edit it into the desired configuration. In the preceding example the front end is of the "pick-and-place" variety. A simulation package is available that tests the circuit and reports on how it would behave if implemented with real logic devices. In addition, a package might contain a **graphics back end** that plots the results of the simulation as timing waveforms or the like. The database package keeps track of the circuit configuration, saves it on disk for later design work, and maintains libraries of similar logic circuits. The main interest of this book is in the graphics portions, but we shall also look at some elementary database issues, as they affect how one represents the "picture" of the circuit and passes it along to a simulator.

- *Interactive architectural design.* A design tool similar to the circuit design application comes from the field of architecture, as shown in Figure 1.15. An architect can construct a model of a building by indicating various floor plans and elevations, and the program fashions these data into a three-dimensional model that is then displayed from

Figure 1.14.
Digital logic design application.

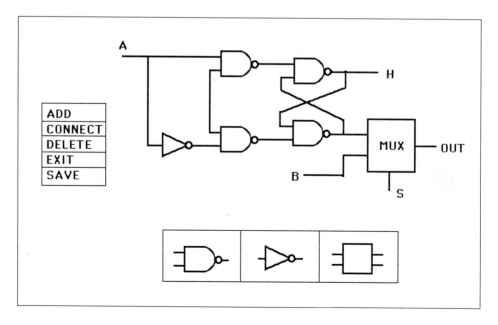

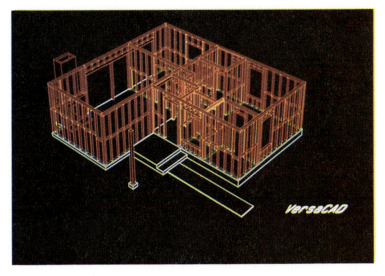

Figure 1.15.
A computer-aided architectural design application. (Courtesy of Versacad Corp.)

various points of view. For example, by selecting window shapes and sizes, the architect can place windows at various trial locations and can even call up different textures, such as brick or stucco, for the outside walls. In this way a building can be "previewed"—perhaps right in front of the client—and different styles can be tried out to see how they might look if the building were actually built.

One of the advantages of computer graphics is its ability to display objects as if they already physically exist, when they really are only models inside a computer.

- *Design of mechanical structures.* Yet another important CAD application that depends on interactive computer graphics is the design and testing of mechanical structures. Figure 1.16 shows a computer model of an electric drill. Figure 1.16a shows a wireframe model (see Chapter 10)

Figure 1.16.
Designing mechanical structures. (Courtesy of Cisigraph Corp.)

(a)

(b)

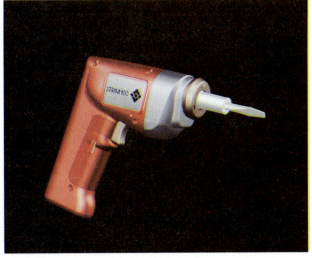

of the drill, and Figure 1.16b shows the drill filled in with color to give a greater sense of solidity. In a wireframe model the shape of the object is suggested by a grid of connected lines. Seen together, the lines give a clear indication of the shape of the structure. Wireframe drawings are particularly useful in interactive design, because they can be drawn rapidly. The designer can shift and rotate the view of the object using a handy input device such as a joystick and see how it looks from every angle. The model can then be tested for strength or strain using a tool such as a finite-element analysis routine. Some elements of constructing and modeling three-dimensional objects are discussed in several chapters beginning with Chapter 10.

- *Mapping and cartography.* Map making is an exacting activity because a huge amount of information and detail must be superimposed with great accuracy. Figure 1.17 shows a detailed map. Map databases are large and complex, and the main task of a map-production application is to gather the proper data from the database and convert them into the desired lines and shapes of the map.

- *Process control.* Processing plants and factories have become more and more complex in recent years, particularly as they have become more automated. Examples are nuclear power plants, hydroelectric facilities, and petroleum refineries. Because of their great complexity, they must be carefully monitored—there must be a "human in the loop" in even automatically controlled environments. The human operator must be given information on a **status display** that is current, precise, and instantly interpretable. For example, the display must report whenever temperatures drift out of their safe range, conveyor belts or valves get stuck, or there are other impending troubles at any point in the system, so that the operator can take appropriate action. The status display can consist of numbers and words, but the information is usually so complex that it is better presented graphically. The display shows a

Figure 1.17.
Producing a complex map.
(Courtesy of Uniras Corp.)

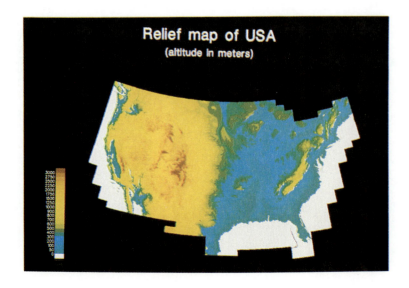

schematic representation for the process, giving the operator the whole picture at a glance. Figure 1.18 shows such a display. It can give the operator an instantaneous picture of the status of the plant and can post warnings by flashing or changing the color of particular graphical elements.

Status displays such as this are controlled from a graphics application program that draws the display based on data collected from various points within the processing plant. The display usually shows the entire plant in some schematic fashion. For example, it can be animated by "bubbles" moving along pipes, or pictures of valves opening and closing, to show exactly what is happening. The user can zoom in on smaller details and can request views of different types of activities within the operation.

- *Flight simulator.* A flight simulator is a system that allows a pilot trainee to sit in a simulated cockpit and safely "fly" a simulated aircraft. The dynamics of the airplane's motion are modeled on a computer, and as the pilot moves the controls in the cockpit, the program responds by calculating new positions and speeds of the simulated plane. The pilot watches a graphics display that shows the view outside the cockpit, and as the plane flies, the display shows what the pilot would indeed see looking out of a real cockpit. Figure 1.19 shows a typical display. Note the degree of realism available, providing the pilot with a real sense of looking out of a cockpit.

  Application programs that produce cockpit displays are among the most demanding and difficult graphics applications to write, because they must respond in real time to changes in the plane's position and orientation and produce the updated display, often computing the new picture 30 times a second. Some important graphics issues that arise in flight simulators are discussed in Chapters 12 through 17.

- *Graphics in image processing.* Computer graphics and image processing are two closely related fields, and they tend to use the same hardware

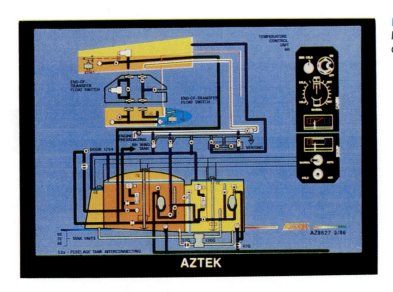

Figure 1.18.
Monitoring a process. (Courtesy of Aztek Corp.)

Figure 1.19.
Simulated view out a cockpit window. (Courtesy of Evans & Sutherland, Inc.)

and many of the same software tools. Whereas computer graphics creates pictures, often from an abstract model of objects, image processing changes already-existing pictures in order to extract new information from them, or for artistic effect. Figure 1.20 shows an example of a processed image. A picture is digitized and entered into the computer using an image scanner, and it is stored in memory as a large array of numbers. The user can invoke various software routines within the application to search for and highlight features in the image. Features can be displayed in different colors to bring out information that might otherwise not be noticed.

1.3   Overview of Graphics Software

The focus of this book is on writing graphics applications. Graphics requires that programs control specialized equipment—graphics displays—but a lan-

Figure 1.20.
A processed image. (Courtesy of Applied Data Systems, Inc.)

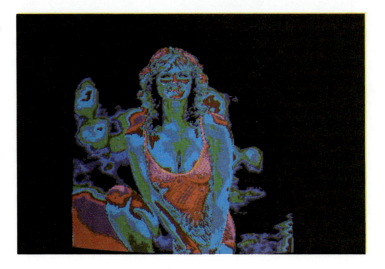

guage such as Pascal does not inherently contain graphics routines. In addition, different graphics devices need different control information. The user must either write the necessary routines or buy them from a vendor. In this section we examine various approaches to this problem.

An example will present some of the basic ideas. Even though it glosses over various issues, it does illustrate some of the problems that arise when designing a graphics application.

Figure 1.21a shows an international symbol to be drawn, perhaps as a first project in a graphics course or as a logo that a company would put on all its documents.

The first job is to "see" what shapes the logo contains, that is, to interpret it geometrically. (See the exercises for other examples of visualizing shapes.) We must construct a precise numerical description of the shapes, so that a sequence of calls to various graphics functions can draw it. At first glance its shape looks rather complex, but Figure 1.21b suggests that the logo can be decomposed into a collection of simple overlapping primitives: in this case, circles and rectangles. When each of the primitives is filled in with black, the desired logo will be complete. Some places may be "painted" two or three times, but on most devices this is equivalent to painting once.

Some sort of circle drawer and rectangle drawer are needed to draw the logo. Suppose the graphics toolbox includes the following routines:

procedure *Circle* (*cx, cy, radius* : *real*; *filled* : *boolean*);
procedure *Rectangle*(*px, py, width, height, angle* : *real*; *filled* : *boolean*).

Circle( ) requires for parameters the location of the circle's center (*cx, cy*), its radius *radius*, and *filled*, which specifies whether the circle should be filled with color. *Rectangle*( ) requires the position of the lower left corner (*px,py*), the dimensions *height* and *width*, and the angle at which the rectangle is tilted, *angle*.

At this point the actual size and placement of the final picture need not be decided—there are tools to scale and position pictures at a later stage. The logo is centered in a convenient *x,y*-coordinate system, as shown in Figure 1.21b, and each of the 15 objects is measured to determine its characteristic coordinates.

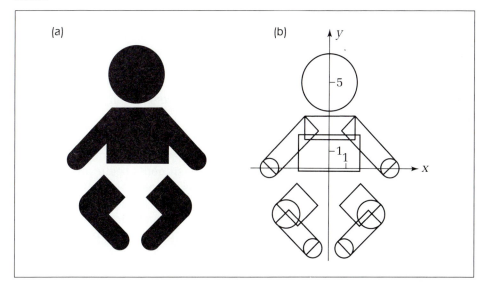

Figure 1.21.
(a) A simple logo to be drawn.
(b) Layout of the logo.

The application that draws the logo might look like the following code fragment:

Code Fragment 1.1. Drawing the Logo

```
procedure DrawLogo;
begin
    Enter_Graphics; {initialize graphics device}
    Set_Color(black); {set the drawing color to black}
    Circle(0.0, 5.0, 1.6, true); {draw the head}
    {other calls to Circle( ) would appear here}
    Rectangle(3.0, −0.4, 3.4, 1.2, 45.0, true); {left arm}
    {other calls to Rectangle( ) would appear here}
    Exit_Graphics {shut down graphics device}
end;
```

The application in which this procedure occurs might do a lot of other drawing, or the logo could be its main task.

The question is how to obtain the procedures *Circle*( ), *Rectangle*( ), and so on that work properly on the given host and the given graphics device. There are several possibilities:

- *Embedded graphics routines.* Some environments contain an assortment of graphics procedures embedded in them, seemingly as extensions to the programming language itself. Macintosh[1] Pascal, for instance, comes with routines such as *Line*( ), *PaintRect*( ), and *Fill_Oval*( ) that are immediately available to draw on the Macintosh screen. Turbo Pascal[2] comes with similar routines, *Line*( ), *FillPoly*( ), *Circle*( ), and so forth, to be used on an IBM personal computer.

  These products are designed to work on a specific host and to draw on a specific graphics device; that is, they are **device dependent**. These embedded routines are convenient tools for producing graphics in a single environment, although an application written for one environment must be adjusted—perhaps even substantially rewritten—to work in a different environment.

For the preceding logo example, the programmer examines (in a manual) the available routines for the environment at hand and accordingly writes the procedures *Circle*( ), *Box*( ), and so on. The most basic graphics primitive needed here is a routine, *Line*( ), that draws a single line. It then is easy to implement *Box*( ) and *Circle*( ) through a few calls to *Line*( ). Most of the early chapters in this book require only a form of *Line*( ), from which we can build an extensive set of drawing routines.

- *Independent graphics package.* When the programming language itself does not support any graphics, one must buy a package of graphics routines from an independent vendor. Many students begin programming on a VAX[3] host, for instance; yet VAX Pascal has tools only for driving character terminals. Thus the users must buy a package that can be linked to an application to produce graphics. Procedures such as *Line*( ) and *Circle*( ) are included, in one form or another, in the package, as are

---

[1]Macintosh is a trademark of Apple Computer Co.
[2]Turbo Pascal is a trademark of Borland International, Inc.
[3]VAX is a trademark of Digital Equipment Corporation.

several device drivers to control the actual graphics devices. A **device driver** is a collection of low-level routines that sends particular codes and commands to a specific graphics device. Each graphics device needs a driver that has been designed for it, and there are hundreds of different drivers in use today.

The application development scenario thus takes the following form:

1. The programmer writes the application—say in Pascal—with a particular graphics package in mind, placing calls to its procedures in the application code.

2. The program is compiled.

3. A graphics terminal is chosen to be used. The application, the graphics package, and the appropriate device driver are linked into an executable program form.

4. The user starts this program running at the chosen terminal and proceeds to use the application.

It is sometimes possible to achieve the following desirable goal: If a different graphics device is to be used, the program does not have to be rewritten or even recompiled. A different driver is simply linked in, and the application is run from the new terminal. Such applications are called **device independent**. Device independence can be achieved by careful design of the graphics package. Suppose it contains the routine $Line(x1, y1, x2, y2 : real)$, whose job is to draw a line between coordinates (x_1, y_1) and (x_2, y_2). What would be found inside the routine $Line(\ )$? It might look like the following:[4]

Pseudocode Fragment 1.2. Looking into a Device-independent Routine

```
procedure Line (x1, y1, x2, y2 : real);
var xa, ya, xb, yb : real;
begin
   <make some tests and adjustments on endpoints>
   ddLine(xa, ya, xb, yb) {pass the burden to ddLine( )}
end;
```

It performs some tests on the endpoints—for "clipping" and the like (see Chapter 3)—and then calls a lower-level procedure, $ddLine(\ )$, with the adjusted arguments. The device driver contains a routine called $ddLine(\ )$ ("device driver Line"), and every driver uses a different version of $ddLine(\ )$. All of the device's idiosyncrasies are kept out of $Line(\ )$ and are instead put in this driver routine. Thus when a different device is to be used, a file with the proper version of $ddLine(\ )$ and the like is linked in, with no changes required in $Line(\ )$.

Graphics software packages are large and costly to develop, whereas device drivers are small and fairly inexpensive. Thus to separate the graphics' algorithms from the device's indiosyncrasies means that the developer has to fashion only one graphics package, with as many device drivers as there are devices to drive.

---

[4]Pseudocode statements surrounded by the symbols $<$ and $>$ are intended only to be suggestive of some action and are used to encapsulate details that are not relevant to the discussion.

On Graphics Standards

The device independence of a software package is a real advantage to the application programmer, allowing many applications to be converted (ported), with modest effort, between graphics devices. All of the programmers in a company can learn how to use the package and can teach it to new programmers.

But the package will eventually become obsolete, for a variety of reasons: The supplier company may no longer support the package; a new package may come along that has more powerful utilities; or key personnel may move to another company, leaving no one skilled in writing drivers for new devices.

Because new graphics packages will always be appearing, a graceful and inexpensive way to port applications from one graphics package to another is needed, which is why graphics **standards** are valuable. If there is a common understanding and agreement regarding graphics functions, then two different packages designed accordingly will enable an application to be adapted from one to the other at a reasonable cost.

The **Graphical Kernel System**, or **GKS**, is an international standards system that specifies what a graphics package should contain and how its ingredients should be organized. Our book uses the GKS perspective. This helps the reader form a mental model of graphics packages that is consistent with GKS and organize applications that can communicate with graphics routines "in the GKS way." Then when the reader encounters an actual GKS package in future programming, it will be more natural to write applications for it.

The Do-It-Yourself Package

Some programmers like to develop their own graphics package, so that they will know exactly what each tool does and also how to **maintain** the package, fixing any bugs that appear, adding new features, or improving the efficiency of the algorithms involved. They then can build a variety of larger applications on top of the graphics package. They can also develop their own device drivers when a new device becomes available.

This is also this book's approach. All of the graphics algorithms and tools are designed to work with a small number of routines such as *ddLine*( ), *EnterGraphics*( ), or *SetPixel*( ). Everything above this level is written in a device-independent fashion. The net result is that the reader learns how graphics algorithms operate and at the same time acquires a fairly complete software package. If a programmer already has a package of routines available—either embedded in a favorite environment or as a file to be linked with the applications—this approach will show how those routines operate. We shall discuss how to develop simple device drivers in Chapter 2 and present several example drivers in Appendix 1.

Exercises

1.1. Surveying the Site.

There is usually a variety of graphics equipment at any college or company site. As a group project, make a survey of the graphics facilities at your site, which includes

- the graphics display devices.
- the graphics software packages.
- the device drivers.
- the hosts on which each operates.
- the available manuals.

1.2   Key Publications in Graphics.

There are many graphics-oriented publications in circulation that are useful for keeping abreast of new ideas and new graphics equipment. Some of the most important of these are

- *ACM SIGGRAPH: Computer Graphics*
- *ACM Transactions on Graphics*
- *Computer Graphics and Image Processing*
- *IEEE Computer Graphics and Applications*
- *NCGA Computer Graphics Today*
- *Eurographics*
- *Computer Graphics World*
- *The Visual Computer*
- *Computer Graphics Forum*

See whether your library has any of these, and look over several issues to get a sense of the material that each offers.

1.3.   Visualizing Figures.

Figure 1.22 shows examples of geometrical figures you might wish to draw using computer graphics. As was done for the logo in Section 1.3, place each in a convenient coordinate system, and specify it in terms of "hollow" or "filled" circles, rectangles, and other simple primitives. Give the parameters that fully describe each graphic primitive that you use.

1.4.   Getting Started in Drawing.

Using the most convenient host and graphics display device available, determine how to program it to draw a simple straight line. Then write a short application that draws a rectangle.

Figure 1.22.
Example geometrical figures to specify.

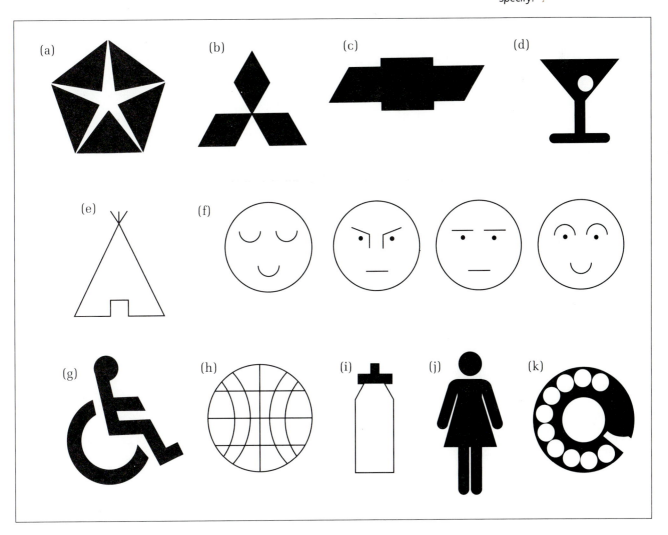

1.5.   Resolution of Devices.
Measure how many dots per inch the various printers at your site can produce. Take as examples a low-cost dot matrix printer and a high-end laser printer.

1.6.   Computing the Resolution.
Assume that the x- and y-coordinates of points are represented within the computer by 10-bit binary numbers. How many different points (x,y) can be represented? If each line segment is characterized by two endpoints, how many line segments can be represented?

1.7.   Sample Applications.
Prepare a list of a dozen applications used routinely at your site that employ graphics. Note which ones are interactive and which simply produce graphical output.

1.8.   Adding Graphics to an Application.
Select an existing application that does not use graphics, and discuss how the addition of graphics could enhance it. Sketch some screens showing menus that might enhance interaction and some screens showing the graphical output that the application might produce.

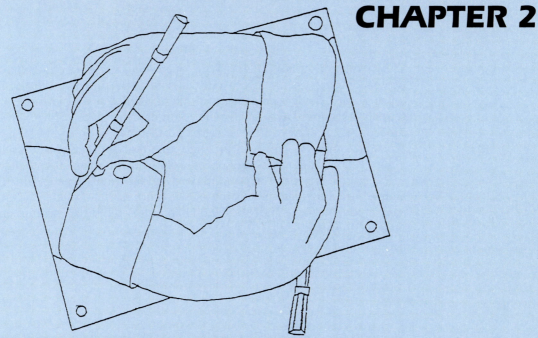

CHAPTER 2

Graphics Devices and Their Control

Goals of the Chapter

- To describe the different types of graphics devices.
- To examine the basic output primitives and primitive attributes that graphics devices draw.
- To examine the various input devices available in graphics equipment.
- To categorize input devices in terms of their logical function.
- To develop elementary examples of device drivers.
- To construct a device-independent procedure that draws a straight line on any device.

23

2.1   Introduction

This chapter describes different types of graphics devices from the point of view of what they can draw and how one can control the drawing. We also look at the types of input devices commonly used today and how they are controlled. With these types in mind, we then develop a fundamental tool, a device-independent procedure that draws a line between two specified endpoints. Using this single procedure, one can create surprisingly rich drawings, such as those shown in Figure 2.1, composed entirely of line segments. Because computer graphics is highly geometric, many important ideas and techniques can be illustrated with simple line drawings such as these. The more realistic shaded images that we shall study later are solidly based on a foundation of line drawings and require many of the same tools.

2.2   Graphics Devices

Chapter 1 showed several examples of graphics displays, categorized as color versus monochrome, hard copy versus soft copy, and so on. Another categorization important to programmers is line drawing versus raster scan. Programming techniques tend to differ significantly for these types, often making it difficult to write purely device-independent programs.

2.2.1 Line-Drawing Displays

Line-drawing displays can draw only lines. There are two major kinds of line-drawing displays: the pen plotter and the vector-refresh display.[1]

Pen Plotters

Pen plotters were described in Chapter 1. The pen plotter provides a useful mental image of the line-drawing process that extends naturally to other line-drawing devices based on video monitors. The pen first moves invisibly to one endpoint of the line to be drawn, then it is "put down" (in the case of a video monitor, the beam is turned on), and finally the pen is moved in a straight line to the second endpoint of the line, thus drawing the line segment. Line-drawing displays have a built-in coordinate system, as suggested in Figure 2.2 for the pen plotter. The pen is directed to a particular position by sending to the plotter the desired x- and y-coordinates of the point. The example shows that the x-coordinate can range from 0 to 1023 and the y-coordinate can range from 0 to 767. Thus the total number of **addressable points** is $1024 \times 768 = 786,452$, and the plotter can draw a line between any two of these points.

Line-drawing devices are built with a basic repertoire of **device commands**. Each of these commands is encoded in some fashion, so that when the device

---

[1]A third kind, the "direct-view storage tube" (DVST), is a CRT display that behaves like a pen plotter: A line is drawn by sweeping the electron beam once between its endpoints, after which special electronics keep the line visible. The only way to erase a line is to erase the entire screen. DVSTs were among the first affordable graphics devices but are seldom used today.

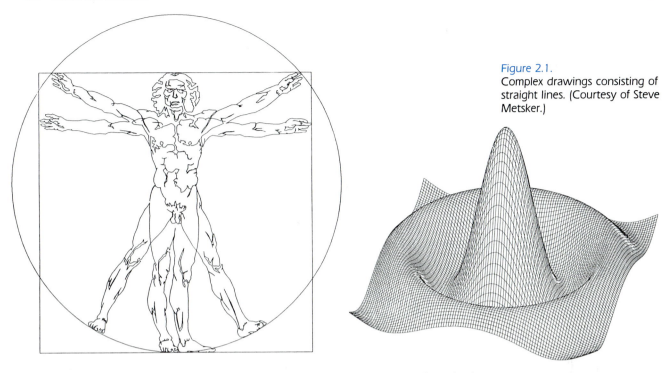

Figure 2.1.
Complex drawings consisting of straight lines. (Courtesy of Steve Metsker.)

receives a command code from the host computer, it can respond with the appropriate action. For example, a suitable basic set of commands for a pen plotter is the following:

Pen_Up;   ← lift pen
Pen_Down;   ← put pen down for writing
Go_To(*x, y*);   ← move pen to (*x, y*) in a straight line
Get_Pen(*i*);   ← exchange current pen with pen #*i*

Notice that commands like these are **mode-setting** commands: Once the device receives them, they alter the "state" of the machine until a subsequent command sets a different mode. For instance, when *Pen_Down* is received, the pen is set in the down mode and remains down until *Pen_Up* is sent. Similarly,

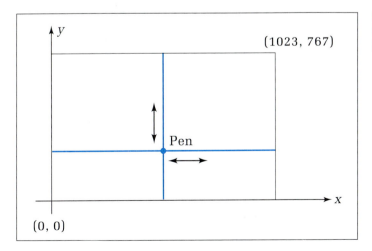

Figure 2.2.
Example coordinate system for a plotter.

Get_Pen(2) sets the current drawing color mode to the color in pen 2. Furthermore, the pen is always at a **current position**, wherever it was last sent by a *Go_To*( ) command. Some other kinds of devices don't automatically keep track of a current position or a current drawing mode. This will affect how we write programs to control them.

A line-drawing device must be sent (*x, y*) values in its own coordinate system, called **device coordinates.** Consider our example plotter. To draw a straight line from (34, 128) to (254, 128), the device would be sent encoded versions of the commands

> *Pen_Up*;
> *Go_To*(34, 128);
> *Pen_Down*;
> *Go_To*(254, 128);

Various device drivers are discussed later and also in Appendix 1.

Vector-Refresh Displays

Another important line-drawing display, based on a CRT, is the **vector-refresh display**. It is so named because in its graphics mode it can draw only line segments, or vectors. Other names for this kind of terminal are "stroke," "random scan," and "calligraphic." Figure 2.3 shows an example. The electron beam is swept in a straight line from one point on the screen to another, with the beam either "on" at one of several possible intensities, or "off." (Some vector-refresh terminals can also draw in colors through the use of three beams, as described in Chapter 1.) When the beam is on, it excites the phosphor along its path and leaves a visible glowing line on the display. This glow rapidly dies out as the beam moves on, and so the entire picture must be redrawn, or **refreshed**, frequently, typically 60 times a second. At these rates the human eye has enough persistence of its own that the user sees no flickering in the image.

Vector-refresh terminals have a built-in coordinate system just as pen plotters do. For instance, the *x*- and *y*-coordinates each might range in value from 0 to 511, with (0, 0) being at the upper left corner and (511, 511) at the lower right corner. The beam may be moved from any addressable point on the screen to any other. Carefully designed (and expensive) electronics within the refresh display ensure that the path of the beam will be straight from one point to the other.

Figure 2.3.
Vector-refresh display. (Courtesy of Evans and Sutherland.)

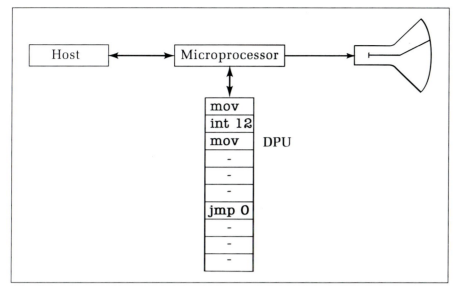

Figure 2.4.
DPU on refresh display.

Refresh displays are used for highly interactive applications, in which the picture must be changed rapidly. For instance, in a computer-aided architectural design (CAAD) application, the user/architect may want to rotate the picture of a house being designed, in order to see it from various angles. Because it is easy to remove one view of the house (just stop refreshing it) and then to display the house from a slightly different angle, it is easy to achieve the visual effect of the house rotating right before the user's eyes.

The host computer running the application must be spared the burden of refreshing the image many times a second; otherwise it would have little time left to run the application. Refresh terminals are therefore commonly built today with an internal **display processing unit (DPU)** that takes care of the refreshing chore. As shown in Figure 2.4, the vector-refresh terminal houses a microprocessor along with a sizable amount of memory for a display file. The **display file** contains primitive instructions such as

```
0 MOV 34, 127 [move to (34, 127)]
1 INT 12      [set intensity to level 12]
2 MOV 56, 213
  .
  .
9 JMP 0        [jump back to instruction 0 to repeat]
  .
  .
```

that move (MOV) the beam to the given x- and y-coordinates (34, 127),[2] set its intensity (INT) to the next desired value (12), and so forth. The microprocessor reads rapidly through these commands and controls the beam accordingly. The last instruction in the sequence is a jump (JMP 0) command, which forces the microprocessor to take its next display command from location 0, the beginning of the display file, and so the whole refresh cycle begins again. The image can be altered by the host running the application. It sends commands to load new data into the display file, and the image changes in the next refresh cycle. Although

[2]Each MOV updates the current position to its new value. The current position is maintained in a memory register within the device.

DPUs can be much more complex than the one described here, the idea is the same: The application sends information about the image once, and the local DPU takes care of the refreshing process.

Line-drawing displays are not well suited to filling areas of the display in a solid color. Because the lines drawn are rather narrow, many must be drawn side by side to fill an area. Usually some form of **cross-hatching** is used to approximate a solid area. In contrast with line-drawing displays, raster-scan devices easily display filled areas.

2.2.2 Raster-Scan Displays

The **raster-scan** (or simply **raster**) display is the other major class of display device. Raster displays construct a picture from individual points of color rather than lines. Each spot is called a **pixel**, short for "picture element." Figure 1.10 shows a picture on a raster video display.

Text characters are formed with patterns of dots. Straight lines and curves are formed by illuminating the appropriate sequence of pixels. And areas of the screen can be filled with solid colors: All of the pixels within the area are simply set to the desired color. Algorithms to accomplish this are discussed in Chapter 13. Figure 2.5 shows how the information stored for an image corresponds to the image for a raster display. In this example the display is bilevel: Each pixel is displayed either "on" (black) or "off" (white). The raster image is stored, or "buffered," in a region of memory called a **frame buffer**. (The term *frame* denotes a single picture, as in a frame of film.) There is a direct correspondence between each pixel in the display and one bit of memory in the frame buffer. If the value stored in a bit is 0, the corresponding pixel will be displayed white, and if the value stored is 1, the pixel will appear black. The application running on the host computer loads the appropriate bit values into each memory location in the frame buffer.

The Scanning Process

Recall that in a vector-refresh display the deflection of the beam is controlled by the local DPU processor. But this is not the case for a raster-scan device, in

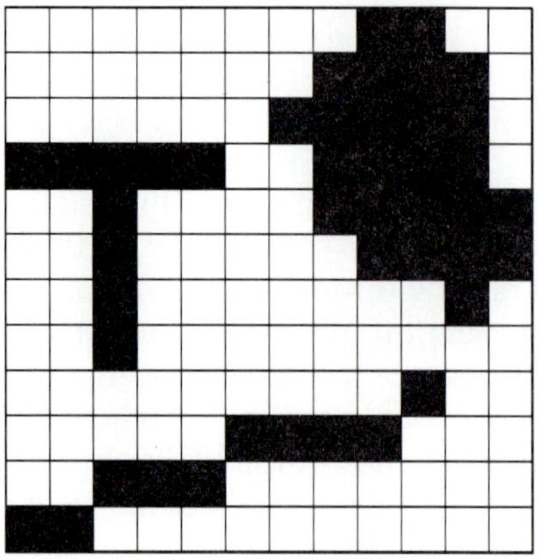

Figure 2.5.
The correspondence between image data and their display.

Bits in Memory

0	0	0	0	0	0	0	0	1	1	0	0
0	0	0	0	0	0	0	1	1	1	1	0
0	0	0	0	0	0	1	1	1	1	1	0
1	1	1	1	1	0	0	1	1	1	1	0
0	0	1	0	0	0	0	1	1	1	1	1
0	0	1	0	0	0	0	0	1	1	1	1
0	0	1	0	0	0	0	0	0	0	1	0
0	0	1	0	0	0	0	0	0	0	0	0
0	0	0	0	0	0	0	0	0	1	0	0
0	0	0	0	0	1	1	1	1	0	0	0
0	0	1	1	1	0	0	0	0	0	0	0
1	1	0	0	0	0	0	0	0	0	0	0

Spots on Screen

which the deflection circuitry runs independently. The image is scanned row by row from top to bottom, just as in an ordinary TV monitor. Figure 2.6 shows the repetitive pattern followed by the CRT beam as it paints out a sequence of **scan lines**, one above the other. Each position of the beam on the screen corresponds to a particular pixel, and the values of these pixels are read out from the frame buffer in synchrony with the beam position. The intensity control on the CRT simply takes bit values from the frame buffer at the correct instants and converts them into intensity values.

For the image to be refreshed, it must be scanned many times a second. Several ingredients, therefore, must be considered when designing the scanning process: the refresh rate, the persistence of the phosphor (how rapidly its glow fades out after being excited by the electron beam), and the scanning method. For high-cost displays, a rapid refresh rate, typically 60 times a second, is used. Rapid refresh rates require expensive electronics within the CRT to control the beam, as well as expensive digital circuitry to access information in the frame buffer sufficiently rapidly. For lower-cost devices the image might be refreshed only 30 times a second. The problem here is that the image near the top of the screen begins to fade out while the lower half of the screen is being scanned, and vice versa, which can lead to a noticeable flicker.

Two partial solutions are available to reduce this flickering on displays having low refresh rates. The first is to use a higher-persistence phosphor, which will still be glowing brightly enough when the pixel is refreshed on the next cycle. But unfortunately, it glows so long that the image can become "smeared" if it is changing rapidly, as when an icon is dragged rapidly across the screen. Bright areas also tend to leave "light tails" behind as they move on

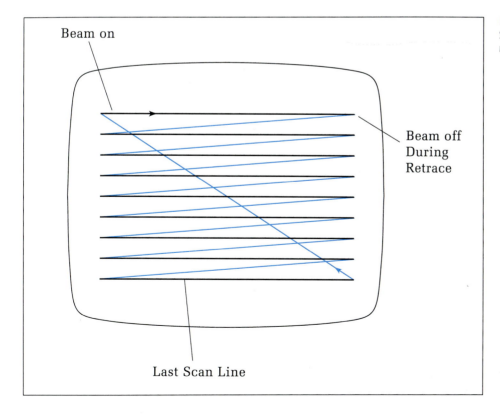

Figure 2.6.
Scanning of CRT beam, noninterlaced.

the screen, which can be distracting to the user. The second partial solution uses an **interlaced** scanning pattern, as shown in Figure 2.7. Here the beam refreshes every other scan line in sequence. For a refresh rate of 30 times a second, it refreshes the even-numbered lines in 1/60 of a second and then the odd-numbered lines in the next 1/60 of a second. Because the eye tends to blend the light in adjacent scan lines, less flickering is observed, even with phosphors of reasonably short persistence. Home TV sets universally use this form of interlacing, and it works well, as TV images usually have somewhat fuzzy boundaries anyway. In computer graphics, however, many synthetic images have sharp boundaries between regions and have horizontal lines only one scan line wide. For these images, interlacing is not particularly satisfactory, because line-to-line "averaging" cannot occur.

Drill Exercise

2.1.   Information Rates for Scanning. Consider a frame buffer consisting of 512 rows of 512 columns each. If the image is refreshed 60 times a second, how fast (in bits/sec) must information be read out from the frame buffer?

Multiple Intensity/Color Raster Displays

In order to create raster images that can support several intensities or colors, more information must be stored for each pixel in the frame buffer. Each pixel color is represented by several bits, and conversion circuitry converts the digital representation of each pixel value into appropriate intensity controls. If a pixel is described by b bits, there will be 2^b possible values for its color. Figure 2.8 shows a situation in which there are six bits of information per pixel. This is called a "6 bit/pixel" frame buffer, or one might say that there are "6 bit planes" of memory in the frame buffer. The six bits that represent the pixel value can

Figure 2.7.
Interlaced scanning.

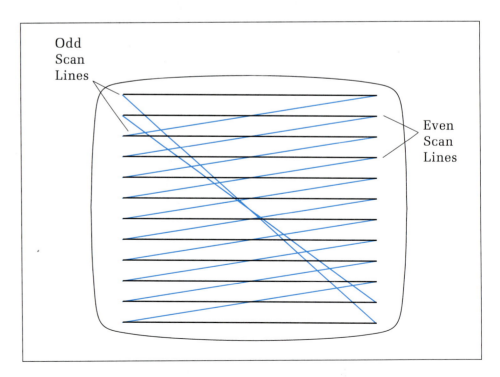

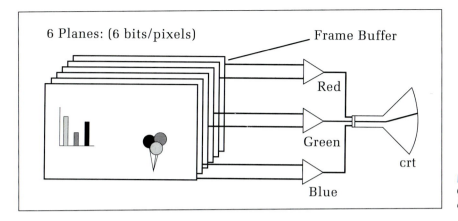

Figure 2.8.
Color raster operation—
6 bits/pixel.

distinguish 64 color values. In this example, two of the bits are routed to the green gun of the CRT, two to the red gun, and two to the blue gun. Thus each of the guns can be driven at four possible intensities; for instance:

Bit Values	Relative Intensity
00	0 (dark)
01	⅓ (dim)
10	⅔ (brighter)
11	1 (brightest)

The digital value (e.g., 10) is converted to the "analog" value ⅔ by means of a **digital-to-analog converter**, or **DAC**, which is an electronic device designed to convert logical values into voltage values. Each gun has a DAC, and the intensity of its beam is driven by the output voltage from the DAC. Because each gun has four possible intensities here, $4 \times 4 \times 4 = 64$ different colors can be displayed.

For example, suppose a given pixel contains the value 011100. The color for that pixel would be determined as

01 ⇒ red level = ⅓
11 ⇒ green level = 1
00 ⇒ blue level = 0

The displayed color is therefore a combination of a bright green and a fairly dim red, which is seen as a tint of yellow. (Color synthesis will be discussed in Chapter 16.)

Some raster displays have a **color lookup table**, or **LUT**, that defines a working set of colors. The LUT, which consists of some memory and electronics within the display, is loaded by the application and is therefore under the programmer's control. An index identifies each color in the table and specifies the amount of red, green, and blue that it contains. To draw in a particular color, the application stores the index of the desired color, rather than the color value itself, in each relevant pixel location in the frame buffer.

Table 2.1 shows an example for the case of 3 bits/pixel, providing ($2^3 = 8$) possible index values. Each color in the table is represented by six bits, two each for the red, green, and blue guns. For the example values shown in the table, if a

Table 2.1 A Typical Color Table

Index	Red	Green	Blue	Result
0	00	00	00	black
1	10	00	00	medium red
2	11	00	10	reddish purple
3	11	00	11	bright magenta
4	00	10	00	medium green
5	00	11	00	bright green
6	10	10	10	gray
7	11	11	11	white

pixel contains value 2, the values sent to the D/A converters will be 11 (bright) for the red gun, 00 (off) for the green, and 10 (brighter) for the blue. The color displayed will therefore be a mix of red and blue.

The number of bits/pixel determines how many different table indices there can be: For b bits/pixel, the table is 2^b long. Many raster terminals support 8 bits/pixel and therefore have LUTs with 256 entries. With a single loading of the LUT by the application, the device can display 256 different colors simultaneously. On the other hand, the **palette** of a terminal is the total number of different colors it can display. This is fixed by the number of bits sent to the D/A converters. In the example, 6 bits feed the D/A converters, and so $2^6 = 64$ colors can be displayed. The LUTs of some terminals can send 8 bits to each gun, so that 24 bits define each color. Such a terminal has a palette of $2^{24} = 16$ million colors, even though only a small number—say 256—can be displayed simultaneously. Some applications of lookup tables are discussed in Chapter 13.

Drill Exercises

2.2. The Size of a LUT. Consider a frame buffer having 4 bits/pixel, and suppose that each of the three DACs is driven by 5 bits. How many entries are there in the LUT? How many bits are there in all in the entire LUT? How many colors can be displayed at one time, and how many colors are in the palette?

2.3. Loading a LUT. Consider a 3 bits/pixel frame buffer and a LUT that drives each DAC with 5 bits. Show the contents of the LUT so that as the pixel value grows from 000 to 111, eight shades of pure red are displayed, from the darkest possible red to the brightest. Make the intensity of each red shade approximately proportional to the value in the pixel.

Hard-Copy Raster Devices

Various hard-copy devices are based on a raster concept. Each draws pictures by transferring frame buffer information dot by dot to the display medium.

- *Film recorders.* In a **film recorder** the "screen" is a strip of photographic film, and the electron beam exposes the film as it sweeps over it in a raster pattern. Sometimes film recorders are separate devices with their own frame buffers, as shown in Figure 2.9, and sometimes they are simply cameras mounted directly on a CRT display. The film can be advanced automatically by the computer once an image has been exposed. This is called a *new frame action.* Film recorders are frequently used to make high-quality 35-mm slides, especially for business applications.

Figure 2.9.
A film recorder. (Courtesy of Lasergraphics, Inc.)

● *Laser printer.* **Laser printers** also can scan out raster patterns from an internal frame buffer, rapidly sweeping a laser beam over an internal drawing surface. At certain spots over which the laser beam is swept, the surface becomes electrically charged, causing "toner" powder to adhere to the spots. The toner is then transferred to the paper to create the picture. Laser printers offer much higher resolution than do matrix printers, capitalizing on the great precision with which a laser beam can be positioned.

● *Ink-jet plotter.* **Ink-jet plotters** produce hard-copy raster images in color. A tiny nozzle sweeps over the paper and squirts the proper ink at each "pixel position." Figure 2.10 shows a colored plot made by using a high-resolution ink-jet plotter.

Figure 2.10.
Example of a plot from an ink-jet plotter. (Courtesy of Ann Marie LeBlanc.)

2.2.3 Controlling the Frame Buffer

The frame buffer represents a large amount of memory: If the image is $r \times c$ (r rows by c columns) and there are b bits/pixel, the memory required will be $r \times c \times b$ bits. A high-quality raster display can have $r = 1024$, $c = 1024$, and $b = 24$, requiring some 25 million bits (or three megabytes) of storage! The question arises: Where does this memory reside, and how is it accessed?

In some raster display systems, the frame buffer is actually part of the computer's memory. These are called **bit-mapped** (or **memory-mapped**) devices: The processor can directly access individual pixels by reads and writes to addresses in its own memory space. A separate logic circuit accesses these same locations to refresh the display. To build an image the application writes the desired color values directly into the appropriate memory locations, so at the lowest software level the control of the display consists of one of the processor's own instructions, such as *load A,B,* that loads the value A into memory location B.

For convenience, however, it is desirable to create a routine, *SetPixel* (*row, col, A*), that computes the memory address for the pixel at *(row, col)* and loads pixel value A into that address.

A routine to draw a line between two given endpoints is more complicated, as it must set many pixels to the desired color. As suggested in Figure 2.11, the routine has to compute which pixels to turn on between the two designated endpoints so that the path of pixels will be the best approximation of the ideal line segment that joins the endpoints. The following example routine *DD_Line( )* accomplishes this. It works directly in device coordinates—rows and columns in the frame buffer—to determine which pixels lie closest to the ideal line. At each column it uses a "rounding" operation to find the row value closest to the ideal line.

Figure 2.11.
Drawing a line on a raster display.

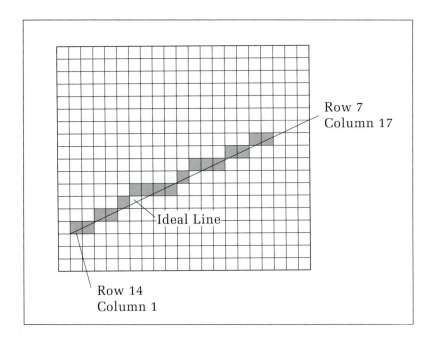

Code Fragment 2.1. Drawing a Line on a Raster Display

procedure *DD_Line(row1, col1, row2, col2, color : integer)*;
{Draw a line from (*col1, row1*) to (*col2, row2*) in the given color}

{Special case: assumes the line has slope between −1 and +1, and that *col1* <= *col2*}

```
var
    dy, dx, y, m : real;
    x : integer;
begin
    dx := col2 − col1;
    dy := row2 − row1;
    m := dy / dx;
    y := row1;
    for x := col1 to col2 do
        begin
            SetPixel(x, Round(y), color);
            y := y + m
        end
end;
```

See the exercises for further ideas about this routine. It is not very efficient because it uses *real* numbers inside the inner loop. We offer in Chapter 13 a much more efficient algorithm to draw a line, which uses only integer variables and performs only additions within its inner loop.

Notice in Figure 2.11 that even the best fit to a straight line has abrupt jumps in it, owing to the discrete nature of the pixels themselves. This **jaggedness** is an inherent property of raster displays, and the phenomenon is known fondly as the **jaggies.** In Chapter 13 we shall describe techniques to soften the visual effect of the jaggies.

Many raster displays are **satellite** (meaning dependent or subservient) displays, in which the frame buffer and video monitor are housed in a box separate from the host computer, and they communicate over a data link. In these cases the application running on the host cannot directly change pixel values in the frame buffer memory, and so it must send other kinds of commands to the display. The display contains its own microprocessor, read-only memory (ROM), and frame buffer memory. The ROM contains many utility routines for controlling the display, including some version of *DD_Line( )*, circle-drawing routines, and the like. Scratch-pad memory associated with the microprocessor can keep track of such things as a current position or a current drawing color. The application program sends commands to the device in a "device language," perhaps in the form of character strings or strings of binary words. The microprocessor acts as an **interpreter** and executes the low-level operations, making the appropriate changes in the frame buffer and hence in the displayed picture.

For instance, some basic commands that the Raster Technologies Model 1/25 terminal interprets include

- **DRWABS x, y**—Draw a line from the current position to *(x,y)*.

- **MOVABS x, y**—Move current position to *(x,y)*.

- **CLEAR**—Fill the screen with the current pixel value.

- **CIRCXY rad**—Draw a circle of radius *rad* about current position.

As another example, a variety of raster devices respond to ReGIS, the Remote Graphics Instruction Set, first developed by Digital Equipment Corporation. When in graphics mode, a ReGIS device responds to character strings such as

$P[230,45]V[280,80]P[100,50]T$'Hello world'

$P[230, 45]$ positions the current position at (230, 45) in device coordinates, and $V[280, 80]$ draws a line (a vector) from the current position to (280, 80) and then updates the current position to this new value. The rest of the string above then writes the text "Hello world" starting at (100, 50). In an application, program routines construct strings such as this and send them to the device, which interprets them and displays the desired graphics. More details on ReGIS may be found in Appendix 1.

If the communications line between the host and the satellite raster display device is slow, the user will want the language sent to the display interpreter to be concise, in order to permit the most rapid communication of instructions possible. An instruction such as DRWABS x, y, for example, requires the transmission of at least 10 characters—more if the values of *x* and *y* require several decimal digits. If the communications line supports transmission at only 120 characters per second, this instruction will take a long time to be received.

2.3   Developing Device Drivers

We encountered a variety of "device commands" while examining different types of devices. For a line-drawing device such as a plotter we might have routines like *Pen_Up*, *Pen_Down*, and *Go_To(x, y)*. For a raster device we might have *SetPixel*, *DD_Line*, or such routines as DRWABS and *P* [..]. In all cases, device coordinates must be sent to the device in question, and each device has its own built-in coordinate system.

This great variety of device commands and coordinate systems causes two difficulties. First, it is hard to discuss fundamental ideas and methods without getting mired in device details. Second, it is difficult to alter an application written for one device so that it can drive a different device. We thus need to "hide" the details of each device inside "driver" routines that offer a uniform interface to applications. Specifically, we need a procedure such as *Draw_Line(x1, y1, x2, y2 : real)*; that draws a line from point *(x1, y1)* to point *(x2, y2)*. A different version of *Draw_Line( )* is written for each device—the code inside *Draw_Line( )* is device specific and refers to the device's coordinate system—but the application does all of its drawing by making calls to *Draw_Line( )* and so views this as a **device-independent** routine. Applications can therefore be written without regard to the specific graphics device doing the drawing. When it is time to run the application on a particular device, the appropriate version of *Draw_Line( )* is inserted, and the program is compiled and run.

Normalized Device Coordinates

What coordinate system is suitable for this device-independent line drawer? The endpoints (*x1, y1*) and (*x2, y2*) are given in terms of real (floating-point) numbers for convenience, but they must be restricted in range to make sure the line "fits" onto the display surface of each device being used. A square region in (*x, y*) space is chosen as a uniform space in which to work. GKS defines **normalized device coordinates**, or **NDC**, space, as the square region with the lower left corner (0, 0) and the upper right corner (1, 1), as shown in Figure 2.12. Thus for every point (*x, y*) in NDC, both *x* and *y* lie between 0 and 1. NDC space serves as the standard working coordinate system for all devices, and *Draw_Line*( ) or its equivalent automatically expands this space as much as possible to fit onto the display surface, no matter how large. Using floating-point numbers for *x* and *y* affords ample precision to specify complicated pictures.

To help keep in mind the space being used, we shall abandon *Draw_Line*( ) and adopt the suggestive name *lineNDC_*( ), defined as

procedure *LineNDC_*(*x1, y1, x2, y2 : real*);
{Draw a line from (*x1, y1*) to (*x2, y2*) in NDC.
Use a different version for each device.
All versions look like this to application}

Figure 2.12 shows that *LineNDC_*( ) takes the coordinate values lying in NDC and draws the corresponding line on the target graphics display. But where on the display should the line be placed? A simple convention for now is that *LineNDC_*( ) "maps" the unit square of NDC onto the largest square region on the device, appropriately centered. Figures drawn inside the NDC square therefore appear within a square on the display surface, in a different size but with no distortion.

A handy example of the use of *LineNDC_*( ) is *Box*( ), which draws a rectangle having opposite corners at (*x1, y1*) and (*x2, y2*). The box has horizontal or vertical sides. *Box*( ) simply joins together the corners of the box with four calls to *LineNDC_*( ).

Code Fragment 2.2. Building a Box Drawer Using LineNDC_( )

procedure *Box*(*x1, y1, x2, y2 : real*);
{draw the box with one corner at (*x1, y1*),
and opposite corner at (*x2, y2*).}

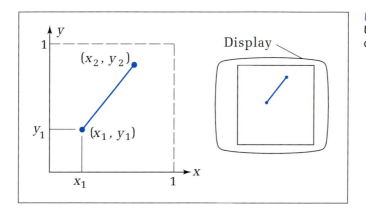

Figure 2.12.
Using normalized device coordinates—NDC.

begin
  LineNDC_(x1, y1, x2, y1);
  LineNDC_(x2, y1, x2, y2);
  LineNDC_(x2, y2, x1, y2);
  LineNDC_(x1, y2, x1, y1)
end; *{Box}*

Mapping NDC onto the Device

Each incarnation of *LineNDC_( )* must map the unit square of NDC to the largest square on the device's surface, which we call the **device square.** That is, given any point $P = (x, y)$ in NDC, we need to compute the corresponding device coordinates $Q = (dx, dy)$ in the device square, as suggested in Figure 2.13. The mapping should be proportional; that is, if x is, say, 40 percent of the way from the left side to the right side of NDC, then dx should also be 40 percent of the way from the left side to the right side of the largest square. Similarly, when $y = 0.1$, dy must be 10 percent of the way from the bottom to the top of the square region. Because a proportional mapping is required, dx must be linearly related to x, so that

$$dx = Ax + B \tag{2.1}$$

for constants A and B, and similarly

$$dy = Cy + D \tag{2.2}$$

for constants C and D.

Now, how are the coefficients A, B, C, and D determined? We shall first solve an example using specific values and then generalize to a mapping from any rectangle to any other. This general mapping will be handy in other contexts throughout the book.

Example of Mapping NDC onto a Device

Suppose the device has horizontal coordinates that range left to right from 0 to the value x_{max}, and vertical coordinates that range bottom to top from 0 to y_{max}.

Figure 2.13.
Mapping an NDC point to a
device point.

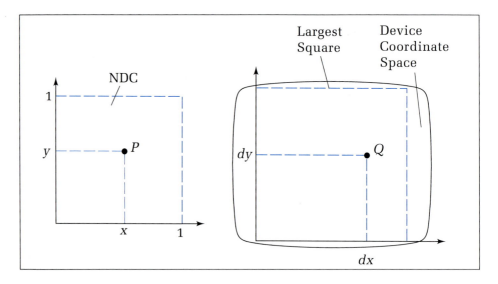

An example that uses $x_{max} = 1023$ and $y_{max} = 767$ is shown in Figure 2.14. (These are the values for a Tektronix 4662 plotter.) What is the largest square that can fit inside this space? The height y_{max} is the smaller dimension for this device and so determines the size of the square: y_{max} by y_{max}. The horizontal center of the square must lie halfway across the device space, at $x_{max}/2$. For a width of y_{max} units, the square reaches $y_{max}/2$ units to the left and $y_{max}/2$ to the right of this center. Thus when $y_{max} < x_{max}$, we find the upper left-hand and lower right-hand corners to be at

$$((x_{max} - y_{max})/2, y_{max}) \text{ and } ((x_{max} + y_{max})/2, 0) \qquad (2.3)$$

respectively. For the device of Figure 2.14, these values round off to (128, 767) and (895, 0). (Check this.)

Now find coefficients A and B in Equation 2.1. Use the fact that $x = 0$ maps to $dx = 128$ to obtain the condition $128 = B$ in Equation 2.1, and similarly obtain $895 = A + B$ from the fact that $x = 1$ maps to $dx = 895$. Combining these we get $A = 767$ and $B = 128$. The same reasoning is used to obtain $C = 767$ and $D = 0$. Therefore NDC point (x, y) maps to

$$dx = 767x + 128$$
$$dy = 767y \qquad (2.4)$$

This checks at each of the corners: For instance, it properly yields $(dx, dy) = (128, 767)$ at $(x, y) = (0, 1)$. It also checks at the center of NDC: $(x, y) = (0.5, 0.5)$ implies $(dx, dy) = (511.5, 383.5)$.

Drill Exercise

2.4.   The Coefficients in Terms of x_{max} and y_{max}. Assuming the corners of the target square are as given in Equation 2.3, show that the mapping equations are

$$dx = y_{max}x + \frac{x_{max} - y_{max}}{2} \qquad (2.5)$$

$$dy = y_{max}y \qquad (2.6)$$

Check that the center of NDC maps to the center of the screen.

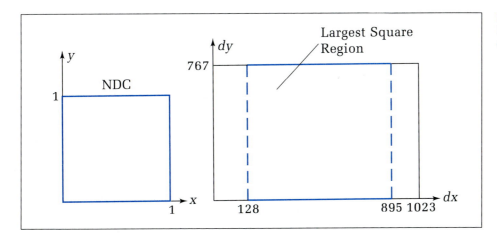

Figure 2.14.
Mapping NDC to an example device.

With this information we can implement a version of *LineNDC_( )* for this common device situation:

- y increases (bottom to top) from 0 to y_{max}

- x increases (left to right) from 0 to x_{max}

- $y_{max} < x_{max}$

The routine is shown in the following code fragment. The first five lines perform the mapping from the NDC to the device coordinates, using device-dependent values for the constants *Maxx* and *Maxy* (which stand for x_{max} and y_{max}, respectively). The drawing uses the low-level routines *Go_To( )* and so on, which are assumed to be available. (Details of these are given in Appendix 1.)

Code Fragment 2.3. Using the Mapping in LineNDC_( )

```
procedure LineNDC_(x1, y1, x2, y2 : real);
{map to largest square. Assume Maxy < Maxx.}
const Maxx = 1023;
       Maxy = 767;
var dx1, dy1, dx2, dy2 : integer;
                offset : real;
begin
   offset := (Maxx − Maxy) / 2.0;
   dx1 := round(Maxy * x1 + offset); {do the mapping to}
   dy1 := round(Maxy * y1);          {the largest square}
   dx2 := round(Maxy * x2 + offset);
   dy2 := round(Maxy * y2);
   Pen_Up;
   Go_To(dx1, dy1);
   Pen_Down;
   Go_To(dx2, dy2)
end;
```

For most devices the general form of *LineNDC_( )* looks much the same. There is a mapping part that converts NDC points to device points, followed by a command part that sends properly encoded instructions and versions of the coordinates to the actual device. Appendix 1 demonstrates several device drivers of this form.

Notice that an application can use this driver routine in a totally device-independent manner. It need know nothing about the geometry of the display surface: All device idiosyncrasies are hidden within the routine itself. The application can be ported to another device simply by substituting a different version of *LineNDC_( )* that also maps to the largest square. Nobody needs to scrutinize the application code and make changes in it.

Using the Entire Display Area

When a driver restricts its drawing to the largest square on the display surface, total device independence is achieved, but precious drawing area can be wasted, as most display surfaces are rectangular rather than square: Some are short and wide, and others are tall and narrow.

The shape of a rectangle is summarized by its **aspect ratio**, the ratio of its height to its width:

$$R = \text{aspect ratio (of a rectangle)} = \frac{\text{height}}{\text{width}} \tag{2.7}$$

For instance, a television screen has an aspect ratio of about $R = 0.75$, and a standard 8½-by-11-inch piece of paper has an aspect ratio of 1.29. Because we often encounter devices with aspect ratios this different from 1, we surely don't want the device driver to waste the area outside the largest square.

Drill Exercise

2.5. How Much Is Wasted? For a rectangle of aspect ratio .75, what fraction of its total area lies outside the largest square that can be drawn in it? Generalize to an arbitrary aspect ratio, R.

To overcome this limitation we may choose to alter $LineNDC\_(\ )$ so that it can draw anywhere on the display surface. Figure 2.15 shows how this can be done for a device having an aspect ratio of less than 1. The basic idea is to restrict the use of NDC to a rectangle, R_{NDC}, having the same aspect ratio R as the device does. The biggest such rectangle extends from 0 to 1 in x, and from 0 to R in y. We can now map all of R_{NDC} to the entire display surface rectangle R_{dev}. Any point within R_{NDC} that is passed to the new $LineNDC\_(\ )$ is drawn in R_{dev}, and any point within R_{dev} can be drawn.

The new mapping also uses these principles. We seek the same relations as in Equation 2.5, but they are even simpler here: $x = 0$ now maps to $dx = 0$, and $x = 1$ to $dx = x_{max}$. Similarly, $y = 0$ maps to $dy = 0$, and $y = R$ to $dy = y_{max}$. (Recall that $R = y_{max}/x_{max}$.) So we obtain

$$dx = x_{max}x \tag{2.8}$$

$$dy = x_{max}y \tag{2.9}$$

(Check this. Specifically, what is dy when $y = R$?)

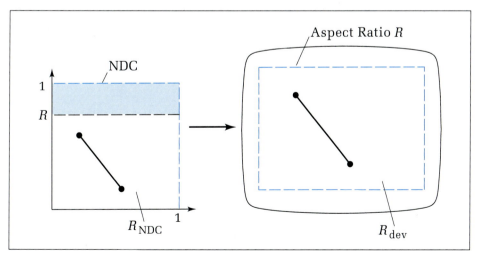

Figure 2.15.
Extending the drawing area on the display.

Drill Exercises

2.6.   Adjusting a Device Driver Rewrite Code Fragment 2.3 so that it can draw on the entire Tektronix plotter surface.

2.7.   And for Devices with $R > 1$ ... When a device has an aspect ratio larger than 1, we restrict drawing in NDC to a rectangle with a lower left corner (0, 0) and an upper right corner ($1/R$, 1). In this case, derive the appropriate mappings that correspond to Equation 2.8 and Equation 2.9. Write code for *LineNDC_( )* for a device whose coordinates range in x from 0 to 600 and in y from 0 to 900.

Notice that some measure of device independence has been lost with this refinement. Now the application must be aware of the device's aspect ratio and restrict its drawing in NDC accordingly! But most programmers feel this is a small price to pay for access to the entire drawing area of each device.

Alternatively, some devices can be interrogated at run time for their values of x_{max} and y_{max}. The application can use these to compute R and pass this information to *LineNDC_( )*, thereby "fine-tuning" it on the fly to the device at hand.

Drill Exercise

2.8.   Run-Time Tuning of *LineNDC_( )* Adjust *LineNDC_( )* so that it can use values of *Maxx*, *Maxy*, and R from the application and adjust its mapping so that the proper portion of NDC is mapped to the entire display surface. It should be able to accommodate both of the cases $R < 1$ and $R > 1$.

The Data Type *point*

Often the programmer wants to bind together the x- and y-coordinate values of each point in a data structure, so that the points are viewed as single entities rather than as two separate values. In Pascal this is easily done using records:

Code Fragment 2.4. Defining the Data Type point

```
type   point = record
                 x, y : real
               end;
```

It is convenient to have a version of *LineNDC_( )* that takes endpoints in this form. To distinguish it we use the slightly different name *LineNDC( )*:

```
procedure LineNDC(p1, p2 : point);
{Draw a line from p1 to p2}
```

Both ways to specify points are convenient and are used in various routines throughout the book. The notational distinction between *LineNDC( )* and *LineNDC( )* is not rigidly adhered to—the version being used should be clear from the context.

Drill Exercise

2.9.   Alternative Form for *LineNDC_( )* Rewrite Code Fragment 2.3 as *LineNDC( )* in the form that accepts two variables of type *point*.

2.4 Graphics Output Primitives and Attributes

Several kinds of complex pictures can be drawn on graphics displays, but programmers think in terms of building up a given picture out of more elementary graphic objects, called **primitives**. An output graphics primitive is a picture element that is directly supported by a graphics package or even by the display hardware. In this section we describe the primitives that are included as part of the GKS standard. We also describe the primitive's **attributes**, or the characteristics that affect how it appears. Typical attributes of a line, for instance, are its

- color
- line width
- line type: dashed, dotted, or solid

For each primitive type we describe the most important associated attributes as specified by the GKS standard.

2.4.1 The GKS Output Primitives

GKS provides six **output primitives** and offers the means to draw them:

- polyline
- polymarker
- text
- fill area
- cell array
- generalized drawing primitive

Polyline

A **polyline** is a connected sequence of straight lines. The sequence of lines need not form a closed figure, and individual lines may cross one another. The point at which two lines meet is a **vertex** of the polyline. The data required to specify a polyline are a list of **vertices**, each given by a coordinate pair:

$$(x_1, y_1,), (x_2, y_2), ..., (x_n, y_n)$$

For example, the polyline shown in Figure 2.16 is described by nine vertices beginning with (0.4, 0.2), (0.4, 0.3), (0.5, 0.3), (0.5, 0.6), . . . (What are the remaining vertices in the polyline?)

Drill Exercise

2.10. Adding to the Polyline. Add more vertices to the polyline in Figure 2.16 to draw a door inside the house, resting on its base.

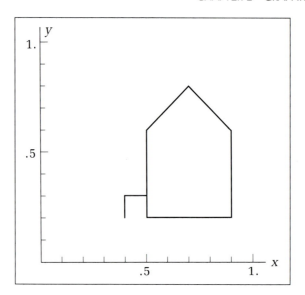

Figure 2.16.
An example polyline.

Figure 2.17 shows several examples of pictures constructed from polylines. (How many different polylines does the face contain?)

A polyline is naturally captured as a list of vertices. We call the data type that describes a polyline a **polypoint**, to stress that it is a list of points; the term *polyline* denotes the corresponding graphics primitive. Following good programming practices, we include in the data structure a count of the number of elements used in the array. The *polypoint* type is therefore defined as

Code Fragment 2.5. Defining the Data Type polypoint

polypoint = **record**
                    num: *0..MaxVert*; {number of points}
                    pt: **array** [*1..MaxVert*] **of** *point*
      end;

The constant *MaxVert* is an agreed-upon largest size for a polyline. It should be declared at the beginning of an application, as in **const** *MaxVert* = 100.

Suppose *poly* is a variable of type *polypoint*. Then *poly.num* = 0 indicates an empty polyline. If *poly.num* = 1 the polyline consists of a single point. The

Figure 2.17.
Several examples of polylines.

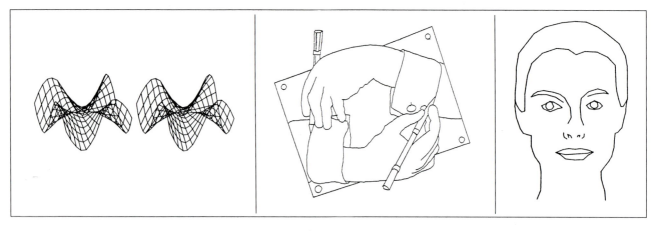

first line segment of *poly* begins at *poly.pt*[1] and ends at *poly.pt*[2]. Thus *poly* contains (*poly.num* − 1) line segments. When *poly.num* = 2, the polyline consists of a single line segment.

GKS provides a polyline-drawing routine, but when a GKS-type package is not available, it is easy to include one's own *polyline* in an application. Such a routine can be implemented in several ways, depending on the basic line-drawing routine at hand. For example, the version based on *LineNDC(p1, p2 : point)* draws a line between each successive pair of points in the polyline.

Code Fragment 2.6. Drawing a Polyline Using LineNDC

```
procedure PolylineNDC(poly : polypoint);
  {draw polyline poly}
var i: integer;
begin
  with poly do if num > 1 then
    for i := 1 to (num − 1) do LineNDC(pt [i], pt [i + 1])
end;
```

This version will draw nothing unless there is at least one line segment. It can be extended to draw a single point when *poly.num* = 1 simply by executing *LineNDC(pt*[1], *pt*[1]).

The principal attributes for a polyline as specified by GKS are

- *Color.* GKS specifies that all lines within a given polyline be given the same color. If you want some of the lines to have different colors, you must put them into separate polylines. GKS provides a function, *Set_Polyline_Color_Index*( ), to establish the color of the line segments (see Enderle et al. 1984). When you are not using GKS, you may add a *color* parameter to *LineNDC*( ) that establishes the desired color of the line segments.

- *Line type.* Lines may be drawn in patterns such as solid, dashed, dotted, or dot-dashed. Most graphics packages offer a set of predefined line types that can be referenced, and they also frequently offer a mechanism for defining one's own line types, perhaps by loading a pattern such as 1111110011111100 into a variable. The stream of ones and zeros forms a "template" of the line type, in this case long dashes separated by short spaces. This approach is discussed further in Chapter 13.

- *Line width.* You may want to make some lines thicker than others, for emphasis. The line width attribute allows this. To make a line three times the normal thickness, for instance, software often simply draws each line segment three times, offsetting the three versions by the thickness of one line. All lines within a single polyline have the same line width.

Polymarker

The **polymarker** primitive places **markers** of the same size and shape at a sequence of desired positions. Figure 2.18 shows some examples of polymarkers. The markers usually have simple shapes such as . + * × 0, but some devices can draw fancy markers such as ♣, △, or electronic symbols. Sometimes an

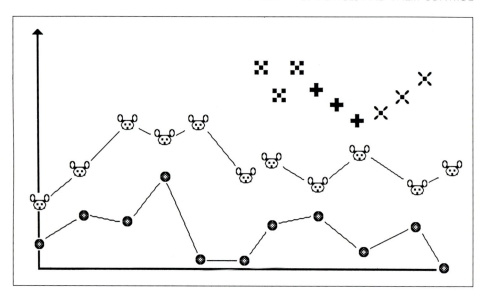

Figure 2.18.
Several examples of
polymarkers.

implementation of *Polymarker* uses the built-in character set of the device, so that *Polymarker* simply "types" the character +, 0, or × at the desired spots. The marker *type* is one of the attributes of a polymarker and is specified before polymarker drawing is done. One can use a list of the same type, *polypoint*, as for a polyline to specify the points at which the markers are to be placed. Hence an appropriate interface to *Polymarker* is **procedure** *Polymarker*(*places* : *polypoint*).

In addition to the polymarket type the polymarker attributes are color and marker size. Markers in a polymarker can be made larger or smaller than their default size by setting the marker size to a number other than one. Display devices that must use the built-in characters to draw markers ignore this attribute.

Text

Most graphics terminals have both a **text mode** and a **graphics mode**. In the text mode they display text using a built-in character generator. The character generator is capable of drawing alphabetic, numeric, and punctuation characters, and some terminals can also draw some special symbols such as π, ♠, ♣, and ©. Usually these characters cannot be placed arbitrarily on the display but must be placed in some row and column of a built-in grid.

If you want to display higher-quality text or want more flexibility in choosing the size and position of your characters, you must use a graphics terminal in conjunction with the appropriate software. The graphic presentation of high-quality text is a complex subject, in which only faintly perceptible differences in detail can spell the difference between pleasing and ugly text. Indeed, we see so much printed material in our daily lives that we subliminally expect characters to be displayed with certain shapes, spacings, and subtle balances. Figure 2.19 shows some examples of text drawn graphically. Also see Figure 1.11.

Many commercial graphics software packages can produce high-quality text, whose appearance is controlled by specifying a large number of attributes. In GKS a string of text *String* such as '*Population of the U.S.A.*' is drawn starting

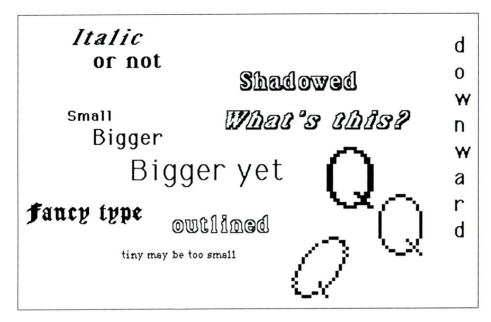

Figure 2.19.
Examples of graphical text.

at some point (x, y) using a routine like *Text(x, y, String)*. The real art of producing visually pleasing text lies in choosing the proper attributes.

There are many text attributes, the most important of which are

- *Color.* The color of a title or a label greatly affects the impact of the associated text. Colors are thus chosen carefully when designing slides for presentation graphics, in order to exploit the subtle message embodied in a color or in combinations of colors.

- *Font.* A font is a specific style and size of characters and special symbols; Figure 2.20 shows various character styles. The shape of each character can be defined by a polyline, as shown in Figure 2.21, or by a pixel pattern, as shown in Figure 2.22. Graphics packages come with a set of

Figure 2.20.
Some examples of fonts.

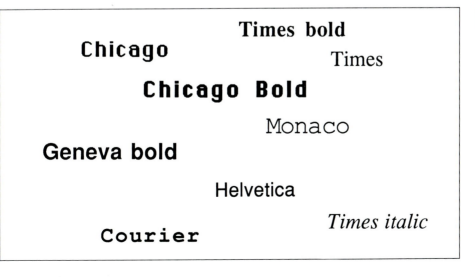

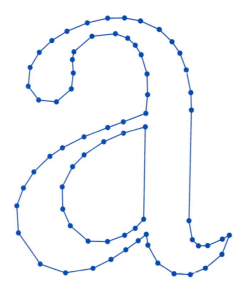

Figure 2.21.
Character shape defined by a polyline.

predefined fonts, and additional fonts can be purchased from companies that specialize in designing and digitizing them.

● *Character size.* Both the height and the width of each character usually can be varied. That is, characters can be made "fat" or "thin" in various sizes for purposes of emphasis and to convey a sense of the word involved. For characters defined as polylines, height and width can be precisely adjusted (as discussed in Chapter 11), whereas adjustments for those defined by pixel patterns are more limited (as discussed in Chapter 13).

Figure 2.22.
Character shape defined by a pixel pattern.

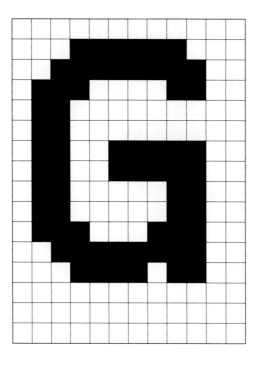

- *Character spacing.* Individual characters can be spread apart or packed closely together by varying the character-spacing attribute, as suggested in Figure 2.23.

- *Text justification.* Text can be fit into particular areas so that the first and/or last characters line up in some fashion. The standard choice is "left-justified" text, but one can also choose "centered" or "right-justified" text:

These lines of text
are centered
on the page,

whereas these
are right-justified, all
pushed up against
the right side of the page.

- *Text path.* A sequence of characters can be displayed using the four different paths: right, down, up, and left, as shown in Figure 2.24. Notice that the characters themselves are not reversed, that just the relative placement of successive characters in a string is changed. The down path is often used to label the y-axis in a graph, and the up and left versions are used mainly for special visual effects.

- *Tilted characters and strings*: Characters may also be drawn tilted along some direction, as shown in Figure 2.25. Tilted strings like this are often used to annotate parts of a graph

Figure 2.23.
Different character spacings.

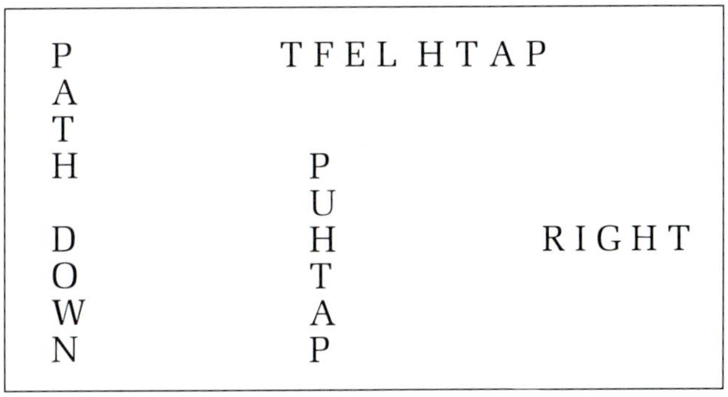

Figure 2.24
Different text paths.

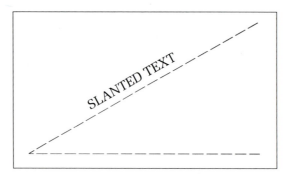

Figure 2.25.
Tilting strings of characters.

This hardly exhausts the attributes associated with text, but it suggests the complexity that confronts the designer and application programmer in producing text. We often design charts and slides iteratively. On the first few passes, we compose the general layout of the graphics and text, using default fonts, sizes, and spacings. Then in subsequent passes we fine-tune the text attributes until we achieve the desired picture.

Fill Area

The **fill-area** primitive is used to draw an area filled with some color or pattern. Figure 2.26 shows several examples. The area is described by a set of vertices.

$$(x_1, y_1,), (x_2, y_2), \ldots, (x_n, y_n)$$

just as a polyline is. The area is defined by connecting the points in sequence with straight lines, with the last point, (x_n, y_n), also connected to the first point, (x_1, y_1). Doing this defines a **polygon**, which figures prominently in graphics. For a fill-area primitive, the enclosed area is filled with the desired pattern. The actual boundary defined by the lines may or may not be drawn.

GKS provides various ways to specify the pattern to be used to fill the polygon. Algorithms to fill a polygonal region, with either a solid color or a pattern, are described in Chapter 13.

Figure 2.26.
Examples of the fill-area
primitive.

Cell Array

The **cell array** is drawn as a rectangular array of rectangular blocks, such as those shown in Figure 2.27. Each rectangle is filled with a color by passing to the *Cell Array*( ) routine an array of color indices. The size of the rectangle, as well as the number of rows and columns, can be controlled by the application. If the correct size and dimensions of the cell array are chosen, each rectangle will correspond to a single pixel in a raster display. In this way GKS can place an entire raster image on a display screen.

Generalized Drawing Primitive

Finally, the **generalized drawing primitive**, or GDP, of GKS allows specific functions to be invoked directly on a workstation. Some workstations have built-in capabilities to draw special curves such as ellipses, circular arcs, or spline curves (see Chapter 14), as suggested by Figure 2.28. The application can send commands and parameters to the suitable workstations to draw these special curves. Using built-in drawing routines in a workstation has two important benefits: It makes the drawing faster and more efficient, and it relieves the programmer from having to build the drawing routines into the application.

Drill Exercise

2.11. Functions in Your Graphics Package. If a graphics package is available at your site, examine its user's manual to determine the arguments required to draw a polyline, a polymarker, or text. Make a list of the attributes of each primitive that the application can control. Also determine what flexibility the fill-area and cell-array primitives provide and whether the package offers any GDPs. If the package does not conform to the GKS standard, discuss how its specification of these primitives and their attributes differs.

Figure 2.27.
Example of the cell array primitive.

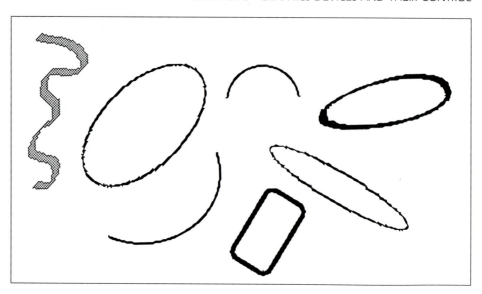

Figure 2.28.
Some examples of generalized
drawing primitives.

2.5   Graphics Input Devices

All graphics applications produce output on some display; interactive graphics applications also accept commands and data from the user. A set of graphics input devices is installed on each workstation, and the user manipulates them to send information back to the application.

There are two important ways to categorize input devices: physically and logically:

- *Physical input devices.* Input devices come in many shapes and forms, such as tablets, mice, and joysticks, and each has both advantages and disadvantages. The user tends to think of these devices physically, in terms of how they are held and controlled.

- *Logical input devices (functions).* Although two devices may be physically handled differently by the user, they may send the same type of data back to the application. Thus the application programmer tends to think of input devices logically as **input functions**, in terms of what data they generate. GKS provides a standard set of six input functions.

When an application is run on a particular graphics workstation, each input function required by the application must be performed by an installed device, and the logical input functions and physical input devices are appropriately associated by the graphics package and various device drivers.

2.5.1 Types of Logical Input Functions

GKS defines six types of **logical input functions:**

- String
- Choice

- Valuator
- Locator
- Stroke
- Pick

String

The **string** device is the most familiar, producing a **string of characters** and thus modeling the action of the usual keyboard of a computer terminal. A GKS package provides a routine such as **procedure** *Get_String*(**var** *str : string*)[3] that behaves much like *readln( )*. When invoked in an application, the program pauses until the user types in a string of characters followed by a termination character. It places the string in *str* and resumes. Later, the characters in *str* can be interrogated by the application to alter its action.

Choice

A **choice** device reports a **selection** from a number of choices. The programmer's model is that of a bank of buttons. The graphics package provides a routine such as **procedure** *Get_Choice*(**var** *button : integer*);. When this routine is invoked, the application pauses until the user presses one of a set of buttons to indicate the desired choice, and then it proceeds. Then *button* takes on the associated value and can be tested, as in the following code fragment:

Code Fragment 2.7. Using the Choice Input Function

```
Get_Choice(button);
case button of
   1: Erase_Display;
   2: Repaint_Display;
   3: SavePicture;
   4: Exit
end; {case}
```

Valuator

A **valuator** produces a **value** of type *real* between 0 and 1, which can be used to fix the length of a line, the speed of an action, or perhaps the size of a picture. The model in the programmer's mind is a knob that can be turned from 0 to 1 in smooth gradations. The graphics package provides a routine such as **procedure** *Get_Valuator*(**var** *trigger : integer*; **var** *value : real*). When invoked, the application pauses as usual. The user adjusts the knob and then *triggers* the action, perhaps by pressing a keyboard key or a special button. The selected value is than available in *value*, along with the trigger value stored in *trigger*.

Locator

A fundamental requirement in interactive graphics is for the user to *point* to a position on the display. The **locator** input device performs this function, as it

---

[3]GKS offers standard names for routines, but the GKS packages vary considerably, as vendors often choose different names. We use simple and suggestive names here.

produces a **coordinate pair**, (x, y), of type *point*. The graphics software package provides a function such as **procedure** *Get_Locator*(**var** *trigger* : *integer*; **var** *pos* : *point*). When invoked, the application pauses. The user manipulates some input device in order to position a visible spot and then triggers the choice. This places the value of the point in *pos*, and the trigger value in *trigger*.

For example, a common use of a locator in interactive graphics is to draw a line: *Get_Locator*( ) is invoked twice, once to get each endpoint of the desired line. Then *LineNDC*( ) or its equivalent is used to draw the line. Leaving details aside, this looks like

Code Fragment 2.8. Using the Locator to Draw a Line

```
Get_Locator(trig, spot1);
Get_Locator(trig, spot 2);
LineNDC(spot1, spot2);
```

We shall discuss this basic technique in more detail later.

The "mouse" shown in Figure 2.29 is a familiar device to most programmers; it is frequently used as a locator. As the user moves the mouse around, a **graphics cursor**—a small dot or cross—follows accordingly on the display. The user moves the mouse until the cursor arrives at the desired location, which is associated with a coordinate pair, say $(0.3, 0.87)$. The choice is triggered by pressing one of the buttons on the mouse. The program resumes with variable *pos* set to $(0.3, 0.87)$.

Stroke

A **stroke** device is an extension of a locator. It produces a **sequence** of several coordinate pairs: (x_1, y_1), (x_2, y_2), ..., and so is equivalent to a succession of *Locate*s. It is often used to input a polyline, as we shall describe in Chapter 6.

Figure 2.29.
A mouse used as a locator.

Pick

The **pick** input device is used to identify a portion of a picture for further processing. As we point out in Chapter 6, a GKS package allows a picture to be defined in terms of **segments**, which are groups of related output primitives and their attributes. The package provides tools to define segments and to give them identifying names. When using *Pick*, the user "points" to a part of a picture with some physical input device, and the package figures out which segment is being pointed to. *Pick*( ) returns the name of the segment to the application, enabling the user to erase, move, or otherwise separate parts of a picture.

2.5.2 Types of Physical Input Devices

Keyboard

All workstations come equipped with a keyboard, the familiar *String* input device—sending strings of characters to the application program upon request. This keyboard is also frequently used as a *Choice* device, as it consists of a set of buttonlike keys. Often a keyboard contains a special set of **cursor keys** and **function keys** that are particularly well suited to the *Choice* function.

Buttons

Sometimes a separate bank of buttons is installed on a workstation. If the bank fits nicely under the user's hand, selections can be made easily without having to look away from the display screen. A bank of buttons invariably performs the *Choice* input function.

Mouse

The **mouse** has become a popular and familiar input device, as it is easy and comfortable to operate. A typical mouse is shown in Figure 2.29. As the user slides the mouse over the desktop, the mouse sends the **changes** in its position to the workstation (or to mouse driver software), which keeps track of the mouse's position and moves the cursor on the screen accordingly. Because the mouse points to a place on the display, it is most often used to perform a *Locate* or a *Pick* function. There are usually one or more buttons on the mouse that the user can press to trigger a *Pick* or *Locate* or to make a *Choice*.

As with any device that indicates an (x, y) position, the mouse may also be used as a *Valuator* logical device. The *Valuator* value is simply one of the values x or y, with the other value ignored. For instance, the user can visualize the left side of the screen as corresponding to value 0 and the right side as corresponding to value 1, and use just the x-coordinate of the mouse to indicate the *Valuator* value.

Tablet

As shown in Figure 2.30, a **tablet** provides an area on which the user can slide and point a stylus. Whereas a mouse can report only its relative position, a tablet can detect the absolute position of its stylus. This position is detected either magnetically or acoustically by electronics within the body of the tablet, and this information is used to move a cursor on the display screen accordingly. The tablet is most often used as a *Locator*, *Stroke*, or *Pick* logical device. The tip of the stylus often contains a microswitch, and by pressing down on the stylus the user can trigger a logical action.

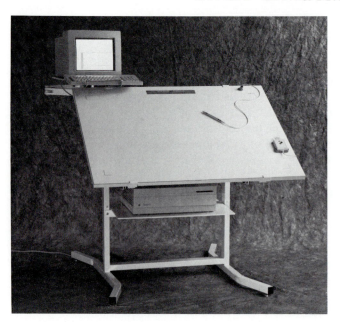

Figure 2.30.
A graphics tablet.
(Courtesy of GTCO Corp.)

The tablet is particularly handy for digitizing drawings, as the user can tape a drawing onto the tablet surface and then move the stylus along the lines of the drawing, pressing down to send each new point to the workstation. Often a menu area is printed on the tablet surface, as in Figure 1.4, and the user *Picks* a menu item by pressing down the stylus inside any one of the menu item boxes. Suitable software associates each menu item box with the function desired for the application. (This is discussed further in Chapter 6.)

Joystick and Trackball

Figure 2.31 shows two similar input devices that control the position of a cursor on the display. The **joystick** (Figure 2.31a) has a lever that can be pivoted in any direction to indicate position. The **trackball** (Figure 2.31b) has a large ball that can be rotated in any direction with the palm of the hand to alter the cursor position. For each of these devices, internal circuitry converts physical motion into electrical signals, just as in the mouse. These devices are used primarily as *Locator* and *Valuator* devices.

(a)   (b)

Figure 2.31.
Joystick and trackball.

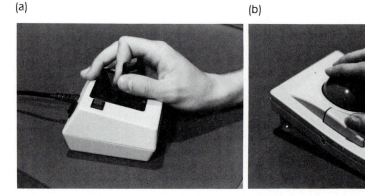

Figure 2.32.
A bank of knobs.
(Courtesy of Tektronix, Inc.)

Knobs

Figure 2.32 shows a bank of knobs that the user can turn to "dial in" a value. Each knob performs a logical *Valuator* function. Banks of knobs such as these are often part of a workstation used for the interactive design of three-dimensional objects. The user can rotate a displayed object in three dimensions by adjusting the position of three separate knobs. Also, two knobs can be used to control the *x* and *y* positions of a cursor on a display, so that the knobs together can perform the *Locator*, *Stroke*, and *Pick* functions.

Thumbwheels and Paddles

Two other popular input devices are thumbwheels and paddles. **Thumbwheels** are usually built into a workstation and are operated by rotating each wheel with the thumb. An internal potentiometer detects the rotational position of each thumbwheel and converts it into an electrical signal.

Paddles (Figure 2.33) became popular in the late 1970s through their use on the Apple II* home computer. The user rotates each paddle knob with a separate hand (or two people each take one paddle in order to compete in some computer game).

Because these devices provide two separate controls, they are actually of the *Valuator* type and may be used for that purpose. Frequently, however, they are used together and so can perform the *Locate*, *Stroke*, or *Pick* functions.

Light Pen

Another device used to *Pick* or *Locate* on refresh displays is the **light pen**. A light pen is actually a light detector. When the user points to a place on the screen and the drawing beam illuminates the phosphor there, the light pen sends an electrical pulse to the workstation. In a refresh display each line is redrawn many times a second, and so the light pen repeatedly receives a pulse as the line passes beneath it. Because the workstation generates each line based on an item in the DPU (see Section 2.2), it "knows" which line is being drawn at

*Apple II is a trademark of the Apple Computer Co.

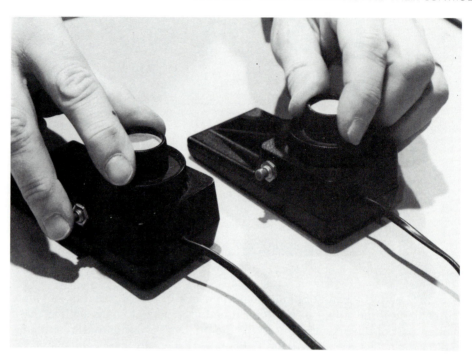

Figure 2.33.
Paddles.

each instant and therefore over which line the light pen is positioned. In this way the workstation identifies the line under the light pen. Light pens are frequently used for highly interactive applications. They require the user to look directly at the screen, and some users find it fatiguing to hold the pen for long periods.

2.6   Summary

This chapter described some of the input and output graphics devices in use today. There are two kinds of output devices: line-drawing and raster displays, both of which were discussed. For both types of displays one needs to be able to draw straight lines, and we examined the fundamental routine *LineNDC*( ). *LineNDC*( ) is part of a device driver utility package. Based on descriptions of lines in a unified coordinate system called normalized device coordinates, *LineNDC*( ) maps the lines into the coordinate system of the relevant device and then draws the line. We looked at two versions of *LineNDC*( ). The simplest and most device independent maps all of the NDC space onto the largest square region of the display surface. A more powerful version sacrifices some device dependence but can draw on the entire display surface. For this type the application requires knowing the device's aspect ratio.

The GKS graphics standard specifies six basic kinds of output primitives that should be provided by any graphics software utility package. We discussed each type of primitive, along with the attributes that affect its appearance on the display. GKS also specifies that graphical input devices be associated with one of six types of logical input devices, and we described their functions.

Programming Exercises

2.12. Pen Exchanges. Add to the repertoire of plotter commands given in Section 2.2 a command that causes the plotter to exchange one pen for another, in order to change its drawing color. What arguments does this command require? What would the programmer expect the pen's position to be immediately after the command is completed?

2.13. Driver for the IBM Hi-Res Screen. Rewrite the procedure *LineNDC*( ) of Section 2.3 for an IBM-PC display with the following device coordinates:

- Upper left-hand corner of display is at (0, 0).

- Lower right-hand corner of display is at (639, 349).

Assume for this procedure that the driver routine *DD_Line*(a, b, c, d) is available that draws a line between device coordinate points (a, b) and (c, d).

2.14. *DD_Line*( ). Describe how the *DD_Line*( ) routine in Code Fragment 2.1 works. Extend it to the case in which the line can have any slope and *row*1 can equal *row*2.

CHAPTER 3

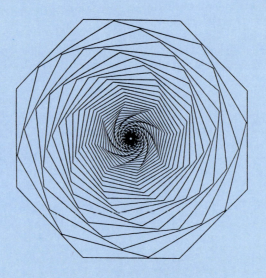

Getting Started
Making Pictures

A picture shows me at a glance what it takes dozens of pages of a book to expound.

Ivan S. Turgenev, *Fathers and Sons*, 1862

Goals of the Chapter

- To introduce the concepts of windows, viewports, and clipping.
- To develop a complete line-clipping tool.
- To develop the generic *Line*( ) that uses *LineNDC*( ) and forms the basis for all subsequent line drawing.
- To introduce the notion of the current position and to build various graphics routines around it.
- To develop tools for relative drawing and turtlegraphics.
- To describe how to draw simple line plots and bar charts.
- To introduce various forms of polygons and to build routines to draw them.

3.1   Introduction

In this chapter we build a bag of software tools for line drawings based on the single device-independent routine *LineNDC*( ) of Chapter 2. It is gratifying to discover how far one can go using just this tool.

To proceed effectively the reader must have a working device driver for at least one display device. The driver needs to have only modest functions.

- *LineNDC_(x1, y1, x2, y2 : real)*. This is the crucial routine, as it draws a line. It is also convenient to have at hand the slight variation *LineNDC(p1, p2 : point)* with parameters of type *point*.[1]

- *StartGraphics*. This routine initializes the display and sets it into a graphics-drawing mode. For many devices it also erases anything appearing on the screen. If it does not, *ClearScreen*, an additional routine, is useful.

- *ExitGraphics*. This routine returns the display to a text mode, so that it can be used for further program development.

These routines might be embedded in the Pascal language designed for a particular graphics device, or they might exist in a graphics package. They usually have slightly different names and may take parameters in somewhat different forms. Such cosmetic adjustments are left to the reader. If no utilities are available, the reader must construct them for a device that is available, using for a guide the examples in Appendix 1 and the manual for the device.

3.2   Simple Line Drawing

Line drawings of some complexity can be constructed using *LineNDC_*( ). We begin with elementary figures and build up powerful tools for drawing elaborate

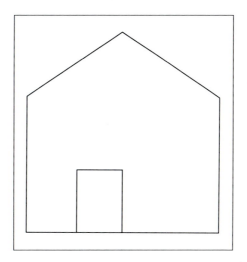

Figure 3.1.
A simple house drawing.

---

[1]A summary of all data types used in this book can be found in Appendix 3.

figures. The simple house shown in Figure 3.1 consists of eight line segments. It might be created using the procedure *House* given by

Code Fragment 3.1 Procedure to Draw a Simple House

```
procedure House;
begin
    LineNDC_(0.5, 0.7, 0.8, 0.5); (*draw outline of house*)
    LineNDC_(0.8, 0.5, 0.8, 0.1);
    LineNDC_(0.8, 0.1, 0.2, 0.1);
    LineNDC_(0.2, 0.1, 0.2, 0.5);
    LineNDC_(0.2, 0.5, 0.5, 0.7);
    LineNDC_(0.35, 0.1, 0.35, 0.3);
    LineNDC_(0.35, 0.3, 0.5, 0.3); (*draw door*)
    LineNDC_(0.5, 0.3, 0.5, 0.1)
end;
```

A complete program to carry out the drawing is very simple:

Code Fragment 3.2. Program to Carry Out the House Drawing

```
program DrawHouse;
    .
<declarations of House, LineNDC, StartGraphics, etc.>
    .
begin {DrawHouse}
    StartGraphics;
    House;
    ExitGraphics
end;
```

Alternatively the data for the house could be stored in a variable, *poly*, of type *polypoint*, as given in Code Fragment 2.5, and drawn using the routine *PolylineNDC(poly)* of Code Fragment 2.6. Notice that because *PolylineNDC(poly)* draws a line for each successive pair of points in *poly*, the points have to be properly ordered in *poly*.

Drill Exercise

3.1   Drawing the House As a Polyline. Find an ordering of the data points given in Code Fragment 3.1 to load into variable *poly*, so that *PolylineNDC(poly)* draws the house properly.

The approach of Code Fragment 3.1 has a major limitation: It can draw only one house—the data are "hard wired" into the routine. It is far better to design tools that can draw **families** of objects, which are distinguished by different parameter values. The following version takes this approach: It specifies the placement and dimensions of the house through four parameters. That is, *corner* gives the (*x,y*) location of the lower left corner of the house, and *width* and *height* fix the house's dimensions. Other dimensions are calculated within the routine, with the door one-half as tall as the house, one-fourth as wide, and so forth.

Code Fragment 3.3. More Flexible House Drawing

```
procedure House2(corner : point; W, H : real);
var
   Right, Top, Roof_Top, Door_Right, Door_Top, Door_Left : real;
begin
   with corner do
   begin
      Right := x + W;
      Top := y + H;
      Roof_Top := Top + H / 2.0; (* make size of roof = H / 2 *)
      Door_Right := x + W /2.0; (* right side of door *)
      Door_Top := y + H / 2.0; (* door ht set by H *)
      Door_Left := Door_Right − W / 4.0; (* door width is W / 4 *)
      LineNDC_(x, y, x, Top);
      LineNDC_(x, Top, Door_right, Roof_Top); {draw house outline}
      LineNDC_(Door_right, Roof_Top, Right, Top);
      LineNDC_(Right, Top, Right, y);
      LineNDC_(Right, y, x, y);
      LineNDC_(Door_Right, y, Door_Right, Door_Top); {draw door}
      LineNDC_(Door_Right, Door_Top, Door_Left, Door_Top);
      LineNDC_(Door_Left, Door_Top, Door_Left, y)
   end {with}
end; {house2}
```

Drill Exercise

3.2.   Parameters for the House. What parameter values should be passed to *House2*( ) in order to draw the house of Figure 3.1? *Answer:* Use (0.2, 0.1), 0.6, and 0.4.

The advantage of a parameterized routine such as *House2*( ) is that it can be reused many times with different data, to generate scenes such as the "village" shown in Figure 3.2. The routine provides a **template** for the basic shape of the object, and the parameters determine its specific size and position.

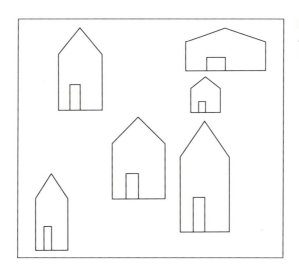

Figure 3.2.
A small "village" drawn using *House2*( ).

3.3   The World Coordinate System

LineNDC_( ) and *PolylineNDC( )* deal with coordinates specified entirely in NDC. This offers a uniform approach for developing device drivers, but it can be unnatural and confining for a programmer designing applications.

One problem is that objects are described using NDC numbers that lie between 0 and 1. But a programmer may want to draw an object that is actually 25 feet wide and 18 feet tall. **Scaling** is thus required to convert the natural dimensions of the object into the enforced dimensions of NDC. The object seems to have one set of dimensions, and the drawing another, which brings up the important distinction between modeling and viewing.

● *Modeling.* **Modeling** is the process of creating and manipulating a model of an object or a system. A model for a dynamic system, for example, might involve a set of differential equations that characterizes its behavior under various conditions.

In graphics we often use a **geometric model**, which is a description of an object that provides a numerical representation of its shape, size, and various other properties. Modeling issues arise frequently—particularly in three-dimensional graphics—in connection with describing shapes of the different bodies we wish to draw.

As an example, consider the following description of a certain thin metal bracket, one view of which is provided in Figure 3.3.

The bracket consists of a rectangle of width 6 inches and height 4 inches. It is 0.1 inches thick. There is a circular hole of radius 1 inch, centered at the center of the bracket. A rectangular piece has been cut from the upper right corner of the bracket. This hole is 1 inch wide and 2 inches high.

This description provides a (somewhat crude) geometric model of the bracket that illustrates some important features. The dimensions of the

Figure 3.3.
A geometric model of a bracket.

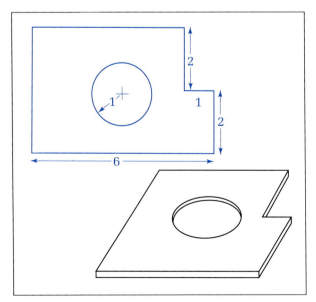

object are given in units—inches—appropriate to the object. The shape of the bracket is described in terms of primitives such as rectangles and circles. There is no particular position specified for the bracket.

● *Viewing.* **Viewing** is the process of drawing a view of a model on a display. The geometric description of the object provided by the model is converted into a set of graphics primitives, which are displayed where desired on the display surface. The same model may be used for many different views, and the choice of view determines the size and position of the primitives.

Modeling therefore describes the object under investigation and its behavior. If a model describes a physical object, it is logical to use dimensions that "fit" the object. Drawing views of the model is a separate task, leading into issues of NDC, primitives, display devices, and the like.

Modeling is most conveniently done in an unbounded **world coordinate system**, the entire two-dimensional plane, not just a square piece of it, as is used for NDC. Figure 3.4 shows a representation of world coordinates, with some convenient scale marked off. Think of it as the usual x,y-plane. Each point is specified as a pair of real numbers such as (3.12968, −634.12), of arbitrary precision. (Within a program such numbers are retained with a high but finite precision, of course, using the floating-point format available.) In the programmer's mind there may be units—feet, micrometers, kiloyards—associated with x,y-values, but these need not be specifically stated in the program code.

Three Viewing Issues

Three questions arise immediately when one wants to produce a view of a model: how much of the model should be drawn, where it should appear on the display, and how the world coordinates are converted to the viewing NDC coordinates. Consider, for instance, a detailed map of the United States, with rivers, coastlines, and state boundaries specified as lists of (longitude, latitude) pairs. The user may want to draw a detailed close-up of only one state. How can the rest of the map be eliminated? And the map may be only part of the total picture;

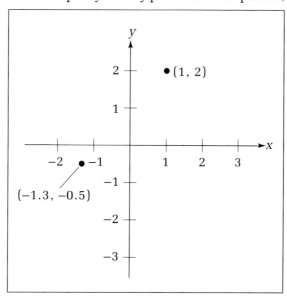

Figure 3.4.
World coordinates.

that is, the user may want to compose a picture with the map in the upper left corner and text or other objects on the right-hand side.

The programmer thus needs more flexibility and control over

- which part of the object to draw.

- where it is drawn.

- how big it is drawn.

3.3.1 Windows and Viewports

Windows and viewports provide just the degree of flexibility needed. Once the part of the program that describes the model has been constructed, the programmer can specify a view. This consists of two rectangles, a window given in world coordinates and a viewport given in NDC, as shown in Figure 3.5. The **window** defines the portion of the model that is to be drawn. The parts that lie inside the window are drawn, but the parts lying outside are **clipped** off and do not appear. A line-clipping algorithm is described next, which examines each line in the model and determines which part of it, if any, will lie within the window.

The **viewport** defines where in NDC the visible parts will be drawn. The viewport must lie within the portion of NDC that the device driver maps to the device (recall Chapter 2). Figure 3.5 shows an example in which the device has an aspect ratio, R, that is less than 1, so that the rectangle with upper right corner $(1, R)$ is available. The viewport can be positioned anywhere within this area.

The geometric elements in the window are mapped proportionally onto the viewport: They are stretched into the size and shape of the viewport and drawn there, as suggested in Figure 3.5. This mapping is similar to the earlier mapping from NDC to the device coordinates that takes place in *LineNDC*( ). We show its details next. Viewports offer control over where an object will be drawn on the display and how big it will be.

Unless stated otherwise, we will assume that windows and viewports are aligned with the coordinate axes; that is, they have horizontal and vertical sides. Windows can have any size and location in world coordinates; viewports must

Figure 3.5.
Windows and viewports.

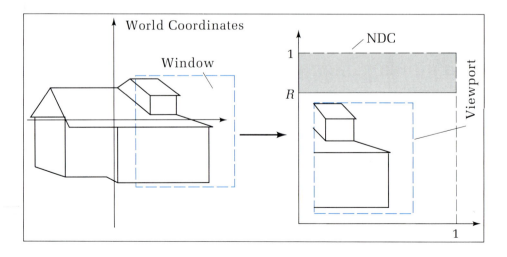

fit within the available rectangle in NDC. The window and viewport need not have the same aspect ratios, and if they are different, there will be some distortion in the picture drawn. Normally, the aspect ratios of the window and viewport are made equal, although distortion can sometimes be used to achieve a special effect.

Example 3.1. Distorting a Picture

Consider the window and viewport shown in Figure 3.6. The window extends from −1 to 3 in x and from −2 to 2 in y, so it is a square—with an aspect ratio of 1. The viewport extends from 0.5 to 0.8 in x and from 0.4 to 0.9 in y, so it has an aspect ratio of 0.5/0.3 = 1.6667. Square S_1 lies outside the window, and so it is clipped. Square S_2 lies inside, so it is drawn, but with distortion—as a rectangle. Rectangle R is partially drawn, and circle C is distorted into an ellipse and drawn.

Example 3.2. A Potpourri of Windows and Viewports

Several windows and viewports are defined and shown in Figure 3.7. Each rectangle is defined by the opposite corners' coordinates (left, top) and (right, bottom):

Region	Left	Top	Right	Bottom
window 1	−4	5	2	2
window 2	−3	4	0	2
viewport 1	.1	.9	.4	.63
viewport 2	.6	.9	.9	.63
viewport 3	.1	.6	.7	.3
viewport 4	.75	.5	.95	.1

Window 1 "sees" more of the object than does window 2. When these windows are mapped to viewports 1 and 2, the effect of the smaller window is to

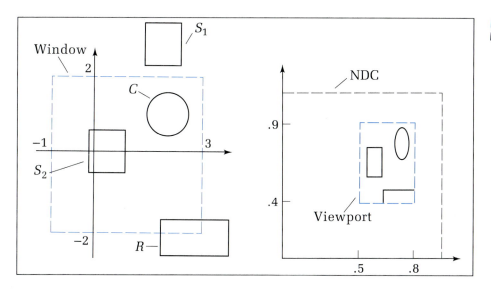

Figure 3.6.
Example window and viewport.

"zoom in" on the object, to get a closer look. Window 1 is shown mapped to the larger viewport 3 in a different part of NDC, producing a second view of the objects. Window 2 is shown mapped to viewport 4, which has a different aspect

Figure 3.7.
Two windows and four viewports.

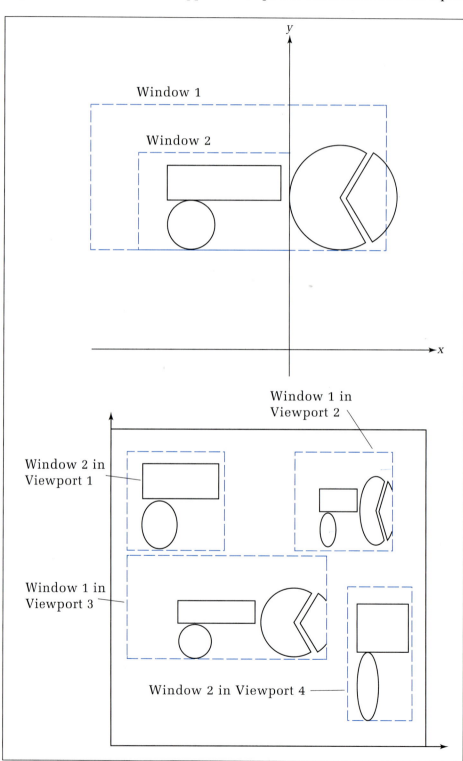

ratio, with some resulting distortion. Window 2 has a height of 2 and a width of 3, and so its aspect ratio is .666. Similarly, viewport 4 has height of .4 and width of .2, with an aspect ratio of 2.

Drill Exercise

3.3.   On Aspect Ratios. Window W has its upper left corner at (1.5, 5.6) and its lower right corner at (4.8, −1.4). Viewport V has opposite corners at (0.3, 0.95) and (0.75, 0.1). Sketch these objects on graph paper.

1.   What are the aspect ratios of W and V? (*Answer:* 2.12 and 1.889.)

2.   If a square appears in W, what will be the aspect ratio of the corresponding rectangle drawn in V? (*Answer:* 0.899.)

3.   If a line has slope 3 in W, what will be its slope when drawn in V? (*Answer:* 2.673.)

The Main Drawing Utility: Line( )

Windows and viewports are used in the main drawing tool $Line(p1, p2 : point)$, which forms the basis of all line-drawing graphics. $Line(\ )$ performs the following functions:

1.   It clips the line from $p1$ to $p2$ at the window boundaries.

2.   If any portion of this line remains inside the window, $Line(\ )$ will map the endpoints of the segment to the viewport in NDC.

3.   It uses $LineNDC(\ )$ to draw the mapped segment in NDC.

There are two fundamental operations here: clipping and mapping. The mapping is simple, and we shall discuss it first and then examine a clipping procedure. $Line(\ )$ can be used even without a clipping routine, as it works properly whenever the window is chosen to encompass the entire object.

What happens when clipping is not performed, yet some of the object lies outside the window? Corresponding parts of the image will also lie outside the viewport. There may be room on the display for these outlaw elements, in which case the picture is displayed as expected. On the other hand, some displays produce "wrap-around," as shown in Figure 3.8. Point B, for instance, is situated so far above the window that its corresponding "image" lies outside the screen space, and so segment AB wraps around and appears to emerge from the bottom of the display at C.

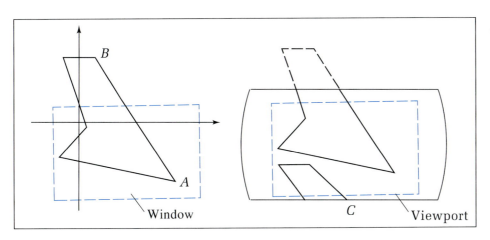

Figure 3.8.
Wrap-around when clipping is not used.

3.3.2 Mapping from a Window to a Viewport

Figure 3.9 shows a window W in world coordinates and a viewport V in NDC. We denote the left, right, top, and bottom positions of window W by W_l, W_r, W_t, and W_b respectively, and similarly for V. For a given point (x, y) within W, we must compute the corresponding point, say (dx, dy) in V. To make corresponding distances between points proportional, we use the same type of linear expressions as in Equations 2.1 and 2.2:

$$dx = s_x x + t_x$$
$$dy = s_y y + t_y \qquad (3.1)$$

in which we must determine suitable values for the coefficients s_x, s_y, t_x, and t_y. First, obtain the mapping from x to dx. When $x = W_l$ we must have $dx = V_l$, so the equation will be $V_l = s_x W_l + t_x$. Similarly, when $x = W_r$ we will want $dx = V_r$, so we obtain the condition $V_r = s_x W_r + t_x$. These two equations for the two unknowns, s_x and t_x, are easily solved. The same reasoning is used to find the two values s_y and t_y (see the exercises). The final results are

$$s_x = \frac{V_r - V_l}{W_r - W_l}$$

$$s_y = \frac{V_t - V_b}{W_t - W_b}$$

$$t_x = \frac{V_l W_r - W_l V_r}{W_r - W_l} \qquad (3.2)$$

$$t_y = \frac{V_b W_t - W_b V_t}{W_t - W_b}$$

Drill Exercises

3.4. Derive and Check the Mapping. Show the steps that solve the linear equations to produce the promised values of s_x, t_x, s_y, and t_y. Then use Equation 3.1 to prove that each of the four corners of W truly maps to the corresponding corner of V. Also show that the center of W maps to the center of V.

3.5. The Inverse Mapping. Find the mapping from the viewport to the window, that is, the inverse mapping to

that in Equation 3.1. In Chapter 6 we shall see how this inverse mapping is used to program graphical input devices.

3.6. Inverting a Picture. Show that one can also easily invert a picture—turn it upside down—by making V_b the position of the top of the desired viewport and V_t its bottom.

Figure 3.9.
Mapping a window to a viewport.

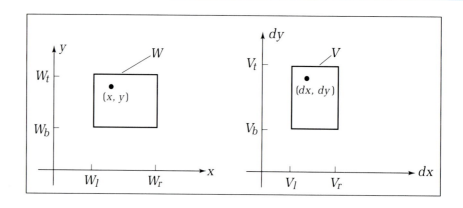

Implementing the Mapping

It is not difficult to implement this mapping in code. The convenient data type *rect* for a rectangle is defined in the following code fragment, which stores the left *l*, top *t*, right *r*, and bottom *b* values for the sides of the rectangle. The sides are assumed by convention to be horizontal and vertical. A useful routine for loading values into a variable of type *rect* is also shown:

Code Fragment 3.4. Setting Up a Rectangle

```
type rect = record
              l, t, r, b : real
            end;

procedure SetRect(left, top, right, bott : real; var r : rect);

{set boundary of rectangle}
begin
  with r do begin
    l := left; t := top; r := right; b := bott
  end
end;
```

In an application the window and viewport are declared as **var** *W, V : rect*. The user specifies values for these, or they can be computed in the application. The window is established by *SetRect(appropriate values. . , W)* and similarly for the viewport. Then a routine such as

Code Fragment 3.5. Build the Window to Viewport Mapping Parameters

---

```
procedure MapRects(W, V : rect; var sx, tx, sy, ty : real);
{compute factors sx, sy, tx, ty from rectangle definitions}
```

computes the variables that correspond to s_x, s_y, and so on of Equation 3.2. For instance, this routine includes the command $sx := (V.r - V.l) / (W.r - W.l)$ to compute s_x. These four variables can be made globally accessible for efficiency, to be used in *Line( )* and other routines. Assuming this has been done, the mapping of a world point *pWorld : point* to an NDC point *pNDC : point* becomes simply

Code Fragment 3.6. Mapping a Point from a Window to a Viewport

---

```
pNDC.x := sx * pWorld.x + tx;
pNDC.y := sy * pWorld.y + ty;
```

With this mapping in hand, the procedure *Line( )* takes the following shape:

Code Fragment 3.7. The Main Line-drawing Routine Line( )

```
procedure Line(p1, p2 : point);
{ Draw a line from p1 to p2 in world coordinates }
var
  pNDC1, pNDC2 : point; {endpoints of the mapped line}
begin
  Clip(p1, p2, vis); {remove if no clipping desired}
  if vis then {remove if no clipping desired}
```

begin
   pNDC1.x := *sx* * *p1.x* + *tx*;
   pNDC1.y := *sy* * *p1.y* + *ty*;
   pNDC2.x := *sx* * *p2.x* + *tx*;
   pNDC2.y := *sy* * *p2.y* + *ty*;
   LineNDC(pNDC1, pNDC2)
   end
end; { *Line* }

A polar coordinate version is discussed in the exercises. Notice that if a clipping routine *Clip(*) is not available or no clipping is desired, the two lines indicated can be removed from *Line(*).

3.4   Clipping a Line

In this section we fashion the clipping routine **procedure** *Clip*(**var** *p1*, *p2* : *point*; **var** *vis* : *boolean*);. *Clip(*) clips the line segment between *p1* and *p2* in world coordinates to the window boundaries. If any portion in the window remains, the new endpoints will be placed in *p1* and *p2*, and *vis* will be set to *true*. If the line has been completely clipped out, *vis* will be set to *false*. Figure 3.10 shows a typical situation covering the range of possible actions for a clipper. *Clip(*) does one of four things to each line:

● *Nothing* if the entire line lies within the window, as for segment *CD*.

● *Eliminates it* if the entire line lies outside the window, as for segment *AB*.

● *Clips one end* if one endpoint of the segment is inside the window and one is outside, as for segment *ED*.

● *Clips both ends* if both endpoints are outside the window but a portion of the segment passes through it, as for segment *AE*.

There are many arrangements possible between a segment and the window. The segment can lie to the left, to the right, above, or below the window. Or it

Figure 3.10.
Clipping lines at window boundaries.

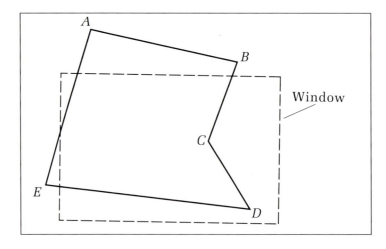

can cut through any one (or two) window edges, and so on. We therefore need an organized and efficient approach that identifies the prevailing situation and computes new endpoints for the clipped segment. Efficiency is important because there may be hundreds or even thousands of line segments in a typical picture, and each must be clipped against the window. The **Cohen–Sutherland algorithm** provides a rapid divide-and-conquer attack on the problem.

3.4.1 The Cohen–Sutherland Clipping Algorithm

The Cohen–Sutherland algorithm quickly detects and dispenses with two common and trivial cases. As shown in Figure 3.11, both endpoints of segment AB lie within window W, and so the whole segment AB must lie within W. Therefore AB can be "trivially accepted": It needs no clipping. This situation prevails when a large window is used that encompasses most of the line segments. On the other hand, both endpoints C and D lie entirely to one side of W, and so segment CD must lie entirely outside. It is "trivially rejected," and nothing is drawn. This situation arises frequently when a small window is used with a dense picture that has many segments outside the window.

To determine whether endpoints are inside or outside W, the algorithm sets up a "half-space code" for each endpoint. Each edge of the window defines an infinite line that divides the whole space into two **half-spaces**, the "inside" half-space and the "outside" half-space, as shown in Figure 3.12 for the right edge of W.

Code Fragment 3.8. Half-Space Code for an Endpoint

type *half_space_code* = **record**
　　　　　　　　l, t, r, b : boolean
　　end;

This is similar to the *rect* type except that the values are *boolean* rather than *real*. The *t* field of a code will be *true* if the point lies above the top edge of W, in the outside half-space determined by the top edge. For example, suppose that point p has code c. If p lies above and to the right of W, its code will have the value $(c.l, c.t, c.r, c.b) = (false, true, true, false)$. If p is inside W, its code will be

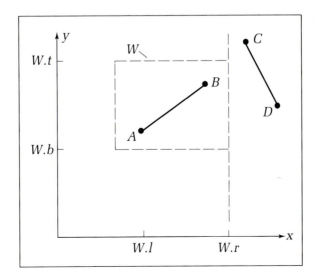

Figure 3.11.
Trivial acceptance or rejection of a segment.

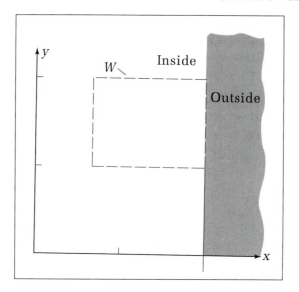

Figure 3.12.
Half-spaces determined by a
window edge.

(*false, false, false, false*), as it doesn't lie in any outside half-space. Figure 3.13
shows the half-spaces for each of the window's edges. Building the code for a
point requires only four simple comparisons: The x-coordinate of the point is
compared with the left edge of W; the y-coordinate with the top edge; and so
forth. These comparisons are easily built into the routine *Encode*( ):

Code Fragment 3.9. Building the Half-Space Code for a Point

```
procedure Encode(p : point; var c : half_space_code);
{build code for point p}
begin
    c.l := (p.x < W.l);
    c.r := (p.x > W.r);
    c.b := (p.y < W.b);
    c.t := (p.y > W.t)
end;
```

Figure 3.13.
Half-space codes for an
endpoint.

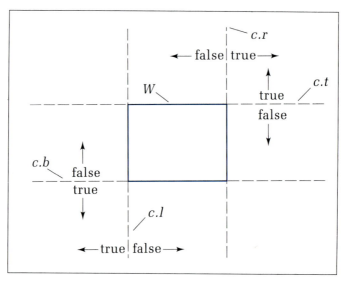

A point *p1* with code *c1* will be inside the window if all of its code fields are *false*, which can be summarized in the boolean variable *in1* :

in1 := (**not** *c1.l*) **and** (**not** *c1.t*) **and** (**not** *c1.r*) **and** (**not** *c1.b*).

Therefore the segment from *p1* to *p2* will be trivially accepted if both endpoints are inside: Accept it if *in1* **and** *in2*. It is just as easy to reject the segment trivially: See whether the codes *c1* and *c2* both have *true* in the same field:

$$reject := \quad (c1.l \textbf{ and } c2.l) \textbf{ or } (c1.r \textbf{ and } c2.r)$$
$$\textbf{or } (c1.t \textbf{ and } c2.t) \textbf{ or } (c1.b \textbf{ and } c2.b);$$

If neither of these tests succeeds, the segment must be analyzed further. A divide-and-conquer strategy is used: The segment is clipped against one of the window edges, and the accept/reject test is repeated to see whether a definite answer has been reached. If not, the segment is clipped against another edge, and the test is performed once more.

Figure 3.14 shows how the segment is clipped against the right edge of *W*. Point *A* must be computed. Its *x*-coordinate is clearly *W.r*, found with no extra calculation. Its *y*-coordinate requires adjusting *p1.y* by amount *d*. But *d* is just the amount *e* times the slope *m* of the segment, and so the new coordinate *p1.y* is found from the old as

$$p1.y := p1.y + (W.r - p1.x) * m;$$

Similar reasoning is used for clipping against the other three edges of *W*.

If the segment is vertical, its slope cannot be computed: It is infinite.[2] Before computing *m*, therefore, this condition is tested (using *p1.x = p2.x*), and if found to exist, a simpler clip is used. If *p1* is above the window, for instance (i.e., *c1.t = true*), then *p1* is clipped to the top edge of *W* simply by setting *p1.y := W.t*. Value *p1.x* is not altered.

These ideas are collected in the routine *Clip*( ). A set of steps is repeated until a trivial accept or reject is detected, at which point *done = true*. Each time

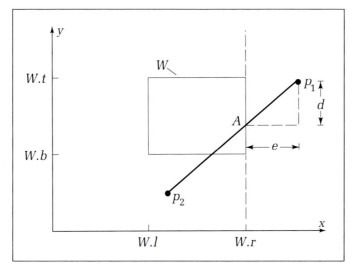

Figure 3.14.
Clipping a segment against an edge.

---

[2]Unlike the physical world in which exactly vertical lines rarely occur, graphics abounds with them, as a program can easily force verticality.

through the *repeat* loop the two endpoints are reencoded and tested. If a clip is required, we will know that one or both of the points must lie outside the window. If *p1* is found to be inside, the endpoints will be swapped so that the remaining operations will guarantee that *p1* is outside. This simplifies the code.

Code Fragment 3.10. Clipping a Line to the Window

```
procedure Clip (var p1, p2 : point; var vis : boolean);
var
    c1, c2, tmp_cd : half_space_code;
    tmp_pt : point;
    m : real; {slope of line}
    in1, in2, done : boolean;
{insert procedure Encode( ) here from Code Fragment 3.9.}
begin {Clip}
    done := false;
    vis := false;
    repeat
        Encode (p1, c1);
        Encode (p2, c2);
        in1 := (not c1.l) and (not c1.t) and
                (not c1.r) and (not c1.b);
        in2 := (not c2.l) and (not c2.t) and
                (not c2.r) and (not c2.b);
        if in1 and in2 then {trivially accept}
        begin
            done := true;
            vis := true
        end {trivially accept}
        else if (c1.l and c2.l) or (c1.r and c2.r)
        or (c1.t and c2.t) or (c1.b and c2.b) then
        begin
            done := true; {trivially reject}
            vis := false
        end
        else begin {at least one endpoint is outside}
            if in1 then
            begin {swap p1, p2 and c1, c2 : ensure p1 is outside}
                tmp_cd := c1; c1 := c2; c2 := tmp_cd;
                tmp_pt := p1; p1 := p2; p2 := tmp_pt
            end;
            if p2.x = p1.x then {line is vertical}
            begin
                if c1.t then p1.y := w.t {p1 is above}
                else if c1.b then p1.y := w.b {p1 is below}
            end
            else begin {not a vertical line}
                m := (p2.y − p1.y) / (p2.x − p1.x); {build slope}
                if c1.l then
```

```
      begin
          p1.y := p1.y + (w.l − p1.x) * m;
          p1.x := w.l
      end
      else if c1.r then
      begin
          p1.y := p1.y + (w.r − p1.x) * m;
          p1.x := w.r
      end
      else if c1.b then
      begin
          p1.x := p1.x + (w.b − p1.y) / m;
          p1.y := w.b
      end
      else if c1.t then
      begin
          p1.x := p1.x + (w.t − p1.y) / m;
          p1.y := w.t
      end
    end {not vertical line}
  end {at least one outside}
until done
end; {Clip}
```

A situation that requires all four clips is shown in Figure 3.15. The first clip changes p1 to A; the second changes A to C; the third alters the other endpoint to B; and the last changes B to D. No matter in what order the clips are performed, there will always be a situation in which all four clips are necessary.

Drill Exercises

3.7.   Hand Simulation of *Clip*( ). Go through the clipping routine by hand for the case of a window W given by (W.l, W.t, W.r, W.b) = (0, 1, 1, 0) and the following line segments:

1.   p1 = (0.5, 0.2), p2 = (0.8, 0.9);

2.   p1 = (0.5, 0.4), p2 = (1.6, 0.7);

3.   p1 = (0.4, −1.6), p2 = (0.4, 2.7);

4.   p1 = (0.4, −1.6), p2 = (0.8, −2.7);

5.   p1 = (−2, −3), p2 = (3, 5);

In each case determine the endpoints of the clipped segment, and for a visual check, sketch the situation on graph paper.

3.8.   Reorganization of Boolean Expressions. Some Pascal compilers stop evaluating boolean expressions as soon as their value is clear. The evaluation of the expression E1 **and** E2 **and** E3, for instance, proceeds from left to right, evaluating first E1, then E2, and so on, but stopping as soon as any expression E1 or E2 is found to be *false*, as then the whole expression must be *false*.

Examine each of the boolean expressions in *Clip*( ) to see whether they can be rewritten in a form that could take advantage of early termination. Would the advantages of this be significant in terms of execution speed?

3.9.   Rotated Windows. In some applications it is desirable to clip against a window that has been rotated through some angle θ, as shown in Figure 3.16. Consider what changes must be made to *Clip*( ) to produce the proper clipping. Would it be simpler first to rotate the segment through −θ, clip against an unrotated window, and then rotate back the clipped segment? Discuss this approach as well.

With *Line*( ) available, we can draw pictures of complex models, taking advantage of the window–viewport mechanism to choose which part to display

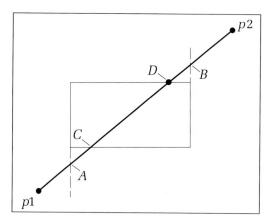

Figure 3.15.
A segment that requires four clips.

and to scale and position the picture as desired. In order to facilitate this, we develop some additional graphics tools, based on *Line( )*.

3.4.2 A Bonus—The Golden Ratio

Over the centuries, one aspect ratio has been particularly celebrated for its pleasing qualities in works of art: the aspect ratio of the **golden rectangle**, considered as the most pleasing of all rectangles, being neither too thin nor too squat. It figures in the Greek Parthenon (see Figure 3.17), Leonardo da Vinci's *Mona Lisa*, Salvador Dali's *The Sacrament of the Last Supper*, and in much of M. C. Escher's works. The **golden ratio** ϕ on which this rectangle is based is also a fascinating quantity and often appears unexpectedly in computer graphics.

Figure 3.18 shows a golden rectangle, with sides of length 1 and the golden ratio $\phi \doteq 1.618$. Its aspect ratio has the unique property that if a square is removed from the rectangle, the piece that remains will again be a golden rectangle! What value must ϕ have to make this work? Note in the figure that the smaller rectangle has height 1 and so to be golden must have width $1/\phi$. Thus

$$\phi = 1 + \frac{1}{\phi} \tag{3.3}$$

which is easily solved to yield

$$\phi = \frac{1 + \sqrt{5}}{2} = 1.618033989. . . \tag{3.4}$$

Figure 3.16.
Clipping against a rotated window.

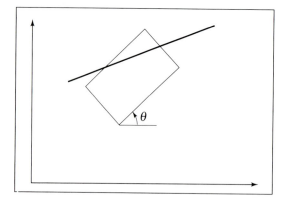

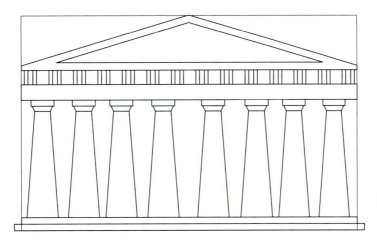

Figure 3.17.
The Greek Parthenon fitting within a golden rectangle.

This is approximately the aspect ratio of a standard 3-by-5 index card. From Equation 3.3 we see also that if 1 is subtracted from ϕ, the reciprocal of ϕ will be obtained: $1/\phi = .618033989. \ldots$ This is the aspect ratio of a golden rectangle lying on its side, as in Figure 3.18.

In many ways, ϕ is remarkable mathematically, two favorites being

$$\phi = \sqrt{1 + \sqrt{1 + \sqrt{1 + \sqrt{1 + \ldots}}}}$$

and

$$\phi = 1 + \cfrac{1}{1 + \cfrac{1}{1 + \cfrac{1}{1 + \ldots}}}$$

These both are easy to prove (how?) and display a pleasing simplicity in the use of the single digit 1.

The idea of a golden rectangle's containing a smaller version of itself suggests a form of "infinite regression" of figures—within figures—within figures—*ad infinitum*. Figure 3.19 shows that the golden rectangle demonstrates

Figure 3.18.
The golden rectangle.

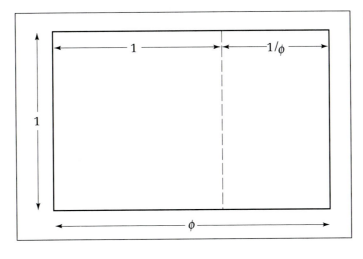

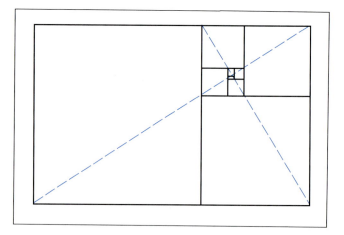

Figure 3.19.
Infinite regressions of the
golden rectangle.

this. Keep removing squares from each remaining golden rectangle. It also is instructive to write a routine that creates this picture using *Line*( )—see the exercises.

There is much more to be said about the golden ratio, and many delights can be found in Gardner (1961), Hill (1978), Huntley (1970), and Ogilvy (1969). For instance, in the next chapter we see golden pentagrams, and in Chapter 11 we see that the golden ratio is an inherent part of a "shear" transformation. Finally, in Appendix 8 we see that two of the "platonic solids," the dodecahedron and the icosahedron, contain three mutually perpendicular golden rectangles!

Drill Exercise

3.10.   On ϕ and Golden Rectangles. First, show that the preceding two formulas for ϕ that involve only ones are true. Second, find the point at which the two dotted diagonals shown in Figure 3.19 lie, and show that this is the point to which the sequence of golden rectangles con- verges. Third, use Equation 3.3 to derive an interesting relation that is used in Appendix 8:

$$\phi^2 + \frac{1}{\phi^2} = 3$$

3.5   Adding More Drawing Tools

3.5.1 The Current Position in World Coordinates

The routines *Line*( ) and *LineNDC*( ) need as arguments both endpoints of each line, which can be excessive, as in the house-drawing example of Code Fragment 3.1. When a succession of connected lines is to be drawn, each endpoint must be passed twice to a line routine: as the second endpoint of one line and as the first endpoint of the next line in the sequence.

We thus add convenience utilities that avoid this redundancy in applications and also provide extra flexibility to the programmer. They use the **current position (CP)**, which is a world coordinate analog of the inherent current position that many devices (such as a pen plotter) maintain: the point most recently drawn to or moved to. The global variable **var** *CP* : *point* is defined and maintained by the application, and two new routines, *MoveTo(p : point)* and *Line-To(p : point)*, are defined.

- *LineTo(p : point)* draws a (clipped) line from *CP* to *p* and then updates *CP* to *p*.

- *MoveTo(p : point)* updates the *CP* to *p*.

Implementations of these routines take the following shape:[3]

Code Fragment 3.11. The MoveTo( ) and LineTo( ) Routines

```
var CP : point; {global variable}
procedure MoveTo(p : point); {Change CP to p}
  begin
    CP := p
  end;
procedure LineTo(p : point); {Draw from CP to p and update CP}
begin
  Line(CP, p); {draw clipped line}
  CP := p; {update CP}
end;
```

Notice that the *CP* can exist outside the window. The clipping routine inside *Line( )* alters the endpoints of the segment that it is given, but because parameters are passed to *Line( )* "by value," this does not alter *p*. Thus *CP* is updated properly through *CP := p*.

The use of a current position and procedures such as *MoveTo( )* and *LineTo( )* may be found in many graphics packages. Some packages maintain their own *CP* so that the application doesn't have to. But the GKS standard does not include it, for several reasons. One is that a routine like *LineTo( )* is not self-contained but requires a separate variable *CP* that seems "hidden" from the programmer, sometimes leading to confusion (Enderle 1984, p. 64). Another reason is that one can confuse the *CP* with a device coordinate current position that is maintained in the hardware by various kinds of devices (such as a pen plotter). But many graphics programmers feel that it is a small burden to define and maintain *CP*. We refer freely to the *CP* and use *LineTo( )* and *MoveTo( )* whenever it is convenient.

Drill Exercise

3.11. Exploring *MoveTo( )*. The definition of *MoveTo( )* just changes the values of some internal variables in a program—it doesn't send any commands to the device. So if the device is a pen plotter, the pen will not move when *MoveTo( )* is called. Is this a problem: will the plotter behave properly on the next call to *LineTo( )*?

3.5.2 Defining *Polyline( )*

Recall from Chapter 2 that a polyline connects a sequence of points with straight lines. *Polyline(poly : polypoint)* is the version that operates on points given in world coordinates. It draws a line segment between each successive pair of points in the sequence, after clipping each to the window. It is the fundamental line-drawing primitive of GKS. Figure 3.20 shows an example. The segments that survive the clipping are shown in color. These segments would be mapped to the viewport and displayed.

[3]The similar forms *LineTo_(x, y : real)* and *MoveTo_(x, y : real)* that use explicit *x*- and *y*-coordinates are also frequently used.

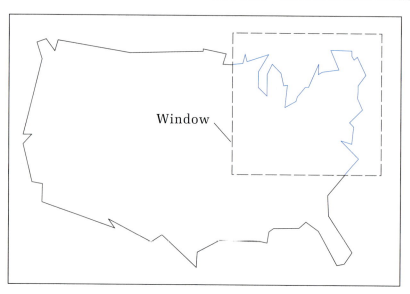

Figure 3.20.
A polyline in world
coordinates.

One can construct *Polyline*( ) from *PolylineNDC*( ) of Code Fragment 2.6 by simply replacing *LineNDC_*( ) with *Line*( ) of Code Fragment 3.7. As we mentioned, the clipping inside *Line*( ) does not affect the original data in the *polypoint* array because the endpoint parameters are passed to *Line* ( ) by value.

A sequence of points can always be placed in a *polypoint* array and then drawn as a polyline, but it may be inconvenient to set up a separate *polypoint* just to draw a few connected lines. The programmer may prefer instead to *MoveTo*( ) the first point in the sequence and then to *LineTo*( ) each of the remaining points in turn.

In fact, it seems logical to implement any polyline as a *MoveTo*( ) followed by *LineTo*( )s rather than in terms of *Line*( ). A polyline based on the sequence of points $p[1], p[2], p[3], \ldots, p[n]$ can be drawn using *MoveTo*($p[1]$) followed by *LineTo*($p[2]$), *LineTo*($p[3]$), . . . , *LineTo*($p[n]$). *Polyline*( ) can easily be written in this form, and it is seen to have a slightly simpler structure. There is no saving in execution time, however, as *LineTo*( ) must call *Line*( ) anyway. However, as discussed in the exercises, an alternative form along these lines can dramatically increase efficiency when sending polyline data to a device that maintains a hardware current position.

Drill Exercise

3.12.   Points Specified in Polar Coordinates. In some applications you may wish to prescribe points in polar coordinate form, as in Equation 3.7. An alternative to *LineTo*( ) can then be formed: *LineToPolar*(*rad, angle : real*). What minor adjustments in *LineTo*( ) are required to do this?

3.5.3 Relative Moves and Draws

Relative moves and draws offer additional variations on *Line*( ) and can have a pronounced effect on applications. Here the arguments specify changes in position. The use of a current position is mandatory: The goal is to free the programmer from specifying where each point is. Instead, the programmer specifies how far to go along each coordinate to the next desired point. Relative moves and draws are not included in the GKS standard, but they are sufficiently useful that many programmers find it valuable to build them into an application.

Two routines are defined, *LineRel(Disp)* and *MoveRel(Disp)*. Both routines take as arguments *Disp*, a displacement or change from the current position *CP*. Because *Disp* is a displacement, it behaves as a vector does, and so we define the data type

> *Code Fragment 3.12. The* Vector *Data Type*

---

type *vector* = **record**
> > *dx, dy : real*
> > **end;**

and define the displacement through *Disp : vector*. The *vector* type has the same form as the *point* type, so nothing really new has been introduced. The fields have names *dx* and *dy* as a reminder that displacements are being used. We shall see in Chapter 7, however, that in order to prevent confusion it is necessary to distinguish carefully between points and vectors, and so this definition is made for consistency.

MoveRel(Disp) produces the same effect as does *MoveTo(new)*, in which *new* is given by[4]

new.x := CP.x + Disp.dx;
new.y := CP.y + Disp.dy;

Therefore *Disp* is simply added to the *CP* to determine the new point. Similarly, *LineRel(Disp)* is exactly the same as *LineTo(new)*. The implementation of these routines is left as an exercise.

Relative moves and draws are particularly well suited to drawing instances of an object at various places on the display, simply by moving the *CP* to the desired spot and drawing the object. The important aspect is that no absolute position information appears in the routine that draws the instance—the routine doesn't "know" where the object is to be drawn. For example, consider the procedure *Arrow( )* that draws a triangular arrow with its point at the *CP, as* shown in Figure 3.21:

> *Code Fragment 3.13. Drawing an Arrow Using Relative Moves and Draws*

```
procedure Arrow(w, h : real);
begin
  LineRel_(w, −h);
  LineRel_(−2 * w, 0.0);
  LineRel_(w, h)
end;
```

It is a good idea to restore the *CP* to its original position as the last task in such a routine, so that the routine will not produce any hidden side effects. This happens automatically in *Arrow( )*. Restoring the *CP* will be useful if relative moves are used after the object has been drawn.

The use of relative moves and draws is a convenient approach to implementing markers (recall Chapter 2), and *Arrow( )* is such a marker. For example,

---

[4]The alternative form *MoveRel_(dx, dy : real)* is assumed to be defined as well.

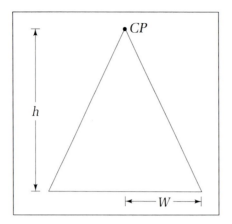

Figure 3.21.
Arrow drawn using *LineRel_( )*.

a picture made up of many arrows of random size, shape, and position can be produced by the repeated execution of

MoveTo_(random, random);
Arrow(random, random);

in which *random* is a function that returns a randomly selected real number (similar to *GetRand* in Appendix 3).

Figure 3.22 shows another example of the use of relative moves and draws. Figure 3.22a shows a "ladder" section consisting of two electrical resistors. We want to draw several repetitions of the section connected in cascade, as shown in Figure 3.22b. This is easily done using relative moves: When one section has been drawn, a relative move through three units in both x and y brings the CP to the starting position for the next section, where it is drawn again (see the exercises). Furthermore, the zigzag representing the resistor can also be drawn, as shown in Figure 3.22c, by the following sequence:

LineRel_(0.1, 0.2);   {short zag}
LineRel_(0.2, −0.4); *LineRel_(0.2, 0.4)*;   {zig-zag}
LineRel_(0.2, −0.4); *LineRel_(0.2, 0.4)*;   {zig-zag}
LineRel_(0.2, −0.4); *LineRel_(0.1, 0.2)*;   {zig–short zag}

3.6   Relative Polar Coordinates: Turtlegraphics

So far we have paid only lip-service to the polar coordinate approach to describing points. But when one combines the notion of relative moves and draws with that of polar coordinates, a powerful technique results. Relative moves and draws are specified in terms of a direction and a distance. The program keeps track of the **current direction, CD,** of the drawing operation (as well as the CP). A turtle provides a vivid mental model.[5] It plays the part of the pen in a pen plotter. It is always at some position (CP) and headed in some direction (CD). We add the commands

[5]The turtle model is found in "Turtlegraphics," which appeared in the popular language LOGO (see Abelson and diSessa 1981). It has been found to be very accessible to children first learning to use computers.

1. *LineForward*(*dist* : *real*) causes a line to be drawn from the CP through a distance *dist* in the current direction CD, after which the CP is updated to the new position.

2. *MoveForward*(*dist* : *real*) does no drawing; it only updates the CP exactly as in *LineForward*( ).

3. *Right*(*angle* : *real*) turns the turtle *angle* degrees more to the right, that is, clockwise (CW). No drawing is done; *angle* degrees is simply added to CD. A left turn is performed by using a negative value for *angle*.

Notice that each of the turtle's moves is specified in polar coordinates (as a direction and distance) from the CP, so that the turtle is operating in a form of relative polar coordinates. Additional turtle routines such as *Left*( ), *TurnTo*( ), and *LineBackward*( ) are suggested in the exercises. Figure 3.23 shows a typical turtlegraphics display, in which a small triangle indicates the turtle's position and direction. The result of executing the following commands is shown, given that the turtle starts at the position shown in the up direction.

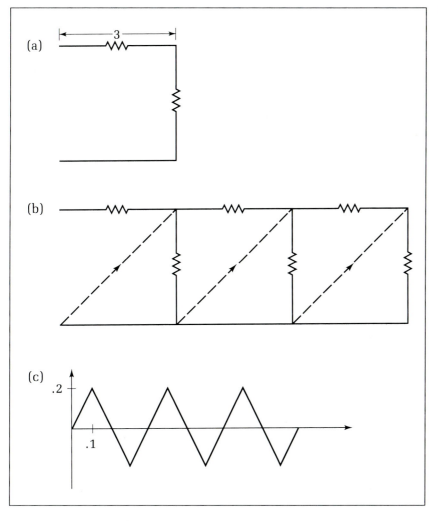

Figure 3.22.
Drawing a ladder network with relative draws.

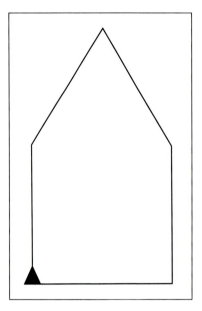

Figure 3.23.
Turtlegraphics example.

Code Fragment 3.14. Example Turtlegraphics Routine

```
procedure Turtle_House;
begin
    LineForward(20.0); {Draw up left wall}
    Right(30.0); {turn right 30 degrees}
    LineForward(20.0); {go up left side of roof}
    Right(120.0); {etc..}
    LineForward(20.0);
    Right(30.0);
    LineForward(20.0);
    Right(90.0);
    LineForward(20.0); {last line drawn}
    Right(90.0) {turn back to original direction}
end;
```

(See the exercises for an extension of this routine to include a size parameter.)
The procedure returns the turtle to its original position and direction so that
there is no net effect on the turtle from drawing the house, that is, no side effects.
What total angle must the turtle turn through in order to return to its starting
direction? This is useful to know when the routine is to be called within some
driving process such as

Code Fragment 3.15. Repeated Use of a Turtle Routine

```
for i := 1 to 6 do
begin
    Turtle_House;
    Right(60.0)
end;
```

that produces Figure 3.24.

Figure 3.24.
Using *Turtle House* repeatedly.

These new routines are easily implemented and are handy to have available. The global variable *CD* is defined in the application along with *CP*. *CD* is the number of degrees measured counterclockwise (CCW) from the *x*-axis. Figure 3.25 shows how the new position is calculated based on elementary trigonometry when *LineForward*( ) is used.

Code Fragment 3.16. Turtle Routines
_____

```
const TWOPI = 6.283185308; {2 pi}
var CD : real;
procedure LineForward(dist : real);
var
   angle : real;
   p : point;
begin
   angle := TWOPI * CD / 360.0; {convert degrees to radians}
   p.x := CP.x + dist * cos(angle);
   p.y := CP.y + dist * sin(angle);
   LineTo(p);
   CP := p
end;
{..............................}
procedure Right(angle : real); {clockwise turn by angle degrees}
begin
      CD := CD − angle
end;
```

MoveForward( ) is almost identical to *LineForward*( ) and is left as an exercise.

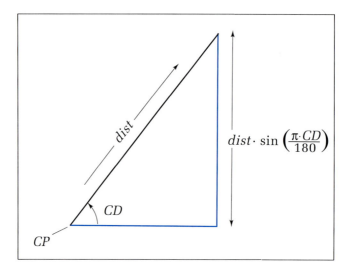

Figure 3.25.
Effect of the *LineForward( )*
routine.

Drill Exercises

3.13. Build *MoveForward( )*. Write the routine *Move-Forward*(*dist* : *real*) in Pascal.

3.14. Using Turtle Commands. List the invocations of *MoveForward( )*, *LineForward( )*, and *Right( )* that produce the figure shown in Figure 3.26. The turtle begins at *T*, heading horizontally to the right. At the end of the drawing the turtle is at its starting position and direction. What must angles A_1, A_2, and A_3 be? What must distance L_1 be?

3.15. *HideTurtle and Showturtle*. Rather than define both *MoveForward( )* and *LineForward( )*, we often use just *Forward( )*. This moves the turtle forward along the CD either visibly (as in "pen-down") or invisibly (as in "pen-up") according to the global variable *turtle_visible*: *boolean* that determines its drawing mode. Routines *Hide-Turtle* and *ShowTurtle* are defined to set the value of *turtle_visible*. Give appropriate definitions of these additional procedures.

Figure 3.26.
Example turtle figure for
Exercise 3.14.

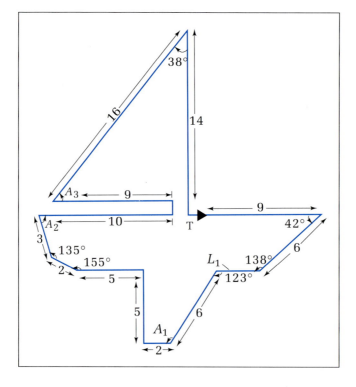

3.6.1 An Application of Turtlegraphics: Polyspirals

Turtlegraphics provides a fine utility for drawing a large and varied family of curves called **polyspirals**, which are excellent learning tools and pleasing to the eye.

    To create a polyspiral, begin at the current position and draw in some initial direction through a given distance *dist*. Then turn right through some angle *angle* and draw forward through a larger (or smaller) distance. The change in distance is governed by a variable *incr*. With these three parameters, you can construct a dazzling array of pictures. Figure 3.27 shows several polyspirals with their associated arguments (*dist*, *angle*, *incr*). If *incr* is set to 0, the figure will neither grow nor shrink. If in addition *angle* has value 360°/*k* for some integer *k*, the figure will repeat after *k* segments.

Figure 3.27.
Examples of polyspirals.

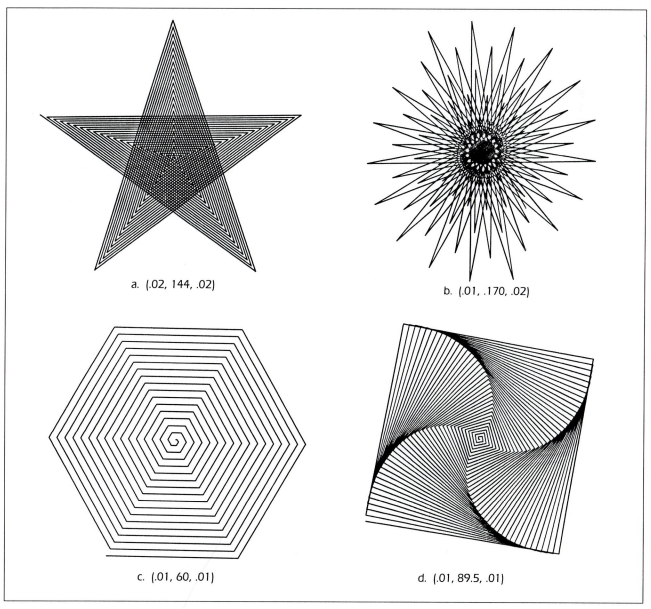

a. (.02, 144, .02)

b. (.01, .170, .02)

c. (.01, 60, .01)

d. (.01, 89.5, .01)

The code to generate polyspirals is given in the following code fragment:

Code Fragment 3.17. Polyspirals

```
procedure Polyspiral(dist, angle, incr : real; num : integer);
{Draw num segments of a spiral with given exterior angle}
var i : integer ;
begin
  for i := 1 to num do
  begin
    LineForward(dist);
    Right (angle);
    dist := dist + incr
  end
end;
```

3.7 Line and Bar Charts

Computer graphics is often used to prepare charts to present data. Indeed, business graphics is largely constructing presentations of data in chart form to make them compelling to the viewer. Of the many forms of charts, two of the most common are **line charts** and **bar charts.**

In this section we see how the preceding tools can be used to produce simple line and bar charts. These first charts present the desired data in raw form; no attempt is made to add professional decorations to the charts such as tick marks, legends, and annotations. In fact, the production of professional quality charts is a complex task requiring sophisticated techniques and is greatly influenced by aesthetic considerations.

Line and bar charts are constructed from lists or tables of numbers, the charts being simply a visual presentation of these numbers in a form the eye can readily understand. These lists of numbers come from mainly three sources:

- *Data obtained by measurements.* For example, a person observes some experiment and jots down a sequence of numbers read from a thermometer, voltmeter, or machine printout. A pollster interviews randomly selected people and builds up lists of numerical responses. (The census is an example of a very large set of such data.) People and machines often track aspects of the stock market and other financial indicators and build massive tables of data. Because tables of figures are difficult to interpret—particularly to see trends and correlations among different lists—plots can be of great service in exposing the data's underlying significance.

- *Mathematical relations.* When studying the behavior of a mathematical function, such as

$$f(x) = \sin(2\pi x) + \cos^5(7\pi x)/x^3$$

it is helpful to visualize its graph, $f(x)$ versus x, as x varies over a range of values. From such a plot one can immediately see the extreme values of the function, how fast it oscillates, where its roots are, and the like. This insight then guides further analytical study of the function. Computer graphics can easily provide plots like this.

- *Computer simulations.* Many computer programs are designed to simulate the workings of a process. The process is often modeled through sets of equations that attempt to describe how the ingredients of the process interact with one another (recall Section 3.3).

As an example of a simulation, the growth in the size of a rabbit population is said to be modeled by the following equation (Gardner 1961):

$$y_k = y_{k-1} + y_{k-2} \tag{3.5}$$

where y_k is the number of bunnies at the k-th generation. This model says that the number in this generation is the sum of the numbers in the previous two generations. The initial populations are $y_0 = 1$ and $y_1 = 1$. Successive values of y_k are formed by substituting earlier values, and the resulting sequence is the well-known **Fibonacci sequence;** 1, 1, 2, 3, 5, 8, 13. . . . A plot of the sequence y_k versus k reveals the nature of this growth pattern (see the exercises).

Another example is the beguiling **hailstone sequence,** in which the value y_k depends on y_{k-1} in a nonlinear way: If y_{k-1} is odd, then $y_k = 3y_{k-1} + 1$; otherwise $y_k = y_{k-1}/2$. For example, the sequence beginning at $y_0 = 17$ is 17, 52, 26, 13, 40, 20, 10, 5, 16, 8, 4, 2, 1 . . . . Once a power of 2 is reached, the sequence falls like a hailstone to 1 and becomes trapped in a short repetitive cycle (which one?). Does the sequence fall to 1 for every starting value? No one knows, but the intricacies of the sequence have been widely studied (Hayes 1984), and plots of y_k versus k have been examined to try to find structure in the hailstone sequence (see the exercises).

Another simple simulation provides a fascinating look into the world of **chaos** (see Gleick 1987, Hofstadter 1985). As in the hailstone sequence, a sequence of values is generated by the repeated application of a function. The function $f(.)$, called the **logistic map,** describes a parabola:

$$f(x) = 4\lambda x(1 - x) \tag{3.6}$$

where λ is some chosen constant between 0 and 1. Beginning at a starting point, x_0, between 0 and 1, the function is applied iteratively to generate the sequence:

$$x_1 = f(x_0)$$
$$x_2 = f(x_1) = f(f(x_0))$$
$$x_3 = f(x_2) = f(f(f(x_0)))$$
etc.

In general, $x_{k+1} = f(x_k)$ for $k \geq 0$. The question is How does this sequence behave? It so happens that a world of complexity lurks in this sequence, a world that is made vivid by displaying its action graphically. Figure 3.28 shows the parabola $y = 4\lambda x(1 - x)$ for $\lambda = 0.7$ as x varies from 0 to 1. The starting point $x_0 = 0.1$ is chosen here, and at $x = 0.1$ a vertical line is drawn up to the parabola, showing the value $f(x_0) = 0.252$. Next we must apply the function to the new value $x_1 = 0.252$. This is shown visually by moving horizontally over to the line $y = x$, as illustrated in the figure. Then to evaluate $f(\ )$ at this new value, a line is again drawn up vertically to the parabola. This process repeats forever: From the previous position (x_{k-1}, x_k) a horizontal line is drawn to (x_k, x_k) from which a

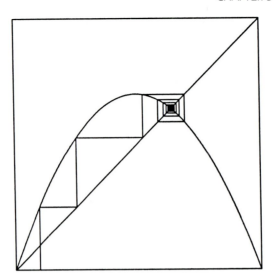

Figure 3.28.
The logistic map for λ = 0.7.

vertical line is drawn to (x_k, x_{k+1}). The figure shows that for $\lambda = 0.7$, the values quickly converge to a stable "attractor," a fixed point so that $f(x) = x$. (What is its value for $\lambda = 0.7$?) This attractor does not depend on the starting point; the sequence always converges quickly to a final value.

If λ is set to small values, the action will be even simpler: There is a single attractor at $x = 0$. But when the "λ-knob" is increased, something strange begins to happen. Figure 3.29a shows what results when $\lambda = 0.85$. The "orbit" that represents the sequence falls into an endless repetitive cycle, never settling down to a final value. There are several attractors here, one at each vertical line in the limit cycle shown in the figure. And when λ is increased beyond the critical value $\lambda = 0.892486418 \ldots$ the process becomes truly chaotic. The case of $\lambda = 0.9$ is shown in Figure 3.29b. For most starting points the orbit is still periodic, but the number of orbits observed between the repeats is extremely large. Other starting points yield truly aperiodic motion, and very small changes in the starting point can lead to very different behavior. Before the truly remarkable character of this phenomenon was first recognized by Mitchell Feigenbaum in 1975, most researchers believed that very small adjustments to a system should produce correspondingly small changes in its behavior and that simple

Figure 3.29.
(a) Cyclic and (b) "chaotic" behavior of the logistic map.

(a) 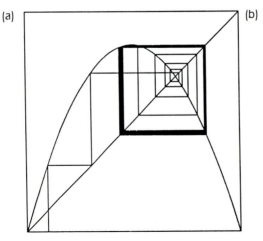   (b)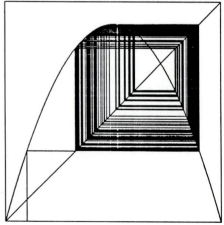

systems such as this could not exhibit arbitrarily complicated behavior. Feigenbaum's work spawned a new field of inquiry into the nature of complex nonlinear systems, known as *chaos theory* (Gleick 1987). It is intriguing to experiment with this logistic map, as is suggested in the exercises.

Another important application is in digital filtering. The output signal from a digital filter is the sequence of numbers y_k for $k = 0, 1, 2, \ldots$ where y_k is related to the input number sequence $x_0, x_1, x_2, \ldots$ through an equation such as:

$$y_k = .4y_{k-1} - .2y_{k-2} + x_k + .3x_{k-1}$$

(The Fibonacci sequence is one example of a digital filter in action.) One can simulate the action of such a filter by calculating each term, $y_0, y_1, \ldots$ in turn for a given input sequence such as $x_k = \sin(2\pi k/14)$ (see the exercises). A computer can do this quite readily and produce a plot of y_k versus k, immediately revealing how the output behaves for this input.

For each of these sources of data, the result is a sequence, $y_1, y_2, \ldots, y_n$, to be plotted. (Sometimes it is desirable to plot y_0 as well.) To capture the values we can define the *sequence* data type, given by the following:

Code Fragment 3.18. Data Type for a Sequence of Values

```
type
    sequence = record
                    num: 0..maxnum;
                    values : array[1..maxnum] of real
               end;
```

The data can be plotted in various ways. For the usual line and bar charts, the values y_i, for $i = 1, \ldots, n$ are taken as y-coordinates, and they are placed at equal increments along the x-coordinate. The values $x_i = i$ are a convenient choice. The distinction between line and bar charts is in how the points are presented and connected. We shall look at each type in turn.

3.7.1 Line Graphs

A **line graph** is just a polyline built out of the data y_i, along with axes and other features if desired. The i-th vertex in the polyline is the point (i, y_i). The position, size, and shape (aspect ratio) of the plot are selected by judicious choices of the window and viewport. Figure 3.30 shows a line graph based on eight values, (4.0, 5.5, 2.6, −2.4, 3.0, 1.2, 2.4, 2.6), with data points joined by straight lines.

How are the window and viewport chosen? There is no inherent shape for the overall plot: It can be tall and skinny or short and fat. The window is therefore chosen to enclose the appropriate part of the polyline, and the viewport is chosen to make the graph look "right."

Choosing the Window

The boundaries of the window are chosen to enclose the polyline, perhaps with a border of extra space surrounding it. The polyline extends in x from 1 to n, and it extends in y from y_{min} to y_{max}, determined by the smallest and the largest data value. These extreme values are computed in the routine *Extremes(data : sequence; var ymin, ymax : real)* that scans the array in *data* and keeps track of

Figure 3.30.
Simple line graph.

the largest and smallest values encountered. This routine is not hard to write and can be found in Appendix 3.

With *ymin* and *ymax* determined, the window parameters can be stored in the global variable *W* using *SetRect*(1.0 − *bord*, *ymax* + *bord*, *data*.num + *bord*, *ymin* − *bord*, *W*); (recall Section 3.3), where an amount *bord* is added to or subtracted from each parameter to add a border around the polyline.

The viewport parameters are usually chosen to achieve a particular look for the graph. For example, perhaps the graph must fit within a certain region of a larger picture, or the user wants it to have a certain size and aspect ratio to achieve some visual effect. This choice depends on the application at hand. If different aspect ratios are used for the window and viewport, the graph will be distorted as always, but because there are no inherent dimensions in the graph, this usually causes no problem.

Text annotation is another issue entirely, and solutions tend to be fairly device dependent. Some graphics packages provide routines such as *Draw-Text*(*str* : *string*) that draw the string of text *str* in world coordinates starting at the CP. Each character of text is fashioned as a set of lines, and each line is mapped from the window to the viewport and then drawn. To prevent such text from being drawn in an overly distorted way, the viewport should be set to have approximately the same aspect ratio as the window. A facility is included in some packages to scale both the height and width of text characters, and the user can perform scaling as needed, both to size the characters and to undo the effects of distortion. This is discussed further in Chapter 11. To achieve high-quality charts one usually must experiment to get the text looking just right.

With the viewport chosen, the window to viewport mapping is set up as before using *MapRects*( ) to build the mapping parameters *sx*, *tx*, *sy*, and *ty*. The polyline is then easily drawn. The following code fragment shows an implementation of this. Instead of building a *polypoint* structure and using *Poly-Line*( ), it is easier to *MoveTo*_( ) the first data value and then do *LineTo*_( )s to the remaining ones. Then a vertical axis is drawn through the first data point at *x* = 1, and a horizontal axis is drawn through *y* = 0. (Some issues concerned with drawing axes are discussed in the exercises.)

Code Fragment 3.19. Plotting a Line Graph

```
procedure LineGraph(data : sequence);
{draw line graph based on a sequence of points.}
{draw horizontal and vertical axes.}
const bord = 0.3; {width of border around window}
var
   ymin, ymax : real;
   i : integer;
begin
   if data.num > 1 then {at least 2 points}
   begin
      Extremes(data, ymin, ymax); {find extreme y-values}
      SetRect(1 − bord, ymax + bord, data.num + bord, ymin − bord, W);
      .
      . {user selects viewport, V}
      .
      MapRects(W, V, sx, tx, sy, ty); {set window−vport mapping}
      with data do
      begin {draw polyline}
            MoveTo_(1.0, values[1]);
            for i := 2 to num do LineTo_(i + 0.0, values[i])
      end;
      Line_(1.0, ymin, 1.0, ymax); {draw vertical axis}
      Line_(1.0, 0.0, data.num, 0.0) {draw horiz. axis}
   end
end;
```

Example: Data Generated by a Mathematical Formula

An important use of line graphs is plotting a function described by a mathematical expression, such as

$$f(x) = x \times \ln^3(2\pi x) + e^{-x^2} \cos^3(7\pi x)/x^3$$

In order to plot it, select a set of values x_i and draw straight lines between successive points $(x_i, f(x_i))$. If the values x_i are closely spaced, the line segments will be short, and the line graph will appear to be a smooth curve.

Normally one chooses to sample $f(x)$ at a succession of values in x equally spaced by some amount δ, beginning at x_{min}. To generate n points, the x-values

$$x_i = x_{min} + (i − 1) \times \delta, \text{ for } i = 1, \ldots, n$$

are used. The array in the sequence *data* is loaded with successive values of the function, that is, *data.values*[i] is set to $f(x_i)$, for $i = 1, \ldots, n$. This sequence is then passed to *LineGraph*( ) to draw the function.

Example: Fourier Series Plot

Fourier analysis plays a central role in fields such as linear system theory and signal processing. It allows a periodic function to be expressed as a sum of

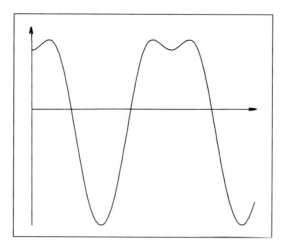

Figure 3.31.
A periodic waveform.

sinusoids having different frequencies. Figure 3.31 shows a plot using the following example:

$$f(x) = \cos(2\pi x) - .3 \cos(4\pi x) - .06 \cos(6\pi x)$$

plotted over the range $x \in (0, 3\pi)$. See Exercise 3.32 at the end of the chapter for more practice with Fourier series plots.

3.7.2 Bar Graphs

Bar graphs offer an alternative format for displaying a sequence of data values. Figure 3.32 uses the preceding sample data to form a bar graph, with each data value determining the height of a bar.

To create simple bar graphs, we fashion a procedure, *BarGraph(data : sequence; width : real)*. The *i*-th bar begins at $x = i$, with its width given by *width*. Each bar is drawn as a rectangle resting on the *x*-axis. The implementation of *BarGraph( )* is called for in the exercises.

Different visual effects can be achieved by using very narrow bars with a *width* of 0.3 or so, or wide ones that abut one another (*width* = 1). The bars can be filled or crosshatched with various colors to convey additional information.

Figure 3.32.
Simple bar graph.

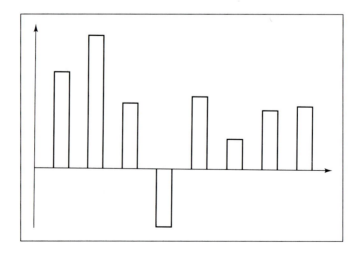

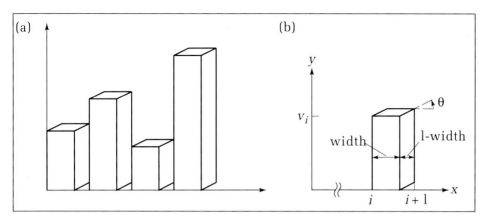

Figure 3.33.
The visual effect of 3D bars.

With a little more effort, one can achieve a three-dimensional illusion where each bar looks "solid." Figure 3.33a shows an example. Instead of a single rectangle, each bar has three parts, representing the front, side, and top of a "block." The height of the block is determined by the data value. Figure 3.33b shows how the blocks can be fashioned, with *width* determining where the front ends and the side begins. The bottom edge of the side face begins at ($i + width$, 0.0) and moves up diagonally at an angle *theta* ending at ($i + 1$, ($1 - width$) * tan(*theta*)). The top edge of the side moves in a similar fashion.

3.8 Summary

This chapter introduced the basic techniques of line-drawing graphics, in order to build up the necessary arsenal of tools to begin doing serious drawing. We made the fewest possible assumptions regarding what kind of graphics devices are available or what kinds of software are installed for them. We used a firm device-independent approach and assumed only that the user has the equivalent of a routine *LineNDC*( ) that can draw lines on the device at hand. The endpoints of a line expressed in NDC are passed to the procedure *LineNDC*( ), and it draws the line in the available region in NDC: either the largest square area on the display or the whole screen if the aspect ratio of the device is used. *LineNDC*( ) hides device dependencies and allows the programmer to focus on the application.

Then we added more capabilities, principally moving to a more user-oriented coordinate system—world coordinates. The designer defines a suitable window in the world that specifies the portion of the overall picture to be drawn. The position at which the picture appears is chosen by specifying a viewport in NDC. If the aspect ratios of the window and viewport are different, the picture will be distorted—stretched relatively more in either the horizontal or the vertical direction—before it is drawn in the viewport. This may or may not be desirable. The portion lying outside the window is clipped out and is not drawn. We also described in detail the simple but powerful Cohen–Sutherland clipping algorithm.

At this point we discussed the fundamental device-independent routine *Line*( ), and for convenience we showed additional routines that maintained a global current position, permitting the programmer to take advantage of the somewhat simpler routines *MoveTo*( ) and *LineTo*( ). To these we added routines to produce relative moves and draws. Relative motion can be described either in Cartesian coordinates through *LineRel*( ) or in polar form, using *LineForward*( ) and *Right*( ).

The rest of the chapter used these tools to build up simple line and bar charts that are based on sequences of numbers, and we demonstrated them with examples that derive their sequences from a list of values or from sampling a mathematical function.

Programming Exercises

3.16.　Instances of a Shape. Devise a building shape such as the house in Figure 3.1 and write a program to draw multiple instances of it.

3.17.　House( )　Revisited. Rewrite the procedure *House*( ) of Section 3.2 using *MoveTo*( ) and *LineTo*( ). Which way is better to pass parameters to *MoveTo*( ) and *LineTo*( ), as *point* or as individual *x*, *y*-components?

3.18.　Using Windows and Viewports. Figure 3.34 shows a triangle and two windows in the world coordinate system, with the triangle having corners at (0, 0), (1, 0), and (0, 2).

Write a program that uses *Line*( ) to generate pictures like those shown in the box. (How is the upside-down one labeled *u* generated?) In a **repeat** loop the user inputs parameters for the next window and viewport desired, and the program draws the triangle. The program can draw any piece of the triangle anywhere on the display device.

3.19.　LineToNDC( ) for Efficient Drawing. Some devices maintain an internal current position in device coordinates and include in their repertoire of commands a device-level "move" and "draw": *DD_LineTo*(*dx*, *dy* : *integer*) and *DD_MoveTo*(*dx*, *dy* : *integer*), which take device coordinate parameters. For this class of device, it is logical to define

driver routines, *LineToNDC*(*p* : *point*) and *MoveToNDC*(*p* : *point*), that require only one point location rather than the two that are required if *LineNDC*( ) is used. Sending fewer data to the device can significantly speed up the drawing process over a slow transmission link, as is often encountered when the device is situated remotely from the host.

Write *LineToNDC*(*p* : *point*) and *MoveToNDC*(*p* : *point*) for a device that maintains a device-level current position. Write them for a device at your site, or if no such device exists, write them for a ReGIS device. These routines maintain a global variable, *CP_ndc* : *point*. They compare the new point, *p*, with the previous one, *CP_ndc*, and draw only if there is a sufficient change.

Then, write a version of *Polyline*(*poly* : *polypoint*) that uses *LineToNDC*( ) and *MoveToNDC*( ) constructed in this way. For a given window and viewport this routine clips each segment in *poly* and produces drawing by calls to *LineToNDC*( ) and *MoveToNDC*( ) as needed. Discuss its advantages over the usual *Polyline*( ) in terms of the data traffic to the device.

3.20.　Positions Given in Polar Coordinates. Sometimes it is convenient to specify a position (*x*, *y*) in polar coordinate form, as a distance *r* from the origin at some angle θ (as-

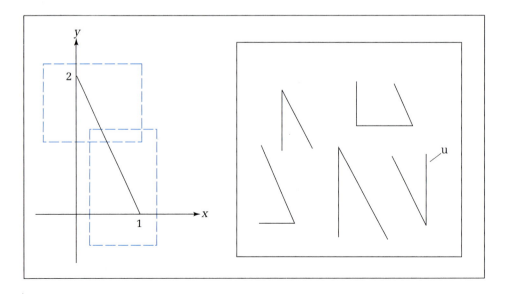

Figure 3.34.
Using different windows and viewports.

sumed to be given in degrees). Using simple trigonometry the point (x, y) is given by

$$(x, y) = \left(r \cos\left(\frac{\pi}{180}\theta\right), r \sin\left(\frac{\pi}{180}\theta\right) \right) \qquad (3.7)$$

Adjust *Line( )* in Code Fragment 3.7 to *LinePolar(rad1, angle1, rad2, angle2 : real)*; which draws a line between the two points specified in polar coordinates.

3.21. Infinite Regressions of Golden Rectangles. Write and exercise a program that draws golden rectangles within golden rectangles until the resolution of the graphics display is exhausted.

3.22. Relative Moves and Draws. Implement the routines *MoveRel(Disp : vector)* and *LineRel(Disp : vector)* which produce relative moves and draws. Use them to draw various elaborate objects.

3.23. *House( )* Using Relative Moves and Draws. Fashion another version of the *House( )* procedure from Section 3.2 that makes no references to any absolute position in world coordinates but draws the house wherever the CP is currently located. Its parameters deal only with the size of the house, not its location.

3.24. Drawing Ladder Networks. Write a routine that draws the type of ladder network shown in Figure 3.22. Implement it using relative moves and draws.

3.25. Implementing *PolyMarker( )*. Write the procedure *PolyMarker(poly : polypoint)*, which draws a marker at the sequence of points specified in *poly*.

3.26. Parameterizing *Turtle_House*. Enlarge *Turtle_House* to *Turtle_House(size : real)* where size determines how large the house is drawn.

3.27. Additional Turtle Routines. Implement other useful turtle routines, *Left(angle : real)*, *LineBackward(dist : real)*, and *TurnTo(angle : real)*. The first two are self-explanatory. The third causes the CD to be set to the given angle.

3.28. Drawing Polyspirals. Write a program that uses *Polyspiral( )* and use it with different parameter sets to get a clear sense of how it operates.

3.29. Recursive Form for *Polyspiral( )*. Rewrite *Polyspiral* in a recursive form, so that *Polyspiral( )* with argument *dist* calls *Polysprial( )* with argument *dist + inc*. Put a suitable stopping criterion in the routine.

3.30. Regular Shapes Using *LineForward( )* and *Right( )*. Write and run a program that draws the set of clustered polygons shown in Figure 3.35, all sharing a common side. Use *LineForward( )* and *Right( )* the proper number of times to draw each *n*-gon.

3.31. Drawing the Axes. Write a routine that adds coordinate axes to a line plot (see Section 3.7). Supposing that data value $y(1)$ is defined, the vertical axis passes through $(1.0, y[1])$. The horizontal axis will pass through $(1.0, 0.0)$ if the data embrace $y = 0$, that is, if some of the data values are negative and some are positive. If this is not the case, have the routine draw the horizontal axis through the middle of the plot, at y-value $\frac{1}{2} \times (y_{\min} + y_{\max})$.

3.32. Drawing Classes of Periodic Waveforms. Write a program that draws a variety of periodic waveforms, based on the **Fourier synthesis waveform** function:

$$f(x) = \sum_{i=1}^{M} a_i \times \cos(2\pi i x + p_i)$$

where the specific choices for the amplitudes a_i and phases p_i determine the resulting waveshape. Test the program on the following examples:

- *Square wave*: for $i = 1, 3, 5, 7, \ldots$, $a_i = 1 / i$, $p_i = -\pi / 2$

- *Triangle wave*: for $i = 1, 3, 5, 7, \ldots$, $a_i = 1 / (i^2)$, $p_i = \pi \times i / 2$

- *Rectified sinewave*: for $i = 1, 2, 3, 4, \ldots$, $a_0 = 0.5$, $a_i = -1 / [(2 \times i - 1)(2 \times i + 1)]$, $p_i = 0$

- *Half-wave rectified sinewave*: $a_0 = 0.5$, $a_1 = \pi / 4$, $p_1 = -\pi / 2$, and for $i = 2, 4, 6, 8, \ldots$, $a_i = -1/ [(i - 1) \times (i + 1)]$, $p_i = 0$

- *Sawtooth wave*: for $i = 1, 2, 3, 4, 5, \ldots$, $a_i = 1/i$, $p_i = \pi/2$

3.33. Drawing a Bar Graph. Write the procedure *BarGraph(data : sequence; width : real)* which draws a bar graph based on the data stored in the sequence *data*. The i-th bar begins at $x = i$, and the width is given by *width*. Each bar is drawn as a rectangle resting on the x-axis. If the available graphics package includes routines for filling or crosshatching rectangles, add parameters to *BarGraph( )* that give the user a choice of interior fill styles.

Figure 3.35.
Polygons sharing a common side.

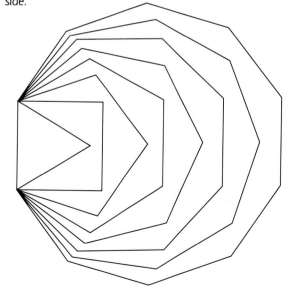

3.34.   Finding the Location of the Extremes. Elaborate *Extremes( )* in Appendix 3 so that it also reports the values of the index *i* at which the minimum and maximum values occur. Why might this be useful information when making plots from arrays of data?

3.35.   Simulation: The Fibonacci Number Sequence. Write a program that draws line graphs and exercise it with the following process:

$$y_k = y_{k-1} + y_{k-2}$$

that generates the famous Fibonacci numbers: 1, 1, 2, 3, 5, 8, . . . , where each element y_k in the sequence is the sum of the previous two. Start the simulation at y_2 using $y_0 = y_1 = 1$, and generate values up through y_N. Adjust the size of the plots appropriately for different N. Also plot the sequence of ratios $p_k = y_k/y_{k-1}$ and watch how quickly this ratio converges to the golden ratio.

3.36.   Sinusoidal Sequences. The following difference equation generates a sinusoidal sequence:

$$y_k = a \times y_{k-1} - y_{k-2} \tag{3.8}$$

$k = 1, 2, . . .$ where a is a constant between 0 and 2; y_k is 0 for $k < 0$; and $y_0 = 1$ (see Oppenheim and Willsky 1983). In general, one cycle consists of S points where $a = 2 \cdot \cos(2\pi/S)$. Figure 3.36 shows the example in which $S = 40$. Write a routine that draws sequences generated in this fashion, and test it for various values of a.

3.37.   Log Log Paper. "Log log" graph paper is useful for plotting curves whose values range over several orders of

Figure 3.36.
A sinusoidal sequence.

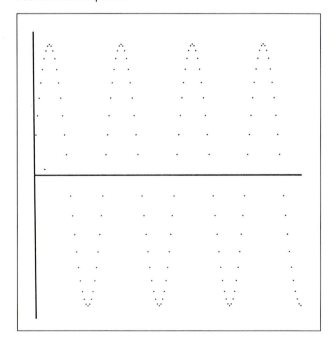

magnitude. In addition, "power-law" functions, $y = x^n$, appear as straight lines, making them easy to identify visually. Log log paper uses a logarithmic scale for each axis. Values marked along an axis are separated by a distance equal to the logarithm of the actual values marked. Thus 1, 10, and 100 are drawn equidistant, as are 2, 4, 8, and so forth.

Write a routine that generates log log graph paper. If appropriate software is available for placing text in a drawing, mark the various lines with their corresponding values. Plot $y = Ax^n$ for a variety of interesting choices of A and n.

3.38.   Plotting a Mathematical Function. Write the following routine:

procedure *FuncPts(x_min : real;* {starting value of x}
delta : real; {increment in x}
N : integer; {num. of points desired}
function *Func : real;* {function to plot}
var *points : sequence);* {resulting points}

that builds the sequence *points* of length N, using samples of function *Func( )* spaced *delta* apart beginning at *x_min*.

3.39.   Amplitude Modulation. The signal transmitted to AM radios uses amplitude modulation of a carrier signal by some speech or music waveform. The carrier is a sinewave at some frequency f_c: $\cos(2\pi f_c t)$, and modulation is effected by multiplying this carrier by the information-bearing signal. Figure 3.37 shows a plot of the waveform $s(t) = \cos(2\pi f_s t) \cos(2\pi f_c t)$, where the modulating signal is itself a

Figure 3.37.
An amplitude modulated signal.

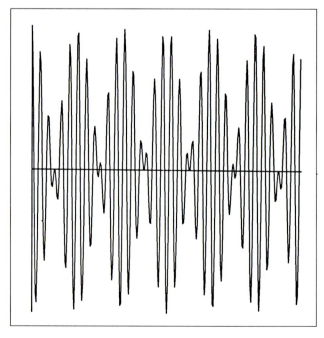

sinusoid at frequency f_s. Write a routine that plots waveforms of this form, and test it with various choices of f_s and f_c. Choose the proper increment in t between samples so that smooth waveforms are drawn.

3.40. Digital Filter Simulations. Write a program that draws line graphs, and exercise it using the process y_0, y_1, y_2, ... described by

$$y_k = .4y_{k-1} - .2y_{k-2} + x_k + .3x_{k-1}$$

where the input process x_k, $k = 0, 1, ...$ is given by

- *A sinusoid*: $x_k = \sin(2\pi k/14)$.

- *A noise process*: $x_k = rand(\ )$, where $rand(\ )$ generates independent random numbers between 0 and 1 (see Appendix 3).

3.41. The Hailstone Sequence. Write a routine, *Hailstone(c : integer)*, that generates the hailstone sequence discussed in Section 3.7, beginning at value c. Also build a driver, *PlotStones(c)*, that draws a line graph of the sequence, showing all values until the final plummet to 1 (if it occurs). The user enters the initial value. Because the largest value reached by the sequence is not known beforehand, how should each graph be scaled? Find the longest sequence that occurs for starting numbers up to 100. There is one impressively long one—which one?

3.42. On the Logistic Map and Chaos. Write and exercise a program that permits the user to study the behavior of repeated iterations of the logistic map, as shown in Figure 3.29. The user gives the values of λ and x_0, and the program draws the limit cycles produced by the system.

3.43. Building and Running Mazes. The task of finding a path through a maze seems forever fascinating (see Ball and Coxeter 1974). Elaborate mazes may be generated on a computer, and graphics allows you to watch them generated and traversed. Figure 3.38 shows a rectangular maze having 100 rows and 150 columns. The goal is to find a path from the opening at the left edge to the opening at the right edge. Trial and error ultimately pays off, but it's more interesting to develop an algorithm to trace a maze automatically.

Write and exercise a program that generates and displays a rectangular maze of R rows and C columns. The program also must find (and display) the path from start to end. The mazes are generated randomly but must be *proper*; that is, every one of the R-by-C cells is connected by a unique, albeit tortuous, path to every other cell. Think of a maze as a graph: A node corresponds to each cell where either a path terminates or two paths meet, and each path is represented by a branch. Figure 3.39 shows a small maze and its associated graph. A node occurs at every cell for which there is a choice of which way to go next. For instance, when Q is reached there are three choices, whereas at M there are only two. The graph of a proper maze is "acyclic" and has a "tree" structure.

How should a maze be represented? One way is to state for each cell whether its north wall is intact and its east wall is intact, suggesting the following data structure:

var *north_wall, east_wall* : **array**[0..*num_rows*, 0..*num_cols*] **of** *boolean*;

If *north_wall*[i, j] is *true*, the *ij*-th cell has a solid upper wall; otherwise the wall is missing. The 0-th row is a phan-

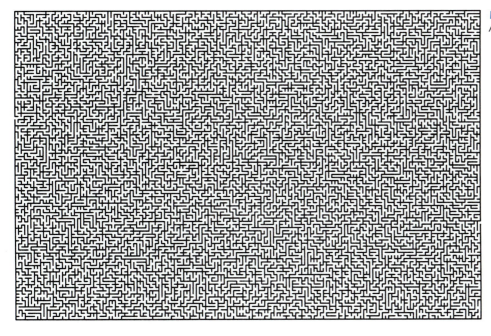

Figure 3.38.
A maze.

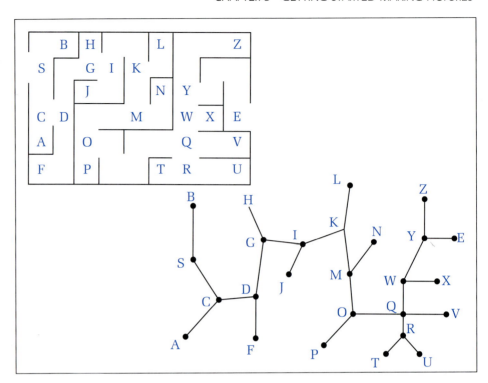

Figure 3.39.
A simple maze and its graph.

tom row of cells below the maze whose north walls comprise the bottom edge. Similarly, *east_wall*[i, 0] specifies where any gaps appear in the left edge of the maze.

Generating a Maze. Start with all walls intact so that the maze is a simple grid of horizontal and vertical lines. The program draws this grid. An invisible mouse is initially placed in a random cell, whose job is to eat through walls to connect adjacent cells. It checks the four neighbor cells (above, below, left, and right) and for each asks whether the neighbor has all four walls intact. If not, the cell has previously been visited and so is on some path. The mouse may detect several candidate cells that haven't been visited: It chooses one randomly and eats through the connecting wall, saving the locations of the other candidates on a stack. The eaten wall is erased, and the mouse repeats the process. When it becomes trapped in a dead end—surrounded by visited cells—it pops an unvisited cell and continues. When the stack is empty, all cells in the maze have been visited. A "start" and "end" cell is then chosen randomly, most likely along some edge of the maze. It is delightful to watch the maze being formed dynamically as the mouse eats through walls. (*Question*: Might a queue be better than a stack to store candidates? How does this affect the order in which later paths are created?)

Running the Maze. Use a "backtracking" algorithm. At each step, the mouse tries to move in a random direction. If there is no wall, it places its position on a stack and moves to the next cell. The cell the mouse is in can be drawn with a red dot. When it runs into a dead end, it can change the color of the cell to blue and backtrack by popping the stack. The mouse can even put a wall up to avoid ever trying the dead-end cell again.

Addendum: Proper mazes aren't too challenging because one can always traverse them using the "shoulder-to-the-wall rule." Trace the maze by rubbing your shoulder along the left-hand wall. At a dead end, sweep around and retrace the path, always maintaining contact with the wall. Because the maze is a "tree," you will ultimately reach your destination. In fact, there can even be cycles in the graph and you still always find the end, as long as both the start and the end cells are on outer boundaries of the maze (why?). To make things more interesting, place the start and end cells in the interior of the maze and also let the mouse eat some extra walls (maybe randomly 1 in 20 times). In this way, some cycles may be formed that encircle the end cell and defeat the shoulder method.

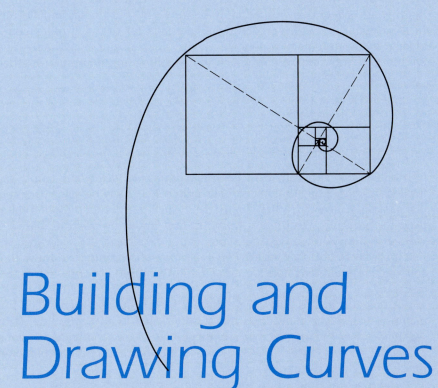

CHAPTER 4

Building and Drawing Curves

Hamlet: Do you see yonder cloud that's almost in shape of a camel?
Polonius: By the mass, and 'tis like a camel, indeed.
Hamlet: Methinks it is like a weasel.

William Shakespeare, *Hamlet*, 1601

Goals of the Chapter

- To introduce various forms of polygons and to build routines to draw them.
- To develop programming tools for drawing curved shapes, including circles and sectors, and to use them to draw pie charts.
- To reveal the power of the parametric representation of curves and to explain how to use it in graphics.
- To describe the properties of various curve shapes and the algorithms for drawing these shapes.
- To develop routines for finding the intersections of line segments.

4.1   Introduction

We now have the tools to draw any polylines that we can dream up, just by figuring out where the vertices are to lie in world coordinates and storing them in a *polypoint* variable. To build up methods for drawing other families of objects, we need tools to generate smoothly varying curves without any apparent corners, and a unified approach to describing and manipulating them.

4.2   Polygons and Their Offspring

Of tremendous importance in computer graphics is the **polygon**,[1] which is formed by connecting the first and last endpoints of any polyline. It is specified just as a polyline is by a list of vertices. Hence the *polypoint* data type is also used for polygons. To draw a polygon, first draw the polyline based on the vertices, followed by an extra segment from the first to the last vertices in the list. It is easy to build a routine, *Polygon(poly : polypoint)*, that draws the polygon, and we shall henceforth assume that this routine is available (see the exercises).

A polygon is closed, with no discernible beginning or end. The line segments in a polygon may cross one another, just as in a polyline. If no two segments cross, the polygon is a **simple polygon**. More elaborate polygons have polygonal "holes" or "islands" in them, but these require more than one polyline for their description.

The most organized polygons are **regular polygons**, defined as

Definition: A Regular Polygon

A polygon is regular if all its sides have equal length and adjacent sides meet at equal interior angles.

An ***n*-gon** is a regular polygon of *N* sides. Familiar examples are the 4-gon (a square), a 5-gon (a pentagon), 8-gon (an octagon), and so on. A 3-gon is an equilateral triangle. Figure 4.1 shows a variety of polygons. The six-sided ones (A, B, C) show a trend toward greater organization, from nonsimple to simple to regular. The square (D) is, of course, regular, but the parallelogram (E) is not. When a regular polygon has many sides, it looks much like a circle, and this is a common way of generating circles. In some drawings, a 30-gon (F) looks very much like a circle, whereas for higher-precision drawings one must use even more sides to get the right effect.

---

[1]Recall from Chapter 2 that GKS defines a primitive based on the polygon called a fill-area primitive.

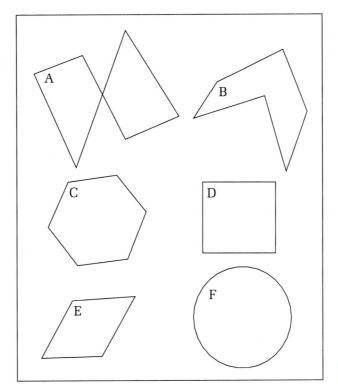

Figure 4.1.
Polygons of various types.

4.2.1 Building and Drawing *n*-gons

It is easy to build and draw regular polygons: We need only compute and store the positions of their vertices. Figure 4.2 shows an octagon. The eight vertices lie at equal intervals around a circle of radius R, separated by angles of $2\pi/8$

Figure 4.2.
Locations of the vertices of an 8-gon.

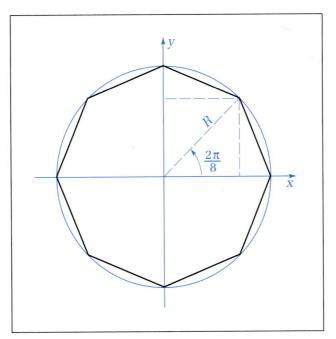

radians. If we set the first vertex on the positive x-axis at $(R, 0)$, the other vertices will lie at multiples of $2\pi/8$. For any given angle A, the position (x, y) of a point on the circle at angle A is found by simple trigonometry to be $(x, y) = (R \cos(A), R \sin(A))$. The i-th vertex v_i of the general n-gon therefore lies at angle $2\pi(i - 1)/N$ and has the position

$$v_i = \left(R \cos\left(\frac{2\pi(i - 1)}{N}\right), \ R \sin\left(\frac{2\pi(i - 1)}{N}\right)\right) \tag{4.1}$$

for $i = 1, 2, \ldots, N$.

The routine *MakeNgon(   )* sets up the vertex locations for a regular n-gon centered at the origin. It will report an error if the value of N is too large (larger than the array size *maxnum*) or is less than 3. The first vertex lies on the x-axis.

Code Fragment 4.1. Building an n-gon

```
procedure MakeNGon(Radius : real; N : integer; var poly : polypoint);
{place vertices of an n-gon in poly}
var
      i : integer;
   angle, del_ang : real;
begin
   if (N < 3) or (N > maxnum) then Report Error {report error if N is bad}
   else begin
      del_ang := TWOPI / N;
         with poly do
         begin
            num := N;
            for i := 1 to num do
            begin
               angle := (i − 1) * del_ang; {begin with angle := 0}
               pt[i].x := Radius * cos(angle);
               pt[i].y := Radius * sin(angle)
            end {for}
         end {with poly}
   end{else}
end;
```

Positioning and Rotating the *n*-gon

The n-gon formed by *MakeNgon(   )* is somewhat restricted in that it is centered at the origin and has one vertex confined to a starting angle of zero—along the positive x-axis. These restrictions are easily removed, if desired, by adding two parameters, *center : point* and *start_angle : real*, to *MakeNgon(   )*. The changes in the routine are simple: *start_angle* is added to the *angle* of each vertex, effectively rotating the n-gon, and *center* is added to the vertices, effectively translating all points through this amount:

```
angle := (i − 1) * del_ang + start_angle; {rotate by start_angle}
pt[i].x := Radius * cos(angle) + center.x;
pt[i].y := Radius * sin(angle) + center.y;
```

4.2.2 Rosettes

With the *n*-gon–building tool in hand, we can draw some interesting shapes. The **rosette** is an *n*-gon with each vertex joined to every other vertex, as shown in Figure 4.3. A rosette is frequently used as a test pattern for computer graphics devices. Its orderly shape readily reveals any distortions, and the resolution of the device can be determined by noting the amount of "crowding" and blurring exhibited by the bundle of lines meeting at each vertex.

Figure 4.3.
Rosettes.

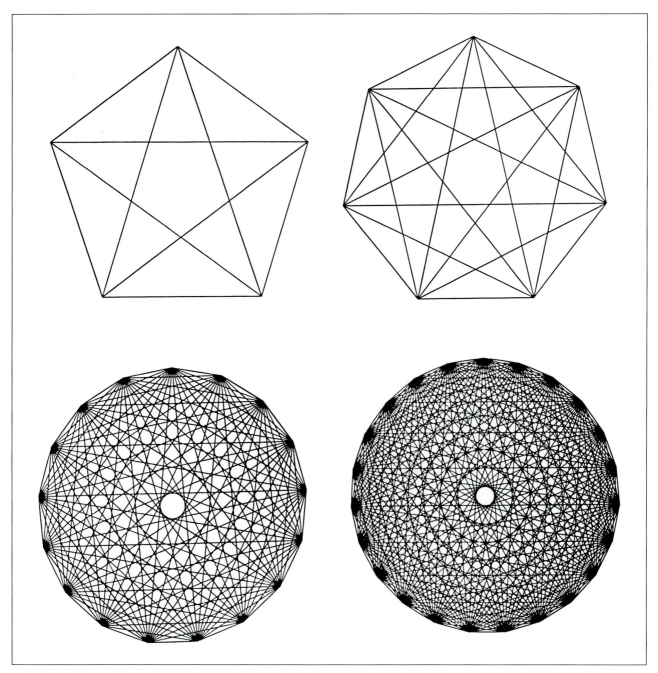

Drill Exercises

4.1. Drawing Rosettes. Write and exercise a program to draw rosettes, in which the user enters the radius and number of sides. *MakeNgon( )* is used to compute the vertices. Then for each vertex v_i a line is drawn to every vertex v_j for which $j > i$. This is easily implemented in two **for** loops.

4.2. How Many Sides in an N-rosette? Show that a rosette based on an *n*-gon, an *N*-rosette, has the following number of sides:

$$\text{number of sides} = \frac{N(N - 1)}{2} \qquad (4.2)$$

This is the same as the number of "clinks" one hears when N people are seated around a table and everybody clinks glasses with everyone else.

Prime Rosettes

If a rosette has a **prime** number N of sides, it can be drawn without "lifting the pen," that is, by using only *LineTo( )* commands. Start at vertex v_1 and draw to each of the others in turn : $v_2, v_3, \ldots, v_N, v_1$ until v_1 is again reached and the polygon is drawn. Then go around again drawing lines, but skip a vertex each time—that is, increment the index by 2—thereby drawing to $v_3, v_5, \ldots, v_1$. This will require going around twice to arrive back at v_1. (A modulo operation is performed on the indices so that their values remain within $1, \ldots, N$.) Then repeat this, incrementing by 3: $v_4, v_7, v_1, \ldots, v_1$. Each repeat draws exactly N lines. Because there are $N(N - 1)/2$ lines in all, the process repeats $(N - 1)/2$ times. Because the number of vertices is a prime, no pattern is ever repeated until the drawing is done. The following routine uses this method to draw prime rosettes:

Code Fragment 4.2. Drawing Prime Rosettes

```
procedure PrimeRosette(radius : real; N : integer);
{draw prime rosette of N sides, where N is prime}
var
    incr, j, index : integer;
    poly : polypoint;
begin
    MakeNgon(radius, N, poly);
    with poly do
    begin
        index := 1;
        MoveTo(pt[index]);
        for incr := 1 to (N − 1)div 2 do
            for j := 1 to N do
            begin {draw N edges}
                index := (index −1 + incr) mod N + 1;
                LineTo(pt[index])
            end
    end
end;
```

Another Golden Figure. The 5-Rosette

The 5-rosette is particularly interesting because it embodies many instances of the golden ratio ϕ. Figure 4.4 shows a 5-rosette with a dotted outer pentagon.

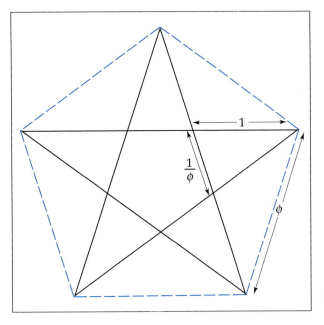

Figure 4.4.
5-rosette and star pentagram.

The Greeks saw a mystical significance in the inner figure, called a **star penta-gram.** In the 5-rosette, the segments have an interesting relationship: Each seg-ment is φ times longer than the next smaller one (see the exercises). Also, because the edges of the star pentagram form an inner pentagon, an infinite regression of pentagrams is possible, as shown in Figure 4.5.

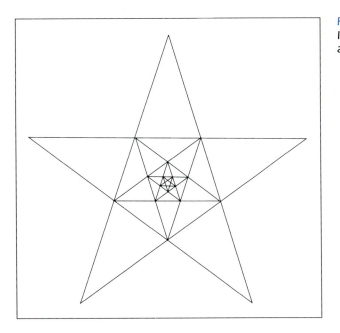

Figure 4.5.
Infinite regressions—pentagons and pentagrams.

Drill Exercise

4.3. The Geometry of the Star Pentagram. Show that the length of each segment in the 5-rosette stands in the golden ratio to that of the next smaller one. One way to tackle this is to show that the triangles of the star pentagram are "golden triangles" with an inner angle of $\pi/5$ radians. Show that $2 \times \cos(\pi/5) = \phi$ and $2 \times \cos(2\pi/5) = 1/\phi$. Another approach uses only two families of similar triangles in the pentagram and the relation $\phi^3 = 2\phi + 1$ satisfied by ϕ.

4.3   Drawing Figures Based on Circles

A circle is a fundamental geometric object in computer graphics. As we showed, it is easily drawn as an *n*-gon with a large number of sides. As the number of sides increases, the individual line segments in the polygon become less visible, and the eye sees a "smooth curve." For high-quality pictures, 50 or more sides are sometimes required.

A routine to draw a circle of radius *rad* centered at the point *center* is given here, which combines the basic operations of *MakeNgon*( ) and *Polygon*( ).

Code Fragment 4.3. A Circle Drawer

```
procedure Circle(center : point; rad : real);
{Draw a circle based on an n-gon with N sides}
const
   N = 50;   {adjust this as required}
var
   p : point;
   i : integer;
   angle, del_ang : real;
begin
   del_ang := TWOPI / N;
   p.x := rad; p.y := 0.0; {initial point}
   MoveTo(p);
   angle := 0.0;
   for i := 1 to N do
   begin
      angle := angle + del_ang;
      p.x := rad * cos(angle) + center.x;
      p.y := rad * sin(angle) + center.y;
      LineTo(p)
   end {for}
end;
```

Circle( ) computes a large number of trigonometric functions and so may operate slowly on some machines. A more efficient method for drawing a circle on a raster display is provided in Chapter 13. It requires no trigonometric computations and uses only integer arithmetic.

In *Circle*( ) a circle is defined by giving its center and radius, but there are other ways to describe a circle, which have important applications in interactive graphics and computer-aided design. Two familiar ones are

1. The center is given, along with a point on the circle. It is simple to find the radius from this information, and so *Circle*( ) can be used at once. If (c_x, c_y) is the center and (p_x, p_y) is the given point on the circle, the radius will be

$$\text{radius} = \sqrt{(p_x - c_x)^2 + (p_y - c_y)^2} \qquad (4.3)$$

2. Three points are given through which the circle must pass. It is known that a unique circle passes through any three points that don't lie in a straight line (see exercise 4.27).

Drill Exercises

4.4 Circle Figures in Philosophy. In Chinese philosophy and religion the two principles of yin and yang interact to influence all creatures' destinies. Figure 4.6 shows the exquisite yin–yang symbol. The dark portion, yin, represents the feminine aspect, and the light portion, yang, represents the masculine. The composition of this symbol is based on two circles touching at the center of a large circle. Each of the inner two circles embraces a small, concentric, inner circle of the opposite shade. Describe the geometry of this symbol when placed in a coordinate system.

4.5 The Seven Pennies. Describe the configuration shown in Figure 4.7, in which six pennies fit snugly around a center penny. Use symmetry arguments to explain why the fit is exact, why each of the outer pennies exactly touches its three neighbors.

Figure 4.6.
The yin–yang symbol.

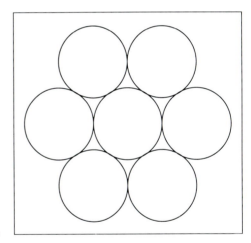

Figure 4.7.
The seven circles.

4.3.1 An Electrical Engineering Application of *Circle*( )

The pattern of circles shown in Figure 4.8 is found in physics and electrical engineering, as the electrostatic field lines around electrically charged wires. It also appears in mathematics in connection with the analytic functions of a complex variable. In Chapter 11 these families also are found when studying a fascinating set of transformations, "inversions in a circle." Here we view it simply as an elegant array of circles and consider how to draw it using *Circle*( ).

In Figure 4.8 there are two families of circles, which we will call A and B. Family A consists of circles that pass through two given points. Suppose the two points are $(a, 0)$ and $(-a, 0)$. The circles in family A can be distinguished by

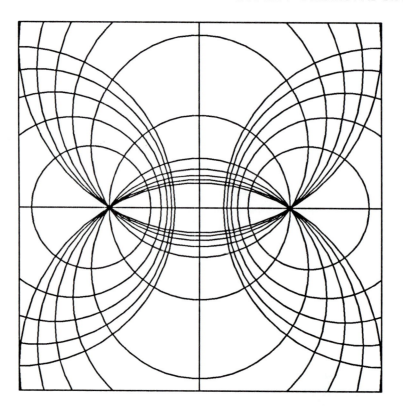

Figure 4.8.
Families of orthogonal circles.

some parameter m, and for each value of m a different circle is generated. The circles have centers and radii given by Pipes (1958):

$$\begin{aligned} Center &= (0, \pm a\sqrt{m^2 - 1}) \\ radius &= am \end{aligned} \qquad (4.4)$$

as m varies from 1 to infinity. Family B is intimately related to family A: Every circle of family B "cuts" through every circle of family A at a right angle. The families of circles are thus said to be **orthogonal** (or perpendicular) to one another. The centers and radii of circles in family B are also distinguished by a parameter n and have the values

$$\begin{aligned} center &= (\pm an, 0) \\ radius &= a\sqrt{n^2 - 1} \end{aligned} \qquad (4.5)$$

as n varies from 1 to infinity. The circles in family B are also known as "circles of Appolonius," and they arise in problems of pursuit. The distances from any point on a circle of Appolonius to the points $(-a, 0)$ and $(a, 0)$ have a constant ratio.

4.3.2 Drawing Pie Charts

With the tools in hand to draw circles, we shall construct another popular type of graph, the **pie chart.** We shall focus on the pie itself and overlook the fancy text and annotations that usually accompany the professionally produced pie charts found in business graphics. A typical example is shown in Figure 4.9. Pie charts are used to illustrate how a whole is divided into parts, as when a pie is

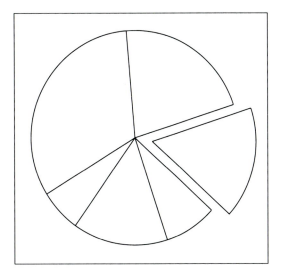

Figure 4.9.
Sample pie chart.

split up and distributed. The eye quickly grasps how big each "slice" is relative to the others. The data for a pie chart might look like

Amount	Color	Exploded	Text
40%	red	no	"milk"
23%	green	no	"honey"
24%	blue	yes	"wheat"
13%	gray	no	"butter"

in which the text would be shown near its corresponding slice. The slices are usually drawn in different colors or with some distinctive cross-hatching.

A pie chart at its simplest is a circle with radial lines delineating the different slices. Often one or more of the slices is "exploded" away from the pack as well, as shown in the figure. In such a case, the pie chart consists of a collection of slices, or sectors. A **sector** consists of an arc of a circle along with two lines joining the arc to the circle's center.

We need a routine, $Arc(\ )$, that draws an arc of a circle. An **arc** is described by the position of the center and radius of the parent circle, along with the beginning and ending angles a_1 and a_2, as shown in Figure 4.10. Because an arc

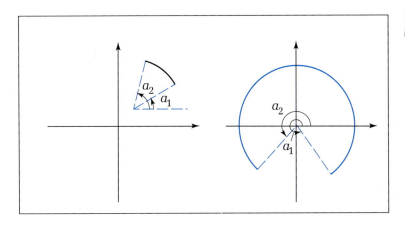

Figure 4.10.
Defining an arc.

is a part of a circle, we expect an arc-drawing routine to resemble *Circle*( )
closely, but with additional parameters to specify angles a_1 and a_2. The procedure *Arc*( ) draws an arc approximated by part of an *n*-gon, using *MoveTo*( )
and *LineTo*( ). This version assumes that *ang2* exceeds *ang1* and uses parameter
anginc to specify the increment in angle between successive points on the *n*-
gon. It draws each segment of the *n*-gon until the angle is within *anginc* of *ang2*
and then draws the last segment exactly to *ang2*.

Code Fragment 4.4. Drawing an Arc

```
procedure Arc(Cent : point; rad, ang1, ang2, anginc : real);
{draw arc—assume ang2 > ang1, and anginc > 0.}
var
    angle : real;
    pt : point;
begin
    pt.x := Cent.x + rad * cos(ang1); {first pt on arc}
    pt.y := Cent.y + rad * sin(ang1);
    MoveTo(pt);       {starting point for sector}
    angle := ang1 + anginc;
    while angle < = ang2 do
    begin
        pt.x := Cent.x + rad * cos(angle);
        pt.y := Cent.y + rad * sin(angle);
        LineTo(pt);                          {draw to next point on arc}
        angle := angle + anginc
    end;
    angle := angle − anginc; {back up to previous angle}
    if angle < ang2 then
    begin
        pt.x := Cent.x + rad * cos(ang2);
        pt.y := Cent.y + rad * sin(ang2);
        LineTo(pt)
    end
end;
```

A sector is easily drawn using *Arc*( ) (how?).

Now to build a pie chart we simply need to know how many slices there
will be and the size of each. Sectors that are exploded are simply shifted slightly
away from the center of the pie chart in the proper direction (see the exercises).

Drill Exercise

4.6   Exploding a Sector of a Pie Chart. Determine how to
draw an exploded sector. The center of the sector is displaced by a small amount radially in the direction of the
middle of the sectors' arc.

4.4 Parametric Representations of Curves

We now introduce a powerful method for expressing the shape of a curve, **parametric representations.** It is of fundamental importance in computer graphics and is used frequently as both a drawing tool and an analytical tool. It is in a sense perfectly matched to the natural way of drawing curves and so fits comfortably in curve-rendering algorithms, avoiding thorny cases that confound other methods. It also is helpful in many intricate geometric explorations, such as finding the unique circle that passes through three points, finding the projection of some point onto a viewing plane, or finding where a ray of light intersects an object. Later we shall see that it works just as well for describing the undulations of curves in three-dimensional space and for characterizing complex surfaces.

Two Ways to View a Curve

There are two useful ways to visualize a curve, as a very thin thread "frozen" in space or as the path of a particle as it moves along the curve. The first view leads us to describe the curve according to the relationship or constraint that its x- and y-coordinates obey. This produces an **implicit form,** as in the equation

$$F(x, y) = 0 \tag{4.6}$$

For example, a circle of radius r has the equation

$$x^2 + y^2 - r^2 = 0 \tag{4.7}$$

and a straight line passing through the points (x_1, y_1) and (x_2, y_2) is captured by the constraint

$$(x_2 - x_1)(y - y_1) - (y_2 - y_1)(x - x_1) = 0 \tag{4.8}$$

Implicit forms are useful at times, but they don't provide much guidance for fashioning an algorithm to draw the corresponding shapes.

Some curves can also be described in **explicit form** through a function, $f(.)$, that specifies the y-coordinate for each value of x: $y = f(x)$. Familiar examples are the straight line $y = mx + b$ (in which m is the slope and b is the y-intercept) and the parabola $y = x^2$. But a function insists that there be one, and only one, value of y for each relevant x, and many curves do not fit this mold. The circle, for instance, is **multivalued**, and so solving Equation 4.7 for y gives two functions, not one: $y = \pm\sqrt{r^2 - x^2}$. There is no single explicit form for the circle. Vertical lines present a similar problem: $y = mx + b$ cannot be used, as $m = \infty$, and so we have to resort to $x = a$ for some a and use a different explicit form for special cases.

A parametric form offers the other way to view a curve and is much more suitable for graphics. It suggests the movement of a point through time, which we can translate into the motion of a pen as it sweeps out the curve. It is called a parametric representation of a curve because a **parameter**—frequently called t and interpreted as "time"—is used to distinguish one point on the curve from another. The path of the particle traveling along the curve is fixed by two func-

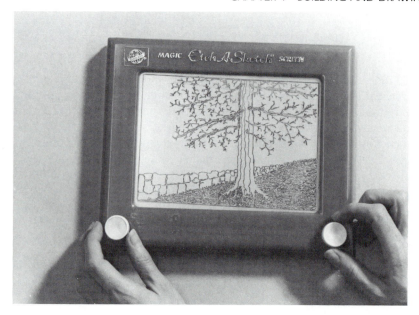

Figure 4.11.
Etch-a-Sketch drawings of parametric curves. (Drawing by Suzanne Casiello.)

tions, $x(\ )$ and $y(\ )$, and we speak of $(x(t), y(t))$ as the position of the particle at time t. The curve itself is the totality of points "visited" by the particle as t varies over some interval, say from 0 to 1. For any curve, therefore, if we can dream up suitable expressions $x(\ )$ and $y(\ )$ they will represent the curve concisely and precisely.

The familiar Etch-a-Sketch[2] shown in Figure 4.11 provides a vivid analogy. As knobs are turned, a stylus hidden in the box scrapes a thin visible line across the screen. One knob controls the horizontal position, and the other directs the vertical position of the stylus. If the knobs are turned in accordance with $x(t)$ and $y(t)$, the parametric curve will be swept out. (Complex curves require significant manual dexterity.)

Parametric forms for curves circumvent all of the difficulties of implicit and explicit forms. Curves can be multivalued; they can self-intersect any number of times; and verticality does not present a special problem. In addition, the approach extends easily to three-dimensional curves. For 3D curves, three functions of t are used, and the point at t on the curve is $(x(t), y(t), z(t))$.

We shall first examine how these ideas work for familiar curves such as lines, circles, and ellipses. Then we shall develop parametric forms for more exotic curves. The result will be a toolbox of interesting and applicable curves, along with the algorithms for drawing them.

4.4.1 Lines, Rays, and Line Segments

Lines, rays, and line segments are fundamental geometric objects in graphics. A **line** is defined by two points, say a and b (see Figure 4.12a). It is infinite in length, passing through the points and extending forever in both directions. A **line segment** (segment for short) is also defined by two points, its **endpoints**, but extends only from one endpoint to the other (Figure 4.12b). A **ray** is "semiinfinite." It starts at a point and extends infinitely far in a given direction (Figure 4.12c).

[2]Etch-a-Sketch is a trademark of Ohio Art.

Lines, rays, and segments all share the same parametric representation. All points on the line segment from $a = (a_x, a_y)$ to $b = (b_x, b_y)$ are represented by the parametric form

$$x(t) = a_x + (b_x - a_x)t$$
$$y(t) = a_y + (b_y - a_y)t \tag{4.9}$$

as t varies from 0 to 1. When $t = 0$, the point $(x(t), y(t))$ is "at" a, and as t increases toward 1, the point moves in a straight line to b. It is midway between the two endpoints when $t = \frac{1}{2}$. It is fraction f of the way from a to b at $t = f$. Recalling the Etch-a-Sketch analogy, the knobs are turned simultaneously at constant speeds. If a "horizontal" speed of $b_x - a_x$ units per second is used, the corresponding vertical speed of $b_y - a_y$ units per second also must be used. If both speeds are doubled, the same line will be swept out, but twice as fast.

The ray that starts at a and passes through b is also given by Equation 4.9, but t is allowed to take on any nonnegative value. The ray "passes through" b at $t = 1$ and then continues forever along the same path. The direction of the ray is given by the vector $(b_x - a_x, b_y - a_y)$, sometimes called its **slope vector**. (Vectors are discussed fully in Chapter 7.) The slope of the segment or ray is given by

$$\text{slope} = \frac{b_y - a_y}{b_x - a_x} \tag{4.10}$$

as long as the denominator is not zero. The slope vector is always well defined mathematically, whereas the slope becomes undefined for vertical lines.

Finally, the line defined by the points a and b is also given by Equation 4.9, but now all real values of t are permitted. Thus segments, rays, and lines differ parametrically only in the values of t that are relevant:

$$\text{segment} : 0 \leq t \leq 1$$
$$\text{ray} : 0 \leq t < \infty \tag{4.11}$$
$$\text{line} : -\infty < t < \infty$$

Drill Exercise

4.7. Lines, Rays, and Segments. Find the parametric form for the segment with endpoints $(2, 3)$ and $(-1, 5)$. Find the midpoint of the segment by using $t = \frac{1}{2}$. Find the slope vector for the ray that begins at $(2, 3)$ and passes through $(-1, 5)$. What is the slope of the segment?

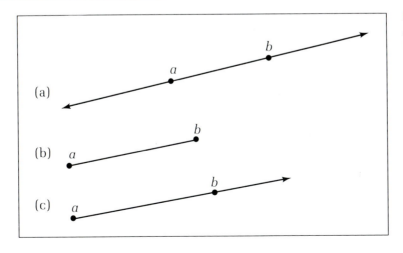

Figure 4.12.
A line (a), segment (b), and ray (c) viewed parametrically.

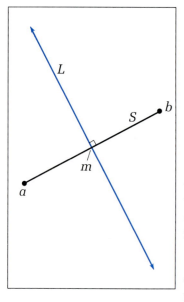

Figure 4.13.
The perpendicular bisector of a
segment.

The Perpendicular Bisector

An important object associated with a line segment is its **perpendicular bisector**, the line that cuts through the midpoint of the segment and is oriented perpendicular to it. Figure 4.13 shows segment S with endpoints a and b. Its perpendicular bisector L is an infinite line that passes through point m that lies halfway from a to b. L and S are orthogonal. According to the preceding discussion, midpoint m is given by

$$m = (m_x, m_y) = \left(\frac{a_x + b_x}{2}, \frac{a_y + b_y}{2}\right) \qquad (4.12)$$

the "mean value" of its endpoints. What is the slope vector of L? Recall that when two lines are perpendicular, their slopes are negative reciprocals of each other. Hence the slope vector of L is found from that of S simply by interchanging the components and negating either one of them:[3]

$$\text{slope vector of } L = (-(b_y - a_y), (b_x - a_x)) \qquad (4.13)$$

The parametric expression for the perpendicular bisector of S is found by combining the following ingredients:

$$\begin{aligned} x(t) &= m_x - (b_y - a_y)t \\ y(t) &= m_y + (b_x - a_x)t \end{aligned} \qquad (4.14)$$

Example

Find the perpendicular bisector L of the segment S having endpoints $a = (3, 5)$ and $b = (9, 3)$.

Solution:

By direct calculation, midpoint $m = (6, 4)$, and because S has slope vector $(6, -2)$, L has representation $L = (6 + 2t, 4 + 6t)$. It is useful to plot both S and L to see this result.

Drill Exercise

4.8.   A Perpendicular Bisector. Find a parametric expression for the perpendicular bisector of the segment with endpoints $a = (0, 6)$ and $b = (4, 0)$. Plot the segment and the line.

The perpendicular bisector is used in Chapter 5 to develop fractal curves, and it also figures prominently in finding the circle that passes through three given points (see the exercises).

4.4.2 Circles and Ellipses

A circle with radius R centered at the origin has the following parametric representation:

$$\begin{aligned} x(t) &= R \times \cos(2\pi t) \\ y(t) &= R \times \sin(2\pi t) \end{aligned} \qquad (4.15)$$

for t between 0 and 1. It is based on simple trigonometry, and in fact we used this

[3]In Chapter 11 we see this "interchange and negate" operation arise naturally in connection with a rotation of 90 degrees.

idea in Figure 4.2 to calculate the vertices of an *n*-gon, as they lie on a circle. For instance, when $t = 0$, the point is at $(R, 0)$, and at $t = 3/4$, it is at $(0, -R)$.

It is useful to visualize drawing the circle on an Etch-a-Sketch. The knobs are turned back and forth in an undulating pattern, one mimicking $\cos(2\pi t)$ and the other $\sin(2\pi t)$. This is surprisingly difficult to do manually.

An **ellipse** is the set of all points for which the sum of the distances to two foci is constant. The ellipse is only a slight generalization of the circle, the $\cos(.)$ and $\sin(.)$ functions being given different scale factors:

$$x(t) = a \times \cos(2\pi t)$$
$$y(t) = b \times \sin(2\pi t) \qquad (4.16)$$

Recall that the ellipse has the implicit formula

$$\left(\frac{x}{a}\right)^2 + \left(\frac{y}{b}\right)^2 = 1 \qquad (4.17)$$

It is easy to check that these expressions are consistent by substituting Equation 4.16 into Equation 4.17 and using the well-known trigonometric fact that $\sin^2(\theta) + \cos^2(\theta) = 1$ for any θ. Figure 4.14 shows the ellipse represented by these equations. Its longer axis has length $2a$, and its shorter axis has length $2b$. The point $(c, 0)$ forms one "focus" of the ellipse, and $(-c, 0)$ forms the other. What is the sum of the distances to the two foci here? Show that a, b, and c are related by $a^2 = b^2 + c^2$. When $a = b$, the ellipse reduces to the circle of radius a, and the two foci coalesce at the origin. (Also note that for $a = b$, Equation 4.17 reduces to Equation 4.7 with $r = a$.)

The **eccentricity**, $e = c/a$, of an ellipse is a measure of how noncircular the ellipse is, being 0 for a true circle. Incidentally, the planets in our solar system have very nearly circular orbits, with e ranging from 1/143(Venus) to 1/4(Pluto). Earth's orbit has $e = 1/60$.

Drill Exercise

4.9. On Eccentricity. As the eccentricity of an ellipse approaches 1, the ellipse flattens into a straight line. But e has to get very close to 1 before this happens. What is the ratio b/a of height to width for an ellipse that has $e = 0.99$?

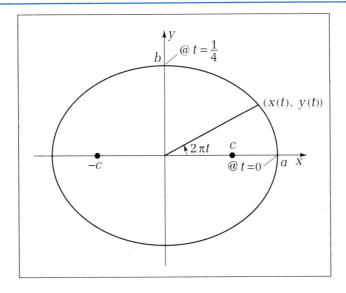

Figure 4.14.
Parametric representation of an ellipse.

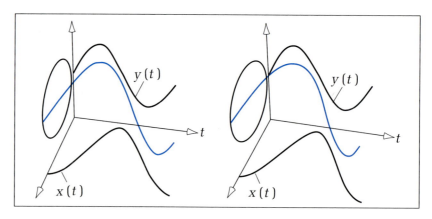

Figure 4.15.
Stereo view of the ellipse in parametric form.

A three-dimensional view of a parametric curve being swept out can be useful in visualizing how the simultaneous undulation of the two functions $x(t)$ and $y(t)$ work together to produce the curve. Figure 4.15 shows a stereo view of the ellipse[4] being swept out as t increases. An extra axis, the t-axis, is shown emanating from the x, y-plane. The shape $x(t) = a \cos(2\pi t) + a_0$ is plotted versus t in the x, t-plane, and the shape $y(t) = b \sin(2\pi t) + b_0$ is shown in the y, t-plane. The offsets a_0 and b_0 have been included to move the ellipse away from the origin in order to clarify the picture. As t increases, both $x(t)$ and $y(t)$ undulate and together with t they sweep out a helix given by $(x(t), y(t), t)$ (shown in blue). The two-dimensional ellipse that is being generated is shown on the x, y-plane.

Drill Exercise

4.10   Other Parametric Forms. Show that the following geometric shapes have the parametric representations specified:

- *Parabola*: $(y^2 - 4ax = 0)$

$$x(t) = a \times t^2$$
$$y(t) = 2a \times t$$

- *Hyperbola*: $((x/a)^2 - (y/b)^2 = 1)$

$$x(t) = a \times \sec(t)$$
$$y(t) = b \times \tan(t)$$

Question: What range in the parameter t is used to sweep out this hyperbola? *Note*: A hyperbola is defined as the locus of all points for which the difference in its distances from two fixed foci is a constant. If the foci here are at $(-c, 0)$ and $(+c, 0)$, a and b must be related by $c^2 = a^2 + b^2$. Contrast this with the ellipse.

Nonuniqueness of a Representation

Note that curves do not have unique parametric representations. For instance, one can surely replace t with $3t$ in the form for the ellipse and still get the same curve. (The moving point traverses the curve three times as t varies from 0 to 1 and does it three times faster, but the same curve is swept out.)

[4]We describe how to view stereo figures in the preface. Producing stereo drawings in an application is discussed in Chapter 12.

Aside for Mathematicians and the Curious

More generally, the t-axis can be warped with any "monotonically increasing" function. That is, $g(t)$ will increase monotonically if it continues to grow, that is, if $t_2 > t_1$ implies that $g(t_2) > g(t_1)$. If a curve C is swept out by the parametric functions $x(t)$ and $y(t)$, the same curve will be swept out by the new functions $x(g(t))$ and $y(g(t))$, possibly using a different interval in t. What matters is that the slope $y'(t)/x'(t)$ (where $'$ denotes the first derivative of the function of C at each value of t) is not altered by the warping. And because the derivative of $y(g(t))$ is simply $y'(t)g'(t)$, and similarly for the derivative of $x(g(t))$, the two $g'(t)$ terms cancel in the ratio, and the slope is unchanged.

In addition to the variety of representations that is produced by "time warps," some curves permit simple representations that differ greatly in character, such as in the next exercise.

Drill Exercise

4.11. Another Parametric Form for the Circle. Show that the following form also generates part of a circle as t varies from 0 to ∞ :

What is its center and radius? What portion is generated as t varies from 0 to 1? Adjust the form in Equation 4.18 so that it represents the ellipse in Equation 4.17.

$$x(t) = a\left(\frac{1-t}{1+t}\right)$$

$$y(t) = 2a\left(\frac{\sqrt{t}}{1+t}\right)$$

$$(4.18)$$

4.4.3 Drawing Curves Represented Parametrically

How do we draw a curve once given its parametric representation? Suppose that two functions, $x(t)$ and $y(t)$, are defined over the interval $[0, 1]$. The curve is swept out continuously as t increases in infinitesimal increments, but in an algorithm we use reasonably sized increments and evaluate $x(t)$ and $y(t)$ at only discrete values of t. That is, we **sample** $x(.)$ and $y(.)$ at a sequence of "times" t_1, $t_2, \ldots, t_n$ and evaluate the position of the point along the curve at each of these moments. The drawing is done simply by connecting these points with a polyline. If the samples are spaced sufficiently close together, the eye will automatically blend together the straight line segments and thus will see a smooth curve.

The algorithm to draw the curve $(x(t)), y(t))$ as t varies from 0 to 1 is given by

- Select N points $t[1], t[2], \ldots, t[N]$ from the interval $[0, 1]$.

- Assign to a variable *curve* of type *polypoint* the following values: *curve.pt*$[i] := (x(t[i]), y(t[i]))$, for $i = 1, \ldots, N$

- Draw the curve using *Polyline(curve)*.

Usually the t-values are chosen to be **equispaced** from 0 to 1, in which case $t_i =$

$(i - 1)/(N - 1)$, so that there is a uniform "unfolding" of the functions $x(t)$ and $y(t)$. (Some other possibilities will be discussed later.) The procedure *Draw-Curve( )* uses equispaced samples to draw the curve based on functions $x( )$ and $y( )$, generalizing the parameter interval from $[0, 1]$ to $[t_1, t_2]$.[5] This version also draws the line segments as they are computed, rather than first building a *polypoint* array and then calling *Polyline( )*. If the curve must be reused at a later point in the application, it will save time to compute the values once and then store them.

Code Fragment 4.5. Drawing a Parametric Curve with Equispaced Samples

```
procedure DrawCurve(function x(t : real) : real;
                    function y(t : real) : real;
                    t_1, t_2 : real;
                    N : integer);
{Draw the curve (x(t), y(t)) using N equispaced samples in [t_1, t_2].}
var
    i : integer;
    t, incr : real;
begin
    if N <= 1 then N := 2; {force at least two points}
    incr := (t_2 - t_1)/(N - 1);
    MoveTo_(x(t_1), y(t_1)); {move to first point}
    t := t_1;
    for i := 1 to (N - 1) do
    begin
        t := t + incr;
        LineTo_(x(t), y(t))
    end
end
```

Drill Exercises

4.12.   An Example Curve. Compute and plot by hand the points that *DrawCurve*(1.0, 2.0, 5) would connect for the case:

$$x(t) = \frac{1}{t^2}, \, y(t) = e^{-t}$$

4.13.   The Circle Again. Compute and plot by hand the eight points that *DrawCurve*(0.0, 5.0, 10) would connect for the functions given in Equation 4.18. Choose $a = 1$.

4.4.4 The Exquisite Superellipse

An excellent variation of the ellipse is the **superellipse**, a family of ellipselike shapes that can produce good effects in many drawing situations. The implicit formula for the superellipse is

$$\left(\frac{x}{A}\right)^n + \left(\frac{y}{B}\right)^n = 1 \tag{4.19}$$

where n is a parameter called the *bulge*. Looking at the corresponding formula for the ellipse in Equation 4.17, the superellipse is seen to become an ellipse

[5]Note: Some Pascal compilers do not support passing parameters of type *function*. In this case $x( )$ and $y( )$ are defined as routines within *DrawCurve( )*.

Figure 4.16.
Family of supercircles.

when $n = 2$. The superellipse has the following parametric representation:

$$x(t) = A \times \cos(t)^{2/n}$$
$$y(t) = B \times \sin(t)^{2/n}$$

(4.20)

for $t \in (-\pi, \pi)$.

Check that Equation 4.20 reduces nicely to Equation 4.16 for the ellipse when $n = 2$. By substituting Equation 4.20 into Equation 4.19 you can see that the formulas are consistent, again using $\sin^2(\theta) + \cos^2(\theta) = 1$.

Figure 4.16 shows a family of **supercircles,** special cases of superellipses for which $A = B$. For $n > 1$ the bulge is outward, whereas for $n < 1$ it is inward. When $n = 1$, it becomes a square. Figure 4.17 shows a scene composed entirely

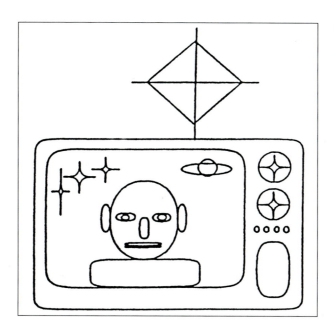

Figure 4.17.
Scene composed of superellipses.

of superellipses, suggesting the range of shapes possible. (Later we shall look at three-dimensional "superquadrics," surfaces that are used in some modern CAD systems to model solid objects.)

Superellipses were first studied in 1818 by the French physicist Gabriel Lamé. More recently in 1959, the extraordinary inventor Piet Hein (best known as the originator of the Soma cube and the game Hex) was approached with the problem of designing a traffic circle in Stockholm. It had to fit inside a rectangle (with $A/B = 6/5$) determined by other roads and had to permit smooth traffic flow as well as be pleasing to the eye. An ellipse proved to be too pointed at the ends for the best traffic patterns, and so Piet Hein sought a fatter curve with straighter sides and landed on the superellipse. He chose $n = 2.5$ as the most pleasing. Stockholm quickly accepted the superellipse motif for its new center. The curves were "strangely satisfying, neither too rounded nor too orthogonal, a happy blend of elliptical and rectangular beauty" (Gardner 1975, p. 243). Since that time, superellipse shapes have appeared in furniture, textile patterns, and even silverware. More can be found out about them in the references, especially in Gardner (1975) and Hill (1979b).

A Mathematical Note

A problem arises in Equation 4.20 when $\cos(t)$ or $\sin(t)$ is negative, as we are attempting to raise a negative number to a fractional exponent, which is illegal. We therefore adopt the interpretation that N^f has the same sign as N and has size $|N|^f$.

Drill Exercise

4.14. Implementation of N_f. Show how the proper interpretation of N^f can be implemented in Pascal so that all cases are evaluated properly, including the case of a negative N and a fractional f.

4.4.5 Polar Coordinate Shapes

Polar coordinates may be used to represent many interesting curves. As shown in Figure 4.18, each point on the curve is represented by an angle θ and a radial

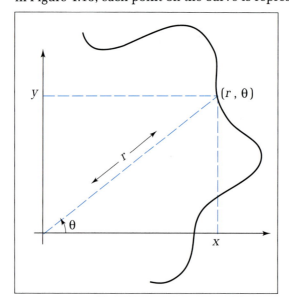

Figure 4.18.
Polar coordinates.

distance r, and the curve is specified by the formula $r = f(\theta)$ that prescribes a particular r for each θ. Here θ is used as a parameter, and a curve is swept out as θ varies. For each point (r, θ) the corresponding Cartesian point (x, y) is given by

$$x = f(\theta) \times \cos(\theta)$$
$$y = f(\theta) \times \sin(\theta) \tag{4.21}$$

Therefore curves given in polar coordinates can be generated and drawn as easily as any others can: The parameter is now θ, which is made to vary over an interval appropriate to the shape. The simplest example is a circle with radius K: $f(\theta) = K$. The form $f(\theta) = 2K \cos(\theta)$ is another simple curve (which one?). Figure 4.19 shows some shapes that have simple expressions in polar coordinates:

1. *Cardioid*: $f(\theta) = K(1 + \cos(\theta))$.

2. *Rose curves*: $f(\theta) = K \cos(n\theta)$, where n specifies the number of petals in the rose. Two cases are shown.

3. *Archimedian spiral*: $f(\theta) = K\theta$.

In each case, constant K gives the overall size of the curve. Because the cardioid is periodic, it can be drawn by varying θ from 0 to 2π. The rose curves are periodic when n is an integer, and the Archimedian spiral keeps growing forever as θ increases from 0. The shape of this spiral has found wide use as a cam to convert rotary motion to linear motion (see Yates 1946).

Figure 4.19.
Examples of curves with simple polar forms.

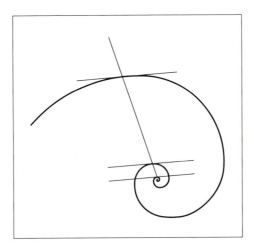

Figure 4.20.
The logarithmic spiral.

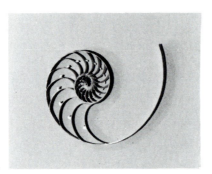

Figure 4.21.
The chambered nautilus.

The **conic sections** (ellipse, parabola, and hyperbola) all share the following polar form:

$$f(\theta) = \frac{K}{1 \pm e \; \cos(\theta)} \tag{4.22}$$

where e is the **eccentricity** of the conic section (Thomas 1953). For $e = 1$ the shape is a parabola; for $0 \le e < 1$ it is an ellipse; and for $e > 1$ it is a hyperbola.

The Logarithmic Spiral

The **logarithmic spiral** (or equiangular spiral) $f(\theta) = Ke^{a\theta}$, shown in Figure 4.20, is also of particular interest (Coxeter 1961). This curve cuts all radial lines at a constant angle α, where $a = \cot(\alpha)$. This is the only spiral that has the same shape for any change of scale: Enlarge a photo of such a spiral any amount, and the enlarged spiral will fit (after a rotation) exactly on top of the original. Similarly, rotate a picture of an equiangular spiral, and it will seem to grow larger or smaller (Steinhaus 1969).[6] This preservation of shape seems to be used by some animals such as the mollusk inside a chambered nautilus (see Figure 4.21): As the animal grows, its shell also grows along a logarithmic spiral in order to provide a home of constant shape (Gardner 1961).

---

[6]This curve was first described by Descartes in 1638. Jacob Bernoulli (1654–1705) was so taken by it that his tombstone in Basel, Switzerland, was engraved with it, along with the inscription *Eadem mutata resurgo*: "Though changed I shall arise the same."

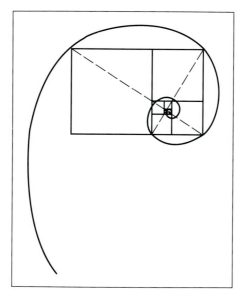

Figure 4.22.
The spiral and the golden
rectangle.

Drill Exercises

4.15. Golden Cuts. Find the specific logarithmic spiral that makes "golden cuts" through the intersections of the infinite regression of golden rectangles, as shown in Figure 4.22 (also recall Chapter 3). How would a figure like Figure 4.22 be drawn algorithmically?

4.4.6 Circles Rolling Around Circles

Another large family of interesting curves can be useful in graphics. Consider the path traced by a point rigidly attached to a circle as the circle rolls around another fixed circle (Thomas 1953, Yates 1946). These are called **trochoids**, and Figure 4.23 shows how they are generated. The tracing point is attached to the

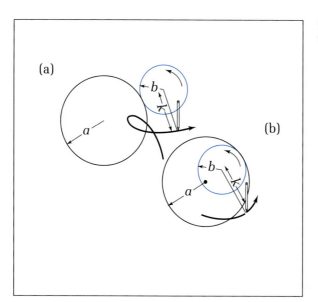

Figure 4.23.
Circles rolling around circles.

rolling circle (of radius b) at the end of a rod k units from the center. The fixed circle has radius a. There are two basic kinds: When the circle rolls externally (Figure 4.23a), an **epitrochoid** is generated, and when it rolls internally (Figure 4.23b), a **hypotrochoid** is generated. The children's game Spirograph[7] is a familiar tool for drawing trochoids, which have the following parametric forms:

● *The epitrochoid:*

$$x(t) = (a + b)\cos(2\pi t) - k \cos\left(2\pi \frac{(a+b)t}{b}\right)$$

$$y(t) = (a + b)\sin(2\pi t) - k \sin\left(2\pi \frac{(a+b)t}{b}\right) \tag{4.23}$$

● *The hypotrochoid:*

$$x(t) = (a - b)\cos(2\pi t) + k \cos\left(2\pi \frac{(a-b)t}{b}\right)$$

$$y(t) = (a - b)\sin(2\pi t) - k \sin\left(2\pi \frac{(a-b)t}{b}\right) \tag{4.24}$$

An ellipse results from the hypotrochoid when $a = 2b$ for any k. The rose curves in Section 4.4.5 are special cases of hypotrochoids in which

$$a = \frac{Sn}{n + 1}$$

$$b = \frac{S(n - 1)}{2(n + 1)} \tag{4.25}$$

$$k = S/2$$

where n is the number of petals and S is an overall sizing constant. When the tracing point lies on the rolling circle ($k = b$), these shapes are called **cycloids**. Some familiar special cases of cycloids are

● *Epicycloids:*

Cardioid: $b = a$

Nephroid: $2b = a$

● *Hypocycloids:*[8]

Line segment: $2b = a$

Deltoid: $3b = a$

Astroid: $4b = a$

Several of these are shown in Figure 4.24.

---

[7] A trademark of Kenner Products.

[8] Note that the astroid is also a superellipse! It has a bulge of 2/3.

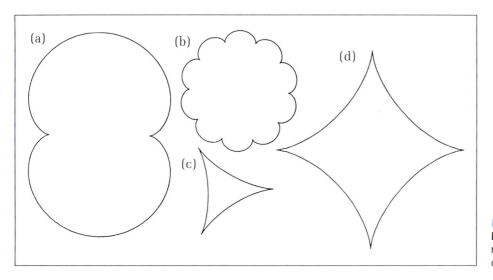

Figure 4.24.
Examples of cycloids: (a)
nephroid, (b) $a/b = 10$, (c)
deltoid, (d) astroid.

Other Orthogonal Families of Curves

Section 4.3 described various families of orthogonal circles, in which each member of one family cuts every member of the other family at right angles. Other family pairs possess this same property; an interesting example is shown in Figure 4.25. Given a pair of foci at $(-c, 0)$ and $(+c, 0)$ we can form all ellipses and hyperbolas that have these foci. From Equation 4.17 the ellipses are given by

$$
\begin{aligned}
x(t) &= a \, \cos(2\pi t) \\
y(t) &= \sqrt{a^2 - c^2} \, \sin(2\pi t)
\end{aligned}
\tag{4.26}
$$

where parameter a distinguishes one confocal ellipse from another. Similarly, the confocal hyperbolas may be distinguished by some parameter d and are given by

$$
\begin{aligned}
x(t) &= d \, \sec(2\pi t) \\
y(t) &= \sqrt{c^2 - d^2} \, \tan(2\pi t)
\end{aligned}
\tag{4.27}
$$

Each ellipse is orthogonal to every hyperbola. Another example, based on "involutes of a circle," is discussed in the exercises.

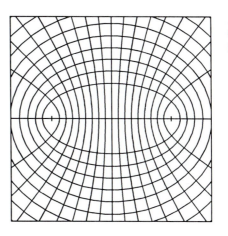

Figure 4.25.
Confocal ellipses and
hyperbolas.

Drill Exercise

4.16. Deriving the Orthogonality Property. Show that the ellipse family is orthogonal to the hyperbola family, that each ellipse cuts through each hyperbola at a right angle.

4.4.7 Playful Variations on a Theme

A wide range of pictures based on parametric representations of curves can be created by varying the way in which the samples are taken and connected. We suggest some possibilities here.

Unevenly Spaced Values of t

Instead of using a constant increment between values of t, when sampling the functions $x(\ )$ and $y(\ )$, we can use a varying increment. It is interesting to experiment with different choices to see what visual effects can be achieved. Some possibilities for the sequence of N t-values between 0 and 1 are

- $t_i = \sqrt{(i-1)/(N-1)}$: The samples cluster closer and closer together as i increases.

- $t_i = (i-1)^2/(N-1)^2$: The samples spread out as i increases.

- $t_i = (i-1)/(N-1) + A \sin(2\pi K(i-1)/(N-1))$: The samples cyclically cluster together or spread apart. Constants A and K are chosen to vary the amount and speed of the variation.

Randomly Selected t-Values

Randomness is often used in computer graphics, both to generate pleasing pictures and to exercise an algorithm thoroughly. Given the functions $x(t)$ and $y(t)$, we choose a succession of random values of t and draw

MoveTo_(x(rand_t), y(rand_t));
for $i := 1$ **to** N **do** *LineTo_(x(rand_t), y(rand_t));*

in which the function *rand_t* returns a randomly generated value between 0 and 1.0 each time it is called. See Appendix 3 for a random number generator. Figure 4.26 shows the polyline generated in this fashion using the functions in Equa-

Figure 4.26.
A random ellipse polyline.

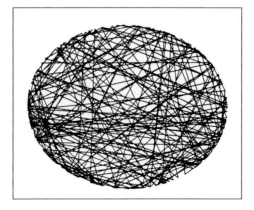

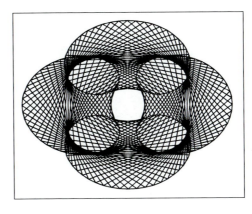

Figure 4.27.
Adding webs to a curve.

tion 4.16 for an ellipse. It is interesting to watch such a picture develop on a display. A flurry of seemingly unrelated lines first appears, but soon the eye detects some order in the chaos and "sees" an elliptical "envelope" emerging around the cloud of lines.

Connecting Vertices in Different Orders

In a popular children's game, pins are driven into a board in some pattern, and a piece of thread is woven around the pins in some order. The N samples of the parametric curve here define the positions of the pins in the board, and *Line-To( )* plays the role of the thread. Suppose the points have been stored in variable *curve* of type *polypoint*. Instead of drawing the points in their natural order from *curve.pt*[1] to *curve.pt*[N], a polyline is wrought by sequencing through the points in a different order:

for $i := 1$ **to** M **do** *LineTo(curve.pt*[*choose(i)*]);

where *choose( )* returns some value between 1 and N. The preceding prime rosette gave one example, where $M = N(N-1)/2$ lines were drawn connecting each point to every other. One can also draw "webs," as suggested in Figure 4.27. Here every k-th point is skipped by setting *choose*(i) $= ((i-1)*k)$ **mod** $N + 1$. Or *choose( )* can return randomly selected values (see the exercises).

4.5   Testing for Intersections of Line Segments

One prevalent task in computer graphics is to calculate where two line segments intersect. It is a crucial part of the clipping algorithm discussed in Chapter 3, and it appears in many other tasks. In addition, it provides an important example of the power of parametric forms: Representing the two lines parametrically helps organize an attack on the problem.

4.5.1 The Problem

Given two line segments, determine whether they intersect, and if they do, find their point of intersection.

Suppose line 1 has endpoints a and b and line 2 has endpoints c and d. As shown in Figure 4.28 the two segments can be disposed in many different ways: They can miss each other (a, b), overlap in one point (c, d), or even overlap over some region (e). They may or may not be parallel. Two lines that are not parallel always intersect, of course, but two segments can be not parallel and still not intersect. An organized approach that tests all these possibilities is crucial.

Set up parametric equations for each of the lines. For line 1:

$$x_1(t) = a_x + (b_x - a_x) \times t$$
$$y_1(t) = a_y + (b_y - a_y) \times t$$

(4.28)

Figure 4.28.
Many cases for two line segments.

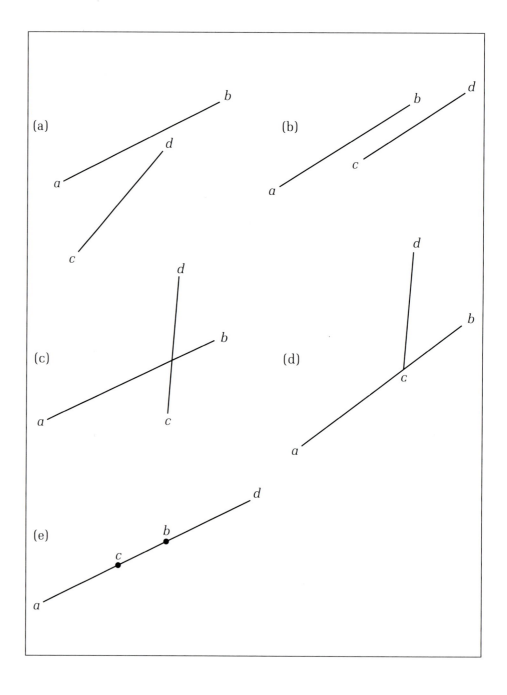

and for line 2:

$$x_2(u) = c_x + (d_x - c_x) \times u$$
$$y_2(u) = c_y + (d_y - c_y) \times u \tag{4.29}$$

It is essential to use different parameters for the two lines, t for one and u for the other, in order to describe different points on the two lines independently. If the same parameter were used, the points on the two lines would be locked together.

Consider the "parent" line of each line segment. This is the infinite line of which the segment is a part. The method first finds where these parent lines intersect and then checks whether the intersection is within both line segments. For the parent lines to intersect, there must be values of t and u—say t_0 and u_0—for which both the x-coordinates agree $(x_1(t_0) = x_2(u_0))$ and the y-coordinates agree $(y_1(t_0) = y_2(u_0))$. Equate the corresponding terms in the preceding equations to obtain two equations in the two unknowns t and u:

$$a_x + (b_x - a_x)t_0 = c_x + (d_x - c_x)u_0$$
$$a_y + (b_y - a_y)t_0 = c_y + (d_y - c_y)u_0 \tag{4.30}$$

These are easily solved: Multiply the first by $(d_y - c_y)$ and the second by $(d_x - c_x)$, and then subtract the second from the first. This eliminates u_0 and gives

$$D \times t_0 = (c_x - a_x)(d_y - c_y) - (c_y - a_y)(d_x - c_x) \tag{4.31}$$

where the term D (short for "denominator") is given by

$$D = (b_x - a_x)(d_y - c_y) - (b_y - a_y)(d_x - c_x) \tag{4.32}$$

There are two principal cases, pivoting on whether D is or is not zero.

D Not Zero

If D is not zero, a definite value exists for t_0 and can be found from Equation 4.31. If this value t_0 lies outside the interval $[0, 1]$, there will be no chance for an intersection: The segment doesn't "reach" the other line. Otherwise an intersection may exist, and so u_0 is found by substituting t_0 into either of the equations in Equation 4.30. If u_0 also lies between 0 and 1, the segments will in fact intersect, and the point of intersection can be found using either Equation 4.28 or Equation 4.29.

Example
Given the endpoints $a = (0, 6)$, $b = (6, 1)$, $c = (1, 3)$, and $d = (5, 5)$, find the intersection.

Solution:
D is found from Equation 4.32 to equal 32, and so the lines are not parallel. Equation 4.31 yields $t_0 = 7/16$, which lies between 0 and 1. Moving on, the first of the equations in Equation 4.30 gives $u_0 = 13/32$ which also lies between 0 and 1, and so the segments do intersect. The intersection is found from Equation 4.28 to be at $(x, y) = (21/8, 61/16)$. This result may be confirmed visually by drawing the segments on graph paper and measuring the observed intersection.

D Is Zero

From Equation 4.32, *D* is zero if

$$\frac{d_y - c_y}{d_x - c_x} = \frac{b_y - a_y}{b_x - a_x} \tag{4.33}$$

which says the slopes are equal, and so the parent lines are parallel. The segments might still overlap, but this can happen only if the parent lines are identical. To test this, see whether *c* lies on the parent line through *a* and *b*. Based on Equation 4.8 the equation for this parent is

$$(b_x - a_x)(y - a_y) - (b_y - a_y)(x - a_x) = 0 \tag{4.34}$$

so substitute c_x for x and c_y for y and see whether the left-hand side is sufficiently close to zero (i.e., its size is less than some tolerance such as 10^{-5}). If not, the parent lines do not coincide, and no intersection exists. If so, the final test is to see whether the segments themselves overlap.

To do this, once again consider the representation for line 1 in Equation 4.28, and find the two values t_c and t_d at which this line reaches *c* and *d*, respectively. Because the parent lines are identical, we can use just the *x*-component (if line 1 is vertical, use the *y*-component instead), and substituting c_x and d_x in turn gives two values:

$$
\begin{aligned}
t_c &= \frac{c_x - a_x}{b_x - a_x} \\[2ex]
t_d &= \frac{d_x - a_x}{b_x - a_x}
\end{aligned}
\tag{4.35}
$$

Line 1 begins at 0 and ends at 1, and by examining the ordering of the four values 0, 1, t_c, and t_d, we can readily determine the relative positions of the two lines. There is an overlap unless both t_c and t_d are less than 0 or larger than 1. If there is an overlap, the endpoints of the overlap can easily be found from the values of t_c and t_d.

Example

Given the endpoints $a = (0, 6)$, $b = (6, 2)$, $c = (3, 4)$, and $d = (9, 0)$, determine the nature of any intersection.

Solution:

D is found to be 0, and so the lines are parallel. Using $(3, 4)$ in the left-hand side of Equation 4.34 also gives 0, and thus the parent lines are identical. Finally, Equation 4.35 yields $t_c = 1/2$ and $t_d = 3/2$, and the segments indeed overlap from $t = 1/2$ to $t = 1$.

The overall algorithm is outlined next using pseudocode. The procedure *Intersect(   )* takes as arguments the four endpoints of the line segments and puts the point of intersection in *int* if there is one. It also puts in *kind* the type of intersection found. Thus *kind* can take one of three values:

- *None* : There is no intersection.

- *One* : There is a point of intersection within both segments.

- *Many* : The segments intersect over an interval.

Other variations are considered in the exercises.

Code Fragment 4.6. Test for the Intersection of Two Line Segments (pseudocode)

```
type intersect_type = (none, one, many);
procedure Intersect(a, b, c, d : point; {endpoints}
                          var int  : point; {pt of intersection}
                          var kind : intersect_type); {type of intersection}
var
   t0, u0, D, tc, td : real;
begin
   kind := none;
   compute D;
   if D <> 0 then
   begin {lines not parallel}
      compute t0, u0;
      if (0 <= t0 <= 1) and (0 <= u0 <= 1) then
      begin {unique intersection exists}
         compute int.x, int.y;
         kind := one
      end
   end {not parallel}
   else {lines parallel} if (c lies on line a, b) then
   begin
      compute tc and td;
      if not (tc, td both < 0 or both > 1) then kind := many
   end
end;
```

Drill Exercises

4.17. Line Segment Intersections. For each of the following segment pairs, exercise the *Intersect( )* algorithm to determine the type of intersection. When it is other than *none*, compute its location.

1. $a=(1, 4)$, $b=(7, 1/2)$, $c=(7/2, 5/2)$, $d=(7, 5)$
2. $a=(1, 4)$, $b=(7, 1/2)$, $c=(5, 0)$, $d=(0, 7)$
3. $a=(0, 7)$, $b=(7, 0)$, $c=(8, -1)$, $d=(10, -3)$
4. $a=(0, 7)$, $b=(7, 0)$, $c=(8, -1)$, $d=(5, 2)$

4.18. Intersections at Endpoints. How should *Intersect( )* handle the case in which an intersection occurs at an endpoint of one or both of the segments?

4.19. The type *segment*. Discuss the value of defining a new data type, *segment*, a record consisting of two *points*. Show how the pseudocode in *Intersect( )* might be enhanced by passing it parameters of type *segment*.

4.6 Summary

This chapter discussed several techniques for creating and drawing curves. We first described drawing polygons and special cases such as *n*-gons and then embellishments such as rosettes. As the number of sides of an *n*-gon increases, the figure approaches a circle, and so we developed algorithms to draw circles.

We also considered several classes of figures based on circles, which led to drawing sectors and putting them together into pie charts.

The chapter introduced the powerful technique of representing a curve parametrically and demonstrated it by means of many examples. The primary advantages to the parametric approach in graphics are

- It is mathematically sound. Vertical portions of curves (where "slopes" become unbounded) need no special attention, and curves that wander back and forth with different y-values for the same x-value are handled automatically.

- It is convenient when drawing curves using a sequence of short line segments, as the parameter can be incremented iteratively and each successive "pen position" can be easily computed.

- It is useful in analytical explorations, such as in calculating where two lines intersect or where the center of a circle defined by three points must lie.

We then studied the intersection of line segments, based on the parametric representation of a line. The need to compute line intersections arises in many parts of computer graphics (such as in clipping and hidden line elimination), and so we must understand both the method and an efficient routine to perform the task.

Programming Exercises

4.20.   The *Polygon( )* Drawing Routine. Write the procedure *Polygon(vertices : polypoint)* which draws the polyline defined by vertices and also connects the first and final vertices with a line.

4.21.   Infinite Regressions of Pentagrams. Write and exercise a routine that draws embedded pentagrams and pentagons.

4.22.   Stellated Polygons. The family of *n*-gons may be enlarged to include "stellated," or starlike, polygons. The sides of an *n*-gon are extended until they meet. Figure 4.29 shows the pentagon in stellated form and two versions of stellated 7-gons. Certain edges of the *n*-rosette are chosen and connected to form a stellation. (What is the Star of David?) Write a routine that draws all possible stellations of the *n*-gon for *n* = 8, 9, 10, and 11. Suggest ways of further generalizing the family of polygons based on *n*-gons.

4.23.   Circle Specified by Its Center and a Point. Write and test a program that uses *Circle( )*. The user specifies the center point and any other point, and the program draws the relevant circle.

4.24.   Rounding Off Corners. Write and test the routine *ArcTo(p, q : point: R : real)*, illustrated in Figure 4.30, which draws a "rounded" corner in the "wedge" formed by the segments L_1 and L_2 defined by the three points *CP*, *p*, and *q*. Think of a circle of radius *R* "snugged" up into this

Figure 4.29.
Some stellated *n*-gons.

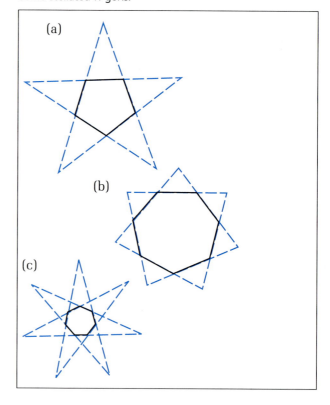

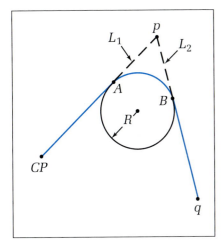

Figure 4.30.
The ArcTo( )
routine.

Here all members of the families pass through a common point $(1, 0)$. Circles in family A have centers at $(1, -m, 0)$ and radii m, and circles in family B have centers at $(1, \pm n)$ and radii n, where both m and n vary from 0 to ∞. Write and exercise a program that draws these families of circles. More challenging: Confine the drawing of each circle to the interior of the unit circle centered at the origin.

4.27. The Excircle. An important way to specify a circle is to give three points through which it must pass. Unless the three points are collinear (i.e., lie in a straight line), there will be exactly one circle that passes through them. In computer-aided design, you often may want to point to three places on a graphics display with some pointing device and see the specified circle appear. Because the three points form a triangle, this is the same as drawing the **circumcircle** (sometimes called the **circumscribed circle** or **excircle**) for the triangle. Figure 4.32 shows some examples.

The main task is to find the center of the excircle. The radius is then easily found as the distance from this center to any of the three points. The key point is that the center of the excircle is equidistant from all three points and so lies on the perpendicular bisector of each side of the triangle. The center is therefore calculated by finding the parametric expression for two of these perpendicular bisectors and then solving them simultaneously.

Develop an algorithm that takes as input three noncollinear points and finds the center and radius of the excircle. Test it by drawing several triangles and their resulting excircles. (How might one test for noncollinearity of the three given points? A method using cross products is given in Chapter 7.)

wedge, which touches the lines at points A and B. Find a way to compute both the location of the circle's center and the points A and B. The routine draws a straight line from CP to A, then the arc from A to B, and finally the straight line from B to q. If R is small, the rounded corner will be very sharp, and if R is large, the corner will be gradual. This routine is useful for drawing various mechanical parts.

4.25. Drawing Orthogonal Circles as in Electrostatic Fields. Write and exercise a program that draws the two families of orthogonal circles described earlier. Choose sets of values of m and n so that the picture will be well balanced and pretty.

4.26. Smith Charts. Another pattern of circles is found in **Smith charts**, familiar in electrical engineering in connection with electromagnetic transmission lines. Figure 4.31 shows the two orthogonal families found in Smith charts.

4.28. Special Points for the Excircle. Show that for any point P on the excircle of a triangle, all the feet of the per-

Figure 4.31.
Orthogonal circles in a Smith chart.

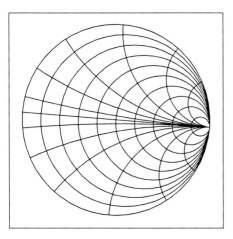

Figure 4.32.
The excircles of various triangles.

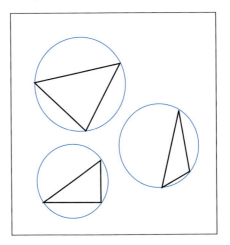

pendiculars from P to the three sides of the triangle lie in a straight line (Coxeter 1961, p. 16). As an addendum to the previous exercise, draw the three perpendiculars and the line on which their feet lie.

4.29.   The Incircle. For any triangle there is a unique circle that just snugs up into it, the **inscribed circle**, or **incircle**, as shown in Figure 4.33. We must find the center of the incircle. Because of symmetry, the center lies on each of the lines that bisect the angles of the triangle. Find the parametric form for two of these lines, and solve for their point of intersection. One way to find the line that bisects an angle is shown in Figure 4.34 for the angle bisector at vertex A. Mark off a unit length along each leg emanating from A, and find the midpoint M of the segment formed. A and M define the desired angle bisector.

Develop an algorithm that takes as input three noncollinear points and finds the center and radius of the incircle. Test it by drawing several triangles and their resulting incircles.

4.30.   Building Pie Charts. Write and exercise a program that takes as input both a list of percentages (e.g., 40, 23, 24, 13) and indications of which slices are to be exploded, and draws the corresponding pie chart. If the graphics device handles color, extend $Line(\ )$ to draw in a specified color, and draw the borders of the slices in color.

4.31.   Superellipses. Write and exercise a program to generate superellipses. Make it flexible enough so that the superellipses can be placed anywhere in world coordinates, with any dimensions and any bulge.

4.32.   Draw the Nautilus. Write a routine that draws the basic curves of the chambered nautilus. Use arcs of circles for the walls between chambers, spacing them at pleasing intervals along the spiral. (It is said that the nautilus spaces its chambers so that their volumes increase according to the golden ratio.)

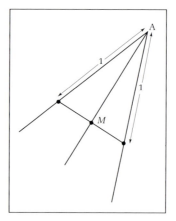

Figure 4.34.
Finding the form for the angle bisector.

4.33.   On Spirals. Consider more general spirals of the form $f(\theta) = K\theta^n$. For $n = 1$ this is the spiral of Archimedes described earlier. For $n = -1$ a hyperbolic spiral $f(\theta) = K/\theta$ results, and when $n = \frac{1}{2}$ a "parabolic spiral" is formed. Exercise a routine that draws various spirals from this class.

4.34.   A Generalization of the Ellipse. An ellipse is formed using a single sine and cosine for the parametric representation (see Figure 4.14). An interesting family of curves may be generated by superimposing several ellipses that are traversed at different speeds. The trochoids discussed earlier are special cases of such curves. This adding together of "harmonics" is similar to the Fourier series plots seen in Chapter 3, but now it is done in two dimensions. We start with two terms and then generalize. Consider the family of curves described by

$$x(t) = X_1 \times \cos(t) + X_2 \times \cos(k \times t)$$
$$y(t) = Y_1 \times \sin(t) + Y_2 \times \sin(k \times t) \qquad (4.36)$$

The first term in each formula represents an ellipse, to which is added a second, "piggyback" ellipse that is traced out k times as fast. In fact, however, as t varies from 0 to 2π, the first ellipse is traced out once, whereas the other is traced out k times. If k is an integer, the figure will close exactly. Figure 4.35 shows an example in which $k = 4$. Write a program that draws such periodic figures, using as input the values of X_1, X_2, Y_1, Y_2, and k. Generalize further by adding more terms to $x(t)$ and $y(t)$.

4.35.   Drawing Trochoids as in Spirographs. Trochoids, popularized in the children's game Spirograph, can be fine-tuned to generate the piggyback ellipses discussed in the preceding exercise. Here the coefficients of the $\sin(\ )$ and $\cos(\ )$ terms must satisfy certain relationships, as discussed in Section 4.4. Write a program that generates spirograph-type figures, and experiment with various values of the parameters.

Figure 4.33.
Finding the incircle.

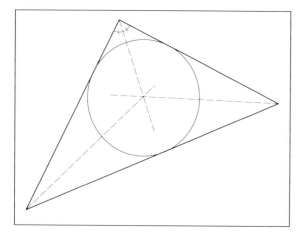

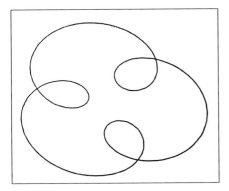

Figure 4.35.
Two piggyback ellipses.

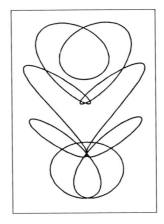

Figure 4.36.
Genie rising.

4.36. The Involute of the Circle. Grab a point P on a piece of thread wound round a broomstick. Keeping the thread taut, unwrap it by circling the broomstick with your hand. The path taken by P is a spiral known as the "involute of a circle." The thread connecting the circle (broomstick) to P forms a tangent to the circle. Apparently this tangent is always perpendicular to the spiral. Also, successive coils of the spiral are parallel and separated by the same distance (which distance?) A family of such spirals is formed by rotating the figure (or by choosing different points P on the thread). Each spiral is orthogonal to all lines tangent to the circle. The parametric form for this curve is

$$x(t) = K(\cos(2\pi t) + 2\pi t \sin(2\pi t))$$
$$y(t) = K(\sin(2\pi t) - 2\pi t \cos(2\pi t)) \qquad (4.37)$$

Write and exercise a program that draws involutes of a circle.

4.37. Other Sinusoidal-Type Curves. Slight alterations in $x(t)$ and $y(t)$ in the earlier exercises can produce remarkably different shapes. For instance, the curve in Figure 4.36 (contributed by Professor Robert Weaver of Mount Holyoke College) results from the following functions:

$$x(t) = \cos(t) + \sin(8 \times t)$$
$$y(t) = 2 \times \sin(t) + \sin(7 \times t) \qquad (4.38)$$

Write a routine that produces this curve, and try other variations as well. Under what conditions on the arguments of the trigonometric functions does the curve always form a closed (periodic) figure?

4.38. Connect the Dots. Write a routine that draws a polyline based on N samples of a parametric curve stored in the variable *curve : polypoint*. Devise various functions *choose(i, N : integer) : integer* that return values between 1 and N. As one example of interest, let *choose( )* perform a "random deal." It produces each of the values $1, 2, \ldots, N$ once in a random order, as if they were being dealt from a shuffled pack of cards.

4.39. Lissajous Figures. A variation on the ellipse of Equation 4.16 is provided if the frequencies of the two sinusoids are allowed to differ:

$$x(t) = \cos(M \times 2\pi \times t + angle)$$
$$y(t) = \sin(N \times 2\pi \times t) \qquad (4.39)$$

where M and N are the new frequencies and *angle* is a "phase offset" between the two components. These shapes are often viewed on an oscilloscope by electrical engineers while studying linear circuits. Write a program that takes M, N, and *angle* as parameters and displays the resulting **Lissajous figures.** Experiment with large increments in t between points chosen on the curves to see the variety of shapes that results. Interesting symmetries can be observed if the values of the x and y variables are swapped (interchanged) after each line is drawn.

4.40. Using Reflections and Symmetry. Mirror images provide a pleasing enhancement of many figures. For any parametric curve $(x(t), y(t))$ it is easy to generate its reflection about the x-axis: simply replace $y(t)$ with $-y(t)$. Further, fourfold symmetry can be attained by drawing the following four curves for any $x(\ )$ and $y(\ )$ functions:

$$\begin{array}{c}(x(t),\ y(t))\\(-x(t),\ y(t))\\(-x(t),\ -y(t))\\(x(t),\ -y(t))\end{array} \qquad (4.40)$$

Similarly, interchanging the coordinates—that is, drawing $(y(t), x(t))$—produces a reflection about a line through the origin and tilted 45 degrees. You can arrange the drawing process so that as each line of $(x(t), y(t))$ is drawn, one or more of these reflections is also drawn. Write a program that allows the user to select one or more of these eight possible symmetries and that draws the corresponding curves.

4.41. Implementation of *Intersect( )*. Flesh out the pseudocode of *Intersect( )*, and exercise it with several examples. In the test application the user inputs four endpoints, and the algorithm determines the nature of any intersection. Both segments are drawn, and if an intersection occurs, it will be highlighted on the display.

4.42. The Four-Bug Problem. First a problem in logic: Four bugs are placed at the corners of a square with sides of length 10. Each bug is turned counterclockwise toward its nearest neighbor and begins to move with the same speed, always turning slightly to aim directly at its neighbor. (It turns out that they describe paths along a logarithmic spiral!) How far will each bug travel before they all collide in the center of the square?

A simple approach to simulating this situation is suggested in Figure 4.37. The bugs lie initially on square *ABCD*. To approximate the initial direction of bug *A*, mark off point *a* that lies some (small) fraction, *f*, of the way from

B to *C*. This point, which we call the *f*-intercept, is easily determined using the parametric form for the segment *BC*. Similarly compute the *f*-intercept points *b*, *c*, and *d* for the other bugs. Suppose the bugs move in jumps, so that bug *A* first jumps fraction *f* of the way along line *Aa*. The others follow suit, at which time they again lie on the corners of another square. At each jump the process is repeated: Each bug jumps fraction *f* of the way from its current position to its *f*-intercept on a side of the previous square. A straight line is drawn from the start to the end of each "jump," so that each bug leaves a "trail" behind it. Write a program that draws the bug trails.

Alternatively, the program can simply draw the successive squares *ABCD*, *abcd*, and so on formed by the bugs. Experiment with different values of *f*, and generalize to *N* bugs situated at the vertices on an *n*-gon. Figure 4.38 shows a typical pattern for the case of five bugs on a pentagon. In Chapter 5 the plane is tessellated with these figures, yielding lovely patterns.

Figure 4.37.
Computing bug motion.

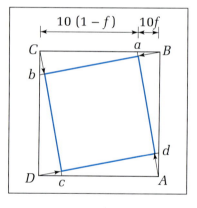

Figure 4.38.
Five converging bugs in a
pentagon.

Approaches to Infinity

So, naturalists observe, a flea
Hath smaller fleas that on him prey;
And these have smaller still to bite 'em;
And so proceed ad infinitum.

Johnathan Swift
"On Poetry, A Rhapsody"

Goals of the Chapter

- To examine the effective use of repetition and recursion in creating figures.
- To extend the ability to visualize complex patterns.
- To examine fundamental tesselations and techniques for creating new tesselations.
- To use recursion to draw space-filling curves.
- To construct fractal curves and trees.
- To construct pictures of Mandelbrot sets.

141

5.1   Introduction

One of the hallmarks of a computer is repetition—not only can it reproduce an earlier computation exactly, but it can also do the same task over and over again without becoming tired. In addition, when coupled with a display device, a computer can produce repetitive patterns that are very pleasing to the eye. People find the right amount of regularity in designs very attractive. Our eyes and brain collaborate to organize an image into understandable pieces and to fit the pieces together, as if they yearn to make geometric sense of a pattern. But we tire quickly of too much regularity and need the jolt of something new and unexpected within a figure. Artists capitalize on this by producing a tension between regularity and surprise.

We created various repetitive patterns in previous chapters. Recall the polyspirals and golden rectangles of Chapter 3 and the rosettes and roulettes of Chapter 4. In this chapter we shall take the next step and examine large classes of patterns, both regular and chaotic. One theme of the chapter is to work toward the very large and very small. Conceptually a process can even proceed to infinity. Simple figures are patched together to form figures that can be extended forever—that is, tilings of the entire infinite plane. And figures can be drawn inside versions of themselves in a recursive fashion that can extend to the smallest speck. Randomness is combined with recursion to generate complex shapes based on the simplest ingredients. We explore self-similarity: the property of a shape to have the same degree of roughness no matter how much it is magnified. And we explore the beguiling Mandelbrot set, considered by some as the most complicated object in mathemetics. No matter how closely one zooms in on it, the pattern is just as gnarled and complex as ever.

We shall develop graphics algorithms for each topic to enable us to generate patterns and create a foundation for further exploration. We can then use these algorithms as computer graphics tools to create special effects in other applications.

5.2   Tiling the Plane

Many of the brightly colored tile-covered walls and floors of the Alhambra in Spain show us that the Moors were masters in the art of filling a plane with similar interlocking figures, bordering each other without gaps. What a pity that their religion forbade them to make images!

M. C. Escher

Interesting patterns arise when a small set of figures is repeatedly drawn over the entire plane. The plane is said to be **tiled** or **tesselated** with the figures if they can be fit together with no gaps. The artist M. C. Escher created many intriguing tesselations, such as those shown in Figure 5.1. Note that a single horseman figure is used in the first example. The horsemen form perfectly interlocking

Figure 5.1.
Two tesselations by M. C. Escher. (© 1988 M. C. Escher Heirs/Cordon Art-Baarn-Holland)

rows, and these rows also interlock with reversed horsemen in adjacent rows. Two figures are used in the fish-and-bird tesselation, but again the whole plane is perfectly tiled. The foreground and background of these figures keep reversing as the eye is drawn from one detail to the next.

First we shall look at tesselations based on a single regular polygon. In this case, only a triangle, square, and hexagon tile the plane. Examples are shown in Figure 5.2. Some variations are possible: Rows of squares can be shifted slightly horizontally in the square tesselation to form layers of "bricks" or other patterns, and bands of triangles can be shifted in one of three directions (which ones?) in the triangle tesselation.

Note that the equilateral triangles must have alternating orientations in order to fit together. Also, because groups of six triangles form a hexagon, the triangular tiling can be made to overlay perfectly the hexagonal tiling.

Hexagonal tesselations appear in beehives and in crystallography, for example (Coxeter 1961), and the game Hex, invented by Piet Hein, is played on a portion of a hexagonal tiling (Berlekamp et al. 1982). (What is seen if lines are drawn from the center of each hexagon to the vertices at 60°, 120°, and 270°?)

The hexagonal network shown in Figure 5.3 is formed by drawing each hexagon of the tesselation at a reduced size and then connecting adjacent hexagons with links (see the exercises). This arrangement has been studied in such diverse fields as computer networks, cellular communication systems for mobile radios, and VLSI design of memory architectures. In computer network-

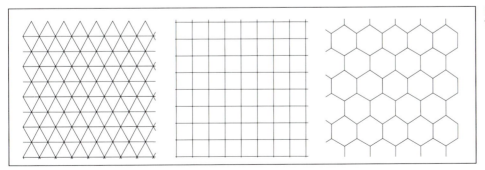

Figure 5.2.
Tiling with *n*-gons.

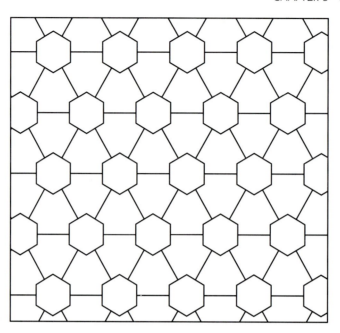

Figure 5.3.
A hexagonal network.

ing, for example, the hexagons represent processors, and the joining lines represent links over which the processors share data. Note that the network of Figure 5.3 is also a tesselation but is based on two different polygons (which ones?)

5.2.1 Drawing Simple Tesselations

Consider how to draw in an application the 3-gon and 6-gon tilings of Figure 5.2. (The 4-gon one is trivial to draw. Why?) For the 3-gon version we draw one row after another of side-by-side equilateral triangles, all in the same orientation (having a horizontal base). Every other row must be offset horizontally by one-half the base of the triangle, and each line segment is drawn only once. For the 6-gon version it is simplest to draw row after row of side-by-side hexagons, again offsetting every other row by one-half the width of the hexagon. Here every line is drawn twice, but on displays that draw lines precisely, the two occurrences are indistinguishable. Clipping can be used to chop off the tilings at the borders of the desired window.

Assume the routines *Triangle(x, y, r : real)* and *Hexagon(x, y, r : real)* are available that draw the desired *n*-gon with the center at (x, y) and radius r. In the following code fragment, suitable values can be provided for the various suggestively named variables so that it produces the 3-gon tiling (see the exercises). A similar form produces the 6-gon version.

Code Fragment 5.1. Drawing the Triangular Tiling

```
for i := 1 to NumRows do
  for j := 1 to NumCols do
  begin
    if Odd(i) then offset := shift else offset := 0;
    Triangle(j * ColWidth + offset, i * RowWidth, 1)
  end;
```

Drill Exercise

5.1. Designing the 3-gon and 6-gon Tesselations. Determine suitable values for *ColWidth*, *RowWidth*, and *shift* for the two types of tilings suggested in the preceding code fragment.

5.2.2 More General Tilings

Insisting that only regular polygons be used in a tesselation is unnecessarily restrictive. What family of tesselations can be based on a single, but not necessarily regular, polygon? An equilateral pentagon can tile the plane, as shown in Figure 5.4. This is called a **Cairo tiling** because many streets in Cairo were paved with tiles using this pattern. Notice that this figure can also be generated by drawing an arrangement of overlapping (irregular) hexagons.

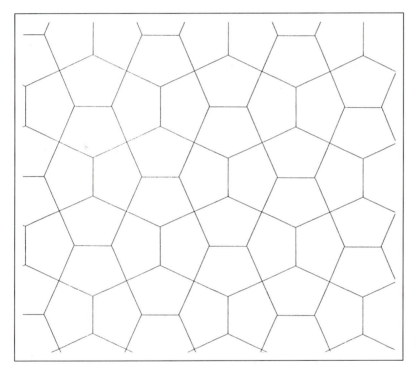

Figure 5.4.
The Cairo tiling.

Drill Exercise

5.2. The Cairo Tile. What are the interior angles of the pentagon in the Cairo tile? What are the relative lengths of the sides of the hexagons involved?

A variety of interesting tilings can be generated by deforming the basic square tiling. For example, by stretching and tilting the square tiling, the squares can be changed into arbitrary parallelograms, as suggested in Figure 5.5. Or an edge can be converted into a zigzag as long as the opposite edge is similarly deformed, as shown in Figure 5.6. The Pegasus example shown in Figure 5.7 was formed in this way, as suggested by McGregor and Watt (1986). Does Escher's horseman in Figure 5.1 fit this model?

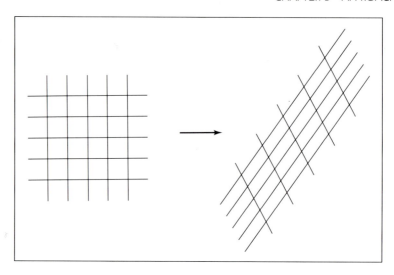

Figure 5.5.
Stretching and tilting the square tiling.

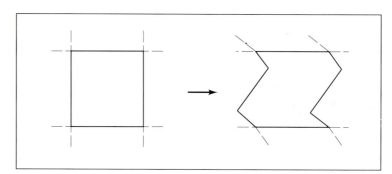

Figure 5.6.
Deforming an edge into a zigzag.

Figure 5.7.
Creating the Pegasus tesselation.

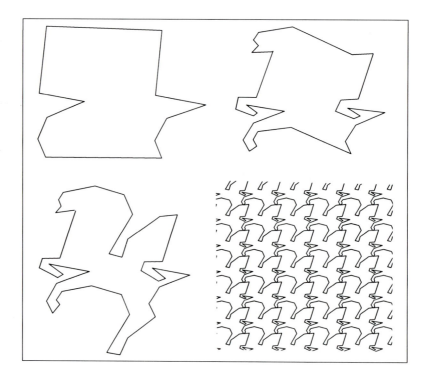

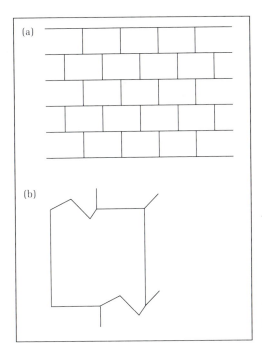

Figure 5.8.
Deforming bricks.

As another possibility, suppose that the rows of the square tiling are first offset to form the brick wall shown in Figure 5.8a. Now a deformation to the left side of the top edge must be matched by a deformation to the right side of the bottom edge, as shown in Figure 5.8b.

Drill Exercises

5.3. Constraints on Deformations. When deforming a square, as shown in Figure 5.5, the 90° angles of each corner may be altered into new angles. What relationship among the angles of the four corners must be maintained?

5.4. Experimenting with Deformations. On graph paper, experiment with deforming the edges of the square tiling to produce interesting figures. Replace each horizontal edge with the same polyline, and do the same for each vertical edge. Experiment also with deformations of the "brick" tiling.

Lovely tesselations can be produced by filling the polygonal tiles with patterns. For instance, recall the "converging bugs" exercise at the end of Chapter 4, which produces a pattern of concentric n-gons that appear to whirl into the center. A pentagonal version is shown in Figure 5.9. Suppose the routine *Draw_Bugs* produces this version. To tile the plane with this (or any other) picture, define a square window as shown and use clipping to eliminate all but the portion lying inside the square.[1] This figure can then be used to tesselate the plane by repeatedly invoking *Draw_Bugs* with a different viewport for each version. The direction of the whirl can be reversed in alternate rows and/or columns to make a prettier pattern, as shown in Figure 5.10. Notice that lines in adjacent viewports meet, so that the eye sees a larger pattern.

[1]Clipping against more general windows such as an n-gon is discussed in Appendix 6.

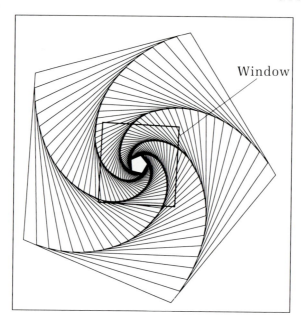

Window

Figure 5.9.
Converging bugs in a window.

Tilings can also be based on more than one polygon. Figure 5.11 shows some tilings based on two *n*-gons (McGregor and Watt 1986, Steinhaus 1969). In some of these examples (which ones?) every vertex is surrounded by the same set of *n*-gons in the same order.

All of these tilings are **periodic**; that is, they are not changed when they are shifted a certain amount in a certain direction. For instance, the horseman tiling in Figure 5.1 can be shifted up vertically by "two horsemen" and will be exactly the same pattern. The hexagons in Figure 5.2 can be shifted either horizontally or vertically by any number of hexagons, without any effect. What shift carries the birds of Figure 5.1 into an identical pattern?

There are many other kinds of tessellations. Later we will discuss some nonperiodic ones based on a single figure in different sizes. Other kinds involve

Figure 5.10.
A six-bug tesselation.

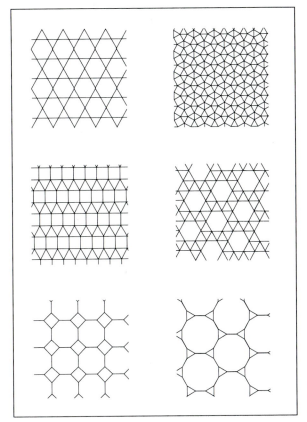

Figure 5.11.
Some tilings based on two n-gons.

a larger number of component shapes (Coxeter 1961, Martin 1982, McGregor and Watt 1986).

We can also go beyond true tesselations to pictures that "migrate" from one pattern to another as the eye sweeps across from left to right. The pattern looks periodic in small regions, but when viewed as a whole, the left side of the figure is totally different from the right (see Hofstadter 1985 for a discussion of such figures). Escher's works also provide many intriguing tesselations as well as migrating patterns.

5.3   Recursively Defined Curves

Many interesting families of patterns are most easily defined recursively. Some give rise to shapes that are both lovely and intriguing; others, such as fractals, produce shapes with useful applications in science and engineering. We examine various examples in this section in order to reveal how they work. Others are suggested in the exercises.

5.3.1 Koch Curves

Perhaps the simplest pattern to generate is the **Koch curve**, discovered in 1904 by the Swedish mathematician Helge von Koch. It stirred great interest because it produces an infinitely long line in a finite area (Gardner 1978).

Successive generations of the Koch curve are shown in Figure 5.12. Begin with a horizontal line of length 1 (Figure 5.12a). To create the first-order curve (call it K_1) divide the line into thirds, and replace the middle section with a triangular "bump" having sides of length $\frac{1}{3}$, as shown in Figure 5.12b. The total line length is evidently $\frac{4}{3}$. The second-order curve K_2 is formed by building a bump on each of the four line segments of K_1, resulting in Figure 5.12c. Because each segment is thereby increased in length by a factor of $\frac{4}{3}$, the total curve length is $\frac{4}{3}$ larger. In general, to form K_{i+1} from K_i, place a bump on every one of its segments. Thus K_i has total length $(\frac{4}{3})^i$, which increases with i as higher generations are formed. As i tends toward infinity, the length of the curve also becomes infinite, yet the curve remains confined to a finite area.

How can we form a Koch curve algorithmically? Suppose that we know how to draw K_8, for which each line segment is of length *len*. Thinking in turtle-graphics terms, we therefore have the proper sequence of *LineForward(len)*, *Left( )*, and *Right( )* commands that make the turtle trace out K_8. In this case, drawing K_9 is simple: Just replace each *LineForward(len)* command for K_8 with four *LineForward(len/3)* commands interspersed with appropriate direction changes. From Figure 5.12b it can be seen that the turtle first turns left through 60°, then right through 120°, and finally left through 60° again.

Thus a Koch curve of order n consists of a four-segment **refinement** of each segment in K_{n-1}. K_0 consists of a single straight line. A Koch curve is defined recursively by requesting refinements of lower-order curves, as seen in the following procedure. This routine draws K_n on a line of length *len* that extends from the current position in the direction *dir*. For example, to draw K_6 on the line from (1, 1) to (4, 5), set *CP* to (1, 1) and execute *Koch*(53.13, 5.0, 6), as this

Figure 5.12.
Three generations of the Koch curve.

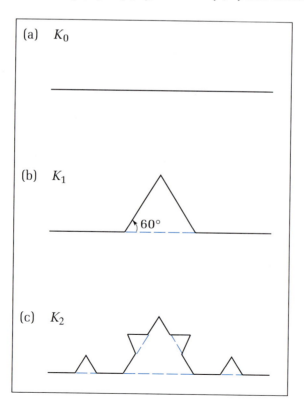

line has length 5 and direction $\tan^{-1}(\frac{4}{3}) = 53.13°$. To keep track of the direction of each segment that may receive a bump, parameter *dir* is passed to subsequent calls to *Koch*( ).

> ### Code Fragment 5.2. Generating a Koch Curve

```
procedure Koch(dir, len : real; n : integer);
{'Koch' the line of length len from CP in direction dir to order n}
const rads = 0.017453293; {convert degrees to radians}
begin
  if n > 0 then
  begin
    Koch(dir, len / 3, n − 1);
    dir := dir + 60;
    Koch(dir, len / 3, n − 1);
    dir := dir − 120;
    Koch(dir, len / 3, n − 1);
    dir := dir + 60;
    Koch(dir, len / 3, n − 1)
  end {if n > 0}
  else LineRel_(len * cos(rads * dir), len * sin(rads * dir))
end;
```

Any line segment can be drawn as a Koch curve. We can invent a verb and speak of "Koch"-ing this line. Figure 5.13 shows the result of koch-ing the three sides of an equilateral triangle with fourth-order Koch curves. This is often called a "Koch snowflake."

Drill Exercises

5.5. Koch-ing an Arbitrary Line. Define the steps needed to draw a Koch curve of order *n* between the points $(a.x, a.y)$ and $(b.x, b.y)$.

5.6. The Length of a Koch Curve. Show that when a line of length L is Koch-ed to order n, the length of each smallest line segment is $(L/3)^n$, and the length of the total Koch curve is $(4L/3)^n$. What is the area enclosed by the snowflake?

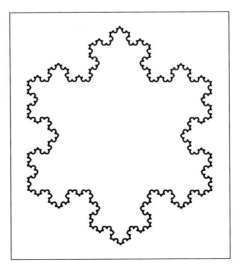

Figure 5.13.
A Koch snowflake.

5.3.2 C-Curves and Dragons

The popular C-curve and dragon illustrated in Figure 5.14 are based on a similar refinement of a line segment. (The origin of their names is apparent from their shapes.) Figure 5.15 shows the refinement process for the C-curve. To progress to the next generation, each line segment is replaced by an "elbow" consisting of two shorter segments joined by a 90° angle. The new segments have length $1/\sqrt{2}$ times that of their parents. Consider a turtle poised at one end of a line segment and aimed along it. To draw the elbow, the turtle turns left through 45°, draws a segment, turns right through 90°, draws the second segment, and then resumes its original course by making a final left turn through 45°. This behavior can be embedded in an algorithm reminiscent of that for the Koch curve.

Code Fragment 5.3. Generating a C-Curve

```
procedure DrawC(dir, len : real; n : integer);
{Draw nth-order C-curve on line from CP len units in direction
dir}
const fct = 0.7071067; {1. / sqrt(2.0)}
begin
  if n > 0 then
  begin
    dir := dir + 45;
    DrawC(dir, len * fct, n − 1);
    dir := dir − 90;
    DrawC(dir, len * fct, n − 1);
    dir := dir + 45
  end
  else LineRel_(len * cos(rads * dir), len * sin(rads * dir))
end;
```

Dragon curves are similar to C-curves except that the direction of the elbow alternates from segment to segment. A dragon curve results from successively folding a thin strip of paper: Lay the strip flat and then fold one end over to meet the other end. Repeat this process forever, always folding over in the same direction. (Only about seven folds are possible in practice.) When the paper is unfolded so that all angles are 90°, a dragon curve emerges.

Figure 5.14.
A C-curve and dragon of the twelfth order.

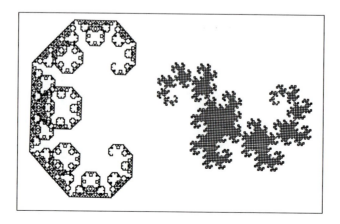

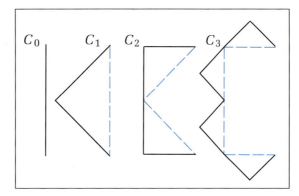

Figure 5.15.
Successive generations of C-curves.

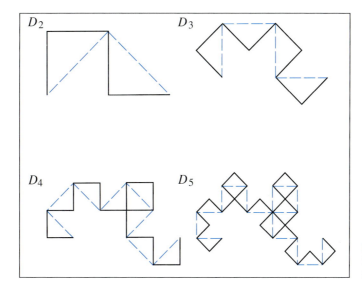

Figure 5.16.
Successive generations of dragons.

Figure 5.16 shows successive generations of dragon curves, with each elbow having a first and a second segment. The rule is this: Replace the first segment with a left-turn elbow and the second segment with a right-turn elbow. A routine to draw dragon curves is discussed in the exercises.

Drill Exercise

5.7. How Large Is a Dragon? Consider a dragon curve of order n based on the line segment from $(0, 0)$ to $(1, 0)$. The dragon lies in a rectangular bounding box, which grows as the order increases. What are the coordinates of the corners of this rectangle as $n \to \infty$? What is the length of this order-n dragon curve?

5.3.3 Space-Filling Curves

The Koch curve is one example of a curve that grows in length without limit yet lies in a bounded region. Other curves do this in such a way that they completely fill the region in which they lie. The two most famous are the Hilbert and Sierpinski curves. A more recent discovery is the Mandelbrot "snowflake," discussed in the exercises.

Hilbert Curves

Hilbert curves, which form very attractive patterns, are named after the great mathematician David Hilbert (1862–1943). A sixth-order Hilbert curve, shown in Figure 5.17, consists of a single unbroken line that starts in the lower left corner and weaves an intricate pattern of left and right turns. What algorithm drives it?

Each Hilbert curve has a certain order, 1, 2, 3, . . ., and one of four orientations, denoted A, B, C, or D. Figure 5.18 shows the four first-order Hilbert curves, A_1, B_1, C_1, and D_1, each a simple three-sided box drawn in a specific direction. These are strung together with some intervening "struts" to form second-order curves, as shown in Figure 5.19. A_2 is composed of the following ingredients: B_1, an "up-strut" (shown dotted), A_1, a "right-strut," A_1 again, a "down-strut" and finally C_1. A recipe for A_2 is therefore B, up, A, right, A, down, C. Similarly, B_2 is seen to be A, right, B, up, B, left, D.

This process continues to all higher orders of Hilbert curve. For instance, B_9 is prescribed by A_8, right, B_8, up, B_8, left, D_8. It is easy to capture this structure in a table that gives the orientations and directions of the subparts for each orientation of a Hilbert curve.[2]

Table 5.1 **Hilbert Curve Definition Table**

A: $BAAC$	A: up right down
B: $ABBD$	B: right up left
C: $DCCA$	C: left down right
D: $CDDB$	D: down left up

These tables are easily constructed and referred to in the drawing algorithm, which is given in the following code fragment.

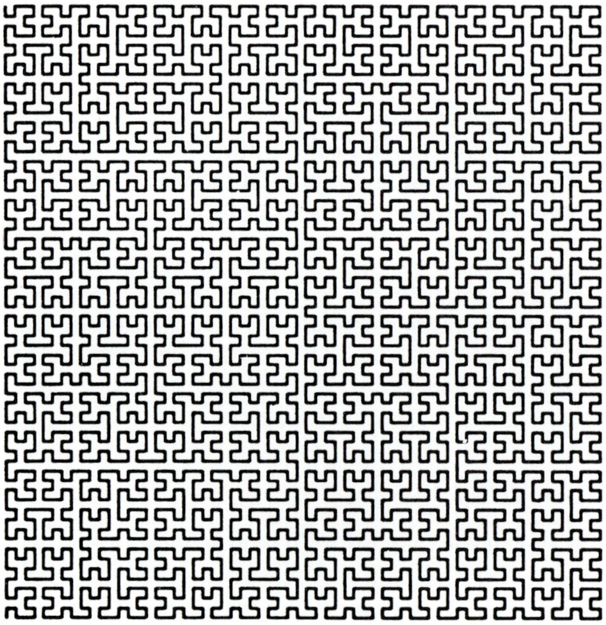

Figure 5.17.
A sixth-order Hilbert curve.

Figure 5.17.
A sixth-order Hilbert curve.

[2]This method was devised by J. G. Griffiths (1983); a similar approach can be found in Wirth (1976).

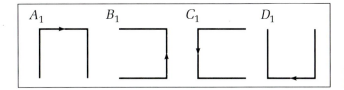

Figure 5.18.
First-order Hilbert curves.

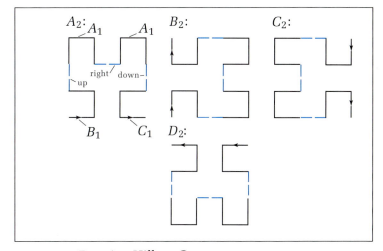

Figure 5.19.
Second-order Hilbert curves.

Code Fragment 5.4. Drawing Hilbert Curves

```
const
    A = 1; B = 2; C = 3; D = 4;
    up = 1; left = 2; down = 3; right = 4;

type
    version = 1..4;
    direction = 1..4;
var
    row : array [version, version] of version;
    dir : array [version, 1..3] of direction;
    dist : real; {length of each line}
<set up values for arrays dir and row>
procedure Hilbert (kind : version; order : integer);
{Draw Hilbert curve of given order}
var j : integer;
begin
    if order > 0 then for j : =1 to 4 do
    begin
        Hilbert (row[kind, j], order − 1);
        if j < 4 then {no extra strut when j = 4}
        case dir[kind, j] of
            up : LineRel_(0, dist);
            down : LineRel_(0, −dist);
            left : LineRel_(−dist, 0);
            right : LineRel_(dist, 0)
        end
    end
end;
```

If *order* = 0, nothing is done, whereas for *order* = 1 only the three struts are drawn, as (*order* − 1) is zero in the recursive call to *Hilbert*( ). For higher orders, the recursive calls draw the proper orientations of the next lower order curve, with intervening struts having the proper direction. Notice that only *LineRel_*( ) is enlisted to draw horizontal or vertical lines. All lines are of length *dist*. If you want to fit the total Hilbert curve of any order into a fixed square, you can make *dist* depend on *order*. For example, the Hilbert curve of order *D* fits in the unit square when

$$dist = \frac{1}{2^D - 1} \tag{5.1}$$

Normalized in this way, Hilbert curves are said to be "space filling." Hilbert proved that as the order tends toward infinity, the infinitely thin, continuous line of the Hilbert curve passes through every point in the unit square!

To draw the A orientation with the lower left corner at (0, 0), first *Move-To_*(0.0, 0.0) and then execute *Hilbert(A, dist)*. Figure 5.20 shows the B orientation of the fifth-order Hilbert curve what should be done for this one?

Sierpinski Curves

Another pleasing and fascinating space-filling curve is the **Sierpinski curve**, which is closed and does not cross over itself. Figure 5.21 shows fourth- and fifth-order Sierpinski curves. Conceptually, each is defined by a succession of "replicate" and "join" operations, as suggested in Figure 5.22. The 0-th order figure S_0 is a square with sides of length *h* standing on a corner (Figure 5.22a). To form S_1, replace this square with four half-size replicas, each moved away from the center by amount *h*. Join these replicas together with horizontal and vertical lines, as shown in color in Figure 5.22b, and erase the four dotted "inner" sides. To create each successive generation, replace each of the squares with four half-size replicas exploded away from its center by the proper amount, draw diagonals, and erase the inner sides. Figure 5.22c suggests the next stage in the process.

This approach is the easiest one to understand, but it requires that certain lines be erased, which is impossible to do on some display devices. An algo-

Figure 5.20.
Hilbert curve of the fifth order.

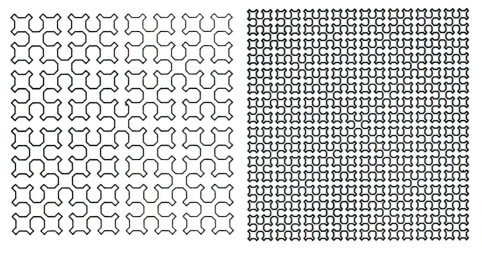

Figure 5.21.
Sierpinski curves S_4 (left) and S_5 (right).

rithm that draws a Sierpinski curve in its final form as one connected line is developed in Wirth (1976).

5.3.4 Reptiles

Reptiles are a class of nonperiodic tilings that are most easily described recursively. Different replicas of a reptile fit together to form a large reptile of the same shape. Thus a large tile can be defined recursively in terms of smaller versions of itself. Figure 5.23 shows various orders of the L-shaped **triomino**, which is just the right shape to embrace four smaller orientations, A, B, C, and D, of itself (Figure 5.23a). Each triomino then can be replaced by these four smaller ones; these can each be replaced by four still smaller ones; and so on. The order

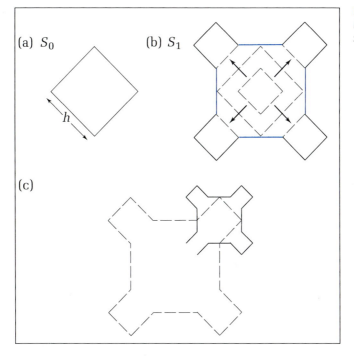

Figure 5.22.
Defining the first- and second-order Sierpinski curves.

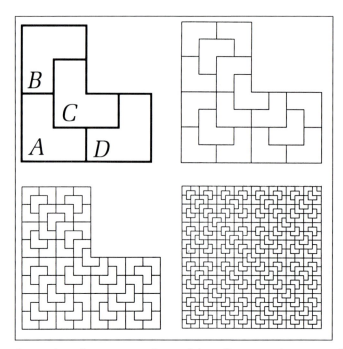

Figure 5.23.
The triomino.

determines how many times this refinement is repeated. An apparent tesselation is created by choosing the window to encompass an inner portion of a
triomino. The following code fragment draws a triomino of a given *height* and
order, with its lower left corner at point *p* and its base rotated counterclockwise
through *angle*. Because the "children" triominos must position and orient
themselves relative to their parents, these parameters are passed to the recursive
calls to *Trio*( ).

Code Fragment 5.5. Drawing Triominos

```
procedure Trio(p : point; height, angle : real; order : integer);
{Draw a triomino}
const
    rads = 0.017453293; {degrees to radians}
    dist = 0.353553391; {sqrt(2) / 4: corner offset for C.}
var
    halfheight : real;
    q : point;
procedure Draw_L(height : real);
{Draw one L in counterclockwise direction at CP in CD.}
var halfheight : real;
begin
    halfheight := height / 2.0;
    LineForward(height); Right(−90.0);
    LineForward(halfheight); Right(−90.0);
    LineForward(halfheight); Right(90.0);
    LineForward(halfheight); Right(−90.0);
    LineForward(halfheight); Right(−90.0);
    LineForward(height); Right(−90.0)
end;
```

begin {*Trio*}
  if *order* <= 0 **then**
  begin {smallest version, draw it}
    CD := *angle*;
    CP := *p*; {initial *CP*}
    Draw_ L(*height*)
  end
  else begin {still too big, call for smaller version}
    halfheight := *height* / 2.0;
    Trio(*p, halfheight, angle, order* − 1); {Do *A*}
    q.x := *p.x* + *height* ∗ *cos*(*rads* ∗ (*angle* + 90.0)); {new corner}
    q.y := *p.y* + *height* ∗ *sin*(*rads* ∗ (*angle* + 90.0));
    Trio(*q, halfheight, angle* − 90.0, *order* − 1); {Do *B*}
    q.x := *p.x* + *dist* ∗ *height* ∗ *cos*(*rads* ∗ (*angle* + 45.0));
    q.y := *p.y* + *dist* ∗ *height* ∗ *sin*(*rads* ∗ (*angle* + 45.0));
    Trio(*q, halfheight, angle, order* − 1); {Do *C*}
    q.x := *p.x* + *height* ∗ *cos*(*rads* ∗ *angle*); {new corner}
    q.y := *p.y* + *height* ∗ *sin*(*rads* ∗ *angle*);
    Trio(*q, halfheight, angle* + 90.0, *order* − 1); {Do *D*}
  end
end;

Because of the various orientations of the tiles within each reptile, these tesselations are nonperiodic. That is, such tesselations do not coincide with any shifted version of themselves. See the exercises for another reptile example, based on the Sphinx.

5.4   Fractals

5.4.1 Self-similarity in Curves

Several of the curves defined so far have been refined by replacing a figure with similar but smaller versions of itself. This leads to the notion of **self-similarity** in a shape: The general level of detail remains the same no matter how closely one looks at it. Consider the Koch curve K_n, for instance. If the refinement process were taken to its limit to create K_∞, one could magnify a portion of the figure a billion times, and the "roughness" of the curve would still appear the same. Similarly, a picture of a Hilbert curve, a dragon, or a triomino (each of infinite order) would look much the same after any amount of magnification. In graphics one never takes the subdivision process to its limit, of course, but the effect of self-similarity is easily approximated.

Nature provides examples that mimic self-similarity. The classic example is a coastline. Seen from a satellite it has a certain level of ruggedness, caused by bays, inlets, and peninsulas. As one flies in for a closer look, more details emerge. A bay is now seen to have a certain ruggedness of its own that was not visible before. Individual boulders and undulations in a beach also give a composite roughness to the view. When one zooms in still farther, smaller rocks and pebbles seem to produce about the same level of ruggedness. This process continues as one looks at individual grains of sand, even through a microscope. Other natural phenomena appear self-similar as well, such as clouds, the cellular structure of a leaf, or the blood vessel system in animals. Indeed, while flying in a airplane it is difficult to judge how large a cloud is. Because it is roughly self-similar, a large cloud situated far away looks much the same as a small cloud nearby.

Benoit Mandelbrot of the IBM Research Center pioneered investigations into the nature of self-similarity. He developed and popularized the field virtually single-handedly and has written extensively on it (e.g., *The Fractal Geometry of Nature*, 1983). We shall discuss several of his inventions and inquiries in this chapter, for they are so well revealed by graphics. Mandelbrot calls various forms of self-similar curves **fractals**, short for "fractional dimensional." A line is one dimensional and a plane is two dimensional, but a curve of infinite length, such as a Koch curve, that fits into a finite region of the plane must have a dimension somewhere between 1 and 2. Accordingly, Mandelbrot devised a method for computing the fractional dimension for such curves (Mandelbrot 1983).

The term *fractal* has become widely associated in graphics with randomly generated curves and surfaces that exhibit a degree of self-similarity. They are used to provide "naturalistic" shapes for representing objects such as coastlines, rugged mountains, grass, and fire.

The simplest fractal is formed by recursively roughening or "fractalizing" a line segment. At each step a line segment is replaced with a "random elbow." Figure 5.24 shows this being done to the line segment S, with endpoints a and b. S is replaced by the two segments from a to c and from c to b. For a fractal curve, c is a randomly chosen point along the perpendicular bisector L of S. Recall from Chapter 4 that L passes through the midpoint m of segment S and is perpendicular to it. According to Equation 4.14 any point c along L has the following parametric form:

$$c = (m_x - (b_y - a_y)t, \ m_y + (b_x - a_x)t) \qquad (5.2)$$

for some value of t. The distance of c from m is proportional to both t and the length of S. The elbow lies on one or the other side of the "parent" segment, depending on whether t is positive or negative. Three stages in the fractalization of a segment are shown in Figure 5.25.

For most fractal curves, t is modeled as a **Gaussian random variable** with a zero mean and some standard deviation. Appendix 3 provides the function

Figure 5.24.
Fractalizing with a "random elbow."

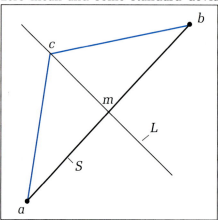

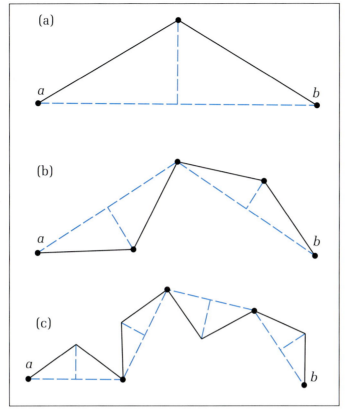

Figure 5.25.
Steps in the fractalization
process.

Gauss that generates such values. Using a mean of zero causes, with equal probability, the elbow to be above or below the parent segment.

Fractal curves are generated by recursively replacing each segment in a random elbow with a smaller random elbow, until some stopping criterion is met. The routine *Fract*( ) generates curves that approximate actual fractals. At each level in the recursion, the length of the segment is tested, and if it is still large enough, the segment will be converted into a random elbow. If it is small enough (that is, if the square of its length, *LenSq*, is smaller than a global value, *MinLenSq*, set by the user), the segment will be drawn using *LineTo*( ). Note that because the offset expressed in Equation 5.2 is proportional to the length of the parent segment, fractal curves are indeed self-similar. At each successive level of recursion, the standard deviation *StdDev* is scaled by a factor f, which is discussed next.

> *Code Fragment 5.6. Fractalizing a Line Segment*

var
    MinLenSq, f : *real*; {global variables}
procedure *Fract*(*a, b* : *point*; *StdDev* : *real*);
{generate a fractal curve from *a* to *b*.}
var
  r, LenSq : *real*;
  n : *point*;

begin
    $LenSq := (a.x - b.x) * (a.x - b.x) + (a.y - b.y) * (a.y - b.y);$
    if $LenSq < MinLenSq$ **then** $LineTo(b)$
    else begin
        $StdDev := StdDev * f;$ {scale $StdDev$ by f}
        $r := Gauss * StdDev;$ {get a random value with mean 0 and std.dev. 1.0.
        Scale it by StdDev to give it the desired std.dev.}
        $n.x := 0.5 * (a.x + b.x) - r * (b.y - a.y);$
        $n.y := 0.5 * (a.y + b.y) + r * (b.x - a.x);$
        $Fract(a, n, StdDev);$
        $Fract(n, b, StdDev)$
    end
end;

The depth of recursion in *Fract*( ) is controlled by the length of the line segment—the recursion stops when the length becomes small enough. Often this length is chosen so that recursion will continue to the limit of the display device's resolution. For a graphics application there is no need to go any further. Alternatively, the parameter *order* can be added to *Fract*( ), giving the maximum depth of recursion, as in the routines for the Koch and dragon curves.

Drill Exercises

5.8.   Controlling the Recursion Depth. Show how to alter *Fract*( ) in order to stop the recursion when a certain depth is reached.

5.9.   Fractalize to the Resolution of the Device. Lines are to be fractalized and displayed on a 515-by-512 pixel display. If you want to fractalize lines so that any horizontal or vertical lines will be fractalized to the resolution of the display, what is the maximum depth of recursion that needs to be used?

Controlling the Persistence of the Fractal Curve

The scaling factor f by which the standard deviation is scaled at each level is based on the **persistence** H of the fractal curve, which determines how "jagged" the curve is. H varies between 0 and 1: Values larger than $\frac{1}{2}$ lead to smoother, more persistent curves, and values smaller than $\frac{1}{2}$ lead to more jagged, "anti-persistent" curves. Factor f depends on H according to Mandelbrot (1983):

$$f = 2^{(\frac{1}{2} - H)} \tag{5.3}$$

Thus, f decreases as H increases. Some sample values are

H	f
0.0	1.4
0.3	1.1
0.5	1.0
0.7	0.9
1.0	0.7

Note that $f = 1$ when $H = \frac{1}{2}$, in which case the standard deviation does not change from level to level. This provides a model of Brownian motion. For persistent curves in which $H > \frac{1}{2}$, we see that $f < 1$, and so the standard deviation diminishes from level to level: The offsets of the elbows become less and less pronounced statistically. On the other hand, when $H < \frac{1}{2}$, antipersistent curves are formed: Factor f is greater than 1, and so the standard deviation increases from level to level, and the elbows tend to become more and more pronounced.

A fractal can be drawn by means of the following steps:

Code Fragment 5.7. Drawing a Fractal Curve

```
procedure DrawFractal(a, b : point);
var
    H, MinLenSq, StdDev : real;
    a, b : point;
begin
    <user inputs H, MinLenSq, and initial StdDev>
    f := exp((0.5 − H) * ln(2.0));
    MoveTo(a);
    Fract(a, b, StdDev)
end;
```

In this routine, factor f is computed using built-in Pascal functions according to Equation 5.3 and the fact that $2^m = e^{m \ln 2}$ for any m.

Some example fractal curves are shown in Figure 5.26 for various values of H, based on a line segment of unit length. (*MinLenSq* was set to .05 and *StdDev* to .2 for these figures.) In each case five fractal curves were generated between the same endpoints to show the possible variations. Note the pronounced effect of changing the persistence H of the fractals.

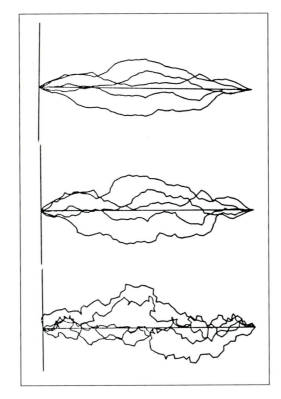

Figure 5.26.
Example fractal curves. (a) $H =$ .7, (b) $H = .5$, (c) $H = .3$.

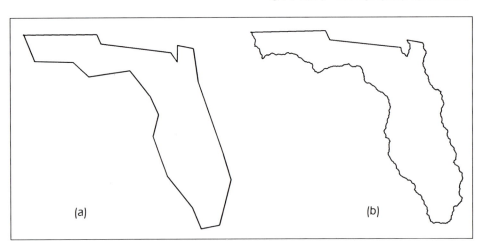

Figure 5.27.
Generating realistic coastlines.

     Arbitrary polylines can be fractalized, as shown in Figure 5.27, providing a
simple means of roughening a shape to make it look naturally rugged. In these
figures the coastline of Florida was crudely digitized, so that Florida is approximated by only 20 points (Figure 5.27a). Then each of the segments on the
coastline of Florida was fractalized, whereas the inland state borders that
should be straight were left unfractalized. It is fascinating to fractalize polygons
that represent known geographic entities such as islands, countries, or conti-
nents, to see how natural their various borders can be made to look. One can also
fractalize other shapes such as animals and the top of a head to give them a
natural appearance.

     One of the features of fractal curves generated by pseudorandom number
generators (as used in *Gauss*( )) is that they are completely repeatable. All that
is required is to use the same seed in the random number generator each time
the curve is fractalized. Each of the three sets of fractals in Figure 5.26 used the
same starting seed, and so they are based on exactly the same sequence of random values (except for a scaling factor based on their different variances). In this
manner a complicated shape such as the fractalized coastline can be completely
described in a database by storing only (1) the polypoint that describes the
original line segments, (2) the values of *MinLenSq* and *StdDev*, and (3) the seed.
From this modest amount of data, a perfect replica of the fractalized curve can
be regenerated at any time.

Fractal Surfaces

Surfaces, as well as lines, can be fractalized in order to generate realistic-looking
mountainous terrain. Plate 1 shows some spectacular examples. The fractalization process is similar to that for a line and is simple conceptually, as suggested
in Figure 5.28. Begin with a triangle, *ABC*, resting on the *x,y*-plane and vertically displace the three edge midpoints, *a*, *b*, and *c*, by a random amount, to
form "pins" rising from the floor. Now join the pinheads to one another and to
the original vertices with lines to form four triangular "facets" (small faces), *ábć*,
ábC, etc. Now repeat this. Each facet is replaced by four new facets by vertically
displacing the midpoints of its edges a random amount and then connecting
them. This process is repeated until the facets are "small enough." Techniques
for the computer representation and realistic display of facets are described in
Chapter 15.

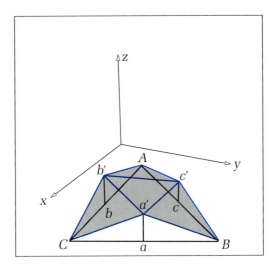

Figure 5.28.
Fractalizing a surface.

5.4.2 Fractal Trees

A fractalization process can be used to generate shapes that resemble trees and shrubs, as suggested in Figure 5.29 (McGregor and Watt 1986). These can be used to ornament various drawings or to be objects of study in themselves. The definition of a tree here is inherently recursive: A tree is a branch with several trees emanating from the end of the branch. Thus at the end of each branch another smaller set of branches is produced, and at the end of each of its branches yet another set is produced. This is most easily done with a recursive routine, *Tree( )*, that calls itself until a certain depth of recursion is reached. Thus one can draw "third-order trees," "fourth-order trees," and the like.

Several additional parameters can be used to characterize the general shape of a tree, as Figure 5.30 suggests. The branch of the tree begins at point p and extends for length L at angle A degrees, terminating at point p_2. At p_2 a new tree is produced, with *num* branches disposed in the "fan-out angle" of F degrees.

Figure 5.29.
Fractal trees.

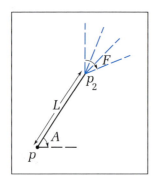

Figure 5.30.
Defining the variables in a tree.

To allow branches in trees to get shorter (or longer) at successive stages, the parameter *LengthRatio* is used, which specifies the ratio of the length of a branch to that of its parent branch. Similarly, *FanRatio* is the ratio of the fan-out angle in a tree relative to that in its parent tree.

Routine *Tree( )* uses this approach to draw a tree. The user specifies values for the listed global variables and then invokes tree drawing with *Tree(start, 90.0, Len, FanoutAngle, order)*. When the recursion depth is reached, the routine *DrawLeaf* can be used to draw, in color, a small circle or other shape at the end of each branch.

Code Fragment 5.8. Drawing a Tree

```
var
    Fanratio, {ratio between fan-out angles}
    LengthRatio : real; {ratio between branch lengths}
    NumBranch : integer; {number of emanating branches}
procedure Tree(p : point; A, L, F : real; n : integer);
{draw order n tree at angle A degrees,
length L, and Fanout Angle F. Start at point p.}
const rads = 0.017453293; {degrees to radians}
var
    i, num : integer;
    p2 : point;
    delang, ang : real;
begin
    if n > 0 then
    begin
        p2.x := p.x + L * cos(rads * A); {find node point}
        p2.y := p.y + L * sin(rads * A);
        Line(p, p2); {draw branch}
        num := NumBranch;
        if num > 1 then delang := F / (num − 1.0) else delang := 0.0;
        ang := A − F / 2.0 − delang; {ready for first branch}
        for i := 1 to num do
        begin
            ang := ang + delang;
            Tree(p2, ang, L * LengthRatio, F * FanRatio, n − 1)
        end
    end
    else DrawLeaf {this routine is left as an exercise}
end; {tree}
```

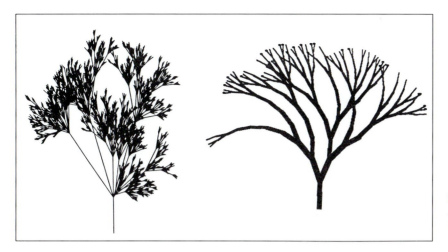

Figure 5.31.
Adding randomness to trees.
[Courtesy of (a) Bill McQuaid
and (b) Adam Lavine.]

Trees generated in this way often look too regular and artificial; a tree will look much more natural if some of its parameters are varied randomly. Figure 5.31 shows examples of trees generated using essentially the same routine *Tree*( ), but with parameters such as the number of branches and the fan-out angle being chosen randomly in each recursive call. See the exercises for these and other variations.

5.5 The Mandelbrot Set

Graphics provides a powerful vehicle for studying the enormously rich **Mandelbrot set**. One view of this set produced on a raster graphic display is shown in Figure 5.32. Each pixel corresponds to a particular point (x, y), and the pixel is colored according to the size that a certain quantity reaches after applying a simple function a large number of times. That is, for each point (x, y) we wish to

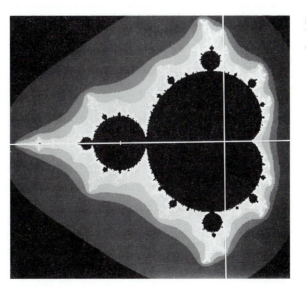

Figure 5.32.
The Mandelbrot set. (Courtesy
of Brett Diamond)

display, a sequence of values, $f_0, f_1, \ldots$, is computed by applying a simple function over and over again. For some points (x, y) the values in the sequence become very large, whereas for others they remain small. Roughly speaking, the Mandelbrot set is the set for which they remain small. It is the black region inside the "wart-covered figure eight" (Dewdney 1988) in Figure 5.32. But as we shall see, the set generated by this simple formulation is incredibly complicated; indeed, it is thought by some to be the most complicated object seen in mathematics.

How is the sequence of points $f_0, f_1, \ldots$ generated for a given point (x, y)? The process is described most elegantly in the complex plane, but readers unfamiliar with complex arithmetic may still experiment with the Mandelbrot set: The following algorithm uses real numbers. Mathematically (x, y) is considered to be the point $c = x + yi$ in the complex plane, where $i = \sqrt{-1}$. A sequence of complex numbers, $d_0, d_1, \ldots$, is formed by iterating the function "square the previous number and add c." Thus $d_{k+1} = d_k^2 + c$. The process always starts with the origin $d_0 = 0 + 0i$, and the first few terms generated are

$$d_1 = c$$
$$d_2 = c^2 + c$$
$$d_3 = (c^2 + c)^2 + c$$
$$d_4 = ((c^2 + c)^2 + c)^2 + c$$
$$\cdots$$

The sequence $f_0, f_1 \ldots$, in whose growth we are interested, is formed simply by taking the magnitude of the complex number d_k: $f_k = |d_k|$.

Example: The Behavior for a Particular c

What happens at $c = -.2 + .5i$? By direct calculation, $d_2 = -.41 + .3i$, $d_3 = -.1219 + .254i$, $d_4 = -.2497 + .4381i$, and so forth. After about 80 iterations the d_k converge to $d_k = -.2499 + .33368i$. This is called a **fixed point** of the function, because squaring it and adding c yields exactly the same value. This fixed point has a finite magnitude, .416479, and so $c = -.2 + .5i$ is in the Mandelbrot set.

For each point (x,y) that represents $c = x + yi$, we wish to compute the sequence f_k for $k = 0, 1, \ldots$ to see whether or not f_k grows arbitrarily large. We can iterate only a finite number of times on a machine, and so only the first N values are computed, for some chosen value of N, say 1000. Often we can get away with fewer iterations. A straightforward result in complex number theory states that if f_k becomes larger than 2 at any point, the sequence will ultimately grow without bound, and (x,y) will not be in the Mandelbrot set. Thus we will stop whenever f_k exceeds 2. If f_k hasn't exceeded 2 by the N-th iteration, we will assume that it never will and conclude that (x,y) is indeed in the Mandelbrot set. The pixel that corresponds to (x,y) is then colored black. If f_k exceeds 2 somewhere in the first N iterations, (x,y) is not in the Mandelbrot set. The corresponding pixel could be colored white to show this, but pictures of the Mandelbrot set are considerably enhanced by using a variety of colors for these "outlying" points. So we choose the color of the pixel according to the number of iterations it takes for f_k to exceed 2. The colors used are purely a matter of taste. For instance, if at (x,y) almost the full N iterations are needed to exceed 2, the point must be close to the Mandelbrot set, and accordingly a light blue might be used. On the other hand, if f_k exceeds 2 after only a few iterations, then (x,y) is far outside the set, and so a fiery red could be used.

The routine *MandelCount* returns the number of iterations required for f_k based on the point (cx,cy) to exceed 2, or N if 2 is never exceeded. (Actually we avoid taking a square root by comparing f_2^k with 4.) A maximum of *num* iterations are performed. The operations performed inside *MandelCount* arise directly from the arithmetic of complex numbers.

Code Fragment 5.9. Generating the Mandelbrot Set

```
function MandelCount(cx, cy : real; num : integer) : integer;
{num is maximum number of iterations.}
const thresh = 4.0; {A larger thresh may yield better pictures.}
var
  x, y, tmp, fsq : real;
  count : integer;
begin
  x := cx; y := cy; fsq :=x * x + y * y;
  count := 1;
  while (count < = num) and (fsq < = thresh) do
  begin
    tmp := x;                    {save old real part}
    x := x * x − y * y + cx;     {new real part}
    y := 2.0 * tmp * y + cy;     {new imaginary part}
    fsq := x * x + y * y;        {square of size of new point}
    count := count + 1
  end;
  MandelCount := count           {number of iterations used}
end;
```

To draw the Mandelbrot set with its "fiery" extensions, a rectangular "window" is chosen in the complex plane, and an array of *numrows* by *numcols* of sample points in the window is examined. For each point *MandelCount* is determined, and based on its value the proper color is assigned to the pixel.

Code Fragment 5.10. Drawing the Mandelbrot Set

```
var
  cx, cy : real;
  i, j, count, num, numcolors, numrows, numcols : integer;
  W : rect;
begin
  <choose num and window>
  <initialize graphics>
  with W do {use window}
  for i := 1 to numrows do
    for j := 1 to numcols do
    begin
      {associate complex number with ij-th pixel}
      cx := left + (right − left) * (j − 1) / (numcols − 1);
      cy := top + (bott − top) * (i − 1) / (numrows − 1);
      count := MandelCount(cx, cy, num);
      if count = num then color := 0 {point is in set; use black}
      else color := trunc(numcolors * (1.0 − count/num));
      set_pixel(i, j, color)
    end
end;
```

What are the properties of the Mandelbrot set and its fiery extensions? It has been studied by a number of mathematicians, and many fascinating facts are known about it (see Mandelbrot 1983, Peitgen and Richter 1986). The boundary of the set is the most interesting place to look and in fact turns out to be a fractal curve. As one zooms in ever closer on a region of interest—by using smaller and smaller windows—new details continually emerge. Plate 2 shows three successive zooms into the region centered at $c = -0.7469 + 0.1073i$. The last picture in the sequence uses the window with the lower left corner at $(-0.74758, 0.10671)$ and the top right corner at $(-0.74624, 0.10779)$. At each zoom a new world of detail becomes visible. For example, what was a single black dot at one zoom becomes an entire new "wart" figure at the next zoom, and it turns out that no two of the miniature warts are exactly alike. Another astonishing fact, proved by John H. Hubbard of Cornell University, is that the Mandelbrot set is connected (Dewdney 1988): Even though the tiny warts seem to float freely in the plane, there is always a wispy tendril of points in the Mandelbrot set that connects them to the parent set.

A practical problem is that to study close-up views of the Mandelbrot set, numbers must be precisely stored and manipulated. Double (or higher) precision arithmetic should be employed. Also, when working close to the boundary of the set, you will need to use a larger number, *num*, of iterations to determine whether a point is inside or outside the set. Therefore, the calculation times for each image will increase as you zoom in. But an image of modest size, say 200 by 200 pixels, can easily be created on a microcomputer in a reasonable amount of time, and the results are well worth the wait. You can also explore the related Julia sets, discussed in the exercises.

5.6   Summary

This chapter examined some approaches to the infinite using repetition and recursion. With certain figures we can move "outward" toward infinity by placing the figures side by side forever, thus tiling the entire infinite plane. It is also possible to go "inward" toward the infinitely small, at least in principle. Recursion provides a simple mechanism for drawing ever smaller "child" versions of a figure inside the "parent" figure, down to the resolution of the display. If the proper class of figures is chosen, the patterns will become self-similar fractals: No matter how closely they are scrutinized, they will exhibit the same level of detail. Randomness can be used to provide an automatic roughness for drawing coastlines, trees, and other natural features. And finally we explored the beguiling Mandelbrot set, whose boundary is itself a fractal curve. As one zooms in on a region near the boundary, new details emerge, and the wart pattern seems to reproduce itself over and over again. This process can continue forever, and so the Mandelbrot set is "infinitely complicated." Computer graphics provides a simple and powerful tool for exploring phenomena such as these. The pictures are generated simply, yet they can reveal enormous complexity.

Programming Exercises

5.10. Honeycombs and Hex Nets. Write a routine that draws a tesselation of the plane using regular hexagons. Can the tiling be drawn without drawing each edge of every hexagon twice? Include the capability of drawing each hexagon at a reduced size and connecting neighboring hexagons with lines as in Figure 5.3.

5.11. Cairo Tiling. Write a routine that draws the Cairo tiling of the plane shown in Figure 5.4. It may be easiest to draw a pattern of overlapping hexagons to form the various pentagons.

5.12. A Pleasing Tesselation. Write a routine that produces the tiling shown in Figure 5.33 (seen in an outside patio in Amherst, Massachusetts). Provide variations on this tiling by adjusting certain points in the basic pattern.

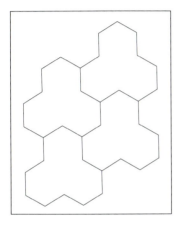

Figure 5.33.
A pleasing patio tiling.

5.13. Whirling Bugs. Write a routine that draws tesselations based on the whirling bug patterns shown in Figure 5.10. Use window clipping to produce a rectangular pattern which is then used to tile the plane. Provide a means to control the direction of the whirl in *Draw_Bugs* so that figures may be drawn in alternating directions.

5.14. Drawing Koch Curves. Implement the *Koch*( ) routine and create pictures such as the Koch snowflake shown in Figure 5.13. Also experiment with drawings of Koch curves on the sides of a regular pentagon and on a complex "interesting" polyline of your choice

5.15. Drawing Dragon Curves. Determine how to alter the C-curve–drawing routine so that it draws dragons. Implement the routine *Dragon(a, b : point; ord : integer)* that draws a dragon of order *ord* on the line segment from *a* to *b*. Apply this routine to the segments of an *n*-gon.

5.16. Generalizations of the C- and Dragon Curves. The angles used previously for the elbows in the C-curves and dragons was 90 degrees. Make this angle a variable in the *DrawC*( ) and *Dragon*( ) routines and experiment with different angles, such as 88 degrees and 92 degrees.

5.17. Sierpinski Curves. Write a routine that draws the Sierpinski curve S_n of order *n*. The curve should fit inside a unit square, with its lower left corner at (0, 0).

5.18. The Mandelbrot Snowflake. Mandelbrot invented a fascinating self-similar fractal curve that fits exactly inside a Koch snowflake. See the cover of *Scientific American*, April 1978, for the third-order Mandelbrot curve, M_3.

The *k*-th-order curve M_k is built up in the following manner, based on subdivisions of an equilateral triangle (Gardner 1978). An equilateral triangle, *ABC*, as shown in Figure 5.34a, has its three sides trisected by points *D* through *I*. Points *JKL* form another equilateral triangle concentric with the first at one-third the size. Point *M* lies halfway between *E* and *J*; *N* lies halfway between *G* and *K*; and *O* lies halfway between *J* and *L*. The Mandelbrot curve M_1 consists of the 13 segments of the polyline: *ADEFGNKM-JOLIHC*. This curve is said to be "built on" segment *AC*. It also has a "left sense" because when looking from *A* to *C* it starts off with a turn to the left.

To form the next generation, M_2, build a curve of the same shape on each of the 13 segments, as shown in Figure 5.36b. The size of each segment determines the size of the

Figure 5.34.
Development of the Mandelbrot snowflake.

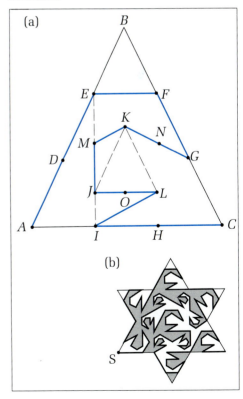

curve. Some of the curves have a left (L) sense, and some have a right (R) sense. Beginning at S, the L, R sequence is *RLLLLRRRLLRRL*. Notice that M_2 fits inside a Koch snowflake of the second order. Write a routine that draws the Mandelbrot curve M_i for $i = 1, 2, 3$. If a display of sufficient resolution is available, also try to draw M_4.

5.19.   The Sphinx Reptile. Write a procedure that draws the Sphinx reptile shown in Figure 5.35. Choose the window to lie completely inside the initial (largest) Sphinx so that the final picture appears to be a tesselation of Sphinxes.

Figure 5.35.
The Sphinx reptile.

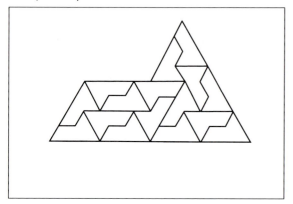

5.20.   Drawing Fractal Shapes. Use the routine *Fract( )* to draw fractalized polylines. Experiment with various polygons that represent islands, states, or countries, and fractalize each to give it a natural appearance.

5.21.   Drawing Random Trees. Adjust the routine *Tree( )* in Section 5.4.2 to introduce some randomness. Have *Tree( )* select randomly the number of branches, *num*, in the range 1 ... *NumBranch* and cause the other parameters also to have a random component. To enable a branch to terminate early, allow the variable *n*, which tracks the depth of recursion, to be decremented randomly. Make the thickness of branches correspond to their order. Also provide for trees that "lean with the wind" by offsetting all initial angles by some amount.

5.22.   Exploring the Mandelbrot Set. Write a program based on *Mandelcount( )* that draws selected portions of the Mandelbrot set. Along with a window, the user specifies the number of rows and columns of pixels to determine, and the program paints the image. Experiment particularly with the regions around $c = -0.75 + 0.02i$ and around $c = -1.25 + 0.02i$.

5.23.   Julia Sets. Julia sets are closely related to the Mandelbrot set. Both of them use iterates of the function $d_{k+1} = d_k^2 + c$ for a given value of c and starting value d_0, and both distinguish inside from outside when f_k is less than 2 or greater than 2, respectively, after N iterations. For the Mandelbrot set, d_0 is always $0 + 0i$, and we determine the color

of the pixel at (x, y) by using $c = x + yi$ in the iteration process. On the other hand, there is a Julia set, $J(c)$, for each value of c! To draw the Julia set $J(c)$, fix c and determine the color of the pixel at (x, y) by using $d_0 = x + yi$ as the starting point. Generate the Julia set $J(-0.7448185 + 0.1050935)$. Experiment with other values of c. Much more can be found in Pietgen and Saupe 1988.

5.24.   Kaleidoscopes. Kaleidoscopes have been popular for centuries (see Walker 1985 for an interesting discussion). As shown in Figure 5.36a, the viewer looks into a cylinder whose walls form an equilateral triangle. Because the inner walls of the cylinder are mirrors, the viewer sees not only the actual objects situated in the "central triangle" at the end of the cylinder but also many replications of them. If high-quality mirrors are used, no boundaries between the three mirror pieces will be visible, and the whole visible "plane" will appear tesselated.

Suppose a coordinate system, as shown in Figure 5.36b, is established in the central triangle. If p is an arbitrary point in this triangle, provide a formula for all of the replicates of p that would be seen. Develop a routine that, given a polyline lying in the central triangle, draws all the replicates as well (that is, that lie within some large window).

Figure 5.36.
Kaleidoscopic tesselations.

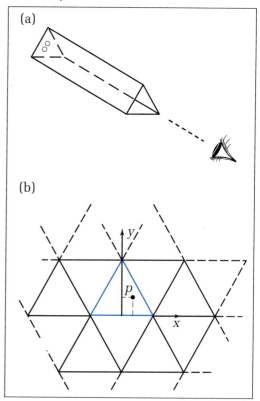

5.25. The Sierpinski Gasket. Generate a picture as a sequence of dots as follows: Form a triangle with three points A, B, and C, and draw any starting point $p[0]$ inside it. Draw a succession of points $p[i]$, each being the midpoint of the previous point and some choice of A, B, or C. That is, $p[i + 1] = (p[i] + R) / 2$, where R is a random selection of A, B, or C. As the number of dots becomes large, the intriguing fractal pattern shown in Figure 5.37, known as the Sierpinski Gasket (Pietgen and Saupe 1988), emerges.

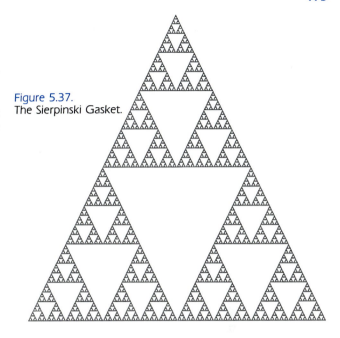

Figure 5.37.
The Sierpinski Gasket.

CHAPTER 6

On Interaction in Graphics

. . . always leave room for the mouse.

Saki, *The Square Egg*, 1924

Goals of the Chapter

- To examine how a user can interact with a graphics application.
- To develop tools for using the *Locate*( ) function.
- To describe the software drivers needed for *Locator* devices.
- To develop an interactive polyline builder and editor.
- To develop techniques for menu building and interaction.
- To examine the basic concepts of picture segments.
- To see how the *Pick* input function interacts with segments.

6.1 Introduction

The concepts and tools we introduced in the last five chapters focused on the pure drawing or plotting of pictures, that is, on the production of output graphical primitives. Little attention was paid to interactive computer graphics. Now we shall develop tools that help a user interact visually with an application. With these tools a user can

- point at objects on the display to edit them.
- select menu items.
- create elaborate polylines and other figures.
- "paint" freehand figures.

With interactive graphics the user works in a natural way—using hand motions and seeing results visually, rather than inputting numbers or typing in character strings to specify an action. The tools are well matched to humans, and so the user is freer to concentrate on the task at hand. The result is vastly enhanced productivity.

The main distinction between physical input devices and logical input devices was discussed in Chapter 2. There are many kinds of physical input devices: tablets, light pens, mice, buttons, knobs, and so forth, but there are only six forms of information that they send back to the application. Recall that the six logical input devices are defined by GKS according to the type of information they return:

Input Function	Data Type Returned
string	*string*
choice	enumeration type
valuator	*real*
locator	*point*
stroke	*polypoint*
pick	segment id

We discussed the *String*, *Choice*, and *Valuator* functions in Chapter 2. We shall introduce here many concepts of interactive graphics programming by focusing on the *Locate* function. A *Locator* is important to much of interactive graphics and is simple to use. Many common physical devices can perform a *Locate* function, and it is reasonably straightforward to devise drivers for them. Thus by focusing on this one input function we can explore many of the ideas of interactive graphics and at the same time develop working tools for applications.

6.2 Introduction to the *Locate* Function

A familiar method for editing text on a word processor is shown in Figure 6.1. When the user moves the mouse around, a cursor makes corresponding moves on the display. Then, when the cursor is positioned over the desired character,

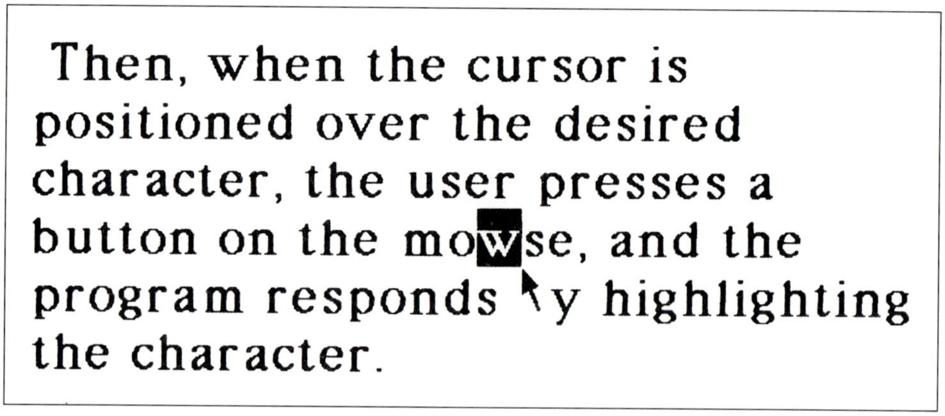

Then, when the cursor is positioned over the desired character, the user presses a button on the mo**w**se, and the program responds ∖y highlighting the character.

Figure 6.1.
Pointing to text in word processing.

the user presses a button on the mouse, and the program responds by highlighting the character. The *Locate* input function operates in much the same way in a graphics environment. The user moves a physical input device and watches a cursor move in response. When the cursor is at the desired spot, the user "triggers" the *Locate*, and the cursor's coordinate position (x,y) is returned to the application for processing. In brief, the application is informed where the user was pointing when the action was triggered. Figure 6.2 shows a light pen being used as a *Locator*. The user points directly at some object on the screen and triggers the action by pressing the light pen against the screen, which closes a microswitch in the pen's tip.

How does one control the *Locator* in an application? Suppose that a graphics package is equipped with a procedure, *Locate*( ), geared to the particular graphics terminal and *Locator* device to be used. Further, suppose that *Locate*( ) has the interface shown at the top of p. 177.

Figure 6.2.
Locate in action.

Code Fragment 6.1. The Interface to Locate( )

type *button = 1..NumButtons;*
procedure *Locate*(**var** *Which_Button : button;* **var** *Location : point),*

NumButtons is a suitably defined constant, giving the number of button choices available. Within an application the *Locate* action is initiated by the statement *Locate(Butt, Spot),* which operates as follows:

- The execution of the application is suspended.

- A cursor appears at some initial position on the display.

- The user manipulates the physical locator to position the cursor at the desired place.

- The user triggers the *Locate( )* by pressing a button or key on the workstation.

- *Butt* is given the value of the button pressed, and *Spot* is replaced with the value of the current location of the *Locator* cursor (in the appropriate coordinate system).

- The application resumes at the next statement following *Locate(Butt,Spot).*

First we shall look at some example applications of the *Locator* that are frequently used in interactive graphics, which will set the stage for a more detailed look at programming and using a *Locator.*

6.2.1 Using *Locate( )* for Instancing

Users often want to draw instances of some graphical object at various places on the display. To draw each instance they point at the desired spot and trigger the action by pressing a command button. The choice of button selects the object to be drawn. The following code fragment lets users draw one of five objects repeatedly or terminate the process by pressing button 6. Figure 6.3 shows an example display after the fragment has been used.

Figure 6.3.
Drawing a collection of objects using *Locate( ).*

Code Fragment 6.2. Draw Instances of Five Objects at the Positions Indicated

```
Locate(Butt, Spot); {indicate first position or quit}
while Butt <>6 do
begin
    CP := Spot; {Set current position to this spot}
    case Butt of
        1: Draw_House;
        2: Draw_Mickey;
        3: Draw_Circle;
        4: Draw_Box;
        5: Draw_Star
    end; {case}
    Locate(Butt, Spot) {get next selection}
end; {while}
```

In this example *Locate*( ) returns a position that becomes that current position (recall Chapter 3) for subsequent drawing. Each of the drawing routines *Draw_House*, *Draw_Mickey*, and the like is assumed to use only relative moves and draws, so that the object is drawn 'at' the specified CP. If a CP is not used, the drawing procedures can be adjusted to accept *Spot* as an explicit argument; for example, *Draw_House(Spot)* would draw the house at location *spot*.

6.2.2 Application: Interactively Creating Polylines

We wish to develop a code fragment that lets users generate freehand polylines by simply moving the cursor around the screen and pressing a button to declare each new point. Figure 6.4 shows an example. We arrange matters so that if button 1 is pressed, the new point will be added to the polyline and a segment will be drawn from the previous point to the current point. If button 2 is pressed, a new polyline is begun. When button 3 is pressed, the process terminates. The following code fragment illustrates the basic ideas involved. Notice the similarities to the previous example.

Figure 6.4.
Drawing polylines interactively. (Courtesy of Susan Verbeck and Chris Russell.)

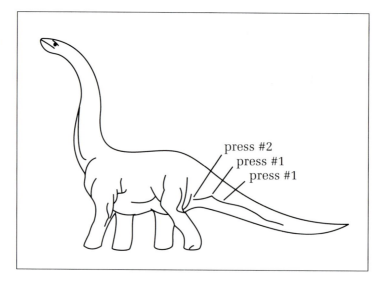

Code Fragment 6.3. Drawing Freehand Polylines

```
repeat
    Locate(Butt, Spot); {send first point or quit}
    case Butt of
        1: LineTo(Spot); {continue the polyline}
        2: MoveTo(Spot); {begin new polyline}
        3: {nothing}
    end {case}
until Butt = 3;
```

More elaborate choices could be incorporated just as easily: $Butt := 4$ could change the line style to dashed, or $Butt := 5$ could change the line color to green.

In this example, the polylines are simply drawn and not retained in memory. More often an application stores the points of each polyline in a data structure so that the polylines can later be edited or filed, as discussed in Section 6.6.

6.2.3 The *Stroke* Input Function

Because the *Stroke* input function is so closely related to *Locate*, we need only look at it briefly and thereafter include it as a simple extension of *Locate*.

The *Stroke* input delivers a sequence of points to the application and so is conceptually equivalent to a succession of *Locate*( )s:

for $i := 1$ **to** *MaxNum* **do** *Locate*(*Butt*, *Spot*[*i*]);

Stroke is usually associated with a tablet or light pen device and is well suited to digitizing lines and curves, as shown in Figure 6.5. Here the user "captures" the shape of a curve taped to the tablet's surface, by moving a tablet "puck" along it. The coordinates of successive points are thereby sent back to the application for storage and subsequent processing. Figure 6.6 indicates with markers a set of

Figure 6.5.
Stroke input performed on a tablet.

Figure 6.6.
A digitized picture.

points that might be sent to the application. (Notice that the user of a tablet does not watch a cursor move on the screen when digitizing a picture but instead watches the tablet's surface. We shall examine other modes of use for a tablet later.) In some situations the user must confirm each point to be sent by pressing a button on the puck. In others the workstation samples the puck's position at specified intervals until the desired number of samples has been sent. One of the advantages of having a separate *Stroke* function within the GKS is that some low-level processing of digitized data can be done within the workstation, invisible to the application. This is useful, because when digitizing a curve, some users crowd samples too closely together, generating excessively redundant data. The workstation then can remove extra points within the *Stroke* function before sending the sequence of points back to the application.

In a call to the *Stroke*( ) input function, the application specifies how many points are to be taken and provides an array to receive the points themselves.

6.2.4 Coordinate Systems Used for *Locate*( ) and *Stroke*( )

In our discussion of the *Locate* and *Stroke* functions, references to the cursor position were given in world coordinates. We assumed that any required conversions among world coordinates, NDC, and device coordinates would be handled transparently within *Locate*( ). This simplified our discussion, but now we must examine the conversion process to clarify several important issues. An understanding of the underlying coordinate systems will facilitate the development of our own device drivers for the *Locator* and simplify writing application programs.

To this end we define a slightly lower level version of *Locate*( ), called *LocateNDC*( ), that returns the cursor coordinates in NDC. The interface is specified as

procedure *LocateNDC*(**var** *Butt* : *button*; **var** *Location* : *point*);

and is illustrated in Figure 6.7. Within *LocateNDC*( ) there is a mapping from device coordinates to NDC, so that all *Location.x* and *Location.y* values returned to the application lie in the range $(0, 0)$ to $(1, 1)$. Actually the range of values may be more restricted. If, as shown in the figure, the device's aspect ratio, R, is smaller than 1, the device driver will arrange matters so that *Location.y* ranges from zero to R. (Alternatively, if $R > 1$, *Location.x* will range from 0 to $1/R$.)

In the application the usual window and viewport are defined as suggested in the figure, using parameters *V.r*, *W.b*, and so on (recall Chapter 3). These parameters are used to map world coordinates to NDC when the application produces output primitives for drawing. They are also used for the input primitives produced by *LocateNDC( )*, but here we work in the opposite direction and build the **inverse transformation** that maps NDC back into world coordinates. By a straightforward rearrangement of Equation 3.1, this mapping from NDC point v to world p is seen to be

$$p_x = \frac{W_r - W_l}{V_r - V_l} \times (v_x - V_l) + W_l$$

$$p_y = \frac{W_t - W_b}{V_t - V_b} \times (v_y - V_t) + W_b \tag{6.1}$$

This transformation can be implemented in the routine

procedure *NDC_to_World*(*NDCpoint* : *point*; **var** *WorldPoint* : *point*)

Note that if the viewport covers only a portion of NDC, *LocateNDC( )* may still pass back points that lie outside the viewport. This occurs whenever the user locates a point outside region V' (see Figure 6.7) that corresponds to the viewport in NDC. No clipping is done at the viewport boundaries for input primitives; rather, the viewport and window definitions are combined to define a transformation that maps any NDC point to its corresponding world point.

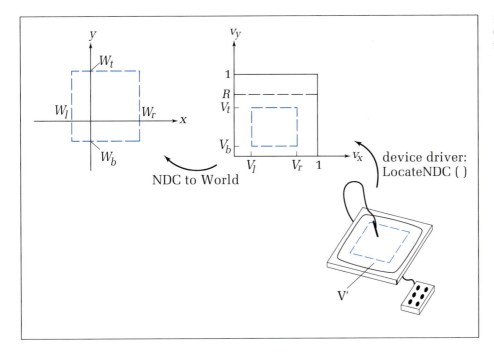

Figure 6.7.
Coordinate system conversions for *Locate( )*.

The original version of *Locate*( ) can now be built around *LocateNDC*( ) simply by incorporating the transformation of Equation 6.1:

Code Fragment 6.4. Building Locate( ) *from* LocateNDC( )

```
procedure Locate(var Butt : button; var Spot : point);
var NDCpoint : point;
begin
    LocateNDC(Butt, NDCpoint);
    NDC_to_World(NDCpoint, Spot)
end;
```

We shall assume for now that *LocateNDC*( ) is available: Later we shall develop some actual *LocateNDC*( ) drivers.

6.3   The Graphics Cursor: Prompts and Echoes

When *Locate*( ) or *LocateNDC*( ) is invoked, a graphics cursor is displayed at some initial position. In this role it is called a **prompt**, for it informs the user that the *Locate* function is active. But as the user manipulates the input device, the cursor moves around and perhaps changes shape. In this role, therefore, the cursor is called an **echo**, for it echoes back to the user an indication of what the user has just done. In this section we shall examine several alternatives for prompts and echoes and see how they can be controlled in the application.

6.3.1 Initial Position of the Cursor

When the graphics cursor is first displayed (as the prompt), it appears at a particular location on the screen. This position can be used in various ways; for example,

- The initial position can suggest which action the user should take next.

- The cursor can reappear where it disappeared when the user triggered the previous *Locate*( ). This is useful for applications like the interactive polyline drawer.

- For a menu, the cursor can appear close to the most likely menu item to be selected next, thus minimizing the distance the user must move it.

One way to control the initial position at the application level is to pass it as a parameter. For instance, it can be passed in the variable *NDCpoint* in **procedure** *LocateNDC*(**var** *Butt* : *button*; **var** *NDCpoint* : *point*); although a better programming practice might be to pass it as a separate parameter. Assuming that we pass it through *NDCpoint*, the higher-level *Locate*(**var** *Butt* : *button*; **var** *Spot* : *point*) procedure could also pass the initial position in world coordinates as *Spot*. Then *Locate*( ) would take the form shown in Code Fragment 6.5.

Note that *Spot* is first converted to NDC using *World_to_NDC*( ) before it is used by *LocateNDC*( ).

Code Fragment 6.5. *Establishing the Initial Position*

```
procedure Locate(var Butt : button; var Spot : point);
   {pass initial cursor position as Spot in world coordinates.}
var NDCpoint : point;
begin
   World_to_NDC(Spot, NDCpoint);
   LocateNDC(Butt, NDCpoint);
   NDC_to_World(NDCpoint, Spot)
end;
```

6.3.2 Cursor Shapes

The cursor shape should help the user *Locate* accurately, and it can also change dynamically as the user proceeds. Figure 6.8 shows some possible shapes.

- *Crosshair.* A crosshair cursor consists of a horizontal and a vertical line extending across the entire display. The cross point is the current cursor location. A crosshair is particularly helpful when the user must line up objects horizontally and vertically, such as when composing a block diagram.

- *Cross.* A cross cursor can have many different shapes, such as ★, ×, ▷, ⊕, ◇, or ⇒. In each case the shape of the cursor points to a specific point on the display, which is the current cursor position. Although the cross is hard to line up horizontally or vertically with other points on the display, it has other advantages: Its shape or size can change depending on the state of the program or the nature of the next item (a circuit element, a menu item, some icon) that should be pointed to. Sometimes an icon or message "sticks" to the cross and is dragged along with it, which makes it easy for the user to keep the message in view when moving the cursor around.

- *Rubber band.* The rubber band cursor changes dynamically as the input device is manipulated. The initial position determines an anchor point (the prompt) which remains stationary. As the user moves the device away from this first position, a line like a rubber band expands and contracts, always joining the anchor point with the current cursor posi-

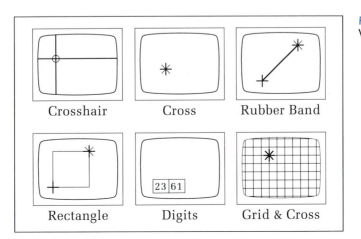

Figure 6.8.
Various useful cursor shapes.

tion (the echo). This moving endpoint can have some cross shape, too, and when *Locate*( ) is triggered, the rubber band disappears. A rubber band cursor gives a preview of a how a line will look joining the anchor with the cross. It is particularly useful with polyline drawing, in which the anchor point is at the endpoint of the previous polyline segment.

- *Rubber rectangle.* The rubber rectangle cursor is similar to the rubber band, except that the anchor point and current cursor position are shown as opposite corners of a rectangle. Like the crosshair cursor, the rubber rectangle is helpful for aligning objects horizontally and vertically.

- *Digits.* Sometimes it is important to be able to read off the exact coordinates of the cursor as it moves around. A pair of digits can be displayed at some position on the screen or can be made "sticky" and follow along with a crosslike cursor.

Other variations are possible as well. For instance, the color of the cursor can be changed at key points within the application, perhaps to alert the user that some system resource is about to be exhausted or that the cursor has moved perilously close to some other object. The cursor can also be confined to a grid or lattice, so that it jumps discontinuously between cross points in a grid. This facilitates lining objects up in a rectangular fashion.

One of the issues in cursor design and control is performance: how rapidly the cursor can be erased and redrawn as the user moves the device around. If the cursor is maintained locally in a graphics terminal using hardware or a firmware microcontroller, very high-speed updates can be attained. On the other hand, if the application must erase and redraw the cursor—as in the following example—then the flow of the entire application can be noticeably retarded.

6.4   A Simple *Locator* Driver

Sometimes an inexpensive graphics terminal has no other input device than its keyboard. In other situations a bare-bones graphics package may support no input functions at all or be missing the necessary drivers. In these cases we must fashion our own driver, and the simplest approach is to use various keys on the keyboard to move a cursor around. We shall develop such a driver in this section as a complete implementation of the procedure *LocateNDC*( ).

As mentioned in Chapter 1, keyboards often come equipped with "arrow keys" labeled ←, ↑, ↓, and →. Some even have additional arrow keys labeled ↗, ↘, and so on. Other keyboards have no special keys at all, in which case we must choose four keys that we will interpret to be arrow keys. For example, we could choose four keys that form a handy cluster, such as i, j, k, and m, to designate up, left, right, and down, respectively.

Whatever the choice, the next step is to determine from the manual for the terminal the specific character code that is transmitted when each of the four keys is pressed.[1] We shall denote these character codes as *char.up*, *char.left*, *char.right*, and *char.down* and assume from now on that they are known.

---

[1] On some terminals, pressing a key sends more than one character. For instance, on the DEC VT240, the ↑ key sends the three characters <ESC>[A. In such cases, the keypress interpreter discussed next must be adjusted accordingly.

A skeleton version of *LocateNDC(   )* is as follows:

Code Fragment 6.6. Skeleton of LocateNDC(   )

Draw cursor at some initial position in NDC;
repeat
  wait for keypress;
  update position of cursor accordingly;
until nonarrow key is pressed;
Erase cursor;
Return current cursor position and code for the key pressed;
Because this version of *LocateNDC(   )* generates and maintains its own cursor, we must build functions *DrawCursor(Curs : point);* and *EraseCursor(Curs : point);* that draw and erase the desired cursor shape (cross, arrow, and so on) at position *Curs* in NDC. We usually can erase the cursor by drawing it in the background color. *LocateNDC(   )* is called with the desired initial cursor position in *Curs*, and the final position is found in *Curs* upon exiting from the procedure.

The full version of *LocateNDC(   )* therefore looks like the following:

Code Fragment 6.7. A Simple Keyboard LocateNDC(   ) *Driver*

```
var stepx, stepy : real; {length of each cursor jump: global}
procedure LocateNDC(var Butt : button; var Curs : point);
{Use keyboard to maneuver cursor and report its final position}
{exit when a nonarrow key is pressed}
var
  ch : char;
  done : boolean;
begin
  DrawCursor(Curs); {display the prompt}
  done := false;
  repeat
    Read(ch); {wait for user to press a key}
    if ch in [char.up, char.left, char.right, char.down] then
    begin
      EraseCursor(Curs); {from previous position}
      case ch of
        char.up:    Curs.y := Curs.y + stepy;
        char.down:  Curs.y := Curs.y − stepy;
        char.right: Curs.x := Curs.x + stepx;
        char.left:  Curs.x := Curs.x − stepx
      end;
      DrawCursor(Curs) {redraw cursor at new position}
    end
    else done := true
  until done;
  Butt := ch;
  EraseCursor(Curs) {don't need it anymore}
end;
```

The global variables *stepx, stepy* determine how far the cursor "hops" at each keystroke. They must be initialized by the application. Sometimes users like to be able to change the hop distance by changing *stepx*, *stepy* on the fly. For instance, the keys d and h can be used in the **if** statement to double and halve *stepx* by inserting commands like

else if *ch* = 'd' **then** *stepx* := *stepx* * 2.0;
else if *ch* = 'h' **then** *stepx* := *stepx* / 2.0;

and similarly for altering *stepy*.

6.5   A Glimpse at a Mouse Driver

Now we shall look briefly at a different kind of driver, this time for a mouse.[2] We shall examine how the mouse sends information to the terminal and see what kinds of software commands are needed to fashion *LocateNDC(   )*.

Because a mouse is picked up and put down at arbitrary locations on the work surface, it cannot report its absolute position. It can report only its changes in position, and the terminal or host must accumulate these changes and maintian the cursor. The mouse has on-board logic that sends a sequence of values Δx and Δy to report its changes in position. It sends 8-bit bytes of data whenever its "state" changes, that is, when the mouse is moved or one of its three buttons is pressed. Thus when its state changes, the mouse sends the following bytes of data:

1. A "synchronization byte," 10000ABC, in which the first five bits, 10000, signify that this is the beginning of a data block, and the three bits ABC denote the state of the three buttons: 0 if depressed and 1 if released.

2. A byte signifying Δx.

3. A byte signifying Δy.

4. Another byte signifying any additional Δx.

5. Another byte signifying any additional Δy.

Consider a *LocateNDC(   )* driver for the mouse that tracks the mouse's movements from some initial position until button C is pressed. A skeleton of such a driver might look like

```
<Initialize position variables pos.x, pos.y;>
<Display cursor at initial position;>
repeat
    <read bytes until synch byte appears;>
    <save button status bits A, B, C;>
    EraseCursor(pos); {make ready to move cursor}
    for i := 1 to 2 do {get two sets of position changes}
    begin
        read dx,dy {read changes from mouse}
```

---

[2]This discussion is based on the Mouse Systems Corporation's PC Mouse, but other mice operate in a similar manner.

$pos.x := pos.x + scalex * dx$; {accumulate new changes}
$pos.y := pos.y + scaley * dy$
end;
   $DrawCursor(pos)$
until $C = 1$;

Scale factors *scalex* and *scaley* are used to convert from the mouse motion counts to NDC. Usually their values are set by the application in order to control the "sensitivity" of the reported values to the mouse's motion.

There are various details with which one must cope when writing such a driver, but this sequence gives the general idea. For instance, because the update process must be rapid, parts of the routine are usually written in assembly language, and in addition, they are interrupt driven to avoid cumbersome polling of the mouse.

With these lower-level concerns in hand, we shall now return to an examination of additional uses of *LocateNDC*( ), in pointing at an item, selecting a menu, and the like.

6.6 Using *Locate* to Select an Object

In the instance-drawer and freehand polyline applications, the user points at an arbitrary spot on the display and causes something to appear there. Another important application is to point to something already displayed in order to identify it. For instance, in a circuit design application, dozens of logic gates may be already positioned on the display, and the user may want to indicate a certain one in order to move or delete it from the circuit.

Selecting a displayed object by pointing at it is often called *picking* an item, and here we shall discuss one form of picking—geometric picking using *Locate*( ). Later we shall look at the GKS input function *Pick* that uses picture segments.

The following sequence of events occurs with geometric picking:

- The application invokes *Locate*(*Butt*, *Spot*).

- The user positions the cursor close to the intended object.

- The user triggers *Locate*(*Butt*, *Spot*) to acquire the value of *Spot*.

- The application then

    Tests each of the displayed objects to determine which is most likely the intended one.
    Highlights its choice in some fashion and asks the user to confirm that it is correct.
    If correct, the application will store some identification of the selected objects; otherwise the user will be prompted to pick again.

The two principal methods for determining which display object is the most likely one are minimum distance and containment. Figure 6.9a illustrates

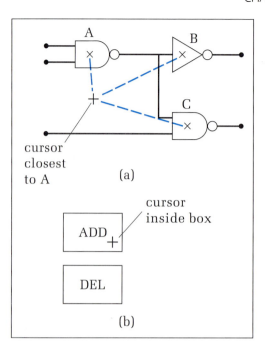

Figure 6.9.
Determining which object is
being pointed to.

the **minimum distance** approach, in which the distance from the cursor to the center of each of a list of objects is measured, and the closest object is the one selected. Figure 6.9b then shows the **containment** method, in which a collection of regions—in this case rectangular boxes—is tested to determine in which region (if any) the cursor resides.

6.6.1 Geometric Picking Using a Distance Criterion

When using the minimum distance approach, the application computes the distance between the cursor and each object and determines the closest one. To do this, the application must keep track of the various objects through some list that specifies where each candidate object lies. The location (in world coordinates) of each object can be stored in a variable, *Center* : *point*, that specifies some central point in the object. Presumably the user points near this center when attempting to designate the object.

Suppose that the user points to a spot and triggers *Locate(Butt, Spot)*. The application then scans the object list to determine the closest object, using some distance-measuring function, **function** *DistSquared(Spot, Center* : *point)* : *Real*. The function *DistSquared(   )* would most likely use the measure

$$DistSquared(a,\ b) = (a_x - b_x)^2 + (a_y - b_y)^2 \qquad (6.2)$$

that yields the square of the Euclidean distance between points a and b. Because we need only compare distances to the various objects, we needn't take the square root to obtain the true distance.

An implementation of this approach is shown in Code Fragment 6.8. The routine *Closest(   )* searches a linked list of objects and returns a pointer to the object whose center is closest to *Spot*. A type *object* is defined, having a *Center* field and a link to the next object in the list. A linked list is usually the most appropriate to an interactive design environment when the number of objects to be encountered is unpredictable and the user frequently inserts and deletes objects.

> *Code Fragment 6.8. Finding the Closest Object to* Spot

```
type
    object_ptr = object;
    object = record
                center : point;
                Info: ... {other data}
                next : object_ptr
            end;

function Closest(Spot : point; Objects : object_ptr) : object_ptr;
var
    LeastDist, NewDist : real;
    p : object_ptr;
begin
    if Objects = nil then Closest := nil {empty object list}
    else begin {search list}
        LeastDist := DistSquared(Spot, Objects^.center);
        Closest := Objects; {closest so far}
        p := Objects^.next;
        while p <> nil do
        begin
            NewDist := DistSquared(Spot, p^.center); {distance to this one}
            if NewDist < LeastDist then
            begin
                LeastDist := New Dist; {update to new best distance}
                Closest := p              {point to best object}
            end;
            p := p^.next
        end {while p}
    end {else}
end; {Find_Closest}
```

One might include some minimum distance tolerance in this routine, so that **nil** will be returned if the user doesn't point close enough to any object.

6.6.2 Programming Project: A Polyline Editor

In Section 6.2 we used the *Locate* function to fashion an interactive polyline builder. This tool allows a user to create polylines by pointing to a sequence of positions on the display. In this section we shall extend that capability to a more complete polyline editor with which the user can alter or edit a polyline after it has been created. This is an important tool when using polylines, of course, because a user is rarely satisfied with the first polylines attempted.

We shall describe the principal functions of a polyline editor we call *Politor* but leave many details for a programming project. Carrying through this project serves two important purposes: A valuable tool is created for future use in graphics, and several central notions are clarified, including the use of *Locate*, the relationship between the picture of an object and its internal representation, and the design of interactive graphical editors in general.

6.6.3 The Functional Specification of *Politor*

Politor must support four activities:

1. The creation of polylines.

2. The insertion of new line segments within an existing polyline.

3. The deletion of line segments from an existing polyline.

4. The filing of polyline data for a later editing session.

The user controls *politor* entirely through a *LocateNDC(Butt, Spot)* command, which selects the next action according to one of seven values for *Butt*:

Butt =   1: Enter the add mode to begin a new polyline, placing the first point at *Spot*. Once in the add mode, concatenate each additional point using *Butt* = 4.

Butt =   2: Delete the closest point to *Spot* in the polyline.

Butt =   3: Enter the insert mode, to insert points after the point closest to *Spot*. Once in the insert mode, insert each additional point using *Butt* = 4.

Butt =   4: Add or insert additional point.

Butt =   5: File (save or recall) the polylines.

Butt =   6: Refresh the display.

Butt =   7: Exit the program.

Figure 6.10a shows the result of pressing button 2 when pointing nearest to point *c* in the polyline. All of the points are tested to see which is nearest *Spot*, and point *c* is identified. Then the two line segments meeting at the point are erased, and a new segment is drawn from *b* to *d*.

Figure 6.10b shows the result of pressing button 3 while pointing to *b*, followed by three more presses of button 4 to insert points *m*, *n*, and *o*, followed by one press of some other button. The first press of button 3 causes a search for the point nearest *Spot*, and *b* is found to be the winner. The program also changes into an insert mode and remains there as long as the button pressed is none other than 4. Because this is an *insert after* function, the user must know in which order the vertices of the target polyline occur, so that the inserted points will appear between this point and the next existing point (*c*). When in an insert mode, each triggering of *Locate*( ) requires no searching for any nearest point: the *Locator* is used instead to "draw at" the indicated point. Note that a vertex of a polyline may be moved by first deleting it and then inserting a new point at the new location.

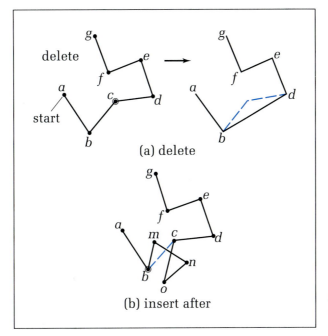

Figure 6.10.
Inserting and deleting points in a polyline.

Data Structures for *Politor*

Because operations are to be performed on polylines, they must be stored in some on-line data structure; it is not sufficient simply to draw the picture of the polyline, because then there would be no way to identify which line segment was which. Arrays can be used to store polyline data, but they are more difficult to manage with inserts and deletes. Therefore, linked lists are recommended. Figure 6.11 shows a possible structure for representing the collection of polylines, and the suggested data types are

Code Fragment 6.9. Suggested Data Types for the Polyline Editor

```
type
    polyptr = ^polylink;
    vertptr = ^vert;
    polylink = record
                    start : vertptr;
                    next : polyptr
                end;
    vert = record
                vertex : point;
                next : vertptr
            end;
```

In the figure, **var** *head : polyptr* points to a linked list containing pointers (of type *vertptr*) to the first vertex in each associated polyline. Each vertex (of type *vert*) contains the (x,y) coordinates of the vertex and a link to the next vertex. Because there is no underlying scale in *Politor*—the polylines are purely artistic creations by hand and eye on the display—there is no need to use world coordinates. All vertices can be generated and stored in NDC.

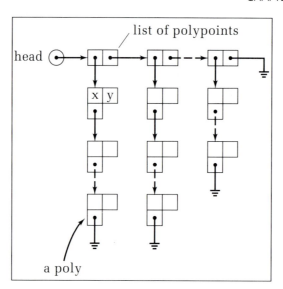

Figure 6.11.
Data structure for the polylines
in *Politor*.

Filing Polylines

When *Butt* = 5 the user is given the choice of S)AVE or R)ECALL and asked for a
file name. If the response is S for SAVE, then the list of polylines will be saved in
the given file. The file will be created if it does not already exist or will be
overwritten if it does exist. If the response is R for RECALL, then the polyline
data will be read from the file and will replace the current polyline data. (Alternatively, the filed polyline data can be added to the data already on line.)

A variety of data formats can be used to save a polyline. A simple one
counts the number of vertices in each polyline in turn and starts each vertex list
with this count. The vertices then follow, using (x,y) pairs in NDC. For example,
the following describes three polylines, of 3, 4, and 2 vertices, respectively:

```
3
.012 .450
.000 .897
.586 .254
4
.342 .213
.246 .678
.344 .777
.121 .589
2
.788 .100
.450 .323
```

When SAVING, the linked list data structure is traversed (scanned) and converted into this format. And when RECALLING, the file is read, and the linked
lists are created in a straightforward manner.

Picture Refreshing

The *Refresh* function occurs often in graphics editors. Most changes such as
moves or deletions corrupt a picture somewhat, as some lines are obscured or

overwritten as part of the editing process. Naturally the user wants to see a picture that accurately portrays the current state of the database. But if each change causes the entire picture to be refreshed (totally erased and then the current lines redrawn), the response speed of the whole program will be reduced, thereby interfering with the user's productivity. Thus it is important to have some control over the refresh process. In *Politor* the user can activate the *Refresh* function at any time, which erases the display and regenerates pictures of all polylines directly from their description in the database. Because this flexibility exists, it is not necessary for every delete to be faithfully shown on the display. Instead, *Politor* uses a faster method of feedback: Instead of erasing a segment, an X is drawn through it to show that it no longer exists in the data set. When many such deletes have been accumulated and the display looks congested, the user performs a *Refresh* and generates an up-to-date display.

6.7   Geometric Picking Using Containment

Geometric picking must use a minimum distance criterion if candidate objects can appear at arbitrary positions on the display. However, when the objects to be picked occur at predictable positions, it is not necessary to search for the closest one. Instead, much simpler tests can be used.

It is easy to determine whether the point *Spot* returned by *Locate(Butt, Spot)* lies in a given rectangle. If *Box* is of type *rect*, the function *Inside( )*

function *Inside(Spot : point*; Box : *rect) : boolean*;
begin
   Inside := false;
  if *Spot.x* < *Box.r* **then**
    if *Spot.x* > *Box.l* **then**
      if *Spot.y* < *Box.t* **then**
        if *Spot.y* > *Box.b* **then** *Inside := true*
end;

easily tests for the containment of *Spot* within *Box*, by checking that *Spot* lies inside each of the four walls of *Box*. Because menu items are often housed inside rectangular boxes, this kind of test is frequently used in menuing, as we shall see in the next section. If the shape of the enclosure is more complex, the containment test will be complex as well. (Chapter 17 discusses tests for containment within a polygon.)

6.8   Menu Design and Selection in Graphics Applications

In this section we introduce the use of menus in graphics applications and show how menuing can be implemented with geometric picking. In Section 6.11 we shall revisit menuing and see how segments and the *Pick* input function are used.

The principal advantage of menus is that they display at each point in an application a list of the possible options. This saves the user from having to remember what options are available and also prevents him or her from choosing a meaningless or damaging one. Many kinds of menus are used in interactive computing, and on ordinary text terminals, the menu items are selected by typing in one or more characters, as in the following examples:

```
    MAKE A CHOICE: A)DD D)ELETE B)EGIN Q)UIT I)NSERT C)LEAR
or
    CHOOSE OPTION: 1) List Names
                   2) Add a New Name
                   3) Remove a Name
                   4) Edit an Entry
                   5) Print the List
                   6) Exit from Program
```

In these cases the user's eyes have to leave the screen to look at the keyboard, and looking away can disrupt the train of thought. In graphics programming, on the other hand, the menu items can be displayed directly on the work surface, and the user can point to and select items with only a slight shift of the eyes. This visual continuity results in less fatigue and greater productivity.

A typical graphical menu is shown in Figure 6.12, illustrating several types of menu items. Some items are represented by words of **text**, whereas others are shown as small geometric shapes, or **icons**, that are readily recognized. Some items are enclosed in "bounding boxes," and some are not.

Figure 6.12 shows the display apportioned into various regions: menu regions, a "prompt-and-feedback" region, and the main "work" region. The work region is where the drawing and editing takes place, and so one usually wants as large an area as possible for this. The prompt-and-feedback region reserves some space for instructions and status reports from the application to the user. The menus in the menu regions show the possible choices the user can make. Ideally only "active" possibilities—those that are legitimate at the current moment in the application—are displayed, but often it is too slow or inconvenient to keep changing the menu items as the state of the application changes.

Figure 6.12.
An example of a graphics menu.

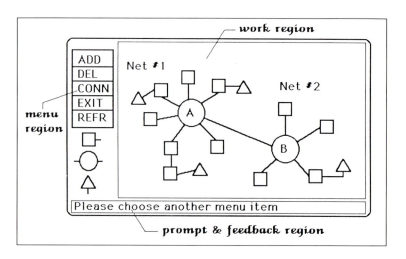

Because having large menus on the screen uses up precious display area, we generally want to keep the menus short and concise. Using short words as the text for menu items can make them difficult to recognize, however, and so we must compromise in designing the human interface to the application. Sometimes multilevel menus are used, in which a selection from the main menu causes the old menu to disappear and a new menu to appear, from which subsequent selections can be made. But too many menu levels can make an application bewildering and unwieldy, demonstrating again that the interface must be carefully designed.

Other alternatives available on raster terminals with some additional software support are pop-up and pull-down menus, as shown in Figure 6.13. A **pull-down** menu is usually activated by the user, who "pulls" it down by pointing to its name. A **pop-up** menu appears automatically to prompt the user in response to some change in the application. These menus do not need precious screen area reserved for them. Instead, when they appear they cover parts of the display already in use, and when they disappear the original graphics must be restored. Some simple algorithms for this are discussed in Chapter 13.

6.8.1 Screen Layout and Menu Design

Although menus can be created in either NDC or world coordinates, they are usually designed as part of the overall "screen layout" task in NDC,[3] as suggested in Figure 6.14. In this example we assume that the aspect ratio, *Ratio*, of the target display device (normally a video screen) is less than one, and so only values of v_y from 0 to *Ratio* in NDC are available.[4] The designer apportions the

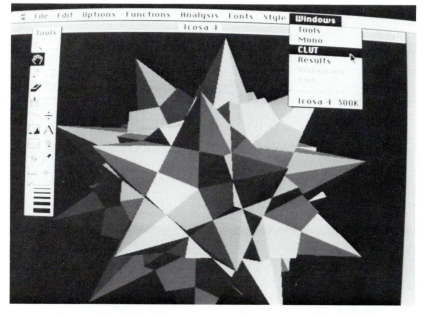

Figure 6.13.
Examples of pop-up and pull-down menus.

---

[3]Menus can also be designed and generated in world coordinates. There are advantages and disadvantages to this, as investigated in the exercises.
[4]Designing a screen layout with a specific aspect ratio makes the application somewhat device dependent, but it allows the designer to use all of the drawing area, instead of just the largest square within the display. In an application all references to these device dependencies should be isolated and annotated to facilitate future porting of the application to a different display.

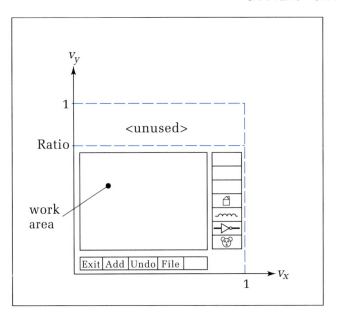

Figure 6.14.
Designing the screen layout in NDC.

available NDC space into the work region, the prompt area, and menu areas. Within the menus, items typically take two forms: text strings and icons.

Text String Menu Items

Text string menu items are usually rectangular boxes with a string of characters drawn snugly inside. Longer text strings require larger surrounding boxes. Sometimes the box itself is not drawn, but the items are arranged so that the user can select one by pointing to any spot within an imaginary bounding box that fits snugly around the text.

If the text characters can have any size desired (see Chapter 2), then the designer can choose the dimensions of the menu regions quite freely and fit the text to each menu item accordingly. For instance, you may choose to put four menu items in the region for which v_x lies between .1 and .6. and v_y lies between .1 × *Ratio* and .2 × *Ratio*. If, on the other hand, you want to use the hardware character generator in the display terminal in order to generate menus as fast as possible, then you must take care to choose the size and position of each menu box so that the text will fit properly. This often requires tedious trial and error, and the result is highly device dependent.

Icon Menu Items

Because it can be hard to capture a lot of suggestive meaning in a short text menu item, a designer can use geometric icons instead. A small figure is drawn on the display, often with its associated bounding box, and the user points anywhere inside this box to select the icon seen there. The icons can be designed directly in NDC if desired, perhaps as a set of polylines drawn using *LineNDC( )*.

Data Structures for Menus

In the layout process the designer generates a list of menu items such as

Id	Type	Figure	Left	Top	Right	Bottom
1	text	add	.10	.20	.14	.10
2	text	del	.14	.20	.18	.10
3	text	exit	.18	.20	.22	.10
4	icon	nand	.80	.90	.90	.75
5	icon	nor	.80	.75	.90	.55
.	.	.	.	.	.	.
.	.	.	.	.	.	.

that specifies for each menu item:

Id: An identification number.

Type: Whether the item is text or an icon.

Box: The position and dimensions of its bounding box.

Figure: The text string to be displayed or a name for the icon shape.

This list specifies where each item will lie but does not tell how to draw it.

Text: To draw text items we must know the position in NDC of the lower left-hand corner of the string's first character. This could be stored in a variable, *corner*, of type *point*. We also need the height and width in NDC of the string's characters. (If hardware text is used, these fields will be replaced by some reference to the font and character size desired.)

Icons: To draw icons we need the set of polylines that comprises it. For this purpose we can use a pointer of type *polylink* (see Section 6.6) to the linked list of relevant polylines. (In Chapter 13 we discuss icons formed as bitmaps.)

To store this list and other necessary information in the application, the designer might use a linked list of records of the type *menu_item*, defined next. Each record must completely characterize its menu item. Because it must describe both text and icon items, it is reasonable to use a variant record type:

Code Fragment 6.10. Suggested Data Types for Menus

```
type
    menu_ptr = ^menu_item;
    menu_item = record
                    id : integer;            {item's id}
                    box : rect;              {item's bounding box}
                    next : menu_ptr;         {next item in list}
                case kind : (text, icon) of
                    text : (word : string;       {item's text}
                            height, width : real; {character size}
                            corner : point);      {where to draw it}
                    icon : (poly : polylink)     {start of polylines}
                end; {case and record}
```

The *id* field holds the item identification that is returned when the item is selected. The *box* field is used for both drawing the bounding box and testing during menu selection. The *next* field points to the next menu item in the list, if any, and the remaining fields are used to draw the menu items. Additional fields can be added to specify color and other attributes of the text, whether the bounding box should be drawn, and the like.

6.8.2 Menu Selection Using *LocateNDC( )*

We wish to implement geometric picking in a function,

function *WhichItem(menu : menu_ptr; Spot : point) : menu_ptr;*

that returns a pointer to the menu item found, or **nil** if none is found. Then *menu* points to the linked list of menu items, and *Spot* is the location returned by *LocateNDC( )*. The item-picking process is as follows:

1. The application invokes *LocateNDC(Butt, Spot)*.

2. The user points to the desired item with the *Locator* and triggers it.

3. *LocateNDC( )* returns *Spot*, and *WhichItem( )* is invoked.

4. Each bounding box in the menu list is tested in turn to see whether *Spot* lies inside it, until the first one is found or the list is exhausted. The containment test uses *Inside( )*, as described in Section 6.7.

The following code fragment shows a possible realization of *WhichItem( )*:

Code Fragment 6.11. Menu Selection Using Geometric Picking

```
function WhichItem(menu : menu_ptr; Spot : point) : menu_ptr;
var
   ptr : menu_ptr;
   Found : boolean;
begin
   ptr := menu; {get first item}
   Found := false;
   while (ptr <> nil) and not Found do
     if Inside(Spot, ptr^.box) then Found := true
     else ptr := ptr^.next; {try next item}
   if Found then WhichItem := ptr
   else WhichItem := nil
end; {WhichItem}
```

Finally, the pointer returned by *WhichItem( )* can be used to access the *id* of the menu item that is picked, in order to invoke the appropriate action. The user is repeatedly prompted to make a selection until a valid menu item is selected. The **until** condition can be extended to include only certain menu items if the application cannot perform certain actions at this point in its course. It is assumed that a procedure is available for each possible menu item.

Code Fragment 6.12. Main Flow of Menu Selection

```
var Item : menu_ptr;
begin
  repeat {keep trying until user selects a menu item}
    LocateNDC(Butt, Spot);
    Item := WhichItem(menu, Spot);
  until Item <> nil;
  case Item^.id of
    1: Add( ); {calls to corresponding routines}
    2: Delete( );
    3: Exit( );
    4: Get_Nand( );
    5: Get_Nor( );
  end {case}
end;
```

6.9 A CAD Application: Creating Networks Graphically

We shall consider here some important graphics techniques frequently used in computer-aided design (CAD). A standard CAD task is to design an object having certain properties and meeting the specified criteria of the application. Many CAD applications involve a **network** of some sort, an interconnection of various elements that form a system. Figure 6.15 shows graphical representations (schematic diagrams) of several examples:

- A logic circuit consisting of logic gates of various sorts interconnected with wire leads.

- An electrical circuit consisting of transistors, resistors, capacitors, and the like, interconnected with leads.

- A graph network of "nodes" interconnected with "branches." This is a general network that can represent many situations, particularly those involving a flow of some quantity or commodity through the network. In the case shown, the branches are "directed," permitting the flow in only one direction. Numerical values can be associated with each branch and/or node, denoting the "costs" or "rewards" for using them. For example: The nodes can be cities and the branches can be roads. The branch costs are distances or fees for traveling between the neighboring cities. Or the nodes are storage tanks and the branches are pipes. The branch costs are the maximum flow rates for each branch.

- A block diagram for a classical feedback system, in which the input signal e is modified as it passes through each processing block and v is the resulting output signal.

- A computer communications network, showing separate processors interconnected by data transmission lines.

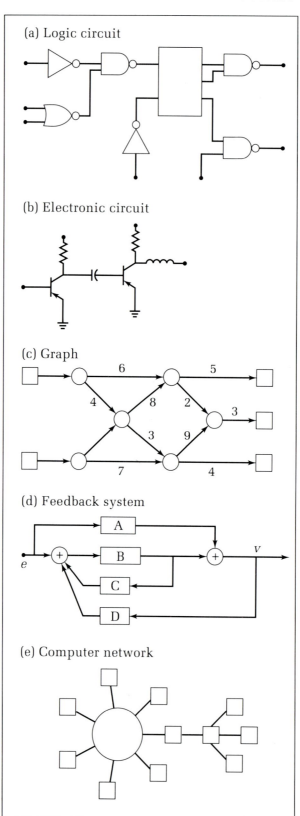

Figure 6.15.
CAD applications: building networks.

The design process has several stages, a simplified version of which might take the following form:

1. The designer creates the network by specifying which elements are in it and how they are connected.

2. The initial design is subjected to analysis and simulation programs that test its operation or characteristics.

3. If it doesn't work well enough, the network will be edited: Elements are rearranged, added, and deleted, and parameter values are changed. Then it is retested (return to Step 2).

4. When it finally meets the design requirements, it is stored in a database and sent to the next phase: manufacturing, quality control, publishing, or whatever is appropriate.

First we shall focus on the first step, the creation of the original network. The designer must describe in some language the elements in the network and how they are interconnected. If graphics are used, this can be done visually, and the resulting system is often called a **graphics front end** to the CAD system. A graphics front end supports highly interactive creation and editing of the desired network. It captures the network in some symbolic form in a database and, in addition, displays it in some intelligible form so the user can operate on it.

6.9.1 Placement of the Elements: Pick and Place

One important capability of a graphics front end allows the user to "pick and place" various elements with a *Locator* to create an initial configuration. (This action is sometimes called *Put That There*.) Figure 6.16 shows a digital logic circuit being built up of four elementary devices. An icon menu with suggestive symbols for the four elements shows what devices are available. The user picks elements and places each in turn at the desired spots in the network. We shall examine how to use *Locate*( ) to do this. Some elements must first be rotated to the desired orientation before they are placed.

The pick-and-place action uses the *Locator* in two roles:

- *Choose*: To do geometric picking in order to select the element.

- *Position*: To indicate the place where the element is to go.

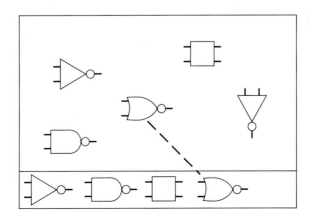

Figure 6.16.
Pick-and-place creation of a logic circuit.

See the exercises for the implementation of an actual pick-and-place routine.

If you want to rotate the element, then different buttons on the *Locator* can indicate them. For instance, buttons 1 through 4 can cause rotations of 0°, 90°, 180°, and 270°, respectively. There may be a separate icon for each of the rotations of the element, but this uses valuable screen area. In Chapter 11 we shall develop a general technique for rotating graphical objects.

Interconnecting the Elements

Once the elements have been placed in the network, the user will want to interconnect them. Each element may have several connect points, or **pads**, that are candidates for connections. Figure 6.17 shows various kinds of elements, with the pads for each indicated by small squares. Some elements may have no pads; others (such as a 40-pin integrated circuit chip) may have several. To make each connection the user will most likely

1. Initiate the *Connect* function by selecting a *Connect* menu item.

2. Point to the first pad.

3. Point to the second pad.

(An alternative approach is described in the exercises.) The connection process has three stages:

1. Determining which pads are to be connected.

2. Drawing the connection.

3. Storing the connection in the database.

After each *Locate* the application must decide which pads are to be connected. Because the elements can be positioned arbitrarily in the work area, a "closest point" criterion is used to determine to which pad the *Locator* is pointing. The distance between each pad of each element and the *Locator* position is computed, and the smallest distance wins.

Each connection must be displayed visually, with the exact techniques to do this depending on the shape and nature of the elements. For a graph consisting of circles and lines, it is easiest to draw straight lines between the centers of the relevant circles, as shown in Figure 6.18a. For a schematic diagram such

Figure 6.17.
Examples of connection pads for elements.

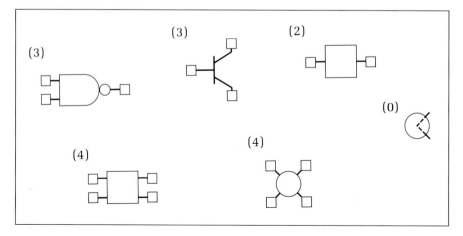

as the logic circuit example, you can connect the appropriate pads with horizontal and vertical lines. There are various ways to do this, some more pleasing than others. Figure 6.18b shows with dotted lines a variety of possibilities. Often the user must intervene and indicate which is the most appropriate.

As each element or connection is added to the network, its description is inserted into the database. The data that must go into the database are application dependent. For a logic circuit, the type, position, and orientation of each gate are recorded, along with information describing which pads are attached to which. For example, the circuit shown in Figure 6.19 can be captured by the data in the following table:

Connection Data for the Logic Circuit Example

Id	Kind	x	y	Rot	L1	L2	L3
1	NOR	0.6	0.65	0	A	D	C
2	NOR	0.6	0.35	0	C	B	D
3	NOT	0.2	0.5	270	A	B	-

The geometry of each element is stored in its center (x, y) and the rotation angle *Rot*, whereas the **connectivity** (or topology) is specified by naming the nodes (A, B, C ....) to which each element lead (L1, L2, L3 ...) is connected. For instance, element 1 is a NOR circuit with lead L1 connected to node A, L2 connected to node D, and L3 connected to node C. There are many ways to store connectivity data, and the best one to choose will depend on the application and the choice of algorithms to be used to simulate the network.

Figure 6.18.
Interconnecting leads in a circuit.

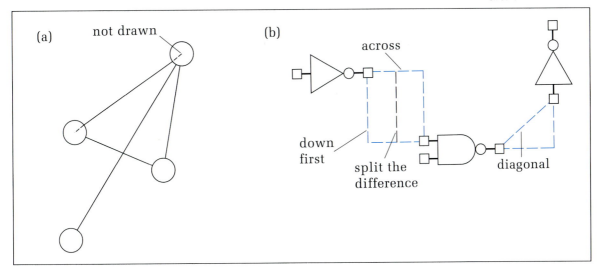

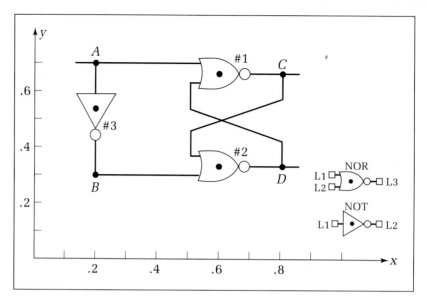

Figure 6.19.
Example of a logic circuit.

6.10 Working with Pictures As Segments

Some graphics packages provide tools to control collections of output primitives and their attributes as if they were single entities. These collections are called **segments**, and various operations can be performed on segments that facilitate interaction with a displayed picture. One of the most common uses of segments is in menuing: A menu or a portion of it is defined as a segment and thereafter is treated as an entity. Here we shall discuss the basic notions of segments and their manipulation in various graphics situations. We follow the GKS approach to segment control, but it should be noted that other standards such as the CORE deal with segments in a similar manner.

6.10.1 What Is a Segment?

A segment is, again, a collection of primitives and attributes stored in memory along with a **name** and some ancillary information. The application begins the definition of a segment by means of an instruction such as *CreateSegment(Name)*, in which *Name* is usually an integer. All of the statements that follow this one up to the instruction *CloseSegment* are associated with segment *Name*. For example, a green polyline, a blue circle, and some text can be placed in segment 21 using statements such as

CreateSegment(21);
SetColor(*green*);
PolyLine(...);
SetColor(*blue*);
Circle(...);
Text('This is a nice segment');
CloseSegment;

Segments are created one at a time, and so a *CloseSegment* must appear before the next *CreateSegment*( ). Thus there is no mechanism to build up segments of segments or other hierarchical pictures within GKS or the CORE. (The Programmar's Hierarchical Interactive Graphics Standard [PHIGS] support hierarchical definitions of pictures, however; see Appendix 7.)

When a segment is created, it is immediately mapped from world to NDC using the current window-to-viewport mapping,[5] and the primitives are stored in memory in their NDC form. Once a segment has been created, its primitives are fixed; they cannot be edited or added to. In this sense a segment is like a graphical snapshot.

Because of these limitations on segments, they may appear primitive and to be of little assistance to the programmer. But this isn't so. They can store complex pictures in a predigested form—already mapped to NDC—that permits rapid redisplay. A segment also has several dynamic segment attributes that can be controlled by the application to facilitate many tasks in interactive graphics. We shall first examine how they are useful when a sequence of pictures is to be drawn in which certain parts do not change. Then we shall discuss the use of segment attributes.

6.10.2 Automatic Redisplay of Segments

Consider the task of drawing several versions of a chart, as suggested in Figure 6.20. Certain portions of the different charts are the same, such as the axes, the annotations, and the background decoration. Only the foreground details change from version to version. Segments can be used here to store the common parts, which need be computed only once and stored in a segment. Then as each picture is produced, only the new parts need be fashioned. The graphics package is usually set up to redraw all segments automatically after each *ClearDisplay* instruction. The user changes the plotter paper, or advances the film in the film recorder, before executing this instruction. The following code fragment illustrates the reuse of a segment (named 3) in several pictures:

Code Fragment 6.13. Using a Common Segment in Several Pictures

```
CreateSegment(3);
{. . .}              {create the segment here}
CloseSegment;       {segment is displayed}

for i := 1 to num_of_pictures do
begin
    <fashion new parts of pictures for the i-th chart>
    <draw new part on top of segment #3>
    <pause to admire, to change plotter paper, etc.>
    ClearDisplay; {erase all, then redisplay segment #3}
end;
```

This use of segments both simplifies the application code and streamlines the chart production. When a great deal of computation is required to generate the

---

[5]GKS allows several window-to-viewport mappings to be defined at the same time. They are called *normalization transformations* (see Chapter 11), and each is given an identifying number. The version that maps a given segment to NDC can be specified by the application.

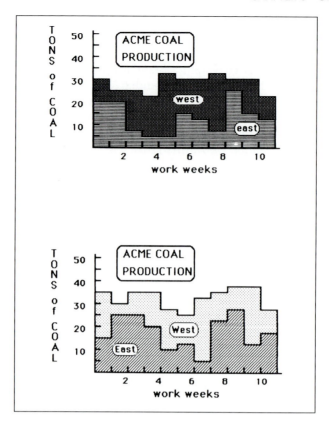

Figure 6.20.
Drawing several versions of a
chart.

segment, it is an advantage to generate it once and store it rather than to have to generate it anew for each chart.

6.10.3 Segment Attributes

The primitives and primitive attributes that are stored in a segment cannot be altered after the segment has been created. Are segments then completely static entities? Can any aspects be altered?

The aspects that can be changed as often as desired are the **dynamic segment attributes**, which are visibility, highlighting, detectability, segment priority, and segment transformation. Each affects a segment in its entirety.

1. *Visibility*. An entire segment may or may not be displayed. For instance, if a menu has been created as segment 15, then it can be "posted" (made visible) with a statement like *SetVisibility*(15, *on*) and similarly "unposted" using *SetVisibility*(15, *off*). In this way the menu can be made to appear only when it is appropriate for the user to make a selection. Also, different menus can come and go in the same place on the display. Because a segment need be created only once and then is retained in memory, it is usually much faster to post a segment such as a menu than it is to recompute it.

2. *Highlighting*. Highlighting a segment makes it distinctive and therefore draws the user's attention to it. A segment can be highlighted in various ways, such as by making it blink, glow more brightly, or

change color, depending on the display's capabilities. A typical instruction is *SetHighlight*(15, *on*). Highlighting is often used to provide feedback to the user. First the user points at an object stored as a segment. Then software within the graphics package tries to determine which segment was pointed to and accordingly highlights its choice. The user confirms the choice if it is indeed the segment intended. Otherwise the user points again, perhaps more carefully.

3. *Detectability*. One of the most important reasons for using segments is that they can be *pick-ed* by a user for further action. This detectability attribute determines whether a segment is sensitive to being picked if it is pointed at by the appropriate input device. Being able to turn on and off the detectability of different segments during an interactive session gives the application and the user greater control over the sequence of events.

4. *Segment priority*. Segment priority sets up a pecking order among segments, by means of a command such as *Set_Seg_Priority*(*Name* : *integer*; **var** *Priority* : *integer*). It is used to cope with segments that overlap on the display in two ways:

   ● *When redrawing segments.*

   ● If two overlapping segments are redrawn on a raster display, the one that is drawn last will automatically conceal the one that was drawn first and appear to be on top of it. The application thus uses segment priority to control the order in which segments are drawn. This is normally used only for raster displays, on which higher-priority segments are drawn after lower-priority segments. Line-drawing displays lack a "paint-over" capability, and so a rather complicated "shielding" mechanism has to be provided. The highest-priority segment is drawn first. Then as each successively lower priority segment is drawn, it is shielded, or clipped, against the union of all the higher-priority primitives so that only its uncovered parts are made visible. This capability is not commonly provided in a workstation or graphics package.

   ● *When* Pick*ing segments.* The user *Picks* a segments by pointing at its display with a suitable input device. If two or more segments are very close together—or even overlap—it may be hard to point accurately at the one desired. A GKS graphics package uses segment priority to make some segments "more *Pick*able" than others. If two segments are pointed at simultaneously, the one with the higher priority will be selected.

5. *Segment transformation*. Each segment can have a transformation associated with it that rotates, scales, and shifts all the primitives in the segment each time it is drawn. In this way the snapshot of primitives in a segment can be oriented, sized, and positioned in different ways. This type of mapping, called an *affine transformation*, is discussed in detail in Chapter 11. The data that define the transformation are stored in memory along with the segment. The application can change the transformation at any time, and whenever the segment is redisplayed, its primitives are retransformed, clipped, and then sent to the device driver for actual drawing.

6.11 The *Pick* Input Function

The *Pick* input function allows the user to point to a displayed object and select it for further action. The objects to be selected must reside in segments, and the *Pick* function returns the name of the segment (and other information) to the application.

When the user points to a primitive and triggers the *Pick* function, the package scans all of the primitives in every (detectable) segment. It checks for those primitives that pass through the so-called pick aperture of the pointing device. This is a rectangular region in NDC, centered at the pointing position, in which primitives can be "seen" by the pointing device. The size of the aperture can often be controlled by the application: a small aperture for delicate, precise picking and a larger one when coarser picking is preferable. For each visible primitive encountered, the package looks up the priority of the associated segment and keeps track of the highest priority yet detected.

Whereas we had to develop our own search method when using *Locate*( ) to pick geometrically, the management of this scanning and testing is performed automatically with Pick. The programmer is thus relieved of having to implement these functions. In addition, some workstations include hardware that assists the scanning and association of *Pick* with stored segments, thereby removing a significant burden from the graphics package.

In some instances a bounding box is associated with certain primitives, in order to facilitate the detection of a primitive within the pick aperture. In the case of text, for instance, the obvious choice is a rectangle that just surrounds all of the characters in the text item. In this way the user need not point directly to a text character but need only point within the vicinity of the item to be chosen.

Besides the name of the segment, *Pick*( ) also returns more precise information about the object pointed to, the **pick-id**. In the case of menu selection the whole menu might be a segment, and individual items within the menu would be given separate pick-ids. The following code fragment shows how pick-ids might be defined for the menu in Figure 6.21:

Code Fragment 6.14. Defining Pick-ids in a Segment

```
CreateSegment(12);
Menu_Box;      {draws menu border}
SetPickId(1);
MoveTo(..,..);
DrawText('Apples'); {the text 'Apples' has Pick_id = 1}
SetPickId(2);
MoveTo(..,..);
DrawText('Oranges'); {Oranges has Pick_id = 2}
SetPickId(8);
MoveTo(..,..);
DrawText('Exit'); {Exit has Pick_id = 8}
CloseSegment;
```

The notion is that primitives are associated with the most recently declared pick-id, and so the lines that make up the characters in the label 'Oranges' are

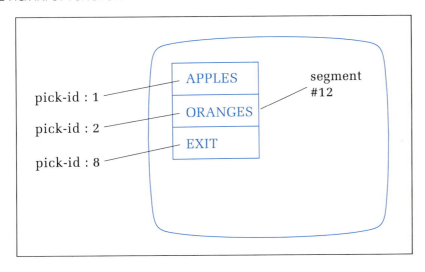

Figure 6.21.
Defining pick-ids.

associated with a pick-id of 2, and those in 'Exit' with a pick-id of 8.

The *Pick* routine provided by the graphics package would have a form such as

procedure *Pick*(**var** *SegName, PickId* : *integer*);

Suppose the application calls *Pick*(*Name, PkId*). The program waits while the user positions the pointing device and triggers it and then receives from the workstation the two values for *Name* and *PkId*. (If no segment is being pointed to, *Name* will receive the value 0.) If the user points close to the word 'Apples' in the preceding example, the application will receive the values *Name* = 12, *PkId* = 1. The application can then take appropriate action. A typical fragment for such menu selection might look like

Code Fragment 6.15. Menu Selection Using Pick( )

```
SetVisibility(12, ON); {make the menu visible}
SetDetectability(12, ON); {make the menu detectable}
Pick(Name, PkId); {user picks item}
while (Name <> 12) do Pick(Name, PkId); {keep trying for menu pick}
case PkId of
   1 : Do_Apples;
   2 : Do_Oranges;
   8 : Do_Exit
end; {case}
SetVisibility(12, OFF); {make the menu disappear}
SetDetectability(12, OFF); {make it insensitive to picks}
```

The menu is first made visible and detectable, and then *Pick*( ) is called repeatedly until the user successfully picks something in segment 12. (The code might include some helpful prompts to the user after an unsuccessful pick, such as "Please pick a menu item.") With the application then reassured that the user is picking some menu item, the **case** statement takes appropriate action based on the value of *PkId*.

6.12 Summary

In this chapter we described some of the tools that allow the user to interact visually and manually with an application. Of the six logical input functions, the *Locator* was singled out as of fundamental importance. When invoked by an application and triggered by the user, it returns a coordinate pair (x, y) to the application for further processing. In this way the user can painlessly specify a position to the program. The user is guided by prompts, seen as cursors of various types and shapes, as well as echoes that confirm that the requested actions were in fact performed.

A simple *LocateNDC*( ) driver was described that uses keystrokes to move the cursor and returns positions in NDC. The mapping from NDC back to world coordinates is carried out by *Locate*( ), so that the application can work in world coordinates.

Locators can be used for many tasks, such as drawing freehand, building and editing polylines, picking menus, and making connections between elements. We examined the process of doing each of these example tasks. In some cases the user will want to "draw that there," which requires picking some icon from a selection and then pointing to the place where it should appear. The picking process can be done geometrically by searching all candidates to find the closest one to the position of the *Locator*. For more predictable kinds of picking, such as from menu boxes situated in fixed locations, simple containment tests can be performed to determine to which item the user is pointing.

Some pictures are best handled as segments, consisting of groups of output primitives and their attributes. Standards such as GKS provide for segment management routines with which the programmer can create named segments for subsequent manipulation. Segments have various types of attributes that can be changed dynamically, offering easy control over their appearance, detectability, and priority for both input and output. Segments are most useful when an application must help the user pick one displayed object versus another. The *Pick* input function identifies to which segment the user is pointing and allows the application to adjust its course accordingly. Segment managers are complex and add significant expense to a graphics package, but when available they offer great power and flexibility to the programmer.

Programming Exercises

6.1. Build a Polyline Creation Routine. Write a program that allows the user to create polylines interactively. Discover how to activate the equivalent of *Locate*( ) that is resident in a workstation/graphics package combination available to you, or build *LocateNDC*( ) if one is not already available.

6.2. Implementing *NDC_to_World*( ). Write and exercise the procedure *NDC_to_World*( ).

6.3. Build a *Locator* Driver. Implement a version of the simple keyboard *LocateNDC*( ) routine on an available graphics terminal. Use a simple + for the cursor shape. If possible, write the routine so that the user needn't press

Enter in order to send a keystroke to the host. Add features that allow the user to alter the cursor's hop distance.

6.4. Designing Cursor Shapes. Redo the previous exercise using a crosshair cursor shape. Also have the driver print out the NDC coordinates of the cursor's current position at a suitable place on the display.

6.5 Implementing *Stroke*( ). Write and exercise a *Stroke*( ) procedure using the interface *Stroke*(*MaxNum* : integer; **var** *points* : *polypoint*). *Stroke*( ) uses a succession of *Locate*( )s to input no more than *MaxNum* points and places them in *points* (using the *points.num* field to capture the number of points obtained). The user presses one button on the *Locator* device to trigger each point, and another button to terminate the *Stroke* sequence.

6.6. Implementing *Politor*. Write the *Politor* application that implements the functions described in Section 6.6.3. Other functions should be added to *Politor* as well, such as a one-step deletion of an entire polyline and a listing of the coordinates of polylines' endpoints.

6.7. Generating Menus in World Coordinates. Menus can be created in world coordinates as well as in NDC. The use of world coordinates permits the choice of a convenient window and viewport for each menu. This can simplify the menu generation process and allow menus to be positioned more freely in the display. Figure 6.22 shows an example. Here the menu extends from 0 to 2 in *x* and from 0 to 5 in *y*, and as before, each item is associated with one of the boxes. The window is set to just enclose this menu rectangle, and a suitable viewport is chosen in NDC, as suggested in the figure. Because a different window and viewport are used for each menu, the application must keep track of several window-to-viewport mappings. If *Locate*( ) is used instead of *LocateNDC*( ), then the appropriate inverse transformation for each menu must be used (in a routine like *Inside*( )) in order to determine which menu item is selected.

Write a program that builds a set of menus defined in world coordinates and that permits the selection of menu items from these menus, using *Locate*( ).

6.8. Menu Building. Write and exercise *BuildMenu*( ), which accesses an array of records of type *menu_item*, as described, and draws the corresponding menu.

6.9. A Pick-and-Place Routine. Develop a routine that effects a pick-and-place action. The icon menu should include at least four elements, and they are picked using the *Locator*. As each one is picked, it can be positioned anywhere in the drawing area, at one of the four orientations 0°, 90°, 180°, or 270°.

6.10. Deleting Elements. Add to the pick-and-place routine the capability to delete any element that is on display.

6.11. Initiating a *Connect*. In Section 6.9, a specific menu item, *Connect*, was used to initiate the *Connect* function. Alternatively, one of the *Locator* buttons can specify the *Connect* function directly. The user at any time simply points at the first pad and presses that button and then points to the second pad and retriggers the *Locator*. Write a code fragment that implements this action.

6.12. Building a General Graph. Write a program that allows a user to build a complex graph. The nodes of the graph should be drawn as circles, and the branches should be drawn as straight lines. A branch between two nodes is oriented as if to connect the centers of the circles representing the nodes, but it is visible only between the circles.

6.13. Adding Arrows for Directed Graphs. Extend the previous exercise to add arrowheads to the branches in a graph to create directed graphs and to allow the user to specify a numerical quantity that represents the "cost" of each branch.

Provide a means for storing the graph in an external file and for reloading it into the application.

6.14. Editing a Graph. Extend the graph-building application so that the graph may be edited; that is, in addition to adding new nodes and branches the user can also delete nodes and branches. The application should check whether a deletion creates any "dangling" (unconnected) nodes or branches, and if so, it should remove them.

6.15 Building Logic Circuits. Write and exercise an application that permits a user to construct a digital logic circuit interactively. An icon menu shows symbols for NAND, NOR, and NOT gates. Instances of these can be placed as desired, and their pads may be interconnected, as described in Section 6.9. All interconnection leads should consist of horizontal and vertical segments. Provide for deleting both interconnections and gates, and arrange for the circuit to be stored in an external file.

6.16. Block Diagrams. Build an application that allows a user to create a block diagram of a system, as in Figure 6.15d. The blocks are drawn as rectangles; "summers" are shown as circles; and parts of the block diagram are con-

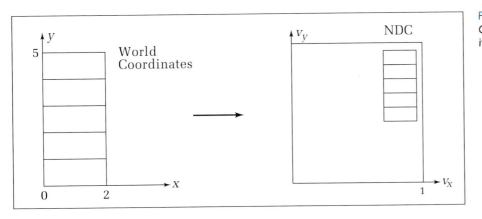

Figure 6.22.
Geometric picking of menu items: world coordinates.

nected by leads composed of horizontal and vertical line segments. Provide for labeling each block with a text string drawn inside it. Provide also for deleting system elements and for storing the system in an external file.

6.17.   Menu Interaction Using Segments. Consider a user interface that involves two types of menus: a function menu and an object menu. The function menu consists of four text items: *Add*, *Delete*, *Move*, and *Exit*, each of which invokes a corresponding function: *Do_Add*, *Do_Delete*, and so forth. This menu is drawn as a rectangle on the left side of the display, with the five text strings stacked one upon another. The object menu consists of four items, each drawn as an icon: a triangle, a tree, a star, and a circle. The four icons are drawn in a rectangle stacked one upon another. This menu occupies the same position on the display as does the function menu.

Write the skeleton of an application that first defines each menu as a segment, assigning different pick-ids to each menu item. It then has a main loop that posts the function menu and requests a *Pick* from it. If *Add* is selected, the object menu replaces the function menu, and a *Pick* of one of the objects is requested, followed by a *Locate* for the position to add the new object. A new segment is created for the added object, and it is drawn. If *Delete* is selected, another *Pick* will be requested to identify an object (*not* a menu item) on the display to be deleted, and the picture of the segment will vanish. If *Move* is chosen, a *Pick* of the object will be requested, followed by a *Locate* to show where it is to appear. The segment for the original object is made invisible, and a new segment is created for the moved object.

If a graphics package is available that supports segments, use this program. Otherwise simply sketch the various instructions, carefully showing how the segments are managed and *Pick*-ed.

CHAPTER 7

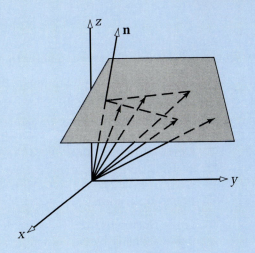

Vectors and Their Use in Graphics

Goals of the Chapter

- To develop the powerful mathematical language of vectors and to relate vectors to many graphical objects of interest.

- To relate geometric concepts to their algebraic representations and their efficient implementation in application code.

- To describe lines and rays parametrically in terms of vectors.

- To introduce and exploit the dot product as an important tool in computer graphics and to use it to compute such quantities as the angle between two lines, the normal direction to a line or plane, the equation for a plane, and the projection of one line onto another.

- To describe the half-spaces defined by lines and planes and to see why dot products are the central tool in clipping algorithms.

- To introduce the vector product and use it to compute such quantities as the area of a polygon and the normal direction to a surface.

- To develop the triple scalar product as a tool to measure volumes, the planarity of a polygon, and the intersection of three planes.

7.1 Introduction: Vectors and Their Manipulation

In the previous chapters we dealt with several kinds of objects:

- *Scalars* are single real numbers that express magnitude, such as 1.5 and π. In programs they are represented by the type *real*.

- *Points* are expressions of geometric positions, and they have several possible representations. For instance, in two dimensions (2D) they are captured by **2-tuples** giving their coordinates relative to a coordinate system. Both the Cartesian form such as $(x, y) = (3.4, -0.56)$ and the polar form $(R, \theta) = (2.4, 45°)$ are commonly used. The type *point* is used in an application.[1]

- *Lines, Segments, and Rays* are described by various linear equations or parametrically by two functions, $(x(t), y(t))$, both of which vary linearly with t. The permitted range of t-values determines whether the object is a line, a ray, or a line segment.

- *Circles and arcs* are described by a quadratic equation or parametrically in terms of trigonometric functions.

Thus far we have said little about such important concepts as the angle between two lines, the length of a line, the direction that a point travels along a line, or the projection of one line onto another. Here we shall develop the concise and elegant language of vectors. Vector arithmetic provides a unified way to express many geometric ideas algebraically. For instance, in graphics we usually work with vectors of two, three, and four dimensions, but many results can be stated once for vectors without referring to their dimensionality or to an underlying coordinate system: The special cases used in graphics are summarized in a single expression. With this unification a few tools can be used for many tasks.

Although the reader is assumed to know something about vectors, he or she should study these sections with some care, as the methods we develop will be used in many contexts throughout the text. For instance, we shall describe in Chapter 8 a simple two-dimensional ray-tracing application based on vector algebra that shows how gas molecules bounce around in a chamber or how a billiard ball moves on an elliptical pool table. It's quite captivating in itself, but more importantly, the same vector ideas are used later when generating realistic images using three-dimensional ray-tracing techniques. We shall also see how a vector-based "inside–outside" test can be used for both 2D and 3D clipping.

When discussing vectors, it is important to remember their dual nature: Whereas they are defined algebraically in tems of certain operations that can be performed on them, they also permit a geometric interpretation in terms of points, lines, directions, and the like. Viewed geometrically, vectors are objects having length and direction, corresponding to several physical entities such as force, displacement, and velocity. Vectors are often drawn as arrows of a certain

---

[1]See Appendix 3 for a summary of all defined data types.

length pointing in a certain direction. We shall denote them by names displayed in boldface, as in **w** and **N**.

When referring to a specific coordinate system, vectors have an algebraic representation given by 2-tuples, 3-tuples, and so on, as appropriate. Thus one of the representations of the two-dimensional vector **a** is an ordered pair of real numbers: $\mathbf{a} = (a_x, a_y)$.

Although vectors have the same form as do points in their representations, they are not the same creature. Whereas a point is a **position**, it is best to think of a vector geometrically as a **displacement**. For example, in a given 2D coordinate system, $\mathbf{a} = (3.5, 1.2)$ indicates a displacement or change in the first coordinate of 3.5 units, and a displacement of 1.2 units in the second coordinate. In programs, vectors are captured by the following data types:

Code Fragment 7.1. Data Types for 2D and 3D Vectors

```
type
   vector = record
                 dx, dy : real
           end;
   vector3D = record
                   dx, dy, dz : real
              end;
```

Here the fields are given names such as *dx, dy* to emphasize that a vector represents a change of a certain amount in each component. Recall the use of this type in Chapter 3 in connection with the *MoveRel( )* and *LineRel( )* functions.

Two points, $P_1 = (x_1, y_1)$ and $P_2 = (x_2, y_2)$, naturally define the vector **v**, with its components given by the difference of the corresponding point coordinates: $\mathbf{v} = (x_2 - x_1, y_2 - y_1)$. This vector is sometimes denoted $P_1 P_2$ and is called "the vector from P_1 to P_2." Figure 7.1 shows an example in which $P_1 = (2, 3)$ and $P_2 = (4, 5)$, so that $\mathbf{v} = (2, 2)$. In the figure, **v** is shown **bound** to P_1. Vectors

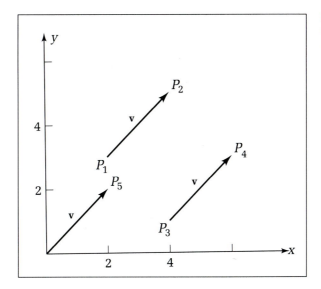

Figure 7.1.
The vector $\mathbf{v} = P_1 P_2$ as a displacement from P_1 to P_2.

themselves do not have fixed locations, although for visual clarity we usually sketch them as emanating from some given point. As shown, **v** is also the vector from P_3 to P_4. A case of particular interest is a vector bound to the origin, as in the vector (also **v**) that emanates from $(0, 0)$ and terminates at P_5. This is often called a **position vector**:

> **Definition**
>
> For any point $P = (P_x, P_y)$ in a coordinate system, the vector **v** bound to the origin with coordinates $\mathbf{v} = (P_x, P_y)$ is the position vector for P.

As long as the coordinate system is not altered, the point P and the position vector **v** are algebraically and geometrically indistinguishable. But keep in mind that in the more general abstract setting that we are initially formulating here, **v** is indeed a vector and P is indeed a point, and so they are not conceptually the same object. We shall discuss this further later.

Three-dimensional (3D) vectors are also of great importance in graphics. Figure 7.2 shows the vector $\mathbf{v} = (2, 3, 4)$ in a 3D coordinate system, in which **v** defines a displacement of two units along the x-axis, three units along the y-axis, and four units along the z-axis. The version of **v** that is the position vector $0B$ for B is shown, with the head of the arrow located at the point $B = (2, 3, 4)$.

7.2   Operations with Vectors

We shall next examine the basic operations that can be performed on vectors and determine their geometric interpretation. We shall develop them once for a vector of n-dimensions: For any positive integer n, an n-dimensional vector **w** is an **n-tuple**

$$\mathbf{w} = (w_1, w_2, \ldots, w_n)$$

where each component w_i is a scalar. The 2D and 3D vectors for which $n = 2$ and $n = 3$ are most often encountered in graphics. We cannot visualize vectors of

Figure 7.2.
Stereo view of
three-dimensional vectors.

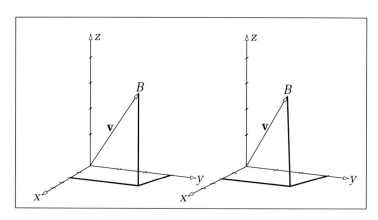

dimension greater than three, of course, but they are extremely valuable entities. In Chapter 11 we shall use 4-tuples to unify transformations of pictures.

The two principal manipulations in vector arithmetic are the addition of two vectors and the scaling of one vector. We state the main facts here for general n-dimensional vectors:

7.2.1 Adding Two Vectors

In terms of their components, the sum $\mathbf{c}$ of two vectors, $\mathbf{a}$ and $\mathbf{b}$, denoted as $\mathbf{c} = \mathbf{a} + \mathbf{b}$, is defined as

$$\mathbf{c} = (c_1, c_2, \ldots , c_n) = (a_1 + b_1, a_2 + b_2, \ldots , a_n + b_n) \qquad (7.1)$$

that is, the addition is performed componentwise : $c_i = a_i + b_i$ for each i. For example, $(3, 1, 6) + (2, 9, -5) = (5, 10, 1)$. Figure 7.3 shows a two-dimensional example, using $\mathbf{a} = (1, -2)$ and $\mathbf{b} = (3, 2)$. We can represent the addition of two vectors graphically in two different ways. In Figure 7.3a we bind one to the other (i.e., place the tail of $\mathbf{b}$ to the head of $\mathbf{a}$) and draw the sum as emanating from the tail of $\mathbf{a}$ to the head of $\mathbf{b}$. The sum "completes the triangle," which is the simple addition of one displacement to another. The components of the sum are clearly the sums of the components of its parts, as the algebra dictates. Alternatively, in Figure 7.3b we bind both vectors to the same point, thereby forming two sides of a parallelogram. The sum of the vectors is then a diagonal of this parallelogram, the diagonal that emanates from the binding point of the vectors. This view—the "parallelogram rule" for adding vectors—is the natural picture for forces acting at a point: The parallelogram gives the resultant force.

The addition of two 2D vectors is easily carried out in code, as suggested by the following procedure:

Code Fragment 7.2. Vector Addition

```
procedure AddVectors(a, b : vector; var c : vector);
begin
    c.dx := a.dx + b.dx;
    c.dy := a.dy + b.dy
end;
```

The general n-dimensional version of this routine follows similarly.

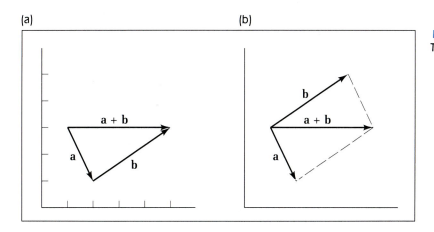

(a)   (b)

Figure 7.3.
The sum of two vectors.

7.2.2 Scaling a Vector

If a vector $\mathbf{a} = (a_x, a_y)$ is added to itself, $\mathbf{b} = \mathbf{a} + \mathbf{a}$, the result is apparently a vector with each component doubled: $\mathbf{b} = (2a_x, 2a_y)$. It seems logical to "factor out" the scale factor and to write $\mathbf{b} = 2\mathbf{a}$, which conveys the notion of scaling a vector. **Scaling** changes the length of a vector and/or reverses its direction. If s is a scalar and $\mathbf{a}$ is a vector, then s times $\mathbf{a}$ is denoted as $s\mathbf{a}$ and is defined as

$$s\mathbf{a} = (sa_1, sa_2, \ldots, sa_n) \tag{7.2}$$

That is, each component of $\mathbf{a}$ is multiplied by the scalar s. For $s = 2.5$ the vector $s\mathbf{a}$ has the same direction as $\mathbf{a}$ but is 2.5 times as long, as shown in Figure 7.4. When s is negative, the direction of $s\mathbf{a}$ is opposite that of $\mathbf{a}$: The case $s = -1$ is shown in the figure. A procedure to carry out the scaling operation $\mathbf{b} = s\mathbf{a}$ might be declared as

procedure *Scale*(s : *real*; a : *vector*; **var** b : *vector*);

and is easy to write—see the exercises.

7.2.3 Subtracting Vectors

From the basic adding and scaling operations, subtraction follows easily: $\mathbf{a} - \mathbf{c}$ is simply $\mathbf{a} + (-\mathbf{c})$, with i-th component $a_i - c_i$. Figure 7.5 shows the geometric interpretation of this operation, that is, forming the difference of $\mathbf{a}$ and $\mathbf{c}$ as the sum of $\mathbf{a}$ and $-\mathbf{c}$. Using the parallelogram rule, this sum is seen to be equal to the vector that emanates from the head of $\mathbf{c}$ and terminates at the head of $\mathbf{a}$. This is recognized as one diagonal of the parallelogram constructed using $\mathbf{a}$ and $\mathbf{c}$. Note too that it is the diagonal opposite from the one that represents the sum $\mathbf{a} + \mathbf{c}$.

7.2.4 The Magnitude (Length) of a Vector

If a vector $\mathbf{w}$ is represented by the n-tuple $(w_1, w_2, \ldots, w_n)$, how might its magnitude (equivalently, length or size) be defined and computed? We define the magnitude of a vector in terms of the distance from its tail to its head. Based on the Pythagorean theorem, this becomes

> **Definition: The Magnitude of a Vector**
>
> The magnitude of vector $\mathbf{w}$ is denoted as $|\mathbf{w}|$ and is given by
>
> $$|\mathbf{w}| = \sqrt{w_1^2 + w_2^2 + \ldots + w_n^2} \tag{7.3}$$

Figure 7.4.
Scaling a vector.

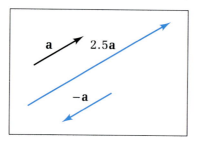

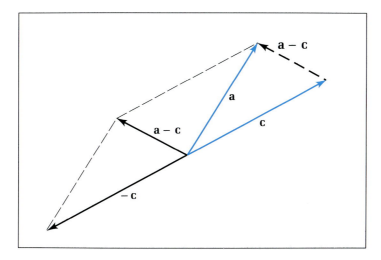

Figure 7.5.
Subtracting vectors.

For example, the magnitude of $\mathbf{w} = (4, -2)$ is $\sqrt{20}$, and that of $\mathbf{w} = (1, -3, 2)$ is $\sqrt{14}$. A vector of zero length is often denoted as $\mathbf{0}$. Note that if $\mathbf{w}$ is the vector from point A to point B, then $|\mathbf{w}|$ will be the distance from A to B. In a program the function $Length(v : vector) : real$ is often needed to compute the length of a vector. (Writing $Length(\ )$ and its 3D version $Length3D(\ )$ is left as an exercise.)

Now that we have defined length, note that an alternative representation of a 2D vector is its "polar" form: (magnitude, direction). That is, if the (x, y) form for vector $\mathbf{a}$ is $(3, 4)$, it will have length 5 and be oriented at $36.8699°$ from the horizontal, so that it has the polar representation $(5, 36.8699°)$. Because vectors are frequently introduced as entities with magnitude and direction but not position, their polar representations are actually very logical.

Normalizing Vectors—Unit Vectors

It is often convenient to scale a vector so that the result has a length equal to one. This is called **normalizing** a vector, and the result is known as a **unit vector**, meaning "unit length" vector. For example, form the normalized version, $\mathbf{u_a}$, of $\mathbf{a}$ by scaling it with the value $1/|\mathbf{a}|$:

$$\mathbf{u_a} = \frac{\mathbf{a}}{|\mathbf{a}|}$$

Clearly this is a unit vector, $|\mathbf{u_a}| = 1$ (why?), having the same direction as $\mathbf{a}$. At times we refer to a unit vector as a **direction**. Note that any vector can be written as its magnitude times its direction: If $\mathbf{u_a}$ is the normalized version of $\mathbf{a}$, it may always be written

$$\mathbf{a} = |\mathbf{a}|\mathbf{u_a}$$

Example

Let $\mathbf{c} = (3, -4)$. Then $|\mathbf{c}| = 5$ and the normalized version $\mathbf{u_c}$ is $\mathbf{u_c} = (\frac{3}{5}, -\frac{4}{5})$.

A routine to normalize a vector might have the interface *Normalize*(v : *vector*; **var** u : *vector*). It forms the unit vector u by scaling each component of v : $u.dx := v.dx / Length(v)$ and similarly for $u.dy$.

Drill Exercise

7.1.   Normalizing Vectors. Normalize each of the following vectors:

$(1, -2, .5)$

$(8, 6)$

$(4, 3)$

7.2.5 Linear Combinations of Vectors

With methods in hand for adding and scaling vectors, it is useful to define a linear combination of vectors. To form a **linear combination** of two vectors, **v** and **w**, scale—or "weight"—each of them by some scalars—say a and b—and add the weighted versions to form the new vector, $a\mathbf{v} + b\mathbf{w}$. More generally:

> **Definition**
>
> A linear combination of the m vectors $\mathbf{v}_1, \mathbf{v}_2, \ldots, \mathbf{v}_m$ is a vector of the form
>
> $$\mathbf{w} = a_1\mathbf{v}_1 + a_2\mathbf{v}_2 + \ldots + a_m\mathbf{v}_m \qquad (7.4)$$

where $a_1, a_2, \ldots, a_m$ are scalars. For example, the linear combination $2(3, 4) + \frac{3}{2}(2, 4)$ forms the vector $(9, 14)$. In later chapters we shall deal with rather elaborate linear combinations of vectors, especially when representing curves and surfaces using spline functions.

The following code fragment forms the linear combination $\mathbf{w} = a\mathbf{u} + b\mathbf{v}$ in two dimensions. Extending the procedure to more than two vectors in n-dimensions is addressed in the exercises.

Code Fragment 7.3. Linear Combination of Two 2D Vectors

```
procedure Combo2D(a, b : real; u, v : vector; var w : vector);
{build w = a * u + b * v}
begin
    w.dx := a * u.dx + b * v.dx;
    w.dy := a * u.dy + b * v.dy
end;
```

Convex Combinations of Vectors

A special class of linear combinations has an important place in mathematics and numerous applications in graphics: the **convex combinations**, or linear combinations for which the coefficients are nonnegative and add up to one.

The linear combination

$$\mathbf{w} = a_1\mathbf{v}_1 + a_2\mathbf{v}_2 + \ldots + a_m\mathbf{v}_m$$

will be a convex combination if the scalars a_i add to 1 and $a_i \geq 0$: They all are nonnegative. Thus $.3\mathbf{a} + .7\mathbf{b}$ is a convex combination of $\mathbf{a}$ and $\mathbf{b}$, but $1.8\mathbf{a} - .8\mathbf{b}$ is not. The set of coefficients $a_1, \ldots, a_m$ is sometimes said to form a **partition of unity**, meaning that a unit amount of "material" is partitioned into pieces.

Convex combinations frequently arise in applications when one is making a unit amount of some brew and can add only positive amounts of the various ingredients. They appear in unexpected contexts. For instance, we shall see in Chapter 14 that "spline" curves are in fact convex combinations of a set of vectors, and in our discussion of color in Chapter 16 we shall find that any color of unit brightness may be considered to be a convex combination of three primary colors!

A Vector Ray As a Convex Combination

A particularly important convex combination is

$$\mathbf{p}(t) = \mathbf{a}(1 - t) + \mathbf{b}t \tag{7.5}$$

in which $\mathbf{a}$ and $\mathbf{b}$ are arbitrary vectors and we restrict t to $0 \leq t \leq 1$. This is reminiscent of the parametric representation of a line seen in Chapter 4. The scalars are $(1 - t)$ and t, which clearly sum to one, and both are nonnegative. In addition, $\mathbf{p}(t)$ is a **vector function** of t, that is, a vector whose length and direction vary with t, as shown in Figure 7.6a. At $t = 0$, $\mathbf{p}(t)$ is just $\mathbf{a}$, and at $t = 1$, it is $\mathbf{b}$. Notice that with the proper choice of t, any vector that lies on the line between $\mathbf{a}$ and $\mathbf{b}$ can be represented by this convex combination.

If we bind $\mathbf{p}(t)$ to a fixed point, then as t increases toward 1, $\mathbf{p}(t)$ "pivots" away from $\mathbf{a}$ toward $\mathbf{b}$, its arrowhead following a straight-line trajectory. If t increases beyond 1, the arrowhead will continue a straight-line course beyond

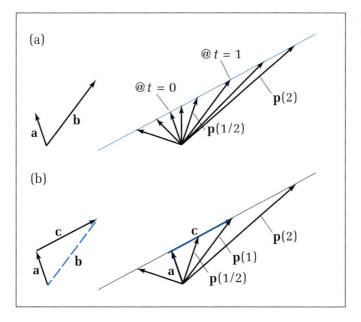

Figure 7.6.
A parametric ray defined using vectors.

b, but for these values of t, $\mathbf{p}(t)$ is no longer a convex combination. Similarly, for $t < 0$, the ray is well defined but no longer a convex combination. Notice that the figure is given independent of any coordinate system and that the vectors can be of any dimension.

Rearranging terms slightly in Equation 7.5, we obtain another useful form for this vector function:

$$\mathbf{p}(t) = \mathbf{a} + (\mathbf{b} - \mathbf{a})t$$
$$= \mathbf{a} + \mathbf{c}t \tag{7.6}$$

where we define $\mathbf{c} = \mathbf{b} - \mathbf{a}$. For t between zero and one, this form is also a convex combination (of **a** and **b**), but it is not as obvious, owing to the rearrangement of the terms. Now t appears as the scalar in only one of the component vectors, and the term $\mathbf{c}t$ acts as an offset or displacement on **a**. As t increases, an increasing amount of offset **c** is added to the fixed **a**, as shown in Figure 7.6b.

As another example, consider a convex combination of three vectors. Choose two parameters α_1 and α_2, both lying between 0 and 1, and form the following linear combination:

$$\mathbf{q} = \alpha_1 \mathbf{v}_1 + \alpha_2 \mathbf{v}_2 + (1 - \alpha_1 - \alpha_2)\mathbf{v}_3 \tag{7.7}$$

This is a convex combination, as none of the coefficients is ever negative and they clearly sum to one. Consider the example of Figure 7.7, in which the three position vectors $\mathbf{v}_1 = (1, 6)$, $\mathbf{v}_2 = (3, 3)$, and $\mathbf{v}_3 = (8, 3)$ are shown. By the proper choice of α_1 and α_2, any vector lying within the shaded triangle of vectors can be represented. The vector $\mathbf{b} = .2\mathbf{v}_1 + .5\mathbf{v}_2 + .3\mathbf{v}_3$, for instance, is shown explicitly as the vector sum of the three weighted ingredients. If $\alpha_2 = 0$, any vector in the set labeled L that joins $\mathbf{v}_1$ and $\mathbf{v}_3$ can be "reached" by the proper choice of α_1. For example, the vector that is 20 percent of the way from $\mathbf{v}_1$ to $\mathbf{v}_3$ along L is given by $.8\mathbf{v}_1 + .2\mathbf{v}_3$.

Figure 7.7.
The set of vectors representable by convex combinations.

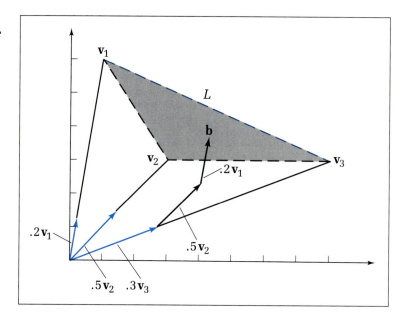

Drill Exercise

7.2. Representing Vectors in Figure 7.7. With reference to Figure 7.7, what values, or range of values, for α_1 and α_2 create the following sets?

a. $\mathbf{v}_1$.

b. The set joining $\mathbf{v}_1$ and $\mathbf{v}_2$.

c. The vector midway between $\mathbf{v}_2$ and $\mathbf{v}_3$.

d. The centroid of the triangle.

7.2.6 Vectors Versus Points

Points seem to have some similarity to vectors. For instance, both a 2D point and a 2D vector can be represented as a 2-tuple of numbers. But the coordinates of a point represent position, whereas those of vectors represent displacement. Vectors have magnitude and direction but no position; points have position but neither magnitude nor direction. Operations have been established for vectors such that arbitrary vectors (of the same dimension) may be added and multiplied by scalars. Any linear combination of a set of vectors is itself a legitimate vector. Can points be combined in the way that vectors are, and can points and vectors ever be mixed?

An important property of vectors is that the value taken on by any linear combination is independent of the choice of origin of the coordinate system. For example, the sum of vectors $\mathbf{u} + \mathbf{v}$ shown in Figure 7.8 does not depend on whether φ_1 or φ_2 is used as the origin of the system, as each vector is simply a displacement within the system. But the location of a point such as P in Figure 7.8 depends on the choice of origin. P has coordinates (9, 8) if the origin is φ_1, whereas if φ_2 is used, it has coordinates (4, 1).

Expressions that add or scale points, such as $P_1 + P_2$ and $2P_1$ are often found in algorithms in the graphics literature, as are expressions such as $P_1 + \mathbf{v}$ that mix points and vectors. Because computer programs compute individual coordinates of points and/or vectors, they have no difficulty operating on, say, $P_1 + P_2$ to produce new coordinates. But the question remains whether a mean-

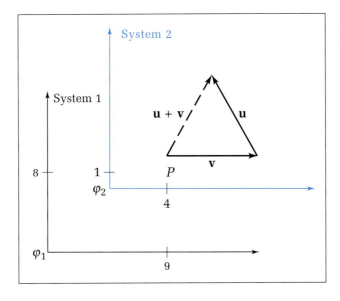

Figure 7.8.
Vectors are independent of the choice of origin.

ingful geometric object is being represented and whether the computed result is still correct in a slightly different geometric context, such as after the origin of the coordinate system has been shifted.

We know that a vector is the difference between two points, in the sense that it is the amount that one point must be displaced to make it coincide with the second point. This can be written as

$$\mathbf{v} = P_2 - P_1 \qquad (7.8)$$

Consider what this relation would become if we set point P_1 to the origin φ of the coordinate system being used. This is the same as binding vector $\mathbf{v}$ to the origin. But then P_2 has the same coordinates as does $\mathbf{v}$ in this coordinate system, and so $\mathbf{v}$ is the position vector for P_2. A position vector is indistinguishable both algebraically and geometrically from a point, as long as we don't change the origin of the system.

Also, when we displace a point so that it is shifted to a new position, it is surely still a point, and so we can assert: A point plus a vector is a point and write:

$$P_2 = P_1 + \mathbf{v} \qquad (7.9)$$

This is clearly consistent with Equation 7.8. Computationally it also makes sense: Add corresponding components of P_1 to those of $\mathbf{v}$ to form components of P_2. Thus there is no conceptual problem in sketching a vector $\mathbf{v}$ bound to a point P_1: It emanates from P_1 and its arrowhead terminates at point P_2, having coordinates given by $P_1 + \mathbf{v}$.

In both of these equations the "+" and "−" operators are different from the usual arithmetic "+" and "−," as they work with points and vectors rather than numbers. But computationally and geometrically they are meaningful statements.

Example: Point–Direction Form for a Ray

Our ability to write a point as the sum of a point and a vector makes immediate sense of the parametric representation for a line (or segment or ray) given by

$$P(t) = A + \mathbf{c}t \qquad (7.10)$$

where A is a point and $\mathbf{c}$ is a vector. As t increases from 0, the point $P(t)$ travels in a straight line from A in the direction $\mathbf{c}$. As we saw in Chapter 4, the allowed range of t-values determines whether $P(t)$ is a line, a segment, or a ray:

$A + \mathbf{c}t$ is a line if all t are allowed.

$A + \mathbf{c}t$ is a ray if nonnegative t are allowed.

$A + \mathbf{c}t$ is a segment if t in (0, 1) are allowed.

Equation 7.10 is called the **point–direction form** of the ray, line, or segment.

Linear Combinations of Points

The difference of two points makes sense, and so does a point plus a vector. Now we want to generalize to an arbitrary linear combination of points. For instance, what is the geometric meaning of $3P_2 + 4P_5 - 6P_6$? Form the object E as the following weighted sum of m points $P_1,...,P_m$:

$$E = \sum_{i=1}^{m} a_i P_i \qquad (7.11)$$

Is it a point, a vector, or nothing at all? The question that sorts this out is: How does E depend on the **choice of origin** of the coordinate system (see Goldman 1985)?

Suppose the origin is shifted, so that each point P_i is altered to $P_i + \mathbf{u}$, where $\mathbf{u}$ represents the shift in origin. If E is a point, it too must be shifted by the same $\mathbf{u}$. On the other hand, if E is a vector, it must *not* be affected by $\mathbf{u}$.

Symbolically E becomes E' given by

$$E' = \sum_{i=1}^{m} a_i(P_i + \mathbf{u})$$

$$= \sum_{i=1}^{m} a_i P_i + \sum_{i=1}^{m} a_i \mathbf{u} \qquad (7.12)$$

$$= E + S\mathbf{u}$$

where S is the sum of the coefficients:

$$S = \sum_{i=1}^{m} a_i \qquad (7.13)$$

We see that the effect of the shift in each P_i is to add an offset to E given by $\mathbf{u}$ times the sum of the coefficients in the linear combination. If E is a point, this offset must be identical to $\mathbf{u}$ itself, and so S must equal 1. If E is a vector, this offset must not amount to anything, and so S must equal 0. Summarizing:

1. E is a point if $S = 1$.

2. E is a vector if $S = 0$.

3. E is meaningless for other values of S.

Examples

The difference between two points:
The object $P_2 - P_1$ is equivalent to $a_2 P_2 + a_1 P_1$, with $a_2 = 1$ and $a_1 = -1$. Hence $S = 0$, and so this object is a vector, as we have already seen.

The midpoint between P_1 and P_2:
Midpoints were discussed in Chapter 3. The object $(P_1 + P_2)/2$ uses coefficients $a_1 = \frac{1}{2}$ and $a_2 = \frac{1}{2}$, having sum $S = 1$, and so it is a legal point.

The parametric line:
$P(t) = P_1(1 - t) + P_2 t$ was used earlier as a parametric expression for the line through P_1 and P_2. It is a linear combination, with $a_1 = (1 - t)$ and $a_2 = t$, which sum to 1. Hence it is indeed a legal point for each value of t.

Any convex combination of points is a point:
This is so because the coefficients in the linear combination sum to 1.

An illegal form:
One cannot simply add two points. The object $P_1 + P_2$ is not valid, and Figure 7.9 shows why. Points P_1 and P_2 are shown represented in two coordinate systems, one offset from the other. Viewing each point as the head of a vector bound to its origin, we see that the sum $P_1 + P_2$ yields two different points in the two systems. Therefore $P_1 + P_2$ depends on the choice of coordinate system. Note that the midpoint $\frac{1}{2}(P_1 + P_2)$ does not depend on this choice.

Scaling a point is not legal:
The object $3P_1$ is also illegal. Shifting the origin does not shift the point by the same amount, but by three times this amount, as $3(P_1 + \mathbf{u}) = 3P_1 + 3\mathbf{u}$.

$5P_1 + 2P_2 - 6P_3$ is legal:
Here the coefficients sum to one, and so this object is a point. This works because we can rearrange terms to form $P_1 + 4(P_1 - P_3) + 2(P_2 - P_3)$, a point plus a vector.

An Application: "Tweening" for Art and Animation

We have seen that the combination

$$P(t) = (1 - t)A + tB \tag{7.14}$$

of the two points A and B is a valid point for any value of t, because the coefficients $(1 - t)$ and t sum to 1. If t lies between 0 and 1, the point $P(t)$ is said to **interpolate** the points A and B. $P(t)$ lies fraction t of the way from A to B.

This can be used to transform one figure into another in a graceful, gradual manner. Figure 7.10 shows a simple example, in which each of nine points of

Figure 7.9.
Adding points is not legal.

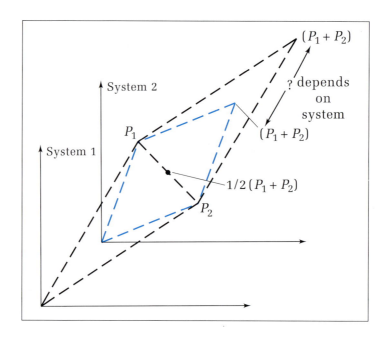

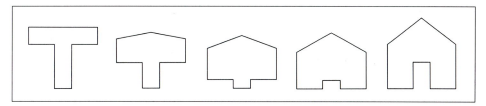

Figure 7.10.
Tweening a "T" into a house.

the letter T is converted into a corresponding point of a house. We begin with two polylines having the same number of vertices. Call the points of the first A_i and those of the second B_i, for $i = 1, \ldots, n$. In the figure, polyline A corresponds to the T and polyline B to the house. Now construct an "in-between" polyline, $P(t)$, or informally a "tween" having vertices $P_i(t)$, where

$$P_i(t) = (1 - t)A_i + tB_i \qquad (7.15)$$

for a given value of t between 0 and 1. If $t = \frac{1}{2}$ is used, for instance, the polyline $P(\frac{1}{2})$ is made up of midpoints between the corresponding vertices in A and B. For $t = .25$, the points of the tween are 25 percent of the way from A to B. Figure 7.10 shows the resulting figures for the set of t-values 0, .25, .5, .75, and 1.

Drill Exercise

7.3. A Limiting Case of Tweening. What is the effect of tweening when all of the points A_i in polyline A are the same? How is polyline B distorted in its appearance in each in-between?

The routine *DrawSequence( )* draws a sequence of n tweens based on the polylines A and B. For each t-value in the sequence 0, $1/(n-1)$, $2/(n-1)$, . . ., 1, *Tween( )* computes the polyline $P(t)$, which is then drawn. The routine *NewFrame* causes a **newframe action**, which is device dependent. In a plotting situation it alerts the user to remove the old piece of paper from the plotter and insert the new piece. In a photo-recording session it automatically advances the film to the next frame, ready for exposure. In an interactive display, *NewFrame* simply erases the polyline, perhaps after a suitable pause (see the exercises).

Code Fragment 7.4. Tweening a Polyline

```
var A, B, poly : polypoint;
procedure Tween(t : real);
{build poly as linear interpolation of A and B at t.}
var i : integer;
begin
  with poly do
  for i := 1 to num do
  begin
    pt[i].x := (1.0 − t) * A.pt[i].x + t * B.pt[i].x;
    pt[i].y := (1.0 − t) * A.pt[i].y + t * B.pt[i].y
  end
end;{Tween}
```

procedure *DrawSequence*(*n* : *integer*);
{draw *n* equispaced versions between *A* and *B*.}
var *k* : *integer*;
begin
   if (*A.num* <> *B.num*) **or** (*A.num* < 2) **or** (*n* < 2) **then** *ReportError*
   else for *k* := 1 **to** *n* **do**
   begin
      Tween((*k* − 1) / (*n* − 1)); {build in-between polyline}
      Polyline(*poly*);
      NewFrame; {go to next frame}
   end {**else**}
end; {*DrawSequence*}

Figure 7.11 shows an artistic use of this technique based on two sets of polylines. Three in-betweens are shown (what values of *t* are used?). Because the two sets of polylines are drawn sufficiently far apart, there is room to draw the in-betweens between them with no overlap, so that all five pictures fit nicely on one frame.

Susan E. Brennan of Hewlett Packard in Palo Alto, California, has produced caricatures of famous figures using this method (see Dewdney 1988). Figure 7.12 shows an example. The second and fourth faces are based on digitized points for Elizabeth Taylor and John F. Kennedy. The third face is a tween, and the other three are based on **extrapolation**. That is, Equation 7.15 is used with values of *t* larger than 1, so that the term (1 − *t*) is negative. Extrapolation can produce caricaturelike distortions, in some sense "going to the other side" of polyline *B* from polyline *A*. Values of *t* less than 0 may also be used, with a similar effect.

Drill Exercises

7.4.   An Extrapolation. Polyline *A* is a square with vertices (1, 1), (−1, 1), (−1, −1), (1, −1), and polyline *B* is a wedge with vertices (4, 3), (5, −2), (4, 0), (3, −2). Sketch (by hand) the shape *P*(*t*) for *t* = −1., −0.5, 0.5, and 1.5.

7.5.   Extrapolation Versus In-Betweening. Suppose that five polyline pictures are displayed side by side. From careful measurement you determine that the middle three are in-betweens of the first and the last, and you calculate the values of *t* used. But someone claims that the last is actually an extrapolation of the first and the fourth. Is there any way to tell whether this is true? If it is an extrapolation, can the value of *t* used be determined? If so, what is it?

Figure 7.11.
From man to woman. (Courtesy of Marc Infield.)

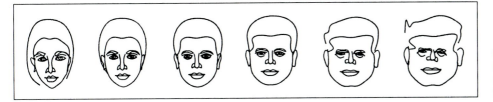

Figure 7.12.
Face caricatures: Tweening and
extrapolation. (Courtesy of
Susan Brennan.)

In-betweening is used in the film industry to reduce the cost of producing animations such as cartoons. In earlier days an artist had to draw 24 pictures for each second of film, because movies display 24 frames per second. With the assistance of a computer, however, an artist need draw only the first and final pictures in certain sequences and let the others be generated automatically. For instance, if the characters are not moving too rapidly in a certain one-half-second portion of a cartoon, the artist can draw and digitize the first and final frames of this portion, and the computer can create 10 in-betweens using linear interpolation, thereby saving a great deal of the artist's time.

7.2.7 Convex Sets and Convex Hulls

We discussed convex combinations of vectors earlier, and now we also know that convex combinations of points are legitimate. They give rise to an important geometric object in graphics, the convex hull of a set of points.

> **Definition: Convex Sets**
>
> A **convex set** of points is a collection of points in which the line connecting any pair in the set lies entirely within the set.

Figure 7.13 shows various examples of two- and three-dimensional sets, in which the ones labeled C are convex. Convex sets must be solid with no holes and no inward-bending corners. Thus the interiors of a circle or rectangle are convex sets, but the letter L is not. In three dimensions, a cone and cylinder are convex, but a doughnut is not.

> **Definition: The Convex Hull of a Set of Points**
>
> Given a collection of points, the **convex hull** is the smallest convex set that contains the points.

For points lying in a plane it helps to visualize the points marked with pins sticking out of the plane. If an elastic band is stretched around the whole set and then released, it will "snap" in against certain pins and take the shape of the convex hull. Figure 7.14a shows a set of points in the plane and its convex hull. For a set of points in three dimensions, you can visualize surrounding the set with a balloon and then releasing the air to let the balloon squeeze down around

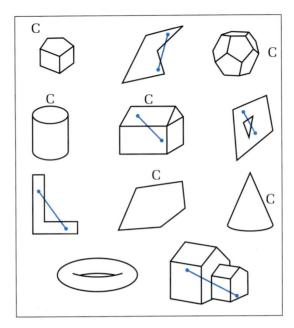

Figure 7.13.
Examples of sets in 2D and 3D, some of which are convex.

the points, thereby forming its convex hull. Figure 7.14b shows a set of points in three dimensions and their convex hull.

Now the convex hull H of a set of points is the set of all convex combinations of the points. That is, given m points P_i, $i = 1, \ldots, m$, build a point P as

$$P = \sum_{i=1}^{m} a_i P_i \tag{7.16}$$

Figure 7.14.
Examples of convex hulls.

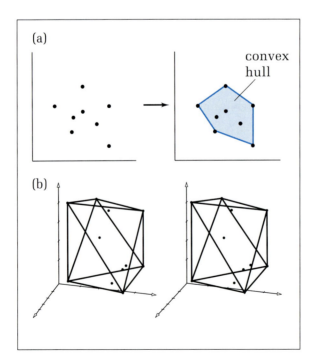

where each coefficient $a_i \geq 0$ and they sum to one. For each such choice of the coefficients we get a point in the convex hull H, and if we take the set of all possible collections of the a_i, the entire hull H will be formed.

Figure 7.15 shows the set of points that are convex combinations of m, given points for $m = 3$ and $m = 5$. All points in the triangle shown (and only those) are formed as various convex combinations of the points P_1, P_2, and P_3. The set of convex combinations certainly forms a convex set. In fact, for any two points in the set, the line joining them is precisely the set of all convex combinations of just those two points. It is also the convex hull for the set of two points. For a convex set based on three points, if one of the three weighting coefficients a_i is zero, then the convex combination will yield a point on one of the sides of the triangle, that is, on the boundary of the convex hull of the set of three points. For four or more points, some may lie inside the convex hull, as suggested in the figure.

In graphics we often use convex combinations and convex sets in association with such topics as spline curves, polygon filling, clipping, hidden surface elimination, and color combinations.

Drill Exercise

7.6. Convex Combinations of Points. Show that the set of convex combinations of any three points is precisely the triangle (along with its interior) formed by the points.

7.3 The Dot Product of Two Vectors

We shall now introduce a simple but extremely powerful tool that is frequently used throughout the book. It provides valuable information about a pair of vectors such as the angle between them (particularly it tells when they are perpendicular) and the projection of one vector onto another. It also gives the equation of a plane described in terms of a point and two vectors.

The **dot product** (also called the **inner product** or **scalar product**) of two vectors is simple to define and compute. For two-dimensional vectors, (a_1, a_2) and (b_1, b_2), it is simply the scalar $a_1 b_1 + a_2 b_2$: Multiply corresponding compo-

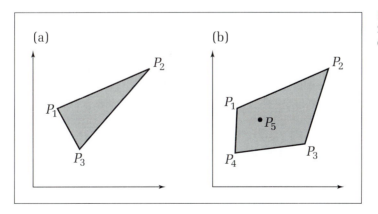

(a)   (b)

P_2

P_1

P_3

P_1

P_5

P_2

P_3

P_4

Figure 7.15.
Set of points covered by convex combinations.

nents of the two vectors, and add the results. For example, the dot product of (3, 4) and (1, 6) is 27, and that of (2, 3) and (9, −6) is 0.

The definition of the dot product generalizes easily to n dimensions:

> **Definition: The Dot Product**
>
> The dot product d of two n-dimensional vectors $\mathbf{v} = (v_1, v_2, \ldots, v_n)$ and $\mathbf{w} = (w_1, w_2, \ldots, w_n)$ is denoted as $d = \mathbf{v} \cdot \mathbf{w}$ and has value
>
> $$d = \mathbf{v} \cdot \mathbf{w} = \sum_{i=1}^{n} v_i w_i$$

Examples

a.   The dot product of (2, 3, 1) and (0, 4, −1) is 11.

b. $(2, 2, 2, 2) \cdot (4, 1, 2, 1.1) = 16.2$.

c. $(1, 0, 1, 0, 1) \cdot (0, 1, 0, 1, 0) = 0$.

d. $(169, 0, 43) \cdot (0, 375.3, 0) = 0$.

It is easy to compute the dot product in code. For two-dimensional vectors we have

Code Fragment 7.5. Forming the Dot Product: 2D Case

```
function Dot(a, b : vector) : real;
begin
   Dot := a.dx * b.dx + a.dy * b.dy
end;
```

Implementations of the n-dimensional version are requested in the exercises.

7.3.1 Properties of the Dot Product

The dot product exhibits four major properties that we frequently exploit and that follow easily (see the exercises) from its basic definition:

1.   *Symmetry*: $\mathbf{a} \cdot \mathbf{b} = \mathbf{b} \cdot \mathbf{a}$

2.   *Linearity*: $(\mathbf{a} + \mathbf{c}) \cdot \mathbf{b} = \mathbf{a} \cdot \mathbf{b} + \mathbf{c} \cdot \mathbf{b}$

3.   *Homogeneity*: $(s\mathbf{a}) \cdot \mathbf{b} = s(\mathbf{a} \cdot \mathbf{b})$

4. $|\mathbf{b}|^2 = \mathbf{b} \cdot \mathbf{b}$

The first states that the order in which the two vectors are combined does not matter. The next two proclaim that the dot product is linear; that is, the dot product of a sum of vectors can be expressed as the sum of the individual dot products, and scaling a vector scales the value of the dot product. The last property is also useful, as it asserts that taking the dot product of a vector with itself yields the square of the length of the vector. It appears frequently in the form $|\mathbf{b}| = \sqrt{\mathbf{b} \cdot \mathbf{b}}$.

The following manipulations show how these properties can be used to simplify an expression involving dot products. The result itself will be used in the next section.

Example: Simplification of $|\mathbf{a} - \mathbf{b}|^2$

Simplify the expression for the length (squared) of the difference of two vectors, $\mathbf{a}$ and $\mathbf{b}$, to obtain the following relation:

$$|\mathbf{a} - \mathbf{b}|^2 = |\mathbf{a}|^2 - 2\mathbf{a} \cdot \mathbf{b} + |\mathbf{b}|^2 \qquad (7.17)$$

The derivation proceeds as follows: Call the expression $|\mathbf{a} - \mathbf{b}|^2$ by the name Φ.

By the fourth property, Φ is the dot product:

$$\Phi = |\mathbf{a} - \mathbf{b}|^2 = (\mathbf{a} - \mathbf{b}) \cdot (\mathbf{a} - \mathbf{b})$$

Use linearity:

$$\Phi = \mathbf{a} \cdot (\mathbf{a} - \mathbf{b}) - \mathbf{b} \cdot (\mathbf{a} - \mathbf{b})$$

Use symmetry and linearity to simplify this further:

$$\Phi = \mathbf{a} \cdot \mathbf{a} - 2\mathbf{a} \cdot \mathbf{b} + \mathbf{b} \cdot \mathbf{b}$$

Recognize the dot product of a vector by itself:

$$\Phi = |\mathbf{a}|^2 - 2\mathbf{a} \cdot \mathbf{b} + |\mathbf{b}|^2$$

which gives the desired result. By replacing the minus with a plus in this relation, we can easily obtain the following similar and useful relation:

$$|\mathbf{a} + \mathbf{b}|^2 = |\mathbf{a}|^2 + 2\mathbf{a} \cdot \mathbf{b} + |\mathbf{b}|^2 \qquad (7.18)$$

7.4   Applications of the Dot Product

Next we shall discuss several important applications of the dot product.

7.4.1 The Angle Between Two Vectors

The most important application of the dot product is in finding the angle between the vectors or between two intersecting lines. Figure 7.16 shows two vectors, $\mathbf{a}$ and $\mathbf{b}$, separated by angle θ. These vectors can have two, three, or any number of dimensions. They form two sides of a triangle, and the third side is $\mathbf{a} - \mathbf{b}$. By the law of cosines the square of the length of $\mathbf{a} - \mathbf{b}$ can be expressed in terms of the lengths of $\mathbf{a}$ and $\mathbf{b}$ and the cosine of θ:

$$|\mathbf{a} - \mathbf{b}|^2 = |\mathbf{a}|^2 + |\mathbf{b}|^2 - 2|\mathbf{a}||\mathbf{b}| \cos(\theta) \qquad (7.19)$$

This equation and Equation 7.17 give two forms for $|\mathbf{a} - \mathbf{b}|^2$. Equating these forms, we see that

$$\mathbf{a} \cdot \mathbf{b} = |\mathbf{a}||\mathbf{b}| \cos(\theta) \qquad (7.20)$$

Divide through both sides by $|\mathbf{a}||\mathbf{b}|$ and use the unit vector notation $\mathbf{u_a} = \mathbf{a}/|\mathbf{a}|$ to obtain

$$\cos(\theta) = \mathbf{u_a} \cdot \mathbf{u_b} \qquad (7.21)$$

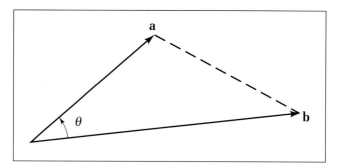

Figure 7.16.
The dot product and the angle between two vectors.

This is the desired result: The cosine of the angle between two vectors **a** and **b** is the dot product of their normalized versions.

Example
Find the angle between **a** = (3, 4) and **b** = (5, 2).

Solution:
Form |**a**| = 5 and |**b**| = 5.385 so that **u$_a$** = (3/5, 4/5) and **u$_b$** = (.9285, .3714). The dot product **u$_a$** · **u$_b$** = .85422 = cos(θ), so that θ = 31.326°. This can be checked by plotting the two vectors on graph paper and measuring the angle between them.

Drill Exercise

7.7.   Find the Angle. Calculate the angle between the vectors (2, 3) and (−3, 1), and check the result visually using graph paper. Then compute the angle between the 3D vectors (1, 3, −2) and (3, 3, 1).

7.4.2 The Sign of **a** · **b**, and Perpendicularity

Recall that cos(θ) is **positive** if |θ| is less than 90°, **zero** if |θ| equals 90°, and **negative** if |θ| exceeds 90°. Because the dot product of two vectors is proportional to the cosine of the angle between them, we can therefore observe immediately that two vectors (of any nonzero length) are

- less than 90° apart if **a** · **b** > 0.
- exactly 90° apart if **a** · **b** = 0.
- more than 90° apart if **a** · **b** < 0.

This is indicated by Figure 7.17. The sign of the dot product is used in a simple hidden surface removal technique, discussed in Chapter 15.

The case in which the vectors are 90° apart, or **perpendicular**, is of special importance.

Definition

Vectors **a** and **b** are perpendicular if **a** · **b** = 0.

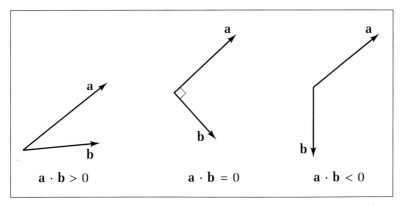

Figure 7.17.
The sign of the dot product.

Other names for perpendicular are **orthogonal** and **normal**, and we shall use all three interchangeably.

Drill Exercises

7.8. Testing for Perpendicularity. Which pairs of the following vectors are perpendicular to one another: $(3, 4, 1)$, $(2, 1, 1)$, $(-3, -4, 1)$, $(0, 0, 0)$, $(1, -2, 0)$, $(4, 4, 4)$, $(0, -1, 4)$, and $(2, 2, 1)$?

7.9. Pythagorean Theorem. Refer to Equations 7.17 and 7.18. For the case in which **a** and **b** are perpendicular, these expressions have the same value, which seems to make no sense geometrically. Show that it works all right, and relate the result to the Pythagorean theorem.

7.4.3 Projecting and Resolving Vectors

It is often useful to **decompose** or **resolve** a given vector into two components: one component in the direction of a second given vector and one that is perpendicular to this second vector. For instance, we might wish to study how the gravitational force **G** acting on the block shown in Figure 7.18a moves it down the incline. To do this it is helpful to resolve **G** into the force **F** acting along the incline and the force **B** acting perpendicular to the incline. In Figure 7.18b, vector **a** is shown resolved into a component **c** along the given vector **b**, and a component **e** that is perpendicular to **b**. By simple vector addition, $\mathbf{e} = \mathbf{a} - \mathbf{c}$, and so once **c** is known, **e** will follow at once. Drop a line from the head of **a** to meet **b** at a right angle. This forms vector **c**, the so-called **perpendicular projec-**

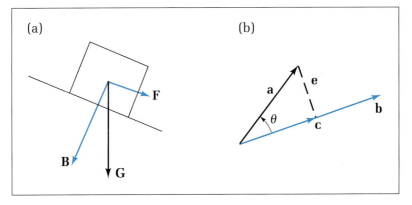

Figure 7.18.
Resolving a vector into two orthogonal vectors.

tion of **a** onto **b**. Evidently, **c** has the same direction as **b**, but a different length. We must find |**c**|. According to simple trigonometry, |**c**| is |**a**| cos(θ), and using Equation 7.20 we obtain

$$|\mathbf{c}| = |\mathbf{a}|\frac{(\mathbf{a} \cdot \mathbf{b})}{|\mathbf{a}||\mathbf{b}|}$$

$$= \mathbf{a} \cdot \mathbf{u_b} \qquad\qquad (7.22)$$

As we would expect geometrically, the length of **c** depends on the length of **a**, but not on that of **b**. Now to form the actual vector **c**, attach the direction of **b** to |**c**| to make $\mathbf{c} = |\mathbf{c}|\mathbf{u_b}$. Then using Equation 7.22 we get the handy forms:

$$\mathbf{c} = (\mathbf{a} \cdot \mathbf{u_b})\mathbf{u_b}$$

$$= \frac{\mathbf{a} \cdot \mathbf{b}}{|\mathbf{b}|^2}\mathbf{b} \qquad\qquad (7.23)$$

This result will not change even if **a** is directed more than 90° away from **b**. In that case, $\mathbf{a} \cdot \mathbf{b} < 0$, and so **c** points in the opposite direction from **b**, just as one expects.

A Two-Dimensional Example
Find the projection of the vector **a** = (6, 4) onto **b** = (1, 2), as shown in Figure 7.19.

Solution:
The projection **c** lies along the extension of **b** at the foot of the perpendicular dropped from **a**. From Equation 7.23 the projection **c** is given by $\frac{(6,4) \cdot (1,2)}{5}(1, 2) = (2.8, 5.6)$. Vector **e** = **a** − **c** = (3.2, −1.6). Note that numerically $\mathbf{c} \cdot \mathbf{e} = 0$, and so **c** and **e** are indeed orthogonal.

A Three-Dimensional Example
Find the projection of the vector **a** = (3, 4, 2) onto **b** = (−1, 2, −1).

Solutions:
Direct calculation yields **c** = (−0.5, 1, −0.5) and **e** = (3.5, 3, 2.5), and **c** is again orthogonal to **e**.

Figure 7.19.
Example of resolving a vector into components.

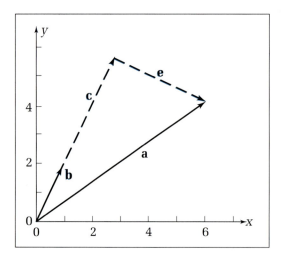

It remains to be proved that **e** is in general perpendicular to **b**. Further, you may sometimes want to compute how far a point is from a line. This distance must be the length |**e**| of **e** (see the next exercises).

Drill Exercises

7.10. Resolving a Vector into Two Orthogonal Components. Show that **e** is perpendicular to **b**. That is, use the expression for **c** and the fact that **e** = **a** − **c** to show that **b** · **e** = 0.

7.11. The Pythagorean Theorem Again. Use Equation 7.23 to show algebraically that $|\mathbf{e}|^2 = |\mathbf{a}|^2 - |\mathbf{c}|^2$.

7.12. The Distance from a Point to a Line. Given point P and a line through point A in the direction **b**, what is the distance from P to the line? *Hint*: Project vector $P - A$ onto **b**. The distance is the length of **e**.

7.4.4 Application of Projection: Reflections

We often want to study what happens as one object bounces off another and to simulate this behavior and display it graphically. This is particularly important in modeling the reflection of light off a surface or in studying how a jumble of moving gas molecules or billiard balls behaves. The case study in the next chapter develops an application that traces a ray of light (or a gas molecule) as it bounces around inside a reflective chamber. At each bounce a reflection is made to a new direction, as derived in this section. In Chapters 15 and 18 we shall study in some depth how light moves in three dimensions and reflects off various surfaces.

Geometric optics dictates that the angle of reflection must equal the angle of incidence. We shall show how to use vectors and projections to compute this new direction easily. We can think in terms of two-dimensional vectors for simplicity, but because the derivation does not explicitly state the dimension of the vectors involved, the same result applies in three dimensions for reflections from a surface.

Figure 7.20a shows a ray in direction **a**, hitting line L, and reflecting in direction **r**. The angle θ_1 between **a** and **n** must equal the angle θ_2 between **n** and **r**, where **n** is the vector perpendicular to the line. How is **r** related to **a** and **n**?

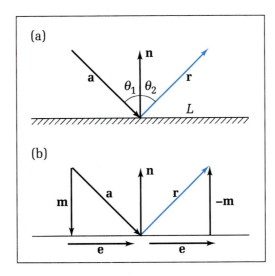

Figure 7.20.
Reflection of a ray from a surface.

Figure 7.20b shows **a** resolved into portion **m** along **n** and portion **e** orthogonal to **n**. Because of symmetry, **r** has the same component **e** orthogonal to **n**, but the opposite component along **n**, and so **r** = **e** − **m**. Because **e** = **a** − **m**, this gives **r** = **a** − 2**m**. Now from Equation 7.23

$$\mathbf{m} = (\mathbf{a} \cdot \mathbf{u_n})\mathbf{u_n} \tag{7.24}$$

and so we obtain the result

$$\mathbf{r} = \mathbf{a} - 2(\mathbf{a} \cdot \mathbf{u_n})\mathbf{u_n} \tag{7.25}$$

Example

Let **a** = (4, −2) and **n** = (0, 3). Then Equation 7.25 yields **r** = (4, 2), as expected. Both the angle of incidence and reflection are equal to $\tan^{-1}(2)$.

Drill Exercises

7.13.   Find the Reflected Direction. For **a** = (2, 3) and **n** = (−2, 1), find the direction of the reflection.

7.14.   Lengths of the Incident and Reflected Vectors. Using Equation 7.25 and properties of the dot product, show that $|\mathbf{r}| = |\mathbf{a}|$.

7.4.5 The Point Normal Form for a Line and a Plane

We shall develop a simple but powerful representation for a line and for a plane based on the dot product. It is used in many parts of graphics such as clipping, hidden line elimination, and polygon filling.

We shall describe the ideas in terms of a line and then see how easily they generalize for a plane. Consider line L that passes through point $A = (A_x, A_y)$ in direction **c** = (c_x, c_y), as shown in Figure 7.21. In some contexts it is useful to find the **normal** direction, **n** = (n_x, n_y), to this line. This is the direction that is perpendicular to **c**, as shown. Now **c** · **n** = 0 is the same as $c_x n_x + c_y n_y = 0$, or

$$\frac{c_y}{c_x} = \frac{-n_x}{n_y} \tag{7.26}$$

(This expresses the familiar fact that perpendicular lines have slopes that are negative reciprocals of one another. This was used in Chapter 4 to find the perpendicular bisector of a segment.)

The condition that **n** be orthogonal to **c** only fixes **n** up to a multiplicative factor; that is, **n** can be any multiple of $(c_y, -c_x)$, as suggested in Figure 7.22. There are two legitimate opposite directions for the normal vector. The equation of the line obtained below is the same, regardless of the version of **n** used.

To obtain an equation for line L, consider an arbitrary point, $R = (x, y)$, on L. The vector $R - A$ must be perpendicular to **n**, and so **n** · $(R - A) = 0$. It is tempting now to write **n** · R = **n** · A, but (speaking formally) we cannot form dot products between a point and a vector, only between two vectors. So to proceed, we replace R with the vector **r** bound to the origin (and having the same coordinate as R) and similarly replace A with **a**. This makes all ensuing calculations dependent on the choice of origin of the coordinate system, but the equation of a line is dependent on it anyway, and so there is no loss. With this replacement we can use linearity and write:

$$\mathbf{n} \cdot \mathbf{r} = D \tag{7.27}$$

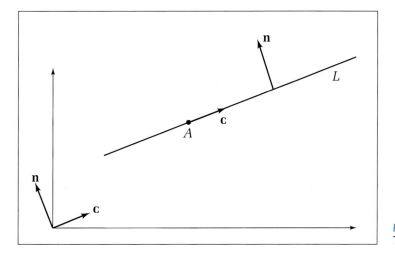

Figure 7.21.
The normal direction to a line.

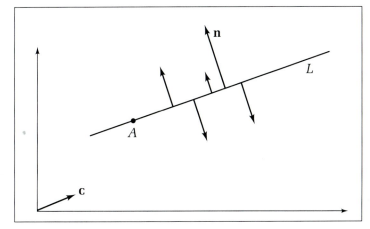

Figure 7.22.
Different normals to the line.

where

$$D = \mathbf{n} \cdot \mathbf{a} = n_x A_x + n_y A_y \qquad (7.28)$$

This is the **point normal** equation for the line. Equation 7.27 may be written in the familiar form for a straight line:

$$n_x x + n_y y = D \qquad (7.29)$$

The coefficients multiplying x and y in this last equation are precisely the components of the normal to the line. Equation 7.27 shows that all points on a straight line (or all vectors from the origin to a point on the line) share the same dot product value with the normal direction! This is obvious from Figure 7.23, as all vectors $\mathbf{r}_1$, $\mathbf{r}_2$, and so on have the same projection (shown as $\mathbf{m}$) onto $\mathbf{n}$, and the term $\mathbf{n} \cdot \mathbf{r}$ is proportional to this projection. The line passes closest to the origin at point B in Figure 7.23, and this closest distance is the length of $\mathbf{m}$. From Equation 7.22 this distance is $D/|\mathbf{n}|$ (why?). This suggests what D is geometrically: D reports the "position" of the line, and D is altered by shifting the line parallel to itself, as suggested in Figure 7.24. A set of lines, $\mathbf{n} \cdot R = D$, having the same normal, $\mathbf{n} = (1, 2)$, but different Ds are shown. As D increases, the lines shift in the direction of $\mathbf{n}$.

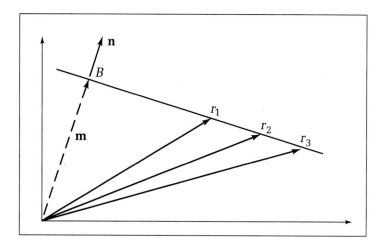

Figure 7.23.
The dot product is constant for all points.

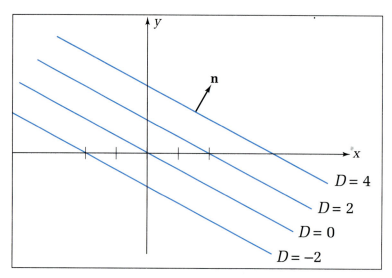

Figure 7.24.
Changing the value of the dot product.

Example

Consider the line through points $A = (2, 3)$ and $B = (4, 4)$. Subtracting one from the other, the vector $\mathbf{c}$ becomes $\mathbf{c} = (2, 1)$. Thus according to Equation 7.26, the normal vector $\mathbf{n}$ is any multiple of $(-1, 2)$, say $\mathbf{n} = K(-1, 2)$. The choice of K is immaterial to the equation for the line. From Equation 7.27 we get the point normal $K(-1, 2) \cdot (x, y) = K(-1, 2) \cdot (2, 3)$, which becomes $-x + 2y = 4$. Of course, point B and any other point on the line satisfies this equation. The normal to the line is instantly spotted from the coefficients of x and y: $(-1, 2)$.

Drill Exercise

7.15. Determining a Line. Find the point normal equation of the line that passes through $(-3, 4)$ and $(6, -1)$. Sketch the line and its normal vector on graph paper.

The point normal form for a line is convenient in many settings, as we shall see next. It also is useful to have a routine such as **procedure** *PointNormal*(*a*, *b* : *point*; **var** *n* : *vector*; **var** *L* : *line*) that computes the normal and *D* given two points on the line (see the exercises). This suggests the definition of the type *line* to capture the point normal form:

Code Fragment 7.6. Data Type for a Line in Point Normal Form

```
type
   line = record
             norm : vector;
             D : real
         end;
```

Extension of the Point Normal Form to the Plane

Planes can also be represented in point normal form, and the classic equation for a plane emerges by a simple extension of the preceding ideas. Planes are also used extensively in 3D graphics, and one must frequently clip objects against planes that define a "view volume." Solid objects are often modeled using collections of small, flat faces called *facets*, and algorithms must determine the plane in which each facet lies, to check whether the facet obscures some other object or to determine its orientation so that the facet may be shaded properly (see Chapters 15 and 17). The plane is the simplest of all surfaces and is easily characterized. More complex surfaces will be discussed in the next chapter.

Figure 7.25 shows a portion of plane *P* in three dimensions. A plane is completely specified by giving a single point, $S = (s_x, s_y, s_z)$, that lies within it and the normal direction to the plane. Just as the normal vector to a line in two dimensions orients the line, the normal to a plane orients it in space. The normal is understood to be perpendicular to any line lying in the plane. Call the normal direction in Figure 7.25 $\mathbf{n} = (n_x, n_y, n_z)$. For an arbitrary point, $R = (x, y, z)$, in the plane, form the vector from *R* to *S*. It must be perpendicular to $\mathbf{n}$, giving:

$$\mathbf{n} \cdot (R - S) = 0 \tag{7.30}$$

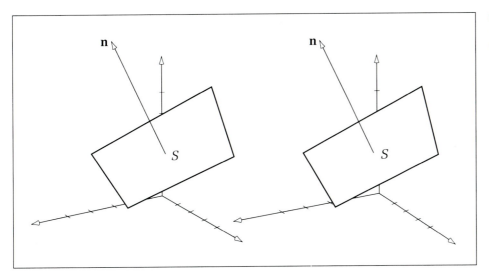

Figure 7.25.
Determining the equation of a plane.

Replace $R - S$ with $\mathbf{r} - \mathbf{s}$ in the usual fashion and use linearity to obtain

$$\mathbf{n} \cdot \mathbf{r} = D \tag{7.31}$$

where

$$D = \mathbf{n} \cdot \mathbf{s} \tag{7.32}$$

This is the point normal equation of the plane. It is identical to that for the line: a dot product set equal to a constant. For the plane the dot product operates on three-dimensional rather than two-dimensional vectors, but the fact is the same: All points in a plane have the same dot product with the normal. Indeed, all points have the same projection onto $\mathbf{n}$, as suggested in Figure 7.26.

Drill Exercise

7.16.   Projecting Points Onto n. Show that the projection of any point $\mathbf{r}$ in the plane $\mathbf{n} \cdot \mathbf{r} = D$ onto $\mathbf{n}$ is the same. How long is this projected vector?

Recall that the equation of a plane P is traditionally written as

$$Ax + By + Cz = D \tag{7.33}$$

where the coefficients A, B, C, and D distinguish one plane from another. By spelling out the dot product in Equation 7.31, we see that the point normal form is actually this very equation:

$$n_x x + n_y y + n_z z = D \tag{7.34}$$

Just equate $A = n_x$, $B = n_y$, and $C = n_z$. This shows that (A, B, C) is the normal direction to the plane.

Example
Find the point normal form of the equation for plane P through $(1, 2, 3)$ with normal vector $(2, -1, -2)$.

Figure 7.26.
Points in a plane share the same projection on **n**.

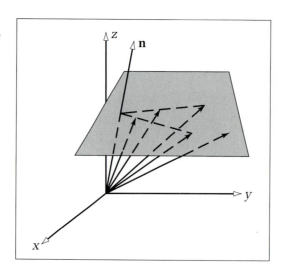

Solution:
The point normal form is $(2, -1, -2) \cdot (x, y, z) = D$, where D is the dot product of $(-2, 1, -2)$ and any chosen point in the plane. Using $(1, 2, 3)$ for this point D is $D = -6$. The equation for the plane may be written out as $2x - y - 2z = -6$.

Example
How close does the plane come to the origin?

Solution:
The point on the plane closest to the origin is the point on the plane pierced by **n** itself. (It's closest because it is the perpendicular projection of the origin onto the plane.) This point is therefore proportional to **n**, say $K\mathbf{n}$, and the distance in question is $|K\mathbf{n}|$. What is K? Because $K\mathbf{n}$ lies on the plane, it satisfies $\mathbf{n} \cdot (K\mathbf{n}) = D$, or $9K = -6$, and so $K = -2/3$. Thus the closest point is $(-4/3, 2/3, 4/3)$ at a distance of 2 from the origin.

7.4.6 Inside–Outside Half-space Test for a Point

In many applications it is meaningful to attach the notion of "inside" and "outside" to the half-spaces defined by a line. When one side of a line is known to be on the inside, we can define the **inward normal** for the line. The **outward normal** then points in the opposite direction.

We often need to test whether a point Q lies outside or inside the half-space of a line. Suppose that line E passes through point A and has outward normal **n**, as shown in Figure 7.27. The angle θ between **n** and vector $Q - A$ must be less than 90° if Q lies on the outside, and so the dot product $\mathbf{n} \cdot (Q - A) > 0$. Similarly, angle θ will be larger than 90° if Q lies on the inside, and so $\mathbf{n} \cdot (Q - A) < 0$. Finally, the angle will be 90° if Q lies on E, in which case $\mathbf{n} \cdot (Q - A) = 0$. This provides a simple test:

Inside–Outside Test

Suppose line E passes through point A and has outward normal **n**. Then for any point Q,

1. Q will lie in the outside half-space of E if $(Q - A) \cdot \mathbf{n} > 0$.

2. Q will lie on E if $(Q - A) \cdot \mathbf{n} = 0$.

3. Q will lie in the inside half-space of E if $(Q - A) \cdot \mathbf{n} < 0$.

If we replace $Q - A$ with the vector $\mathbf{q} - \mathbf{a}$ and call $\mathbf{a} \cdot \mathbf{n} = D$, then line E is given by the equation $\mathbf{n} \cdot \mathbf{p} = D$, and the test may be rewritten:

Inside–Outside Test (alternative form)

Suppose line E has outward normal **n** and equation $\mathbf{n} \cdot \mathbf{p} = D$. Then point Q with vector representation **q** will lie

1. in the outside half-space of E if $\mathbf{q} \cdot \mathbf{n} > D$.

2. on E if $\mathbf{q} \cdot \mathbf{n} = D$.

3. in the inside half-space of E if $\mathbf{q} \cdot \mathbf{n} < D$.

For example, the origin $(0, 0)$ will lie in the outside half-space of a line if, and only if, $D < 0$ (why?).

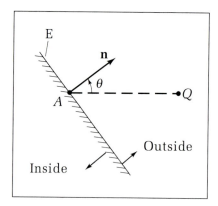

Figure 7.27.
In which half-space does Q lie?

Drill Exercise

7.17.   Working with Half-spaces of Lines. Given that line E passes through points $(5, 5)$ and $(2, 1)$ and that point $(1, 2)$ lies in its outside half-space:

a.   Find the outward normal vector for line E. *Answer:* $\mathbf{n} = (-\frac{4}{5}, \frac{3}{5})$.

b.   Find the equation of the line. *Answer:* $-4x + 3y = -5$.

c.   Determine whether each of the following points lies in the inside or outside half-space of E: $(4, 4)$, $(2, 0)$, $(8, 7)$, $(0, -5/3)$. *Answer:* out, in, in, on.

Extension to Planes

The preceding ideas extend immediately to testing the position of a point Q relative to a plane. Suppose that in an application, the notion of inside and outside is available, and plane P is known to pass through point A and to have the outward normal vector $\mathbf{n}$. Then point Q will be in the outside half-space of P if the vector Q–A makes an angle of less than 90° with $\mathbf{n}$ or if the quantity $T = (\mathbf{q} - \mathbf{a}) \cdot \mathbf{n}$ is positive. Even though all the points and vectors here are three dimensional instead of two dimensional, this is the same test as for the line above, and so we can say immediately that Q lies on

1.   the outside half-space of P if $T > 0$.

2.   on P if $T = 0$.

3.   the inside half-space of P if $T < 0$.

This uniformity of method is one of the most pleasing aspects of the dot product: A little effort pays off in several contexts and for any number of dimensions.

Example

If the equation of plane P is $x - 2y + 3z = 4$ and it is known that $(-2, 2, 1)$ is in its outside half-space, find the outward normal and determine whether point $(-1, -2, 1)$ is on the inside or outside half-space of P.

Solution:
By inspection a normal to the plane is $(1, -2, 3)$, for which $D = 4$. Is this an outward or inward normal? We are given that $(-2, 2, 1)$ is outside, and so if $(1, -2, 3)$ is indeed an outward normal, then according to the inside–outside test $(-2, 2, 1) \cdot (1, -2, 3)$ must be greater than 4. But it is not; it is -3. Therefore the outward normal has the opposite direction: $(-1, 2, -3)$, and when all terms in the equation are negated to reflect this, $D = -4$. Now reapply the test to the

uncertain point $(-1, -2, 1)$: $(-1, -2, 1) \cdot (-1, 2, -3) = -6$, which is smaller than -4, and so the point lies inside the plane.

We next return to two dimensions and show how the inside–outside test forms the basis for a powerful clipping algorithm.

7.4.7 Application: Line Clipping to Convex Windows

The Cohen–Sutherland clipping algorithm, discussed in Chapter 3, clips away those parts of a line that lie outside a window. This algorithm, however, requires the window to be a rectangle and to be oriented so that its edges are aligned with the coordinate axes. But the simple inside–outside test can be applied to fashion an even more powerful clipping tool, one that works for any convex polygon window. It easily clips a line to a rotated window, as shown in Figure 7.28, and also clips a line to a triangle, a parallelogram, a convex hexagon, and so on. This tool was originally developed by Cyrus and Beck (1978), and a rather efficient clipper for rectangular windows based on similar ideas was also devised by Liang and Barsky (1984).

Window W, consisting of a convex polygon, is shown in Figure 7.29, along with a line segment, L, extending from P_1 to P_2. We wish to identify the "visible" part of segment L, the part lying in the interior of W. But because W is convex, its interior is defined as the region in the inside half-space of every edge of W. This is the key to the algorithm. Segment L is tested against each edge of W in turn, and pieces lying in outside half-spaces are "chopped off." When all edges have been processed, the piece of L that remains must lie in the interior of W and so is visible.

If L is treated parametrically, it will be particularly easy to keep track of which part still lies in W after each edge has executed its chop. We represent L in the form

$$P(t) = P_1 + \mathbf{c}t \qquad (7.35)$$

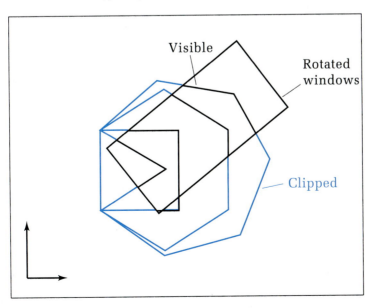

Figure 7.28.
Clipping against a rotated window.

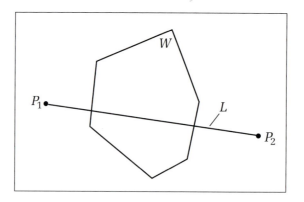

Figure 7.29.
Clipping a line to a convex
polygon.

where $\mathbf{c} = P_2 - P_1$. At $t = 0$, $P(t)$ is "at" P_1, and at $t = 1$, it is at P_2. As is customary, we say informally that it "moves" from P_1 to P_2 as t increases from 0 to 1 and that $\mathbf{c}$ is the "direction" in which it moves.

As each edge of the window is processed, we use two values, t_{in} and t_{out}, to keep track of the range in t for which the segment might be in the window. That is, based on the edges tested so far, the segment definitely does not enter W until $t = t_{in}$ and definitely exits no later than $t = t_{out}$, and so it must be invisible outside (t_{in}, t_{out}). In addition, t_{in} and t_{out} start with values 0 and 1, respectively. This interval is continually whittled away as new edges are tested and new parts of the segment are found to be invisible. If after some chop the interval becomes empty, the clipper will immediately exit, as the segment must be totally invisible. This is called an **early out.** If there is no early out by the time all edges have been tested, the remaining interval (t_{in}, t_{out}) will define the portion of L that lies within the window.

Consider how the chopping process uses dot products and inside–outside tests. Because W is convex, each of its edges, E, may be given as a line in the point normal form:

$$\mathbf{n} \cdot \mathbf{p} = D \tag{7.36}$$

where $\mathbf{n}$ is chosen to be the outward normal for the edge. Now edge E can be situated in a number of ways relative to the line segment L:

E Is Parallel to L

E will be parallel to L if $\mathbf{n}$ is perpendicular to $\mathbf{c}$; that is, $\mathbf{n} \cdot \mathbf{c} = 0$. In this case, L lies either wholly inside or wholly outside the window. To see which of these is in force, choose any point on L, say P_1, and use the inside–outside test. Let $\mathbf{p}_1 = P_1 - 0$ be the vector from the origin to P_1. Then L will be wholly inside if

$$\mathbf{p}_1 \cdot \mathbf{n} < D \tag{7.37}$$

In this case L is trivially visible, and neither t_{in} nor t_{out} is altered. In the opposite case, in which L is totally outside, it is trivially invisible, and the clipping algorithm terminates.

E Is Not Parallel to the Segment

If E is not parallel to the segment, $\mathbf{n} \cdot \mathbf{c}$ will be either positive or negative, and L must intersect edge E at some time t_i. To find this time, substitute Equation 7.35

into Equation 7.36 to find the intersection time t_i:

$$t_i = \frac{D - \mathbf{n} \cdot \mathbf{p}_1}{\mathbf{n} \cdot \mathbf{c}}$$ (7.38)

One of the two cases shown in Figure 7.30 applies to t_i: The segment is entering the inside half-space of E (case a) or it is exiting it (case b).

If its direction, $\mathbf{c}$, is less than 90° away from $\mathbf{n}$ (that is, if $\mathbf{n} \cdot \mathbf{c} > 0$), the segment must be exiting. Otherwise it is entering.

If it is entering, then the portion for $t < t_i$ is definitely invisible, and so the lower limit, t_{in}, is increased to t_i (if it isn't already this large). On the other hand, if it is exiting, then the portion for $t > t_i$ will be invisible, and so limit t_{out} will be reduced to t_i (if it isn't already this small).

Example: Clip L Against a Triangle

The segment L from $P_1 = (-1, -1)$ to $P_2 = (9, 12)$ is to be clipped against the triangular window W having vertices (3, 2), (6, 12), and (12, 5), as shown in Figure 7.31. Clip against each edge in turn. An outer normal for E_1 is $\mathbf{n} = (3, -9)$ (why?), for which choice $D = -9$. Now $\mathbf{n} \cdot \mathbf{c} = (3, -9) \cdot (10, 13) = -87$, and so the segment is entering, and the intersection time is $t_i = (-9 - (3, -9) \cdot (-1, -1))/(-87) = 15/87$. Thus t_{in}, which originally equaled 1, is set to 15/87. Now clip against E_2, for which $\mathbf{n} = (-10, 3)$ and $D = -24$. For this edge, $\mathbf{n} \cdot \mathbf{c} = -61$, and so L is again entering and $t_i = 31/61$; thus more chopping is done: t_{in} is now $31/61 = 0.508$. Finally, clip against E_3. Here $\mathbf{n} \cdot \mathbf{c} = (7, 6) \cdot (6, 12) = 114$, and so L is exiting, with intersection time $t_i = 91/114 = 0.798$. The visible portion of the line therefore has $(t_{in}, t_{out}) = (0.508, 0.798)$. Use these in Equation 7.35 to obtain the endpoints (4.08, 5.604) and (6.98, 9.374) for the clipped line.

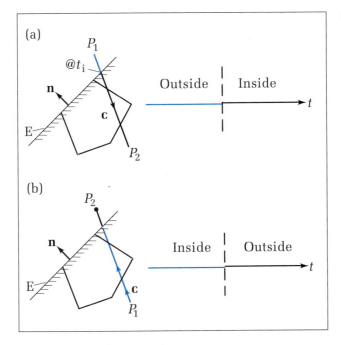

Figure 7.30.
The segment enters or exits the inside half-space of E.

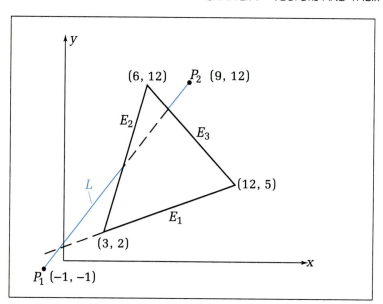

Figure 7.31.
A clipping example.

Drill Exercise

7.18. Find the Clipped Line. Find the portion of the segment with endpoints (2, 4) and (20, 8) that lies within the quadrilateral window with corners at (0, 7), (9, 9), (2, 2), and (14, 4).

We shall develop a skeleton of the Cyrus–Beck clipper here, relegating a complete implementation of it to Appendix 6. The variables t_{in} and t_{out} are initialized to 0 and 1, respectively, and then each edge of the window in turn chops away at the interval (t_{in}, t_{out}) until we run out of windows or the interval vanishes.

Because the chopping action is the same for each edge, we hide its details in a function, *Chop(numer, denom : real) : boolean*. Parameters *numer* and *denom* are the numerator and denominator of t_i in Equation 7.38, respectively, and they capture the relative position of the segment through the values

$$numer = \mathbf{n} \cdot \mathbf{c}$$
$$denom = D - \mathbf{n} \cdot \mathbf{p}_1$$

(7.39)

Chop( ) implements these tests: It increases t_{in} or decreases t_{out} as required. It answers the question, Has the entire segment been chopped out? by returning *true* if the chop annihilates the segment and *false* if any visible piece remains (see Appendix 6).

The Cyrus–Beck clipper then takes the following form:

Code Fragment 7.7. Skeleton of Cyrus–Beck Clipper for a Convex Window

```
t_in := 0.0; t_out := 1.0; {initialize interval}
<set c := P2 − P1;> {direction of segment}
i := 1;
gone := false; {some of segment L is still visible}
```

repeat
　　<*get norm and D for* i-*th edge of window;*>
　　$a := Dot(norm, c)$;
　　$b := D - Dot(norm, P1)$;
　　$i := i + 1$;
　　$gone := Chop(a, b)$; {is there an 'early out'?}
until *gone* **or** ($i > num\_edges$);

When finished, *gone* tells whether there is anything left of segment *L* to draw. If so, the final values of t_{in} and t_{out} will be substituted into the parametric form of the segment, $P_1 + \mathbf{c}t$, to obtain the endpoints of the clipped line.

In Chapter 12 we shall see that this algorithm works in three dimensions in this same form. The edges of the window become planes defining a convex region in three dimensions, and the segment *L* is suspended in space.

In addition to filling in details of the Cyrus–Beck clipping algorithm, Appendix 6 examines two other clipping algorithms that are widely used in advanced applications. The Sutherland–Hodgman clipper is similar to the Cyrus–Beck method, performing clipping against a convex polygon. But instead of clipping a single line segment, it clips an entire polygon (which needn't be convex) against the window. Most importantly, its output is again a polygon (or a set of polygons if the clipping breaks the original polygon into several pieces). The reason for wanting to retain the polygon structure after clipping is that the display device may need to fill the clipped polygons with some color or pattern (as discussed in Chapter 13), and this would not be possible if the edges of the polygon were clipped individually.

Also in Appendix 6 we describe the Weiler–Atherton clipping algorithm, which clips any polygon *P* against any other polygon *W*, convex or not. It can output the part of *P* that lies inside *W* (**interior clipping**) or the part of *P* that lies outside *W* (**exterior clipping**). In addition, both *P* and *W* can have "holes" in them. As might be expected, this algorithm is somewhat more complex than the others we have examined, but its power makes it a welcome addition to one's toolbox in a variety of applications.

The Liang–Barsky Clipper

Liang and Barsky offered a refinement of the Cyrus–Beck approach for a rectangular window having horizontal and vertical edges. For a horizontal edge the normal vector is $(0, \pm1)$, and for a vertical edge it is $(\pm1, 0)$, and so no multiplications are required in the dot product computations in Equation 7.39 (why?). This leads to highly efficient code (see the exercises). Liang and Barsky also provided solutions for clipping in three dimensions and in "homogeneous coordinates," as we shall see in Chapter 12.

7.5　Using Three-Dimensional Vectors

We shall continue our development of vector tools with an emphasis on three-dimensional vectors. Two additional tools, defined for 3D vectors only, round out our arsenal for vector operations: the cross product and the triple scalar product.

7.5.1 Left-Handed Versus Right-Handed Coordinate Systems

There are two ways to define a three-dimensional coordinate system—as a **right-handed** system or as a **left-handed** system. Figure 7.32a shows the two versions. The difference between them lies in the "sense" (forward or backward) of the z-axis. To determine the sense of a coordinate system, do an experiment with each hand: Rotate your fingers around the z-axis from the positive x-axis around to the positive y-axis, and see whether your thumb points along the positive or the negative z-axis. Determine the hand for which your thumb points along the positive z-axis. In a right-handed system it is the right hand, and in a left-handed system it is the left hand, as seen in the figure.

Right-handed systems are more familiar and are conventional in mathematics, physics, and engineering. In this text we use a right-handed system when setting up models for objects, and so we define world coordinates in a right-handed system (Figure 7.32b). In some modeling contexts the z-axis instead of the y-axis is pointed "upward."

But left-handed systems also have a natural place in graphics. Think of viewing the x, y, z-system as one views an x, y-graph, with the y-axis pointed up and the x-axis to the right. Then for a left-handed system, the z-axis points "away" from the viewer (Figure 7.32c). Therefore larger values of z correspond to greater distances away, or larger "depths," which is intuitively the way things should work. In later chapters we shall capitalize on this naturalness and use a left-handed system for a **viewing coordinate system**. To minimize confusion in our discussions, we shall make it clear which is being used and what difference it makes.

Figure 7.32.
Left- and right-handed
coordinate systems.

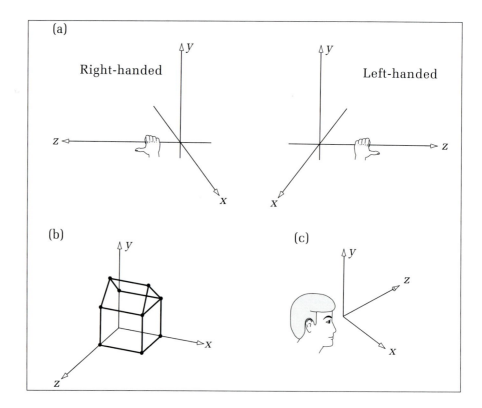

The Standard Three-Dimensional Unit Vectors

Some special three-dimensional unit vectors appear so frequently that they have been given names: $\mathbf{i}$, $\mathbf{j}$, and $\mathbf{k}$, each directed along one of the coordinate axes of the coordinate system being used. That is, $\mathbf{i}$ is directed along the positive x-axis, $\mathbf{j}$ along the y-axis, and $\mathbf{k}$ along the z-axis. Thus in terms of coordinates of the x, y, z-system, the vectors are given by

$$\mathbf{i} = (1, 0, 0), \mathbf{j} = (0, 1, 0), \text{ and } \mathbf{k} = (0, 0, 1) \tag{7.40}$$

Using these definitions any 3D vector such as (a, b, c) can be written in an alternative form:

$$(a, b, c) = a\mathbf{i} + b\mathbf{j} + c\mathbf{k} \tag{7.41}$$

Example

Notice that $\mathbf{v} = (2, 5, -1)$ is clearly the same as $2(1, 0, 0) + 5(0, 1, 0) - 1(0, 0, 1)$, which is recognized as $2\mathbf{i} + 5\mathbf{j} - \mathbf{k}$.

Because this form presents a vector as a sum of separate elementary component vectors, it simplifies various pencil-and-paper calculations. It is particularly convenient when dealing with the cross product, discussed next.

Note that in a left-handed system, the unit vector $\mathbf{k}$ is aimed in the opposite direction from $\mathbf{k}$ in a right-handed coordinate system, as $\mathbf{k}$ is (by definition) always directed in the positive z-direction.

7.6   The Cross Product of Two Vectors

The **cross product** (also called the **vector product**) of two vectors is another vector. It has many useful properties, but the one we use most often is that it is perpendicular to both of the given vectors. The cross product is defined only for three-dimensional vectors, yet it can be applied as well to several important problems in graphics concerned with two-dimensional polygons.

Given the 3D vectors $\mathbf{a} = (a_x, a_y, a_z)$ and $\mathbf{b} = (b_x, b_y, b_z)$, their cross product is denoted as $\mathbf{a} \times \mathbf{b}$. It is defined in terms of the standard unit vectors $\mathbf{i}$, $\mathbf{j}$, and $\mathbf{k}$ by

Definition of $\mathbf{a} \times \mathbf{b}$

$$\mathbf{a} \times \mathbf{b} = (a_y b_z - a_z b_y)\mathbf{i} + (a_z b_x - a_x b_z)\mathbf{j} + (a_x b_y - a_y b_x)\mathbf{k} \tag{7.42}$$

(It can actually be derived from more fundamental principles. See the exercises.) As this form is rather difficult to remember, it is often written as an easily remembered determinant (see Appendix 2 for a review of determinants).

$$a \times b = \begin{vmatrix} \mathbf{i} & \mathbf{j} & \mathbf{k} \\ a_x & a_y & a_z \\ b_x & b_y & b_z \end{vmatrix} \tag{7.43}$$

As long as you remember the rules for evaluating determinants, you will be able to find the cross product. The implementation of the procedure *Cross(a, b : vector3D;* **var** *c : vector3D)* to compute the cross product is discussed in the exercises.

From this definition one can easily show the following algebraic properties of the cross product:

1. $\mathbf{i} \times \mathbf{j} = \mathbf{k}$
    $\mathbf{j} \times \mathbf{k} = \mathbf{i}$
    $\mathbf{k} \times \mathbf{i} = \mathbf{j}$

2. $\mathbf{a} \times \mathbf{b} = -\mathbf{b} \times \mathbf{a}$ (antisymmetric)

3. $\mathbf{a} \times (\mathbf{b} + \mathbf{c}) = \mathbf{a} \times \mathbf{b} + \mathbf{a} \times \mathbf{c}$ (linear)

4. $(s\mathbf{a}) \times \mathbf{b} = s(\mathbf{a} \times \mathbf{b})$ for any scalar s (homogeneous)

These results are true in both left-handed and right-handed coordinate systems. Note the logical ordering of ingredients in the fact $\mathbf{i} \times \mathbf{j} = \mathbf{k}$, which also provides a handy mnemonic device for the direction of cross products.

Drill Exercises

7.19.   Demonstrate the Four Properties. Prove each of the preceding four properties given for the cross product.

7.20.   Derivation of the Cross Product. The form in Equation 7.42 given as a definition can actually be derived from more fundamental ideas. We need only assume that

a.   The cross product operation is linear.

b.   The cross product of a vector with itself is **0**.

c. $\mathbf{i} \times \mathbf{j} = \mathbf{k}$, $\mathbf{j} \times \mathbf{k} = \mathbf{i}$, and $\mathbf{k} \times \mathbf{i} = \mathbf{j}$.

By writing $\mathbf{a} = a_x\mathbf{i} + a_y\mathbf{j} + a_z\mathbf{k}$ and $\mathbf{b} = b_x\mathbf{i} + b_y\mathbf{j} + b_z\mathbf{k}$, apply these rules to derive the proper form for $\mathbf{a} \times \mathbf{b}$.

7.6.1 Geometric Interpretation of the Cross Product

By definition the cross product $\mathbf{a} \times \mathbf{b}$ of two vectors is another vector, but how is it related geometrically to the others, and why is it of interest? Figure 7.33 gives the answer. The cross product $\mathbf{a} \times \mathbf{b}$ has the following useful properties (whose proofs are requested in the exercises):

1. $\mathbf{a} \times \mathbf{b}$ is perpendicular to both $\mathbf{a}$ and $\mathbf{b}$.

2.   The length of $\mathbf{a} \times \mathbf{b}$ equals the area of the parallelogram determined by $\mathbf{a}$ and $\mathbf{b}$. This area is equal to

$$|\mathbf{a} \times \mathbf{b}| = |\mathbf{a}||\mathbf{b}| \sin(\theta) \tag{7.44}$$

where θ is the angle between $\mathbf{a}$ and $\mathbf{b}$, measured from $\mathbf{a}$ to $\mathbf{b}$ or $\mathbf{b}$ to $\mathbf{a}$, whichever produces an angle of less than 180 degrees. As a special case, $\mathbf{a} \times \mathbf{b} = 0$ if, and only if, $\mathbf{a}$ and $\mathbf{b}$ have the same or opposite directions or if either has zero length. What is the magnitude of the cross product if $\mathbf{a}$ and $\mathbf{b}$ are perpendicular?

3.   The sense of $\mathbf{a} \times \mathbf{b}$ is given by the right-hand rule when working in a right-handed system. For example, twist the fingers of your right hand from $\mathbf{a}$ to $\mathbf{b}$, and then $\mathbf{a} \times \mathbf{b}$ will point in the direction of your thumb. (*Note*: When working in a left-handed system, use your left hand in this technique.)

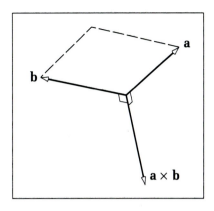

Figure 7.33.
Interpretation of the cross product.

Example

Let $\mathbf{a} = (1, 0, 1)$ and $\mathbf{b} = (1, 0, 0)$. These vectors are easy to visualize, as they both lie in the x, z-plane. (Sketch them.) The area of the parallelogram defined by $\mathbf{a}$ and $\mathbf{b}$ is easily seen to be 1. Because $\mathbf{a} \times \mathbf{b}$ is orthogonal to both, we expect it to be parallel to the y-axis and hence be proportional to $\pm\mathbf{j}$. In either a right-handed or a left-handed system, sweeping the fingers of the appropriate hand from $\mathbf{a}$ to $\mathbf{b}$ will reveal a thumb pointed along the positive y-axis. Direct calculation based on Equation 7.42 confirms all of this: $\mathbf{a} \times \mathbf{b} = \mathbf{j}$.

Drill Exercise

7.21. Vector Products. Find the vector $\mathbf{b} = (b_x, b_y, b_z)$ that satisfies the cross product relation $\mathbf{a} \times \mathbf{b} = \mathbf{c}$, where $\mathbf{a} = (2, 1, 3)$ and $\mathbf{c} = (2, -4, 0)$. Is there only one such vector?

7.22. Proving the Properties. Prove each of the preceding three properties given for the cross product.

7.23. Nonassociativity of the Cross Product. Show that the cross product is not associative. That is, that $\mathbf{a} \times (\mathbf{b} \times \mathbf{c})$ is not necessarily the same as $(\mathbf{a} \times \mathbf{b}) \times \mathbf{c}$.

7.24. Another Useful Fact. Show that

$$|\mathbf{a} \times \mathbf{b}| = \sqrt{|\mathbf{a}|^2|\mathbf{b}|^2 - (\mathbf{a} \cdot \mathbf{b})^2}$$

7.6.2 The Scalar Triple Product

Before discussing applications using the cross product, we shall combine it with the dot product to provide the final tool we need. Given three vectors, $\mathbf{a}$, $\mathbf{b}$, and $\mathbf{c}$, combine them to create the scalar S defined by

$$S = \mathbf{a} \cdot (\mathbf{b} \times \mathbf{c}) \tag{7.45}$$
$$= a_x(b_yc_z - b_zc_y) + a_y(b_zc_x - b_xc_z) + a_z(b_xc_y - b_yc_x)$$

This can also be written conveniently as the determinant:

$$S = \begin{vmatrix} a_x & a_y & a_z \\ b_x & b_y & b_z \\ c_x & c_y & c_z \end{vmatrix} \tag{7.46}$$

Interchanging the rows of a determinant causes only a change in sign (see Appendix 2), and so if we do it twice, there will be no change at all. Hence a cyclic permutation in the vectors has no effect on the value of S, and it has the following three equivalent forms:

$$S = \mathbf{a} \cdot (\mathbf{b} \times \mathbf{c})$$
$$= \mathbf{b} \cdot (\mathbf{c} \times \mathbf{a}) \tag{7.47}$$
$$= \mathbf{c} \cdot (\mathbf{a} \times \mathbf{b})$$

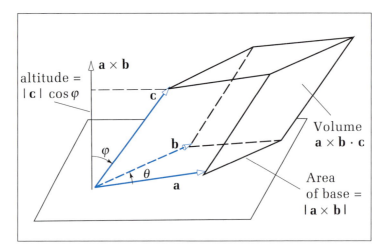

Figure 7.34.
The scalar triple product measures volume.

Geometrically the scalar triple product has a simple interpretation. Its magnitude is the volume of the parallelepiped formed by the vectors **a**, **b**, and **c** all applied to the same point, as shown in Figure 7.34. To see why this is so, recall that the magnitude of **a** × **b** yields the area of the base of this parallelepiped. Remember the dot product is the product of this magnitude and the altitude |**c**| cos(ϕ) of the parallelepiped. This value is the volume as claimed. The sign of the triple scalar product follows that of cos(ϕ): positive if $\phi < 90°$ and negative if $\phi > 90°$. (*Question*: Does the sign of the triple scalar product depend on the use of a right-handed versus a left-handed system?)

Note that if the three vectors lie in the same plane, the scalar triple product will be zero, as the volume of the parallelipiped then degenerates to zero. Suppose that none of **a**, **b**, or **c** is the zero vector. Then the triple scalar product **a** · (**b** × **c**) = 0 if, and only if, the three vectors are coplanar. (*Corollary*: The three vectors will be coplanar if any two of them are parallel.) This property can be used to determine how nearly planar a polygon is.

The triple scalar product can be used to find a simple expression for the point at which three (nonparallel) planes intersect. This in turn gives rise to a closed-form expression for the center and radius of the circle that passes through three given points. (In Chapter 4 we derived this excircle algorithmically.) An intermediate quantity of interest, the "triple vector product," emerges in the derivation. (See the exercises for discussions of these results.)

7.7   Applying the Cross Product and the Scalar Triple Product

With these properties in hand we shall apply these products to a collection of geometric problems involving planes and polygons. When objects and scenes in graphics are modeled as collections of polygonal facets, or "faces," it can be important to compute how large a polygon is, how it is oriented, and whether it is convex. These results are used later in such problems as hidden surface elimination, clipping, and shading.

7.7.1 Finding the Normal to a Plane

We begin with the classic application of the cross product: finding the normal vector to a plane. The equation $\mathbf{n} \cdot \mathbf{r} = D$ completely describes a plane once its normal $\mathbf{n}$ and the parameter D are known. But if we are told only that the plane passes through three specific points, how can $\mathbf{n}$ and D be computed? The cross product provides the tool.

First, find the plane that passes through three points. Any three points, P_1, P_2, P_3, determine a unique plane, as long as they don't lie in a straight line. Figure 7.35 shows this situation. To find the normal vector, build two vectors, $\mathbf{a} = P_2 - P_1$ and $\mathbf{b} = P_3 - P_1$. Their cross product, $\mathbf{a} \times \mathbf{b}$, must be normal to every line in the plane and so is the desired normal vector. Any scalar multiple of this cross product is also a normal, including $\mathbf{b} \times \mathbf{a}$, which points in the opposite direction. For whichever choice is made, use one of the three points P_1, P_2, or P_3 as $\mathbf{r}$ in $\mathbf{n} \cdot \mathbf{r} = D$ to compute D, thereby creating the point normal form for the plane. (*Question*: What will happen here if the three points do lie in a straight line?)

Example

Find the equation of the plane that passes through the points $(1, 0, 2)$, $(2, 3, 0)$, and $(1, 2, 4)$.

Solution:
By direct calculation, $\mathbf{a} = (2, 3, 0) - (1, 0, 2) = (1, 3, -2)$, and $\mathbf{b} = (1, 2, 4) - (1, 0, 2) = (0, 2, 2)$, and so their cross product $\mathbf{n} = (10, -2, 2)$. Now find D by using $\mathbf{r} = (1, 0, 2)$ in $\mathbf{n} \cdot \mathbf{r} = D$ to obtain $D = 14$, yielding the equation $10x - 2y + 2z = 14$.

Example Revisited

Will we get the same plane if we use the points in a different order, instead building the cross product out of, say, $\mathbf{a} = (1, 0, 2) - (2, 3, 0) = (-1, -3, 2)$ and $\mathbf{b} = (1, 2, 4) - (2, 3, 0) = (-1, -1, 4)$? Then $\mathbf{a} \times \mathbf{b} = (-10, 2, -2)$. This time use, say, $(1, 0, 2)$ in the dot product with $\mathbf{n}$ to get $D = -14$. This gives the equation $-10x + 2y - 2z = -14$, which is clearly the same plane.

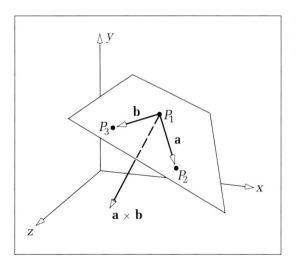

Figure 7.35.
Finding the plane through three given points.

Drill Exercise

7.25   Finding Some Planes. For each of the following triplet of points, find if possible the equation of the plane that passes through the triplet. Assuming that the origin is in the inside half-space of the plane, find the outward normal vector.

a. $P_1 = (1, 1, 1)$, $P_2 = (1, 2, 1)$, $P_3 = (3, 0, 4)$

b. $P_1 = (8, 9, 7)$, $P_2 = (-8, -9, -7)$, $P_3 = (1, 2, 1)$

c. $P_1 = (6, 3, -4)$, $P_2 = (0, 0, 0)$, $P_3 = (2, 1, -1)$

d. $P_1 = (0, 0, 0)$, $P_2 = (1, 1, 1)$, $P_3 = (2, 2, 2)$

7.7.2 The Simplest Polygons: Triangles

Three (noncollinear) points, P_1, P_2, and P_3, in three dimensions determine a simple triangle, and the preceding method finds the plane in which the triangle lies. Other results are also easily obtained for a triangle:

1.   The polygon is always convex.

2.   The triangle's area is easily found:

$$\text{area of triangle} = \frac{1}{2}|\mathbf{a} \times \mathbf{b}| \qquad (7.48)$$

where, as before, $\mathbf{a} = P_2 - P_1$ and $\mathbf{b} = P_3 - P_1$. This follows because we know that the magnitude of the cross product gives the area of the enclosed parallelogram, and the triangle's area is just one-half of this.

When a polygon with more than three points is given, these properties are not as easily established. Polygons are not necessarily convex; their points may not all lie in one plane; and the area of the polygon is not immediately obvious. We shall next examine how the cross product and the triple scalar product can be used to determine the nature and size of a more general polygon.

7.8   Applications to Polygons

For the following methods we assume that a polygon is given by a list of m vertices, P_1, P_2,...,P_m. In an application the data might well be stored in a variable, *poly : polypoint3D*, in which *polypoint3D* is a simple extension of the familiar *polypoint*:

Code Fragment 7.8. Data Type for Storing a Polygon

```
type
     polypoint3D = record
                      NumVerts : 0..maxnumverts;
                      pt : array[1..maxnumverts] of point3D
              end;
```

The constant *maxnumverts* prescribes the largest number of vertices to be encountered.

7.8.1 Testing the Planarity of a Polygon

A polygon is **planar** if all its vertices lie in one plane. In that case any three (noncollinear) vertices may be used to determine its specific plane. When there are more than three vertices it may happen that not all the points will lie in a plane. That is, a user may make errors while inputting data for the polygons, as may a modeling routine as it generates the faces from some general description of an object. Therefore some applications must test the polygons to ensure that they are indeed planar.

From the vertices P_i, for $i = 1,...,m$, choose one vertex, say P_1, as a "pivot" point, and form the $(m - 1)$ **pivot vectors** $\mathbf{v}_i = P_i - P_1$, for $i = 2,...,m$. These vectors will lie in the same plane if, and only if, the vertices P_i lie in the same plane. We have seen that three vectors are coplanar if, and only if, their triple scalar product vanishes. Then form the $(m - 3)$ scalar triple products: $\mathbf{v}_i \cdot (\mathbf{v_3} \times \mathbf{v_2})$, for $i = 4,...,m$. If any of them is not zero, the polygon will be nonplanar. (Owing to round-off errors, quantities that are theoretically zero often are computed to have a small but nonzero value. So here a small positive tolerance value, *eps*, should be chosen, and the polygon will be planar if the triple scalar products reveal values smaller than *eps*.)

Example

Consider the four points shown in Figure 7.36—$(0, 0, 0)$, $(1, 0, 0)$, $(1, 0, 1)$, and $(0, a, 1)$—where a is any real value. The first three points lie in the x,z-plane, but the fourth is suspended a units above the plane. We can see that the polygon will be planar only if $a = 0$, but what does the triple scalar product reveal? Direct calculation gives $\mathbf{u}_1 \cdot (\mathbf{u}_3 \times \mathbf{u}_2) = a$, confirming that the polygon will be planar if, and only if, $a = 0$.

Drill Exercise

7.26.   Are These Points Planar? Determine which four of the following five points are coplanar: $P_1 = (1, 3, 4)$, $P_2 = (2, 0, 3)$, $P_3 = (2, -2, 0)$, $P_4 = (3, 0, 6)$, $P_5 = (1, 1, 1)$. Find the plane through which the four coplanar points pass, and sketch it along with the noncoplanar point.

7.27.   Find Four Coplanar Points. Find a point that is coplanar with $(1, 3, 2)$, $(1, 1, -1)$, and $(0, 2, 1)$ and one that is not.

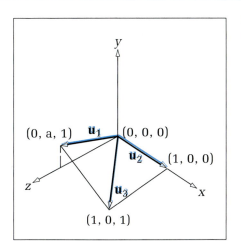

Figure 7.36.
Testing the planarity of a polygon.

7.8.2 Find the Normal to a Polygonal Face

If a polygon is planar we can choose any three noncollinear points and use the preceding method to compute the normal to their plane. This appears to solve the problem of finding the plane of a polygon: Choose a triple of points and form the cross product. But what if the choice of triple happens to be collinear? Or worse, what if the polygon is nonplanar?

A robust method devised by Martin Newell can be used to compute the components (n_x, n_y, n_z) of the normal vector (see Newman and Sproull 1979, Sutherland et al. 1974). It takes different triples of points from the polygon, each triple defining a constituent triangle in the polygon. It then finds the normal vector to the plane of each triangle in the usual fashion. Finally, these normals are simply added together. Collinear triples contribute a zero vector to this sum and so have no effect. The sum is proportional to an "average" normal vector that is taken as an estimate of the normal to the polygon. For a planar polygon, the exact normal is found; for a "nearly planar" polygon, there is no true normal, but the sum can be used as an approximate normal. The specific algorithm follows.

The Newell Method

Call the coordinates of $P_i = (x_i, y_i, z_i)$. Let index j depend on index i as follows: **if** $i = m$ **then** $j := 1$ **else** $j := i + 1$;. Thus P_j is the next vertex after P_i, taking into account that P_1 follows P_m. Then the average normal has the following components:

$$n_x = \sum_{i=1}^{m} (y_i - y_j)(z_i + z_j)$$

$$n_y = \sum_{i=1}^{m} (z_i - z_j)(x_i + x_j) \tag{7.49}$$

$$n_z = \sum_{i=1}^{m} (x_i - x_j)(y_i + y_j)$$

The computation requires only one multiplication per edge for each of the components of the normal, and no testing for collinearity is needed.

Example

Consider the polygon with vertices $P_1 = (6, 1, 4)$, $P_2 = (7, 0, 9)$, and $P_3 = (1, 1, 2)$. Direct use of the cross product gives $((7, 0, 9) - (6, 1, 4)) \times ((1, 1, 2) - (6, 1, 4)) = (2, -23, -5)$. Application of the Newell method yields the same result: $(2, -23, -5)$.

Drill Exercise

7.28.　Using the Newell Method. For the three vertices (6, 1, 4), (2, 0, 5), and (7, 0, 9), compare the normal found using the Newell method with that found using the usual cross product. Then use the Newell method to find (n_x, n_y, n_z) for the polygon having the vertices (1, 1, 2), (2, 0, 5), (5, 1, 4), (6, 0, 7). Is the polygon planar? If so, find its true normal using the cross product, and compare it with the result of the Newell method.

7.8.3 Detecting a Left Versus a Right Turn

In various algorithms, we must traverse a polygon, "visiting" each vertex and/or edge in turn to make a calculation. We think of "moving along" an edge from one vertex to the next and then "turning onto" the next edge. It can be important whether this is a left turn or a right turn.

For example, if P_1, P_2, and P_3 are three adjacent vertices of the polygon, construct the **edge vectors** $\mathbf{a} = P_2 - P_1$ and $\mathbf{b} = P_3 - P_2$. Figure 7.37a shows the case in which a and b lie in the x, y-plane, for simplicity, and a left turn is made as we switch directions from **a** to **b**. A right turn is shown in Figure 7.37b.

Now how is the sense of the turn related to the cross product and the triple scalar product? Suppose a right-handed system is assumed in Figure 7.37, so that the z-axis (or, equivalently, the **k** direction) is pointed outward toward us from the page (denoted by the point of the arrow seen at the origin). Using the right-hand rule, the cross product $\mathbf{a} \times \mathbf{b}$ is pointed out of the page with a positive **k** component. If we form the dot product of this vector with **k** itself, we will obtain a quantity whose sign reveals the sense of the turn, positive for a left turn and negative for a right turn. The terms *positive* and *negative* are less closely tied to the viewer's vantage point than are *left* and *right*, particularly when the vectors lie in an arbitrary plane. We therefore adopt the terminology *positive* and *negative*, tying it to the sign of a mathematical expression.

> **Definition**
>
> For vectors **a** and **b** in the x, y-plane, the turn from **a** to **b** will be **positive** if
>
> $$T = \mathbf{k} \cdot (\mathbf{a} \times \mathbf{b}) \geqslant 0 \qquad (7.50)$$
>
> and will be **negative** otherwise. This result will not change if a left-handed system is used instead of a right-handed system. In Figure 7.37, positive indicates a left turn, and negative a right turn. The next exercise shows how simple this calculation is.

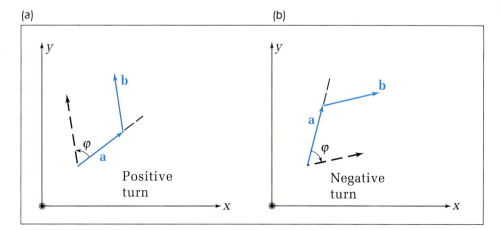

(a)

(b)

Positive turn

Negative turn

Figure 7.37.
Detecting left or right turns in traversing a polygon.

Example

Consider three vertices of a polygon having positions $(2, 3, 0)$, $(4, 1, 0)$, and $(5, 5, 0)$ in the x, y-plane. For the first edge, $\mathbf{a} = (2, -2, 0)$, and for the second, $\mathbf{b} = (1, 4, 0)$. The scalar triple product T has value 10, and so a positive (counterclockwise) turn is made from the first to the second edge.

Drill Exercises

7.29.   Computing the Sense of a Turn. Show that for vectors lying in the x, y-plane the computation of T is particularly simple, requiring only two multiplications:

$$T = \mathbf{k} \cdot (\mathbf{a} \times \mathbf{b}) = a_x b_y - a_y b_x \qquad (7.51)$$

This test can easily be implemented in code as **function** *PositiveTurn(a, b: vector): boolean*, which will return *true* if the turn is positive (see the exercises).

7.30.   Generalization to Turns in Any Plane. We wish to generalize the result in Equation 7.50 to vectors lying in an arbitrary plane. Suppose the plane has equation $\mathbf{n} \cdot \mathbf{r} = D$, where $\mathbf{n}$ is the outward normal, as suggested in Figure 7.38. The meaning of *positive* has to be to extended here to "positive when viewed along vector $\mathbf{n}$." Show that a meaningful definition of a positive turn is that the triple scalar product T must be positive:

$$T = \mathbf{n} \cdot (\mathbf{a} \times \mathbf{b}) \qquad (7.52)$$

7.8.4 Testing the Convexity of a Polygon

The positive-versus-negative turn test provides a straightforward way to find whether a simple polygon is convex. Figure 7.39 shows several polygons lying in a plane; consider what happens as each is traversed. For a convex polygon, all of the turns are in the same direction, as for polygons A and B. But if the polygon is not convex, as in the case of C, both kinds of turns will occur, which leads to

Figure 7.38.
Positive and negative turns for
arbitrary vectors.

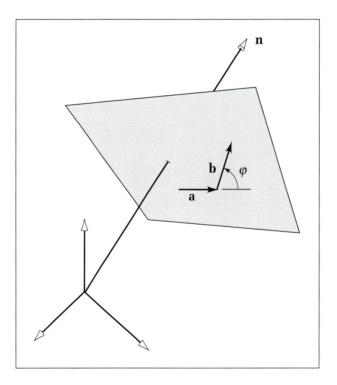

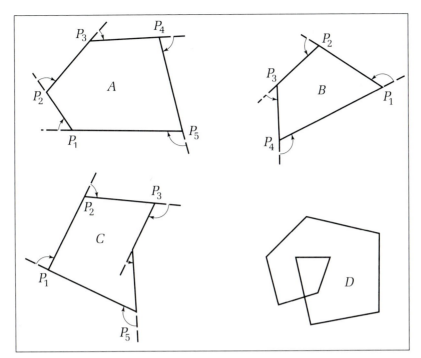

Figure 7.39.
Traversing polygons to test for convexity.

the convexity test. That is, a simple polygon is convex if, and only if, all turns have the same sign as it is traversed.

We must restrict this test to simple polygons, however, because a more complicated (self-intersecting) polygon such as D in the figure can pass the sign test and still not be convex. It is easy to implement the convexity test in a routine such as **function** *IsConvex(poly : polypoint3D) : boolean;* which will return *true* if the (simple) polygon in *poly* reveals all turns as being of the same sign (see the exercises).

7.8.5 Computing the Area of a Polygon

Computer-aided design systems often must compute properties of geometric objects, both to use in further calculation and to report them to the user. An important property of a polygon is its area.

Because the area of a triangle is easily computed from Equation 7.48, we need only decompose a polygon into a collection of triangles and sum the areas of these triangles. Figure 7.40 shows an example of a convex polygon. One of the vertices, say P_m, is chosen as a pivot, and the $m - 1$ pivot vectors $\mathbf{a}_1 = P_1 - P_m$, $\mathbf{a}_2 = P_2 - P_m, \ldots, \mathbf{a}_{m-1} = P_{m-1} - P_m$ are constructed. These pivot vectors are used to find the area of each triangle. Two sides of triangle i are given by vectors $\mathbf{a}_i$ and $\mathbf{a}_{i+1}$, and there are $m - 2$ triangles in all. For a convex polygon, as in Figure 7.40, the area of the i-th triangle is given by Equation 7.48: $\frac{1}{2}|\mathbf{a}_i \times \mathbf{a}_{i+1}|$, and these contributions are summed to form the total area of the polygon.

If the polygon is not convex, however, not all the successive triangles will contribute "positive" area. Figure 7.41 shows a seven-sided polygon decomposed into five triangles by the pivot vectors. Some of the triangles do make a positive turn from the first to the second pivot vector, but others make a negative

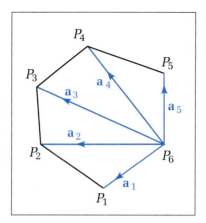

Figure 7.40.
A convex polygon as a union of triangles.

turn. Those based on a positive turn (the first, third, and fifth) contribute positive area, whereas those based on a negative turn (the second and fourth) contribute negative area. It is not hard to see that if all the positive and negative areas are summed, the actual area of the polygon will be determined. Take the absolute value of the net area at the end, as there could be more negative area than positive area, depending on the order in which the vertices are labeled. This method works also for convex polygons such as that of Figure 7.40. In that case, all of the turns are negative so that all of the areas are negative, but they add up properly.

Now how is this done algorithmically? To form this signed area we need a slight variation of Equation 7.48: Instead of using the magnitude of the cross product, it is dotted with $\mathbf{u_n}$, the (unit-length) outward normal to the plane of the polygon. (If the polygon lies in the x, y-plane $\mathbf{u_n}$ is simply $\mathbf{k}$.) The dot

Figure 7.41.
Finding the area of a general polygon.

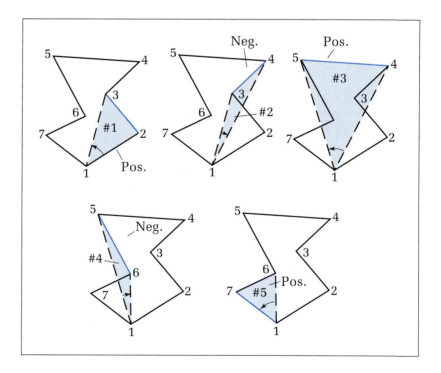

product with $\mathbf{u_n}$ simply sorts out the positive and negative signed areas. It does not affect the individual areas themselves, as it has unit magnitude. Note that this quantity is almost identical to that used for the left-right turn test in Equation 7.52. Specifically, for the i-th triangle the **signed area** SA_i is

$$SA_i = \tfrac{1}{2}\, \mathbf{n} \cdot \mathbf{a}_i \times \mathbf{a}_{i+1} \tag{7.53}$$

and the true area is

$$\text{area} = \left| \sum_{i=1}^{m-2} SA_i \right| \tag{7.54}$$

A routine to compute the area of a polygon is discussed in the exercises.

Example

Find the area of the polygon having vertices $(0, 0)$, $(4, 0)$, $(3, 2)$, $(6, 3)$, and $(0, 8)$.

Solution:

By direct calculation the three scalar triple products are

i	Subarea
2	$\tfrac{1}{2}\,\mathbf{k} \cdot (8\mathbf{k})$
3	$\tfrac{1}{2}\,\mathbf{k} \cdot (-3\mathbf{k})$
4	$\tfrac{1}{2}\,\mathbf{k} \cdot (48\mathbf{k})$

and so the triangle has area $(1/2)(8 - 3 + 48) = 53/2$.

Drill Exercises

7.31. Calculating the Area. The vertices of several polygons are as follows. Use the preceding method to calculate the area for each of them, and check your answers by plotting the polygons on graph paper and finding the area.
a. $(1, 2)$, $(2, 5)$, $(8, 4)$, $(7, -2)$, $(1, -4)$
b. $(0, 4)$, $(4, 0)$, $(0, 0)$
c. $(0, 0)$, $(0, 8)$, $(10, 8)$, $(5, 4)$, $(10, 0)$

7.32. The Intersection of Three Planes. Two planes intersect in a line, and a third plane intersects this line at a single point. The scalar triple product provides a closed-form expression for this point (Faux and Pratt 1979). Show that the point of intersection of the three planes, $\mathbf{n}_i \cdot \mathbf{r} = D_i$, for $i = 1, 2, 3$, is given by

$$\mathbf{r} = \frac{D_1(\mathbf{n}_2 \times \mathbf{n}_3) + D_2(\mathbf{n}_3 \times \mathbf{n}_1) + D_3(\mathbf{n}_1 \times \mathbf{n}_2)}{\mathbf{n}_1 \cdot (\mathbf{n}_2 \times \mathbf{n}_3)} \tag{7.55}$$

provided that the denominator is not zero.

Do this by testing to see that $\mathbf{r}$ lies in each of the three planes: Substitute the expression for each plane in this formula, and use the properties of the triple scalar product to show that an equality results. Explain the geometric meaning of a zero denominator in Equation 7.55.

Show that the common point of the three planes

$$3x + 2y - z = 5$$
$$x - 4y + 2z = 3$$
$$2x + 2y + 3z = 1$$

is $\mathbf{r} = (104/56, -31/56, -30/56)$. What geometric quantity has the value of the denominator (56) here?

7.33. Some Useful Geometric Relations. The next four exercises are based on four points, A, B, C, and D, in space, with corresponding vectors bound to the origin, $\mathbf{a}$, $\mathbf{b}$, $\mathbf{c}$, and $\mathbf{d}$. It may be helpful to use the geometric interpretation of the scalar triple product.

1.   Show that the volume of the tetrahedron whose vertices are A, B, C, D is

$$\frac{1}{6}|(\mathbf{b} - \mathbf{a}) \cdot (\mathbf{c} - \mathbf{a}) \times (\mathbf{d} - \mathbf{a})|$$

Compute this volume for $A = (1, 1, 1)$, $B = (0, 0, 2)$, $C = (0, 3, 0)$, and $D = (4, 0, 0)$.

2. If $\mathbf{b} \neq \mathbf{c}$, show that the perpendicular distance from A to the line through B and C is

$$\frac{|(\mathbf{a} - \mathbf{b}) \times (\mathbf{c} - \mathbf{b})|}{|\mathbf{b} - \mathbf{c}|}$$

Compute this distance if $A = (1, -2, -5)$, $B = (-1, 1, 1)$, and $C = (4, 5, 1)$.

3. If B, C, and D determine a plane, show that the perpendicular distance from A to this plane is

$$\frac{|(\mathbf{a} - \mathbf{b}) \cdot (\mathbf{c} - \mathbf{b}) \times (\mathbf{d} - \mathbf{b})|}{|(\mathbf{c} - \mathbf{b}) \times (\mathbf{d} - \mathbf{b})|}$$

Compute this distance for $A = (1, 0, 0)$, $B = (0, 1, 1)$, $C = (1, -1, 1)$, and $D = (2, 3, 4)$.

4. If $\mathbf{a} \neq \mathbf{b}$ and $\mathbf{c} \neq \mathbf{d}$ and if $P = (\mathbf{b} - \mathbf{a}) \times (\mathbf{c} - \mathbf{d}) \neq 0$, show that the shortest distance between the line through A and B and the line through C and D is

$$\frac{|(\mathbf{c} - \mathbf{a}) \cdot (\mathbf{b} - \mathbf{a}) \times (\mathbf{c} - \mathbf{d})|}{P}$$

Compute this distance when $A = (4, 5, 1)$, $B = (1, -1, 3)$, $C = (1, -2, -5)$, and $D = (-1, 1, 1)$.

7.34. The Triple Vector Product. The triple vector product (TVP) of three vectors, $\mathbf{a}$, $\mathbf{b}$, and $\mathbf{c}$, is given by $TVP = \mathbf{a} \times (\mathbf{b} \times \mathbf{c})$. It often arises during pencil-and-paper calculations involving cross products. Sketch typical vectors $\mathbf{a}$, $\mathbf{b}$, and $\mathbf{c}$ and then sketch the TVP. Show that it can be written as the difference of the two scaled vectors: $TVP = (\mathbf{a} \cdot \mathbf{c})\mathbf{b} - (\mathbf{a} \cdot \mathbf{b})\mathbf{c}$ (Faux and Pratt 1979). Do this by simplifying the x-component of TVP, and then use cyclic permutation of the vectors to obtain the other components. Finally, put the three component results together.

7.35. The Circle Through Three Points. Given the three points A, B, and C in space, find the circle that passes through them. Suppose that without loss of generality the points have been shifted so that D lies at the origin, A has position vector $\mathbf{a}$, and B has position vector $\mathbf{b}$. Call the center of the circle C with position vector $\mathbf{c}$. Sketch this situation. Now C must lie at the intersection of three planes (Faux and Pratt 1979):

1. The plane through A, B, and D.

2. The plane that bisects line AD perpendicularly (*Hint*: the plane $\mathbf{p} \cdot \mathbf{a} = |\mathbf{a}|^2/2$).

3. The plane that bisects BD perpendicularly.

Use the result of Exercise 7.34 to build an expression for $\mathbf{c}$, and then simplify it using the preceding triple vector product result. The final result should be (calling $|\mathbf{b}| = b$ and $|\mathbf{a}| = a$)

$$\mathbf{c} = \frac{b^2(a^2 - \mathbf{a} \cdot \mathbf{b})\mathbf{a} + a^2(b^2 - \mathbf{a} \cdot \mathbf{b})\mathbf{b}}{2|\mathbf{a} \times \mathbf{b}|^2} \qquad (7.56)$$

with radius

$$|\mathbf{c}| = \frac{ab|\mathbf{a} - \mathbf{b}|}{2|\mathbf{a} \times \mathbf{b}|} \qquad (7.57)$$

7.36. The Centroid of a Set of Points. Let $\mathbf{p}_i$, for $i = 1, \ldots, k$ be vectors bound to the origin corresponding to points P_i. If mass m_i (positive, negative, or zero) is located at P_i, we shall define the **centroid** of the system to be the point $\mathbf{C}$ given by

$$\mathbf{C} = \frac{\displaystyle\sum_{i=1}^{k} m_i \mathbf{p}_i}{D}$$

where

$$D = \sum_{i=1}^{k} m_i$$

is not zero. Show that the position of the centroid is independent of the location of the origin.

7.37. A Familiar Trigonometric Identity. By forming the dot product of $\mathbf{a} = \cos(\alpha)\mathbf{i} + \sin(\alpha)\mathbf{j}$ and $\mathbf{b} = \cos(\beta)\,\mathbf{i} + \sin(\beta)\,\mathbf{j}$, derive the trigonometric identity $\cos(\alpha - \beta) = \cos(\alpha)\cos(\beta) + \sin(\alpha)\sin(\beta)$.

7.38. Derivation of the Dot Product Properties. Derive the three properties of the dot product given in Section 7.3.1 using the fact that multiplication of scalars is commutative, $p \times q = q \times p$, and distributive, $(p + q) \times r = p \times r + q \times r$.

7.39. A Family of Vectors. Find a unit vector orthogonal to $(1, 3, 4)$. How many such vectors are there?

7.9   Summary

In this chapter we reviewed the fundamental ideas of vector arithmetic and related them to geometric objects and properties frequently encountered in computer graphics. We showed how vectors unify the treatment of points, lines, lengths, angles, and directions, marrying geometric concepts to algebraic tools. In addition, vector arithmetic provides a framework for translating many geometric concepts into program code.

The basic operations available for vectors are the addition of two vectors and the scaling of a vector by a scalar. Vectors are interpreted geometrically as entities having length and direction but not position. One can view a vector as a displacement and hence as the difference between two points. If vectors are "applied to the origin," they will become indistinguishable from points as long as one stays within the given coordinate system, and this gives rise to the notion of "linear combinations of points."

We introduced the dot product to measure the angle between two vectors. In particular, it tells when two vectors of any dimension are perpendicular, leading to the notion of the normal vector to a line, curve, or surface. Lines and planes can then be represented in the convenient point normal form. The dot product also computes the projection of one vector into another, which among other things allows one to find the direction of reflection of a ray from a surface.

The sign of the dot product also reveals when two vectors are pointed less than or more than 90 degrees from each other, which can be combined with the notion of an outward normal to a line to determine whether a point is in the inside or outside half-space of the line. The very same test applies equally well to half-spaces determined by a plane. This test gives rise to the powerful Cyrus–Beck clipping algorithm for clipping against convex windows in two or three dimensions.

We rounded out our arsenal of vector tools in this chapter by introducing the cross product. The cross product yields a new vector perpendicular to both of the argument vectors. The size of the cross product can be used to obtain the area of the triangle formed by the vectors, which is useful for calculating the area of complicated polygons. The scalar triple product combines the dot and cross products and measures the volume inside a parallelepiped, which can be used to measure coplanarity, the intersection of three planes, areas of polygons lying in arbitrary planes, and so forth. We shall have several occasions to use each of these tools in the remaining chapters.

Programming Exercises

7.40. Scaling a Vector. Develop the routine **procedure** $Scale(v : vector; f : real; \mathbf{var}\ w : vector)$ that performs $\mathbf{w} = f\ \mathbf{v}$.

7.41. The Length of a Vector. Write **function** $Length$ $(v : vector) : real$ that computes the length of a 2D vector. Extend the definition to a general n-dimensional vector.

7.42. Normalizing a Vector. Write the routine $Normalize(v : vector3D; \mathbf{var}\ u : vector3D)$ that normalizes vector $\mathbf{v}$ to produce unit vector $\mathbf{u}$. Make the computation as efficient as possible.

7.43. n-Dimensional Vector Addition. Write a routine that produces an n-dimensional vector by adding two n-dimensional vectors. Define appropriate data types for n-dimensional vectors.

7.44. More General Linear Combinations. Write the procedure $LinCombo(v : VectArray; f : ScalarArray; \mathbf{var}\ w : Ntuple)$ that fashions a linear combination of m n-tuples:

$$\mathbf{w} = \sum_{i=1}^{m} f_i\ \mathbf{v_i}$$

where $VectArray$ and $ScalarArray$ are the types

type
  $VectArray = \mathbf{array}[1..m]\ \mathbf{of}\ Ntuple;$
  $ScalarArray = \mathbf{array}[1..m]\ \mathbf{of}\ real$

7.45. Animation with Tweening. Devise two interesting polylines with the same number of points, and use the routines $InBetween(\ )$ and $DrawSequence(\ )$ to fashion a simple animation on an interactive graphics terminal. Construct $NewFrame$ so that after a short pause the old polyline is erased, in preparation for the next one. If your terminal has more than one page of display memory, draw the "next" polyline off screen while the "current" one is being viewed, and then switch pages to view the new picture.

This allows for smoother animation.

7.46. Back and Forth. In the preceding animation exercise, *DrawSequence( )* causes parameter *t* to progress steadily from 0 to 1. Adjust this so that in some fashion, *t* varies back and forth, first moving from 0 to 1 and then back to 0 again. Also try the case in which *t* does not change uniformly but in a sinusoidal fashion, so that the *i*-th value of *t* is $\sin((i-1)\pi/(n-1)2)$ instead of $(i-1)/(n-1)$.

7.47. The Convex Hull. Given a set *S* of *m* points P_i in the plane, invent an algorithm that computes the convex hull of *S*.

7.48. Computing Dot Products. Write **function** *Dot_n(a, b : vector_n) : real* that computes the dot product of two *n*-dimensional vectors. Provide a suitable data type definition for an *n*-tuple.

7.49. Building the Point Normal Form. Fashion **procedure** *PointNormal(a, b : point;* **var** *L : line)* which computes variable *L : line*, consisting of a normal vector **n** and the coefficient *D* for the line that passes through the two points *a* and *b*. What should the routine do if the two points are the same?

7.50. On the Liang–Barsky Clipper. Consider the case of a rectangular window stored in a variable of type *rect*. Optimize the Cyrus–Beck algorithm given in Appendix 6, taking advantage of the simpler calculations required for this class of window. Adjust the code for the most efficient execution possible.

7.51. A Routine to Compute the Equation of a Plane. Write and test **procedure** *Plane(n : vector3D; P : Point3D;* **var** *A, B, C, D : real)*; which returns the values of the coefficients *A, B, C,* and *D* of the plane, given the normal vector **n** to the plane and some point *P* lying in the plane.

7.52. Calculation of the Cross Product. Create **procedure** *Cross(a, b : vector3D;* **var** *c : vector3D)*; which computes the cross product of two vectors. Base the calculation on Equation 7.42, and note that it requires six multiplications.

7.53. The *PositiveTurn* Test. Develop and test **function** *PositiveTurn( )* which determines whether a positive or negative turn is taken as one moves from direction **a** to direction **b**.

7.54. Testing Convexity. Use the *PositiveTurn( )* function from the previous exercise to construct the function *IsConvex(poly : polypoint3D) : boolean* which will return *true* if, and only if, the simple polygon *poly* is convex.

7.55. Finding the Area of a Polygon. Develop **function** *Area(polyn : polypoint3D) : real* which calculates the area of a polygon by summing signed areas for its component triangles.

CHAPTER 8

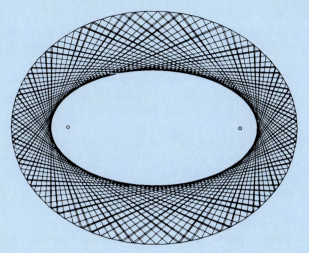

Two-Dimensional Ray Tracing: Reflections in a Chamber

Goals of the Chapter

- To see how the tools—particularly the dot product—developed in the previous chapter can be used in practical situations.
- To see how a graphics application of moderate size can be devised to display an interesting simulation that requires successive reflections of an object from a boundary.
- To introduce some of the central ideas of ray tracing in two dimensions, in which they are much more easily visualized than in three dimensions. The methods, however, are easily extended later to three dimensions.

8.1   A Ray-Tracing Experiment

The goal of this short chapter is to apply many of the tools and ideas introduced earlier to a fascinating yet simple simulation. We shall develop a complete graphics application step by step to illustrate how the geometric notions that arise in the simulation can be translated into routines to carry it out.

The simulation performs a kind of ray tracing, based in a two-dimensional world for easy visualization. **Ray tracing** has become an important tool in computer graphics for synthesizing realistic images, and accordingly we shall devote Chapter 18 to it. In image synthesis, several hypothetical rays of light are "cast" or "traced" through a three-dimensional world containing various objects. The path of each ray is traced as it bounces off various mirrorlike surfaces or passes through transparent objects, until it is stopped by some object. The color of that object is then determined and used to set the color of a corresponding pixel on the graphics display.

This simulation traces the path of a single tiny "pinball" as it bounces off various objects inside a "chamber." Figure 8.1 shows a cross section of a chamber that has five walls and contains three circular "pillars." The pinball begins at a point given by position vector **s** and moves in a straight line in direction **c** until it hits a barrier, whereupon it "reflects" off the barrier and moves in a new direction, again in a straight line. It continues doing this forever. The path of the pinball is therefore a long polyline. Alternatively, one can envision the polyline as the path of a ray of light as it moves within the chamber reflecting off shiny walls and barriers. It can be called interchangeably either a ray or a pinball. Figure 8.2 shows an example of the path that a ray traverses.

Our first task is to devise an algorithm that determines which object the ray will hit first and where it will hit. This hit point is then the starting point for the

Figure 8.1.
A ray-tracing experiment.

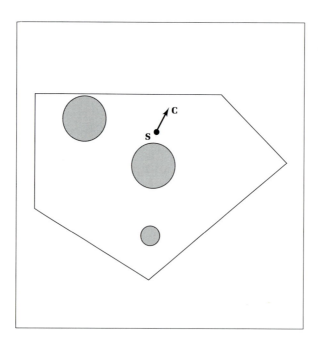

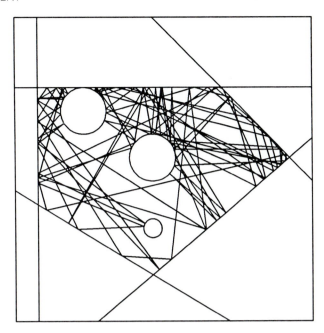

Figure 8.2.
An example path for the ray.

next segment of the path, and we can find the direction for this new ray using Equation 7.25.

For this experiment the ray will hit two types of objects, pillars and walls. A pillar is given by a circle. A wall can be defined by a line segment joining two endpoints, but it is more convenient to represent it by an infinite straight line. When the form of Equation 7.5 is used, we obtain a compact expression for the "hit time" and the "hit point." Because all expressions are in terms of dot products, they apply equally well to the three-dimensional case in which a wall becomes a plane and a circle becomes a sphere (see Chapter 18).

The Chamber As a Collection of Half-spaces

In this approach, the polygonal chamber is modeled by a collection of lines. Each wall is an infinite straight line: The vertices of the polygon are prescribed only implicitly by the relative positions of the lines where they intersect one another. This simplicity imposes some restrictions on the shapes of the chambers in the experiments; that is, they are always convex. Each line divides the entire plane into two infinite half-spaces: The "inside" occupies half of the plane on one side of the line, and the "outside" occupies the half on the other side. Figure 8.3a shows a line, L, coinciding with one edge of polygon P, with L dividing the plane into two half-spaces. The outside half-space, S, is shown shaded. Note that when an inside and outside are so defined, it becomes meaningful to talk about an **inward normal** vector, whose direction is indicated by the arrows. (The **outward normal** vector, of course, points in the opposite direction.) Note that lines don't have inward and outward normals by themselves. Rather, inwardness is a property we attach in the context of the problem, and so it is the modeler's job to specify which direction is inward and which is outward.

The chamber is therefore modeled by a collection of lines in the form $\mathbf{n}_i \cdot \mathbf{p} = D_i$, where $\mathbf{p} = (x, y)$ and $\mathbf{n}_i$ is taken to be the inward normal for the i-th

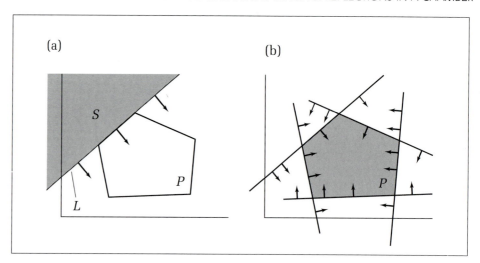

(a)   (b)

Figure 8.3.
L divides the plane into two
half-spaces.

edge. D_i specifies where the line lies. Together the lines and their notions of inward and outward define the interior of a convex polygon—in this case, our reflecting chamber. Figure 8.3b shows that the interior of the convex polygon is the set of points that is simultaneously on the inside of every edge.

8.1.1 The Intersection of a Ray with a Line

With the chamber defined, we next must compute where a ray hits a wall. Consider the ray

$$\mathbf{r}(t) = \mathbf{s} + \mathbf{c}t \tag{8.1}$$

which starts at $t = 0$ at the point represented by vector $\mathbf{s}$ and moves in direction $\mathbf{c}$. At what time, t_h, and at which point, $\mathbf{p}_h$, does it "hit" the line L given by

$$\mathbf{n} \cdot \mathbf{p} = D \tag{8.2}$$

By definition, $\mathbf{p}_h$ is the spot where the ray and the line have the same coordinates. To get a condition on this point, simply substitute Equation 8.1 into Equation 8.2 to obtain

$$\mathbf{n} \cdot (\mathbf{s} + \mathbf{c}t) = D \tag{8.3}$$

This puts a constraint on the single unknown t: The t that satisfies this equation is the desired hit time, t_h. Using linearity we get

$$(\mathbf{n} \cdot \mathbf{s}) + (\mathbf{n} \cdot \mathbf{c})t = D \tag{8.4}$$

a linear equation in t. If $\mathbf{n} \cdot \mathbf{c} \neq 0$, the solution will be

$$t_h = \frac{D - \mathbf{n} \cdot \mathbf{s}}{\mathbf{n} \cdot \mathbf{c}} \tag{8.5}$$

On the other hand, if $\mathbf{n} \cdot \mathbf{c} = 0$, the ray will be traveling parallel to the line ($\mathbf{c}$ is perpendicular to $\mathbf{n}$) and so will never hit it. When there is a hit, we can find the exact coordinates of the hit point, $\mathbf{p}_h$, by substituting t_h into Equation 8.1:

$$\mathbf{p}_h = \mathbf{r}(t_h) = \mathbf{s} + \mathbf{c}t_h \tag{8.6}$$

Example

When and where does ray $(1, 4) + (3, -1)t$ intersect line $(2, -1) \cdot \mathbf{p} = 6$?

Solution:

Direct calculation in Equation 8.5 gives $t_h = 8/7$, and using this in Equation 8.6 yields $\mathbf{p}_h = (31/7, 20/7)$. It is instructive to plot the ray and the line on graph paper and to compare the intersection with this numerical result.

These results can be put into the form of a procedure that computes the intersection time of the ray, as suggested in the following code fragment.

Code Fragment 8.1. Find the Intersection of a Ray with a Line

```
procedure Ray_with_Line(s, c, n : vector; D : real; var time : real);
{find time t at which ray s + ct hits line n.p = D}
var denom : real;
begin
        denom := Dot(n, c); {test if ray is parallel to line}
        if denom = 0.0 then time := -1.0 {impossible value}
        else time := (D - Dot(n, s)) / denom
end;
```

When the ray is parallel to the line (*denom* = 0), the procedure reports this by setting *time* to an "impossible" value. Any negative value is impossible because the ray begins each segment of its journey at $t = 0$.

To see how this procedure is used in the ray-tracing experiment, consider the simplest case, in which the chamber is empty: There are no circles present, and so the ray encounters only walls. Figure 8.4 shows an empty chamber having five walls, shown as a pentagon, and the ray $\mathbf{s} + c\mathbf{t}$. The ray is intersected with each of the walls in turn, to determine which wall it will hit first.

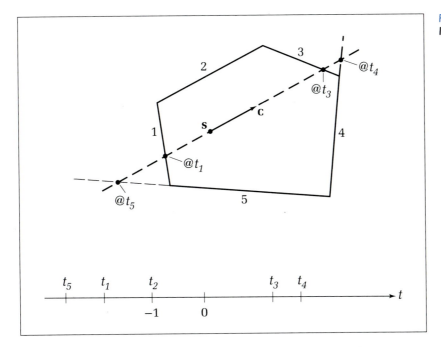

Figure 8.4.
Intersections with walls only.

To see which wall the ray will hit first, we invoke *Ray_with_Line*( ) for each wall in turn and keep track of the hit times. Walls that are intersected in the forward path of the ray return positive hit times, and those intersected "behind" the ray return negative hit times. The "impossible" value $t_h = -1$ is also returned for a wall parallel to the ray. Suppose wall 1 returns t_1; wall 2 returns t_2; and so on. The time line in the figure shows how the hit times are ordered in this example. There are two positive hit times here, t_3 and t_4. The smaller of these is the one of interest. Therefore the winning hit time is the smallest positive value returned when scanning the walls.

Once the first hit time, t_h, has been identified, the hit point of the ray is computed as $\mathbf{p} = \mathbf{s} + \mathbf{c}t_h$, and *LineTo(p)* is employed to draw the ray from its starting point to this new hit point. Now the process repeats with a new ray emanating from $\mathbf{p}$, moving in the reflected direction. The direction, $\mathbf{r}$, of the reflected rays is found from Equation 7.25:

$$\mathbf{r} = \mathbf{c} - 2(\mathbf{c} \cdot \mathbf{u}_n)\mathbf{u}_n \tag{8.7}$$

where $\mathbf{u}_n$ is the normalized version of normal to the wall hit by the ray. The algorithm keeps track of which wall yielded the first hit time so that this normal can be accessed from the chamber description. Wall descriptions can be stored in the data type *line* defined earlier. The whole chamber is conveniently stored in a linked list of walls, or as an array, *walls* : **array**[1..*NumWalls*] **of** *line*.

The skeleton code for the experiment looks like

Code Fragment 8.2. Skeleton of Ray-Tracing Experiment—Walls Only

---

```
<set up data for walls>
<give initial ray position s and direction c>
begin
    repeat
        <scan walls and find smallest positive hit time t_h>
        <get hit point as p = s + c * t_h>
        LineTo(p); {draw ray}
        s := p; {update start point for next ray}
        <get normal for the hit wall>
        <compute reflected direction as r>
        c := r; {update direction for next ray}
    until bored
end;
```

Note that as each new ray is created, its start point is always *on* some wall, the previous "first-hit" wall. If that same wall is now tested for an intersection with this new ray, it will return a hit time of 0.0. Check this out in *Ray_with _Line*( ). Owing to round-off errors, the computed hit time could have a very small positive value, and so this same wall would win the competition for the first wall struck the next time. The ray could never escape. Therefore the previous first-hit wall should not be among those tested by the new ray. It is easy to remember the previous first-hit wall and to skip over it when scanning the wall list.

Figure 8.5 shows an example for a hexagonal chamber, in which the ray began at *S* traveling vertically and made 100 reflections. The implementation of this project is discussed in the exercises.

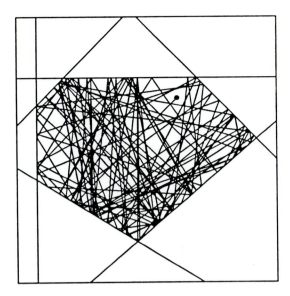

Figure 8.5.
An example ray path.

8.1.2 The Intersection of a Ray with a Circle

Now we shall make the situation more interesting by adding pillars to the chamber. Consider a circle with radius R and center $\mathbf{h}$. Does the ray $\mathbf{r}(t) = \mathbf{s} + \mathbf{c}t$ intersect this circle? If so, at what point does the hit occur?

The circle is the set of all points, $\mathbf{p} = (x, y)$, at distance R from $\mathbf{h}$, given neatly in vector form by

$$|\mathbf{p} - \mathbf{h}| = R \tag{8.8}$$

Again we substitute the ray into this equation to obtain a constraint on the hit time. Squaring both sides for convenience, we obtain

$$|\mathbf{s} + \mathbf{c}t - \mathbf{h}|^2 = R^2 \tag{8.9}$$

This may be expanded using properties of the dot product (see Equation 7.18):

$$|\mathbf{s} - \mathbf{h}|^2 + 2(\mathbf{s} - \mathbf{h}) \cdot \mathbf{c}t + |\mathbf{c}|^2 t^2 = R^2 \tag{8.10}$$

This is in the form of a quadratic equation in t:

$$At^2 + 2Bt + C = 0 \tag{8.11}$$

with[1]

$$
\begin{aligned}
A &= |\mathbf{c}|^2 \\
B &= (\mathbf{s} - \mathbf{h}) \cdot \mathbf{c} \\
C &= |\mathbf{s} - \mathbf{h}|^2 - R^2
\end{aligned}
\qquad
\begin{aligned}
&(8.12) \\
&(8.13)
\end{aligned}
$$

The solution is the familiar

$$t_h = -\frac{B}{A} \pm \frac{\sqrt{B^2 - AC}}{A} \tag{8.14}$$

[1]Note that the middle term here is $2B$ rather than B. This is a slightly less familiar form, but its solution is more compact.

Note that A is never 0 for a reasonable ray (why?). If the "discriminant" $B^2 - AC$ is negative, there are no real solutions, and so the ray must miss the circle entirely. If $B^2 - AC = 0$, there is one solution, and so the ray just grazes the circle, touching it at one point. If $B^2 - AC > 0$, there are two solutions and two points of intersection. Because the ray moves forward as t increases, the smaller solution is the true hit time: the time at which the ray first intersects and enters the circle. The larger solution is the t at which the ray would exit from the circle.

This computation is easily implemented, as follows:

Code Fragment 8.3. Find the First Intersection of a Ray with a Circle

```
procedure Ray_with_Circle(s, c, h : vector; R : real; var time : real);
{find time at which ray s + ct first hits circle}
var
    AA, BB, CC, discrim : real;
    w : vector;
begin
    AA := Dot(c, c);
    w.dx := s.dx − h.dx; w.dy := s.dy − h.dy;
    BB := Dot (w, c);
    CC := Dot(w, w) − R * R;
    if AA = 0 then Error {should never happen}
    else begin
        discrim := BB * BB − AA * CC;
        if discrim < 0.0 then time := −1.0 {ray misses}
        else time := (−BB − sqrt (discrim)) / AA {smaller solution}
    end
end;
```

Once the hit time t_h is known, the hit point is simply given by $\mathbf{p}_h = \mathbf{s} + \mathbf{c}t_h$. What is the normal to the circle at this point? According to Figure 8.6, it must be

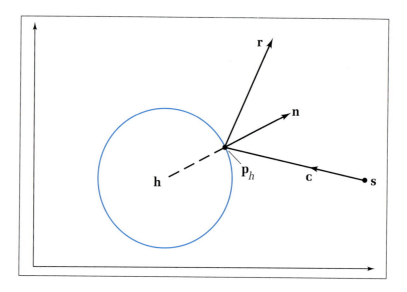

Figure 8.6.
A ray reflecting from a circle.

pointed radially out from the center of the circle to the hit point, and so it has direction $\mathbf{p}_h - \mathbf{h}$. Its length is immaterial, as the reflection calculation normalizes it anyway.

8.1.3 Building the Ray-Tracing Experiment

The skeleton of Code Fragment 8.2 needs only a minor adjustment to include intersections with pillars as well as walls. To the list of walls must be added a list of pillars. Conceptually it is simplest to have a single list that includes both walls and pillars, which is easily done by defining the type *object* based on a variant record:

Code Fragment 8.4. Data Types to Describe the Walls and Pillars

```
type
  object_ptr = ^object;
  object = record
              next : object_ptr; {for linked list}
              case kind : boolean of {true for circle}
                true : (cent : vector; radius : real);
                false : (norm : vector; D : real)
           end;
```

When *kind* is **true**, the record holds a description of a circle: the center *cent* and the radius. When *kind* is **false**, it holds data for a wall.

For each ray beginning at *s* and moving in direction *c*, the entire object list is scanned. Pointer *p* of type *object_ptr* moves through the list, and for each object the intersection time is determined. As each new positive intersection time is found, it is compared with the earliest hit time found so far, and if it is still earlier, it will become the new best candidate.

Code Fragment 8.5. Finding the First Hit Time

```
if p <> last_best then {skip object if ray is on it}
with p^ do
begin
  if kind then                          {object is a circle}
    Ray_with_circle(s, c, cent, radius, time)
  else                                  {object is a wall}
    Ray_with_Line(s, c, norm, D, time);
  if (time > 0) and (time < best_time) then {new best time}
  begin
    best_time := time; {update best yet}
    best_object := p
  end
end;
```

Here *p* is first compared with *last_best*, which points to the object on which the current ray begins its path. (It was the first-hit object for the previous ray.) There is no need to test it for the current ray.

When the first hit point is found, the ray is drawn from **s** to it. The normal to the surface and the new reflection direction are found using

Code Fragment 8.6. The Normal to the Surface of the Object

```
if kind then            {the object is a circle}
begin
    n.dx := s.dx − cent.dx; {normal to circle at hit point}
    n.dy := s.dy − cent.dy
end
else n := norm;         {the object is a wall; use inward normal}
{find new reflection direction—put it in c}
coeff := 2.0 * Dot(c, n) / Dot(n, n);
c.dx := c.dx − coeff * n.dx; {new direction}
c.dy := c.dy − coeff * n.dy;
```

Finally, *last_best* is updated to *best_object* to prepare for the next cycle. A complete implementation of this ray tracer is requested in the exercises.

8.2   Variation on a Theme: Elliptipool

It is interesting to consider other shapes for chambers. Elliptical pool tables went on sale in the United States in 1964 under the name Elliptipool (Gardner 1971, Steinhaus 1969). We can simulate Elliptipool by tracing rays bouncing inside an elliptical chamber, as suggested in Figure 8.7. The curved wall of the chamber introduces two new ingredients: finding the intersection of a ray with an ellipse and finding the direction of motion of a ray after it reflects from an elliptical wall.

Suppose the ellipse is given as in Chapter 4 by

$$\left(\frac{x}{a}\right)^2 + \left(\frac{y}{b}\right)^2 = 1 \tag{8.15}$$

having its two foci at $(\pm\sqrt{a^2 - b^2}, 0)$. As before, the intersection of the ray with this wall is found by substituting the ray's form, $\mathbf{s} + \mathbf{c}t$, into the equation, yielding a quadratic equation in t. If the ray starts out in the interior of the chamber, one of the solutions is positive and one is negative (why?). Use the positive one.

To find the direction of the reflected ray, we must compute the normal to the wall. Unlike the earlier polygonal chambers, this normal varies from point to point: we must find the normal at this point of intersection. To find the normal at (x, y), first find the slope of the curve at (x, y). Elementary calculus gives it: View y in Equation 8.15 as a function of x and take the derivative of both sides of this equation with respect to x to obtain

$$\frac{2x}{a^2} + \frac{2yy'}{b^2} = 0 \tag{8.16}$$

where $y' = dy/dx$, and so the slope y' is seen to be the ratio of $-b^2x$ to a^2y. Hence the tangent vector is $(a^2y, -b^2x)$. The normal vector is perpendicular to this tangent vector and is found by interchanging the components and negating one of them. The normal is therefore proportional to (b^2x, a^2y). Now we want the

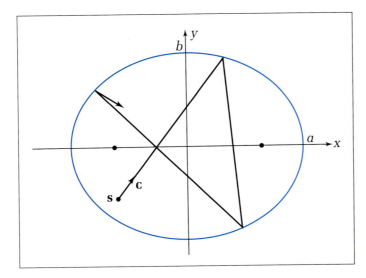

Figure 8.7.
Example simulation of Elliptipool.

inner normal, as the ray bounces off the inside wall of the ellipse. By inspection of Figure 8.7, both the x and y components of the inner normal are negative when x and y are positive, so use the form

$$\mathbf{n} = (-b^2x, -a^2y) \tag{8.17}$$

This may be used in Equation 7.25 to find the direction of the reflected ray.

A simulation of Elliptipool reveals some fascinating behavior: there are only three types of ray paths (Steinhaus 1969).

- If the ray passes over either focus, it will rebound and pass over the other focus. This is due, of course, to the well-known reflection property of ellipses. The ray will pass over alternating foci forever. After a few passes the path will become indistinguishable from the x-axis.

- If the ray does not pass between the foci on its initial path, it will never pass between them thereafter. Instead, it will move along paths that are tangent to a smaller ellipse having the same foci (Figure 8.8).

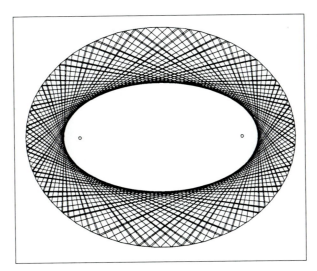

Figure 8.8.
Rays tangent to a second ellipse.

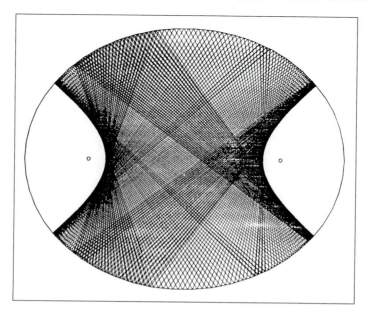

Figure 8.9.
Rays tangent to a hyperbola.

- If the ray starts off passing between the foci, it will trace out an endless path that will never get closer to the foci than a hyperbola with the same foci (Figure 8.9).

An implementation of the Elliptipool simulation makes an interesting and rewarding project and is requested in the exercises. Chambers of other shapes (perhaps superellipses?) should be experimented with as well. For each type one must find ray–wall intersections and the normal vector at any point on the wall.

Programming Exercise

8.1.   Building a 2D Ray Tracer—Walls Only. Write and exercise a program that traces a ray as it reflects off the shiny inner walls of a chamber. The chamber is a convex polygon represented by lines, as discussed in Section 8.1. Arrange to read in the line data from an external file and to have the user specify the ray's starting position and direction.

8.2.   Building a 2D Ray Tracer—Walls and Pillars. Add pillars to the chamber in Exercise 8.1, and run various reflection experiments.

8.3.   Implementing Elliptipool. Write and exercise a program that simulates Elliptipool as described in Section 8.2. The user indicates the starting position and direction of the ray in some fashion, and the ray is traced for a large number of bounces. Allow the user to specify the case of the ray

passing through a focus. (Beware that for this situation, an arithmetic round-off error may cause some unpredicted effects. How can it be counteracted?)

Have the ray change color occasionally so that its current path remains apparent as the display fills in with paths. Experiment with ellipses of different eccentricity, including circular pool tables.

Enhance the experiment by placing circles or other barriers (ellipses?) inside the elliptical pool table. Do any recognizable patterns emerge in the ray paths in this case?

8.4.   SuperElliptipool. Repeat this experiment except make the shape of the pool table a superellipse (see Chapter 4). Determine how to compute ray–wall intersections and the inner normal vector to the wall at any point on it.

CHAPTER 9

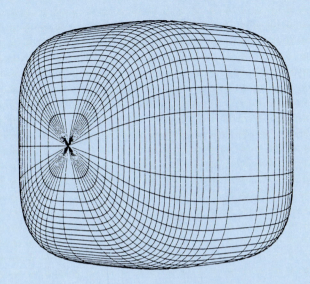

Modeling Surfaces

On the outside grows the furside, on the inside grows the skinside;
So the furside is the outside, and the skinside is the inside.

Herbert George Ponting, *The Sleeping Bag*

Goals of the Chapter

- To survey a large class of surfaces that are used in modeling and graphics.
- To develop parametric representations of surfaces and patches in terms of vectors.

9.1   Introduction

The solid objects we wish to model and draw using computer graphics are bounded by various surfaces, which form the "skin" of the object. Often an object is modeled as having a skin composed of a number of faces, each of which is a (planar) polygon and which can be characterized and drawn using vector tools developed in Chapter 7. In other cases the skin of an object consists of one or more smoothly curved surfaces. The surface of an object can be modeled as a "patchwork quilt" of pieces of different surfaces called *patches*, which fit together to form its total skin. Very complex objects can be modeled in this way.

Many useful surface shapes have simple mathematical representations, and so they are easy to analyze. The vector tools previously developed can be of great help in this, particularly when the surfaces are represented parametrically. We shall set the stage by discussing the parametric representation of the familiar plane.

Next we shall build a repertoire of simple but interesting curved surface shapes and see how the cross product can be used to characterize the normal vector to a curved surface. The normal vector must be found when one wants to shade or color a surface properly or when it is important to determine the direction in which light reflects from the surface at a particular point.

This chapter will examine surface description and modeling rather than surface drawing, in order to focus on the nature of the surfaces themselves. Techniques to draw these surfaces will be presented in Chapter 10, once we have formulated the required tools.

9.2   Parametric Representations for Surfaces

In earlier chapters parametric representations proved their worth for two-dimensional curves, and for three-dimensional curves the same is true. A 3D curve is described by $P(t) = (x(t), y(t), z(t))$. The position of each point on the curve depends on a single parameter t: To each value of t correspond three coordinate values, $x(t)$, $y(t)$, and $z(t)$. For instance, recall the example of the helix in Chapter 4, in which $P(t) = (\cos(t), \sin(t), t)$. Where is this point, at $t = 0$ or at $t = \pi$? Visualize it as the path of a particle as it moves through time or as a one-dimensional "thread" that is frozen in space.

It should be no surprise that parametric forms are also a potent tool for representing surfaces. A surface is a two-dimensional object, and so its parametric form requires two parameters. Any point on a surface is given as a function, $P(u, v)$, of two variables, u and v. The value of $P(u, v)$ is a point in 3D space having three components, (X, Y, Z), and when it clarifies things we say that the components depend on u and v: $P(u, v) = (X(u, v), Y(u, v), Z(u, v))$. Different surfaces are characterized by different functions, $X(\ )$, $Y(\ )$, and $Z(\ )$. The notion is that the surface is "at" $(X(0, 0), Y(0, 0), Z(0, 0))$ when both u and v are zero, that is, "at" $(X(1, 0), Y(1, 0), Z(1, 0))$ when $u = 1$ and $v = 0$, and so on.

It frequently is useful to describe the position of the surface at (u, v) by means of a position vector, $\mathbf{p}(u, v)$, and to write out the components of the vector as $\mathbf{p}(u, v) = (X(u, v), Y(u, v), Z(u, v))$. In terms of the standard unit vectors $\mathbf{i}$, $\mathbf{j}$, and $\mathbf{k}$ this becomes

$$\mathbf{p}(u, v) = X(u, v)\mathbf{i} + Y(u, v)\mathbf{j} + Z(u, v)\mathbf{k} \qquad (9.1)$$

We move back and forth freely between these equivalent forms.

A surface also has an **implicit equation** given by

$$f(x, y, z) = 0 \qquad (9.2)$$

for some function $f(x, y, z)$. The equation constrains the way that values of x, y, and z must interact to confine the point (x, y, z) to the surface. It is not always easy to find the function $f(x, y, z)$ when given a parametric form, nor is it always easy to go the other way and find a parametric form given $f(x, y, z)$. But given both the parametric form of Equation 9.1 and the implicit form of Equation 9.2 it is simple to determine whether they describe the same surface. Simply substitute $X(u, v)$, $Y(u, v)$, and $Z(u, v)$ for x, y, and z, respectively, in Equation 9.2 and see whether the equation is satisfied.

Example: A Sphere

A sphere of radius R centered on the origin has the familiar implicit form

$$f(x, y, z) = x^2 + y^2 + z^2 - R^2 \qquad (9.3)$$

We discuss the following sphere as a special case of a larger family of surfaces and show that one of its parametric forms is

$$\mathbf{p}(u, v) = R \cos(v) \cos(u)\mathbf{i} + R \sin(v)\mathbf{j} + R \cos(v) \sin(u)\mathbf{k} \qquad (9.4)$$

To make sure that these are consistent, substitute terms of Equation 9.4 into corresponding terms of Equation 9.3: $f(x, y, z) = (R \cos(v) \cos(u))^2 + (R \sin(v))^2 + (R \cos(v) \sin(u))^2 - R^2$. This is easily seen to be identically 0 for every value of u and v.

For some surfaces it is meaningful to define an "inside" region and an "outside" region. For surfaces like a sphere that enclose a portion of space, it is obvious which is the inside. Other surfaces like a plane clearly divide 3D space into two regions, but one must refer to the context of the application to tell which half-space is the inside and which the outside. The function $f(x, y, z)$ of the implicit form is sometimes called the **inside–outside** function for the surface, because it is meaningful to say that a point (x, y, z) is

$$\text{inside the surface if } f(x, y, z) < 0$$
$$\text{on the surface if } f(x, y, z) = 0 \qquad (9.5)$$
$$\text{outside the surface if } f(x, y, z) > 0$$

For the sphere above this clearly makes sense. For convenience, therefore, we shall hereafter call $f(x, y, z)$ the inside–outside function for each surface of interest, but in an application we must check to see whether this interpretation is meaningful. When it is, we have available a quick and simple test for the disposition of a given point, (x', y', z'), relative to the surface: Just evaluate $f(x',$

y', z') and test whether it is positive, negative, or zero. This is seen in Chapter 17 to be useful in hidden line and hidden surface removal algorithms.

9.3   The Parametric Form for a Plane

The simplest surface is a plane. We studied it earlier based on the point normal form $(n_x, n_y, n_z) \cdot (x, y, z) = D$. This is an implicit equation, reporting a condition that any point (x, y, z) must obey in order to lie on the plane. The point normal equation is easily rearranged to an explicit form describing, for instance, how y varies as a function of x and z: $y(x, z) = (D - n_x x + n_z z)/n_y$. One of the issues with explicit forms like this is the special cases with which one must deal separately. Here, for instance, the explicit form will fail if $n_y = 0$. A parametric form that doesn't require special cases is more desirable, particularly when it facilitates rendering pictures of the plane. We shall now develop such a form.

A plane can be specified by giving one of its points, the position vector $\mathbf{c}$, along with two (noncollinear) directions, $\mathbf{a}$ and $\mathbf{b}$, as shown in Figure 9.1. This information clearly suffices, as the normal is given by $\mathbf{a} \times \mathbf{b}$, so the point normal form follows immediately. (The context of an application would be needed to tell which of the two normal directions is the outward normal.) To construct a parametric form for this plane, note that any point in the plane can be represented by a vector sum: $\mathbf{c}$ plus some amount of $\mathbf{a}$ plus some amount of $\mathbf{b}$. Use parameters u and v to specify the "amounts" u and v of $\mathbf{a}$ and $\mathbf{b}$, respectively, so we have $\mathbf{c} + u\mathbf{a} + v\mathbf{b}$. This provides the desired parametric form

$$\mathbf{p}(u, v) = \mathbf{c} + \mathbf{a}u + \mathbf{b}v \qquad (9.6)$$

Given any values of u and v we can identify the corresponding point on the plane. For example, the position "at" $u = v = 0$ is $\mathbf{c}$ itself, and that at $u = 1$ and $v = -2$ is $\mathbf{p}(1, -2) = \mathbf{c} + \mathbf{a} - 2\mathbf{b}$.

Figure 9.1.
Defining a plane parametrically.

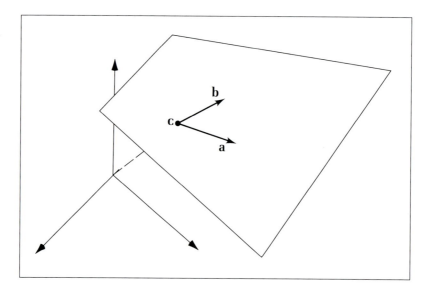

Note that if one of the parameters is fixed, say $u = 3$, the position vector will be a function of one variable and will represent a straight line: $\mathbf{p}(3, v) = (\mathbf{c} + 3\mathbf{a}) + \mathbf{b}v$. This is the same form as the ray in Equation 7.5, where the parameter was called t instead of v.

The parametric form of Equation 9.6 can be rearranged into the "component" form of Equation 9.1 by collecting terms

$$\mathbf{p}(u, v) = (c_x + a_x u + b_x v)\mathbf{i} + (c_y + a_y u + b_y v)\mathbf{j} + (c_z + a_z u + b_z v)\mathbf{k} \qquad (9.7)$$

so that in Equation 9.1 the function $X(u, v) = c_x + a_x u + b_x v$, and the forms for $Y(u, v)$ and $Z(u, v)$ follow similarly. Each of these functions is linear in both u and v. The following examples show how to convert the specifications of a plane from one form to another.

Example

Consider the plane passing through $(1, 2, 4)$ so that both $\mathbf{a} = (2, 1, -1)$ and $\mathbf{b} = (4, 3, 3)$ are perpendicular to its normal. Find both versions of the parametric form for this plane, as well as its point normal form.

Solution:

The parametric form of Equation 9.6 can be written directly: $\mathbf{p}(u, v) = (1, 2, 4) + (2, 1, -1)u + (4, 3, 3)v$. Rearrange this to the other version: $\mathbf{p}(u, v) = (1 + 2u + 4v)\mathbf{i} + (2 + u + 3v)\mathbf{j} + (4 - u + 3v)\mathbf{k}$. Find the normal as $\mathbf{n} = \mathbf{a} \times \mathbf{b} = (6, -10, 2)$ and D as $D = \mathbf{n} \cdot \mathbf{c} = -6$, so that the point normal form is $6x - 10y + 2z = -6$.

Example

Find a parametric form for the plane $2x - y + 3z = 8$.

Solution:

By inspection the normal is $(2, -1, 3)$. There are many parametrisations; we need only find one. For $\mathbf{c}$, choose any point that satisfies the equation; $\mathbf{c} = (4, 0, 0)$ will do. Find two (noncollinear) vectors, each having a dot product of 0 with $(2, -1, 3)$; $\mathbf{a} = (1, 5, 1)$ and $\mathbf{b} = (0, 3, 1)$ are seen to work. Thus the plane has parametric form $\mathbf{p}(u, v) = (4, 0, 0) + (1, 5, 1)u + (0, 3, 1)v$.

Drill Exercises

9.1. Is This Really a Plane? Show that every point having the form of Equation 9.6 satisfies the point normal form $\mathbf{n} \cdot \mathbf{p}(u, v) = D$. Use $\mathbf{n} = \mathbf{a} \times \mathbf{b}$ for $\mathbf{n}$ and $\mathbf{n} \cdot \mathbf{c}$ for D. The point normal form shows that all points on a plane must share the same value for a certain triple scalar product. Give a geometric interpretation of this.

9.2. Alter the Parametric Form. For the same plane as in the preceding second example find another parametric form with $\mathbf{c}$ the point on the plane closest to the origin and $\mathbf{a}$ and $\mathbf{b}$ the mutually perpendicular unit vectors.

9.3. Find the Plane. Find a parametric form for the plane coincident with the y, z-plane.

9.3.1 Planar Patches

In the parametric form of Equation 9.6 the values for u and v can range from $-\infty$ to ∞; thus the plane can extend forever. In some situations we want to deal with only a "piece" of a plane, such as a parallelogram lying in it. Such a piece is called a **planar patch**, a term that invites us to imagine the plane as a quilt of many patches joined together. Much of the practice of modeling solids is piecing together patches of various shapes to form the skin of an object.

A planar patch is formed by restricting the range of allowable u and v values in Equation 9.6. For instance, one often restricts u and v to lie only between 0 and 1. The patch is positioned and oriented in space by appropriate choices of **a**, **b**, and **c**. Figure 9.2a shows the available range of u and v as a square in **parameter space**, and Figure 9.2b shows the patch in **object space**, which results from this restriction. To each point in parameter space there corresponds one 3D point in the patch given by Equation 9.6. The patch is a parallelogram whose corners correspond to the four corners of parameter space and are situated at

u	v	Corner
0	0	**c**
0	1	**c** + **b**
1	0	**c** + **a**
1	1	**c** + **a** + **b**

The vectors **a** and **b** determine both the size and the orientation of the patch. If **a** and **b** are perpendicular, the grid will become rectangular, and if in addition both **a** and **b** have unit length, the grid will become square. Changing **c** just slides the patch parallel to itself without changing its shape.

Figure 9.2.

Mapping between two spaces to define a planar patch.

Example

Let **c** = (1, 3, 2), **a** = (1, 1, 0), and **b** = (1, 4, 2). Find the corners of the planar patch.

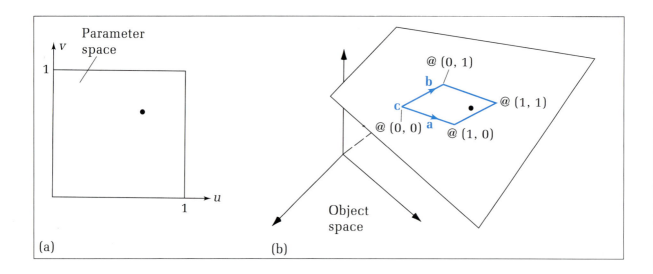

(a)   (b)

Solution:
From the preceding table we obtain the four corners: $\mathbf{p}(0, 0) = (1, 3, 2)$, $\mathbf{p}(0, 1) = (2, 7, 4)$, $\mathbf{p}(1, 0) = (2, 4, 2)$, and $\mathbf{p}(1, 1) = (3, 8, 4)$. These points should be coplanar. Are they? Yes, if the triple scalar product of $\mathbf{a}$, $\mathbf{b}$, and $\mathbf{a} + \mathbf{b}$ is zero (why?). But $(\mathbf{a} + \mathbf{b}) \cdot \mathbf{a} \times \mathbf{b}$ is clearly zero (why?), and so the four corners are indeed coplanar.

Example: Characterize a Patch
Find the $\mathbf{a}$, $\mathbf{b}$, and $\mathbf{c}$ vectors that create a square patch of length 4 on a side centered at the origin and parallel to the x, z-plane.

Solution:
The corners of the patch are at $(2, 0, 2)$, $(2, 0, -2)$, $(-2, 0, 2)$, and $(-2, 0, -2)$. Choose any corner, say $(2, 0, -2)$, for $\mathbf{c}$. Then $\mathbf{a}$ and $\mathbf{b}$ each have length 4 and are parallel to either the x- or the z-axis. Choose $\mathbf{a} = (-4, 0, 0)$ and $\mathbf{b} = (0, 0, 4)$.

Drill Exercise

9.4. Find a Patch. Find some vectors, $\mathbf{c}$, $\mathbf{a}$, and $\mathbf{b}$, that create a patch having the four corners $(-4, 2, 1)$, $(1, 7, 4)$, $(-2, -2, 2)$, and $(3, 3, 5)$.

9.4 Introduction to Curved Surfaces

Flat planes and patches are simple and form a good starting point, and it is surprisingly easy to extend our modeling capabilities to a much larger class of curved surfaces.

Curved surfaces can have complex shapes, particularly when many "patches" with different representations are pieced together. Here, however, we shall examine families of surfaces that have a simple implicit form or parametric form. In Chapter 14 we shall extend these notions to more complicated surfaces with far less simple parametric forms based on splines.

Five important classes of surfaces are

1. *Ruled surfaces.* Surfaces generated by "sweeping" a straight line through space in some fashion.

2. *Surfaces of revolution.* Surfaces generated by "sweeping" a curved line about an axis.

3. *Quadric surfaces.* Surfaces defined by quadratic equations in x, y, and z.

4. *Superquadric surfaces.* An extension of quadric surfaces modeled on the generalization used in Chapter 4 to extend the ellipse to the superellipse.

5. *Surfaces defined by mathematical functions.*

These are not disjoint families. For instance, some quadric surfaces are also surfaces of revolution, and some surfaces of revolution are also ruled. But it is conceptually illuminating to categorize a vast range of surface shapes in this way. For each surface we give both its implicit form (based on its inside–outside function) and its parametric form. The parametric form is a natural tool for drawing a surface, as we shall see later. We also present formulas for the normal vector at each point of a surface. Being able to evaluate the normal direction is essential to shading surfaces realistically and to determining how light reflects off the surface.

9.5   Ruled Surfaces

The family of ruled surfaces is simple to describe yet provides a wide range of useful and interesting shapes. They are swept out by moving a straight line along a particular trajectory and are composed of a collection of straight lines in the following sense:

Definition

A surface is **ruled** if through every one of its points passes at least one line that lies entirely on the surface.

Because ruled surfaces are based on a family of lines, it is not surprising to find buried in them something akin to the familiar parametric form, $\mathbf{p}(v) = (1 - v)\mathbf{p}_0 + v\mathbf{p}_1$, where $\mathbf{p}_0$ and $\mathbf{p}_1$ are vectors. But for ruled surfaces the vectors $\mathbf{p}_0$ and $\mathbf{p}_1$ become functions of another parameter u: $\mathbf{p}_0$ becomes $\mathbf{p}_0(u)$, and similarly $\mathbf{p}_1$ becomes $\mathbf{p}_1(u)$. Thus ruled surfaces have the parametric form

$$\mathbf{p}(u, v) = (1 - v)\mathbf{p}_0(u) + v\mathbf{p}_1(u) \qquad (9.8)$$

The functions $\mathbf{p}_0(u)$ and $\mathbf{p}_1(u)$ define curves lying in 3D space. Each is described by three component functions, as in $\mathbf{p}_0(u) = (x_0(u), y_0(u), z_0(u))$. Both $\mathbf{p}_0(u)$ and $\mathbf{p}_1(u)$ are defined on the same interval in u, say from u_{start} to u_{end}. The ruled surface consists of one straight line joining each pair of corresponding points, $\mathbf{p}_0(u')$ and $\mathbf{p}_1(u')$, for each u' in (u_{start}, u_{end}), as indicated in Figure 9.3. At $v = 0$ the surface is "at" $\mathbf{p}_0(u')$, and at $v = 1$ it is at $\mathbf{p}_1(u')$. The straight line at $u = u'$ is often called the **ruling at** u'.

For a particular fixed value, v', of v the contour of constant $v = v'$, or **v-contour at** v' is some blend of the two curves $\mathbf{p}_0(u)$ and $\mathbf{p}_1(u)$. It is a linear combination of them, with the first weighted by $(1 - v')$ and the second by v'. When v' is close to 0, the shape of the v-contour is mainly determined by $\mathbf{p}_0(u)$, and when v' is close to 1, the curve $\mathbf{p}_1(u)$ has the most influence. If v lies between 0 and 1, we effectively have an "in-between" curve, just as we had in-between points in Chapter 7.

If v is restricted to lie between 0 and 1, only the line segment between corresponding points on the curves will be part of the surface. On the other hand, if v is not restricted, each line will continue forever in both directions, and the surface will resemble an unbounded curved "sheet." When v is less than 0 or larger than 1, v-contours are based on an extrapolation from one defin-

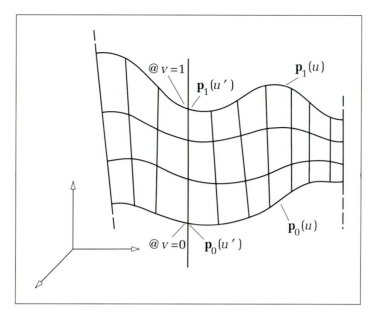

Figure 9.3.
A ruled surface as a family of
straight lines.

ing curve to the other. A curved "ruled patch" is formed by restricting the range
of both u and v, say between 0 and 1.

Some examples of ruled surfaces will show their nature as well as their
versatility. We discuss three important ruled surfaces, the cylinder, cone, and
bilinear patch.

9.5.1 Cylinders

Figure 9.4 shows a cylinder. A **cylinder** results when a line, L, called the **generator**, is swept along a curve, $p_0(u)$, called the **directrix** that lies in some plane.
As L is swept, it is always kept parallel to itself.

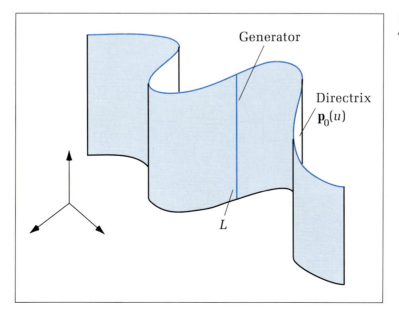

Figure 9.4.
A cylinder.

To see how to incorporate the requirement that line L remain parallel to itself as it sweeps, rearrange the terms in Equation 9.8 to get an alternative parametric form for a ruled surface:

$$\mathbf{p}(u, v) = \mathbf{p}_0(u) + v\mathbf{d}(u) \qquad (9.9)$$

where we have simply set $\mathbf{d}(u) = \mathbf{p}_1(u) - \mathbf{p}_0(u)$. This is like the point direction form for a line: At each value u' of u the line emanates from $\mathbf{p}_0(u')$ in the direction $\mathbf{d}(u')$. Now to keep L parallel to itself, simply make $\mathbf{d}$ a constant, so that the form of a cylinder is

$$\mathbf{p}(u, v) = \mathbf{p}_0(u) + v\mathbf{d} \qquad (9.10)$$

To be a true cylinder, the directrix $\mathbf{p}_0(u)$ is confined to lie in a plane. The direction $\mathbf{d}$ need not be perpendicular to this plane, but if it is, the surface is called a **right cylinder**.

A familiar example of a cylinder is a **circular cylinder**, for which the directrix is a circle. For instance, if the circle lies in the x, y-plane, we have $\mathbf{p}_0(u) = (\cos(u), \sin(u), 0)$.

Example: A Circular Cylinder

Consider the cylinder shown in Figure 9.5a, with a circular directrix lying in the x, y-plane: $(\cos(u), \sin(u), 0)$. Let us suppose the generator is parallel to the z-axis: $\mathbf{d} = (0, 0, 1)$. From Equation 9.10 the parametric form is then

$$\mathbf{p}(u, v) = (\cos(u), \sin(u), 0) + v(0, 0, 1) \qquad (9.11)$$
$$= \cos(u)\mathbf{i} + \sin(u)\mathbf{j} + v\mathbf{k}$$

where u varies from 0 to 2π and v can be any real value. Note that v affects only the $\mathbf{k}$ component and that the circular cross section is easily recognized in $\cos(u)\mathbf{i} + \sin(u)\,\mathbf{j}$. For instance, at $(u, v) = (0, 0)$ the surface lies at $(1, 0, 0)$ and as u increases a circle in the x, y-plane is swept out. As v changes, the surface point moves back and forth along z accordingly. If we limit the range of v, the cylinder will be of finite length.

It is not hard to find the inside–outside function, $f(x, y, z)$, for this cylinder. We need an expression in x, y, and z that evaluates to zero when $\cos(u)$ is substituted for x, $\sin(u)$ for z, and v for y. It must yield 0 for any u and v. For this

Figure 9.5.
Two circular cylinders.

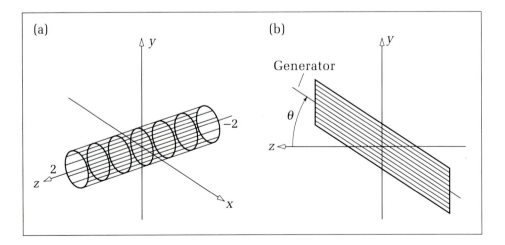

surface the choice $f(x, y, z) = x^2 + y^2 - 1$ works. No term in z appears, as z is completely unconstrained for this cylinder. Figure 9.5a shows the cylinder using ten rulings between $v = -2$ and 2, and seven curves of constant v.

As a generalization the axis of the cylinder can be "tilted" by some angle, θ, as shown in Figure 9.5b, so that the generator has direction $\mathbf{d} = (0, \sin(\theta), \cos(\theta))$. The directrix has not been tilted here: It is still $(\cos(u), \sin(u), 0)$. The cylinder has the parametric form

$$\mathbf{p}(u, v) = \cos(u)\mathbf{i} + (\sin(u) + v\sin(\theta))\mathbf{j} + v\cos(\theta)\mathbf{k} \qquad (9.12)$$

For $\theta = 0$ this agrees with that of the preceding vertical cylinder. What is it for $\theta = \pi/2$? Now v affects both the $\mathbf{i}$ and $\mathbf{k}$ components, and so as v varies, the surface point moves parallel to the tilted axis. If we hold v constant at some v_0 we will obtain a curve that represents the vertical **cross section**: $(\cos(u), \sin(u) + v_0\sin(\theta), v_0\cos(\theta))$. What is the shape of this cross section?

9.5.2 Cones

Cones form another class of ruled surface. A **cone** is generated by a line that moves along a given plane curve, but the lines are constrained to pass through a fixed point (the vertex of the cone). We use Equation 9.8 and force $\mathbf{p}_0(u)$ to be a constant:

$$\mathbf{p}(u, v) = (1 - v)\mathbf{p}_0 + v\mathbf{p}_1(u) \qquad (9.13)$$

In this case all lines pass through $\mathbf{p}_0$ at $v = 0$. The plane curve through which all lines pass is $\mathbf{p}_1(u)$, and they pass through it at $v = 1$, as suggested in Figure 9.6. Just as in the case of the cylinder, certain special cases are familiar. A **circular cone** results when $\mathbf{p}_1(u)$ is a circle, and a **right circular cone** results when the circle lies in a plane that is perpendicular to the line joining the circle's center to $\mathbf{p}_0$.

Drill Exercises

9.5.   Tilted Directrix. Alter the preceding cylinder that has a tilted axis so that the directrix is also tilted by θ. Then the cylinder becomes a right circular cylinder. What is the parametric form for this object? Sketch it. What shape does a horizontal cross section have now? What is its inside–outside function?

9.6.   Ribbon Candy. Find the parametric form and sketch the cylinder whose generator is parallel to the z-axis and whose directrix is a sinusoid $y = 2\sin(2\pi x/5)$.

9.7.   Double Helix. As discussed earlier, a helix that winds about the z-axis has the form $\mathbf{p}(u) = (\cos(u), \sin(u), u)$. Find expressions for two helices, $\mathbf{p}_0(u)$ and $\mathbf{p}_1(u)$, both of which wind around the y-axis yet are $180°$ out of phase so that they wind around each other. If these curves are used to define a ruled surface, it will look like a length of twisted ribbon. Sketch it by hand.

9.8.   The Right Circular Cone. Consider a right circular cone whose vertex is at the origin, whose axis coincides with the y-axis, and whose horizontal cross sections are circles, with the radius equal to the height of the section above the origin. Show that the parametric form for this cone is $\mathbf{p}(u, v) = v(\cos(u), 1, \sin(u))$. Also show that the inside–outside function is $f(x, y, z) = x^2 + z^2 - y^2$.

9.9.   A Pyramid. What shape should $\mathbf{p}_1(u)$ have to create a ruled surface that is a pyramid with a square base? Give specific expressions for the curve and the point $\mathbf{p}_0$ so that the square base of the pyramid lies in the x, z-plane, centered at the origin, with sides of length 2. The pyramid should have height 1.5.

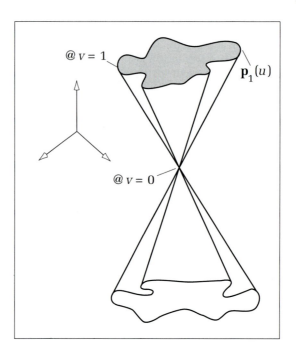

Figure 9.6.
A cone.

9.5.3 Bilinear Patches

In Section 9.3 we constructed planar patches by working with the form for a plane, $\mathbf{p}(u, v) = \mathbf{c} + \mathbf{a}u + \mathbf{b}v$, and restricting u and v to lie between 0 and 1. This produced a planar patch with four edges and four corners. Because of the construction the four corners automatically lie in the same plane.

But what if we are given four arbitrary points, $\mathbf{p}_{00}$, $\mathbf{p}_{01}$, $\mathbf{p}_{10}$, and $\mathbf{p}_{11}$, in space and asked to fashion a patch with these four corners? If the points are not coplanar, what shape will the patch have?

We need to define some surface shape, $\mathbf{p}(u, v)$, that passes through the four given points. The simplest approach is to make the surface ruled. Define its $v = 0$ edge, $\mathbf{p}_0(u)$, as the straight line through $\mathbf{p}_{00}$ and $\mathbf{p}_{10}$, and its $v = 1$ edge, $\mathbf{p}_1(u)$, as the straight line through $\mathbf{p}_{01}$ and $\mathbf{p}_{11}$. The patch then has the form

$$\mathbf{p}(u, v) = (1 - v)((1 - u)\mathbf{p}_{00} + u\mathbf{p}_{10}) + v((1 - u)\mathbf{p}_{01} + u\mathbf{p}_{11}) \qquad (9.14)$$

Figure 9.7.
A bilinear patch (a stereo view).

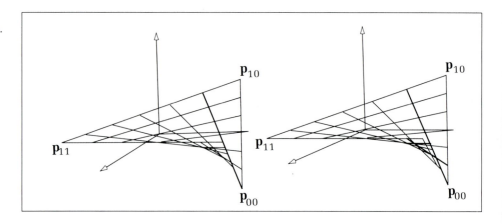

Because this expression is linear in both u and v, it is often called a **bilinear patch**. By direct calculation the surface $\mathbf{p}(u, v)$ passes through the four given points at its corners, when (u, v) is $(0, 0)$, $(1, 0)$, $(0, 1)$, and $(1, 1)$. If the four points are not coplanar, the patch must "twist" in space as it progresses from the $v = 0$ edge to the $v = 1$ edge. An example is shown in Figure 9.7. The $v = 0$ edge is vertical, defined by the points $(0, 2, 3)$ and $(0, -2, 3)$, and the $v = 1$ edge is horizontal, defined by $(5, 0, 4)$ and $(5, 0, -4)$. Therefore the patch makes a 90° twist.

9.6 The Normal Vector to a Surface

A plane, $\mathbf{n} \cdot \mathbf{p} = d$, has the fundamental property that its normal vector $\mathbf{n}$ is the same at every point on the plane. But what about curved surfaces? Can we define a normal direction to the surface at a point, and if so, can we calculate it?

The normal direction to a surface can be defined at a point, $\mathbf{p}(u_0, v_0)$, on the surface by considering a very small region of the surface around (u_0, v_0). If the region is small enough and the surface varies "smoothly" in the vicinity, the region will be essentially flat. Thus it behaves locally like a tiny planar patch and has a well-defined normal direction. Figure 9.8 shows a surface patch with the normal vector drawn at various points. The direction of the normal vector is seen to be different at different points on the surface. We give the name $\mathbf{n}(u, v)$ to the normal at (u, v).

How is it calculated? We present two formulas that yield the normal vector. One is suitable when the surface is given parametrically, the other for a surface given implicitly.

The Normal Vector for a Surface Given Parametrically

Not surprisingly, $\mathbf{n}(u_0, v_0)$ takes the form of a cross product between two vectors that lie in the tiny planar patch near (u_0, v_0), as it is then guaranteed to be perpendicular to them both. The two vectors in the plane (indicated as $\mathbf{t}_u$ and $\mathbf{t}_v$ in the figure) are certain **tangent** vectors. Calculus texts show that they are sim-

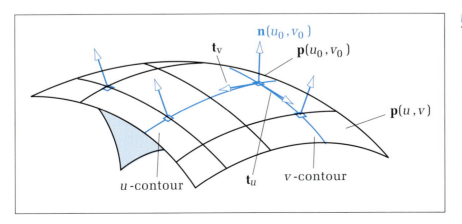

Figure 9.8.
The normal vector to a surface.

ply related to partial derivatives of $\mathbf{p}(u, v)$ evaluated at the point in question (Thomas 1953). An expression for the normal vector is then

$$\mathbf{n}(u_0, v_0) = \left(\frac{\partial \mathbf{p}}{\partial u} \times \frac{\partial \mathbf{p}}{\partial v} \right)\Bigg|_{u=u_0, v=v_0} \tag{9.15}$$

where the vertical bar | indicates that the derivatives are evaluated at $u = u_0$, $v = v_0$. Now $\mathbf{n}(u_0, v_0)$ so formed is not automatically a unit length vector, but it can be normalized to unit magnitude in the usual fashion if desired. The partial derivatives of $\mathbf{p}(u, v)$ exist if the surface is "smooth enough." The surfaces of interest here have the necessary smoothness and have simple enough mathematical expressions so that finding the required derivatives is not difficult. Because $\mathbf{p}(u, v) = X(u, v)\mathbf{i} + Y(u, v)\mathbf{j} + Z(u, v)\mathbf{k}$, the derivative of a vector is just the vector of the individual derivatives $(\partial X(u, v)/\partial u, \partial Y(u, v)/\partial u, \partial Z(u, v)/\partial u)$.

For example, consider the plane given parametrically by $\mathbf{p}(u, v) = \mathbf{c} + \mathbf{a}u + \mathbf{b}v$. The partial derivative of this with respect to u is just $\mathbf{a}$, and that with respect to v is $\mathbf{b}$. Thus according to Equation 9.15, $\mathbf{n}(u, v) = \mathbf{a} \times \mathbf{b}$, which is recognized to be the correct result.

The Normal Vector for a Surface Given Implicitly

An alternative expression is used if the surface is given by an implicit form, $f(x, y, z) = 0$ (Faux and Pratt 1979). The normal direction at the surface point, (x, y, z), is found using the **gradient**, ∇f, of the inside–outside function f:

$$\mathbf{n} = \nabla f = \frac{\partial f}{\partial x}\mathbf{i} + \frac{\partial f}{\partial y}\mathbf{j} + \frac{\partial f}{\partial z}\mathbf{k} \tag{9.16}$$

where each partial derivative is evaluated at the desired point, (x, y, z). This version of $\mathbf{n}(u_0, v_0)$ has the same direction as that in Equation 9.15, but not necessarily the same length. Again, it can be normalized if desired. For example, the plane $\mathbf{n} \cdot \mathbf{p} = d$ has the inside–outside function $f(x, y, z) = n_x x + n_y y + n_z z - d$ which has the gradient $\nabla f = (n_x, n_y, n_z)$, as we expect. Note that this form based on the gradient gives the normal vector as a function of x, y, and z, rather than of u and v.

Sometimes for a surface we know both the inside–outside function, $f(x, y, z)$, and the parametric form, $\mathbf{p}(u, v) = X(u, v)\mathbf{i} + Y(u, v)\mathbf{j} + Z(u, v)\mathbf{k}$, In such cases it is frequently simplest to find the parametric form, $\mathbf{n}(u, v)$, of the normal at (u, v) by a two-step method: (1) Use Equation 9.16 to get the normal at (x, y, z) in terms of x, y, and z, and then (2) substitute the known functions $X(u, v)$ for x, $Y(u, v)$ for y, and $Z(u, v)$ for z. The examples below illustrate this method.

Example: The Circular Cylinder

Consider the circular cylinder given by Equation 9.11: $\mathbf{p}(u, v) = \cos(u)\mathbf{i} + \sin(u)\mathbf{j} + v\mathbf{k}$. The inside–outside function for this cylinder was shown to be $f(x, y, z) = x^2 + y^2 - 1$. We find the normal using two routes:

- *The gradient.* The gradient of $f(x, y, z)$ is $(2x, 2y, 0)$. Substitute $X(u, v) = \cos(u)$ for x and $Y(u, v) = \sin(u)$ for y to get $\mathbf{n}(u, v) = (2\cos(u), 2\sin(u), 0)$. The 2 may be factored out if desired, as it does not affect the direction of the normal.
- *The cross-product.* The partial derivatives of $\mathbf{p}(u, v)$ are easily found to be

$$\frac{\partial p}{\partial u} = -\sin(u)\mathbf{i} + \cos(u)\mathbf{j}$$

$$\frac{\partial p}{\partial v} = \mathbf{k} \tag{9.17}$$

and the cross product has value

$$\mathbf{n}(u, v) = \cos(u)\mathbf{i} + \sin(u)\mathbf{j} \tag{9.18}$$

This agrees with the first result.

Note that for this cylinder the normal is exactly the directrix vector. Conse-quently, it always points outward radially from the axis of the cylinder. A radial direction is expected, as the normal to a circle points radially. The normal does not change with v, and so it is constant along each ruling of this surface. If the range in v is limited to, say $(-2, 2)$, we understand that there are no surface points beyond this range, and so it is not meaningful to evaluate the normal there. Also, there are no "caps" on this cylinder at its ends: It is open because we have defined only the cylindrical walls.

A surface has no inherent inward versus outward normal, but if we are considering this cylinder to be a geometric object with an inside enclosed by the surface, we tend to say that the normal is an **outward** normal.

Example: The Right Circular Cone

Consider the right circular cone of Exercise 9.8. We first find the normal using partial derivatives of the parametric form:

$$\mathbf{n}(u, v) = v(-\sin(u), 0, \cos(u)) \times (\cos(u), 1, \sin(u)) \tag{9.19}$$
$$= v(-\cos(u)\mathbf{i} + \mathbf{j} - \sin(u)\mathbf{k})$$

The direction of the normal does not vary with v, and its length is proportional to v. This is generally true—see the following exercises. The direction of the normal for this cone is determined by the vector $(-\cos(u), 1, -\sin(u))$ which can be seen to be pointed radially inward and up at an angle of 45 degrees. The outward normal would point radially outward and down at 45 degrees.

Now we find the normal using the gradient of the inside–outside function. According to Exercise 9.8, this function is $x^2 + z^2 - y^2$, which has gradient $(2x, -2y, 2z)$. This is seen to be consistent with Equation 9.19 by substituting the parametric forms to obtain $-2(-v\cos(u), v, -v\sin(u))$.

Drill Exercises

9.10.   The Normal to a Bilinear Patch. For the bilinear patch of Equation 9.14, the normal is the cross product of the two partial derivatives, $\dfrac{\partial p(u, v)}{\partial u}$ and $\dfrac{\partial p(u, v)}{\partial v}$, where, for instance,

$$\frac{\partial p(u, v)}{\partial u} = (1 - v)(\mathbf{p}_{10} - \mathbf{p}_{00}) + v(\mathbf{p}_{11} - \mathbf{p}_{01}) \tag{9.20}$$

If all four points lie in the same plane, this normal vector should not depend on u and v. Show that this is so.

9.11.   The Tilted Cylinder. Find the normal vector to the tilted cylinder of Equation 9.12 and also to the right cylinder with the tilted axis discussed in Exercise 9.5. Should the normal be perpendicular to all rulings of the cylinder? Is it?

9.12.   Normals for Cylinders. Show that for all cylinders given by Equation 9.10 the normal does not depend on parameter v. Give a geometric justification for this. Also show that the normal is always perpendicular to the generator, and give a geometric justification.

9.13. Normals to Cones. Show that the direction of the normal vector to the general cone of Equation 9.13 is independent of v, with a magnitude that is proportional to v.

9.14. The Normal to a Patch. Find the normal vector at each u, v to the patch shown in Figure 9.7.

9.7   Surfaces of Revolution

Another large and interesting family of surfaces are those modeled as a **rotational sweep** of a given plane curve, C, around an axis. Figure 9.9 shows an example[1] in which C lies in the x, z-plane and the rotation is about the z-axis. C is often called the *profile* of the surface and is given parametrically by $\mathbf{c}(v) = (x(v), z(v))$ as v varies over some range $(v_{\text{start}}, v_{\text{end}})$.

For the surface of revolution, each point $(x(v), z(v))$ of the profile is swept around the axis under control of the u parameter, with u specifying the angle that each point has been rotated about the axis. The different positions of the curve C around the axis are called **meridians**. When the point $(x(v), 0, z(v))$ is rotated by u radians, it becomes $(x(v) \cos(u), x(v) \sin(u), z(v))$. Sweeping it completely about the axis generates a full circle, and so contours of constant v are circles, called **parallels** of the surface. The meridian "at" v has radius $x(v)$ and lies at height $z(v)$ above the x, y-plane. Thus the general point on the surface has position vector

$$\mathbf{p}(u, v) = (x(v) \cos(u), x(v) \sin(u), z(v)) \tag{9.21}$$

For example, let the curve $\mathbf{c}(v)$ be a straight line parallel to the z-axis and lying a unit distance from it, so that $\mathbf{c}(v) = (1, v)$. When this line is swept around the z-axis, a cylinder is generated. Equation 9.21 dictates that the parametric form is $(\cos(u), \sin(u), v)$. This agrees with Equation 9.11.

Figure 9.9.
A surface of revolution.

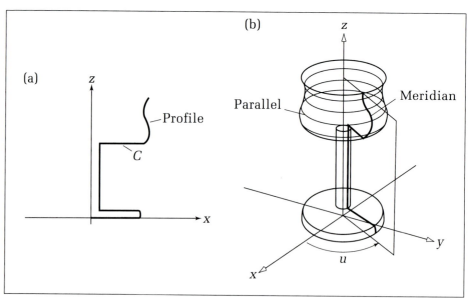

[1]Following modeling convention, this object is shown in a right-handed coordinate system with the z-axis pointing upward.

Drill Exercise

9.15. Rotation About Other Axes. Give the parametric form for a surface of revolution in which a curve, $\mathbf{c}(v) =$ $(x(v), z(v))$, lying in the x, y-plane is rotated about the y-axis. Repeat for a curve rotated about the x-axis.

A surface of revolution modeled by Equation 9.21 can be drawn by drawing appropriate sets of u-contours and v-contours. A list $u_1, u_2, \ldots, u_n$ of u-values is chosen, and for each value the u_i-contour $(x(v) \cos(u_i), x(v) \sin(u_i), z(v))$—a rotated profile—is drawn. Then a similar list, $v_1, \ldots, v_m$, of v-values is selected, and for each v_i the v_i-contour—a circle—is drawn. Routines to do this will be discussed in Chapter 10.

Example: The Sphere

The sphere is a familiar surface of revolution. The profile curve, $\mathbf{c}(v)$, is a semi-circle given by $(R \cos(v), R \sin(v))$ as v varies from $-\pi/2$ to $\pi/2$, as shown in Figure 9.10a. Therefore the sphere (Figure 9.10b) has representation

$$\mathbf{p}(u, v) = (R \cos(v) \cos(u), R \cos(v) \sin(u), R \sin(v)) \tag{9.22}$$

for $-\pi/2 \leq v \leq \pi/2$ and $0 \leq u \leq 2\pi$.

Because the globe is so familiar, one often equates u with longitude and speaks of the meridian at a certain longitude. Similarly, v is associated with latitude: $v = 0$ at the equator and $v = \pi/2$ at the North Pole.

The normal to the sphere, $\mathbf{p}(u, v)$, is found by direct calculation using Equation 9.15. It is the cross product of $(-R \cos(v) \sin(u), R \cos(v) \cos(u), 0)$ with $(-R \sin(v) \cos(u), -R \sin(v) \sin(u), R \cos(v))$, yielding

$$\mathbf{n}(u, v) = -R \cos(v) \mathbf{p}(u, v) \tag{9.23}$$

This normal is proportional to $\mathbf{p}(u, v)$ itself: as we expect, it is directed radially out from the center. Notice that with this parametrization the scaling factor—$R \cos(v)$—causes the normal to vanish at the North and South poles, whereas we know geometrically that the true normal should have a constant length everywhere. An algorithm that needs the normal direction at each (u, v) would use Equation 9.23 without the scaling factor.

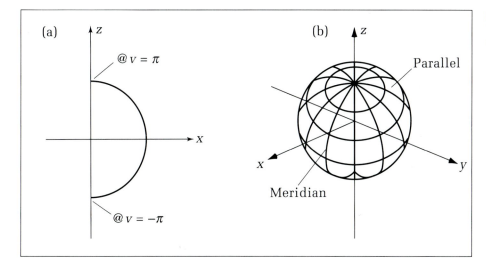

(a) @ $v = \pi$ ... @ $v = -\pi$

(b) Parallel ... Meridian

Figure 9.10.
The sphere as a surface of revolution.

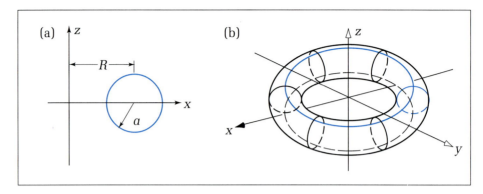

Figure 9.11.

As before, the normal can be found from the gradient of the inside–outside function for the sphere. We already saw that this function is $x^2 + y^2 + z^2 - R^2$. It has gradient $2(x, y, z)$ which is also directed radially out from the center.

Example: The Torus

Another familiar shape is the doughnutlike **torus**, which is generated by sweeping a displaced circle about the z-axis (Figure 9.11a). The circle has radius a and is displaced along the x-axis by R, so that the profile has parametric representation $(R + a \cos(v), a \sin(v))$. Therefore the torus (Figure 9.11b) has representation

$$\mathbf{p}(u, v) = ((R + a \cos(v)) \cos(u), (R + a \cos(v)) \sin(u), a \sin(v)) \qquad (9.24)$$

Both its u-contours and v-contours are circles.

Drill Exercises

9.16. The Normal to the Torus. Show that the normal vector to the torus has the form

$$\mathbf{n}(u, v) = a[\cos(v)(\cos(u)\mathbf{i} + \sin(u)\mathbf{j}) \\ + \sin(v)\mathbf{k}](R + a \cos(v)) \qquad (9.25)$$

Also, find the inside–outside function for the torus, and compute the normal using its gradient.

9.17. An Elliptical Torus. Find the parametric representation for the following two surfaces of revolution:

a.   The ellipse of Equation 4.16 is first displaced R units along the x-axis and then revolved about the y-axis.

b.   The same ellipse is revolved about the x-axis.

9.18. A "Genie of Revolution." Sketch what the surface would look like if the genie of Equation 4.38 were revolved about the y-axis.

9.19. Revolved n-gons. Sketch the surface generated when a square having vertices $(1, 0, 0)$, $(0, 1, 0)$, $(-1, 0, 0)$, $(0, -1, 0)$ is revolved about the y-axis. Repeat for a pentagon and a hexagon.

9.8   The Quadric Surfaces

An important family of surfaces, the **quadric surfaces**, are the 3D analogs of conic sections (the ellipse, parabola, and hyperbola—see Chapter 4), because the intersection of a quadric surface with a plane yields a conic section. Some of the quadric surfaces have beautiful shapes and are often used in graphics.

The inside–outside functions for the quadrics are quadratic in x, y, and z:[2]

$$Ax^2 + By^2 + Cz^2 + D = 0 \qquad (9.26)$$

for some choices of the coefficients A, B, C, and D.

The six basic quadric surfaces of interest are illustrated in Figure 9.12.

a. Ellipsoid

b. Hyperboloid of one sheet

c. Hyperboloid of two sheets

d. Elliptic cone

e. Elliptic paraboloid

f. Hyperbolic paraboloid

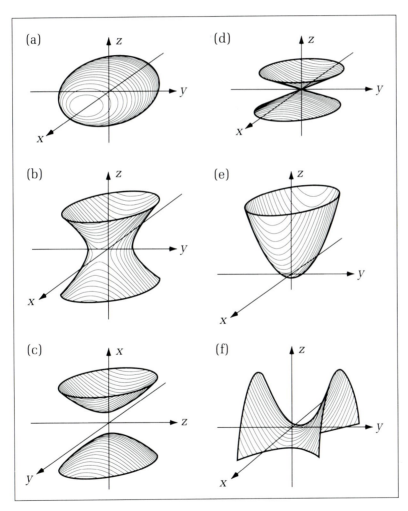

Figure 9.12.
The six principal quadric surfaces.

---

[2]Terms in x, y, and z alone, as well as those in xy, xz, and yz, sometimes appear in expressions for quadric surfaces. Analytic geometry texts show how these terms may be eliminated by suitable orientation and positioning of the surface (e.g., Apostol 1961). (Tools to do this are also developed in Chapter 11 but are not needed at this point.) We shall deal with these oriented versions here for simplicity.

Table 9.1 gives the inside–outside function, $f(x, y, z)$, and the parametric form, $\mathbf{p}(u, v) = X(u, v)\mathbf{i} + Y(u, v)\mathbf{j} + Z(u, v)\mathbf{k}$, for each surface.

Note that a change of sign in one term of the inside–outside function causes a cos( ) to be changed to sec( ) and a sin( ) to be changed to tan( ) in the parametric forms. Both sec( ) and tan( ) grow without bound as their arguments approach $\pm\pi/2$, and so when drawing u-contours or v-contours the relevant parameter is restricted to a smaller range.

9.8.1 Normal Vectors to Quadric Surfaces

Because the inside–outside function for each quadric surface is quadratic in x, y, and z, it is particularly easy to find normal vectors. The gradient vector for each term is linear in its own variable, and so substitution of $X(u, v)$ for x, and so on is straightforward. For instance, the gradient of $f(x, y, z)$ for the ellipsoid is

$$\nabla f = \left(2\frac{x}{a^2},\ 2\frac{y}{b^2},\ 2\frac{z}{c^2} \right) \tag{9.27}$$

Table 9.1
The Quadric Surfaces

Name of Quadric	Inside–Outside Function	$X(u,v)$
Ellipsoid:	$\left(\frac{x}{a}\right)^2 + \left(\frac{y}{b}\right)^2 + \left(\frac{z}{c}\right)^2 - 1$	$a \cos(v) \cos(u)$
Hyperboloid of one sheet:	$\left(\frac{x}{a}\right)^2 + \left(\frac{y}{b}\right)^2 - \left(\frac{z}{c}\right)^2 - 1$	$a \sec(v) \cos(u)$
Hyperboloid of two sheets:	$\left(\frac{x}{a}\right)^2 - \left(\frac{y}{b}\right)^2 - \left(\frac{z}{c}\right)^2 - 1$	$a \sec(v) \cos(u)$
Elliptic cone:	$\left(\frac{x}{a}\right)^2 + \left(\frac{y}{b}\right)^2 - \left(\frac{z}{c}\right)^2$	$av \cos(u)$
Elliptic paraboloid:	$\left(\frac{x}{a}\right)^2 + \left(\frac{y}{b}\right)^2 - z$	$av \cos(u)$
Hyperbolic paraboloid:	$-\left(\frac{x}{a}\right)^2 + \left(\frac{y}{b}\right)^2 - z$	$av \tan(u)$

Name of Quadric	$Y(u,v)$	$Z(u,v)$	v-range	u-range
Ellipsoid:	$b \cos(v) \sin(u)$	$c \sin(v)$	$(-\pi/2, \pi/2)$	$(-\pi, \pi)$
Hyperbloid of one sheet:	$b \sec(v) \sin(u)$	$c \tan(v)$	$(-\pi/2, \pi/2)$	$(-\pi, \pi)$
Hyperbloid of two sheets:	$b \sec(v) \tan(u)$	$c \tan(v)$	$(-\pi/2, \pi/2)$	sheet# 1: $(-\pi/2, \pi/2)$ sheet# 2: $(\pi/2, 3\pi/2)$
Elliptic cone:	$bv \sin(u)$	cv	any real	$(-\pi, \pi)$
Elliptic paraboloid:	$bv \sin(u)$	v^2	$v \geq 0$	$(-\pi, \pi)$
Hyperbolic paraboloid:	$bv \sec(u)$	v^2	$v \geq 0$	$(-\pi, \pi)$

and so the normal in parametric form is (after deleting the 2)

$$\mathbf{n}(u, v) = \left(\frac{X(u, v)}{a^2}, \frac{Y(u, v)}{b^2}, \frac{Z(u, v)}{c^2}\right)$$

$$= \frac{1}{a}\cos(v)\cos(u)\mathbf{i} + \frac{1}{b}\cos(v)\sin(u)\mathbf{j} + \frac{1}{c}\sin(v)\mathbf{k}$$

(9.28)

Normals for the other quadric surfaces follow just as easily, and so they need not be tabulated.

9.8.2 Some Notes on the Quadric Surfaces

We shall summarize briefly various useful properties of each quadric surface. One such property of a quadric is the nature of its principal traces. A **trace** is the curve formed when the surface is "cut" by a plane. The principal traces are those cut by the planes $z = k$, $y = k$, or $x = k$, respectively, where k is some constant.

- *Ellipsoid.* Compare the inside–outside function and parametric form for the ellipsoid with Equations 4.16 and 4.17 to see how they extend the 2D ellipse to this 3D ellipsoid. Parameters a, b, and c give the extent of the ellipsoid along each axis. When two of the parameters are equal, the ellipsoid is a surface of revolution (if $a = b$, what is the axis of revolution?). When a, b, and c all are equal, the ellipsoid becomes a sphere. For this choice of parametrization, the parallels lie in planes parallel to the plane $z = k$, and the meridians lie in planes that pass through the z-axis. All principal traces of the ellipsoid are ellipses.

- *Hyperboloid of one sheet.* When $a = b$, the hyperboloid becomes a surface of revolution. The principal traces for the planes $z = k$ are ellipses, and those for the planes $x = k$ and $y = k$ are hyperbolas. The hyperboloid of one sheet is particularly interesting because it is a ruled surface, as suggested in Figure 9.13a. If a thread is woven between two parallel ellipses, as shown, this surface will be created. Formulas for the rulings are discussed in the exercises. (The patch in Figure 7.36 is also a hyperboloid of one sheet. Why?)

- *Hyperboloid of two sheets.* No part of the surface lies between $x = -a$ and $x = a$ (why?). When $a = b$, it becomes a surface of revolution. The traces for planes $x = k$ when $|k| > a$ are ellipses, and the other principal traces are hyperbolas.

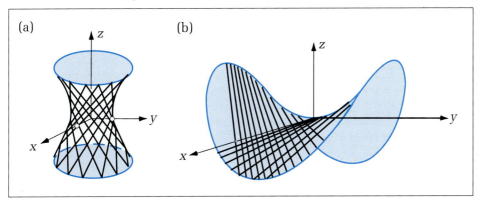

Figure 9.13.
Two ruled quadric surfaces.

- *Elliptic cone.* The elliptic cone is a special case of the general cone treated earlier: Its generator lines trace an ellipse. This cone is, of course, a ruled surface, and the principal traces for planes $z = k$ are ellipses. What are traces for planes that contain the z-axis? When $a = b$, this quadric is a surface of revolution: It becomes a right circular cone.

- *Elliptic paraboloid.* The traces of an elliptic paraboloid for planes $z = k > 0$ are ellipses, and the other principal traces are parabolas. When $a = b$, it is a surface of revolution.

- *Hyperbolic paraboloid.* The hyperbolic paraboloid is sometimes called a "saddle-shaped" surface. Its traces for planes $z = k \neq 0$ are hyperbolas, and for planes $x = k$ or $y = k$ they are parabolas. (What is the intersection of this surface with the plane $z = 0$?) This is also a ruled surface (see Figure 9.13b).

Drill Exercises

9.20.   Finding Normals to the Quadrics. Find the normal vector in parametric form for each of the six quadric surfaces.

9.21.   The Hyperboloid As a Ruled Surface. Suppose $(x_0, y_0, 0)$ is a point on the hyperboloid of one sheet. Show that the vector

$$\mathbf{r}(t) = (x_0 + a^2 y_0 t)\mathbf{i} + (y_0 - b^2 x_0 t)\mathbf{j} + abct\mathbf{k} \quad (9.29)$$

describes a straight line that lies everywhere on the hyperboloid and passes through $(x_0, y_0, 0)$. Is this sufficient to make the surface a ruled surface? Why or why not?

9.22.   The Hyperbolic Paraboloid As a Ruled Surface. Show that the intersection of any plane parallel to the line $y = \pm bx/a$ cuts the hyperbolic paraboloid along a straight line.

9.9   The Superquadrics

Following the work of Alan Barr (1981), we can extend these quadric surfaces to a vastly larger family, in much the way we extended the ellipse to the superellipse in Chapter 4. This also greatly increases the repertoire of surface shapes we can use as models in applications.

The 2D superellipse curve was defined in Equation 4.19 by the implicit equation $f(x, y) = 0$ with

$$f(x, y) = \left(\frac{|x|}{a}\right)^n + \left(\frac{|y|}{b}\right)^n - 1 \quad (9.30)$$

where n is a parameter called a **bulge**. The superellipse is symmetrical about both axes: $f(-x, y) = f(x, -y) = f(-x, -y) = f(x, y)$. For $n = 2$, it coincides with the ellipse. As n increases more and more beyond 2, it bulges outward. For very large values of n, it becomes boxlike. Its sides are nearly straight, and its "corners" rather sharp (see Figure 4.16). On the other hand, as n decreases below 2, there is less and less bulge outward, so that at $n = 1$ the sides are straight lines. For $n < 1$, it bulges inward, with a look of being pinched.

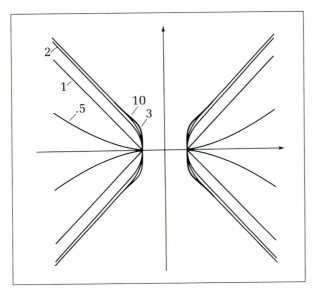

Figure 9.14.
The superhyperbola family.

The superellipse has the parametric representation

$$x(u) = a \, \cos(u)^{2/n}$$
$$y(u) = b \, \sin(u)^{2/n}$$
(9.31)

for $u \epsilon (-\pi, \pi)$. See the note following Equation 4.20 for the proper interpretation of this form when $2/n$ is fractional.

The **superhyperbola** can also be defined (Barr 1981). It is the curve having the parametric form

$$x(u) = a \, \sec(u)^{2/n}$$
$$y(u) = b \, \tan(u)^{2/n}$$
(9.32)

When $n = 2$, the familiar hyperbola is obtained. Figure 9.14 shows example superhyperbolas. As the bulge n increases beyond 2, the curve bulges out more and more, and as it decreases below 2, it bulges out less and less, becoming straight for $n = 1$ and pinching inward for $n < 1$.

Barr defines four **superquadric solids** as extensions of the first three quadric surfaces, as well as an extension of the torus. The extension involves introducing two "bulge factors," n_1 and n_2, to which various terms are raised. These bulge factors affect the surfaces much as n does for the superellipse. When both factors equal 2, the first three superquadrics revert to the quadric surfaces catalogued previously. Example shapes for the four superquadrics are shown in Figure 9.15.

1. Superellipsoid

2. Superhyperboloid of one sheet

3. Superhyperboloid of two sheets

4. Supertoroid

Their inside–outside functions and parametric forms are given in Table 9.2.

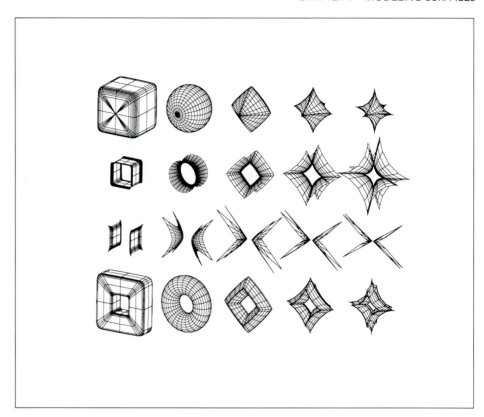

Figure 9.15.
Examples of the four superquadrics. n_1 and n_2 are (left to right): 10, 2, 1.11, .77, and .59. (Courtesy of Jay Greco.)

Table 9.2 The Superquadric Surfaces

Name of Quadric	Inside–Outside Function	$X(u,v)$
Superellipsoid:	$\left(\left(\frac{x}{a}\right)^{n_2} + \left(\frac{y}{b}\right)^{n_2}\right)^{n_1/n_2} + \left(\frac{z}{c}\right)^{n_1} - 1$	$a\cos^{2/n_1}(v)\cos^{2/n_2}(u)$
Superhyperboloid of one sheet:	$\left(\left(\frac{x}{a}\right)^{n_2} + \left(\frac{y}{b}\right)^{n_2}\right)^{n_1/n_2} - \left(\frac{z}{c}\right)^{n_1} - 1$	$a\sec^{2/n_1}(v)\cos^{2/n_2}(u)$
Superhyperboloid of two sheets:	$\left(\left(\frac{x}{a}\right)^{n_2} - \left(\frac{y}{b}\right)^{n_2}\right)^{n_1/n_2} - \left(\frac{z}{c}\right)^{n_1} - 1$	$a\sec^{2/n_1}(v)\sec^{2/n_2}(u)$
Supertorus:	$\left(\left(\left(\frac{x}{a}\right)^{n_2} + \left(\frac{y}{b}\right)^{n_2}\right)^{1/n_2} - d\right)^{n_1} + \left(\frac{z}{c}\right)^{n_1} - 1$	$a(d + \cos^{2/n_1}(v))\cos^{2/n_2}(u)$

Name of Quadric	$Y(u,v)$	$Z(u,v)$	v-range	u-range
Superellipsoid:	$b\cos^{2/n_1}(v)\sin^{2/n_2}(u)$	$c\sin^{2/n_1}(v)$	$[-\pi/2, \pi/2]$	$[-\pi,\pi]$
Superhyperboloid of one sheet:	$b\sec^{2/n_1}(v)\sin^{2/n_2}(u)$	$c\tan^{2/n_1}(v)$	$(-\pi/2, \pi/2)$	$[-\pi, \pi]$
Superhyperboloid of two sheets:	$b\sec^{2/n_1}(v)\tan^{2/n_2}(u)$	$c\tan^{2/n_1}(v)$	$(-\pi/2, \pi/2)$	sheet# 1: $(-\pi/2, \pi/2)$; sheet# 2: $(\pi/2, 3\pi/2)$
Supertorus:	$b(d + \cos^{2/n_1}(v))\sin^{2/n_2}(u)$	$c\sin^{2/n_1}(v)$	$[-\pi, \pi)$	$[-\pi, \pi)$

Drill Exercises

9.23. Extents of Superquadrics. What are the maximum x, y, and z values attainable for the superellipsoid and the supertoroid?

9.24. Special Cases of Superquadrics. For each of the preceding superquadrics, write $f(x, y, z)$ for the following cases:

a. $a = b = c$

b. $n_1 = n_2 = 2$

c. both $a = b = c$ and $n_1 = n_2 = 2$

In each case determine whether the surface is a surface of revolution about some axis, and if so, specify which axis. Describe also any other symmetries in the surfaces.

9.9.1 Normal Vectors for the Superquadrics

The normal vectors $\mathbf{n}(u, v)$ can be computed for each superquadric in the usual two ways, by a cross product of partial derivatives or by the gradient, but because the calculation is tedious, we shall give the results here.

The normal vectors for the superellipsoid and the supertoroid are the same:

$$\mathbf{n}(u, v) = \frac{1}{a} \cos^{2-2/n_1}(v) \cos^{2-2/n_2}(u)\mathbf{i} + \frac{1}{b} \cos^{2-2/n_1}(v) \sin^{2-2/n_2}(u)\mathbf{j} + \qquad (9.33)$$
$$\frac{1}{c} \sin^{2-2/n_1}(v)$$

For the superhyperboloid of one sheet, it is easiest to say how the form for the normal vector differs from that of the superellipsoid. It's a simple replacement of one trigonometric function by another: Replace all occurrences of $\cos(v)$ with $\sec(v)$ and those of $\sin(v)$ with $\tan(v)$. Do not alter $\cos(u)$ or $\sin(u)$ or any other term.

For the superhyperboloid of two pieces, the trigonometric functions in both u and v are replaced : Replace all occurrences of $\cos(v)$ with $\sec(v)$, those of $\sin(v)$ with $\tan(v)$, those of $\cos(u)$ with $\sec(u)$, and those of $\sin(u)$ with $\tan(u)$.

Drill Exercise

9.25. Deriving the Normal Vectors. Derive the formula of Equation 9.33 using Equation 9.15, and repeat this using Equation 9.16.

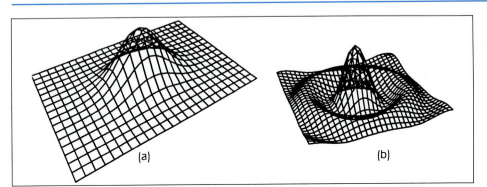

(a)   (b)

Figure 9.16.
Example functions of two variables.

9.10 Mathematical Functions of Two Variables

In Chapter 3 we discussed plotting line graphs based on a mathematical function, $f(.)$, of one variable. To reveal the shape of the function, we plotted $y = f(x)$ versus x by connecting closely spaced points, $(x_i, f(x_i))$, with straight-line segments.

In some scientific investigations you may want to reveal the shape of the surface defined by some function, $g(.\,,.)$, of two variables. The surface could be plotted as $z = g(x, y)$, as $y = g(x, z)$, and so forth. We shall use $z = g(x, y)$ here. The functions are often given by formulas such as

$$g(x, y) = e^{-ax^2 - by^2} \tag{9.34}$$

(for some parameters a and b) or

$$g(x, y) = \frac{\sin(\pi(x^2 + y^2))}{\pi(x^2 + y^2)} \tag{9.35}$$

9.11 Summary

In this chapter we introduced techniques for describing simple surfaces parametrically and also examined the general plane and planar patch. We also studied a general technique for computing the normal vector to a surface at any desired point. Finding the normal vector plays an important role in realistic image synthesis and the hidden line problem, as we shall see later. Along with surfaces of revolution and ruled surfaces, we also saw how the quadric surfaces are represented and how, with little extra effort, this family can be enlarged to the superquadrics. Finally, we discussed how the parametric representation of a mathematical function can be written directly from the function.

Because these surfaces are defined by functions, they are necessarily **single valued**: For each value of (x, y) there is one, and only one, value for $g(x, y)$. (Contrast this with the sphere, for which (x, y) yields two values.) Because functions are single valued, they permit a simple parametric form:

$$\mathbf{p}(u, v) = (u, v, g(u, v)) \tag{9.36}$$

That is, u and v can be used directly as the dependent variables for the function, and the first components of the position vector are simply $X(u, v) = u$ and $Y(u, v) = v$. Thus u-contours lie in planes of constant x, and v-contours lie in planes of constant y. Figure 9.16a shows a view of the example in Equation 9.34, and Figure 9.16b shows the function of Equation 9.35. Also see Figure 2.1b for this function drawn with the hidden lines removed. Each line is a trace of the surface cut by a plane, $x = k$ or $y = k$, for some value of k. Plots such as these can help illustrate the behavior of a mathematical function.

CHAPTER 10

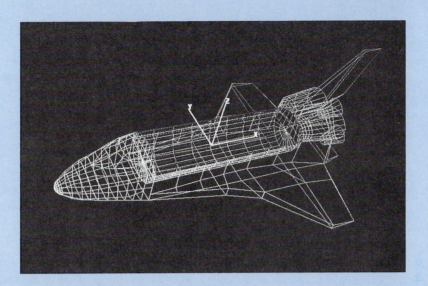

Three-Dimensional Graphics

As lines, so loves oblique, may well
Themselves in every angle greet;
But ours, so truly parallel,
Though infinite, can never meet.

Andrew Marvell, *The Definition of Love*

Goals of the Chapter

- To introduce wireframe models for surfaces and solids and to learn how to construct them.
- To develop techniques for drawing simple three-dimensional objects.
- To use these techniques to draw pictures of wireframe models.
- To study the properties of simple parallel and perspective projections.
- To see how to apply these drawing techniques to the surfaces introduced in Chapter 9.

10.1 Introduction

In this chapter we enter into one of the most fascinating areas in computer graphics: modeling and displaying three-dimensional objects. How does one describe and then display solid objects such as an airplane, a human face, or a wrench? How can an architect model a house on a computer so that a client can view it from all angles and with different exteriors? How might an application be organized that gives a user the illusion of flying around a town and between buildings? Such programs have many ingredients, and we first must construct a set of tools to draw simple three-dimensional objects. Later we shall combine these tools to fashion more elaborate applications.

In this chapter we shall discuss techniques for making simple line drawings of two kinds of objects: the surfaces discussed in the last chapter and solids modeled by wireframes. A **wireframe model** consists of a collection of points (vertices) and a set of edges that connects pairs of points. Together the points and edges define the shape of the object. The vertices and edges are typically stored in a database that is accessed during the drawing process. A computer graphic rendering of a wireframe model consists of a straight line drawn for each edge of the model; Figure 10.1 shows an example.

Drawings of wireframes tend not to be realistic: The object appears hollow and can be hard to interpret. The use of shading (Chapter 15) and hidden surface removal (Chapter 17) techniques improve the renditions dramatically. But wireframes can be drawn rapidly and so are often used for previewing objects in an interactive scenario.

Although we model and draw wireframes as collections of wires connecting vertices, we often think of them as being an underlying solid object whose shape is suggested by the wireframe. The piston, for instance, is naturally thought of as a solid object. Certain sets of edges seem to define different "faces" of the object, and together these faces form the "skin" of the object. Wireframes are often used to model **polyhedra**, which are solid objects whose faces consist of planar polygons. As we shall discuss in more detail in Chapter 15, polyhedra can have very complex shapes, and even contain holes. The wireframe model captures the geometry of the object through vertices and edges, and later we shall define a polyhedron according to its faces.

Many of the mathematical surfaces introduced in Chapter 9 can also be drawn as a collection of straight lines connecting various points, as in Figure 9.7. The major difference is that the locations of the points are computed, based on a formula or algorithm, rather than stored in a database. One might say that such surfaces are algorithmically based, whereas the wireframe models are data based. Certain objects are defined by a blend of data and algorithms, however, and so the distinction can become blurred.

For both wireframe models and mathematical surfaces, the points and edges lie in 3D space, and so to render pictures of them something must be projected onto the drawing surface. This chapter introduces some projection techniques, and we shall see how to make complex drawings of a wide variety of objects. But to keep things simple, we shall discuss viewing an object only from a restricted set of directions. More complicated drawings are made possible by rotating objects in space (Chapter 11) and by a general viewing mechanism embodied in a "synthetic camera" (Chapter 12).

Figure 10.1.

A wireframe piston.

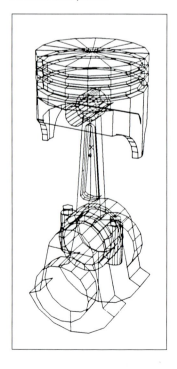

10.2 Wireframe Models

A wireframe model captures the shape of a 3D object in two lists, a vertex list and an edge list. We shall examine the main ideas of wireframe models using a polyhedron we call the **basic barn**, shown in Figure 10.2. The **vertex list** specifies geometric information: where each corner is located. The vertices of the barn are defined here in a right-handed coordinate system with the z-axis upward, in accordance with modeling conventions. The **edge list** provides connectivity information, specifying (in arbitrary order) the two vertices that form the endpoints of each edge. Sample lists are shown in Table 10.1. Two extra edges have been added to the back side to make it easier to distinguish the front and back of the barn in a drawing.

Table 10.1 **Vertex and Edge Lists for the Basic Barn**

Vertex List				
vertex	*x*	*y*	*z*	
1	0	0	0	back side
2	0	1	0	
3	0	1	1	
4	0	.5	1.5	
5	0	0	1	
6	1	0	0	front side
7	1	1	0	
8	1	1	1	
9	1	.5	1.5	
10	1	0	1	

Edge List		
edge	*vertex1*	*vertex2*
1	1	2
2	2	3
3	3	4
4	4	5
5	5	1
6	6	7
7	7	8
8	8	9
9	9	10
10	10	6
11	1	6
12	2	7
13	3	8
14	4	9
15	5	10
16	2	5
17	1	3

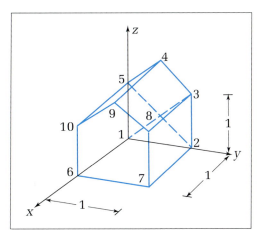

Figure 10.2.
Introducing the basic barn.

Drill Exercises

10.1.   Add a Door. What additional data should be inserted in the vertex and edge lists to define a door centered halfway between vertex 7 and 2? Give it a width of .25 and a height of .5.

10.2.   The Unit Cube. Provide a vertex list and an edge list for a wireframe model of the unit cube defined by the eight vertices (i, j, k) where i, j, and k each can take on the values 0 and 1.

How is a wireframe model stored in an application? Many possibilities exist, such as arrays and linked lists, and each has its advantages in certain situations. Here we adopt a simple record structure based on two arrays.

Code Fragment 10.1. A Data Type for Wireframe Models

```
const
    MaxNumVerts = 50; {allowable number of vertices}
    MaxNumEdges = 100; {allowable number of edges}
type
    wireframe = record
                    numverts : 0..MaxNumVerts;
                    vert : array[1..MaxNumVerts] of point3D;
                    numedge : 0..MaxNumEdges;
                    edge : array[1..MaxNumEdges, 1..2] of 1..MaxNumVerts
                end;
```

A record **var** *barn : wireframe* would contain the actual positions of the *numverts* vertices as an array of 3D points. For instance, *barn.vert*[3] would contain the value (0.0, 1.0, 1.0). Each edge specifies the indices of the vertices that define its endpoints: *barn.edge*[13, 1] is 3, and *barn.edge*[13, 2] is 8. The two endpoints of the i-th edge lie in three-dimensional world coordinates at *barn.vert*[*barn.edge*[i, 1]] and *barn.vert*[*barn.edge*[i, 2]].

10.3   Drawing Wireframes: Introduction to Projections

Treat them in terms of the cylinder,
the sphere, the cone, all in perspective.

Paul Cézanne, 1925

To draw a wireframe object, we simply draw each edge defined in its edge list. Thus the real issue is how to draw a line defined in three-dimensional space on a two-dimensional drawing surface. That is, we must remove a dimension in some fashion, and there are two simple types of projection from 3D to 2D to do this. The drawings they allow are restricted in their point of view, but this defect will be removed later.

The general technique to be used for drawing a 3D line segment is

1.   Project each of its two endpoints to a 2D point.

2.   Draw a straight line between the two projected endpoints.

This works because the projections we use preserve straight lines: If 3D point P lies on the line between 3D points A and B, the projection of P will always lie on the line between the projection of A and that of B. This property is easily proved, and it makes line drawings very simple indeed. If it were not true, we would have to project each point on the 3D line segment separately—a clearly impossible task!

The problem has now been reduced to finding the projection of a single point in three dimensions. We shall first examine how to do this orthographically.

10.3.1 The Simplest Orthographic Projections

Consider the problem of projecting 3D point $P = (P_x, P_y, P_z)$ onto some plane. There are many ways to do this. The simplest is just to discard one component, say the z-component, so that P projects to $P' = (P_x, P_y)$. As shown in Figure 10.3, this is equivalent to projecting the point onto the x, y-plane. Each point is projected by finding where a ray (called a **projector**) drawn through the point and parallel to the z-axis hits the x, y-plane. In this case the x, y-plane is called the **viewplane**. This is a special case of a **parallel projection**, in which all projectors are parallel to one another. It is called **orthographic** because all the rays are orthogonal to the viewplane.

It is easy to show that this projection preserves straight lines: Any 3D line, $(s_x + g_x t, \; s_y + g_y t, \; s_z + g_z t)$, projects as $(s_x + g_x t, \; s_y + g_y t)$, which is again the form for a (2D) straight line. Lines that are parallel in three dimensions project to lines that are also parallel (see the exercises).

When drawing lines in an application, the viewplane acts like the familiar 2D world coordinates. A window is defined in the usual manner on this plane; the projected line is clipped against the window and mapped to the viewport; and it is finally drawn by the device. The code to draw the projected line between 3D points A and B of type *point3D* is simply

Line_(A.x, A.y, B.x, B.y);

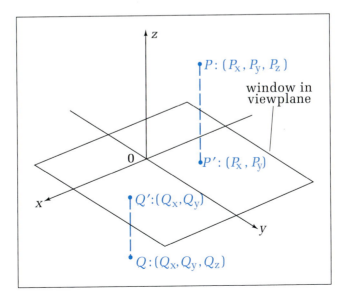

Figure 10.3.
The simplest orthographic projection.

The following code fragment draws a wireframe object using this projection:

Code Fragment 10.2. Drawing an Orthographic View of a Wireframe Object

```
procedure ObjectInOrthogView(object : wireframe);
{draw wireframe object—deleting z-component}
var
   i : integer;
   v1, v2 : point3D;
begin
   with object do if numedge >0 then
   begin
      for i := 1 to numedge do
      begin
         v1 := vert[edge[i, 1]]; v2 := vert[edge[i, 2]];
         Line_(v1.x, v1.y, v2.x, v2.y)
      end
   end
end;
```

Other Orthographic Projections

The preceding orthographic projection is often called a *top* (or *bottom*) view. There are two other popular orthographic projections: The *front* view uses projectors parallel to the *x*-axis and has the viewplane coincide with the *y*, *z*-plane. This projection discards the *x*-component of *P*. The *side* view uses projectors parallel to the *y*-axis along with a viewplane lying in the *x*, *z*-plane. When *P* is projected, its *y*-component is discarded.

Figure 10.4 shows the three orthographic projections of the basic barn. Note in the front view that the front and rear walls are indistinguishable: They lie right on top of each other. Similarly, the left and right walls cannot be distinguished in the side view. Orthographic views can be hard to interpret, although for some objects the three orthographic views taken together provide enough information for a complete understanding of the object's shape (do they here?). Some people become very skilled in constructing a mental image of the object from these views.

Orthographic views are usually too restrictive, however, and thus some additional views of an object from different angles are needed in order to understand a drawing. A better view can be obtained by first rotating the object so that more detail is visible; an approach we discuss in Chapter 11. Another approach is to use perspective views of objects, which are more realistic, as they retain some sense of depth.

Drill Exercises

10.3.   Three-Dimensional Curves. As a point moves through space, it traces out a curve that can be represented parametrically by some position vector, $\mathbf{f}(t) = (x(t), y(t), z(t))$. An example is the helix, $(\cos(t), \sin(t), t)$, which spirals about the *z*-axis as it moves down it. Sketch by hand the top, front, and side orthographic views of this helix.

10.4.   Parallelism Is Preserved. Show that an orthographic projection preserves parallelism: Any two lines that are parallel in three dimensions project to parallel lines.

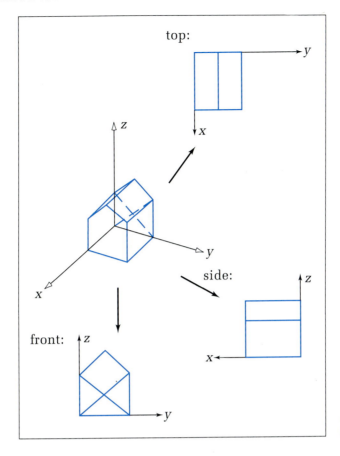

Figure 10.4.
Orthographic projections of the barn.

10.3.2 Simple Perspective Projections

Perspective projections are also simple to perform, and they give a more natural view of a 3D object than do orthographic projections. We are accustomed to viewing objects in perspective in everyday life, and the form of mathematical perspective we set up here produces quite faithful drawings of objects. A complete treatment of perspective projections is given in Chapter 12.

A perspective projection depends on the relative positions of two objects, an **eye** and a viewplane. Figure 10.5 shows the simplest arrangement, in which the viewplane is the y, z-plane and the eye is E units away along the x-axis at $(E, 0, 0)$. E is often called the **eye distance**. To determine the projection of a 3D point, $P = (x, y, z)$, onto the viewplane, connect P to the eye with a straight line, and see where the line intersects the viewplane. The intersection point, $P' = (y', z')$, is the point actually drawn. Thus the projectors for a perspective projection are not parallel but converge on a single point, the eye.

We shall suppose for now that the point P is not "behind the eye." That is, we shall insist that $x < E$. P can be on the far side of the viewplane from the eye, in the viewplane itself, or between the eye and viewplane, but it must not be behind the eye. We shall remove this restriction later.

Analytically, it is simple to find the projected point P'. The ray from the eye to P has the form

$$\mathbf{r}(t) = (E, 0, 0)(1 - t) + (x, y, z)t \qquad (10.1)$$

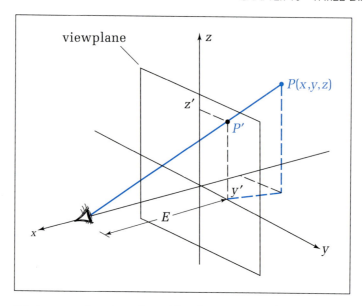

Figure 10.5.
A simple perspective projection.

It intersects the viewplane (the plane $x = 0$) when its x-component is zero. Equation 10.1 shows that the x-component of the ray is $E(1 - t) + xt$, which is zero when

$$t' = \frac{1}{1 - x/E} \qquad (10.2)$$

This hit time is necessarily positive, as we have assumed that $x < E$. Using this time in Equation 10.1 we see that the projected point is

$$y' = \frac{y}{1 - x/E} \qquad (10.3)$$

$$z' = \frac{z}{1 - x/E} \qquad (10.4)$$

This perspective projection is similar to the earlier orthographic projection, except that both the y- and z-coordinates are scaled by the hit-time factor, $t' = 1/(1 - x/E)$. This factor introduces **perspective foreshortening**: That is, objects farther away from the eye appear smaller. For a point far from the eye (at a large negative value of x), this factor is small, and so (x, y, z) is projected to a small value (y', z'), nearer the origin. For a point right on the viewplane, (x, y, z) projects to (y, z) itself, just as with an orthographic projection. At the other extreme, a point, (x, y, z), near the eye (x only slightly less than E) projects to a very large (y', z'): The screen is far behind the point, and so there is a dramatic enlargement.

Drill Exercises

10.5.   Computing a Perspective Projection. Find the 2D point to which each of the following points will project if $E = 5$:

a.   (3, 4, −5)

b.   (4, 8, 0)

c.   (2, 8, 3)

d.   (1, 8, 4.99)

10.6.   The Helix Viewed in Perspective. Sketch by hand a perspective view of the helix defined in Exercise 10.3.

Perspective Projections Preserve Straight Lines

Happily, perspective projections preserve straight lines, just as orthographic ones do. The 3D line $(s_x + g_xt, s_y + g_yt, s_z + g_zt)$ projects as

$$y(t) = \frac{s_y + g_yt}{1 - s_x - g_xt}$$

$$z(t) = \frac{s_z + g_zt}{1 - s_x - g_xt}$$

$$(10.5)$$

This is a parametric form for a straight line, as may be shown by writing out the forms of $y(t_2) - y(t_1)$ and $z(t_2) - z(t_1)$. Each of these quantities has a numerator proportional to $t_2 - t_1$, and they have the same denominator.

Therefore the ratio

$$\frac{z(t_2) - z(t_1)}{y(t_2) - y(t_1)}$$

$$(10.6)$$

is constant. The following exercise requests further exploration of this proof.

Drill Exercise

10.7. Proving That the Projection Is a Straight Line. By direct algebraic manipulations, show that the ratio in Equation 10.6 is a constant for any choice of t_1 and t_2. Show that this guarantees that the curve $(y(t), z(t))$ is a straight line.

Because straight lines are preserved, we need only project the endpoints of a 3D line and then can draw a 2D line between the two projected endpoints.

Wireframe models can be drawn in perspective, as shown in Figure 10.6 for the basic barn. Here the eye is placed at $E = 4$, and the perspective foreshortening of the rear side is quite apparent. Because it is farther from the eye, it projects to a smaller image. The parallelism in the lines is no longer preserved, unless they happen to be parallel to the viewplane. As we shall see, any parallel lines that recede at all from the eye, such as edges 13 and 14, point to a "vanishing point" (in this case the origin).

Note that the orthographic projection is actually a limiting case of the perspective projection. If we make the eye distance E larger and larger, the projec-

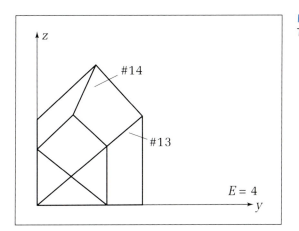

Figure 10.6.
The basic barn in perspective.

tors through the eye will become more and more parallel, and the factor $1/(1 - x/E)$ will become closer and closer to 1. As $E \to \infty$, the projectors become parallel and the factor becomes one, and so the perspective projection becomes identical to the orthographic projection.

A routine to perform a perspective projection is simple and is given next. It is a direct implementation of Equations 10.3 and 10.4. It tests for conditions that would cause nonsensical results, and if one is found, the error-reporting routine *ReportError* will be invoked. Otherwise the projected point will be placed in *p_out*.

> *Code Fragment 10.3. Finding the Perspective Projection of a Point: Eye on the x-Axis*

```
procedure Persp_x(p_in : point3D; E : real; var p_out : point);
{project p_in to p_out using perspective projection—eye on x-axis}
var t_hit : real;
begin
    if (p_in.x > = E) or (E = 0.0) then ReportError
    {point is behind eye or eye is on viewplane}
    else begin
        t_hit := 1.0 / (1.0 − p_in.x/E);
        p_out.x := p_in.y * t_hit;
        p_out.y := p_in.z * t_hit
    end
end; {project}
```

It is not hard to draw wireframe models in perspective; Code Fragment 10.2 need only be adjusted slightly to include scaling by the hit time (see the exercises).

Looking from Other Directions

This perspective view places the eye on the x-axis and uses the y, z-plane as the viewplane. But just as with orthographic projections, we can interchange axes and obtain other views.

One commonly used setup puts the eye on the z-axis and uses the x, y-plane as the viewplane. Then we see the x-axis pointing to the right and the y-axis pointing up, which is a familiar orientation for many charts. It is a simple matter to adjust *Persp_x*( ) to a version *Persp_z*( ) that handles this case (see the exercises). The eye lies at $(0, 0, E)$, and the viewplane is given by $z = 0$. For a point, $P = (x, y, z)$, the ray from P to the eye is given by $(0, 0, E)(1 − t) + (x, y, z)t$ (contrast this with Equation 10.1), so this ray strikes the viewplane when its z-component $E(1 − t) + zt$ is zero, at the hit time t' given by

$$t' = \frac{1}{1 - z/E} \tag{10.7}$$

Thus it hits the plane at

$$x' = \frac{x}{1 - z/E}$$

$$y' = \frac{y}{1 - z/E} \tag{10.8}$$

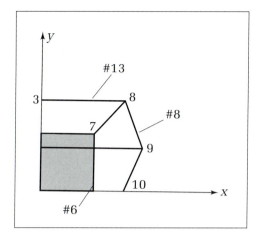

Figure 10.7.
A view of the barn with the eye on the z-axis.

Figure 10.7 shows the barn of Figure 10.2 from such a point of view, using $E = 4$. The floor of the barn (shaded) is farther away from the roof and thus appears smaller. Some edges and vertices are labeled to help interpret this view.

Drill Exercises

10.8.   Sketch a Cube in Perspective. Cube C has sides of length 2, is centered at the origin, and has its sides aligned with the three coordinate axes. Draw (by hand) the perspective view of cube C when the eye is at $E = 5$ on the z-axis. Repeat when C is shifted so that its center is at $(1, 1, 1)$.

10.9.   Putting the Eye on the y-Axis. Sketch by hand the perspective projection of the basic barn when the eye is on the y-axis at $(0, 2, 0)$. Label each edge using Figure 10.2 as a guide.

10.4   Further Wireframe Modeling of Objects

The preceding vertex and edge lists for the barn are easy to fashion by hand. A sketch of the desired object is made in a coordinate system; each of the vertices is labeled and its position is jotted down; and for each edge the indices of the endpoints are noted. Vertex and edge lists can be stored in an external file and loaded into an application when needed.

In more complex modeling situations, we must procedurally fashion models of polyhedra. A **procedural model** uses an algorithm of some sort to compute the locations of the vertices and loads data automatically into a record of type *wireframe*. Two families of such objects are discussed here, to provide examples that may be used immediately for drawing wireframes. A third family appears later in the discussion of surfaces of revolution.

10.4.1 Modeling a Prism

A **prism** is a polyhedron that is a "swept" solid. The base is a polygon, P. It initially lies in the x, y-plane and is swept along the z-axis to some height, H. A vertical edge is created for each vertex of P as P is swept along. A typical result is shown in Figure 10.8. If P has n vertices, the final prism must have $2n$ vertices and $3n$ edges (why?).

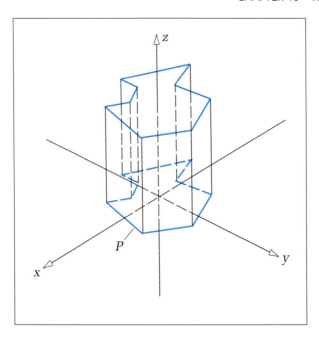

Figure 10.8.
Modeling a prism.

Drill Exercises

10.10.   The Prism in Perspective. Sketch by hand how a prism would be drawn using a perspective projection with the eye at (4, 0, 0) when the base of the prism is a 6-gon (see Chapter 3) of radius 1 centered at the origin. Make the prism of height $H = 2$.

10.11.   The Unit Cube As a Prism. Does the unit cube of Exercise 10.2 belong in this prism family? Specify the base polygon of the prism.

Suppose that polygon P is stored in the variable *poly* of type *polypoint*, and we wish to fill in values for the *wireframe* type variable *prism*.

The Vertex List

The first n vertices are simply those of P but positioned in 3D in the x, y-plane. For instance, if *poly.pt*[i] is (2.2, 4.1), *prism.vert*[i] must be (2.2, 4.1, 0). The next n vertices replace the z-coordinate of 0 with H.

The Edge List

The endpoints of the edges must, of course, be keyed to the arrangement of vertices just chosen. The first n edges can be those of the vertical sides of the prism, so that *prism.edge*[i, 1] and *prism.edge*[i, 2] are just i and $i + n$, respectively. The next n edges can be those of the polygon lying in the x, y-plane. So *prism.edge*[$i + n$, 1] is i, and *prism.edge*[$i + n$, 2] is $i + 1$ (except when $i = n$, in which case it is 1 to close up the polygon). The final n edges are those of the top face of the prism. The details are left as an exercise.

10.4.2 The Platonic Solids

If all of the faces of a polyhedron are identical and each is a regular polygon, the object is a **regular polyhedron**. These symmetry constraints are so severe that only five such objects can exist, the **platonic solids** shown in Figure 10.9. They

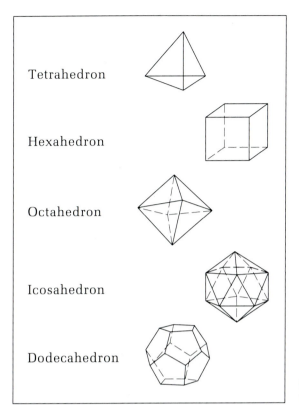

Tetrahedron

Hexahedron

Octahedron

Icosahedron

Dodecahedron

Figure 10.9.
The five platonic solids.

have fascinating properties and arise often in graphics: Appendix 8 describes them in greater detail and provides vertex and edge lists for each. They are also discussed further in connection with shading faces and ray tracing. To build elementary views of them, see the exercises.

10.5 Drawing Surfaces

We have seen how to produce orthographic and perspective drawings of wireframe models. Such a drawing shows a rather hollow-looking object, but it is usually easy to imagine the object as in fact being solid: Sets of the edges are seen as forming faces that together enclose some amount of space.

In Chapter 9 we examined the mathematical description of a rather different entity, the surface. Surfaces can be "open" in the sense that they do not enclose space, or they can be "closed," in which case they are often viewed as the outer surface of a solid object. Here we shall examine how to produce drawings of the surfaces studied earlier.

10.5.1 Drawing Surface Patches

Consider the plane $\mathbf{p}(u, v) = \mathbf{c} + \mathbf{a}u + \mathbf{b}v$ of Equation 9.6, in which $\mathbf{a}$, $\mathbf{b}$, and $\mathbf{c}$ are vectors. A finite piece of this plane is obtained by restricting the parameters u and v to lie in the range 0 to 1.

A planar patch can be depicted by drawing a **grid** of straight lines on it, most easily by drawing a set of **u-contours** and **v-contours**. Recall from Chapter 9 that the u-contour at u' is a curve formed when u is held fixed at value u' and v varies from 0 to 1. This is the curve (in three dimensions) given by $\mathbf{c} + \mathbf{a}u' + \mathbf{b}v$ for $v \in (0, 1)$. For a planar patch this is a straight line. The two cases $u = 0$ and $u = 1$ define two borders of the patch. Similarly, the v-contour at v' holds v constant at v' and lets u vary from 0 to 1. (What is its formula?) It is also a straight line here. The lines $v = 0$ and $v = 1$ define the other two edges of the patch.

As an example, Figure 10.10 shows an orthographic projection (along the z-axis) of the patch specified by $\mathbf{c} = (0, 1, 0)$, $\mathbf{a} = (3, 1, -2)$, and $\mathbf{b} = (2, 5, 2)$. The patch has corners at $(0, 1, 0)$, $(3, 2, -2)$, $(2, 6, 2)$, and $(5, 7, 0)$. The projected patch is, of course, another parallelogram. (What are its corners?) A grid is shown on the patch, consisting of five projected u-contours (using u values 0, .25, .5, .75, and 1) and six projected v-contours (using v values 0, .2, .4, .6, .8, and 1). Note that as we expect, the projected u-contours and v-contours are parallel.

Figure 10.11 shows the same patch drawn using a perspective projection. The eye is on the z-axis at distance $E = 4$. Each of the four corners (x, y, z) projects to the point (x', y') as shown in the following table:

The Four Corners of the Patch and Their Projections

x	y	z	t'	x'	y'
0	1	0	1	0	1
3	2	-2	2/3	2	4/3
2	6	2	2	4	12
5	7	0	1	5	7

Notice how each hit-time factor t' affects the final position of its projected point. Two of the corners lie on the viewplane and so are not altered. One corner lies far from the eye and has both its coordinates reduced. And one point is close to the eye, so that its coordinates are increased. Also note that the u-contours and

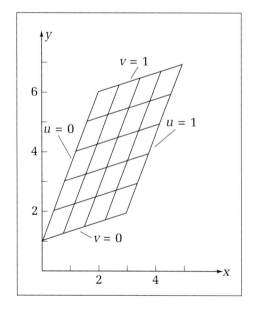

Figure 10.10.
An orthographic projection of a planar patch.

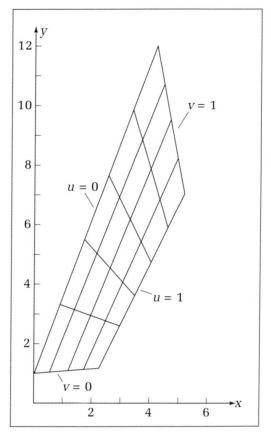

Figure 10.11.
The patch drawn using a
perspective projection.

v-contours are not parallel when a perspective projection is used. Although these lines are parallel in three dimensions, they appear closer together as they recede from the eye. The eye takes visual cues from this nonparallelism and interprets it as changing depth.

Drawing grids on planar patches amounts to drawing a sequence of straight lines. It is not hard to compute the endpoints of each line in three dimensions, and then an orthographic or perspective projection reduces it to a 2D line. A routine to draw such patches is discussed in the exercises.

Example: The Horizontal Infinite Plane in Perspective

One can draw grids on an infinite plane as well as on a patch. Conceptually an infinite number of u- and v-contours are drawn to "cover" the entire plane. But because all lines outside the window are clipped anyway, the programmer arranges to draw only enough lines to cover the window.

The classic perspective projection shows a grid on an infinite horizontal plane in such a way that **vanishing points** and a **horizon** are visible. Figure 10.12 shows a grid drawn on the horizontal plane $y = -2$. The plane is parametrized as $\mathbf{p}(u, v) = u\mathbf{i} - 2\mathbf{j} - v\mathbf{k}$, so that lines of constant v sweep across to the right with increasing x, and lines of constant u recede directly back parallel to the z-axis. Integer increments are used in both u and v.

How do these lines appear in the perspective view? Set $E = 1$. According to Equation 10.8, the point $\mathbf{p}(u, v)$ projects to $(u/(1 + v), -2/(1 + v))$, and lines of constant $v = v_0$ project to horizontal lines passing through $y = -2/(1 + v_0)$

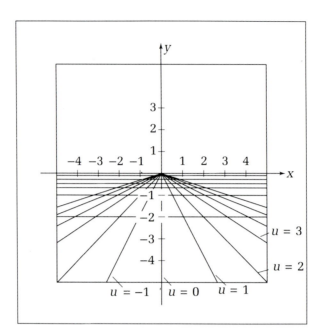

Figure 10.12.
Vanishing points and the horizon.

(why?). These lines become more crowded for larger values of v_0. Lines of constant $u = u_0$ project as straight lines that pass through the point $(u_0, -2)$ when $v = 0$ (why?), and they all converge on the vanishing point $(0, 0)$ as $v \to \infty$. As we shall discuss more thoroughly in Chapter 12, the horizon lies at $y = 0$: All lines in any horizontal plane that recede at all will end up on the horizon.

Drill Exercises

10.12.   Variations on the Theme. Carefully draw by hand the same picture as in Figure 10.12, but with $E = 4$. What is the effect of changing the horizontal plane from $y = -2$ to $y = -4$? What happens at $v = -4$?

10.13.   Other Grids in Perspective. Consider the reparametrization of this plane to $\mathbf{p}(u, v) = (u + v)\mathbf{i} - 2\mathbf{j} - v\mathbf{k}$. If integer values of u and v are used, will the grid still be square? Lines of constant u no longer recede parallel to the z-axis. What is their vanishing point now? What do lines of constant v project to? Do they have a vanishing point now? Sketch the grid for $E = 1$, and generalize this to an arbitrary unit square grid on a horizontal plane.

10.5.2 Drawing Curved Surfaces Using Contours

Chapter 9 presented parametric representations for a variety of surfaces such as cones, superquadrics, and mathematical functions of two variables. The general form for a surface is

$$\mathbf{p}(u, v) = X(u, v)\mathbf{i} + Y(u, v)\mathbf{j} + Z(u, v)\mathbf{k} \tag{10.9}$$

in which one surface is distinguished from another by the choices of functions $X(., .)$, $Y(., .)$, and $Z(., .)$ and by the permissible ranges $(u_{\min}, u_{\max})$ and $(v_{\min}, v_{\max})$ of the parameters u and v.

Here we examine how to make drawings of surfaces. The approach is to draw a collection of u-contours and v-contours in order to reveal the shape of the surface. We also see how models akin to wireframes can be fashioned using this same technique.

Suppose that we have implemented for the surface of interest the routine **function** $X(u, v : real) : real$ that evaluates $X(u, v)$ for any relevant values of u and v. Similarly, we have $Y(u, v : real) : real$ and $Z(u, v : real) : real$. These might be simple evaluations of formulas, or they could involve complex algorithms.

To draw the u-contour at u' as v varies from v_{min} to v_{max}, do the following:

1. At a set of (usually equispaced) values v_i between v_{min} and v_{max}, compute the location $P_i = (X(u', v_i),\ Y(u', v_i),\ Z(u', v_i))$.

2. Project each point, P_i, to its 2D counterpart, p_i, using an orthographic or perspective projection.

3. Draw the polyline based on the 2D points $p_1, p_2, \ldots$

A similar approach is used for drawing v-contours.

We shall now consider briefly the issues in drawing the various types of surfaces discussed in Chapter 9.

Surfaces of Revolution

Recall from Chapter 9 that a surface of revolution has the parametric form

$$\mathbf{p}(u, v) = x(v)\cos(u)\mathbf{i} + x(v)\sin(u)\mathbf{j} + z(v)\mathbf{k} \qquad (10.10)$$

in which the "profile" is defined by the curve $(x(v), z(v))$. We depict a surface of revolution by drawing a set of parallels and a set of meridians. Parallels are v-contours and are circles in three dimensions. Meridians are u-contours and are rotated versions of the profile. The case in which the profile is a half-circle, $(x(v), z(v)) = (R\cos(v), R\sin(v))$, was shown in Figure 9.10a. When rotated about the z-axis, it generates a sphere or globe. We can't yet draw the globe from the general point of view shown in that figure, but we can draw perspective projections with the eye on, say, the y-axis. Such a view is shown in Figure 10.13.

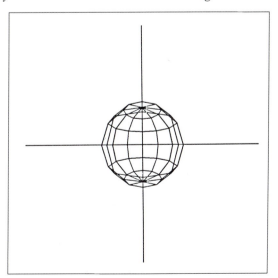

Figure 10.13.
Perspective view of a globe.

Five parallels at $v = -60°$, $-30°$, $0°$, $30°$, and $60°$ are shown, along with ten meridians at multiples of $36°$. The globe has radius 5, and the eye distance is $E = 10$, so there is noticeable perspective foreshortening.

Drill Exercises

10.14. The Torus. Determine a reasonable set of u- and v-contours to be used in drawing the torus of Figure 9.11.

10.15. Define the Profile. Provide specific definitions, $(x(v), z(v))$, for each of the 13 segments of the goblet profile. For v between 0 and 1, $(x(v), z(v))$ "spells out" segment A; for v between 1 and 2, it spells out B; and so forth.

A goblet such as that in Figure 9.9 is also interesting to draw. A mathematical expression is found that approximates the desired shape of the profile, and a set of parallels and meridians is drawn. The profile function may have to be defined "piecewise" to achieve the desired shape. Figure 10.14 shows an example design for the profile made of 13 segments: A, C, E, G, K, and M are straight lines; B, D, F, H, and L are quarter-circles; J is a half-circle; and I is a portion of a sinewave.

For a complicated profile such as this, some experimentation is usually required to find the best values of v at which to draw parallels.

Modeling the Surface As a Wireframe

As an alternative to defining the profile mathematically, we can model it as a sequence of points (x_1, z_1), (x_2, z_2), . . . , (x_n, z_n), as suggested in Figure 10.15.

Figure 10.14.
Designing the profile for the goblet.

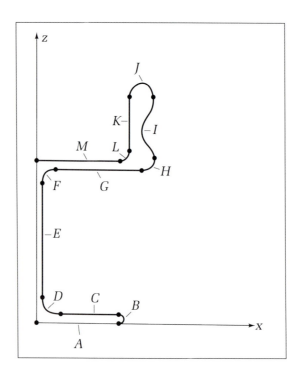

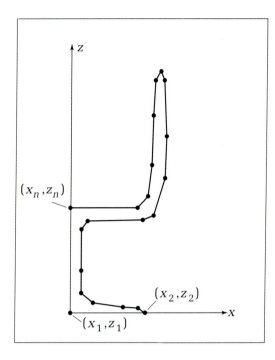

Figure 10.15.
The profile modeled by data points.

This leads to a wireframe model for the surface of revolution. Versions of the profile are placed at, say, m different angles of rotation u_j for $j = 1, 2, \ldots, m$ about the z-axis. The one at angle u_j therefore has vertices $P_{ij} = (x_i\cos(u_j), x_i \sin(u_j), z_i)$ for $i = 1, 2, \ldots, n$.

The meridian for the version at u_j is the set of edges joining these vertices (where j is fixed and i varies from 1 to n). Other edges are added to form the parallels: For each i the P_{ij} for $j = 1, 2, \ldots, m$ are joined. The wireframe model contains a total of nm vertices. (How many edges are there in all?) This can easily be put into code—see the exercises.

Mathematical Functions of Two Variables

Recall from Chapter 9 that to plot the function $g(., .)$ as $z = g(x, y)$ the appropriate parametric form is $\mathbf{p}(u, v) = (u, v, g(u, v))$. With this formulation, u-contours are the same as contours of constant x, and v-contours are contours of constant y. Equispaced contours are usually used, and they should be spaced closely enough so that no important undulations in the function are skipped over.

Example

Suppose we wish to plot the function $g(x, y) = e^{-x^2 - 2y^2}$ over the range $x \in (-3, 3)$ and $y \in (-2, 2)$. We choose a perspective view with the eye at $(6, 0, 0)$ on the x-axis.

Figure 10.16 shows the result of using 31 u-contours and 21 v-contours. The general shape of the function is apparent, but the details are somewhat jumbled owing to the restricted point of view as well as the presence of lines that should be hidden by closer parts of the surface. This figure clearly points to the need for being able to view surfaces like this from better angles (as we do in Chapter 12).

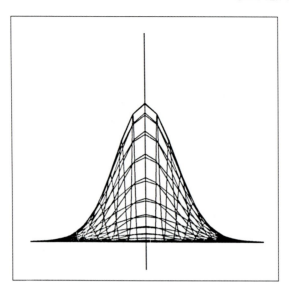

Figure 10.16.
Perspective view of a function
of two variables.

Quadrics and Superquadrics

To draw these surfaces we can take the same approach of drawing several u- and v-contours. Tables 9.1 and 9.2 provide the required functions, $X(u, v)$, $Y(u, v)$, and $Z(u, v)$, as well as the ranges of u and v. The same problem arises here from the restricted point of view: It fails to reveal the surface shape clearly. Also, particularly for the superquadrics, the use of equispaced u- and v-contours causes lines to be "bunched" together in some places (see Figure 9.15) and spread out in others. Therefore one must experiment to achieve the best and most revealing drawings of these surfaces.

When more than one drawing is to be made of a surface or when a model of it is needed for other purposes, a wireframe model can be constructed in the same way as for a surface of revolution. A selection of values $u_1, u_2, \ldots$ and $v_1, v_2, \ldots$ is made, and the vertices are defined at each $\mathbf{p}(u_i, v_j)$. These are placed in a vertex list in a variable of type *wireframe*. Following this, edges are added to the model by tracing along in u for each v_j and then tracing along in v for each u_i. Once formed, the wireframe object can be drawn as always, any number of times.

10.6 Summary

We first introduced the notion of a wireframe model that captures the shape of an object by means of a set of vertices and edges. Wireframes are used extensively in interactive modeling situations, for they permit very rapid drawing of a model, thus allowing a designer to see the object from various angles and to edit it. Later, faces are added to such models, and the faces are filled with appropriate colors. This makes the images much more realistic, but the drawing process also takes longer.

In order to draw a three-dimensional object such as a wireframe, each edge must be projected in some fashion from three dimensions to two dimensions. To help develop geometric intuition, only the simplest projections were introduced. An orthographic projection just deletes one of the three coordinates of each point. Parallel projectors are used: The projector from each point is directed parallel to the axis of the deleted coordinate.

We also described perspective projections. The projector from each point moves toward a fixed point called the eye, and the projected point is the intersection of the projector and a viewplane. Because the projectors converge at the eye, more remote objects appear smaller—a phenomenon known as perspective foreshortening. For simplicity, we considered only a restricted class of perspective projections, for which the eye is constrained to lie on one of the coordinate axes. This often, however, produces drawings that are sterile and unrevealing, pointing to the need for a more general projection scheme.

We showed that both orthographic and perspective projections preserve straight lines, which is a boon to graphics applications, as we need only find the projection of the two endpoints of a 3D line and draw the line between these projections.

Finally, we addressed the problem of drawing several of the surface types introduced in Chapter 9 and described the general technique of drawing u-contours and v-contours.

Programming Exercises

10.16. Drawing 3D Curves. Develop a routine that draws orthographic and perspective views of the curve $\mathbf{f}(t) = (x(t), y(t), z(t))$ for given functions $x(\ )$, $y(\ )$, and $z(\ )$. To draw such a curve, compute the position vector of the curve at a set of closely spaced values of t; project each point; and join them in a polyline. Exercise the program on the helix $(\cos(t), \sin(t), t)$ and some additional shapes of your choice.

10.17. Drawing Wireframes in Perspective. Adjust Code Fragment 10.2 so that it draws an object of type *wireframe* in a perspective projection. Parameter E for eye distance must be supplied to the routine. Make the routine flexible enough so that the eye can be placed on any of the axes.

10.18. Adjusting *Persp_z*( ) for the New Viewing Direction. Write out the code for *Persp_z*( ) that performs a perspective projection of an arbitrary point onto the viewplane $z = 0$ with the eye at $(0, 0, E)$.

10.19. Putting the Eye on the *y*-Axis. Derive the necessary projection for the case in which the eye is on the y-axis and the x, z-plane is the viewplane. Also consider what changes must be made if the eye is on the negative x-, y-, or z-axis. In Chapter 12 we generalize by putting the eye at any position whatsoever.

10.20. Modeling the Prism. Write routine *BuildPrism* (*poly* : *polypoint*; H : *real*; **var** *prism* : *wireframe*) which builds a wireframe model based on a polygon stored in *poly*. The routine fills in values for the vertex list and edge list.

10.21. Drawing Platonic Solids. After studying Appendix 8 on the platonic solids, write a routine, *BuildDodeca*, that sets up a record of type *wireframe* for the dodecahedron described there. Then draw the dodecahedron using various perspective projections. Repeat for the icosahedron.

10.22. Drawing Patches in Perspective. Write the procedure *DrawPatch*(*c, a, b* : *vector3D*; *num_u, num_v* : *integer*) which draws a perspective projection of the patch $\mathbf{c} + \mathbf{a}u + \mathbf{b}v$ for u and v between 0 and 1, with *num_u* and *num_v* grid lines drawn on the patch in u and v, respectively. Exercise the routine by drawing a variety of patches on planes having different directions.

10.23. Modeling Surfaces of Revolution As Wireframes. Write and exercise **procedure** *BuildSurfRev*(*poly* : *polypoint*; m : *integer*; **var** *obj* : *wireframe*); which constructs a wireframe, *obj*, from a polypoint, *poly*. The routine places m versions of the polypoint rotated about the z-axis, as described in Section 10.5.2, and connects edges to form meridians and parallels.

10.24. Drawing Ruled Surfaces. Write and exercise an application that draws various ruled patches in perspective. Among other surfaces, draw the "ribbon candy" and "double helix" of Exercises 9.6 and 9.7.

10.25. Drawing Fields of Normals to Surfaces. Write a routine that draws short line segments at a grid of points on a given surface to represent the size and direction of the normal vector to the surface at each grid point. Exercise the routine on several types of surfaces.

10.26. Drawing Surfaces of Revolution. Implement routines to draw the u-contours (rotated profiles) and v-contours (circles) of a surface of revolution. To exercise the program, choose example shapes for the profile curve, including a half-circle and a polyline, and draw perspective views of the surface.

10.27. Drawing Quadric Surfaces. Write an application that produces perspective projections of each of the quadric surfaces introduced in Section 9.8. For each example, adjust the various parameters to create as revealing a picture of the surface as possible.

10.28. Drawing Superquadrics. Repeat the previous exercise, but draw the four superquadrics instead. Produce examples that show the effect of changing the bulge factors n_1 and n_2.

10.29. Drawing Mathematical Functions. Write a routine that plots u-contours and v-contours for functions with position vector $\mathbf{p}(u, v) = (u, v, g(u, v))$ in a perspective projection. Put the eye on the x-axis and define a window in the y, z-plane. Exercise the routine with the functions in Equations 9.34 and 9.35, as well as the following two functions:

The Starr beauty:[1]

$$g(x, y) = \frac{xy(x^2 - y^2)}{x^2 + y^2} \qquad (10.11)$$

A black hole:

$$g(x, y) = \frac{-1}{x^2 + y^2} \qquad (10.12)$$

[1]Named for Professor Norton Starr of Amherst College, who made exquisite plots of this function in the early days of graphics.

CHAPTER 11

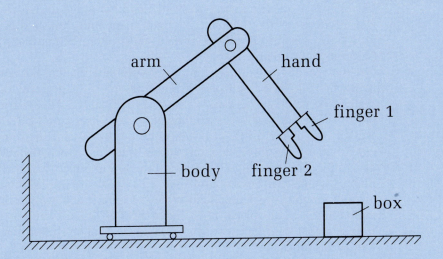

Transformations of Pictures

Goals of the Chapter

- To discuss the principal concepts and tools for transforming one picture into another.
- To study the main ideas of affine transformations in two and three dimensions.
- To develop procedures for building affine transformations and for applying them to representations of objects.
- To introduce and explore the use of homogeneous coordinates.
- To examine some nonlinear transformations that are useful in graphics.

11.1   Introduction

The objects dealt with in graphics and computer-aided design are given numerical descriptions that characterize their shape and dimensions. The numbers used refer to some coordinate system, most often the familiar x, y- or x, y, z-Cartesian coordinates.

But we often need more than one coordinate system. For convenience, we might first describe each part of some assembly in its own local coordinate system. We can then "assemble" the parts by specifying the relationship of each of the local frames of reference. Sometimes objects exhibit certain symmetries, so that only a part of them needs to be described and the remainder can be constructed by appropriate reflections, rotations, or translations. During a design process the designer may want to view an object from different vantage points, which can be accomplished by either rotating the object or moving around a hypothetical camera to achieve the desired views. And in a computer animation several objects must move relative to one another from frame to frame, so that their local coordinate systems must be shifted and rotated as the animation proceeds.

In this chapter we shall examine a set of tools that allow applications to manipulate graphical objects and their coordinate systems in an organized and efficient manner. Our emphasis is on the affine transformations, which are widely used in graphics. One important and familiar example is the window-to-viewport transformation, used to adjust the size and position of a picture.

There are two ways to view a transformation: as an object transformation or as a coordinate transformation. An **object transformation** alters the coordinates of each point according to some rule, leaving the underlying coordinate system unchanged. A **coordinate transformation** produces a different coordinate system and then represents all original points in this new system. The two views are thus closely connected, and each has advantages. To avoid confusion, we shall first develop the central ideas in terms of object transformations and then in Section 11.4 relate them to coordinate transformations.

11.2   Two-Dimensional Transformations

Although the same transformation approach is used for 3D objects as for 2D objects, it is easier to visualize effects and build intuition in the 2D case, and so we shall start there.

The possibilities for transforming graphical objects range from the simple to the complex. Figure 11.1 shows a simple example: A shape is enlarged, rotated slightly, and moved to a new position. Such transformations are common in graphics, in which parts of a picture are shifted, resized, and reoriented until they fit properly and harmoniously in the display area. Figure 11.2, on the other hand, shows a much more complicated warping of one figure (see Figure 2.1) into another, used for visual effect and to emphasize certain geometric features.

A 2D object transformation alters each point, P, in the plane into a new point, Q, using a specific formula or algorithm. More precisely, it alters the

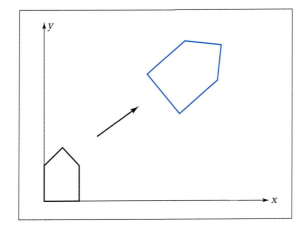

Figure 11.1.
A picture before and after a
transformation.

coordinates of P into new values that specify point Q. This can be expressed using some function, T, that maps coordinate pairs into coordinate pairs:

$$T(P_x, P_y) = (Q_x, Q_y) \qquad (11.1)$$

or, more succinctly,

$$Q = T(P) \qquad (11.2)$$

where $P = (P_x, P_y)$ and $Q = (Q_x, Q_y)$. Figure 11.3 illustrates this process: An arbitrary point P in the plane is mapped to Q. Q is the image of P under the mapping T. In program code the procedure $T(\ )$ could be declared as **procedure** $T(P : point;$ **var** $Q : point)$; and the code in $T(\ )$ would compute the new coordinates Q_x and Q_y based on those of P.

Keep in mind that each point P of interest in the plane is subjected to the same mapping. Because of this, we can talk of mapping whole collections of

Figure 11.2.
A complex warping of a figure.

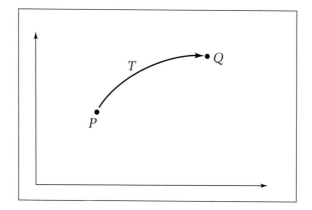

Figure 11.3.
Mapping points into new
points.

points, such as lines or circles, at once. The image of line L under T is the set of all images of the individual points of L. For most mappings of interest, this image is still a connected curve of some shape, but it may no longer be a straight line. Affine transformations, however, do preserve lines: The image of a straight line under T is also a straight line. Most of this chapter will focus on affine transformations, but we shall also introduce several examples of mappings that do not preserve lines.

11.3 The Affine Transformations

The most common transformations used in computer graphics are the **affine transformations**, all of which admit a particularly simple matrix representation, and a succession of affine transformations can easily be combined into one overall affine transformation.

Affine transformations have a simple form. If the 2D affine transformation T maps $P = (P_x, P_y)$ into the image $Q = (Q_x, Q_y)$, Q_x and Q_y will be related to $P = (P_x, P_y)$ by the simple equations

$$Q_x = aP_x + cP_y + tr_x$$
$$Q_y = bP_x + dP_y + tr_y$$
(11.3)

for some six constants a, b, c, d, tr_x, and tr_y. (As discussed later, to avoid degeneracies we insist that $ad \neq bc$.) Thus the new components are linear combinations of the old ones, along with offsets tr_x and tr_y (the name tr suggests a translation). Affine transformations are simply linear transformations plus added offsets. Both Q_x and Q_y are linear mixes of P_x and P_y. This "cross fertilization" between the x- and y-components gives rise to rotations and shears.

The affine transformation of Equation 11.3 has a useful matrix representation that helps organize one's thinking.[1] By direct calculation it is easy to see that Equation 11.3 can be written using a matrix:

$$(Q_x, Q_y) = (P_x, P_y) \begin{pmatrix} a & b \\ c & d \end{pmatrix} + (tr_x, tr_y)$$
(11.4)

[1]See Appendix 2 for a review of matrices.

This can be written more compactly as

$$Q = PM + \mathbf{tr} \qquad (11.5)$$

where $P = (P_x, P_y)$, $Q = (Q_x, Q_y)$, $\mathbf{tr} = (tr_x, tr_y)$ is the offset vector, and M is the 2-by-2 matrix:

$$M = \begin{pmatrix} a & b \\ c & d \end{pmatrix} \qquad (11.6)$$

The form of Equation 11.5 suggests a "signal flow" visual aid that proves useful when discussing affine transformations. Figure 11.4 shows the point P "feeding into" a block labeled M, as if it were a physical signal. When passing through the block, P is multiplied by matrix M. The result of this (the point PM) then passes through a "summer" in which the vector $\mathbf{tr}$ is added to it. The final signal that emerges from this system is the transformed point $Q = PM + \mathbf{tr}$. Note that it is clear from this diagram that an affine transformation is a matrix multiplication followed by a translation. Various forms of this flow diagram are used to make the succession of point operations clearer and more vivid.

Drill Exercise

11.1. Reversing the Order of the Elements. Suppose the summer is placed before the matrix multiplication in the signal flow diagram of Figure 11.4. If point P is fed into the system, provide an expression for the point Q that is produced.

Because the whole point of using a transformation is to convert one graphical object into another, we must explore the variety of geometric effects offered by affine transformations. Affine transformations produce arbitrary combinations of four **elementary transformations**: (1) a translation, (2) a scaling, (3) a rotation, and (4) a shear. Figure 11.5 shows an example of the effect of each type. We shall first look at each one individually and then examine more general properties when they are used in combination.

11.3.1 Translation

One often must translate a picture into a different position on a graphics display. The **translation** part of the affine transformation of Equation 11.5 arises

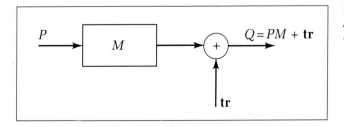

Figure 11.4.
A signal flow visualization for affine transformations.

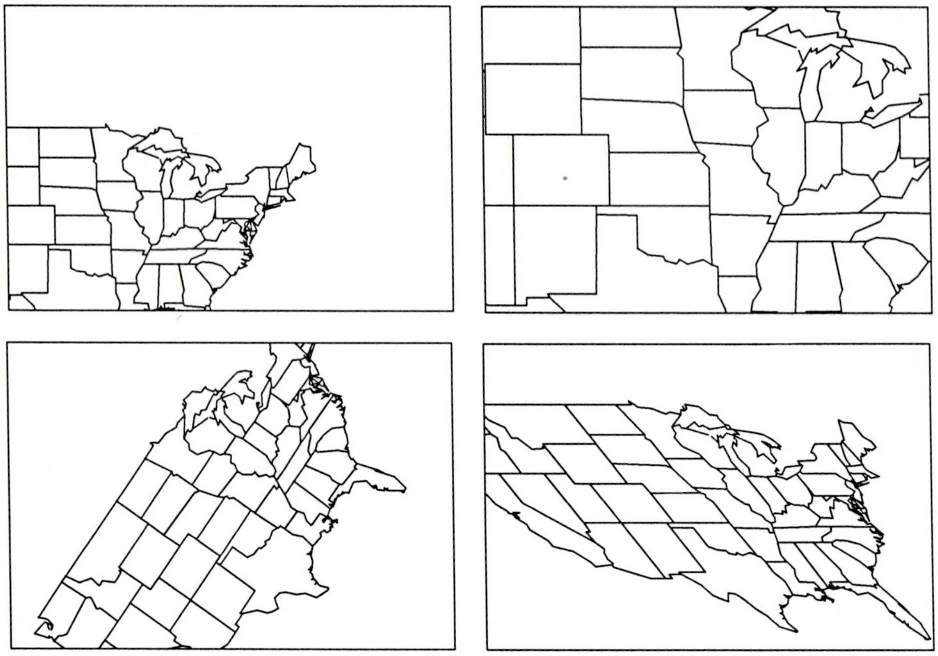

Figure 11.5.
Elementary transformations of a
map.

from the offset vector $\mathbf{tr} = (tr_x, tr_y)$. For a translation alone, PM must equal P itself, and so M must be the **identity matrix**:

$$M = \begin{pmatrix} 1 & 0 \\ 0 & 1 \end{pmatrix} \qquad (11.7)$$

and Equation 11.5 becomes $Q = P + \mathbf{tr}.$[2] In component form:

$$(Q_x, Q_y) = (P_x + tr_x, P_y + tr_y) \qquad (11.8)$$

Each point is translated over the plane by the amount (tr_x, tr_y), in the same manner that vector addition is performed. For example, if the translation vector is $(2, 3)$, every point will be altered into one that is two units farther to the right and three units above the original point. The point $(1, -5)$ is thus transformed into $(3, -2)$, and the point $(0, 0)$ is transformed into $(2, 3)$.

The signal flow diagram for a pure translation is shown in Figure 11.6. The multiplication by the matrix M is omitted because M is the identity matrix.

11.3.2 Scaling

Figure 11.6.
Signal flow diagram for a pure
translation.

A **scaling** changes the size of a picture and involves two scale factors, S_x and S_y, for the x- and y-coordinates, respectively:

$$(Q_x, Q_y) = (S_x P_x, S_y P_y) \qquad (11.9)$$

and so the matrix for a scaling is simply

$$M = \begin{pmatrix} S_x & 0 \\ 0 & S_y \end{pmatrix} \qquad (11.10)$$

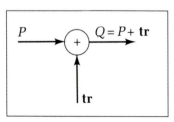

[2]We saw in Chapter 7 that adding a vector to a point is a meaningful operation, as it causes a displacement.

and vector **tr** is **0**. The signal flow diagram in this case contains a matrix multiplication only: The summer is absent.

Scaling in this fashion is more accurately called **scaling about the origin**, because each point P is moved S_x times farther from the origin in the x-direction, and S_y times farther from the origin in the y-direction. If a scale factor is negative, then there is also a **reflection** about a coordinate axis (recall Exercise 4.40.). There are also "pure" reflections, for which both of the scale factors are $+1$ or -1. An example is $T(P_x, P_y) = (-P_x, P_y)$. This transformation produces a mirror image of a picture by "flipping" it about the y-axis, replacing each occurrence of x with $-x$. Figure 11.7 shows an example in which the scaling $(S_x, S_y) = (-1, 2)$ is applied to a collection of points. Each point is both reflected about the y-axis and scaled by 2 in the y-direction.

If the two scale factors are the same, $S_x = S_y = s$, the transformation will be a **uniform scaling**, or a magnification about the origin, with magnification factor $|s|$. If s is negative, there will also be reflections about both axes. A point is moved radially to a position $|s|$ times farther away from the origin. If $|s| < 1$, the points will be moved closer to the origin, a "demagnification." If the scale factors are not the same, the scaling is called a **differential scaling**. The simplest differential scaling occurs when one of the factors S_x or S_y is one. This is known as a **strain**.

11.3.3 Rotation

In regard to the **rotation** of a figure about a given point through some angle, Figure 11.8 shows a set of points rotated about the origin through an angle of $\theta = 60°$. We shall show next that when $T(\ )$ is a rotation about the origin, the offset vector **tr** is zero and $Q = T(P)$ has the form

$$Q_x = P_x \cos(\theta) - P_y \sin(\theta)$$
$$Q_y = P_x \sin(\theta) + P_y \cos(\theta) \qquad (11.11)$$

This form assumes that positive values of θ denote a counterclockwise (CCW) rotation. By inspection, the matrix form for a pure rotation about the origin is

$$M = \begin{pmatrix} \cos(\theta) & \sin(\theta) \\ -\sin(\theta) & \cos(\theta) \end{pmatrix} \qquad (11.12)$$

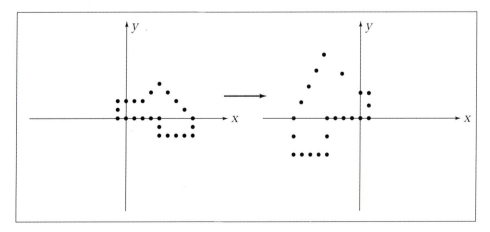

Figure 11.7.
A scaling and reflection.

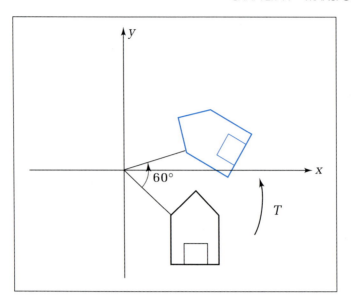

Figure 11.8.
Rotation of points through
angle $\theta = 60°$.

Example

Find the transformed point, Q, caused by rotating $P = (3, 5)$ about the origin through an angle of 60°.

Solution:

For an angle of 60°, $\cos(\theta) = .5$ and $\sin(\theta) = .866$, and Equation 11.11 yields

$$Q_x = 3 \times .5 - 5 \times .866 = -2.83$$
$$Q_y = 3 \times .866 + 5 \times .5 = 5.098$$

Check this on graph paper by swinging an arc of 60° from (3, 5) and reading off the position of the mapped point. Also check numerically that Q is at the same distance, 5.831, as P is from the origin.

Derivation of the Rotation Mapping

Figure 11.9 shows how to compute the new components, (Q_x, Q_y), of an original point, (P_x, P_y), after it has been rotated about the origin through an angle θ. If P is at a distance R from the origin, at some angle ϕ, Q must be at the same distance as P is and at angle $\theta + \phi$. Using trigonometry, from Figure 11.9 the coordinates of Q are

$$Q_x = R \cos(\theta + \phi)$$
$$Q_y = R \sin(\theta + \phi) \tag{11.13}$$

Substitute into Equation 11.13 the two familiar trigonometric relations:

$$\cos(\theta + \phi) = \cos(\theta) \cos(\phi) - \sin(\theta) \sin(\phi)$$
$$\sin(\theta + \phi) = \sin(\theta) \cos(\phi) + \cos(\theta) \sin(\phi) \tag{11.14}$$

and use $P_x = R \cos(\phi)$ and $P_y = R \sin(\phi)$ to obtain Equation 11.11.

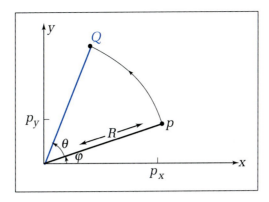

Figure 11.9.
Derivation of the rotation mapping.

Drill Exercise

11.2   Rotate a Point. Use Equation 11.11 to find the image of each of the following points after rotation about the origin:

a.   (2, 3) through an angle of −45 degrees

b.   (1, 1) through an angle of −180 degrees

c.   (60, 61) through an angle of 4 degrees

In each case check the result on graph paper, and compare numerically the distances of the original point and its image from the origin.

11.3.4 Shearing

An example of **shearing** is illustrated in Figure 11.10, which is a shear in the x-direction. In this case the y-coordinate of each point is unaffected, whereas each x-coordinate is translated by an amount that increases linearly with y. A shear in the x-direction is given by

$$\begin{aligned} Q_x &= P_x + hP_y \\ Q_y &= P_y \end{aligned} \qquad (11.15)$$

where coefficient h specifies what fraction of the y-coordinate of P is to be added to the x-coordinate. The quantity h can be positive or negative. Note that shearing can be used to make italic letters out of regular letters.

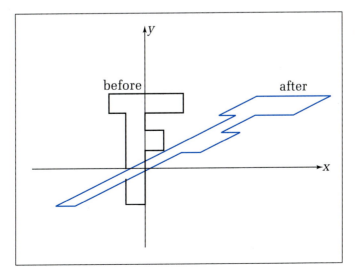

Figure 11.10.
An example of shearing.

Example

Into what point does (3, 4) shear when $h = .3$?

Solution:
$Q = (3 + .3 \times 4, 4) = (4.2, 4)$.

More generally, a simultaneous shear in both the x- and y-directions is effected according to the form

$$Q_x = P_x + hP_y$$
$$Q_y = gP_x + P_y \qquad\qquad (11.16)$$

in which a shear in the y-direction is brought about by a nonzero value of the constant g, which specifies what fraction of P_x is to be added to the y-component of P_y to form Q_y. A shear has the following matrix representation:

$$M = \begin{pmatrix} 1 & g \\ h & 1 \end{pmatrix} \qquad\qquad (11.17)$$

If h is zero, the shear will reduce to a pure shear in the y-direction.

Example

Let $g = .2$ and $h = .5$. To what point does $(6, -2)$ map?

Solution:
$Q = (6 - .5 \times 2, .2 \times 6 - 2) = (5, -.8)$.

Drill Exercise

11.3. Shearing Lines. Consider the shear for which $g = .4$ and $h = 0$. Experiment with various sets of three collinear points to build some assurance that the sheared points are still collinear. Assuming that lines do shear into lines, determine into what objects the following line segments shear:

a.   the horizontal segment between $(-3, 4)$ and $(2, 4)$

b.   the horizontal segment between $(-3, -4)$ and $(2, -4)$

c.   the vertical segment between $(-2, 5)$ and $(-2, -1)$

d.   the vertical segment between $(2, 5)$ and $(2, -1)$

e.   the segment between $(-1, -2)$ and $(3, 2)$

Into what does the square with corners $(-1, -1)$, $(-1, 1)$, $(1, -1)$, and $(1, 1)$ shear?

11.3.5 The Inverse of an Affine Transformation

It is always reassuring to be able to undo the effect of a transformation, and it is particularly easy with affine transformations. If point P is mapped into point q according to

$$Q = PM + \mathbf{tr}$$

then subtracting $\mathbf{tr}$ from both sides will yield $PM = (Q - \mathbf{tr})$. If matrix M is non-singular (i.e., if its determinant is nonzero—see Appendix 2), postmultiply both sides by the inverse M^{-1} of M and write

$$P = (Q - \mathbf{tr})M^{-1} \qquad\qquad (11.18)$$

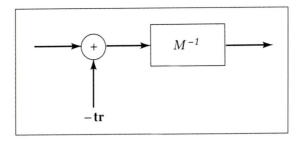

Figure 11.11.
Signal flow diagram for the
inverse transformation.

Figure 11.11 shows the signal flow diagram for this inverse transformation. Because the combined quantity $Q - \mathbf{tr}$ is multiplied by the matrix, the summer must come first, and it adds the offset $-\mathbf{tr}$. The result is then multiplied by matrix M^{-1}.

When it exists, the inverse of M is given by

$$M^{-1} = \frac{1}{ad - bc}\begin{pmatrix} d & -b \\ -c & a \end{pmatrix}$$ (11.19)

For pure rotations, translations, and shearing (along one axis), det $M = 1$ so that M^{-1} exists. For scaling, M^{-1} exists except in the degenerate case, in which one of the scaling factors, S_x or S_y, of Equation 11.10 is zero. From Equation 11.19 we therefore obtain the following useful facts:

- *Rotation* (use M in Equation 11.12):

$$M^{-1} = \begin{pmatrix} \cos(\theta) & -\sin(\theta) \\ \sin(\theta) & \cos(\theta) \end{pmatrix}$$ (11.20)

- *Scaling* (use M in Equation 11.10):

$$M^{-1} = \begin{pmatrix} \dfrac{1}{S_x} & 0 \\ 0 & \dfrac{1}{S_y} \end{pmatrix}$$

- *Shearing* (use M in Equation 11.17):

$$M^{-1} = \frac{1}{1 - gh}\begin{pmatrix} 1 & -g \\ -h & 1 \end{pmatrix}$$

- *Translations*: The inverse transformation simply subtracts the offset $\mathbf{tr}$ rather than adds it.

Drill Exercises

11.4.   What Is the Inverse of a Rotation? Show that the inverse of a rotation through θ is a rotation through $-\theta$. Is this reasonable geometrically? Why?

11.5.   Inverting a Shear. Is the inverse of a shear also a shear? Show why or why not.

11.6.   An Inverse Matrix. Compute the inverse of the matrix

$$M = \begin{pmatrix} 3 & 2 \\ -1 & 1 \end{pmatrix}$$

11.4 Some Useful Properties of Affine Transformations

We have examined only the four elementary affine transformations so far and must go on to complex combinations of these, as well as to three-dimensional transformations. But several important properties of general affine transformations can be established with little difficulty, and it is convenient to do this first. Because no reference to the dimension of the transformation is made in the arguments, the properties hold for 3D as well as 2D affine transformations.

Affine Transformations Preserve Lines

As we noted, affine transformations preserve collinearity, and so the image of a straight line is another straight line. In computer graphics this vastly simplifies drawing transformed line segments: We need only compute the image of the two endpoints of the original line and then draw a straight line between them!

To show this property we use the parametric representation for a straight line passing through point A at $t = 0$ and through point B at $t = 1$:

$$P(t) = A(1 - t) + Bt \tag{11.21}$$

Now subject the general point, $P(t)$, on this line to an arbitrary affine transformation according to Equation 11.5 to produce point $Q(t)$:

$$Q(t) = (A(1 - t) + Bt)M + \mathbf{tr} \tag{11.22}$$

But linearity of matrix multiplication allows us to rearrange this to the form

$$Q(t) = (AM + \mathbf{tr}) + (B - A)Mt \tag{11.23}$$

which is clearly also the parametric representation of a straight line; thus an affine transformation does preserve collinearity! The new line passes through $AM + \mathbf{tr}$ and moves in the direction $(B - A)M$.

Preservation of collinearity guarantees that polygons will transform into polygons; in particular, triangles will transform into triangles. As discussed in a later exercise, a 2D affine transformation is completely determined when its effect on a triangle is specified, and any triangle can be transformed into any other by choosing the proper affine transformation. This is not entirely surprising, however, when we recall that a 2D affine transformation involves six constants and therefore has six degrees of freedom, which is enough to specify how each of the three vertices of a triangle is to be mapped.

Affine Transformation of Vectors and Rays

Another fact emerges by simply reinterpreting the lines above as rays. We can view the line of Equation 11.21 as the ray that emanates from point A at $t = 0$ and moves in the direction $\boldsymbol{\beta} = B - A$. The parametric form of this ray is

$$A + \boldsymbol{\beta} t \tag{11.24}$$

Equation 11.22 then shows that the image of this ray is

$$(AM + \mathbf{tr}) + \boldsymbol{\beta} Mt \tag{11.25}$$

which emanates from $AM + \textbf{tr}$ and moves in the new direction $\boldsymbol{\beta}Mt$. The important point is that the vector $\boldsymbol{\beta}$ is transformed into the vector $\boldsymbol{\beta}M$, unaffected by the offset vector $\textbf{tr}$. So when points and lines are transformed, the offset vector $\textbf{tr}$ shifts them, but when a vector is transformed, the offset vector is omitted.

Parallelism of Lines Is Preserved

If two lines are parallel, their images under an affine transformation will also be parallel. Represent the two parallel lines as rays: $L_1(t) = A_1 + \boldsymbol{\beta}t$ and $L_2(t) = A_2 + \boldsymbol{\beta}t$. They have the same direction, $\boldsymbol{\beta}t$, but emanate from different points. Equation 11.25, however, states that after being transformed, they both have direction given by $\boldsymbol{\beta}M$, and so they are parallel. An important consequence of this property is that parallelograms map into other parallelograms.

Coordinate Transformations

We can use the fact that affine transformations map parallelograms into parallelograms to get an idea of what an arbitrary affine transformation T can do. Apply T to a unit square grid, as in Figure 11.12. T maps the square grid to another grid consisting of two sets of parallel lines. This is what an affine transformation can do: Warp figures in the way that one grid is mapped into another. The new lines can be tilted at any angle; they can be any (fixed) distance apart; and the two sets need not be perpendicular. The whole grid can be positioned anywhere in the plane.

From the figure it is apparent that T maps one coordinate system into another. The system with origin O and axes $\textbf{i}$ and $\textbf{j}$ is converted into a system with origin O' (given in terms of the first system by $\textbf{tr}$), and axes we call $\textbf{u}$ and $\textbf{v}$.

How are $\textbf{u}$ and $\textbf{v}$ related to matrix M? We find that $\textbf{u}$ is the result of transforming vector $\textbf{i} : \textbf{u} = \textbf{i}M$. When M is multiplied by $\textbf{i}$, the result is the top row of M. Similarly, $\textbf{v}$ is the result of transforming $\textbf{j}$; thus $\textbf{v} = \textbf{j}M$. We therefore can write M in "partitioned" form (see Appendix 2) as $\textbf{u}$ "placed over" $\textbf{v}$:

$$M = \begin{pmatrix} \textbf{u} \\ \textbf{v} \end{pmatrix} \qquad (11.26)$$

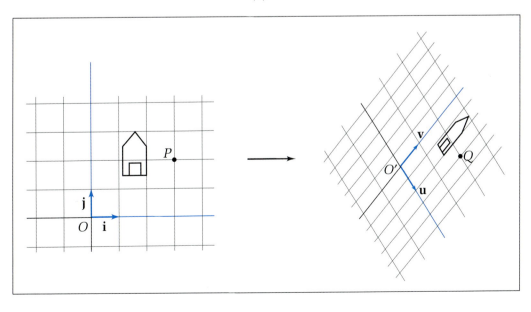

Figure 11.12.
A transformed grid.

The transformation maps the coordinate system with axes **i** and **j** into one having its origin at **tr**, its first axis given by the top row of M and its second axis given by the bottom row of M.

Representing Positions in the New Coordinate System

Suppose that a coordinate System II is derived from System I by matrix M and offset vector **tr**. If point P is given by position vector $\mathbf{p} = (x, y)$ in System I, what will its representation, (a, b), in System II be? One might even call (a, b) the alias of P in terms of the coordinate System II. The situation is shown in Figure 11.13, with **u** and **v** the axis vectors for System II. Thus in terms of System I quantities, **p** has representation $\mathbf{p} = \mathbf{tr} + a\mathbf{u} + b\mathbf{v}$. But because **u** and **v** are the top and bottom rows of M, it is easy to show that $a\mathbf{u} + b\mathbf{v} = (a, b)M$ (why?). Thus we have

$$\mathbf{p} = (a, b)M + \mathbf{tr} \tag{11.27}$$

Simply subtract **tr** from both sides, and then postmultiply both sides by M^{-1} to get the desired System II representation:

$$(a, b) = (\mathbf{p} - \mathbf{tr})M^{-1} \tag{11.28}$$

The expression on the right side is seen to be the inverse transformation of the mapping from System I to System II. This is not surprising, as coordinate transformations operate in just the reverse sense from object transformations. That is, if System II is derived from System I by means of an affine mapping based on transformation T (based on matrix M and offset **tr**), (1) the axes of System II will be the rows of M, and (2) point P with representation in System I of **p** will have representation with respect to System II of **p** applied to the inverse transformation; that is, $(\mathbf{p} - \mathbf{tr})M^{-1}$.

This ability to move between representations in two coordinate systems is particularly useful for general viewing techniques. The most common case involves rigid motions only—when the two coordinate systems are related by rotations and translations, as in the following example. In such a case the mapped axis vectors **u** and **v** are also perpendicular to each other, and both have unit length.

Figure 11.13.
Representing a point in System II.

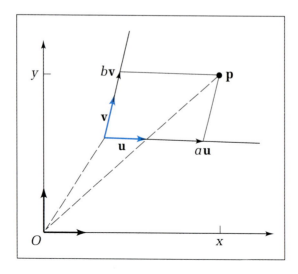

Example

Let the transformation consist of a rotation of 30° followed by an offset by (3, 2). What is the representation of point (6, 7) in the new coordinate system?

Solution:
For a 30° rotation, the top row of M is $\mathbf{u} = (.866, .5)$, and the bottom row is $\mathbf{v} = (-.5, .866)$. M has inverse

$$M^{-1} = \begin{pmatrix} .866 & -.5 \\ .5 & .866 \end{pmatrix}$$

Thus according to Equation 11.28 the representation is $(a, b) = ((6, 7) - (3, 2))M^{-1} = (5.1, 2.83)$. Check this out on graph paper.

Proportional Distances Are Preserved

Affine transformations have yet another useful property. If point U is fraction t of the way between two given points, A and B, before the transformation $T(\ )$ is applied, the transformed point, $T(U)$, will be the same fraction t of the way between the images $T(A)$ and $T(B)$. In Equation 11.21, point $P(t)$ is fraction t of the way between A and B, and this point maps to

$$(AM + \mathbf{tr})(1 - t) + (BM + \mathbf{tr})t \tag{11.29}$$

which is clearly also fraction t of the way from the first image point to the second. Once again these results are a straightforward consequence of the linearity of the transformation.

A special case of the preservation of proportional distances is that midpoints of lines map into midpoints. Thus, because the diagonals of a square bisect each other, the diagonals of any parallelogram must also bisect each other. Also, it is well known that the three medians of an equilateral triangle intersect with its legs in a ratio of 1:2. Because an equilateral triangle can be converted into any triangle by means of an affine transformation, as discussed, the three medians of any triangle must intersect in the ratio 1:2!

Interesting Aside

In addition to preserving lines, parallelism, and proportional distances, affine transformations also preserve ellipses! See the exercises.

Effect of Transformations on the Areas and Volumes of Figures

In CAD applications it is often important to compute and keep track of the area or volume of an object. We saw in Chapter 7 how to compute the area of a polygon. The question naturally arises: How is the area of a polygon affected when all of its vertices are subjected to an affine transformation? It is clear geometrically that neither translations nor rotations have any effect on the area of a figure, but scalings certainly do, and shearing might.

The result is simple, and is developed in the exercises: When the transformation with matrix M is applied to an object, its area is multiplied by the magnitude of the determinant det M (see Appendix 2) of M:

$$\frac{\text{area after transformation}}{\text{area before transformation}} = |\det M| \tag{11.30}$$

The determinant of M in Equation 11.6 is det $M = ad - bc$, and so the ratio of areas is $|ad - bc|$.

Thus for a pure scaling, the new area is $S_x S_y$ times the original area, whereas for a shear along one axis only, the new area is the same as the original area! Equation 11.30 also confirms that a rotation does not alter the area of a figure, as we know that $\cos^2(\theta) + \sin^2(\theta) = 1$.

Example: The Area of an Ellipse

What is the area of the ellipse of Equation 4.17?

Solution:

This ellipse can be formed by scaling the unit circle $x^2 + y^2 = 1$ by the scale factors $S_x = a$ and $S_y = b$, a transformation for which the matrix M has determinant det $M = ab$. The unit circle is known to have area π, and so the ellipse must have area πab.

Drill Exercises

11.7.   Ellipses Are Invariant. It is obvious that rotations and translations do not destroy the property of being an ellipse, but it is also true that scaling and shearing do not, either. In graphics one frequently draws ellipses using a circle-drawing routine, by first stretching the circle in one dimension. Any ellipse can be mapped into a circle or any other ellipse by using the proper affine transformation.

Show that ellipses are invariant under an affine transformation. That is, if $P(t)$ is the parametric form for an ellipse (see Equation 4.16) and if T is an affine transforma-tion, then $Q(t) = T(P(t))$ will also be the parametric representation of an ellipse.

11.8.   Effect on Area. Show that an affine transformation causes the area of a figure to be multiplied by the factor given in Equation 11.30. *Hint*: View any figure as made up of many very small squares, each of which is mapped into a parallelogram, and then find the area of this parallelogram.

11.5 Creating and Applying Affine Transformations

How are affine transformations dealt with in a program? From Equation 11.3 one can see that an affine transformation is specified by six numbers and that four multiplications and four additions are required to perform it. The following code fragments set up a simple data type, *affine*, to capture an affine transformation, and then carry out the operations required. A matrix field, *mat*, is used to store the matrix coefficients a, b, c, and d, and a field of type *vector* contains the offset. See the exercises for an alternative form that avoids matrices in the interest of slightly improved computational efficiency.

Code Fragment 11.1. Computing Affine Transformations

```
type
   affine = record
              mat : array[1..2, 1..2] of real;
              tr : vector
            end;
```

```
procedure Transform(Tran : affine; P : point; var Q : point);
{map point P into Q with transformation Tran}
begin
  with Tran do begin
    Q.x := mat[1, 1] * P.x + mat[2, 1] * P.y + tr.dx;
    Q.y := mat[1, 2] * P.x + mat[2, 2] * P.y + tr.dy
  end
end;
```

Transform assumes that the proper six values in *Tran* have previously been computed. Thus for each of the elementary affine transformations, we need a procedure that builds these appropriate values. For example, the following code fragment shows how a rotation is established.

Code Fragment 11.2. Creating Affine Transformations

```
procedure Set_Rotate(theta : real; var Tran : affine);
{set Tran to effect a rotation through theta radians}
var s, c : real; {store sin( ), cos( ) values}
begin
  c := cos(theta); s := sin(theta);
  with Tran do begin
    mat[1, 1] := c; mat[1, 2] := s;
    mat[2, 1] := -s; mat[2, 2] := c;
    tr.dx := 0.0; tr.dy := 0.0
  end
end;
```

Routines to establish the other three transformations are considered in the exercises and are assumed to be available hereafter.

Drill Exercise

11.9. Building the Other Three Elementary Transformations. Write the following three routines

```
procedure Set_Translate(offset : vector; var Tran : af-
fine);
procedure Set_Scale(sx, sy : real; var Tran : affine);
procedure Set_Shear(g, h : real; var Tran : affine);
```

which build the appropriate values in the record *Tran*. Note that some of the fields in the record *Tran* are zero for each of these transformation types, but this is not the case when several affine transformations are combined.

11.5.1 Transforming Polylines

So far we have applied transformations to individual points only, but frequently a long polyline must be transformed. Fortunately, this is easy to do: Because affine transformations preserve straight lines, we need only transform each of the vertices of the polyline and then draw straight lines between the transformed vertices. This is one of the reasons that affine transformations are so prevalent in graphics.

One proceeds differently depending on whether the transformed polyline is to be drawn once and then forgotten or is to be saved for future use. The following pseudocode fragment builds and stores the transformed polyline. It simply transforms each vertex of *InPoly* in turn and stores it in the corresponding vertex of *OutPoly*. (What tests should be performed before the loop begins?)

Code Fragment 11.3. Transforming a Polyline

```
var InPoly, OutPoly : polypoint;
var i : integer;
begin
    OutPoly.num := InPoly.num;
    for i := 1 to InPoly.num do Transform(Tran, InPoly.pt[i], OutPoly.pt[i])
end
```

If, on the other hand, the transformed polyline is to be drawn once and then forgotten, just transform each vertex in turn, but *MoveTo*( ) the first and *Line-To*( ) each subsequent one. (See the exercises.) The speed at which this can be done is often an important issue, as one might want to control the orientation of a figure interactively. For instance, a routine might use the value returned by a *Valuator* input device (see Chapter 6) to control the rotation of a figure on the display: 0° if the valuator returns 0, 360° if it returns 1, and so forth. The user wants to turn the valuator "knob" and see the properly rotated figure appear instantly. (See the exercises.)

11.6 Composing Affine Transformations

It's rare that we want to perform just one elementary transformation; usually the application requires that we build a complex transformation out of several elementary ones. For example, we may want to

- translate by (3, −4)

- then rotate through 30 degrees

- then scale by (2, −1)

- then translate by (0, 1.5)

- and finally rotate through −30 degrees

These individual transformations combine into one overall transformation in some fashion, and we need an organized approach for building such transformations within an application. The process of applying several transformations in succession to form one overall transformation is called **composing** the transformations. As we shall see, when two affine transformations are composed, the resulting transformation is also affine!

Consider what happens when two transformations, $T_1( )$ and $T_2( )$, are composed. As suggested in Figure 11.14, $T_1( )$ maps P into Q, and $T_2( )$ maps Q into point W.

What is the transformation, $T( )$, that maps P directly into W? That is, what is the nature of $W = T_2(Q) = T_2(T_1(P))$?

Suppose that both $T_1( )$ and $T_2( )$ are affine transformations. $T_1( )$ uses matrix M_1 and offset $\mathbf{tr}_1$, and $T_2( )$ uses matrix M_2 and offset $\mathbf{tr}_2$. The corresponding signal flow diagram is shown in Figure 11.15a. Then we can write

$$Q = PM_1 + \mathbf{tr}_1 \qquad\qquad (11.31)$$

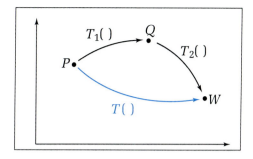

Figure 11.14.
The composition of two transformations.

and so

$$W = QM_2 + \mathbf{tr}_2$$
$$= (PM_1 + \mathbf{tr}_1)M_2 + \mathbf{tr}_2 \qquad (11.32)$$
$$= P(M_1M_2) + (\mathbf{tr}_1M_2 + \mathbf{tr}_2)$$

where we have used linearity to simplify the equation. This shows that the composition (or product) of two affine transformations is indeed an affine transformation, with the composite matrix

$$M = M_1M_2 \qquad (11.33)$$

and the composite offset

$$\mathbf{tr} = \mathbf{tr}_1M_2 + \mathbf{tr}_2 \qquad (11.34)$$

as suggested in Figure 11.15b. The new matrix is just the product of the component matrices, multiplied in the order in which the transformations are applied. The composite offset is a more complex mix of offsets and matrices. The signal flow diagram in Figure 11.15a makes it easy to remember what this offset is: $\mathbf{tr}_1$ is "injected" into the system, is multiplied by M_2, and finally is added to offset $\mathbf{tr}_2$.

This argument extends immediately to the product of any number of affine transformations $T_1, T_2, \ldots, T_n$ (why?). For example, the composition of three such transformations has matrix $M_1M_2M_3$ and offset $\mathbf{tr}_1M_2M_3 + \mathbf{tr}_2M_3 + \mathbf{tr}_3$. The signal flow diagram helps keep things straight.

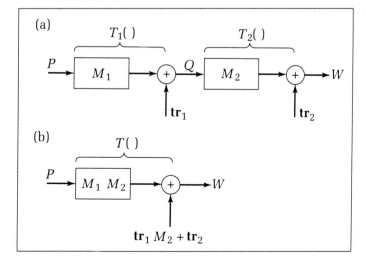

Figure 11.15.
Signal flow when two affine transformations are composed.

Drill Exercises

11.10.   Two Successive Rotations. Suppose that $T_R(\theta)$ denotes the transformation that produces a rotation through angle θ. Show that applying $T_R(\theta 1)$ followed by $T_R(\theta 2)$ is equivalent to applying the single rotation $T_R(\theta 1 + \theta 2)$. Thus successive rotations are additive.

11.11.   Some Transformations Commute. Show that uniform scaling commutes with rotation, in that the resulting transformation does not depend on the order in which the individual transformations are applied. Show that differential scaling does not commute with rotation.

11.12.   Composing Four Affine Transformations. Write out the composite matrix and the composite offset that represent the composition of four affine transformations.

11.13.   A Succession of Shears. Find the composition of a pure shear along the x-axis followed by a pure shear along the y-axis. Is this the same as a simultaneous shear along both axes, as in Equation 11.16? Sketch by hand an example of what happens to a square centered at the origin when subjected to a simultaneous shear versus a succession of shears along the two axes.

A routine to construct the composition of two affine transformations stored in *Tr1* and *Tr2* follows directly from the mathematics. The following code fragment forms the new transformation *TrNew*. It uses a matrix multiplication utility, *MatMult2( )*, which is provided in Appendix 3.

Code Fragment 11.4. Composing Two Affine Transformations

```
procedure ComposeTransf(Tr1, Tr2 : affine; var TrNew : affine);
{compose Tr1, Tr2 to form TrNew}
begin
   with TrNew do
   begin
      MatMult2(Tr1.mat, Tr2.mat, mat);
      tr.dx := Tr1.tr.dx * Tr2.mat[1, 1] + Tr1.tr.dy * Tr2.mat[2, 1] + Tr2.tr.dx;
      tr.dy := Tr1.tr.dx * Tr2.mat[1, 2] + Tr1.tr.dy * Tr2.mat[2, 2] + Tr2.tr.dy
   end
end;
```

One of the main reasons for composing transformations is computational efficiency. To see this, suppose that you want to apply two affine transformations to each of the N vertices of a polyline. It requires 12 multiplications to compose the transformations (why?) and 4 multiplications to apply a transformation to a point. Therefore the "compose-then-apply" route requires a total of $4N + 12$ multiplications. If instead we applied the first transformation to each of the points and then applied the second to each of the N images, $8N$ multiplications would be required. For polylines of practical sizes, $8N$ far exceeds $4N + 12$, and so it behooves the programmer first to compose the two transformations. (*Question*: For which values of N is it quicker to apply the two transformations separately?)

Rotating About an Arbitrary Point

So far all rotations have been about the origin. But suppose we wish instead to rotate points about some other point in the plane. As suggested in Figure 11.16, the desired "pivot" point is $V = (v_x, v_y)$, and we wish to rotate points such as P through angle θ to position Q. To do this we relate the rotation about V to an elementary rotation about the origin. Figure 11.16 shows that if we first translate all points so that V coincides with the origin, then a rotation about the origin (which maps P' to Q') will be appropriate. Once done, the whole plane is shifted

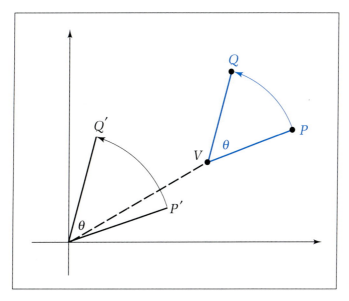

Figure 11.16.
Rotation about point V.

back to restore V to its original location. The rotation therefore consists of the following three elementary transformations:

1. Translate all points through $(-v_x, -v_y)$.

2. Rotate about the origin through angle θ.

3. Translate all points back through (v_x, v_y).

Direct calculation of the transformations produces the mapping from (p_x, p_y) to (q_x, q_y) given by

$$(q_x, q_y) = ((p_x, p_y) + (-v_x, -v_y)) \begin{pmatrix} c & s \\ -s & c \end{pmatrix} + (v_x, v_y)$$

$$= (p_x, p_y) \begin{pmatrix} c & s \\ -s & c \end{pmatrix} + (t_x, t_y) \tag{11.35}$$

where $c = \cos(\theta)$, $s = \sin(\theta)$, and the net offset vector is $(t_x, t_y) = (v_x(1 - c) + v_y s, -v_x s + v_y(1 - c))$.

Example

Find the transformation that rotates points through 30° about $(1, 2)$. To what does the point $(2, 3)$ map?

Solution:
A 30° rotation uses $c = .866$ and $s = .5$. The offset vector is then $(1.134, -.232)$, and so the transformation applied to any point (p_x, p_y) is

$$(q_x, q_y) = (p_x, p_y) \begin{pmatrix} .866 & .5 \\ -.5 & .866 \end{pmatrix} + (1.134, -.232) \tag{11.36}$$

and applying this to $(2, 3)$ yields $(1.366, 3.366)$. This is the correct result, as can be checked by sketching it on graph paper.

Drill Exercises

11.14. Alternative Form for a Rotation About a Point. Show that the transformation

$$q_x = c(p_x - v_x) - s(p_y - v_y) + v_x$$
$$q_y = s(p_x - v_x) + c(p_y - v_y) + v_y$$

(11.37)

is the same as that of Equation 11.35. This form clearly

reveals that the point is first translated by $(-v_x, -v_y)$, rotated, and then translated by (v_x, v_y).

11.15. Reflection About a Tilted Line. Find the transformation that reflects all points about the line $\mathbf{a} + \mathbf{b}t$.

More General Scaling and Shearing

In a similar manner we often want to scale all points about some pivot point other than the origin. Because the elementary scaling operation of Equation 11.10 scales points about the origin, we do the same "shift-transform-unshift" sequence as for rotations. This and generalizing the shearing operation are explored in the following exercises.

Drill Exercises

11.16. Scaling About an Arbitrary Point. Fashion the affine transformation that scales points about a pivot point, (p_x, p_y). Test the overall transformation on some sample points, to confirm that the scaling operation is correct. Compare this with the transformation for rotation about a pivot point.

11.17. Shearing Along a Tilted Axis. Fashion the transformation that shears a point along the axis u tilted at angle θ, as shown in Figure 11.17. Point P is shifted along u an amount that is fraction f of the displacement d of P from the axis.

Example

Find the affine transformation that converts triangle C with vertices $(-3, 3)$, $(0, 3)$, and $(0, 5)$ into equilateral triangle D with vertices $(0, 0)$, $(2, 0)$, and $(1, \sqrt{3})$, as shown in Figure 11.18.

Solution:
We do this by a sequence of three elementary transformations:

1. Translate C down by 3 and right by 3 to place vertex c at $\hat{c}$.

2. Scale in x by 2/3 and in y by $\sqrt{3}/2$ to make the width and height of C the same as that of D.

3. Shear by $1/\sqrt{3}$ in the x-direction to align the top vertex of C with that of D.

Figure 11.17.
Shearing along a tilted axis.

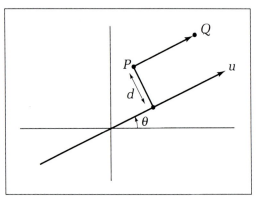

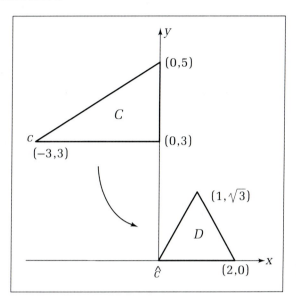

Figure 11.18.
Converting one triangle into another.

Composing these effects by means of direct calculation gives for the overall transformation that carries P into Q:

$$Q = (P + (3, -3)) \begin{pmatrix} \frac{2}{3} & 0 \\ 0 & \frac{\sqrt{3}}{2} \end{pmatrix} \begin{pmatrix} 1 & 0 \\ -\frac{1}{\sqrt{3}} & 1 \end{pmatrix}$$

$$= P \begin{pmatrix} \frac{2}{3} & 0 \\ -\frac{1}{2} & \frac{\sqrt{3}}{2} \end{pmatrix} + \left(\frac{7}{2}, -\frac{3\sqrt{3}}{2} \right) \qquad (11.38)$$

It is simple to check that this transformation does in fact transform triangle C into triangle D. It is a useful exercise to find the inverse of this transformation and to see that it converts triangle D back into triangle C.

Windows and Viewports Revisited

The mapping of a point from world coordinates into NDC was developed in Chapter 3. This mapping is central to the use of windows and viewports and is a component part of the *Line( )* routine in a graphics package. Here we shall look at the window-to-viewport mapping as an affine transformation and see how it is treated in a GKS context.

Equations 3.1 and 3.2 report the window-to-viewport transformation as mapping (x, y) into (dx, dy) according to

$$(dx, dy) = (x, y) \begin{pmatrix} s_x & 0 \\ 0 & s_y \end{pmatrix} + (t_x, t_y) \qquad (11.39)$$

in which the quantities s_x, s_y, t_x, and t_y depend on the window and viewport boundaries. Hence the window-to-viewport mapping is simply a scaling followed by a translation. It is easy to derive this transformation as a sequence of three elementary mappings:

1. A translation from the center, $[(W_r + W_l)/2, (W_t + W_b)/2]$, of the window to the origin. The window is now centered at the origin, and its sides are already aligned with the axes.

2. A scaling by the ratios of the viewport and window dimensions:

$$\left(\frac{V_r - V_l}{W_r - W_l}, \frac{V_t - V_b}{W_t - W_b} \right)$$

This rectangle now has the same dimensions as the viewport but is in the wrong position.

3. A translation from the origin to the center of the viewport.

Drill Exercises

11.18. Is This Correct? Check that the composition of these three mappings does indeed fashion the transformation of Equation 11.39.

11.19. The Viewport-to-Window Mapping. Find the inverse mapping to the transformation of Equation 11.39, and decompose it into a translation followed by a rotation followed by another translation.

The window-to-viewport transformation is known in GKS parlance as a **normalization transformation**. Because we may want to have several window–viewport pairs defined at any one time in an application, GKS maintains a list of normalization transformations, each with its own identification number. The application would include statements like

Set_Window(4, *wxmin, wxmax, wymin, wymax*);
Set_Viewport(4, *vxmin, vxmax, vymin, vymax*);

to specify the boundaries of the window and viewport for normalization transformation 4 and

Select_Normalization_Transformation(4);

to make transformation 4 the active one for subsequent drawing.

When building your own graphics package, therefore, you may wish to mimic this capability by using a table of normalization transformations. This table could take the form of an array of records, one for each transformation. Each record could store the window and viewport specifications as fields of type *rect*, along with the parameters of the resulting transformation in a field of type *affine* (see the exercises).

11.6.1 Decomposing Affine Transformations

Some affine transformations can be **decomposed** (or **factored**) into the product of other, simpler, affine transformations. For instance, the general shear in the

x-direction is easily shown to be the product of a scaling, a unit shear, and another scaling:

$$\begin{pmatrix} 1 & 0 \\ h & 1 \end{pmatrix} = \begin{pmatrix} 1/h & 0 \\ 0 & 1 \end{pmatrix} \begin{pmatrix} 1 & 0 \\ 1 & 1 \end{pmatrix} \begin{pmatrix} h & 0 \\ 0 & 1 \end{pmatrix} \qquad (11.40)$$

Can the unit shear itself be decomposed further? Remarkably it can, and the result is inextricably tied to the golden ratio ϕ (see Chapter 3)! The unit shear is the product of a rotation, a scaling, and another rotation:

$$\begin{pmatrix} 1 & 0 \\ 1 & 1 \end{pmatrix} = \begin{pmatrix} \cos(\alpha) & -\sin(\alpha) \\ \sin(\alpha) & \cos(\alpha) \end{pmatrix} \begin{pmatrix} \phi & 0 \\ 0 & 1/\phi \end{pmatrix} \begin{pmatrix} \cos(\beta) & \sin(\beta) \\ -\sin(\beta) & \cos(\beta) \end{pmatrix} \qquad (11.41)$$

where

$$\begin{aligned} \alpha &= \tan^{-1}(\phi) &\doteq 58.28° \\ \beta &= \tan^{-1}(1/\phi) &\doteq 31.72° \end{aligned} \qquad (11.42)$$

Drill Exercises

11.20. Show These Results. By multiplying these various matrices, show that each of the results of Equation 11.40 and Equation 11.41 is true. *Hint*: For Equation 11.41 use $\cos(\alpha) = 1/\sqrt{1 + \phi^2}$, $\sin(\alpha) = \phi/\sqrt{1 + \phi^2}$, and similarly for the other terms, and also use properties of ϕ such as $\phi^2 = \phi + 1$.

11.21. Seeing It Graphically. Draw a rectangle on graph paper; rotate it through $-58.28°$; scale it by $(\phi, 1/\phi)$; and finally rotate it through $31.72°$. Sketch each intermediate result, and show that the final result is the same parallelogram obtained when the original rectangle undergoes a unit shear.

You can go even further. The matrix that appears in the general affine transformation of Equation 11.4 can be written

$$\begin{pmatrix} a & b \\ c & d \end{pmatrix} = \begin{pmatrix} 1 & 0 \\ (ac + bd)/Q^2 & 1 \end{pmatrix} \begin{pmatrix} Q & 0 \\ 0 & (ad - bc)/Q \end{pmatrix} \begin{pmatrix} a/Q & b/Q \\ -b/Q & a/Q \end{pmatrix} \qquad (11.43)$$

where $Q = \sqrt{a^2 + b^2}$. The last matrix is seen to correspond to a rotation (why?). This factorization, which can be checked by multiplying the matrices, shows that any affine transformation is a shear followed by a scaling, a rotation, and then a translation. Because we know that a shear consists of rotations and a scaling, this result shows that every affine transformation is composed of various scalings and rotations, following by a translation. Although in graphics it is most convenient to think in terms of these three elementary transformations, one can decompose even these into more primitive operations, such as reflections and strains (Martin 1982).

Drill Exercise

11.22. Decompose a Transformation. Decompose the transformation

$$\begin{aligned} Q_x &= 3P_x - 2P_y + 5 \\ Q_y &= 4P_x + P_y - 6 \end{aligned} \qquad (11.44)$$

into a product of rotations, scalings, and translations.

11.7 A Valuable Unification: Homogeneous Coordinates

Equation 11.6 states that an affine transformation is made up of a linear transformation followed by a translation. It is unfortunate that the translation portion is not a matrix multiplication but must instead be added as an extra term.

It is possible to adjust matters slightly so that translations do fit the matrix multiplication form. This provides a satisfying conceptual unity to affine transformations, as then they all are represented by a matrix. They are also easily composed by pure matrix multiplication. We shall first see how to use this method in an application. Later we shall show that the method is based on a general approach used in the field of projective geometry known as homogeneous coordinates.

From Equation 11.4 the linear transformation portion of an affine transformation is given by the following two equations:

$$(Q_x, Q_y) = (P_x, P_y)\begin{pmatrix} a & b \\ c & d \end{pmatrix} \tag{11.45}$$

As can be checked by direct calculation, the truth of these equations is in no way affected by appending an additional component of 1 to both P and Q and also a third row and column to M, consisting of zeros and a 1:

$$(Q_x, Q_y, 1) = (P_x, P_y, 1)\begin{pmatrix} a & b & 0 \\ c & d & 0 \\ 0 & 0 & 1 \end{pmatrix} \tag{11.46}$$

This is the **homogeneous coordinate** form of the equations. The notation $\hat{P} = (P_x, P_y, 1)$ denotes the homogeneous coordinate version of P, and similarly for $\hat{Q}$. By contrast, the versions P, Q, and M given in Equation 11.45 are in **ordinary coordinates**. Now the translation components (tr_x, tr_y) of Equation 11.4 may be inserted directly into the third row of this matrix:

$$(Q_x, Q_y, 1) = (P_x, P_y, 1)\begin{pmatrix} a & b & 0 \\ c & d & 0 \\ tr_x & tr_y & 1 \end{pmatrix} \tag{11.47}$$

yielding three equations: one for Q_x, one for Q_y, and one that simply states $1 = 1$. The first two equations are identical to Equation 11.4. Check this result by multiplying out the right-hand side: Note that the translation values are multiplied by the third component 1 of $\hat{P}$. In this way the entire affine transformation is captured in the single enlarged matrix $\hat{M}$:

$$\hat{M} = \begin{pmatrix} a & b & 0 \\ c & d & 0 \\ tr_x & tr_y & 1 \end{pmatrix} \tag{11.48}$$

The six parameters of a two-dimensional affine transformation appear inside one 3-by-3 matrix. The matrix is said to represent or specify the transformation.

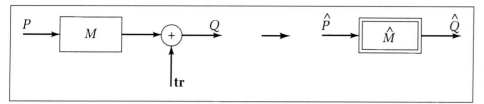

Figure 11.19.
Signal flow diagram in homogeneous coordinate form.

The signal flow diagram for applying a transformation in terms of homogeneous coordinates is shown in Figure 11.19. The operation consists of a single matrix multiplication: $\hat{P}$ is mapped to $\hat{Q}$ according to

$$\hat{Q} = \hat{P} \begin{pmatrix} a & b & 0 \\ c & d & 0 \\ tr_x & tr_y & 1 \end{pmatrix} \qquad (11.49)$$

Once $\hat{Q}$ has been formed, one can simply drop the last component, 1, to recover the normal form of the point.

To summarize, the process of applying the affine transformation represented by the matrix in Equation 11.49 to point P is

- Build the triple $(P_x, P_y, 1)$ from (P_x, P_y) by adding a component.

- Multiply the triple by the transformation matrix.

- Delete the third component of 1.

The following code fragment implements this process using a 3-by-3 matrix M of type $matrix3 = $ **array** $[1..3, 1..3]$ **of** $real$. It assumes that the last column of the matrix has the proper entries, 0, 0, 1.

> Code Fragment 11.5. Transforming a Point with a Transformation Matrix

---

procedure $TransfHomog(M : matrix3; In_pt : point; $**var**$ Out_pt : point)$;
{transform In_pt to Out_pt using 3×3 matrix M}
begin
   $p.x := In\_pt.x * M[1, 1] + In\_pt.y * M[2, 1] + M[3, 1]$;
   $p.y := In\_pt.x * M[1, 2] + In\_pt.y * M[2, 2] + M[3, 2]$
end;

The elementary affine transformations are represented as follows:

- *Translation:*

$$\hat{M}_T = \begin{pmatrix} 1 & 0 & 0 \\ 0 & 1 & 0 \\ tr_x & tr_y & 1 \end{pmatrix} \qquad (11.50)$$

- *Scaling:*

$$\hat{M}_S = \begin{pmatrix} S_x & 0 & 0 \\ 0 & S_y & 0 \\ 0 & 0 & 1 \end{pmatrix} \qquad (11.51)$$

● *Rotation*:

$$\hat{M}_R = \begin{pmatrix} c & s & 0 \\ -s & c & 0 \\ 0 & 0 & 1 \end{pmatrix} \tag{11.52}$$

● *Shearing*:

$$\hat{M}_{SH} = \begin{pmatrix} 1 & g & 0 \\ h & 1 & 0 \\ 0 & 0 & 1 \end{pmatrix} \tag{11.53}$$

The power of using homogeneous coordinates is best revealed when two or more affine transformations are composed. Suppose the two transformations are represented by matrices $\hat{M}_1$ and $\hat{M}_2$. Thus $\hat{P}$ is first transformed to the point $\hat{P}\hat{M}_1$ which is then transformed to $(\hat{P}\hat{M}_1)\hat{M}_2$. By associativity this is just $\hat{P}(\hat{M}_1\hat{M}_2)$, and so the overall transformation is represented by only the single matrix $\hat{M} = \hat{M}_1\hat{M}_2$ (see Figure 11.20).

By the same reasoning, any number of affine transformations can be composed simply by multiplying their associated matrices. In this way, transformations based on an arbitrary succession of rotations, scalings, shears, and translations can be formed and captured in a single matrix.

Example

Build a transformation that

1. rotates through 45 degrees.

2. scales by $S_x = 1.5$ and $S_y = -2$.

3. translates through (3, 5).

Construct the three matrices and multiply them in the proper order to form

$$\begin{pmatrix} .707 & .707 & 0 \\ -.707 & .707 & 0 \\ 0 & 0 & 1 \end{pmatrix} \times \begin{pmatrix} 1.5 & 0 & 0 \\ 0 & -2 & 0 \\ 0 & 0 & 1 \end{pmatrix} \times \begin{pmatrix} 1 & 0 & 0 \\ 0 & 1 & 0 \\ 3 & 5 & 1 \end{pmatrix} = \begin{pmatrix} 1.06 & -1.414 & 0 \\ -1.06 & -1.414 & 0 \\ 3 & 5 & 1 \end{pmatrix}$$

Now to transform point (1, 2), build the triple (1, 2, 1), multiply it by the preceding matrix to obtain (1.94, .758, 1), and drop the one to form the image point (1.94, .758). It is instructive to use graph paper to see how (1, 2) is mapped as it undergoes each of the three transformations.

Figure 11.20.
Composing two transformations using homogeneous coordinates.

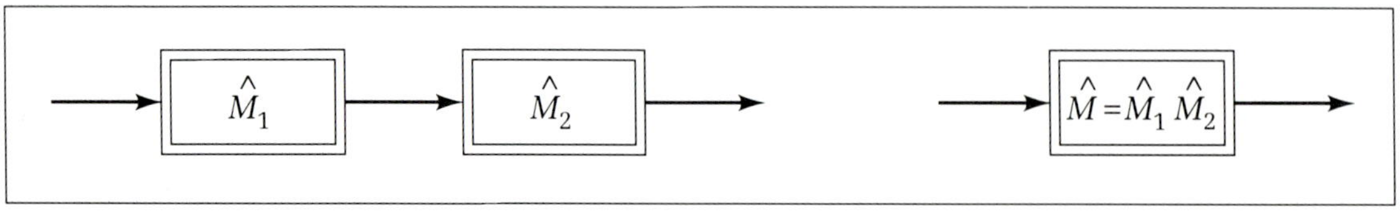

Plate 1.
Realistic terrain based on fractal surfaces. (By R. F. Voss. Reproduced by permission from Mandelbrot (1983). Copyright 1982 by B. B. Mandelbrot.)

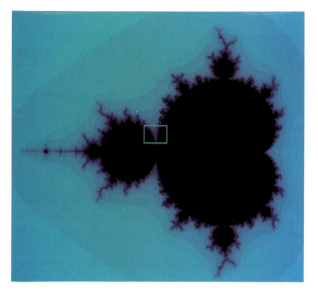

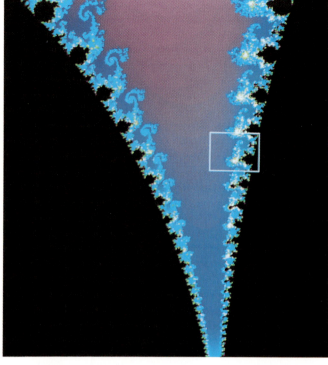

Plate 2.
Successive zooms into the
Mandelbrot set. (Courtesy of
Brett Diamond.)

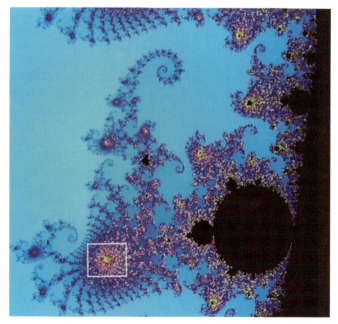

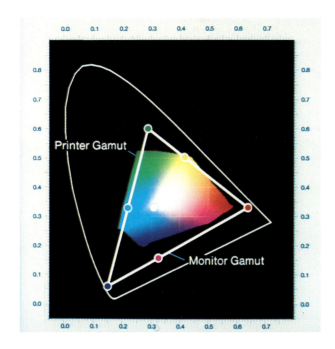

Plate 3.
Color gamuts. (Courtesy of Maureen Stone, Xerox Palo Alto Research Center, 1987.)

Plate 4.
Ray-traced image of a sphere-scene. (Courtesy of Eric Graham.)

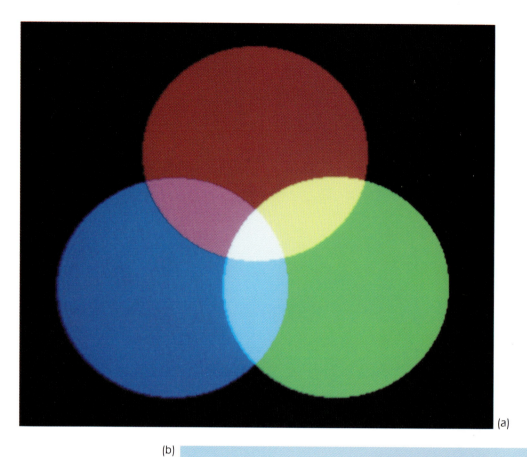

(a)

(b)

Plate 5.
The (a) additive and (b) subtractive primaries. (Courtesy of Brett Diamond.)

Drill Exercise

11.23.   On the Form of the Transformation Matrix. The matrices $\hat{M}_T$, $\hat{M}_S$, $\hat{M}_R$, and $\hat{M}_{SH}$ for the elementary affine transformations all have a third column of 0, 0, 1. Show that the product of any collection of such matrices also has a third column of 0, 0, 1. Hence all transformations built up out of elementary ones can be represented by a matrix with third column 0, 0, 1.

Rotation About an Arbitrary Point—Revisited

Consider again, this time in homogeneous coordinates, the transformation of Equation 11.35 that rotates a point about the pivot point (v_x, v_y). Multiplying the extended matrices for the translation, rotation, and translation, we get

$$
\hat{M} = \begin{pmatrix} 1 & 0 & 0 \\ 0 & 1 & 0 \\ -v_x & -v_y & 1 \end{pmatrix} \times \begin{pmatrix} c & s & 0 \\ -s & c & 0 \\ 0 & 0 & 1 \end{pmatrix} \times \begin{pmatrix} 1 & 0 & 0 \\ 0 & 1 & 0 \\ v_x & v_y & 1 \end{pmatrix}
$$

$$
= \begin{pmatrix} c & s & 0 \\ -s & c & 0 \\ v_x(1-c) + v_y s & -v_x s + v_y(1-c) & 1 \end{pmatrix}
$$

(11.54)

Note that this is equivalent to a rotation through θ about the origin followed by a single translation.

Drill Exercises

11.24.   Rotate About (2, 3) Through 30 Degrees. Build the matrix $\hat{M}$ that performs this transformation, and apply it to several points in the plane. For each such point, draw the intermediate points that would result from performing the three elementary transformations individually.

11.25.   Finding Matrices. Give the explicit form of the 3-by-3 matrix representing each of the following transformations:

a.   Scaling by a factor of 2 in the x-direction and then rotating about (2, 1).

b.   Scaling about (2, 3) and following by translation through (1, 1).

c.   Shearing in x by 30 percent, scaling by 2 in x, and then rotating about (1, 1) through 30°.

11.26.   The Inverse Transformation in Homogeneous Coordinates. Show that if $P = (Q - \mathbf{tr})M^{-1}$, as in Equation 11.18, then $\hat{P} = \hat{Q}\hat{M}^{-1}$, where $\hat{M}$ is given by Equation 11.48.

11.27.   Normalizing a Box. Find the affine transformation that maps the box with corners (0, 0), (2, 1), (0, 5), and (−2, 4) into the square with corners (0, 0), (1, 0), (1, 1), and (0, 1).

11.28.   Effect on Area. In Exercise 11.27, what is the ratio of the areas of the boxes before and after transformation?

To recapitulate, there are two principal benefits of using the homogeneous coordinate approach. One is the uniformity that all affine transformations acquire: Any affine transformation is represented by a single matrix. The second is that affine transformations can be composed by means of simple matrix multiplications. This uniformity helps organize our thinking about specific transformations and simplifies encoding transformation operations in programs. The same benefits apply when dealing with three-dimensional transformations.

11.7.1 The Underlying Notion of Homogeneous Coordinates

The method of enlarging a 2D point from (a, b) to $(a, b, 1)$ and capturing a transformation in a 3-by-3 matrix is above suspicion: It clearly works, as we have shown. But it seems like a clever trick that someone stumbled on. However, it is based on an alternative representation of a point's coordinates that is well rooted in projective geometry, called the **homogeneous coordinate representation.** It dramatically simplifies many mathematical methods and concerns by eliminating troubling special cases, and therefore we shall pause to consider how it operates.

The idea is to give a point P with ordinary coordinates (a, b) not one but an infinite number of equivalent representations! We say that any triple of numbers, (aw, bw, w), represents P just as well, where w can be any nonzero number. So any (nonzero) multiple of $(a, b, 1)$ represents the ordinary point (a, b). For example, the point $(3, 4)$ has the equivalent homogeneous coordinate representations $(3, 4, 1)$, $(6, 8, 2)$, $(.000012, .000016, .000004)$, $(-360, -480, -60)$, and many others. Thus the representation of a point is no longer unique, in much the same way as the coefficients c, d, and g of the equation of a straight line, $cx + dy + g = 0$, are not unique.

It is simple to convert from ordinary coordinates to homogeneous ones: Just append a 1, as we did, and if desired, multiply all three components by some (nonzero) number. To convert back to ordinary coordinates, we first divide all three components by the third component (making the third component equal to 1) and then delete the 1. Summarizing the conversion process:

- *Ordinary to homogeneous:* (a, b) becomes $(a, b, 1)$.

- *Homogeneous to ordinary:* (c, d, w) becomes $(c/w, d/w)$.

We transform points in homogeneous coordinates in the same way, but now complete the process by scaling all three components so that the third component becomes 1.

Example

Suppose the transformation has matrix M given by:[3]

$$M = \begin{pmatrix} 1 & 2 & 1 \\ 3 & 4 & 1 \\ 2 & 5 & 3 \end{pmatrix} \qquad (11.55)$$

What is the image of the point $(3, -1)$?

Solution:

Enlarge $(3, -1)$ to $(3, -1, 1)$ and multiply it by M to get $(2, 7, 5)$. Now convert back to ordinary coordinates: $(2, 7, 5) = (2/5, 7/5, 1)$, which is therefore the point $(0.4, 1.4)$.

In order to understand homogeneous coordinates better, it is helpful to view 2D ordinary points as if they lie in three-dimensional space, as shown in Figure 11.21. Each 2D point, (a, b), is associated with the ray through the origin having parametric form $(x, y, z) = (aw, bw, w)$, using w as the parameter. A single 2D point is thus represented equally well by any 3D point on the ray, except the one at $w = 0$. Hence one ordinary point, (a, b), is distinguished from another, (c, d),

---

[3]Although the affine transformations seen so far always use 0, 0, 1 for the third column, when we later examine projections, we will encounter matrices with arbitrary values in the last column.

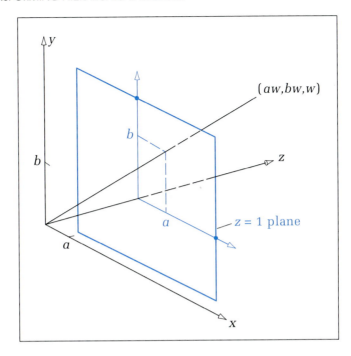

Figure 11.21.
Viewing 2D points in homogeneous coordinates.

only by the direction of its ray in homogeneous coordinates: The two-dimensional points correspond to directions in three-dimensional space. Because ordinary coordinates have a w-component of 1, the ordinary coordinate version of the 2D point is found where the ray penetrates the $z = 1$ plane. Dividing the three components of (aw, bw, w) by w is identical to projecting (aw, bw, w), where all projectors pass through the "eye" at $(0, 0, 0)$, onto the $z = 1$ plane.

Mathematical Aside for the Curious

Although for graphics we do not need to deal with infinitely remote points, homogeneous coordinates do give meaning to such notions. It turns out that a point of the form $(a, b, 0)$ is a mathematically meaningful object: Roughly speaking, it's the point in the x, y-plane residing in the direction, (a, b), "at infinity" (Ayers 1967, Semple and Kneebone 1952). Attaching such points at infinity to the plane removes many awkward special cases. For instance, two lines then will always intersect, even if they are parallel.

11.8 Application: Transforming Hierarchical Objects

Some objects are made up of several parts that are linked together and can move relative to one another. Figure 11.22 shows a (2D) robot consisting of several movable parts: a body that can slide back and forth along the floor, an arm that can pivot about a point on the body, a hand that can pivot about the arm, and finally two fingers that slide together and apart at the end of the hand.

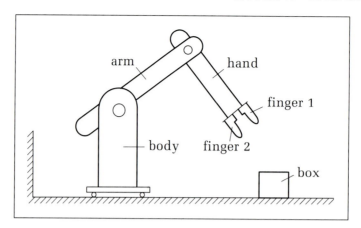

Figure 11.22.
A robot as an assembly of
linked parts.

In a robot design we might want to draw this object again and again with different pivot angles and slide positions, in order to test algorithms for picking up and placing a box. A user might turn one knob on the workstation to control the position of the body, another to control the pivoting of the arm, and a third to move the fingers back and forth. Each knob determines a certain transformation, and at each turn of a knob the robot is erased and redrawn with the new transformations in effect. If this can happen quickly enough, the robot might even appear to be in smooth, continuous motion!

Figure 11.23 shows an abstraction of the various parts of the robot. The body is a vertical line situated at distance L_1 from the wall (origin), and the arm is a line connected to the body and rotated through angle θ_1 from the vertical. We call the arm a "child" of the body, because the position of the arm depends not only on angle θ_1 but also on the position of the body. The transformation that offsets the body by amount L_1 is passed on to the child object by the "parent" object—the body. Similarly, the hand is a child of the arm, and the two fingers are each children of the hand. Where the hand is to be drawn depends on three transformations: the translation through amount L_1 and the two rotations through θ_1 and θ_2. Assemblies such as this are often called **hierarchical objects**, because the whole is made up of parts, the parts consist of subparts, and so on, and dependencies of position and orientation are passed down from parent to child.

Organizing the Transformations

How do we organize the application of the various transformations when drawing the robot? Consider each of the parts in its own separate "master" coordinate

Figure 11.23.
Abstraction of the robot parts.

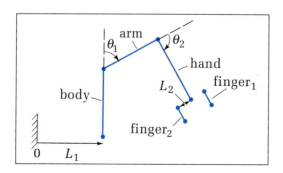

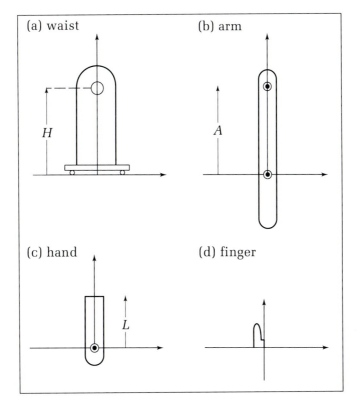

Figure 11.24.
Each part in its own coordinate

system, as shown in Figure 11.24. Each part is positioned for maximum convenience. For instance, the pivot point for the arm is placed at the origin, and the arm points upward so that it is oriented properly when $\theta_1 = 0$.

To draw the robot we need only apply the proper transformation to each of the coordinates in each routine. What transformations are required? The body is easy: Use a translation through L_1:

$$
\hat{M}_{\text{body}} = \begin{pmatrix} 1 & 0 & 0 \\ 0 & 1 & 0 \\ L_1 & 0 & 1 \end{pmatrix}
\tag{11.56}
$$

For the arm we must first shift and orient its coordinate system into place and then draw it in the transformed system. Each primitive must be rotated through angle $-\theta_1$ about its pivot (negative, as it is a clockwise rotation) and then raised vertically distance H, yielding

$$
\hat{M}_{\text{arm}} = \begin{pmatrix} c_1 & s_1 & 0 \\ -s_1 & c_1 & 0 \\ 0 & H & 1 \end{pmatrix}
\tag{11.57}
$$

where $c_1 = \cos(\theta_1)$ and $s_1 = \sin(\theta_1)$. This properly positions it to be attached to the body when the body is in its generic position, but because the body has been transformed, the arm must finally be transformed in the same way. The total transformation applied to each of the arm's graphics primitives is thus the composition of the arm transformation followed by the body transformation. Hence matrix $\hat{M}_{\text{arm}}$ is postmultiplied by $\hat{M}_{\text{body}}$ to form the overall matrix for the arm. The rule is this:

The parent transformation is applied after the child transformation: $\hat{M}_{\text{child}}$ is postmultiplied by $\hat{M}_{\text{parent}}$.

For the remaining parts, each child is transformed so that it is properly positioned relative to the generic position of its parent. M_{hand} produces a rotation through $-\theta_2$ followed by a vertical shift through A. M_{finger1} causes a vertical translation through L and a horizontal one through $-L_2$. M_{finger2} does a reflection about the x-axis followed by a vertical shift by L and a horizontal one by L_2. This allows us to use the same routine, *DrawPart(finger)*, for both of the fingers.

Maintaining the Current Transformation

To draw the robot we must subject the graphic primitives in each part to the proper transformation. Based on our discussion, the composite transformation required for each part is as shown in Table 11.1.

Table 11.1 **Transformations to Be Applied to Each Part**

Object	Transform Primitives to
body	*M_body*
arm	*M_arm M_body*
hand	*M_hand M_arm M_body*
finger 1	*M_finger1 M_hand M_arm M_body*
finger 2	*M_finger2 M_hand M_arm M_body*

It is convenient to maintain a **current transformation matrix** in the global variable **var** *CTM : matrix3* and to load the appropriate parameters into CTM before drawing each robot part. For instance, *CTM* is set to $\hat{M}_{\text{hand}}\hat{M}_{\text{arm}}\hat{M}_{\text{body}}$ just before drawing the hand.

The organization of the robot transformations in Table 11.1 can be represented graphically by a treelike structure,[4] as in Figure 11.25. Each node represents an individual transformation for a part, along with a pointer to the graphical description of the object in master coordinates. At each node, *CTM* is the product of all the matrices in the graph above the node, as indicated.

The robot can be drawn by a preorder traversal of this structure (Kruse 1984). As each node is reached from above, *CTM* is updated by premultiplication by the node transformation, and the object is drawn. This can be viewed as "pushing" the transformation onto a transformation stack: Suppose the procedure *Push(M : matrix3)* causes *CTM* to be replaced with $M * CTM$. As the traversal passes back up through a node, the transformation is "popped," removing its effect from *CTM*. That is, *Pop(M : matrix3)* replaces *CTM* with *Minverse* $* CTM$ in which *Minverse* is the inverse matrix of *M*.

To start the traversal we simply set *CTM* to the identity matrix, using the procedure *Init_CTM*. Then the robot can be drawn using the following code, which utilizes *DrawPart( )* to draw each transformed part:

---

[4]Actually the structure is a **directed acyclic graph**, or **dag**, a graph with directed branches and no cycles. Because two nodes can point to the same object, as in the fingers of the robot, the structure is not a tree. Each node in a dag has a single identifiable parent.

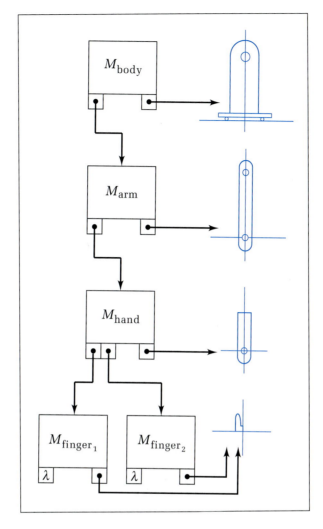

Figure 11.25.
The treelike structure (dag) for the robot.

Code Fragment 11.6. Drawing the Robot

```
procedure DrawRobot;
begin
    Init_CTM;
    Push(M_body);
    DrawPart(body);
    Push(M_arm);
    DrawPart(arm);
    Push(M_hand);
    DrawPart(hand);
    Push(M_finger1);
    DrawPart(finger);
    Pop(M_finger1);
    Push(M_finger2);
    DrawPart(finger)
end;
```

Notice that the transformation for *finger_1* is popped to eliminate it from the stack and then the transformation of *finger_2* is pushed.

One restriction of the approach in Code Fragment 11.6 is that the structure of this robot is hard wired into the code: Altering the robot requires that a procedure must be rewritten and recompiled. A more flexible utility would read the structure of the robot from a data file and construct an actual dag data structure that could be traversed. This issue is addressed in the exercises.

Drawing a Transformed Polyline

The routine *DrawPart*( ) draws the graphic primitives for a part after transforming them using *CTM*. Suppose, for simplicity, that each part can be drawn as a single polyline (see the exercises for extensions). We suppose that a set of records, *Body*, *Arm*, *Hand*, and *Finger*, of type *polypoint* have been created and saved. If the polyline for each object were drawn directly, it would appear as in its master coordinate system. Instead, *CTM* is applied to each vertex of the polyline using *TransfHomog*( ), as shown in the following code fragment:

Code Fragment 11.7. Drawing a Transformed Part

```
procedure DrawPart(part : polypoint);
{draw part using global CTM}
var
i : integer;
  newpt : point;
begin
  with part do
  begin
    if num > 0 then for i := 1 to num do
    begin
      TransfHomog(CTM, pt[i], newpt);
      if i = 1 then MoveTo(newpt) else LineTo(newpt)
    end; {for}
  end {with}
end;
```

Drill Exercises

11.29. Embedding Transformations Inside *Line*( ). Some graphics packages have a provision for embedding a transformation directly in the routine *Line*( )! Routines are provided for setting up the CTM, and then it is understood that this transformation is automatically applied to every primitive that is drawn. The application is thereby relieved of the burden of performing the transformation explicitly. Show how this operation could be introduced in *Line*( ) of Code Fragment 3.7. Discuss the advantages and disadvantages of using this embedded transformation approach.

11.30. Parts of an Object Described by Multiple Polylines. Some parts of the robot of Section 11.7 are described graphically by more than one polyline. What changes must be made in Code Fragment 11.7 to draw parts made up of several polylines?

11.9   Three-Dimensional Affine Transformations

With the groundwork laid for 2D affine transformations, extending the ideas to transformations in three dimensions is straightforward. Visualizing 3D objects and transformations can be difficult at first, but working through the following sections provides valuable practice. By using 3D affine transformations one can scale, rotate, translate, and shear points in three dimensions. Rotations are particularly useful, as they allow us to view objects from different directions. Such views make much more intelligible and pleasing drawings of the wireframes, patches, superquadrics, and the like introduced earlier.

We specify 3D affine transformations by a 3-by-3 matrix and a 3D offset. Later we shall recast them in a 4-by-4 matrix version to simplify composing a sequence of transformations.

A 3D affine transformation of point P into Q has the form

$$Q = PM + \mathbf{tr} \tag{11.58}$$

where $Q = (Q_x, Q_y, Q_z)$, $P = (P_x, P_y, P_z)$ and M is a 3-by-3 matrix:

$$M = \begin{pmatrix} m_{11} & m_{12} & m_{13} \\ m_{21} & m_{22} & m_{23} \\ m_{31} & m_{32} & m_{33} \end{pmatrix} \tag{11.59}$$

Now $\mathbf{tr} = (tr_x, tr_y, tr_z)$ is a "translation vector" in three dimensions. Similar to the 2D case, each of the components of the point (Q_x, Q_y, Q_z) is a linear combination of the P_x, P_y, and P_z plus an offset, and matrix M performs combinations of rotations, scalings, and shears.

After reviewing some of the general properties of affine transformations, we shall examine each of the elementary transformations in three dimensions.

11.9.1 Properties of Three-Dimensional Affine Transformations

Section 11.4 discussed several useful properties of affine transformations. The development of those properties did not refer specifically to the dimensionality of the transformation, and so the properties still hold for 3D affine transformations. Summarizing them for the 3D case:

- Lines are preserved. A straight line lying in 3D space transforms into another straight line.

- Parallelism is preserved. Two parallel lines transform into two other parallel lines.

- Proportional distances are preserved. The image of a point lying fraction f of the way between two points, A and B, transforms into a point that also lies fraction f of the way between the images of A and B.

- Volumes of 3D objects are scaled by the determinant of matrix M:

$$\frac{\text{volume after transformation}}{\text{volume before transformation}} = |\det M| \tag{11.60}$$

Drill Exercise

11.31.   Prove the Properties. By referring to the arguments made for the 2D situation, show that the first three properties do indeed hold in the 3D case.

11.9.2 Translation

The offset vector has an easily visualized effect: Each point is shifted by the amount **tr**. For a pure translation, matrix M would be set to the identity matrix. According the form of Equation 11.58 this translation is performed after the point has been multiplied by matrix M.

For the other pure transformations of scaling, shearing, and rotation in three dimensions, we set the offset vector to the vector **0**.

11.9.3 Scaling

Scaling in three dimensions is a direct extension of the 2D case:

$$Q = P \begin{pmatrix} S_x & 0 & 0 \\ 0 & S_y & 0 \\ 0 & 0 & S_z \end{pmatrix} \tag{11.61}$$

where the three constants S_x, S_y, and S_z cause scalings of the corresponding coordinates. Scaling is about the origin, just as in the 2D case. Figure 11.26 uses the "basic barn" wireframe (see Figure 10.2) to illustrate scaling. Each of the scaling constants is set to the golden ratio 1.618 (recall Chapter 3) to produce three "golden barns."

11.9.4 Three-Dimensional Shears

Three-dimensional shears are somewhat richer than their two-dimensional counterparts: a shear along any pair of axes can be governed by a third axis. The shear matrix has the form

$$M = \begin{pmatrix} 1 & h_{xy} & h_{xz} \\ h_{yx} & 1 & h_{yz} \\ h_{zx} & h_{zy} & 1 \end{pmatrix} \tag{11.62}$$

and so, for instance, the x-coordinate Q_x is related to P by

$$Q_x = P_x + h_{yx}P_y + h_{zx}P_z \tag{11.63}$$

Figure 11.26.
Scaling the basic barn.

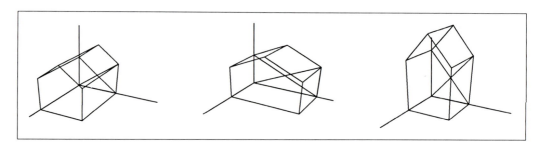

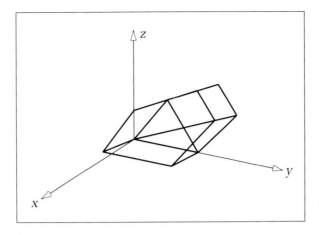

Figure 11.27.
Shearing the basic barn.

The notation is suggestive: h_{yx} tells the amount that the y-coordinate of P affects the x-coordinate of Q, or the amount of the shear "due to y along x." Figure 11.27 shows the basic barn sheared simultaneously by 50 percent due to z along y and by 30 percent due to x along z, using matrix

$$M = \begin{pmatrix} 1 & 0 & .3 \\ 0 & 1 & 0 \\ 0 & .5 & 1 \end{pmatrix}$$

Aside: How Is a Three-Dimensional Shear Like a Two-Dimensional Translation in Homogeneous Coordinates?

Consider the specific shear:

$$Q = P \begin{pmatrix} 1 & 0 & 0 \\ 0 & 1 & 0 \\ t & s & 1 \end{pmatrix} \tag{11.64}$$

which alters 3D point P by shearing it along x with factor t owing to z and along y with factor s owing to z. If P lies in the $z = 1$ plane, so that it has coordinates $P = (p_x, p_y, 1)$, it will be transformed into $(p_x + t, p_y + s, 1)$. Hence it is simply shifted in x by amount t and in y by amount s. So for any point in the $z = 1$ plane, this shear is equivalent to a translation. In fact, the matrix in Equation 11.64 is identical to the homogeneous coordinate form for a pure translation in two dimensions. This correspondence helps reinforce how homogeneous coordinates operate.

11.9.5 Rotation

Rotations in three dimensions are common in graphics, for we often want to rotate an object or a camera system in order to obtain different views. There is a much greater variety of rotations in three than in two dimensions, as we must specify an axis about which to rotate, rather than just a single point. One helpful approach is to decompose a rotation into a sequence of simpler ones, those about a single coordinate axis.

Rotation About a Coordinate Axis

First we present individually the matrices that produce rotations about the x-, y-, and z-axes. In each case the rotation is through an angle, A, about the given axis. We use a right-handed coordinate system and adopt the convention that positive values of A cause a counterclockwise (CCW) rotation about the axis in question as one looks inward along the positive axis toward the origin. The three basic positive rotations are illustrated in Figure 11.28.[5] This formulation is also consistent with the preceding 2D rotations:

A positive rotation in two dimensions is equivalent to a rotation about the z-axis.

Notice what happens with this convention when a 90° angle is used: Any point on one positive axis is rotated into a point on another axis in a cyclic ($x \rightarrow y \rightarrow z \rightarrow x \rightarrow y \ldots$) pattern:

- About the z-axis, the x-axis rotates to the y-axis.

- About the x-axis, the y-axis rotates to the z-axis.

- About the y-axis, the z-axis rotates to the x-axis.

Drill Exercises

11.32. Visualizing the 90° Rotations. Draw a right-handed 3D system and convince yourself that a 90° rotation (CCW looking toward the origin) about each axis rotates the other axes into one another, as specified in the preceding list. What is the effect of rotating a point on the x-axis about the x-axis?

11.33. Rotating the Basic Barn. Sketch the basic barn after it has been rotated 30° about the x-axis. Repeat for the y- and z-axes.

The following three matrices represent transformations that rotate points through angle A about a coordinate axis. We use the suggestive notation $R_x(\ )$,

Figure 11.28.
Positive rotations about the three axes.

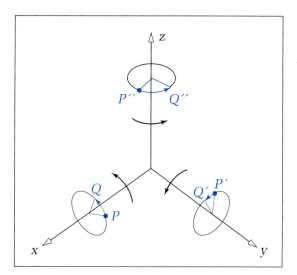

[5]In a left-handed system, using the following matrix forms, the sense of a rotation through a positive A would be CCW looking outward along the positive axis from the origin. This formulation is used by some authors.

$R_y(\ )$, and $R_z(\ )$ to denote rotations about the x-, y-, and z-axes, respectively. The parameter is the angle through which points are rotated, given in radians, and c stands for $\cos(A)$ and s for $\sin(A)$.

1. About the x-axis:

$$R_x(A) = \begin{pmatrix} 1 & 0 & 0 \\ 0 & c & s \\ 0 & -s & c \end{pmatrix} \qquad (11.65)$$

2. About the y-axis:

$$R_y(A) = \begin{pmatrix} c & 0 & -s \\ 0 & 1 & 0 \\ s & 0 & c \end{pmatrix} \qquad (11.66)$$

3. About the z-axis:

$$R_z(A) = \begin{pmatrix} c & s & 0 \\ -s & c & 0 \\ 0 & 0 & 1 \end{pmatrix} \qquad (11.67)$$

Note that five of the terms in each matrix are the zeros and ones of the identity matrix. They occur in the row and column that correspond to the axis about which the rotation is being made. They guarantee that the corresponding coordinate of the point being transformed will not be altered. The c and s terms always appear in a rectangular pattern in the other rows and columns.

Example:
Rotate the point $P = (3, 1, 4)$ through $30°$ about the y-axis. Using Equation 11.66 with $c = .866$ and $s = .5$, P is transformed into

$$(Q_x, Q_y, Q_z) = (3, 1, 4)\begin{pmatrix} c & 0 & -s \\ 0 & 1 & 0 \\ s & 0 & c \end{pmatrix} = (4.6, 1, 1.964)$$

As expected, the y-coordinate of the point is not altered.

Drill Exercises

11.34. Do a Rotation. Find the image Q of the point $P = (1, 2, -1)$ when it is rotated through $45°$ about the y-axis. Sketch P and Q in a 3D coordinate system and show that your result is reasonable.

11.35. Orthogonal Matrices. A matrix is **orthogonal** if its columns are mutually orthogonal unit-length vectors. Show that each of the preceding three rotation matrices is orthogonal. What is the determinant of an orthogonal matrix? An orthogonal matrix has a splendid property: Its inverse is identical to its transpose (also see Appendix 2).

Show why the orthogonality of the columns guarantees this. Find the inverse of each of the preceding rotation matrices, and show that the inverse of a rotation is simply a rotation in the opposite direction.

11.36. Testing 90° Rotations of the Axes. This exercise provides a useful mnemonic device for remembering the form of the rotation matrices. Apply each of the three rotation matrices to each of the standard unit position vectors, **i**, **j**, and **k**,[6] using a $90°$ rotation. In each case discuss the effect of the transformation on the unit vector.

---

[6]The operation of applying a transformation to a vector was justified in Section 11.4.

11.9.6 Building and Using Three-Dimensional Affine Transformations

Three-dimensional affine transformations are constructed and used in much the same way as are their two-dimensional counterparts. The transformation can be stored in a structure of the following type:

> Code Fragment 11.8. Storing Three-Dimensional Affine Transformations

---

type
  affine3D = **record**
        mat : **array**[1..3, 1..3] **of** *real*;
        tr : *vector3D*
      end;

We also need a routine to transform point P into Q, such as **procedure** *Transform3D*(*Tran* : *affine3D*; P : *point3D*; **var** Q : *point3D*). It is simply a 3D version of **procedure** *Transform*( ) in Code Fragment 11.1—see the exercises. We shall assume hereafter that *Transform3D*( ) is available.

Routines to load values into variables of type *affine3D* are also needed. Following the lead of Code Fragment 11.2 we can define

> Code Fragment 11.9. Creating Three-Dimensional Affine Transformations

---

procedure *Set_Translate3D*(*offset* : *vector3D*; **var** *Tran* : *affine3D*);
procedure *Set_Scale*(*sx, sy, sz* : *real*; **var** *Tran* : *affine3D*);
procedure *Set_Rotate3D*(*RotAxis* : *axis*; *angle* : *real*; **var** *Tran* : *affine3D*);

For a rotation we must specify an axis, *axis*, which should be an enumerated type such as **type** *axis* = (x, y, z). *RotAxis* is the axis about which the rotation is to be performed. For a shear we must specify several values such as h_{xz} and h_{yx}, as in Equation 11.62. This can be done in several ways—see the exercises.

Finally, we need a routine, *ComposeTransf3D*(*Tr1, Tr2* : *affine3D*; **var** *TrNew* : *affine3D*), that composes two 3D affine transformations. Constructing such a routine is a straightforward extension of Code Fragment 11.4 and is left as an exercise.

Rotations About an Arbitrary Axis

Rotations about a coordinate axis are certainly useful, but we need a mechanism for a more general rotation about an arbitrary axis passing through the origin. As shown in Figure 11.29, the axis is represented by the position vector **u**, and some point P is to be rotated through angle A to produce point Q.

Because **u** can have any direction, this task at first looks formidable. But we can decompose the required rotation into a sequence of known steps:

1. Perform some rotations so that **u** becomes aligned with the z-axis.

2. Do a rotation about the z-axis through angle A.

3. Undo the alignment rotations to restore **u** to its original direction.

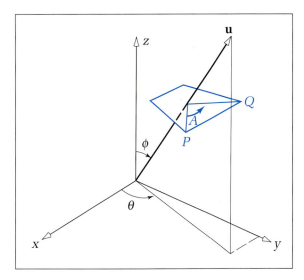

Figure 11.29.
Rotation about an axis through
the origin.

This is reminiscent of rotating about a point in two dimensions: The first step prepares the situation for a simpler known operation; the simple operation is done; and finally the preparation step is undone.

What rotations cause **u** to become aligned with the z-axis? Suppose the direction of **u** is given by the angles θ and ϕ, as indicated in Figure 11.29. Here ϕ is the angle between **u** and the z-axis, and θ is the angle between the x-axis and the plane defined by the combination of **u** and the z-axis. Then ϕ can range from 0 to π, and θ can range from 0 to 2π. (Recall that this is a standard description of direction in terms of **spherical coordinates**. See Appendix 5.)

It's important to use only elementary rotations (those about a coordinate axis) to align **u** with the z-axis, and these are the only ones we know how to do. First, it can be seen from Figure 11.29 that a rotation through $-\theta$ about the z-axis will swing **u** into the x, z-plane to form the new axis, **u'**, as shown in Figure 11.30. (The angle is $-\theta$ because it is a clockwise angle of θ seen looking toward the origin.) From Equation 11.67 the matrix

$$R_z(-\theta) = \begin{pmatrix} \cos(-\theta) & \sin(-\theta) & 0 \\ -\sin(-\theta) & \cos(-\theta) & 0 \\ 0 & 0 & 1 \end{pmatrix} \tag{11.68}$$

accomplishes this. Second, a rotation through $-\phi$ about the y-axis completes the alignment process. The required matrix is

$$R_y(-\phi) = \begin{pmatrix} \cos(-\phi) & 0 & -\sin(-\phi) \\ 0 & 1 & 0 \\ \sin(-\phi) & 0 & \cos(-\phi) \end{pmatrix} \tag{11.69}$$

With **u** aligned along the z-axis, we do the desired rotation about the z-axis through angle A, using matrix

$$R_z(A) = \begin{pmatrix} \cos(A) & \sin(A) & 0 \\ -\sin(A) & \cos(A) & 0 \\ 0 & 0 & 1 \end{pmatrix} \tag{11.70}$$

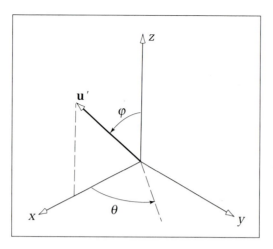

Figure 11.30.
Aligning **u** with the z-axis.

Finally, the alignment rotations must be undone to restore the axis to its original direction. This is easily done using the **inverse matrices** to $R_y(-\phi)$ and $R_z(-\theta)$. According to Exercise 11.35, it is trivial to invert a rotation: Just rotate through the negative of the original angle. We first undo the rotation about the y-axis and then the one about the z-axis, just as if we were "popping" them from a transformation stack, as in the robot discussion. Thus five transformations in all must be composed. Because no translations are involved, we can simply multiply the transformation matrices to obtain one matrix, $R_u(A)$, that captures the desired process. This matrix is given by

$$R_u(A) = R_z(-\theta)R_y(-\phi)R_z(A)R_y(\phi)R_z(\theta) \qquad (11.71)$$

Example

Find the matrix that performs a rotation through angle 35° about the axis situated at $\theta = 30°$ and $\phi = 45°$.

Solution:
The first three rotation matrices involved are

$$R_z(-\theta) = \begin{pmatrix} .866 & -.5 & 0 \\ .5 & .866 & 0 \\ 0 & 0 & 1 \end{pmatrix}$$

$$R_y(-\phi) = \begin{pmatrix} .707 & 0 & .707 \\ 0 & 1 & 0 \\ -.707 & 0 & .707 \end{pmatrix}$$

$$R_z(A) = \begin{pmatrix} .819 & .574 & 0 \\ -.574 & .819 & 0 \\ 0 & 0 & 1 \end{pmatrix} \qquad (11.72)$$

The fourth and last matrices are just transpositions of the first and second. Multiply the five together to obtain the overall result:

$$R_u(35\pi/180) = \begin{pmatrix} .887 & .445 & -.124 \\ -.366 & .842 & .396 \\ .281 & -.306 & .910 \end{pmatrix} \qquad (11.73)$$

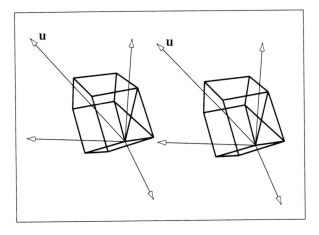

Figure 11.31.
The basic barn rotated about an axis.

Figure 11.31 shows the basic barn after being subjected to this rotation.

Drill Exercise

11.37.   The Matrix Is Orthogonal. Show that the complicated rotation matrix in Equation 11.73 is orthogonal—see Exercise 11.35 for definitions.

11.9.7 Using Rotations for Better Views of Three-Dimensional Objects

An important application of 3D rotations is to provide more flexible views of 3D objects. In Chapter 10 we developed a way to produce perspective views of a scene, but the eye was forced to lie on one of the coordinate axes, making most pictures hard to interpret. Now we want to produce drawings as if the eye were positioned along some axis, **u**, as shown in Figure 11.32a. We also suppose that the viewer's head is oriented "up" in the positive z-direction, and so we call **k** the *up* vector.

To achieve the desired view, we rotate the object so as to align axis **u** with the z-axis and then perform a perspective projection with the eye on the z-axis, as in Section 10.3. The final picture will show the barn's projection on the x, y-plane, with the y-axis pointing upward and the x-axis to the right.

Suppose, as before, that **u** makes angles θ and ϕ with coordinate axes, as shown in the figure. We first perform the rotation $R_z(-\theta - \pi/2)$ about the z-axis. This swings the barn around so that the transformed **u** axis lies in the y, z-plane. This choice of plane ensures that the up vector has been swung so that it points partially along the positive y-direction, in order to make the final picture "up-right." The barn is now rotated using $R_x(-\phi)$, to align the **u** axis with the z-axis, as shown in Figure 11.32b. The rotated object now looks the same from the z-axis as the original object looks from the **u**-axis, and the sense of up has been preserved.

The eye is placed at point $(0, 0, E)$ on the z-axis and the projection given by Equation 10.8 is performed. We assume that the routine *Persp_z*(P : *point3D*; E : *real*; **var** Q : *point*) is available to project point P to Q for an eye at $(0, 0, E)$.

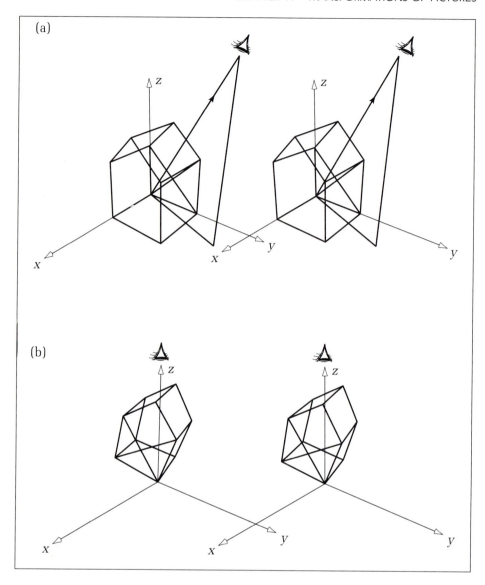

Figure 11.32.
Placing the eye along axis **u**.

The required rotation can be set up using the following:

Code Fragment 11.10. Setting Up the Rotation

Set_Rotate3D(z, −theta − TWOPI/4.0, Tran1);
Set_Rotate3D(x, −phi, Tran2);
ComposeTransf3D(Tran1, Tran2, Tran); {rotation now built}
　　The next code fragment shows how to use this rotation (or any transformation stored in *Tran*) to draw a perspective projection of an arbitrary wireframe model. Each of the vertices *vert[i]* in the wireframe is rotated and projected, with the resulting 2D point stored as *pt[i]* (having the same index) in a temporary array. Then to draw each edge the indices of its two endpoints are retrieved and used to index into the *pt[ ]* array.

Code Fragment 11.11. Rotate and Project a Wireframe Object

```
procedure ViewWireframe(object : wireframe; Tran : affine3D; E : real);
{draw transformed and projected wireframe with eye distance E}
var
   i : integer;
   Q : point3D;
   pt : array[1..MAXNUMVERTS] of point; {hold projected vertices}
begin
   with object do
   begin
      for i := 1 to numverts do
      begin
         Transform3D(Tran, vert[i], Q); {rotate point in 3D}
         Persp_z(Q, E, pt[i]); {project point}
      end;
      for i := 1 to numedges do Line(pt[edge[i, 1]], pt[edge[i, 2]])
   end
end;
```

Figure 11.33 shows the basic barn seen from different points of view (each floor is shaded to assist interpreting the views):

1. $\theta = 45°$, $\phi = 35.264°$ and $E = 4$: This view shows the barn from above at a revealing angle. The eye is quite distant, and so there is little perspective distortion.

2. $\theta = 135°$, $\phi = 30°$ and $E = 2.5$: This is a back view achieved by using $\theta > 90°$. E is smaller here, and so there is more perspective distortion.

3. $\theta = 30°$, $\phi = 120°$ and $E = 1000$: This is a view from below the barn, since $\phi > 90°$. E is so large that there is negligible perspective distortion: It is essentially a parallel projection.

The extra degrees of freedom provided by θ and ϕ allow much greater flexibility in drawing 3D objects, and therefore much improved views. This capability is enhanced further in Chapter 12.

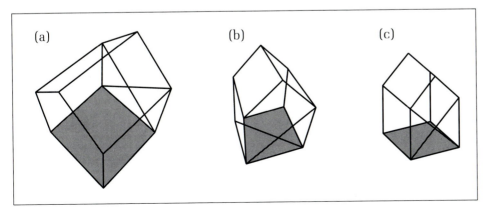

(a) (b) (c)

Figure 11.33.
Three views of the barn.

11.10 Unified Composition of Three-Dimensional Affine Transformations

In order to compose several affine transformations, we want a unified matrix multiplication form that incorporates translations, just as for 2D transformations.

We use the same technique of homogeneous coordinates as employed in two dimensions. An equivalent form for the transformation in Equation 11.58 is

$$(Q_x, Q_y, Q_z, 1) = (P_x, P_y, P_z, 1)\hat{M} \tag{11.74}$$

where the extended matrix $\hat{M}$ is given by

$$\hat{M} = \begin{pmatrix} m_{11} & m_{12} & m_{13} & 0 \\ m_{21} & m_{22} & m_{23} & 0 \\ m_{31} & m_{32} & m_{33} & 0 \\ tr_x & tr_y & tr_z & 1 \end{pmatrix} \tag{11.75}$$

The process follows the same pattern as in the 2D case. The matrix is enlarged from 3 by 3 to 4 by 4 by inserting the translation offset as a fourth row and by appending a fourth column of 0, 0, 0, and 1. Point P is enlarged to $\hat{P}$ by appending a 1 to its coordinates. Then $\hat{P}$ is multiplied by $\hat{M}$ to produce $\hat{Q}$, and finally the fourth coordinate of 1 is dropped from $\hat{Q}$ to restore it to Q. It is easy to check that this form produces the same transformation as does Equation 11.58: Simply write out both expressions and see that they are identical.

Later, when we encounter 4-by-4 matrices with a more complex last column than 0, 0, 0, 1, the fourth component of $(P_x, P_y, P_z, 1)\hat{M}$ will not be 1. In that case we do the same as in Section 11.7.1 and divide through by the fourth component and then delete the 1.

Just as for 2D transformations, if $\hat{M}_1$ maps P into Q, and $\hat{M}_2$ maps Q into S, then $\hat{M}_1\hat{M}_2$ will map P into S, and so we must only multiply the 4-by-4 matrices to form the matrix that represents the composition of the two transformations. As always, the matrices are multiplied in the order in which the transformations are performed.

Drill Exercise

11.38. Composing Transformations. Choose two arbitrary 3D affine transformations, involving any 3-by-3 matrices, M_1 and M_2, and any translation 3-tuples, T_1 and T_2. Carry out (symbolically) the manipulations $Q = PM_1 + T_1$ followed by $S = QM_2 + T_2$ to obtain an expression for S. Then build the two extended (homogeneous coordinates) matrices $\hat{M}_1$ and $\hat{M}_2$ and again obtain the components of $\hat{S} = \hat{P}\hat{M}_1\hat{M}_2$ by direct manipulation. Show that both routes will result in the same transformed point S.

Planes and Quadric Surfaces Are Preserved

Because "straightness" is preserved under an affine transformation, it is not surprising that planes are preserved as well. This can most easily be shown using the parametric form for a plane, given in Equation 9.6, as

$$\mathbf{p}(u, v) = \mathbf{c} + \mathbf{a}u + \mathbf{b}v \tag{11.76}$$

If the general point $\mathbf{p}(u, v)$ is used for P in Equation 11.58, the image point will be

$$\begin{aligned} \mathbf{q}(u, v) &= (\mathbf{c} + \mathbf{a}u + \mathbf{b}v)M + \mathbf{tr} \\ &= (\mathbf{c}M + \mathbf{tr}) + (\mathbf{a}M)u + (\mathbf{b}M)v \end{aligned} \tag{11.77}$$

which is clearly also the parametric representation for a plane. Planes thus transform into other planes. Both the "directions," $\mathbf{a}$ and $\mathbf{b}$, are multiplied by matrix M. The normal to the transformed plane is the cross product of these new directions: $(\mathbf{a}M) \times (\mathbf{b}M)$.

Another approach is to work from the point normal form given in Equation 7.31. Suppose plane P is given by

$$\mathbf{n} \cdot \mathbf{r} = D \tag{11.78}$$

To what plane S does this transform? Consider any point $\mathbf{q}$ on S, in which $\mathbf{q}$ results from applying the transformation to some $\mathbf{r}$ on P, and so $\mathbf{q} = \mathbf{r}M + \mathbf{tr}$. Thus $\mathbf{r} = (\mathbf{q} - \mathbf{tr})M^{-1}$. Because $\mathbf{r}$ is on P, the new surface consists of all points $\mathbf{q}$ that satisfy $\mathbf{n} \cdot (\mathbf{q} - \mathbf{tr})M^{-1} = D$, or

$$\mathbf{n} \cdot (\mathbf{q}M^{-1}) = D + \mathbf{n} \cdot (\mathbf{tr}M^{-1}) \tag{11.79}$$

Now the dot product form, $\mathbf{n} \cdot (\mathbf{q}M^{-1})$, can be rewritten as $(\mathbf{n}M^{-T}) \cdot \mathbf{q}$ (see the exercises), and Equation 11.79 becomes

$$(\mathbf{n}M^{-T}) \cdot \mathbf{q} = D + (\mathbf{n}M^{-T}) \cdot \mathbf{tr} \tag{11.80}$$

which is the point normal form for plane S. Thus S has normal vector $\mathbf{n}M^{-T}$.

Another fact of considerable interest is that quadric surfaces (recall Chapter 9) are transformed into quadric surfaces by means of an affine transformation. Thus ellipsoids transform into ellipsoids, hyperboloids into hyperboloids, and so forth. (A brief discussion of this is given in the exercises.)

Drill Exercises

11.39.   Prove the Fact About Dot Products. Appendix 2 shows a way to write a dot product as a matrix multiplying a vector. Use this to show, for any 3D vectors, $\mathbf{a}$ and $\mathbf{b}$, and any 3-by-3 matrix, Q, that $\mathbf{a} \cdot (\mathbf{b}Q) = (\mathbf{a}Q^T) \cdot \mathbf{b}$, where T denotes the transpositions. Does this result extend to vectors and matrices of other dimensions?

11.40.   Simple Transformations of a Plane. Show that rotating a plane also rotates its normal by the same amount. Discuss what a shear does to a plane. Also, if a plane is scaled differentially, say by scale factor vector $(1, 3, 2)$, how will its normal be affected?

11.41.   Find the Transformed Plane. Consider plane P, given by Equation 11.78, where $\mathbf{n} = (1, 2, 1)$ and $D = 4$. P is transformed into plane Q by the transformation with matrix

$$M = \begin{pmatrix} 1 & 2 & -1 \\ 1 & 1 & 3 \\ 2 & 4 & -1 \end{pmatrix} \tag{11.81}$$

and translation vector $\mathbf{tr} = (3, 4, -1)$. Find the equation and the parametric form for Q beginning with P in the form of Equation 11.76. Repeat, beginning with P in the point normal form of Equation 11.78. Show that the two point normal forms for Q agree, as do its two parametric forms.

11.42.   Quadric Surfaces Transform to Quadric Surfaces. In Chapter 9 we saw that a quadric surface, S, was defined by four values, A, B, C, and D, and that S consists of all points, (x, y, z), that satisfy $Ax^2 + By^2 + Cz^2 + D = 0$. Defining the extended vector, $\mathbf{P} = (x, y, z, 1)$ (as in homogeneous coordinates), this equation can be put into the so-called quadratic form:

$$\mathbf{P}\hat{R}\mathbf{P}^T = 0 \tag{11.85}$$

where $\hat{R}$ is the matrix:

$$\hat{R} = \begin{pmatrix} A & 0 & 0 & 0 \\ 0 & B & 0 & 0 \\ 0 & 0 & C & 0 \\ 0 & 0 & 0 & D \end{pmatrix} \tag{11.86}$$

and $\mathbf{P}^T$ is the transpose of $\mathbf{P}$: the column vector with four rows, x, y, z, and 1. Show that these two forms for surface S are equivalent.

Now consider applying the (nonsingular) 4-by-4 transformation matrix $\hat{M}$ to each point on S, thereby creating the new surface S'. Point $\hat{Q}$ will lie on S' if, and only if, the point from which it came, $\hat{Q}\hat{M}^{-1}$, lies on the original surface S, that is, if

$$(\hat{Q}\hat{M}^{-1})\,\hat{R}(\hat{Q}\hat{M}^{-1})^T = 0 \qquad (11.87)$$

Equivalently, surface S' consists of all points $\hat{Q}$ that satisfy

$$\hat{Q}\hat{R}'\hat{Q}^T = 0 \qquad (11.88)$$

where

$$\hat{R}' = \hat{M}^{-1}\hat{R}\hat{M}^{-T} \qquad (11.89)$$

Thus S' is also a quadric surface, with defining matrix $\hat{R}'$.

Next find the matrix $\hat{R}'$ for an ellipsoid with $(A, B, C, D) = (1, 2, 2, -1)$ when the transformation involves (a) scaling by scale factor vector $(2, 2, 3)$, (b) rotation about the y-axis through $45°$, and (c) translating through $(4, 2, 3)$.

Finally, explore whether there is any transformation that can convert an ellipsoid into a hyperboloid of two sheets.

11.11   Some Interesting Nonaffine Transformations

Although affine transformations are by far the most widely used in graphics, other, more complex transformations are sometimes used to good effect. They typically cause much greater distortion of an object's shape. Lines do not map into lines; ellipses become quite different shapes altogether; and so on.

11.11.1 Fish-Eye Transformation

A fish-eye (2D) transformation simulates what one sees through a "fish-eye" camera lens or through a peephole in a hotel door. Geometrically it is an "angle-halver," as suggested by Figure 11.34. Any point, P, in the x, y-plane is mapped to point Q situated along the line OP but closer to the origin O. Q is thus just a scaled version of P: $Q = sP$. To determine s, imagine a point, E, at unit distance along the z-axis, and note the angle ϕ subtended at E by OP. Hence $\phi = $ arctan

Figure 11.34.

The geometry of the fish-eye transformation.

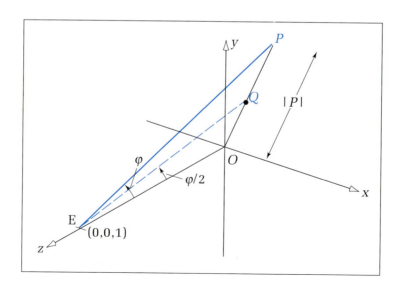

($|P|$), where $|P| = \sqrt{P_x^2 + P_y^2}$ is the length of OP. Now place Q so that OQ subtends an angle only half as large, that is, so that $|Q| = \tan(\phi/2)$. The required scaling is therefore

$$s = \frac{\tan(\arctan(|P|)/2)}{|P|} \qquad (11.82)$$

Although Q is just a scaled version of P, the transformation is highly nonlinear because the scale factor depends on P. With this transformation, points very far away from the origin—for which ϕ is close to $90°$—are mapped to points at around only $45°$. This transformation maps the entire x, y-plane into the interior of the unit circle (why?). This is suggested by Figure 11.35a, which shows the image of a grid under the fish-eye transformation. Figure 11.35b shows a map similarly distorted.

11.11.2 Inversion in a Unit Circle

Inversion in a unit circle has interesting geometrical properties (Dodge 1972, Hill 1980a, 1980b) and can be used to solve a number of problems in mathematics and physics. Let point P have polar coordinates ($|P|$, θ), as shown in Figure 11.36. Its "inverse," Q, must have polar coordinates ($1/|P|$, θ). Thus P and

(a)

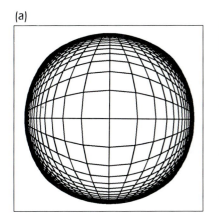

(b)

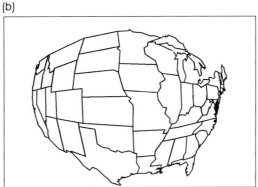

Figure 11.35.
Fish-eye distortions of a grid and a map.

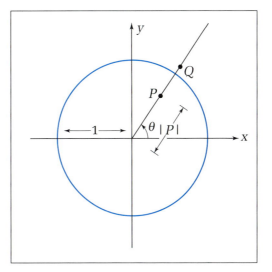

Figure 11.36.
The geometry of an inversion in the unit circle.

Q lie at the same angle, and their distances from the origin have the constant product 1. As in the fish-eye transformation, Q is just a scaled version of P. Here the scaling factor varies as $1/|P|^2$, and the mapping is

$$
\begin{aligned}
Q_x &= \frac{P_x}{|P|^2} \\
Q_y &= \frac{P_y}{|P|^2}
\end{aligned}
\qquad (11.83)
$$

Clearly, any point on the circle of radius 1—the unit circle—maps into itself. Points inside the unit circle, ($|P| < 1$), map into points outside ($|Q| > 1$), and vice versa. The origin is the only point having no inverse. Straight lines that pass through the origin also map into themselves (why?). Figure 11.37 shows how simple figures become distorted: Circle A is mapped into circle A', line B into B', and so forth. Figure 11.38 shows the United States inverted in the unit circle.

Inversions enjoy a host of general properties that are less obvious but not difficult to prove:

- Circles and straight lines that do not pass through the origin map into circles.

- The mapping is "conformal," that is, angles between intersecting lines are preserved under the mapping. In particular, tangency and perpendicularity are preserved.

- Any circle that intersects the unit circle at a right angle maps into itself!

Many more properties, as well as ways to construct inverses to figures, are discussed in (Hill 1980a, 1980b). Also see the exercises at the end of this chapter.

Figure 11.37.
Example inversions.

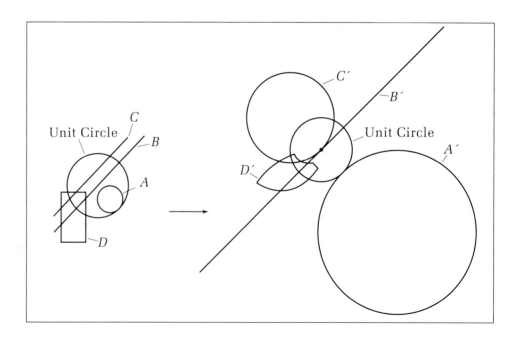

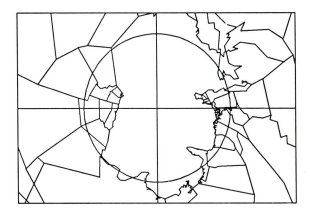

Figure 11.38.
The inversion of a map.

11.11.3 False Perspective

Perspective projections introduced in Chapter 10 involve a division by the "depth" of a point—its distance from the "eye." For example, when the eye is on the z-axis at $(0, 0, 1)$, the 3D point (P_x, P_y, P_z) projects to $[x/(1 - z), y/(1 - z)]$ (see Equation 10.8).

We can create interesting perspectivelike illusions of 2D objects by concocting a "pseudodepth" for each point, (x, y), and inserting it into the transformation. Calling the pseudodepth function $z(x, y)$, the transformation is

$$Q_x = \frac{P_x}{1 - z(P_x, P_y)}$$

$$Q_y = \frac{P_y}{1 - z(P_x, P_y)} \tag{11.84}$$

This is yet another example of Q's being a scaled version of P, with scaling factor $1/(1 - z(P_x, P_y))$. At points for which $z(P_x, P_y)$ is less than but close to 1, the scaling factor is large—a magnification about the origin. On the other hand, a demagnification occurs where $z(P_x, P_y)$ is negative.

An example is shown in Figure 11.39. A knight is drawn before and after using the pseudodepth function $z(x, y) = \frac{1}{2} \exp(-ax^2 - by^2)$ for constants a and b. The scaling factor varies from 2 at the origin to 1 at the outskirts of the image. Other cases are examined in the exercises.

Figure 11.39.
Knight drawn with false perspective. (Courtesy of Susan Verbeck.)

11.12 Summary

This chapter described important tools for transforming pictures and coordinate systems. We introduced affine transformations, which were shown to have a simple form based on a matrix and an offset vector. Affine transformations can perform many of the important picture manipulations required in graphics, and because they preserve straight lines, they make it easy to produce line drawings of transformed objects. Affine transformations can be composed to combine many of the desired effects in a single transformation, and by using homogeneous coordinates, all affine transformations can be represented by a single matrix. This provides a desirable unity of form when performing transformations in an application. This unity also makes it relatively easy to manipulate hierarchical objects using a transformation "stack."

The ideas of 2D transformations are easily extended to the 3D case. Three-dimensional transformations may be harder to visualize, but they can readily be used in applications, and they provide great power in manipulating 3D objects, viewing cameras, and the like.

We also discussed some nonaffine transformations. Whereas affine transformations can only convert parallelograms into parallelograms, these more general transformations can warp the shapes of objects dramatically, which can be useful for achieving certain visual effects.

Chapter Exercises

11.43.   Reflections Revisited. Exercise 4.40 considered a transformation in which the x- and y- coordinates were interchanged, yielding a reflection about a line through the origin tilted at 45°. Does this correspond to a rotation, say through some multiple of 90°? If so, what is the exact rotation involved? If not, is it a combination of a rotation and some other transformation? Specify it, and develop the matrix that represents it.

11.44.   Finding a Normal Direction. A rotation through 90° is represented by the matrix

$$M = \begin{pmatrix} 0 & 1 \\ -1 & 0 \end{pmatrix}$$

Assuming that $A + \beta t$ is the parametric form of a line, transform the line using this matrix. Show that the directions of the line before and after the transformation are orthogonal (use the dot product). What are the slopes of the two lines? Recall that the slopes of two perpendicular lines are negative reciprocals of each other. Show that these two lines satisfy this condition.

11.45.   Mapping Three Points. An affine transformation is completely specified by its effect on three points in the plane, that is, how it maps one triangle into another. Find the affine transformation that maps the three points $(2, 3)$, $(1, 2)$, and $(3, -1)$ into $(5, 4)$, $(4, -2)$, and $(1, 0)$.

11.46.   Inverting a Shear. For an arbitrary shear transformation, find the form of the inverse matrix. Is the inverse of a shear another shear?

11.47.   Lines That Are Invariant Under an Affine Transformation. What set of points and what set of lines are left invariant (unchanged) by the following transformation?

$$M = \begin{pmatrix} 1 & 0 & 0 \\ 0 & 1 & 0 \\ h & k & 1 \end{pmatrix}$$

11.48.   Rotation About an Axis Not Through the Origin. If a given axis of rotation does not pass through the origin, we first translate it to the origin, perform the rotation about it as described, and then translate it back. Define the matrix and offset that accomplish this.

Programming Exercises

11.49. Orthogonal Families of Circles. Figure 4.8 shows two families of circles, with each member of one family orthogonal to every member of the other family. Such families are easy to generate by means of inversions in the unit circle. Invert selected members of the following two simple families: (a) all lines through a given point, P, other than the origin and (b) all circles having P as their center. Because these two families are obviously orthogonal, their inversions are also orthogonal. Write a program that accepts a point P as input and draws the two orthogonal families that result.

11.50. Drawing Polylines. Build the routine **procedure** *DrawTransPoly(Tran : affine; InPoly : polypoint)* which draws a polyline as it is transformed from *InPoly* by the transformation stored in *Tran*.

11.51. Avoiding Matrices in Affine Transformations. Define type *affine*, which is slightly different from that in Code Fragment 11.1 in that it does not use a matrix or a *vector*. It captures the six coefficients a, b, c, d, trx, try as simple fields of type *real*. Discuss why this might improve computational efficiency when performing transformations.

11.52. Draw Transformed Polygons. Write and exercise a program that can draw polygons subjected to any combination to affine transformations. The user can choose each component transformation, and the program composes each choice with the previous transformation and then draws the transformed polygon.

11.53. *Line( )* Revisited—Again. Provide another version of *Line( )* from Chapter 3 that accesses a normalization transformation table to obtain data for the window-to-viewport mapping and that does the appropriate scaling and translation on the world coordinate point.

11.54. Attaching a Polyline to a Valuator. Write a routine that rotates a polyline according to the value returned by an input valuator device (recall Chapter 6). The valuator returns values between 0 and 1, and for each value returned, the polyline is redrawn after rotating it to the corresponding fraction of a full circle.

11.55. Spinning Polygons. Add to the program in Exercise 11.52 the capability of drawing a polygon that "spins along a trajectory," as suggested in Figure 11.40. The trajectory is defined as some form of parametric spiral, $\mathbf{p}(t)$, as in Chapter 4, and is used as an offset vector at a succession of t-values to draw the polygon at its various locations. At each new location the polygon is also rotated and possibly scaled or sheared.

11.56. Data Types for Normalization Transformations. Define an appropriate data structure for storing a list of normalization transformations, as discussed in Section

Figure 11.40.
A polygon spinning along a trajectory.

11.6, and write code to compute the parameters of the transformation from the definitions of the window and viewport.

11.57. Using Homogeneous Coordinates. Rewrite the routines *Transform( )*, *CreateTransf( )*, *Compose-Transf( )*, and *DrawPolyline( )* in a form that uses homogeneous coordinates throughout and captures affine transformations in 3-by-3 matrices. A transformation is achieved with an explicit matrix multiplication by the point being transformed, and two transformations are composed by a simple matrix multiplication. Compare the space and time requirements using this approach with those when ordinary coordinates are employed.

11.58. Dag for an Enhanced Robot. The robot of Section 11.8 has only one arm. Show the directed acyclic graph for a robot that has two identical arms, each with a hand and two fingers. Also give the robot a head that can swivel back and forth.

11.59. Data Structure for a Hierarchical Object. Define an appropriate data structure for describing the nodes in a directed acyclic graph that is to represent a hierarchical object. Each node holds a transformation matrix as well as the inverse transformation matrix, a pointer to a *polypoint* (or list of *polypoint*s that describe the shape of the part), and pointers to "child" nodes of the same type. Design and implement a routine, *DrawDAG( )*, that traverses this structure and draws the represented hierarchical object.

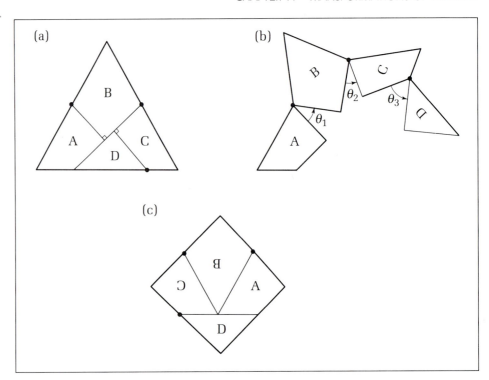

Figure 11.41.
A triangle pivoting into a
square.

11.60.   Triangle into Square. Figure 11.41 shows that an equilateral triangle can be partitioned into four pieces that may be pivoted about one another to fashion a square! Write and exercise a routine that can draw the linked pieces for any set of pivot angles $\theta_1 \ldots \theta_3$. Use the composition of transformations to determine the overall transformation of each part. Have the angles input via three valuator devices if such are available on the workstation.

11.61.   Implementation of *Transform3D( )* and Its Kin. Write and exercise the routine **procedure** *Transform3D(Tran : affine3D; P : point3D;* **var** *Q : point3D)*, which maps 3D point *P* into 3D point *Q* using the transformation stored in *Tran*. Also construct versions of the routines in Code Fragment 11.9 that build the various transformations. Invent a concise set of parameters for specifying the various constants h_{xy}, h_{zx}, and so on to produce simultaneous shears. Also write the routine *Compose-Transf3D( )*, which composes two 3D affine transformations.

11.62.   Drawing with False Perspective. Write a program that draws various objects in the plane, with selected pseudodepth functions. The user selects the object to be drawn (square grid, family of concentric circles, polyspirals, and the like) and the pseudodepth function, and the picture is produced.

11.63.   The Hyperbolic Ellipse Transformation. Show that the transformation

$$Q_x = \sinh(P_x) \cos(aP_y) \qquad (11.$$
$$Q_y = \cosh(P_x) \sin(aP_y) \qquad 90)$$

(where *a* is a constant) maps vertical lines into segments of ellipses and horizontal lines into hyperbolas. Implement this transformation and test it on various polylines.

11.64.   Inverse Transformations. Write routines that create inverse transformations to those fashioned by *CreateTransf( )*.

11.65   Iterated Affine Transformations. The Sierpinski gasket of Exercise 5.25 was generated by placing dots at a sequence of points P_i. Each new point P_{i+1} is found as the midpoint between the previous point P_i and a random selection of one of three vertices *A*, *B*, and *C*.

If we view this process in terms of affine transformations we obtain a fascinating generalization (Demko et al. 1985, Barnsley et al. 1988). Form each P_{i+1} from P_i by subjecting it to one of three affine transformations, T_A, T_B, and T_C, again chosen randomly each time. All of these transformations use the same matrix *M* with entries (a,b,c,d) (see Equation 11.6) given by $(1/2, 0,0,1/2)$, while their offsets are $(A_x/2,A_y/2)$, $(B_x/2,B_y/2)$, and $(C_x/2,C_y/2)$, respectively. Show that this process is equivalent to the "midpoint" selection process used for the Sierpinski gasket.

One can use a different set of affine transformations and obtain other beguiling pictures. The "fern" of Figure 11.42 was formed using an iterative application of the following four transformation:

T_1: (0,0,0,.16), (0,0)
T_2: (.2, .23,−.26, .22), (0, 1.6)
T_3: (−.15, .26, .28, .24), (0, .44)
T_4: (.85,−.04, .04, .85), (0, 1.6)

where again the first four values are the a,b,c,d entries of matrix M and the final two are the offset vectors. At each iteration, T_1, T_2, T_3, or T_4 is selected randomly with probabilities .01, .07, .07, and .85, respectively, and applied to the previous point. Write a routine to generate the fern. (See Barnsely et al. 1988 for other examples.)

Figure 11.42.
The Fern—see Exercise 11.65

CHAPTER 12

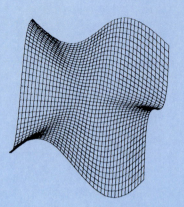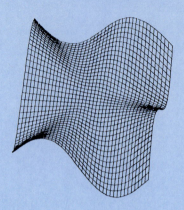

Three-Dimensional Viewing with the Synthetic Camera

I am a camera with its shutter open, quite passive, recording, not thinking.

Christopher Isherwood, *A Berlin Diary*

It adds a precious seeing to the eye.

William Shakespeare, *Love's Labours Lost*

Goals of the Chapter

- To establish with the synthetic camera a more powerful viewing method
- To develop the viewing coordinate system and to describe objects in it
- To devise a means for producing stereo views of objects
- To examine the general perspective transformation
- To study various types of projections and their properties
- To build tools for clipping 3D objects

12.1 Introduction

The 3D viewing methods discussed in Chapter 10 use a rather restricted point of view: Perspective projections require that the eye lie on a coordinate axis (e.g., the z-axis), and the viewplane must coincide with a coordinate plane (e.g., the x, y-plane). Thus if we want to view an object from a different point of view, we must rotate the model of the object. This causes an unfortunate mixing together of modeling (describing and manipulating the objects to be viewed) and viewing (rendering a picture of the objects). And still the pictures are too restricted.

In this chapter we shall develop more flexible methods for a kind of viewing that is completely separate from modeling. One such method is a synthetic camera that is free to move around in space and to point in any direction. The previous projection schemes are seen to be special cases of this new approach, and so the ideas generalize easily. Furthermore, a by-product of the synthetic camera approach is a simple tool for creating stereo views; in fact, all the stereo views in this book were created using this tool. We shall examine a variety of viewing examples and develop techniques for rapid clipping of 3D primitives against a viewing volume. Finally, we shall introduce a powerful perspective transformation that greatly simplifies both clipping and the hidden surface removal process.

12.2 The Synthetic Camera Approach

The synthetic camera concept provides a general viewing approach that has strong intuitive appeal. It grew up in the CORE System (Bergeron 1978) and has been maintained in both the GKS3D and PHIGS approaches (Brown 1985; see Appendix 7). A "synthetic" camera is a way to describe a camera positioned and oriented in three-dimensional space. It has three principal ingredients: a viewplane in which a window is defined, a coordinate system called the viewing coordinate system, and an eye defined within this system.

Figure 12.1 shows such a camera poised in world coordinates. The eye "looks through" the window in the viewplane and "sees" a certain portion of the world, which is the part that is finally drawn.

The viewing coordinate system is sometimes called the **UVN system** after the names traditionally given to its axes. The viewplane coincides with the U, V-plane. Although we let the eye assume more general positions later, in the figure it is positioned on the N-axis. This is, of course, reminiscent of our earlier method in which the viewplane is the x, y-plane and the eye is on the z-axis. In fact, we can view the synthetic camera at this point as just a clone of the world coordinate system that has been pried loose and set free to move around in space, carrying the viewplane and eye with it.

Either a left-handed or right-handed viewing coordinate system can be used. (Both are used by different graphics packages.) We use a left-handed version, as shown in the figure. As mentioned in Section 7.5, a left-handed system seems most natural for viewing: From the eye's point of view, the positive U- and V-directions are to the right and up, as in a standard plot, and the "depth" of a point from the eye increases in the positive N-direction.

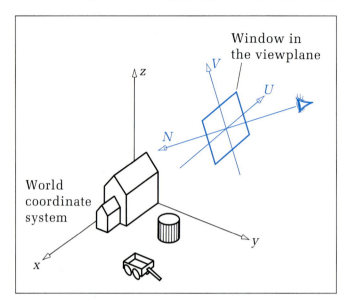

Figure 12.1.
The synthetic camera placed in world coordinates.

12.2.1 Quantitative Description of the Synthetic Camera

We need a mathematical description of each entity in the synthetic camera, which requires specifying the viewing coordinate system, the position and orientation of the viewplane, the window borders, and the position of the eye. We start by specifying the viewplane. A point called the **view reference point (VRP)** is chosen on the viewplane. The VRP becomes the origin of the coordinate system, and it is at (r_x, r_y, r_z) in world coordinates. We often say that the VRP is "at **r**," where **r** is the position vector $\mathbf{r} = (r_x, r_y, r_z)$ (see Figure 12.2).

The normal direction to the viewplane, called the **viewplane normal (VPN)**, is set next and is given as a unit vector, **n**. The components, (n_x, n_y, n_z), of **n** are specified in world coordinates. The VPN establishes the N-axis of the UVN system.

Figure 12.2.
Specifying the viewing coordinate system.

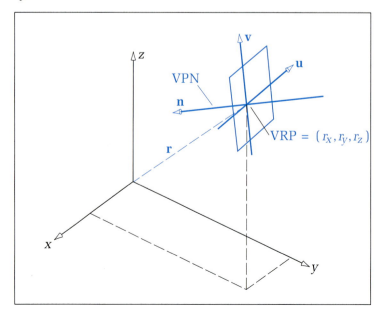

The direction of the V-axis is described by another unit vector, **v**, which is given a direction perpendicular to **n** and pointing in a direction that intuitively corresponds to "upward," as we shall discuss later. The direction of the U-axis is given by a third unit vector, **u**. Once **v** is set, **u** can have only two possible directions, as it must be perpendicular to both **n** and **v**. It is computed as the cross product of **v** and **n**. As we shall see, the system is made left-handed by setting $\mathbf{u} = \mathbf{n} \times \mathbf{v}$.

Example

To help understand these ideas, suppose we wish to look directly onto the center of the right-hand wall of the basic barn of Figure 10.2, as shown in Figure 12.3. The side wall has its center at (1/2, 1, 1/2), which is a natural location for the view reference point. Thus make $\mathbf{r} = (1/2, 1, 1/2)$. The viewplane should be oriented parallel to this wall, so the viewplane normal points in the negative y-direction: $\mathbf{n} = (0, -1, 0)$. A natural "up" direction is along the z-axis, and we choose $\mathbf{v} = (0, 0, 1)$.

Finally the window and the eye must be specified. Whereas the preceding quantities were given in world coordinates, the window and eye are specified in viewing coordinates. This makes sense, as the window and eye are "carried along" with the viewing coordinate system as its position and orientation are changed. The window lies in the viewplane, and its left, top, right, and bottom borders are given by the values (W_l, W_t, W_r, W_b). That is, the window extends from $U = W_l$ to $U = W_r$ in the "horizontal" direction and from $V = W_b$ up to $V = W_t$ in the "vertical" direction. Usually the window is centered near the origin, and so we typically set $W_l = -W_r$ and $W_t = -W_b$. But the window can also be offset from the origin to achieve certain visual effects, as we shall see later.

The eye can be given any position, $\mathbf{e} = (e_u, e_v, e_n)$, in the viewing coordinate system. Often it is positioned on the N-axis at some signed distance E from the VRP, at $\mathbf{e} = (0, 0, E)$. It can also be placed away from the axis to achieve certain "oblique" views or to aid in creating stereo images. These will be discussed later.

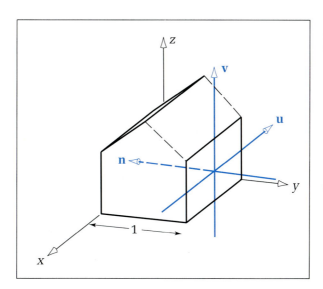

Figure 12.3.
Setup for a particular view of the barn.

Example

We want to define a reasonable eye position and window boundaries for a good view of the barn, as in Figure 12.3. We opt for a perspective view that does not have too much foreshortening and so choose an eye position far back from the VRP on the N-axis, say at $e = (0, 0, -10)$. We also want the window to be large enough to see the whole barn. A reasonable choice is $(W_l, W_t, W_r, W_b) = (-2, 3, 2, -2)$.

12.1.   Other Views and Windows. Specify the VRP and VPN for a view of the barn looking directly down on the center of the roof. For the eye at $(0, 0, -10)$, what is an appropriate window? Repeat for a view looking from below directly up at the origin of the world coordinate system.

Flexibility of the Synthetic Camera Model

The ingredients of the synthetic camera allow the user to control viewing in a manner that corresponds well with our head motion. Thus changing any one ingredient causes an easily understood effect. For example, some common effects used with television, movies, and animation are the following:

- *Fly-by*: The VRP specifies the position of the viewer, and thus altering it is akin to moving your head without changing your direction of looking. If pictures are drawn of a model at a succession of positions and then played back, the sequence of pictures will show a "walk-through" or "fly-by" of the object such as in roaming through a building or flying over some terrain.

- *Looking around*: The VPN determines the direction in which the head is looking. Swiveling the viewplane normal is the same as pivoting your head to get various views of a scene.

- *Head tilting*: Changing the up direction is akin to keeping your eye fixed on an object while tilting your head. When the head is tilted in one direction, the object appears to be rotated in the other direction.

12.3   How Does a User Specify the Camera?

To position and orient the synthetic camera, we must have three elements:

1.   The VRP, $\mathbf{r}$

2.   The VPN, $\mathbf{n}$

3.   The "upward" vector, $\mathbf{v}$

Often a user wants to be able to specify a view interactively, perhaps by typing in the components of these three vectors. The VPR $\mathbf{r}$ is quite easy to choose, as it is usually placed near the center of the part of the object to be viewed.

In a similar manner, one can develop intuition about how **n** should be chosen to achieve a certain view. It is inconvenient to worry about whether a vector is normalized, and the user thus would enter some vector, **norm**, and let the machine find **n** as

$$\mathbf{n} = \frac{\mathbf{norm}}{|\mathbf{norm}|} \qquad (12.1)$$

For instance, the N-axis can be made to point directly at the world coordinate origin by setting **norm** = $-\mathbf{r}$ (why?). Or to point directly down, make **norm** = $(0, 0, -1)$, so that it points in the negative z-direction. To point up at the bottom of an object, use **norm** = $(0, 0, +1)$.

Another, rather intuitive, way for the user to establish **norm** is to give some point of interest, **scene**, in the scene and to define **norm** as the vector from **r** to **scene**: **norm** = **scene** − **r**. This is then normalized to form **n**.

12.3.1 An Alternative: Using Angles to Specify Direction

Some people find it more convenient to specify a direction in terms of angles. As shown in Appendix 5, the spherical coordinate representation of a direction is through the **colatitude** ϕ and the **azimuth** θ. To achieve a VPN that points downward in a certain fashion, the user might say that **n** should have an azimuth of 220° and a colatitude of 120°. (Sketch this direction.) According to Appendix 5, the components of a unit vector having colatitude ϕ and azimuth θ are

$$\begin{aligned} n_x &= \sin(\phi)\,\cos(\theta) \\ n_y &= \sin(\phi)\,\sin(\theta) \\ n_z &= \cos(\phi) \end{aligned} \qquad (12.2)$$

The application would include a routine such as *BuildVPN(theta, phi : real;* **var** *n : vector3D)* to create **n**, given ϕ and θ (see the exercises).

Example
Find the **n** having colatitude 120° and azimuth 220°.

Solution:
Use Equation 12.2 directly to obtain **n** = $(-.6634, -.5567, -.5)$.

Once **r** and **n** have been chosen, there remains the problem of setting **v**. The user might want "up" to be the same as "up" in world coordinates and might be tempted to set **v** = $(0, 0, 1)$. But **v** must be perpendicular to **n**, and if **n** is tilted downward at all, this choice won't work. It's even harder if the user wants the viewer's head tilted at, say, 45°! One should be able to enter a vector, say **up**, as a meaningful suggestion of up and let the application figure out a proper **v** that is perpendicular to **n** and as close as possible to the suggested up direction.

An effective way to find **v** is to project **up** onto the viewplane along the **n** direction to form **up**′, as suggested in Figure 12.4, because **up**′ is the closest vector to **up** that lies in the viewplane. Using Equation 7.23, **up**′ is found to be

$$\mathbf{up}' = \mathbf{up} - (\mathbf{up} \cdot \mathbf{n})\mathbf{n} \qquad (12.3)$$

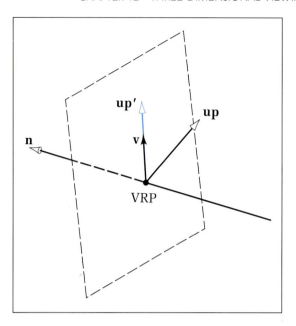

Figure 12.4.
Fashioning the V-axis.

The normalized version **v** of **up**′ is then easily computed:

$$\mathbf{v} = \frac{\mathbf{up}'}{|\mathbf{up}'|} \tag{12.4}$$

Thus the user can input a vector, **up**, that is in approximately the desired up direction, and the application can find the closest appropriate axis vector, **v**.

Notice that this approach will fail if **up** happens to be chosen identical to **n**, for then **up**′ will also be zero (why?). Therefore, in situations in which the user wants to "look" straight up or straight down, care must be taken to choose an **up** that is not also straight up or down.

Finally, because the u-axis vector is perpendicular to both **n** and **v**, it is given by the cross product:

$$\mathbf{u} = \mathbf{n} \times \mathbf{v} \tag{12.5}$$

This form makes the UVN system left-handed. (Setting **u** to the negative of this would make it right-handed). Vector **u** is automatically normalized (why?). Note: **v** and **n** are defined in the right-handed world system, so use the right hand to tell which way a cross product points.

The UVN coordinate system is now completely specified in terms of world coordinates.

Drill Exercise

12.2.   Derive the Expression of up′. Show that Equation 12.3 is the correct form for **up**′ and also that **up**′ is orthogonal to **n**.

12.3.   The Simplest Case. Consider a "default" view in which the VRP is at the origin, the VPN points along the y-axis, and **up** points along the z-axis. Thus **r** = (0, 0, 0), **norm** = (0, 1, 0), and **up** = (0, 0, 1). These formulas should yield **u**, **v**, and **n** equal to **i**, **k**, and **j**, respectively. Show that they do.

Example

Using $\mathbf{n} = (0, -3/5, 4/5)$, find $\mathbf{u}$ and $\mathbf{v}$ when $\mathbf{up}$ is given as $(0, 1, 0)$.

Solution:
First evaluate $\mathbf{up} \cdot \mathbf{n} = -3/5$, and use it in Equation 12.3: $\mathbf{up}' = (0, 1, 0) - (-3/5)(0, -3/5, 4/5) = (0, 16/25, 12/25)$, which normalizes to $\mathbf{v} = (0, 4/5, 3/5)$. *Check:* Is $\mathbf{v}$ indeed normal to $\mathbf{n}$? Now $\mathbf{u} = \mathbf{n} \times \mathbf{v}$ yields $\mathbf{u} = (-1, 0, 0)$, which is clearly normal to both $\mathbf{v}$ and $\mathbf{n}$, and has unit length.

The following procedure, *BuildUVN( )*, constructs $\mathbf{u}$, $\mathbf{v}$, and $\mathbf{n}$ from **norm** and **up**. It uses the vector routines *Normalize( )* and *Cross( )*, as developed in Chapter 7. Also see Appendix 3.

Code Fragment 12.1. Computing $\mathbf{u}$, $\mathbf{v}$, and $\mathbf{n}$

```
procedure BuildUVN(norm, Up : vector3D; var u, v, n : vector3D);
{build u, v, n from norm and Up}
var
  upp : vector3D;
  dotprod : real;
begin
  Normalize3(norm, n); {normalize norm to n}
  dotprod := Dot3D(Up, n);
  upp.dx := Up.dx - dotprod * n.dx;
  upp.dy := Up.dy - dotprod * n.dy;
  upp.dz := Up.dz - dotprod * n.dz;
  Normalize3(upp, v);
  Cross(n, v, u); {build u}
end;
```

12.4 Describing Object Points in Viewing Coordinates

We have developed a method for specifying where the synthetic camera is and how it is "pointing." Given the quantities **norm** and **up**, we can find the $\mathbf{u}$, $\mathbf{v}$, and $\mathbf{n}$ vectors, expressed in world coordinates. Along with the VRP, $\mathbf{r}$, this characterizes the UVN system completely.

We now want to use this capability to draw projections of models. This is greatly facilitated by being able to represent all points of interest in viewing coordinates, because the eye position and window boundaries are given in this system. Therefore, all further work can be done in this single coordinate system, simplifying things both conceptually and computationally.

How do we find the viewing coordinates, (a, b, c), of a world coordinate point, $\mathbf{p} = (x, y, z)$? We harken back to Section 11.4 and use a version of Equation 11.28. View the UVN system as being formed from the world coordinate axes by a rotation and a translation. Recall that if one coordinate system is formed from another by a coordinate transformation, and if we know how to express the new axes in terms of the original system, it will be easy to write the transformation matrix M. The 3D version of Equation 11.26 states that the rows of M are simply the vectors $\mathbf{u}$, $\mathbf{v}$, and $\mathbf{n}$ themselves!

$$M = \begin{pmatrix} \mathbf{u} \\ \mathbf{v} \\ \mathbf{n} \end{pmatrix} = \begin{pmatrix} u_x & u_y & u_z \\ v_x & v_y & v_z \\ n_x & n_y & n_z \end{pmatrix} \tag{12.6}$$

The rest of the transformation is a translation by the VRP, $\mathbf{r}$. Thus if P is a point with viewing coordinates (a, b, c), P must have world coordinates given by $(x, y, z) = (a, b, c)M + \mathbf{r}$. Subtract $\mathbf{r}$ from both sides and multiply by M^{-1} to obtain the desired viewing coordinates for $\mathbf{p}$:

$$(a, b, c) = (\mathbf{p} - \mathbf{r})M^{-1} \tag{12.7}$$

The inverse of M is easy to find because it represents a pure rotation. The rows of M are mutually perpendicular unit vectors (why?); thus, according to Exercise 11.35, the inverse of M is just its transposition, M^T. The three columns of M^T are simply $\mathbf{u}$, $\mathbf{v}$, and $\mathbf{n}$ written as column vectors, which leads to the nice form shown in the following exercise.

Drill Exercise

12.4.   Do It with Dot Products. Show that each of the three components a, b, and c in Equation 12.7 can be found as the dot products:

$$\begin{aligned} a &= (\mathbf{p} - \mathbf{r}) \cdot \mathbf{u} \\ b &= (\mathbf{p} - \mathbf{r}) \cdot \mathbf{v} \\ c &= (\mathbf{p} - \mathbf{r}) \cdot \mathbf{n} \end{aligned} \tag{12.8}$$

It is handy to have the homogeneous coordinate form for this transformation. A single 4-by-4 matrix will capture it. Because the matrix converts world coordinates into viewing coordinates, we name it $\hat{A}_{WV}$ and have

$$(a, b, c, 1) = (x, y, z, 1)\hat{A}_{WV} \tag{12.9}$$

What is the form for $\hat{A}_{WV}$? Its upper left 3-by-3 submatrix is just M^T, and its bottom row is the translation. We must first write Equation 12.7 as a matrix multiplication followed by a translation (see Figure 11.15):

$$(a, b, c) = \mathbf{p}M^T - \mathbf{r}M^T \tag{12.10}$$

The translation is therefore $-\mathbf{r}M^T$. Call $-\mathbf{r}M^T = \mathbf{r}'$. When writing it out, notice that each of its components is the dot product of $\mathbf{r}$ and one of the vectors $\mathbf{u}$, $\mathbf{v}$, or $\mathbf{n}$:

$$\mathbf{r}' = (-\mathbf{r} \cdot \mathbf{u}, -\mathbf{r} \cdot \mathbf{v}, -\mathbf{r} \cdot \mathbf{n}) \tag{12.11}$$

Place this vector in the fourth row of the homogeneous coordinate form matrix. Thus, we obtain

$$\hat{A}_{WV} = \begin{pmatrix} u_x & v_x & n_x & 0 \\ u_y & v_y & n_y & 0 \\ u_z & v_z & n_z & 0 \\ r'_x & r'_y & r'_z & 1 \end{pmatrix} \tag{12.12}$$

Example

Suppose $\mathbf{u} = (-1, 0, 0)$, $\mathbf{v} = (0, 4/5, 3/5)$, $\mathbf{n} = (0, -3/5, 4/5)$, and $\mathbf{r} = (2, 3, -1)$. (Is this system left-handed?) Find the viewing coordinates of the world point $(4, 7, 2)$.

Solution:

The components of the translation $\mathbf{r}'$ are found by evaluating three dot products. The first is $-\mathbf{r} \cdot \mathbf{u} = 2$, and the others are $-9/5$ and $13/5$. The matrix is therefore

$$\hat{A}_{WV} = \begin{pmatrix} -1 & 0 & 0 & 0 \\ 0 & 4/5 & -3/5 & 0 \\ 0 & 3/5 & 4/5 & 0 \\ 2 & -9/5 & 13/5 & 1 \end{pmatrix} \tag{12.13}$$

and multiplying by $(4, 7, 2, 1)$ yields $(-2, 5, 0, 1)$. It is helpful to visualize and sketch this situation, to become convinced that the point $(4, 7, 2)$ in world coordinates does indeed have representation $(-2, 5, 0)$ in viewing coordinates. Why, for instance, is the third component 0?

The following procedure, *WorldtoView( )*, converts any world coordinate point, *WorldPt*, into its corresponding viewing system version, *ViewPt*. For efficiency, it does it using dot products, as in Equation 12.8. *Difference3( )* forms a vector as the difference of two 3D points.

Code Fragment 12.2. Conversion of World into Viewing Coordinates

```
procedure WorldtoView(WorldPt : point3D;
u, v, n, r : vector3D; var ViewPt : point3D);
    var temp : vector3D;
begin
   Difference3(WorldPt, r, temp); {temp : = WorldPt − r}
   ViewPt.x := Dot3(temp, u);
   ViewPt.y := Dot3(temp, v);
   ViewPt.z := Dot3(temp, n)
end;
```

An alternative form for this procedure that uses the 4-by-4 matrix $\hat{A}_{WV}$ is requested in the exercises. The matrix form is preferred when the viewing transformation is combined with other transformations, as we shall see.

12.4.1 Representing Objects in Viewing Coordinates

The main point of this conversion process is to simplify the remaining operations of clipping, projection, and rendering pictures of a scene. Once the synthetic camera has been defined and $\mathbf{u}$, $\mathbf{v}$, $\mathbf{n}$, and $\mathbf{r}$ have been computed, the vertices of all objects in the scene are transformed to viewing coordinates. Figure 12.5 shows the situation. The UVN system is shown with the window defined in the U, V-plane, and the eye resides at position vector $\mathbf{e}$ in this system. The vertices of the barn have been converted into the UVN system. For instance, vertex $\mathbf{p}_9$, which had world coordinates (1, .5, 1.5) (see Table 10.1), now has UVN coordinates such as $(u, v, n) = (2.3, 4.6, 9.75)$. *Note*: The coordinates of a point in the UVN system are u, v, and n. Do not confuse the real number u with the vector $\mathbf{u}$, which is drawn in boldface.

What is the conversion process? Recall that the barn data are stored in variable *barn* of type *wireframe* (see Code Fragment 10.1). The vertex list in *barn* is traversed once, and each vertex is transformed using *WorldtoView*( ). The transformed vertices could be placed back in the array *barn.vert*[ ], but this would cause an undesirable mixing of modeling and viewing. It is better to build a new list, say *UVNvert* : **array**[1..*MaxNumVerts*] of *point3D*, so that the model itself remains uncorrupted. In this way many different views can be drawn using the original barn data. The transformation process is simply **for** $i := 1$ **to** *barn.numverts* **do** *WorldtoView(barn.vert[i], u, v, n, r, UVNvert[i])*;. The edgelist in *barn* doesn't need to be altered (why?). From this point on, all references to the vertices of the barn will use *UVNvert*[ ] instead of *vert*[ ].

12.5   Viewing the Object

Now we want to construct a picture of the object, and for a wireframe object this involves drawing each edge in turn.

Figure 12.6 shows a single arrangement through which we can study both types of planar projections at once. We shall develop ideas in terms of perspective projections and then show that parallel projections arise in the limit as the eye "moves off to infinity." The eye is at $\mathbf{e}$, and we wish to draw the perspective

Figure 12.5.
Everything converted to viewing coordinates.

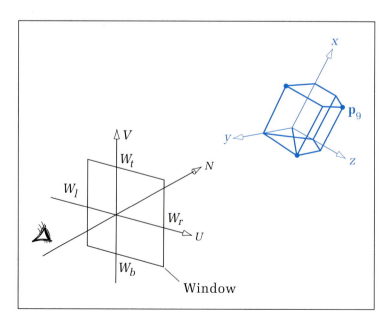

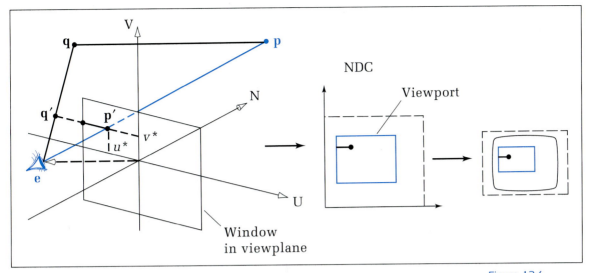

Figure 12.6.
The geometry of perspective projections.

projection onto the viewplane of the edge from **p** to **q**. Because we have seen that perspective projections preserve straight lines, we need only project the endpoints **p** and **q**. The projected edge from **p**′ to **q**′ is clipped to the window, and the endpoints of the portion that lies inside the window are, as always, mapped to the viewport and are finally mapped to the display by the device driver.

In terms of the wireframe *object*, it is most efficient to project all of its vertices, *UVNvert[ ]*, once, and then for each edge to connect the proper pair of projected vertices in two dimensions. Suppose we store the projected vertices in the array *vert2D[ ]*. Then the edges can be drawn using

for *i* := 1 **to** *numedge* **do**
   Line(vert2D[object.edge[i, 1]], vert2D[object.edge[i, 2]]);

much as in Code Fragment 10.2. *Line( )* takes care of the clipping and mapping to NDC, as before. Later we shall see a more powerful approach to clipping.

It is possible to enlarge the type *wireframe* to include the projected vertices, *vert2D[ ]*, directly in the data structure, so that they remain part of the object description. The pros and cons of this are addressed in the exercises.

12.6   The Geometry of Perspective Projections

Referring to Figure 12.6, we must find the location, (u^*, v^*), of the projection of point $\mathbf{p} = (p_u, p_v, p_n)$ onto the viewplane. The coordinates of all points and vectors are given in terms of the UVN system. For a perspective projection, recall that the projector through **p** passes through the eye, also called the **center of projection**.

We follow the same line of thinking as in Section 10.3.2 to develop a general expression for the projected point. Vector arithmetic makes it easy. The ray from the eye at $\mathbf{e} = (e_u, e_v, e_n)$ to **p** has the familiar parametric form:

$$\mathbf{r}(t) = \mathbf{e}(1 - t) + \mathbf{p}t \qquad (12.14)$$

It emanates from the eye at $t = 0$ and reaches $\mathbf{p}$ at $t = 1$. It pierces the view-plane at the hit time t' when its n-component is zero or when $e_n(1 - t') + p_n t' = 0$. This yields

$$t' = \frac{e_n}{e_n - p_n} \tag{12.15}$$

(Under what geometric condition is the denominator zero? Exclude this case for now.) Note that in the usual case in which $e_n < 0$ and $p_n > e_n$, this hit time lies between 0 and 1, as we would expect. Using this in Equation 12.14, the u and v components are

$$u* = \frac{e_n p_u - e_u p_n}{e_n - p_n}$$

$$v* = \frac{e_n p_v - e_v p_n}{e_n - p_n} \tag{12.16}$$

This is the desired projection point. All cases of interest are captured in this single form. The calculation can easily be implemented in the procedure *Persp(p : point3D; e : vector3D;* **var** *pt : point)* (see the exercises).

We shall first examine in detail the most important special case—in which the eye lies on the N-axis—to gain insight into the general result.

12.6.1 Eye on the *N*-Axis

In this most common case for perspective projections, both e_u and e_v are zero, thereby simplifying the projected point to

$$u* = \frac{p_u}{1 - p_n/e_n}$$

$$\tag{12.17}$$

$$v* = \frac{p_v}{1 - p_n/e_n}$$

as long as the eye is not on the viewplane, causing $e_n \neq 0$. Make $e_n < 0$ (again the normal case) for this discussion. Also, we have already excluded from consideration the case of $p_n = e_n$, for which the point lies in the plane through the eye and parallel to the viewplane. Note that the form of Equation 12.17 is reminiscent of Equation 10.7, in which the eye lies on the z-axis. The projected point, $(u*, v*)$, is a version of (p_u, p_v) scaled by the foreshortening factor $1/(1 - p_n/e_n)$. When $\mathbf{p}$ is in front of the eye, $(p_n > e_n)$, the foreshortening term decreases as the "depth" $p_n - e_n$ of $\mathbf{p}$ from the eye increases, making objects appear smaller. For points behind the eye this term is negative.

Example

For $\mathbf{e} = (0, 0, -10)$, what does $\mathbf{p} = (3, -4, 6)$ project to?

Solution:

Using the preceding formulas, the hit time is $t' = \frac{5}{8}$, and the projected point is $\frac{5}{8}(3, -4) = (1.875, -2.5)$.

Drill Exercise

12.5. Find the Projection. For $\mathbf{e} = (0, 0, -4)$, find the hit time and the projection for each of the following points: (a) $\mathbf{p} = (-6, 9, 2)$, (b) $\mathbf{p} = (-6, 9, 0)$, (c) $\mathbf{p} = (-6, 9, -2)$, and (d) $\mathbf{p} = (-6, 9, -6)$. Repeat for $\mathbf{e} = (2, 3, -4)$.

Example

A perspective view of the barn is shown in Figure 12.7 that uses the parameters $\mathbf{r} = (.5, .5, .5)$, **norm** $= (-1, 4, -2)$, **up** $= (0, 0, 1)$, and $\mathbf{e} = (0, 0, -5)$. The world coordinate axes have also been drawn. We are looking slightly downward onto the barn from the negative-y half-space: The y-axis is receding from view. Notice too the visual ambiguity: Our eyes sometimes "flip" the image so that the y-axis appears to be pointing toward us. The back side of the barn can be seen in this figure, with its extra edges (the view would be much easier to intepret if the hidden lines were eliminated). The eye is close enough so that there is a mild but noticeable perspective distortion: Lines parallel in three dimensions project to nonparallel lines.

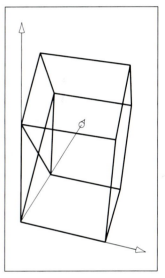

Figure 12.7.
A perspective view of the barn.

12.6.2 Rays Through the Eye, and Pseudodepth

Clearly a perspective projection destroys information: The depth of a point is lost in the process. Every point on a ray that passes through the eye projects to the same point on the viewplane. To see this, consider how points on a ray that passes through the eye project onto the viewplane. Such a ray is given by $\mathbf{p}(t) = \mathbf{e}(1 - t) + \mathbf{a}t$, where $\mathbf{a}$ is any fixed point. (Make $a_n > e_n$ for simplicity, so that $\mathbf{a}$ is in front of the eye.) Choosing different values of t chooses different points on the ray. As t increases, so does the depth of the point being considered.

Simply substitute the components of the ray into Equation 12.17. Notice that (using $e_u = 0$) the term p_u there becomes $a_u t$. Then simplify the expression. Both $u*$ and $v*$ are independent of t, thus proving that all points on the ray project to the same point. This point has coordinates $[a_u/(1 - a_n/e_n), a_v/(1 - a_n/e_n)]$. This is, of course, the point where the ray pierces the viewplane (why?). The following exercise should not be skipped.

Drill Exercise

12.6. Show That These Points Really Do Project to the Same Point. Carry out the manipulations just described to calculate forms for $u*$ and $v*$. Show that the given ray pierces the viewplane at $(u*, v*, 0)$.

Because t disappears, all sense of the depth of the point is lost. In addition, points behind the eye—all those for which $t < 0$—project to the same point as those in front of the eye. Later we shall take some pains to ensure that points behind the eye are properly eliminated in our viewing algorithms.

In later applications (especially hidden surface removal, discussed in Chapter 17), it is useful to compute and carry along an additional quantity that retains a measure of the depth of a point. We call it the **pseudodepth** of the point and denote it by $n*$. We choose it so that as t grows, the pseudodepth does so as well. Therefore, it preserves the **depth ordering** of points that project to the same point. Any quantity that grows as t grows captures this ordering. A particularly harmonious choice that preserves straight lines in three dimensions is modeled on the preceding forms for $u*$ and $v*$. For the given eye position we therefore define the pseudodepth of point $\mathbf{p}$ to be

$$n* = \frac{p_n}{1 - p_n/e_n} \tag{12.18}$$

For $e_n < 0$, as we have supposed, the pseudodepth grows **monotonically** with p_n (i.e., an increase in p_n causes an increase in n^*), as required.

Drill Exercise

12.7.   Plot Pseudodepth. Sketch a plot of $n*$ versus p_n for $e_n < 0$ and observe the monotonic behavior. Repeat for $e_n > 0$. Does this satisfy your geometric intuition?

Because pseudodepth $n*$ is typically computed along with $u*$ and $v*$ for each edge endpoint, we can say loosely that (p_u, p_v, p_n) "projects to"

$$(u*, v*, n*) = \left(\frac{p_u}{1 - p_n/e_n}, \frac{p_v}{1 - p_n/e_n}, \frac{p_n}{1 - p_n/e_n} \right) \tag{12.19}$$

Its computation fits nicely into the process; $n*$ isn't used to locate the projection, as only $u*$ and $v*$ are needed for this. But it provides valuable information to assist hidden line and hidden surface elimination algorithms.

The Perspective Transformation

The value of $(u*, v*, n*)$ in Equation 12.19 is seen to have an interesting and useful form in homogeneous coordinates:

$$\hat{p}* = \left(p_u, p_v, p_n, \frac{e_n - p_n}{e_n} \right) \tag{12.20}$$

because to convert back to ordinary coordinates, we must divide through all terms by the last component. The perspective foreshortening term therefore is set by the fourth component of the projected point! We can write $\hat{p}*$ as an affine transformation on $\mathbf{p}$ (check it by direct calculation):

$$\hat{p}* = (p_u, p_v, p_n, 1)\, \hat{M}_P \tag{12.21}$$

where matrix $\hat{M}_P$ represents a transformation called the **perspective transformation**:

$$\hat{M}_P = \begin{pmatrix} 1 & 0 & 0 & 0 \\ 0 & 1 & 0 & 0 \\ 0 & 0 & 1 & -1/e_n \\ 0 & 0 & 0 & 1 \end{pmatrix} \tag{12.22}$$

This shows a nonzero term, $-1/e_n$, appearing in the last column. The first three terms of the last column of all 4-by-4 matrices encountered up to now have always been zero. Now we finally see what effect a nonzero term has here: It produces prospective foreshortening! This perspective transformation is put to good use later. The pseudodepth term arises by placing one, instead of zero, in the third row and third column. Besides providing pseudodepth, it also makes the perspective transformation nonsingular.

Drill Exercise

12.8. How Is the Eye Itself Affected? Show that applying the perspective transformation to the eye causes it to be moved off to infinity along the N-axis.

Effect of the Eye Located Off the N-Axis

The general case for which the eye is not on the N-axis also has a revealing matrix form. We use the same form for the pseudodepth, $n*$, as before (Equation 12.18). The numerators of both $u*$ and $v*$ in Equation 12.16 are linear combinations of the coordinates of p, suggesting the matrix form

$$\hat{p}* = (p_u, p_v, p_n, 1)\hat{M}_S\hat{M}_P \tag{12.23}$$

where

$$\hat{M}_S = \begin{pmatrix} 1 & 0 & 0 & 0 \\ 0 & 1 & 0 & 0 \\ -e_u/e_n & -e_v/e_n & 1 & 0 \\ 0 & 0 & 0 & 1 \end{pmatrix} \tag{12.24}$$

Again, check this by direct calculation. $\hat{M}_S$ is seen to be a shear, and thus the effect of moving the eye off the N-axis is to shear the image. Suppose that $e_v > 0$ and $e_n < 0$. The effect of this positive e_v is to shift the projected point upward—in the positive v-direction, by an amount proportional to the depth, p_n, of the point. Figure 12.8 shows the effect on the v-coordinate of the projection of p for two placements of the eye. When the eye is shifted up by e_v, the projection shifts up from v_1 to v_2.

Drill Exercise

12.9. Does the Shift Distort the Picture? What is the visual effect of moving the eye? Does the shear caused by moving the eye away from the N-axis distort the projected image in some way?

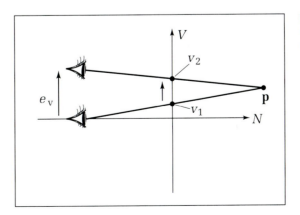

Figure 12.8.
Effect of shifting the eye upward.

Stereo Views

All of the stereo views in this book were generated using the following technique. Two drawings were made, one with the eye at some positive e_u and the other with the eye at $-e_u$, as suggested in Figure 12.9, along with $e_v = 0$ for both eyes. By proper choice of two viewports, the two views are placed side by side in a single picture, with the view seen by the left eye placed on the left, as in Figure 12.10. The preface describes a method for looking at the two pictures simultaneously and fusing them into a single image that reveals the relative depths of the different parts of the object. Some experimentation is usually necessary to pick the best "interocular distance," e_u, and the best spacing of the two images.

Figure 12.10 shows the same view of the barn as in Figure 12.7, but in stereo. To accomplish this, the left eye was set to $(-.4, 0, -5)$ and the right eye to $(.4, 0, -5)$. By fusing the images, the visual ambiguity of Figure 12.7 is eliminated. Figure 12.11 shows a view in which the head has been tilted. Here the viewing system is prescribed by $\mathbf{r} = (.5, .5, .5)$, $\mathbf{norm} = (-5, -3, -2)$, $\mathbf{up} = (0, 1, 1)$, and the left eye is at $(-.4, 0, -10)$. (What are $\mathbf{u}$, $\mathbf{v}$, and $\mathbf{n}$?) Note that the orientation of the barn is difficult to comprehend without the stereo effect. Figure 12.12 shows a close-up of one corner of the barn, with its attendant strong perspective distortion. Here, $\mathbf{ref} = (1, 1, 1)$, (at the corner of the barn) $\mathbf{norm} = (-2, -2, -1)$, and the left eye is at $(-.2, 0, -1)$. The eye offset was reduced to 0.2 here because the eye is so close to the object.

Figure 12.9.
Creating stereo views.

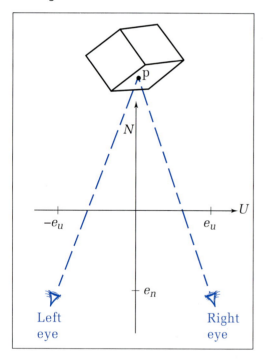

Figure 12.10.
Placing images side by side.

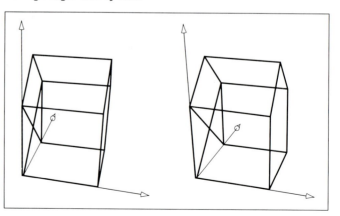

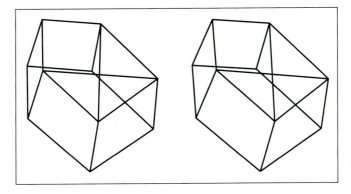

Figure 12.11.
Head tilted.

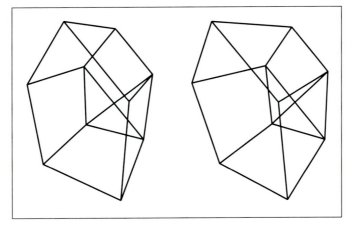

Figure 12.12.
Close-up of corner of barn.

Projections of Parallel Lines

As noted in Chapter 10, a perspective projection of a straight line in three dimensions is still a straight line. However, parallel lines in three dimensions do not always project as parallel lines, which leads to some interesting properties of these projections.

Let $e_u = e_v = 0$ for convenience. Consider the line $\mathbf{p}(t) = \mathbf{q} + \mathbf{dt}$. The "starting point" $\mathbf{q}$ determines the position of the line, and $\mathbf{d}$ determines its direction. From Equation 12.16 we see that it projects to $(u(t), v(t))$, where

$$u(t) = \frac{e_n(q_u + d_u t)}{(e_n - q_n) - d_n t}$$
$$v(t) = \frac{e_n(q_v + d_v t)}{(e_n - q_n) - d_n t}$$

(12.25)

This is a straight line because its slope, given by

$$\text{slope} = \frac{v(t_2) - v(t_1)}{u(t_2) - u(t_1)} = \frac{d_v(e_n - q_n) + d_n q_v}{d_u(e_n - q_n) + d_n q_u}$$

(12.26)

is a constant. (Check this calculation.) Note that if the line is parallel to the viewplane, $(d_n = 0)$, this will reduce to

$$\text{slope} = \frac{d_v}{d_u}$$

(12.27)

which does not depend on the starting point $\mathbf{q}$. Therefore, lines parallel to the viewplane do project as parallel lines. On the other hand, if $d_n \neq 0$, the slope will depend on the starting point, and so receding parallel lines will not project as parallel.

Drill Exercises

12.10.   Lines That Are Still Parallel. Show that the only effect of a perspective projection on a 3D line that is parallel to the viewplane is to scale it.

12.11.   Does Pseudodepth Make Sense? Consider the line $\mathbf{p}(t)$ above. If the line recedes from the viewer as t increases ($d_n > 0$), will the pseudodepth of the point $\mathbf{p}(t)$ also increase? Prove your answer.

Vanishing Points

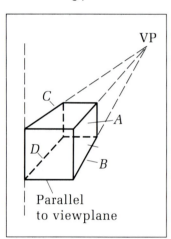

Figure 12.13.
Infinite parallel lines meet at their vanishing point.

Consider the infinite straight line $\mathbf{p}(t) = \mathbf{q} + \mathbf{d}t$ where $d_n > 0$ so that the line recedes from the eye as t increases. What is the behavior of the projected point $(u(t), v(t))$ in Equation 12.25 as $t \to \infty$? The terms containing t dominate in both the numerators and denominators (e.g., the numerator of $u(t)$ becomes just $e_n d_u t$ because $e_n d_u t$ grows so much larger than $e_n q_u$), and the "limiting point" is

$$\left(\frac{e_n d_u}{-d_n}, \frac{e_n d_v}{-d_n} \right) \tag{12.28}$$

This is called the **vanishing point** for this line and for this view. It doesn't depend on the starting point, $\mathbf{q}$, of the line, only its direction, $\mathbf{d}$. Therefore, the projections of all parallel lines (which share the same $\mathbf{d}$) finally terminate at this vanishing point. The classic example is that of parallel railroad tracks receding into the distance and meeting at the horizon (recall Figure 10.12).

Figure 12.13 shows a cube oriented so that edges A, B, C, and D recede from the viewer. If these edges are extended forever in three dimensions, all their projections will meet at the vanishing point. On the other hand, because the vertical edges of the cube are parallel to the viewplane, ($d_n = 0$), according to Equation 12.28 their vanishing points are at infinity. Indeed, if these edges of the cube were extended, their projections would extend forever also.

Drill Exercises

12.12.   Effect of the Eye Position on the Vanishing Point. Because Equation 12.28 is based on Equation 12.25, it gives the position of the vanishing point when the eye is on the N-axis. Show that for a general eye position, the vanishing point is at $(e_u - e_n d_u/d_n, e_v - e_n d_v/d_n)$.

12.13.   Pseudodepth Again. Does the pseudodepth of a point increase without limit as the point moves off to infinity along a line? Find the behavior of $n*$ for this line as $t \to \infty$.

How Realistic Are Perspective Projections?

Perspective projections seem to be a reasonable model for the way we see. But there are some anomalies, owing to the spherical nature of our visual "viewscreen," the retina of the eye. The problem occurs for very long objects. Consider, for example, looking up at a pair of parallel telephone wires, as suggested in Figure 12.14. To create a perspective projection of the scene, the viewplane is placed horizontally before the viewer's eye. Because the wires lie parallel to the

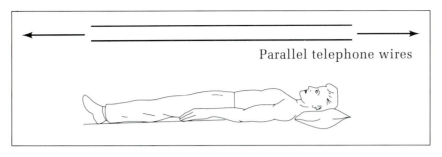

Parallel telephone wires

Figure 12.14.
Viewing very long parallel lines.

viewplane, their perspective images are also parallel. But this is clearly not what is seen. The wires appear "bent," as they converge to vanishing points in both directions! Some artists incorporate this curvature in their drawings by making straight sides of buildings appear curved as they recede from view. The lithograph *Up and Down* by M. C. Escher (Figure 12.15), which has a vanishing point playing a dual role in the center of the drawing, emphasizes this curvature. Escher claimed that he drew such walls curved simply because that was how he saw them (Ernst 1976).

In practice this anomaly is not visible because the window limits the field of view to a reasonable region. (Later we shall use the window and some planes to define a view volume that specifies how the field of view is controlled.)

12.6.3 Parallel Projections

In a parallel projection all projectors from points through the viewplane are parallel. This situation is achieved as a limiting case of the perspective projection in Figure 12.6, by letting the eye move off to infinity in some direction. The eye is at $\mathbf{e} = (e_u, e_v, e_n)$. Let each of these components grow very large while holding their ratios

$$\begin{aligned}\alpha_u &= e_u/e_n \\ \alpha_v &= e_v/e_n\end{aligned} \tag{12.29}$$

constant. More concretely, parameterize the eye position as $(\alpha_u t, \alpha_v t, t)$ and let t grow very large. As t grows, the projectors from different points in the scene become more and more parallel, and in the limit they are exactly parallel, with direction $(\alpha_u, \alpha_v, 1)$ (why?).

The parallel projection of the point $\mathbf{p}$ is still given by Equation 12.23:

$$p* = (p_u, p_v, p_n, 1)\hat{M}_S\hat{M}_P \tag{12.30}$$

in which the shear matrix $\hat{M}_S$ is the same as that in Equation 12.24, because its terms depend only on the ratios α_u and α_v. The big change is in the matrix for the perspective transformation given in Equation 12.22. Because the term $-1/e_n$ is now vanishingly small, $\hat{M}_P$ is the identity matrix! Thus for a parallel projection, $\mathbf{p}$ projects to

$$(u*, v*) = (p_u - \alpha_u p_n, p_v - \alpha_v p_n) \tag{12.31}$$

The perspective foreshortening term has vanished, and only the shear remains. Now parallel lines always project to parallel lines (why?). In this general form it is called an **oblique parallel projection** because the projectors are not perpendicular to the viewplane, as shown in Figure 12.16a. Figure 12.16b shows an oblique projection of a cube whose front face is parallel to the viewplane. In this

Figure 12.15.
Straight walls appearing curved.
(© 1988 M.C. Escher
Heirs/Cordon Art-Baarn-Holland.
Used by permission.)

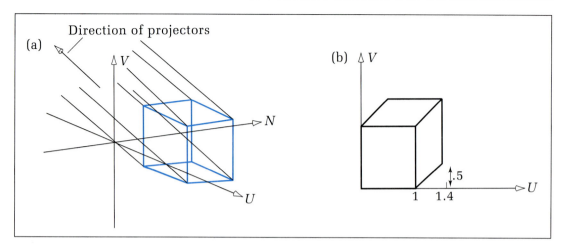

Figure 12.16.
An oblique parallel projection.

example the projectors move up and to the right ($\alpha_u = .4$ and $\alpha_v = .5$ here), and so the top and side of the cube are visible but have been sheared in the projection. For instance, the vertex at (1, 0, 1) in UVN space projects to (1.4, .5). Properties of oblique projections and the motivation for using them will be examined in Section 12.8.

An even simpler form occurs for **orthographic projections**, in which the projectors are perpendicular to the viewplane. This occurs when $\alpha_u = \alpha_v = 0$. Because Equation 12.31 becomes

$$(u* \ v*) = (p_u, \ p_v) \tag{12.32}$$

the projected point is given by the first two components of **p**, and the projection simply discards the *n*-component. We encountered this same effect in Chapter 10 when the projectors were parallel to the *z*-axis.

Example

Figure 12.17 shows the barn from the same point of view as in Figure 12.7, but the eye has been moved far back to **e** = (0, 0, 400). The eye is so remote that we effectively have a parallel projection: Lines that are parallel in three dimensions appear parallel in the drawing.

Figure 12.17.
Barn from way back.

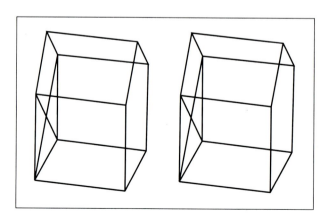

12.7 Taxonomy of Projections

With the mathematics of planar projections now in hand, we shall look at how the various cases fit together and also see how to create some of the classical views used in art, architecture, and engineering drawings.

Planar projections fall naturally into the tree structure shown in Figure 12.18 (Carlbom and Paciorek 1978). Each child of a projection type represents a special case of its parent in the tree. The first fundamental split is between parallel and perspective projections. Even though one is a special case of the other, they have traditionally been treated separately. We shall first examine classes of perspective projections.

12.7.1 One-, Two-, and Three-Point Perspective

Perspective projections divide nicely into the three classes: one-point, two-point, and three-point, depending on the orientation of the viewplane relative to the world coordinate system. The names derive from the situation of viewing the unit cube shown in Figure 12.19. The unit cube is nestled into the positive x-, y-, z-octant with one corner at the origin. Most important, its edges are aligned with the world coordinate axes, which in this discussion are called **principal axes**. Similarly, the three planes $x = 0$, $y = 0$, and $z = 0$ are called the **principal planes**, and the cube has its six faces aligned with them.

One-Point Perspective

Perspective projections are named according to how many finite vanishing points the cube has. Figure 12.20 shows a one-point perspective in which only the receding lines along the x-axis converge to a finite vanishing point. Those along the y- and z-axes do not converge to a vanishing point (or we can say that their vanishing point is "at infinity"). These lines appear horizontal or vertical.

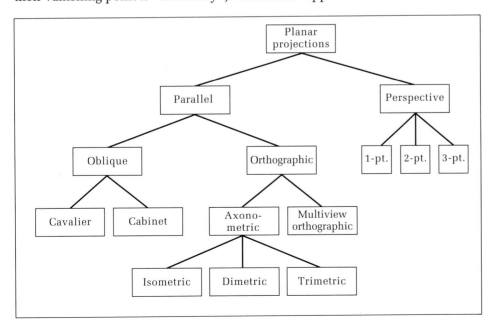

Figure 12.18.
A taxonomy of popular projections.

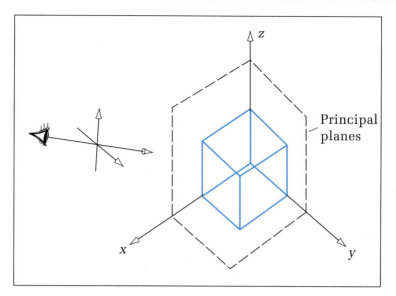

Figure 12.19.
The unit cube and principal axes.

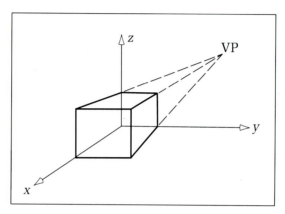

Figure 12.20.
A one-point perspective.

This view is achieved by making the viewplane parallel to the plane $x = 0$. In general, to create a one-point perspective, make the viewplane parallel to one of the principal planes. Thus make $\mathbf{n} = \pm\mathbf{i}, \pm\mathbf{j},$ or $\pm\mathbf{k}$, so that two of the components, (n_x, n_y, n_z), are zero. As we shall show more formally later, only the direction $\mathbf{n}$ matters: Changing the eye position or the direction of the $\mathbf{u}$ and $\mathbf{v}$ axes (the head tilt) affects the position of the vanishing point, but the view is still one-point perspective. (Where is the vanishing point if the eye is kept on the N-axis?)

Drill Exercises

12.14.   Setting the VPN for a One-Point Perspective. An application might set the viewplane normal *norm* using simply *norm.dx* := .., *norm.dy* := .., and so forth. Give appropriate assignments for **norm** that produce four different one-point perspective views. Then suppose instead that *BuildVPN( )* is available (see Equation 12.2). Give the corresponding spherical angles to cause the same four views.

12.15.   Position of the Vanishing Point. Draw by hand the unit cube and the world coordinate axes in one-point perspective with $\mathbf{n} = (0, -1, 0)$ and $\mathbf{e} = (2, 3, -4)$.

Figure 12.21 shows several blocks in one-point perspective. (Arrows point to edges that are parallel to the viewplane.) The blocks have been shifted and rotated, but because of their orientation, all are seen in one-point perspective (why?).

Two-Point Perspective

For a two-point (or "angular") perspective the unit cube has two finite vanishing points, as in Figure 12.22. Here the viewplane has been reoriented so that it is parallel to only a principal axis (rather than a plane). For the principal axis, $\mathbf{k}$ is usually chosen so that the "vertical" remains unchanged. In the figure both $\mathbf{i}$ and $\mathbf{j}$ pierce the viewplane. In general, for a two-point perspective the condition for $\mathbf{n}$ is that it must be perpendicular to exactly one of $\mathbf{i}$, $\mathbf{j}$, or $\mathbf{k}$. Thus two components of $\mathbf{n} = (n_x, n_y, n_z)$ are nonzero, and one must be zero.

Drill Exercise

12.16. Creating Two-Point Perspective Views. Give three examples of calls to *BuildVPN( )* (see Exercise 12.14) that produce two-point perspective views.

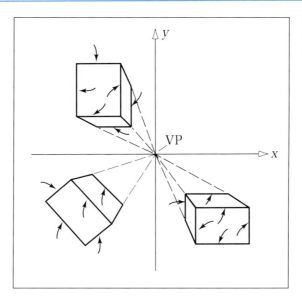

Figure 12.21.
Several blocks in one-point perspective.

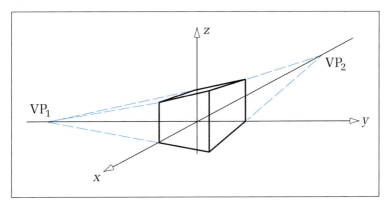

Figure 12.22.
Two-point perspective.

Three-Point Perspective

Figure 12.23 shows the cube in three-point perspective. The viewplane is parallel to none of the principal axes: Equivalently all three axes pierce it. All three components of **n** are nonzero. Artists often use vanishing points in perspective drawings, in order to highlight features or to increase dramatic effect. The beguiling lithograph by M. C. Escher in Figure 12.24 shows the sense of scope afforded by a three-point perspective. (Where are the three vanishing points in this drawing?)

Figure 12.23.
Three-point perspective.

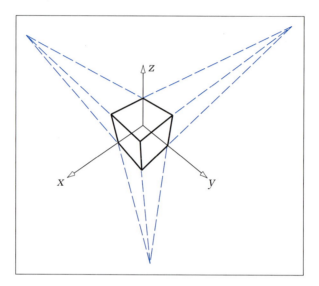

Figure 12.24.
M. C. Escher's *Ascending and Descending*: a three-point perspective. (© 1988 M. C. Escher Heirs/Cordon Art-Baarn-Holland. Used by permission.)

Drill Exercise

12.17. Piercing the Viewplane. We know that for a k-point perspective, in which $k = 1, 2,$ or 3, the unit cube has exactly k finite vanishing points. Show that for such a projection, exactly k of the principal axes pierce (are not par-allel to) the viewplane. Thus the number of piercing principal axes is an equivalent way to characterize perspective projections.

Identifying k-Point Perspective in Homogeneous Coordinates

We will gain additional insight if we examine the homogeneous form of a point's transformation during the projection process. Because we are specifically interested in how the orientation of the viewplane affects the projection, we go back to world coordinates and ask where the projection of the world coordinate point, $\mathbf{q} = (q_x, q_y, q_z)$, lies. In homogeneous coordinates, $\mathbf{q}$ is denoted by $\hat{q}$ and is converted into point $\hat{q}\hat{A}_{WV}$ in (homogeneous) viewing coordinates, according to Equation 12.12. Then, according to Equation 12.23, it projects to the point

$$\hat{p}* = (q_x, q_y, q_z, 1)\hat{A}_{WV}\hat{M}_S\hat{M}_P \qquad (12.33)$$

in which the shear $\hat{M}_S$ and the perspective transformation $\hat{M}_P$ are given by Equation 12.24 and Equation 12.22, respectively. We then assemble the product of the three matrices into a single matrix to reveal the total effect of the transformations that map the world coordinate point $\mathbf{q}$ onto the viewplane:

$$\hat{M} = \hat{A}_{WV}\hat{M}_S\hat{M}_P \qquad (12.34)$$

Shifting the eye away from the N-axis has only an unimportant effect (see the exercises), and so we fix it on the N-axis for simplicity. This eliminates the shear so that $\hat{M}_S$ becomes the identity matrix. We then get

$$\hat{M} = \hat{A}_{WV}\hat{M}_P = \begin{pmatrix} u_x & v_x & n_x & -n_x/e_n \\ u_y & v_y & n_y & -n_y/e_n \\ u_z & v_z & n_z & -n_z/e_n \\ r'_x & r'_y & r'_z & 1 - r'_z/e_n \end{pmatrix} \qquad (12.35)$$

Combining the viewing and perspective transformations places terms depending on $\mathbf{n}$ in the last column of the matrix. When $\mathbf{q}$ is transformed and then converted back into ordinary coordinates, the term that multiplies all three components is

$$\frac{1}{(1 - r'_z/e_n) - (q_x n_x/e_n) - (q_y n_y/e_n) - (q_z n_z/e_n)} \qquad (12.36)$$

If the term $q_x n_x/e_n$ is present, it indicates that there is perspective foreshortening "in the x-direction": Points "more remote in x" are drawn smaller. There will be similar foreshortening in y and z if the terms $q_y n_y/e_n$ or $q_z n_z/e_n$ are present. For each term that is present, a corresponding finite vanishing point exists. If k terms are nonzero, the view will be k-point perspective. A k-point perspective is achieved by making nonzero k of the components of $\mathbf{n}$.

Drill Exercise

12.18.   Move the Eye off the *N*-Axis. Recalculate Equation 12.34 for the general case in which the eye does not lie on the *N*-axis. Show that the shear does not affect the last column of $\hat{M}$.

12.8 | More on Parallel Projections

We shall continue exploring the taxonomy of projections with parallel projections. They split into two types:

1. *Orthographic*: The eye is on the *N*-axis.

2. *Oblique*: The eye is not on the *N*-axis.

12.8.1 Orthographic Projections

For orthographic projections, all the projectors are perpendicular to the viewplane, and from Equation 12.32 the projection simply deletes the third component of the point.

The classification of orthographic projections again depends on the orientation of the viewplane with respect to the world coordinate system, or equivalently to the unit cube nestled within it. **Multiview orthographic projections** are traditionally presented as the top, front, and side views of an object, as we saw in Figure 10.4. The viewplane normal is set in turn to $-\mathbf{k}$, $-\mathbf{i}$, and $-\mathbf{j}$, and the object of interest is drawn. Figure 12.25 shows an example. These views are useful for engineering drawings, as one can measure dimensions of an object directly.

Figure 12.25.
A multiview orthographic drawing.

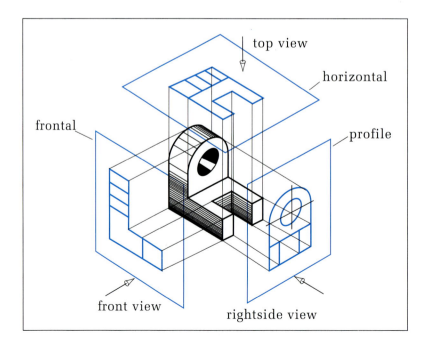

12.8.2 Axonometric Views

Because orthographic projections do not reveal the 3D nature of an object particularly well, axonometric views are also widely used. In an **axonometric view**, the viewplane normal is usually not parallel to any principal axis; rather, it is oriented so that three adjacent faces of the (cubelike) object are visible. The choice of which faces to make visible depends on which faces of the object are important and need to be emphasized. In addition, one of the principal axes is usually chosen to be vertical. Parallel lines in the object are viewed as parallel, but those that recede are equally foreshortened by some factor. Figure 12.26 shows a principal axis (the Y-axis) directed at angle α with respect to the viewplane normal **n**. A line of unit length in this direction is seen to be viewed as having a length of $\sin(\alpha)$, and so the **foreshortening factor** is $\sin(\alpha)$.

Drill Exercises

12.19.   Foreshortening Ratios in Vector Terms. The components of **n** are by definition given by dot products, as in $n_x = \mathbf{n} \cdot \mathbf{i}$. Each therefore measures the cosine of the angle between **n** and its corresponding world coordinate axis. (It is a "direction cosine" of **n**.) Express each of the three foreshortening ratios in terms of a dot product.

12.20.   Finding n. Determine the components of **n** that produce foreshortening ratios for the X-, Y-, and Z-axes of .6, .4, and .7, respectively. How many possible **n** directions are there?

12.21.   n in Spherical Coordinates. Find the three foreshortening ratios for the **n** having colatitude 30° and azimuth 125° (see Appendix 5).

Axonometric projections fall into three classes, depending on how many principal axes are foreshortened by equal amounts:

1. *Isometric*: All three are equally foreshortened.

2. *Dimetric*: Two are foreshortened equally.

3. *Trimetric*: No two are foreshortened equally.

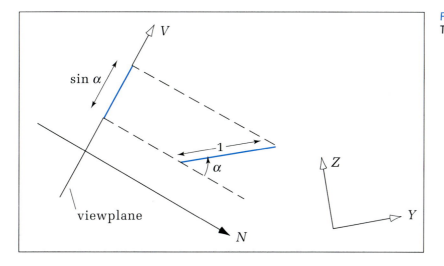

Figure 12.26.
The foreshortening factor.

Isometric Views

An **isometric** view of a cube is shown in Figure 12.27, looking in a direction along one of the cube's eight diagonals. All three axes are foreshortened by the same amount (*iso* means "same," *metric* means "measure"); therefore the three direction cosines of **n** must have the same size. The condition for an isometric view thus is $n_x = \pm n_y = \pm n_z$. In an isometric view the angles between the projections of the principal axes are equal. The lengths of sides of an object that are parallel to a principal axis can be measured directly from a drawing, and all can be scaled the same amount (how much?) to obtain the proper dimensions.

Example

What are the possible colatitudes and azimuths for **n** in an isometric view?

Solution:
According to Equation 12.2, the components of **n** are

$$(\sin(\phi)\cos(\theta),\ \sin(\phi)\sin(\theta),\ \cos(\phi))$$

which must be equal in size. Assume at first that they all are positive. Equating the first two yields $\cos(\theta) = \sin(\theta)$, and so $\theta = 45°$. This rotation of "halfway" between the axes is intuitively satisfying. There are three other values of θ that also achieve $\cos(\theta) = \pm\sin(\theta)$. Now equating the second and third components gives $.707\sin(\phi) = \cos(\phi)$ or $\tan(\phi) = \sqrt{2}$. Thus $\phi = 54.7356°$. Why isn't this 45° also? (Remember that the *X*- and *Y*-axes are already foreshortened by the 45° rotation.) What other value of ϕ makes the second and third components of **n** have the same size?

Dimetric Views

When only two of the axes make the same angle with the *N*-axis, the view is called **dimetric**—two measures are involved. For a dimetric view two of the direction cosines must have the same size, so that $n_x = \pm n_y$, $n_x = \pm n_z$, or $n_y = \pm n_z$. A sequence of dimetric views is shown in Figure 12.28; the third one is almost isometric. For each view, $n_x = n_y$, and both are negative. (What is n_z approximately in the first figure? In the last one?) Alternatively, these views use an **n** having azimuth 225° and varying colatitudes. For each view the angles indicated are equal. The different orientations place differing amounts of emphasis on the faces.

Figure 12.27.
An isometric view of a cube.

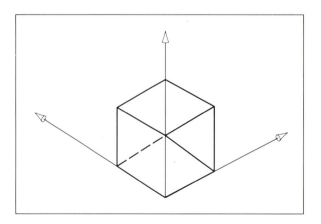

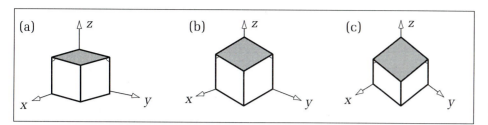

Figure 12.28.
Several dimetric views of a cube.

Drill Exercise

12.22. Sketch a Cube. Sketch a sequence of dimetric views of the cube for which $n_y = -n_z$ and n_x increases from 0 to 1.

Trimetric Views

Finally, if the three axes make different angles with the N-axis, the view is called **trimetric**. Figure 12.29 provides an example, in which there is almost complete freedom of choice for the components of **n**. When the proper orientation is chosen, a trimetric view can look the most natural.

12.8.3 Oblique Projections

We have seen that orthographic projections preserve the exact shape of one face of an object but do not reveal its 3D nature very well. On the other hand, axonometric projections show the 3D quality but do not yield the exact shape for any of the faces. Oblique projections—recall Figure 12.16—are an attempt to combine the useful properties of both orthographic and axonometric projections. They usually present the exact shape of one face of an object (the most important face) and simultaneously show the object's general 3D appearance.

Recall that oblique projections result when the eye is removed from the N-axis to $(\alpha_u t, \alpha_v t, t)$ for very large t. Equation 12.31 specifies the projected point: The image is sheared in the projection. The shear is used to make visible additional sides of a cubelike object. Figure 12.30 shows several views of the cube created by different values of α_u and α_v. The first and last examples are popular and have been given names. The first is a **cavalier** projection, because it uses $\alpha_u = \alpha_v = 1$, and so the shear makes the side and top project with the same length as the front. The last is a **cabinet** projection and uses $\alpha_u = \alpha_v = .5$, so that

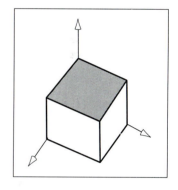

Figure 12.29.
A trimetric view.

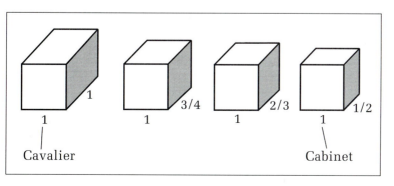

Figure 12.30.
Several oblique projections of a cube.

the side and top appear to have one-half the length of the front. Some people feel that the cavalier version looks too elongated and the cabinet a little too squat, but their numerical simplicity makes them useful nonetheless.

12.9   Clipping Lines to the View Volume

Clipping has been only flirted with in our discussion. It is often ignored with no ill effect when 3D viewing is first tackled. In simple cases the entire object lies in front of the camera and its projection fits nicely within the window so that clipping would have no effect anyway. So far we have performed clipping (if at all) in only two dimensions after the edges were projected.

For the general viewing case, however, we want more control over the parts of the object that are drawn. Imagine the camera "positioned" in the middle of a large model, perhaps a data set representing downtown Chicago. There are buildings in front, to the sides, and behind the camera. Only a small fraction of all the edges of the buildings fall within the field of view of the camera: The rest should be clipped. Because points "behind the eye" project onto the viewplane in the same way as do points in front (see Section 12.6), they must be eliminated too.

12.9.1 The View Volume

We must define precisely the region in space that is to be projected and drawn. This is called the **view volume**. It is shown for a perspective view in Figure 12.31. It is part of the synthetic camera and so is defined in viewing coordinates. The eye and the window together define a double-sided rectangular pyramid that extends forever in both directions. The eye is at $\mathbf{e}$, and the window is the portion of the viewplane specified by the usual rectangular extent (W_l, W_t, W_r, W_b). In general, the eye can lie away from the N-axis, as can the center of the window.

To limit the view volume to a finite size, we can define a **front plane** at $n = F$ and a **back plane** at $n = B$ (sometimes called the "hither" and "yon" planes). These both are parallel to the viewplane and chop off the pyramid into a **frustum** that becomes the view volume. The clipping algorithm to be developed clips off any parts of the object that lie outside this frustum. The effect of clipping against the front plane at $n = F$ is to chop off those parts for which $n < F$: parts that lie behind the eye or in front of it but too close to it. F is chosen to place the front plane in front of the eye, and so the user chooses $F > e_n$. Similarly, the back plane $n = B$ eliminates any parts for which $n > B$, and so the user chooses B to place the back plane beyond the front plane: $B > F$.

In some situations the user adjusts the front and back planes so that F is only slightly less than B. Then only a thin "slice" of the object is seen. This produces "cutaway" drawings of complex objects, such as an internal slice through a jet engine or a building. In other circumstances the user does not specify a front and back plane, in order to see objects through the window no matter where they lie, as long as they are in front of the eye. We shall see later that proper clipping can still take place in the absence of a front plane to remove points behind the eye.

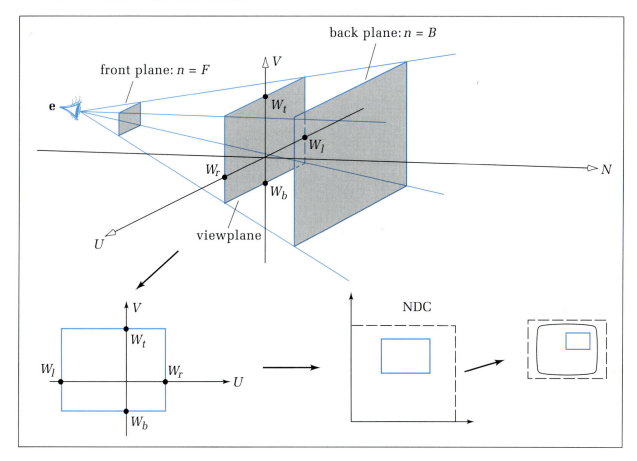

Figure 12.31.
The view volume.

Each edge, E, of each object is clipped against the six walls of the frustum. The endpoints of the part of E that lie within the view volume are found and projected onto the viewplane, as described. Their projections are then mapped to the viewport in NDC and finally to the appropriate device coordinates, as suggested in Figure 12.31.

For a parallel projection the pyramid becomes a **parallelepiped**: As the eye recedes to infinity along the direction $\mathbf{e}$, the sides of the pyramid become more and more parallel.

Drill Exercises

12.23.   Degrees of Freedom for the View Volume. How many different parameters are required to define completely the view volume? What are they?

12.24.   Sketch the View Volume. Sketch the view volume for a perspective projection when $\mathbf{e} = (0, 0, -5)$, the window is given by $(W_l, W_t, W_r, W_b) = (-3, 2, 3, -2)$, $B = 4$, and $F = 3$. What is its actual volume? Draw the projection of the line $(1, 1, 1)(1 - t) + (-1, -2, -3)t$, properly clipped to the view volume.

12.25.   Equations for the View Volume Walls. The front and back planes of the view volume are clearly given by $n = F$ and $n = B$, respectively. It is of some interest also to characterize the four side walls. The top wall, for instance, passes through point $\mathbf{e}$ as well as the points $(W_l, W_t, 0)$ and $(W_r, W_t, 0)$. Find the equation of its plane. As a check, the second component of its normal should be 0 (why?). Repeat for the other three walls.

12.26.   View Volume for a Parallel Projection. Sketch the view volume for the case $(W_l, W_t, W_r, W_b) = (-3, 2, 3, -2)$, $B = 4$, and $F = 3$, when the eye moves off to infinity as $\mathbf{e}(t) = (t, 0, -2t)$.

12.9.2 Summary: What Have We Accomplished So Far?

Before moving to the clipping process, let us summarize where we are. Consider how the world coordinate point $\mathbf{q} = (q_x, q_y, q_z)$ is "seen"—what point does it project to, and what is its pseudodepth? Here $\mathbf{q}$ has the homogeneous coordinate representations $\hat{q} = (q_x, q_y, q_z, 1)$. According to Equation 12.34, the viewing system converts this to point $\hat{p} = (p_u, p_v, p_n, 1) = \hat{q}\hat{A}_{WV}$. (Check that the fourth component of $\hat{p}$ is always 1.) The projection process causes $\hat{p}$ to be seen at the point with homogeneous coordinates $\hat{g} = (g_u, g_v, g_n, g_w)$ given by

$$\hat{g} = (g_u, g_v, g_n, g_w) = \hat{q}\hat{A}_{WV}\hat{M}_S\hat{M}_P \tag{12.37}$$

where $\hat{M}_S$ and $\hat{M}_P$ are given by Equation 12.24 and Equation 12.22, respectively. (One can show—see the exercises—that g_w always has the simple form $g_w = 1 - p_n/e_n$, and so it is positive if, and only if, the point is in front of the eye. This fact proves useful when clipping is considered. When $\hat{g}$ is converted back to ordinary coordinates, by dividing through each term by g_w, the result is

$$(u*, v*, n*) = (g_u/g_w, g_v/g_w, g_n/g_w) \tag{12.38}$$

yielding the projected point $(u*, v*)$ and the pseudodepth $n*$.

This tells us that to compute the required values, $(u*, v*, n*)$, each endpoint must undergo, in one way or another, processing equivalent to multiplication by these three matrices. (Additional matrices might also appear in the computation, as we shall see later.) Because the three matrices must ultimately be accounted for, it is clearly most efficient to apply them all at once: Each endpoint of each edge in the object is multiplied by the single matrix

$$\hat{A}_{WV}\hat{M}_S\hat{M}_P \tag{12.39}$$

It costs only a single matrix multiplication to include the perspective transformation. Then the thousands of object vertices undergo one matrix multiplication. After this we need only recover ordinary coordinates from homogeneous coordinates to get both the projected point $(u*, v*)$ and the pseudodepth $n*$. (Clipping must also be done somewhere in this process.)

The effect of applying the "extra" transformations, $\hat{M}_S\hat{M}_P$, is called **prewarping**. This prewarping moves each vertex of the object in three dimensions so that its u and v coordinates are actually in their final position to be drawn. This is indicated in cross section in Figure 12.32. The eye sees a wireframe "block" lying within the view volume. The front of the block is lying on the viewplane, and so its projection is just itself. The rear of the block appears smaller because it is more remote from the eye. The vanishing point for all horizontal lines in the block is the origin. Points such as P_1 and P_2 along a ray through the eye project to the same point.

When all points are prewarped, the result is as shown in Figure 12.32b. The eye has moved off to $n = -\infty$ and so will "see" a parallel projection. The front of the block is unaffected, but all other points have been brought closer to the origin (the vanishing point). This prewarped block now appears the same in a parallel projection as the original appears in a perspective projection.

Once objects have been prewarped, we need only perform an **orthographic projection** of the prewarped points—which amounts to setting the n-component to zero—in order to obtain the final projected points. (Recall that before being set to zero the n-component is stored separately as the pseudodepth.) Thus we have effectively decomposed a perspective projection into (1) a per-

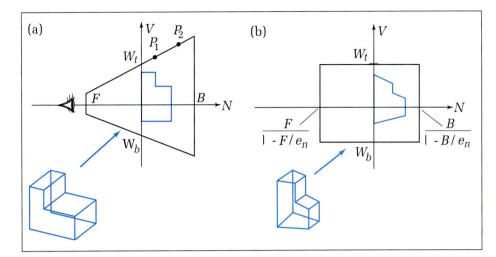

Figure 12.32.
Effect of prewarping.

spective transformation, (2) a division (to recover ordinary coordinates), and (3) an orthographic projection.

Figure 12.32 also indicates what happens to the view volume when it is prewarped: It is transformed into a parallelepiped, a much simpler shape! As shown in the exercises,

1. Prewarping preserves planes.

2. Planes parallel to the viewplane are just shifted. The front and back planes are prewarped to the planes $n = F/(1 - F/e_n)$ and $n = B/(1 - B/e_n)$, respectively.

3. The four side walls of the view volume are warped into the four parallel planes, $u = W_l$, $u = W_r$, $v = W_t$, and $v = W_b$.

Drill Exercises

12.27. Showing How the View Volume Becomes Warped. We know from Chapter 10 that a perspective projection preserves every straight line (except some degenerate cases). First, use this to prove that the perspective transformation also preserves planes. Second, show that the plane $n = A$, where A is a constant, is only shifted by the transformation, and find the new plane. Third, use the fact that a ray through the eye is converted to a ray parallel to the N-axis to show that the side walls of the view volume are transformed into parallel planes, and find their positions.

12.28. What Becomes of Points Behind the Eye? If the perspective transformation moves the eye off to $-\infty$, what will happen to points of the object that lie behind the eye? Consider a line, $\hat{p}(t)$, that begins at a point in front of the eye at $t = 0$ and moves to one behind the eye at $t = 1$. Find its parametric form in homogeneous coordinates after undergoing the perspective transformation, and interpret it geometrically. We shall examine this behavior further when discussing clipping. A valuable discussion of this phenomenon is given in Blinn 1978.

12.9.3 The Normalization Transformation

Because it costs so little to include transformations—just one matrix multiplication while setting up the viewing process—we shall look around to see whether any additional simplifications might be made. The prewarped view volume is now a parallelepiped with the six planes, $u = W_l$, $u = W_r$, $v = W_t$, $v = W_b$, $n = F/(1 - F/e_n)$, and $n = B/(1 - B/e_n)$, for its walls. After clipping and projection the edges that lie in the window must finally be mapped to the desired viewport, given in NDC by (V_l, V_t, V_r, V_b), and then drawn using *LineNDC( )*. Why not combine the window-to-viewport mapping with this matrix multiplication rather than perform a separate transformation later? It will also be handy for depth calculations to normalize the n-components so that they always lie between 0 to 1. We shall thus apply one more matrix and normalize the prewarped view volume into its final configuration, called the **canonical view volume**, as shown in Figure 12.33.[1]

To accomplish the normalization, we need a scaling and translation in each of the three dimensions. The window-to-viewport mapping for u and v is familiar (see Equation 3.1), and the mapping for n is also straightforward. Putting these together yields the normalization transformation matrix given by

$$\hat{N} = \begin{pmatrix} S_u & 0 & 0 & 0 \\ 0 & S_v & 0 & 0 \\ 0 & 0 & S_n & 0 \\ r_u & r_v & r_n & 1 \end{pmatrix} \tag{12.40}$$

where $S_u = (V_l - V_r)/(W_l - W_r)$, $S_v = (V_t - V_b)/(W_t - W_b)$, $S_n = [(e_n - B)(e_n - F)]/e_n{}^2(B - F)$, $r_u = (V_r W_l - V_l W_r)/(W_l - W_r)$, $r_v = (V_b W_t - V_t W_b)/(W_t - W_b)$, and $r_n = F(e_n - B)/e_n(F - B)$. This matrix is easily created in an application and can be multiplied by the others to form the overall matrix:

$$\hat{M}_{\text{tot}} = \hat{A}_{WV} \hat{M}_S \hat{M}_P \hat{N} \tag{12.41}$$

Therefore, as a preparation for clipping, we use the single matrix $\hat{M}_{\text{tot}}$ to transform all object vertices $\hat{q}$ from world coordinates to prewarped and normalized viewing coordinates. Call these new vertices $\hat{g}$:

$$\hat{g} = \hat{q}\hat{M}_{\text{tot}} \tag{12.42}$$

When convenient, we can also express $\hat{g}$ in terms of the points expressed in viewing coordinates $\hat{p}$ as $\hat{g} = \hat{p}\hat{M}_S\hat{M}_P\hat{N}$.

Figure 12.33.
The normalized view volume.

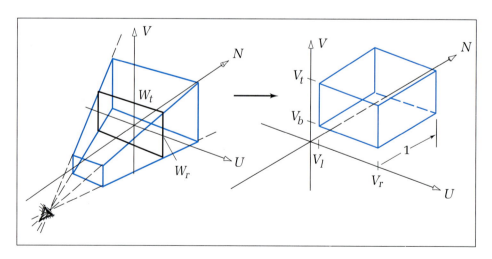

---

[1]Sometimes a unit cube is used for the canonical view volume (Foley and Van Dam 1983). The unit cube extends from 0 to 1 in u and v as well as in n. This is a special case of our canonical view volume: Just set the viewport to all of NDC.

Drill Exercises

12.29. Mapping the Eight Corners. Show that $\hat{N}$ does in fact map each of the eight corners of the prewarped view volume to the corresponding promised corner of the canonical view volume. Does this prove that the transformation of Equation 12.40 performs the required scaling and positioning of the prewarped view volume?

12.30. The Homogeneous Component and Points Behind the Eye. Show by direct calculation that the fourth "homogeneous" component, g_w, in Equation 12.37 is always given by

$$g_w = 1 - \frac{p_n}{e_n} \qquad (12.43)$$

where p_n is the position of the point along the N-axis in viewing coordinates. Argue why this shows that g_w is positive if, and only if, point p lies in front of the eye.

12.31. What If a Parallel Projection Is Desired? How does $\hat{M}_{\text{tot}}$ simplify when a parallel projection is desired? Show the forms of the matrices for the case of a cavalier projection when viewing an object along the negative X-axis.

12.32 Including Modeling Transformations Too. As discussed in Chapter 11, a "generic" object such as a cube is often first scaled, rotated, and positioned to place it properly in the scene. This is done using some matrix, $\hat{M}_{\text{mod}}$, as discussed in Chapter 11. Show how to include this modeling transformation into matrix $\hat{M}_{\text{tot}}$ so that a single matrix can be used for the entire transformation sequence.

12.9.4 The Clipping Process

All object edges must be clipped against the view volume at some point in the process. Because object vertices $\hat{g}$ have been prewarped and normalized, we must clip edges against the canonical view volume. This is most conveniently performed in homogeneous coordinates. Once the clipping is done, we convert each endpoint of each surviving edge back to ordinary coordinates (by performing the perspective division) and use the first two components as the viewed endpoint. The third component is the pseudodepth. If an edge is clipped out entirely, there will be no need to perform any perspective division. This can save time when many object edges lie entirely outside the view volume.

Consider point $\hat{g} = (g_u, g_v, g_n, g_w)$, corresponding to 3D point $(g_u/g_w, g_v/g_w, g_n/g_w)$. It will lie in the canonical view volume if it lies simultaneously on the proper side of each of the six planes of the view volume: "to the right of the left wall," "to the left of the right wall," "above the bottom wall," and so forth. This provides six conditions, which may be written as six inequalities:

$$V_l \leq \frac{g_u}{g_w} \leq V_r$$

$$V_b \leq \frac{g_v}{g_w} \leq V_t \qquad (12.44)$$

$$0 \leq \frac{g_n}{g_w} \leq 1$$

The third inequality is true only when the point is farther from the eye than the front wall and closer than the back wall.

Consider testing whether the individual point $\hat{g}$ is visible. According to Exercise 12.30, if $g_w \leq 0$, the point is behind the eye and therefore is invisible. On the other hand, if $g_w > 0$, these inequalities are equivalent to

$$V_l g_w \leq g_u \leq V_r g_w$$
$$V_b g_w \leq g_v \leq V_t g_w \qquad (12.45)$$
$$0 \leq g_n \leq g_w$$

These tests can easily be implemented in code—see the exercises.

Clipping an Edge

These tests work for a single point, but we want to test an entire edge to find the new endpoints of the clipped line. We follow a version of the Cyrus–Beck algorithm (Cyrus and Beck 1978) reported by Liang and Barsky (1984) (recall Chapter 7 and Appendix 6) and view the (prewarped and normalized) edge E parametrically as $\mathbf{g}(t)$:

$$\hat{g}(t) = (g_u(t),\, g_v(t),\, g_n(t),\, g_w(t)) = (h_u,\, h_v,\, h_n,\, h_w) + (d_u,\, d_v,\, d_n,\, d_w)t \quad (12.46)$$

It begins at endpoint $\hat{g}(0) = (h_u, h_v, h_n, h_w)$ at $t = 0$ and reaches endpoint $\hat{g}(1) = (h_u + d_u, h_v + d_v, h_n + d_n, h_w + d_w)$ at $t = 1$. It is inside the view volume for all t that satisfy the six inequalities of Equation 12.44.

Each of the six inequalities is tested in turn to see at what value of t the edge "enters into" or "exits from" the view volume. We keep track of two variables, t_{in} and t_{out}, initialized to 0 and 1, respectively. The interval $(t_{\text{in}}, t_{\text{out}})$ reports the interval in t over which E might be inside the view volume; that is, it is definitely outside for $t < t_{\text{in}}$ and for $t > t_{\text{out}}$. When an inequality shows that E enters "later" than does the current t_{in}, the value of t_{in} is increased to "chop" off the interval. Similarly, t_{out} can be decreased by some of the inequalities. If any chop eliminates the entire interval (an "early out"), the edge has been eliminated and the next edge is tested. If there is anything left of the interval after all six chops have been performed, the edge is known to enter the view volume at t_{in} and exit at t_{out}. The actual endpoints are found using these values in Equation 12.46.

Each of the six inequalities in Equation 12.44 has a denominator of $g_w(t)$. To obtain a simpler form for the constraints, we wish to multiply each one through by $g_w(t)$, as in Equation 12.45. But if $g_w(t)$ is negative, we should reverse the direction of each inequality. Now $g_w(t)$ will be negative if the point is behind the eye (recall Exercises 12.30). Because arbitrary camera positions are allowed, some edges of the objects may well lie behind the eye, and so negative values of $g_w(t)$ must be coped with.

Can we work with the inequalities in Equation 12.45 anyway? Yes, because at the very least the constraint $g_n(t) > 0$ chops out any troublesome range of t for which the denominator $g_w(t)$ is negative. For instance, suppose that the edge begins somewhere in front of the eye at $t = 0$ and moves in some path that takes it past the eye at $t = t_{\text{eye}}$. It must first pass through the front plane, where $g_n(t)$ becomes negative, so that the constraint $g_n(t) > 0$ will produce a t_{out} smaller than t_{eye}. Thus the troublesome range of t-values in which $g_w(t)$ is negative is chopped out. A similar argument will apply to t_{in} if the edge begins behind the eye or if both endpoints are behind the eye. Thus we can use the forms of Equation 12.45.

Place the terms of Equation 12.46 into these constraints and collect all terms that multiply t to obtain

$$
\begin{aligned}
(V_l d_w - d_u)t &\leq h_u - V_l h_w \\
(d_u - V_r d_w)t &\leq V_r h_w - h_u \\
(V_b d_w - d_v)t &\leq h_v - V_b h_w \\
(d_v - V_t d_w)t &\leq V_t h_w - h_v \\
-d_n t &\leq h_n \\
(d_n - d_w)t &\leq h_w - h_n
\end{aligned}
\qquad (12.47)
$$

Each of these inequalities has the form

$$denom\ t \leq numer \qquad (12.48)$$

The values of *numer* and *denom* are read from Equation 12.47. For instance, the first inequality in Equation 12.47 tests where the edge hits the left wall, with *numer* and *denom* set to $h_u - V_l h_w$ and $V_l dw - d_u$, respectively.

The function *Chop(numer, denom : real) : boolean* of Code Fragment 6.1 in Appendix 6 may be used directly to implement these tests. *Chop(,)* finds the *t* value at which the edge encounters the relevant wall, adjusts t_{in} or t_{out} as appropriate, and returns *true* if the entire edge has been chopped out.

The following pseudocode indicates how the clipper might be implemented. It operates on the edge with endpoints *G1* and *G2*, using an obvious type definition for a point in homogeneous coordinates. If any piece of the edge survives the clipping, the new endpoints will be stored in *G1* and *G2*, and *vis* will be set to *true*.

> *Code Fragment 12.3. Skeleton of the Edge Clipper in Homogeneous Coordinates*

```
type
    point4D = record x, y, z, w : real end;
var
    V : rect; {global viewport}
procedure Clip4(var G1, G2 : point4D; var vis : boolean);
{clip edge from G1 to G2 against canonical view volume}
{if edge survives, vis := true and new endpoints are in G1, G2}
var
    t_in, t_out : real;
    < define function Chop(numer, denom : real) : boolean; >
begin {Clip4}
    vis := false;
    < initialize t_in, t_out, etc. >
    if not Chop(,) then {to right of left wall}
        if not Chop(,) then {to left of right wall}
            if not Chop(,) then {above bottom wall}
                if not Chop(,) then {below top wall}
                    if not Chop(,) then {beyond front wall}
                        if not Chop(,) then {closer than back wall}
    begin {edge survived}
        vis := true;
        if t_out < 1 then {update G2 if it changed}
        begin
            G2.x := . . .; etc.
        end;
        if t_in > 0 then {update G1 if it changed}
        begin
            G1.x := . . .; etc.
        end
    end {survived}
end; {Clip4}
```

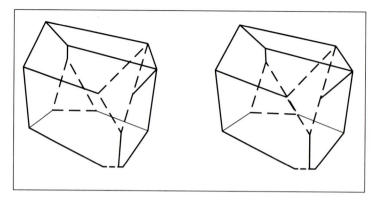

Figure 12.34.
Front and back clipping of the barn.

Figure 12.34 shows this algorithm applied to the barn for a particular view. Three instances of clipping may be seen: The front plane has chopped off the corner of the barn nearest the eye; the back plane has removed a region near the origin of world coordinates; and a corner of the barn has been clipped by the bottom of the window. Dashed lines have been added to emphasize the clipped portions.

Clipping When No Front or Back Planes Are Specified

Sometimes the user wants to draw all points that lie in the window in front of the eye, so that no front or back plane is specified. Then the view volume is a parallelepiped that extends to infinity in both directions along n. What changes must be made? The normalization transformation still maps the window into the viewport, but no mapping of the n-component is performed, and in matrix $\hat{n}$ of Equation 12.40 we simply set $S_n = 1$ and $r_n = 0$ to preserve pseudodepth. Further, because the view volume has only four walls, Equation 12.45 reduces to the following four inequalities:

$$V_l g_w \le g_u \le V_r g_w$$
$$V_b g_w \le g_v \le V_t g_w \tag{12.49}$$

Are there any problems with the sign of $g_w(t)$ changing because of a part of the edge passing behind the eye? We first test which endpoints of the edge are in front of the eye: Use Equation 12.46 and test the signs of $g_w(0)$ and $g_w(1)$. If both are negative, the edge will be wholly behind the eye and will be discarded. If one or both are positive, the same reasoning will show that some t_{in} or t_{out} will chop off the t-interval in which $g_w(t) < 0$, and so all is well.

12.10   Summary

In this chapter we developed tools for defining a synthetic camera in world coordinates that takes "snapshots" of the wireframe model. The camera consists of a viewplane and an eye, and the application defines it in a logical way through a handful of parameters that describe its position and orientation. The result is a second coordinate system, the viewing coordinate system, "suspended" in world coordinates. A window is described in the viewplane, and a view volume is defined by the eye position in viewing coordinates and the window, as well as the front and back planes. All edges are clipped to the six planes of this view volume. Surviving edges are projected onto the viewplane, then transformed to NDC, and finally drawn on the device.

A valuable unification was created, in which all of the necessary transformations are performed in homogeneous coordinates using a single matrix multiplication. This matrix combines (1) the transformation from world coordinates to viewing coordinates, (2) the perspective transformation that prewarps edges so that they may be viewed using a parallel projection, and (3) a normalization of the view volume to a parallelepiped in three-dimensional NDC. Clipping is done in homogeneous coordinates as well. The composite transformation allows edges to be projected trivially and also provides a pseudodepth for each endpoint that will prove very useful when removing hidden lines and surfaces (see Chapter 17).

The tools we examined in this chapter are used in Chapter 15 with only minor changes when drawing models based on many "faces." There each face is a polygon suspended in three dimensions, which is mapped, clipped, and projected onto the viewplane much as edges are here. Once projected, the face can be filled with a suitable color, yielding more realistic views of models than can be achieved using wireframes.

Drill Exercise

12.33. Derivation of the Overall Normalization Matrix. Derive matrix $\hat{N}$ that normalizes the view volume.

Programming Exercises

12.34. Using Angles to Specify Direction. Write **procedure** *BuildVPN(theta, phi : real;* **var** *n : vector3D)* discussed in Section 12.3.1 to compute the view plane normal vector given its colatitude *phi* and azimuth *theta*.

12.35. Building *Set_View( ).* Write the procedure *Set_View( )* that we discussed that computes the vectors **u**, **v**, and **n**, given **e** and **r**.

12.36. Tilting the Head. Generalize the procedure *Set_View( )* to compute **u**, **v**, and **n** for the case in which the camera can be tilted through an angle α. Note that this requires a rotation about the **n** axis (see Chapter 11).

12.37. *WorldtoView( )* in Homogeneous Form. Write a version of the procedure *WorldtoView( )* that does the same thing as does Code Fragment 12.2 but takes as the argument the 4-by-4 matrix $\hat{A}_{WV}$ and uses matrix multiplication.

12.38. The Procedure *ViewtoWorld( ).* Write the procedure

ViewtoWorld(ViewPt, R, u, v, n : vector3D; **var** *Worldpt : vector3D)*

which converts the point *ViewPt* expressed in viewing coordinates into the point *WorldPt* expressed in world coordinates.

12.39. Enlarging the *wireframe* Type. Redefine type *wireframe* to include a second array, *vert2D[ ]*, of vertices. Then *vert2D[ ]* is built by transforming and projecting each of the object's vertices once the viewing system has been specified. Adjust the Code Fragment in Section 12.5 to handle this situation, and discuss the pros and cons of including this extra array as part of the model.

12.40. Implementing *Persp( ).* Write the code for procedure *Persp(p : point3D; e : vector3D;* **var** *pt : point)* which performs a general perspective projection, as in Equation 12.16.

12.41. Drawing Wireframes. Write a program that draws wireframe objects using a synthetic camera model. The program accepts the view reference point, viewplane normal, up direction, and eye distance, along with window boundaries. From these the **u**, **v**, and **n** vectors are computed. Then the vertex and edge lists of the object are read from a file; each vertex is transformed to the viewing coordinate system and projected; and each edge is drawn. Exercise this program by producing several views of the barn from different points in space and different viewing directions.

12.42. Locate the Eye. Given any **r**, **up**, **norm**, and **e**, where in world coordinates is the eye?

12.43.   Drawing _k_-Point Perspectives. Write and exercise a program that draws wireframe objects in one-, two-, and three-point perspective. For each drawing, rotate the object using the techniques of Chapter 11 to orient the objects appropriately.

12.44.   Drawing Parallel Projections. Write and exercise a program that draws wireframe objects in both oblique and nonoblique parallel projections. The user specifies the degree of obliqueness by inputting the foreshortening ratio. The user also inputs the angles θ and ϕ to determine how much to rotate the object in order to obtain each view desired.

12.45.   Determining the Visibility of a Point in Homogeneous Coordinates. Write a routine, _IsVisible_(_g_ : _point4D_, _V_ : _rect_) : _boolean_, that uses Equation 12.45 to determine whether homogeneous coordinate point _g_ lies within the canonical view volume, in which case it will return _true_.

12.46.   Building a Clipper for Three-Dimensional Lines. Write a routine that clips an edge in homogeneous coordinates using the preceding method, and test it on sample edges.

CHAPTER 13

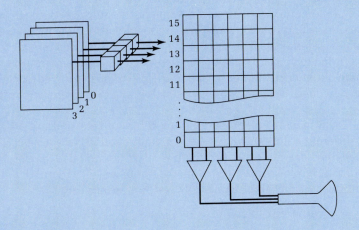

Raster Graphics Techniques

Goals of the Chapter

- To develop tools for the scan conversion of lines and circles
- To build tools for filling regions
- To examine aliasing and methods for reducing it
- To see how off-screen memory can be used for windowing
- To study the various BitBlt operations and their uses

13.1   Introduction

In this chapter we shall examine an assortment of important techniques for generating pictures on a raster graphics device. Chapter 2 introduced the fundamentals of raster displays. Recall that there is a close correspondence between memory elements in a frame buffer and pixels on the display, as summarized in Figure 13.1. The frame buffer consists of R rows of C columns each of memory elements. The data in the frame buffer are repeatedly scanned and converted to spots of light in the display by the refresh circuitry. Each row of the frame buffer corresponds to one scan line in the displayed image, and scan lines are refreshed from left to right starting at the top and moving down line by line.

Each memory element contains B bits of information, which can generate 2^B different colors or intensities for each pixel. Pixel values are translated into intensities or indices according to a color lookup table, as described in Chapter 2. In the simplest case there is one bit per pixel ($B = 1$) and the display is **bilevel**. We speak of the pixel being "off" or "on" according to

- (value = 0) $\Rightarrow$ (pixel is off) black
- (value = 1) $\Rightarrow$ (pixel is on) white

For simplicity we associate here an off pixel with a dark color (black) and an on pixel with a light color (white). This is consistent with many popular bilevel video displays. Keep in mind, however, that the correspondence can be just the opposite on some devices, such as laser printers. On these an on pixel causes a black dot to be printed, and an off pixel leaves white paper unchanged.

Because of the close correspondence between frame buffer elements and pixels, we often suppress the distinction and talk about the "pixel at (c, r)". By this we mean both the contents of the memory in column c and row r of the frame buffer, and the light intensity/color of the resulting spot on the screen. Further, we often speak of the pixel at (x, y). This capitalizes on the familiar orientation of an x, y-coordinate system and associates a pixel's column with a horizontal coordinate and its row with a vertical coordinate. As row numbers normally increase from 0 at the top scan line to some maximum row number at the bottom, the y-axis is sometimes portrayed as pointing downward. Whenever the direction of the y-axis matters in a discussion, we shall reestablish the

Figure 13.1.
The frame buffer and corresponding pixels.

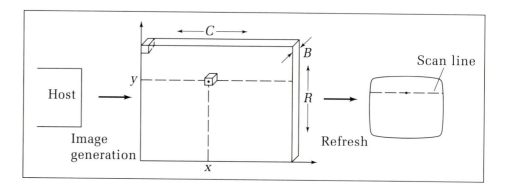

intended correspondence. As in Chapter 2, we shall assume that two routines, *SetPixel*( ) and *GetPixel*( ), are available, with which the host can "drive" the frame buffer. Suitable declarations for these routines are given in the following code fragment for the example of a frame buffer with 480 scan lines, each of 640 pixels, in which each pixel value is represented by 8 bits and hence can take on 256 different values:

Code Fragment 13.1. Declarations for Frame Buffer Routines

```
const
   MaxColumn = 639; {MaxColumn is C − 1}
   MaxRow    = 479; {MaxRow    is R − 1}
   MaxColor  = 255; {MaxColor  is number of colors − 1}
type
   col   = 0..MaxColumn;
   row   = 0..MaxRow;
   color = 0..MaxColor;
procedure SetPixel(c : col; r : row; value : color); {load frame buffer}
function GetPixel(c : col; r : row) : color; {read frame buffer}
```

These routines make the necessary translations between actual memory locations and array positions (c, r). They contain (and therefore "hide") all of the device dependencies, and so our subsequent algorithms can be device independent.

   To increase speed, one may also want to implement a variation of *SetPixel*( ) and *GetPixel*( ). Frame buffers are usually organized so that a single computer word (8, 16, or perhaps 32 bits) can be set or read with one instruction. Particularly in the case of "one bit per pixel" devices, this group of bits often corresponds to a portion of a row of pixels, that is, a part of one scan line. For instance, each full row of 512 pixels might be stored in memory as 16 words of 32 pixels each, laid side by side. Thus for some frame buffers, groups of pixels along a scan line (i.e., adjacent horizontally) can often be set and obtained simultaneously rather than individually, with a dramatic increase in speed. We may decide that it is worth adding routines such as *SetPixelWord*(*col1* : *col*; r : *row*; *value* : *word*) and *GetPixelWord*(*col1* : *col*; r : *row*) : *word*, in which type *word* corresponds to the word size of the machine. Exploiting the particular architecture of the display's frame buffer in this way of course sacrifices some device independence.

13.2   Introduction to Scan Conversion

The principal task of a raster graphic system is **scan conversion**, converting an implicit description of a geometric object such as a line or circle into an explicit pattern of pixel values. For example, the implicit description "straight line from (4, 7) to (16, 10)" must be translated into an explicit set of pixels that are "on" in the frame buffer. An example is shown in Figure 13.2.

   Because of the fundamental nature of straight lines in graphics, we shall first discuss how to scan convert lines, and then we shall discuss the generation of other important geometric objects, such as circles.

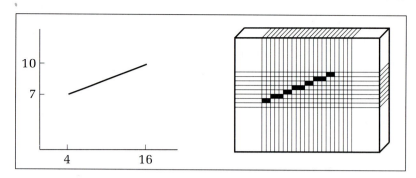

Figure 13.2.
Scan conversion of a line
segment.

13.2.1 Line-Drawing Algorithms

A scan conversion algorithm for a line takes as "data" the two endpoints of the line, say (x_a, y_a) and (x_b, y_b). Its job is to turn on a proper set of pixels in between these endpoints so that a good approximation to the ideal line can be seen.

What properties should we require of a line-drawing algorithm? The lines should be as straight as possible and should reliably pass through both of the given endpoints. The lines should be "smooth" and have uniform brightness along their length. Lines of different slopes should have the same brightness. The process should also be repeatable: If at a later time we apply the algorithm to the same endpoint data, it should produce exactly the same pixels. This is important for erasing the line, which is accomplished by redrawing it in the background color. It also shouldn't matter in which direction the line is drawn. If drawn from (x_b, y_b) to (x_a, y_a), exactly the same pixels should be turned on. This relieves the application from having to remember which direction a line was previously drawn in when erasing a line.

Chapter 2 introduced the simple routine *DD_Line( )*. This method uses real-number arithmetic to find for each horizontal pixel position x between x_a and x_b the ideal y-value and then rounds this off to the nearest pixel position. Because of the use of real arithmetic as well as the *Round( )* operation, it suffers from being quite slow. Also, for steep lines with a large slope, the on pixels tend to be spread quite far apart vertically, which can make steep lines appear less bright than the more horizontal lines do.

We shall present next a much more efficient method that has become the standard line generator in raster graphics. We find that it satisfies most of the desired properties of a line-drawing algorithm.

13.2.2 Bresenham's Line Algorithm

Bresenham's line algorithm uses only integer values and avoids any multiplications (Bresenham 1965). It has a tight and efficient innermost loop that generates the proper pixels. It also is an important example of an **incremental** algorithm that computes the location of each pixel on the line based on information about the previous pixel. Finally, it is representative of a number of curve generation methods.

Suppose that we are given the integer-valued endpoints (x_a, y_a) and (x_b, y_b) (corresponding to column and row positions in the frame buffer). We want to determine the best sequence of intervening pixels. The ideal line segment satisfies

$$y = m(x - x_a) + y_a \tag{13.1}$$

The slope of the line m can be any real number and is given by

$$m = \frac{\Delta y}{\Delta x} \tag{13.2}$$

where

$$\begin{aligned} \Delta y &= y_b - y_a \\ \Delta x &= x_b - x_a \end{aligned} \tag{13.3}$$

To simplify our discussion, we shall examine the special case in which $x_a < x_b$ and the slope lies between 0 and 1. In this case, as x increases from x_a to x_b, the corresponding y increases from y_a to y_b, but y increases less rapidly than does x because $\Delta x > \Delta y$. As x steps across in unit increments from x_a to x_b, the best integer y value will sometimes stay the same and sometimes increment by one. Bresenham's algorithm quickly determines which of these should occur. (Note that y need never either decrement or increment by more than 1. Why?)

Figure 13.3 represents a portion of the frame buffer. Each intersection in the grid represents the center of a pixel. Suppose we somehow know that at x_{i-1} the best y-value is y_{i-1}. We wish to know whether the line at x_i is closer to the point $T_i = (x_i, y_{i-1})$ or to $S_i = (x_i, y_{i-1} + 1)$. At x_i the ideal line has y-value $y* = m(x_i - x_a) + y_a$. One possible position of the ideal line is shown in the figure, but it could also pass slightly below T_i or slightly above S_i. (Why?) Bresenham used the following measures of the error between the candidate points and the ideal line at x_i:

$$\begin{aligned} e(T_i) &= y* - y_{i-1} \\ e(S_i) &= (y_{i-1} + 1) - y* \end{aligned} \tag{13.4}$$

indicated in the figure. For the ideal line shown, both of these errors are positive, and $e(T_i) < e(S_i)$ if the line passes closer to T_i than to S_i. If the line passes below T_i, the error $e(T_i)$ becomes negative, and if it passes above S_i, the error $e(S_i)$ becomes negative (see the exercises). In all of these cases the difference, $e(T_i) - e(S_i)$, can be used to determine which candidate is closer, using the following rule:

Choose T_i if, and only if, $e(T_i) - e(S_i) < 0$.

Thus we don't increment y if this error term is negative and do increment y if the error is positive. The rest is algebra. Use $y*$ in Equation 13.4 to obtain

$$e(T_i) - e(S_i) = 2m(x_i - x_a) + 2(y_a - y_{i-1}) - 1 \tag{13.5}$$

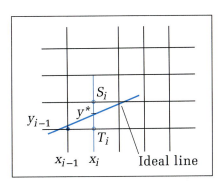

Figure 13.3.
The configuration for deriving Bresenham's algorithm.

The only noninteger number here is m, which is equal to the ratio of two positive integers, Δy and Δx. Multiply Equation 13.5 by Δx (which won't change the sign of the error, as $\Delta x > 0$) to form the final error measure e_i:

$$e_i = \Delta x(e(T_i) - e(S_i)) = 2(\Delta y)(x_i - x_a) + 2(\Delta x)(y_a - y_{i-1}) - \Delta x \quad (13.6)$$

Thus the decision rule is

$$\text{If } e_i < 0, \text{ then choose } y_i = y_{i-1}; \text{ otherwise choose } y_i = y_{i-1} + 1 \quad (13.7)$$

Drill Exercise

13.1. The Signs of $e(T_i)$ and $e(S_i)$. Show that the error measures $e(T_i)$ and $e(S_i)$ have the signs as claimed in all possible cases of an ideal line that (a) has a slope between 0 and 1 and (b) passes closer to $y = y_{i-1}$ at x_{i-1} than to either its neighbor above or its neighbor below.

To see how to iterate with this test, write Equation 13.6 in terms of e_{i+1}: Just replace i by $i + 1$ everywhere to obtain

$$e_{i+1} = 2(\Delta y)(x_{i+1} - x_a) + 2(\Delta x)(y_a - y_i) - \Delta x \quad (13.8)$$

Write e_{i+1} in terms of e_i to get the amount by which the error term must be updated at each step:

$$e_{i+1} = e_i + 2(\Delta y)(x_{i+1} - x_i) - 2(\Delta x)(y_i - y_{i-1}) \quad (13.9)$$

Recognize that $x_{i+1} - x_i = 1$ to simplify this even further. So at each step on the way from x_a to x_b we test the sign of e_i, choose y_i accordingly, and then compute the next error term, e_{i+1}. If y is not incremented, then $y_i = y_{i-1}$, and so $e_{i+1} = e_i + 2(\Delta y)$. Otherwise, $e_{i+1} = e_i + 2(\Delta y - \Delta x)$.

The only question remaining is how to start the process at $i = 0$. Now $x_0 = x_a$ and $y_0 = y_a$; thus, according to Equation 13.6, with $i = 1$ we get $e_1 = 2(\Delta y) - \Delta x$. Putting all this together, we get Bresenham's algorithm (for this special case):

Code Fragment 13.2. Bresenham's Algorithm—Special Case

```
procedure Bresenham(xa, xb : col; ya, yb : row; col_val : color);
{draw line in color = col_val from (xa, ya) to (xb, yb)}
{special case: xa < xb and 0 < (slope of line) < 1}
var
    x : col;
    y : row;
    dx, dy,
    e_inc,      {change in error when y increments}
    e_noinc,    {change in error when no increment in y}
    e : integer; {current error term}
begin
    y := ya;
    dx := xb - xa;
    dy := yb - ya;
    e_noinc := dy + dy; {initialize error terms}
    e := e_noinc - dx;
    e_inc := e - dx;
    for x := xa to xb do {the main loop}
```

```
begin
    SetPixel(x, y, col_val);
    if e < 0 then e := e + e_noinc
    else begin
        y := y + 1;
        e := e + e_inc
    end; {else}
    end; {for}
end; {Bresenham}
```

This algorithm is extremely simple, with an inner loop that has only a few comparisons and a few additions. It is easily implemented in assembly language to achieve the greatest speed. Special-purpose graphic controller integrated circuits are also available that implement Bresenham's algorithm in hardware for even higher performance.

Example

It is instructive to watch the values e_i vary in a specific example. Let $(x_a, y_a) =$ (4, 1) and $(x_b, y_b) = (16, 4)$. Then $\Delta x = 12$ and $\Delta y = 3$. Because this line has a slope of $m = 1/4$, we expect the y-value to increment only every fourth step or so in x. Each time x is incremented, we either add 6 to e_i if e_i is negative, or otherwise we subtract 18 from e_i and increment y.

The resulting sequence of values is

i :	0	1	2	3	4	5	6	7	8	9	10	11	12
x :	4	5	6	7	8	9	10	11	12	13	14	15	16
y :	1	1	2	2	2	2	3	3	3	3	4	4	4
e :	−6	0	−18	−12	−6	0	−18	−12	−6	0	−18	−12	−6

The behavior of the algorithm for this example is shown in Figure 13.4, which illustrates both the resulting line and the variation in e_i. The "jaggies" are clearly visible for the line, where each short horizontal line segment breaks to the next higher one.

The preceding algorithm copes only with the special case $x_a < x_b$ and $0 < m < 1$. The remaining cases are easily handled as well:

- $x_a > x_b$: Test for this condition at the start of the algorithm, and interchange x_a and x_b (and y_a, y_b also) so that x is always incremented from the lower to the higher value.

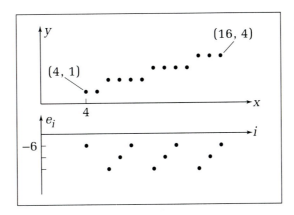

Figure 13.4.
An example of Bresenham's algorithm in action.

- $m > 1$: Simply interchange the roles of x and y, step in y from y_a to y_b, and use the same test to determine when to increment (the less rapidly changing) x.

- *Negative slopes*: If $0 > m > -1$, replace dy with $-dy$. Step in x using exactly the same e_i and tests, but decrement the dependent variable rather than increment it. If $m < -1$, replace dx with $-dx$, and interchange the roles of x and y, as in the case $m > 1$.

- *Horizontal and vertical lines*: These occur so frequently in graphics that it may increase performance to test for them and to use a simplified algorithm when they occur. The improvement for a vertical line would be marginal; most of the time is spent in *SetPixel*( ), anyway. For a horizontal line you might use a form of *SetPixelWord*( ), as discussed in Section 13.12, to write many bits along a scan line at a time, thereby significantly increasing the drawing speed.

See the exercises for implementing these generalizations.

Because the algorithm reinitializes itself for each new line and depends on only the endpoint data, it is completely repeatable: Redrawing a line in a different color completely replaces the first line, and using the background color totally erases the line. The line that is drawn is also independent of the direction chosen, (x_a, y_a) to (x_b, y_b), or vice versa, as it swaps endpoints if necessary to draw from the smaller x to the larger. It also draws steep lines as well as nearly horizontal lines, as it interchanges x and y if required to make the effective slope of a line less than 1. Lines at 45° are still the smoothest, however, because their pixel patterns are so regular.

Drill Exercise

13.2. Numerical Example. For endpoints (8, 23) and (21, 11) show the sequences of x, y, and e_i that evolve as Bresenham's algorithm is applied. Demonstrate that the same pixels are illuminated when the algorithm is started from the opposite endpoint.

Drawing in Patterns

You may on occasion want to draw lines that are dotted or dashed using some pattern. Patterns can be stored as sequences of bits, such as

long dash: 0011111100111111

short dash: 0011001100110011

     solid: 1111111111111111

   dotted: 0101010101010101

A pattern such as 00111111 indicates a dash that is off for two pixels and on for 6. It is simple to incorporate such patterns in Bresenham's algorithm. In Code Fragment 13.2, for instance, each time x is incremented, a pointer into the pattern can be incremented as well, and the corresponding bit value can be used as *value* in *SetPixel*(x, y, *value*). For long lines the pattern is used repeatedly by incrementing cyclically from the end of the pattern back to its beginning.

When a dashed polyline is drawn, you may want the pattern to be continuous from segment to segment. To do this, the pattern and the pointer into it are made globally available to Bresenham's algorithm so that it can be accessed during successive calls to the algorithm. See the exercises for other issues concerning drawing in patterns.

13.2.3 Scan Converting Circles and Ellipses

Circles and ellipses are also frequently needed in applications, and we need a fast way to generate their corresponding pixel patterns from implicit information such as (*center* : *point*, *radius* : *real*). We shall examine here another efficient incremental algorithm that generates circles. See the exercises for an ellipse algorithm.

Circle Generation

Consider drawing a circle centered at $(0, 0)$ with radius R, where R is an integer. We want the set of pixels that is turned on to provide the best approximation to the ideal circle and to be uniformly disturbed along its circumference so that all parts of the circle have uniform brightness. A circle is governed by a quadratic relationship, $(y^2 = R^2 - x^2)$, between x and y, and we expect that the algorithm will be more complicated than that for a straight line. But we can reduce the amount of computation required by capitalizing on the symmetry of a circle, as shown in Figure 13.5. We need only compute the (x, y) values in one octant of the circle, say from A to B in the figure. Given (x, y), there are seven other points along the circle whose coordinates can be easily found. Simply negating and/or interchanging x and y produces the seven locations, $(-x, y)$, $(-x, -y)$, $(x, -y)$, (y, x), $(-y, x)$, $(-y, -x)$, and $(y, -x)$, with the positions shown in the figure.

Bresenham's Circle Generation Algorithm

Consider the best pixels, $P = (x, y)$, to illuminate in the octant from A to B. P should lie at distance R from the origin, so a reasonable measure of the error exhibited by P is the difference between the square of its true distance and R^2:

$$e(P) = (x^2 + y^2) - R^2 \qquad (13.10)$$

Error $e(P)$ will be positive if P is too far from the origin, and negative otherwise.

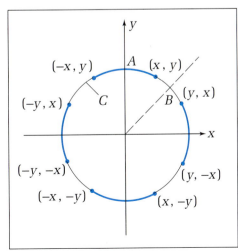

Figure 13.5.
Using eightfold symmetry in the circle.

We follow the same line of reasoning as for Bresenham's line algorithm. Suppose we have determined that the best point at step i-1 is $P_{i-1} = (x_{i-1}, y_{i-1})$. See Figure 13.6. Now increment x_{i-1} by 1 and ask which of the points, $S_i = (x_{i-1} + 1, y_{i-1})$ or $T_i = (x_{i-1} + 1, y_{i-1} - 1)$, is closer to the circle. (These are the only two candidates because the true circle has a slope between 0 and -1 in the octant under consideration.) We can form the errors $e(S_i)$ and $e(T_i)$ for these candidates, but we want to find a way to combine them into a single error quantity, say d_i, whose sign can be used to make the best choice, as in *Choose S_i if $d_i < 0$ else choose T_i.*

The three cases that can occur are suggested in Figure 13.7: The (true) circle C lies above (or on) S_i, between S_i, and T_i, or below (or on) T_i. Consider the second case. If C lies between the two points, the two errors will have opposite signs: $e(S_i) > 0$, whereas $e(T_i) < 0$. Therefore, it appears that we can use the sign of their sum as the error quantity: $d_i = e(S_i) + e(T_i)$. If C is nearer T_i the size $|e(T_i)|$ will be dominated by $e(S_i)$, and the sum d_i will be positive. On the other hand, if S_i is closer to C, $|e(T_i)|$ will be larger than $e(S_i)$, and the sum will be negative. So the test: "Choose S_i if $d_i < 0$; otherwise choose T_i," works for this case. For the case in Figure 13.7a in which we should choose S_i, both errors are negative, and so their sum d_i is negative, and the same test works. For the case of Figure 13.7c in which T_i must be chosen, d_i is positive because both errors are positive: Again it works. Therefore, the decision variable d_i does the job.

All that remains is to fashion an efficient way to update d_i and to start the algorithm on the right foot. Straightforward manipulations (see the exercises) show that d_{i+1} can be written in terms of d_i, as

$$d_{i+1} = d_i + 4x_{i-1} + 6 + 2(y_i^2 - y_{i-1}^2) - 2(y_i - y_{i-1}) \qquad (13.11)$$

So if $d_{i+1} < 0$ then y does not change and the update is

$$d_{i+1} = d_i + 4x_{i-1} + 6$$

Otherwise $y_i = y_{i-1} - 1$ and the update is

$$d_{i+1} = d_i + 4(x_{i-1} - y_{i-1}) + 10$$

The amount that d_i is updated is linear in x here. It appears to be a form of derivative or "first difference" of the error, which is quadratic for the circle. We saw something similar with the straight line, for which the error was linear, thus having a constant first difference.

Figure 13.6.
Derivation of the circle
algorithm.

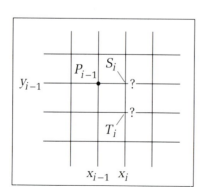

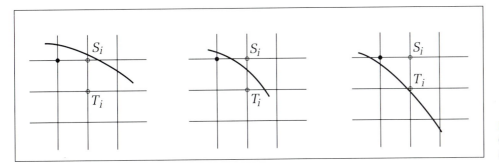

Figure 13.7.
Cases of a circle passing by the next point.

To start the algorithm, notice that $x_0 = 0$ and $y_0 = R$, so that $S_1 = (1, R)$ and $T_1 = (1, R - 1)$, yielding

$$d_1 = 3 - 2R \qquad (13.12)$$

These arguments are easily fashioned into the following algorithm, which is usually called Michener's algorithm because Michener based its details on Bresenham's work. The algorithm draws a circle of radius *Rad* placed at center point (xc, yc). The circle is shifted to this center simply by offsetting the x and y values in calls to *SetPixel( )*.

Code Fragment 13.3. Michener's Circle Algorithm

```
procedure MichCirc(xc : col; yc : row; Rad : integer; value : color);
{draw circle centered at (xc, yc) with radius Rad in color = value}
var
  x : col;
  y : row;
  d : integer;
begin
  x := 0; y := Rad;
  d := 3 − 2 * Rad;
  while x <= y do
  begin
    SetPixel(xc + x, yc + y, value); {draw 8 points}
    SetPixel(xc − x, yc + y, value); {based on (x, y)}
    SetPixel(xc + x, yc − y, value);
    SetPixel(xc − x, yc − y, value);
    SetPixel(xc + y, yc + x, value);
    SetPixel(xc − y, yc + x, value);
    SetPixel(xc + y, yc − x, value);
    SetPixel(xc − y, yc − x, value);
    if d < 0 then d := d + 4 * x + 6 {update error term}
    else begin
      d := d + 4 * (x − y) + 10;
      y := y − 1
    end; {else}
    x := x + 1
  end {while}
end; {MichCirc}
```

Drill Exercises

13.3. Michener Derivation. Show that error term d_{i+1} has the form given in Equation 13.11, for each of the three cases illustrated in Figure 13.7.

13.4. Hand Simulation of Michener's Algorithm. Hand simulate *MichCirc*(40, 30, 20, 1). For each x-coordinate encountered in the algorithm, compute the error term d and plot it versus x.

13.5. Michener's Algorithm for Ellipses. Extend the Michener algorithm to draw the following ellipse:

$$\left(\frac{x - x_c}{A}\right)^2 + \left(\frac{y - y_c}{B}\right)^2 = 1 \qquad (13.13)$$

where A and B are integers. Work out the algorithm so that it deals only with integer quantities.

13.3 │ Methods for Filling Regions

As discussed in Chapter 2, one of the most valuable characteristics of a raster graphics device is that it can display regions filled with a solid color. In this section we shall examine a variety of ways for doing this efficiently.

13.3.1 Defining Regions

Regions can be defined in several different ways, using a variety of data structures, (Ballard and Brown 1982). These different representations are important to areas such as pattern recognition and computer vision that require algorithms that can obtain information about an image by examining the contours or interiors of regions. For our purposes, there are two kinds of regions that we wish to fill, pixel-defined and polygonal regions.

Pixel-Defined Regions

When a set of checkers is placed on a checkerboard, or white and black stones are put down on a *go* board, a collection of **pixel-defined** regions is created. (It is useful to have such a visual aid handy when studying region-fill algorithms.) Regions are defined according to the colors of the pixels, and these colors reveal where each region's interior, exterior, and boundary are. To tell where a region begins and ends, we must agree on the definition of two pixels being "adjacent" or "connected."

There are two basic types of connectedness:

- *4-connected.* Two pixels are considered connected if they are adjacent horizontally or vertically. Thus the pixel at (23, 35) is 4-connected to the one at (23, 36) but not to that at (24, 36).

- *8-connected.* Two pixels are considered connected if they are adjacent horizontally, vertically, or diagonally. Thus pixels at (23, 35) and (24, 36) are 8-connected.

We also distinguish ways to define regions as either interior defined or boundary defined.

- *Interior defined.* All of the pixels inside the region have a given color, *inside-color*, and no boundary pixels have this color. An interior-defined region can have "holes" in it, consisting of pixels of any colors other than *inside-color*.

- *Boundary defined.* The region is defined by a set of pixels of color *boundary-color*, and no interior pixels have this color. Pixels of color *boundary-color* can appear inside the region, thereby forming holes.

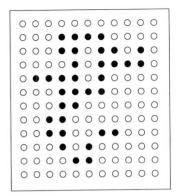

Figure 13.8 shows an example. What is meant by the interior of the region depends on both the type of connectedness and the definition type. If the figure is interpreted as an 8-connected, interior-defined region, its interior contains 35 pixels and its interior has a 3-pixel hole. If, instead, connected means 4-connectedness, there is not one region but three (what are they?). If we say that this is a boundary-defined region (either 4- or 8-connected), its interior is the 3-pixel area surrounded by boundary pixels near the top. Notice here that in some places the boundary is more than one pixel "thick." Such thick boundaries are fine for many algorithms but can confuse certain others, as we shall see later.

Figure 13.8.
Defining regions with pixel colors.

Often we need to manipulate a region that is defined only within the frame buffer itself; there is no higher-level description available. Therefore, any algorithm that is to operate on the region must be able to access the pixel values in the frame buffer, using *GetPixel( )*.

Polygonal Regions

Polygonal regions are described symbolically by reporting the vertices of the associated polygon:

$$p_i = (x_i, y_i), \qquad \text{for } i = 1, \ldots, N \qquad (13.14)$$

perhaps using the *polypoint* data type (see Appendix 3). Figure 13.9 shows some examples. When examining algorithms for filling such regions, we must carefully distinguish classes of polygons: convex versus concave, self-intersecting versus non-self-intersecting, and so on, as some algorithms work for one class but not another.

13.3.2 A Recursive Flood-Fill Algorithm

We begin by presenting two simple filling algorithms that work with pixel-defined regions. The first operates on interior-defined, 4-connected regions. It changes every interior pixel of *int_color* to the new color, *new_color*. It is called a **flood-fill** algorithm because it begins with a "seed" pixel in the interior of the region and floods the region with the new color. It is often used in interactive paint systems because the user can specify the seed by pointing to the interior of the region and then initiate the flood operation.

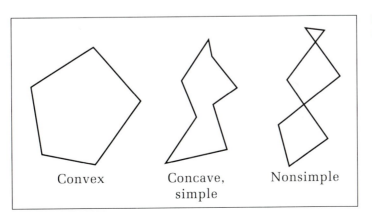

Convex   Concave,   Nonsimple
                          simple

Figure 13.9.
Defining polygonal regions.

The idea of the algorithm is this: If the pixel at (x, y) is part of the interior (i.e., still has color *int_color*), change it to *new_color*, and apply the same process recursively to each of its four neighbors. Otherwise do nothing to this pixel.

Code Fragment 13.4. Recursive Flood Fill for Interior-Defined Regions

```
procedure FloodFill(x : col; y : row; {seed pixel}
                     int_color, new_color : color);
{starting at (x, y), change all pixels of int_color to new_color}
{4-connected version}
begin
  if GetPixel(x, y) = int_color then
  begin
    SetPixel(x, y, new_color); {change its color}
    FloodFill(x − 1, y, int_color, new_color);
    FloodFill(x + 1, y, int_color, new_color);
    FloodFill(x, y + 1, int_color, new_color);
    FloodFill(x, y − 1, int_color, new_color)
  end
end;
```

Note that the process starts afresh at each pixel address that appears in a call to *FloodFill*( ): There is no account taken of **region coherence**, the likelihood that a pixel adjacent to an interior pixel is also an interior pixel. The algorithm proceeds "blindly," testing nearest neighbors with no memory of what has been tested before. For this reason, many pixels are tested several times, requiring a very large number of procedure calls.

Example

Consider the interior-defined region shown in Figure 13.10, consisting of only 5 pixels. Suppose that the seed for filling the region is at $(4, 2)$, marked S. When *FloodFill*(4, 2, *white, black*) is called, the sequence of addresses with which *FloodFill*( ) is called begins with

$(3, 2), (2, 2), (1, 2), (3, 2), (2, 3), (2, 1), (4, 2), (3, 3), (2, 3), (4, 3), \ldots$

In all there are 21 calls to the procedure (see the exercises), involving many repeated tests of the same pixel, such as $(2, 3)$.

Figure 13.10.
An example interior-defined region for filling.

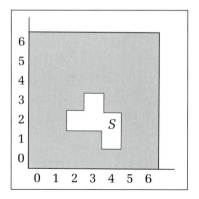

Because of the highly recursive and blind nature of this algorithm, the recursion stack can become very deep—many hundreds for a rather simple region! There is thus a good chance that the algorithm will cause a stack overflow and fail even on regions of modest size. In addition, overhead is required to manage the recursion, which slows the filling process to some degree. More efficient (but more complex) methods that capitalize on coherence are discussed later.

To extend this to an 8-connected version, simply add four instructions that try the four diagonal neighbors, such as *FloodFill*(*x* + 1, *y* − 1, *int_color*, *new_color*).

This recursive method can also be adapted to boundary-defined regions. Only the **if** statement must be changed. As before, the seed must lie in the interior of the region, not on its boundary. A pseudocode skeleton might look like:

if pixel at (*x*, *y*) is neither of *boundary_color* nor of *new_color*
then
1. Set it to *new_color*;
2. Recursively call the procedure, using as seed each of the
   4 (or 8) neighbors of (*x*, *y*).

This algorithm works properly when *boundary_color* = *new_color*. If these are not the same colors, then if any interior pixels happen to be of *new_color*, there will be certain geometrical patterns on which the algorithm can get hung up and terminate before the entire region is filled. (What are some example patterns?) Because of the highly recursive and blind nature of this routine, it suffers from the same defects as does the previous one.

Drill Exercise

13.6.   Hand Simulation of Flood Fill. Exercise by hand the algorithm of Code Fragment 13.4 on a region whose interior is defined by the pixels (1, 1), (2, 1), (2, 2), (3, 2), (2, 3), and (1, 3). The seed is taken to be (2, 2). Repeat when the algorithm is adapted to 8-connected regions, in which the additional four calls are taken in the order (*x* − 1, *y* − 1), (*x* + 1, *y* − 1), (*x* − 1, *y* + 1), (*x* + 1, *y* + 1).

13.7.   Recursive Region Filling. For the interior-defined region shown in Figure 13.10, display the "tree of proce-dure calls" that results when a seed beginning at (4, 2) is used. That is, draw a tree, each node of which contains the address of the pixel being tested by the **if** *GetPixel*( ) statement in Code Fragment 13.4. When the test succeeds, four subtrees of procedure calls are spawned.

What is the depth of this call tree? What is the worst arrangement of four interior pixels for the algorithm, in the sense that the largest number of recursive calls to the procedure is made?

13.3.3 Using Coherence: Region Filling Based on Runs of Pixels

In order to improve on the performance of the previous algorithms and to prevent stack overflow, we shall examine a slightly different approach that efficiently fills in "runs" of pixels. A **run** of pixels is a horizontally adjacent group of interior pixels. To see how the method operates, consider the boundary-defined, 4-connected region shown in Figure 13.11. The s marks the initial seed pixel. The run from a to b in which s resides is filled first. Then the row above is scanned from a to b looking for additional runs. One is found, and its rightmost pixel, c, is saved (its address is placed on a stack) to be dealt with later. Then the row below is scanned from a to b; a run is found; and its rightmost pixel, d, is saved on the stack. Figure 13.11b shows the situation at this point.

Now the stack is popped to produce the new seed, d, and the process is repeated. The run from d to e is filled; the row above is scanned—finding no run—and the row below is scanned between d and e, finding three runs. Pixels f, g, and h are pushed onto the stack. Pixel h is then popped; its run is filled; and the two additional runs, i and j, are identified. At this stage the situation is as shown in Figure 13.11c. The process continues until the stack is empty, at which point all interior pixels "reachable" from the initial seed will have been filled. The reader should follow through this example to develop an understanding of the algorithm. (How can this be extended to 8-connected regions? See the exercises.)

The main flow of this algorithm is as follows:

Code Fragment 13.5. Skeleton of Region-Filling Algorithm

Push address of seed pixel on the stack;
while *stack* **not** *empty* **do**
begin
   Pop the stack to provide the next seed;
   Fill in the run defined by the seed;
   Examine the row above for runs reachable from this run;
   Push the addresses of the rightmost pixels of each such run;
   Do the same for row below the current run;
end; {**while**}

Figure 13.11.
An example region to be
filled using runs.

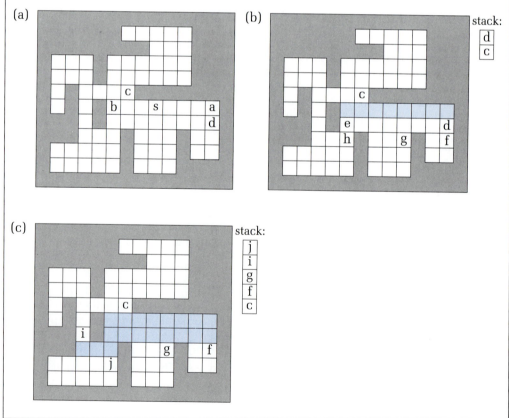

Note that because of region coherence, most runs are apt to consist of many pixels. Because runs are horizontal, the filling process for each run is orderly and can be made efficient. The left and right ends of the run are found by detecting pixels of the boundary color, and then the whole run is filled with the new color without having to read its pixel values again. Groups of pixels can even be filled simultaneously when *SetPixelWord( )* (recall Section 13.1) is available.

GetPixel( ) is used repeatedly when looking for runs above and below the current run. Scanning from right to left, a new run above or below is found, only when the pixel color there changes from *boundary_color* to *old_color*. (Will anything go awry if the region initially happens to have a "sprinkling" of pixels of *new_color*?)

Drill Exercises

13.8. Simulating the Run-Fill Algorithm. Lay out a region on a sheet of graph paper that approximates the shape of the letter B and contains at least 14 interior pixels. Hand simulate the operation of the proceding run-fill algorithm, noting the contents of the stack before each pop.

13.9. Worst-Case Regions. What region shape of 20 interior pixels is the worst for the run-fill algorithm, in the sense that the most pops of the stack are required? Is the count of pops a reasonable measure of how long the algorithm takes? Discuss other measures.

13.3.4 Filling Polygon-Defined Regions

The preceding algorithms must read the frame buffer pixel by pixel in order to identify each pixel's color, and they take action accordingly. In this way they "feel their way" across a region. One suspects that if the application had access to a higher-level description of the region and did not have to refer to existing pixel values, a fill algorithm could perform much faster. Next we shall develop some algorithms that work efficiently with polygon-defined regions.

Suppose that the region to be filled is described by a set of pixel addresses, $p_i = (x_i, y_i)$, for $i = 1, \ldots, N$, that specifies the sequence of a polygon's vertices. For this we need additional data types that mimic *point* and *polypoint* but use integer values for their coordinates, suitably restricted to the size of the frame buffer:

type
   pixel = **record**
           x : *col*;
           y : *row*
      end;

   polypixel = **record**
           num : 0..*MaxNumVerts*;
            pt : **array** [1..*MaxNumVerts*] **of** *pixel*
      end;

The process of clipping a polygon defined in world coordinates against a window is discussed in Appendix 6. We assume that the subject polygon has already been clipped and mapped to the frame buffer coordinates. Its description is stored in a variable, *poly*, of type *polypixel*.

To fill polygon *poly* we progress through the frame buffer scan line by scan line, filling in the appropriate portions of each line. As shown in Figure 13.12,

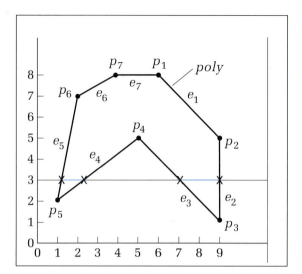

Figure 13.12.
Filling proper portions of a scan line.

the proper portions are determined by finding the intersections of the scan line with all the edges of the polygon. The pixels that lie between pairs of edges must lie in the polygon and are filled with the desired color. The process is

for each scan line **do begin**
Find the intersections of the scan line with all edges of the polygon;
   Sort the intersections by increasing x-value;
   Fill pixels between consecutive pairs of intersections
end;

For example, in Figure 13.12 the scan line at $y = 3$ intersects the four edges e_2, e_3, e_4, and e_5. The four intersection x-values are rounded to integers and sorted to yield the sequence 1, 2, 7, 9, and so the pixel run from column 1 to 2 and that from column 7 to 9 are filled.

Note that taking the sorted edge intersections in pairs uses a form of "parity" or inside–outside test. At each intersection a scan line passes either into or out of the polygon; that is, its parity changes. If it passes to the inside, the subsequent pixels will be filled; if to the outside, they will not. We assume scan lines begin outside polygons. The algorithm exploits **scan-line coherence**, the tendency for several consecutive pixels along a scan line to be interior to the polygon. Hence it can fill whole runs with little testing. (We shall capitalize on additional forms of coherence later.)

Some special cases must be considered:

1. Horizontal edges in the polygon need not be included in the process, as they are automatically filled when their adjacent edges are dealt with.

2. When a scan line passes through the endpoint of an edge—a vertex—it produces two intersections, one for each edge that is adjacent to the vertex. This changes the inside–outside parity twice at a single point. As shown in Figure 13.13, this is fine if the vertex is at a local minimum or maximum (i.e., a local "extremum"), because pixels to the left and right of the vertex will have the same parity. But if the vertex is not at a local extremum,

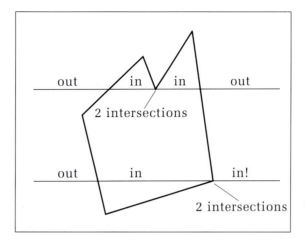

Figure 13.13.
Two intersections found at a vertex.

pixels to the left and right should have opposite parity, even though the algorithm gives them the same parity.

It is not hard to resolve this problem. Before beginning the filling process, test each vertex of the polygon. If its (integer) y-value does not lie at a local extremum, shorten one of the edges slightly, as shown in Figure 13.14. Because vertex $p_6 = (x_6, y_6)$ is not at a local extremum, edge e_5 is altered: Its upper endpoint is changed to $p_{new} = (x_6, y_6 - 1)$. (We shall see later that the slight change in the edge's slope caused by this shortening does not affect the accuracy of the filling process.) Edge e_6 is not changed. Now only one edge is discovered by the scan line, and the parity problem is avoided.

It is not difficult to implement this process of checking and shortening edges: Traverse the polygon edge by edge. Whenever the slopes of two successive (nonhorizontal) edges have the same sign, their common vertex is not a local extremum, and so lower the upper endpoint of the lower edge by one pixel (see the exercises).

Consider the example polygon *poly* of Figure 13.12, in which *poly* is characterized by the following vertex list:

poly : (6, 8), (9, 5), (9, 1), (5, 5), (1, 2), (2, 7), (4, 8)

Figure 13.14.
Shortening an edge.

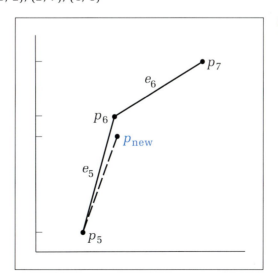

While traversing *poly*, one edge is deleted and two are shortened, yielding the following edges:

e_1: (6, 8) **to** (9, 5)
e_2: (9, 4) **to** (9, 1)
e_3: (9, 1) **to** (5, 5)
e_4: (5, 5) **to** (1, 2)
e_5: (1, 2) **to** (2, 6)
e_6: (2, 7) **to** (4, 8)

Now *poly* can be filled for each of the scan lines 1 through 8. For each scan line, the first edge encountered from the left "turns on" the filling; the next turns it off; and so on.

Note that the algorithm fills self-intersecting polygons, such as the third example in Figure 13.9, as well as simple polygons and polygons with holes. (*Question*: How does it fill a polygon that has a "hole within a hole"?)

Drill Exercises

13.10. Hand Simulation for Sample Polygons. On graph paper sketch several "interesting" polygons, some simple, some self-intersecting, some with holes, and so forth. Include one or more horizontal edges in each. Then hand simulate the edge shortening and filling process for each, and show the results.

13.11. What If an Edge Becomes Horizontal? In the process of traversing *poly* and shortening edges, some edges may become horizontal (when?). Should they then be ignored, as other horizontal ones are, or treated specially? Sketch various situations showing how to cope with this.

Improving the Algorithm's Performance

As with any time-critical algorithm, we look for the most time-consuming parts. Here it is the large number of intersections with edges that must be calculated, several for each scan line passing through the polygon. It helps somewhat that the scan lines are horizontal, but there is still significant effort involved, as the next exercise reveals.

Drill Exercise

13.12. Do It for *poly*. Find all intersections of the scan line at row 3 with the six shortened edges of *poly*.

To reduce this burden, we build and maintain a simple list so that we can locate intersections incrementally. The list, called the *Active Edge List* (AEL), allows the algorithm to capitalize on **edge coherence**, which is (1) the tendency for many of the edges intersected by scan line y to be intersected also by scan line $(y + 1)$, and (2) the property (of a straight line) that the x-value of the intersection migrates predictably from scan line to scan line.

During the filling process, the appropriate runs of pixels along each scan line are filled simply by referring to the AEL. The AEL contains the x-values of all the edge intersections for the "current" scan line, the line currently being filled. The x-values are maintained in sorted order so that according to the parity rule its first two x-values define the first run; its next two define the next run; and so on. The AEL also contains information about each currently intersected edge so that the AEL can be quickly updated to be used for the next scan

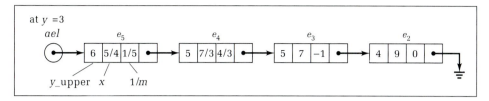

Figure 13.15.
The active edge list (AEL) for a scan line.

line. Figure 13.15 shows a linked-list version of the AEL for the example polygon *poly* when the current scan line is $y = 3$. Three facts are stored for each intersected edge:

1. The y-value y_{upper} of the upper endpoint of the edge (after shortening).

2. The x-value of the intersection with the current scan line.

3. The reciprocal $1/m$ of the edge's slope m. Note that $1/m$ is computed for each edge before any edges are shortened during the preprocessing of *poly*, so that it accurately represents the true polygon edge.

These data are conveniently stored in a linked list using records of the type *edge_info*:

type
   edge_ptr = ^*edge_info*;
   edge_info = **record**
                     y_upper   : *row*; {y at upper endpoint}
                     x_int   : *real*; {x-value of intersection}
                     recip_slope : *real*; {$1/m$}
                     next   : *edge_ptr* {to next edge}
                  end;

Because the AEL contains edge intersections sorted by x-value, each pair of x-values in turn defines a run of pixels, which is easily filled in a simple loop. As each pair of x-values is accessed, the two *x_int* values are rounded to the nearest column in the frame buffer. Assuming *ael* points to the head of the AEL, the following code fragment fills the proper runs along scan line y:

   Code Fragment 13.6. Filling Runs in Scan Line at Row y

```
var
  tmp : edge_ptr;          {moving pointer through the AEL}
  x, x1, x2 : col;
begin
  tmp := ael;        {start at head of AEL}
  while tmp <> nil do
  begin
    x1 := round(tmp^.x_int); {closest column, 1st edge in pair}
    tmp := tmp^.next;
    x2 := round(tmp^.x_int); {closest column, 2nd edge in pair}
    tmp := tmp^.next;
    for x := x1 to x2 do SetPixel(x, y, value); {fill the run}
  end; {while}
end;
```

Notice the scan-line coherence here: Many pixels are filled at the same time in the **for** loop. We shall see in later chapters that this algorithm is easily extended to incorporate "shading" for realism (Chapter 15) and "hidden surface elimination" (Chapter 17).

The only issue remaining is how to update the AEL as we move to each successive scan line, in order to exploit the edge coherence. Suppose we have just filled along scan line y using the preceding code fragment. Four things can happen as we update the AEL to the scan line at $(y + 1)$:

1. The new scan line may now lie just beyond (above) some of the edges represented in the AEL. Find if this is so by comparing the new y-value with each y_upper value in the AEL and deleting any edge for which y exceeds y_upper.

2. The x-value of each intersection may change. We can update this value directly from the information in each edge record. Upon moving up one scan line, the intersection must move over by the amount $1/m$, the inverse slope of the edge. Each intersection value x_int in the AEL is updated to $x\_int + recip\_slope$. Note that the x_int value must be stored as a real number, because accuracy would be lost if updates were rounded off to integers. This incremental adjustment to obtain the new intersection is fast, requiring only one addition.

3. A new pair of edges may be encountered, as y becomes equal to the y-value of the lower endpoint of some edges in the polygon. Edge records for such edges are added to the AEL, as we shall describe later.

4. The order of x_int values of edge intersections may become reversed if two edges cross (for nonsimple polygons). The list must be resorted if this happens, as we shall describe later, as well.

To find which edges must be added, we could test each vertex in the polygon for this condition, but this is inefficient. Instead, an **edge table** is created before the filling process begins, which is used for rapid access to the required information during the AEL's updating.

Building the Edge Table

The edge table is formed while traversing the polygon to eliminate horizontal edges and shorten others. Each edge is characterized by a record of the same type, *edge_info*, as used in the AEL. The *y_upper* and *recip_slope* fields are loaded with the proper values, and the *x_int* field is loaded with the x-value of the lower endpoint of the edge in question. As we mentioned, the reciprocal slope of an edge is based on the original edge data stored in *poly*, even if the edge is shortened during this preprocessing.

The edge table is built as an array of lists, *edge_table*: **array** [*row*] **of** *edge_ptr*, one entry for each scan line. Figure 13.16 shows the edge table for polygon *poly* of Figure 13.12. Edge records are inserted into the edge list corresponding to the y-value of their lower endpoint; that is, *edge_table*[*y*] points to a list of all edges having their lower endpoint on scan line y.

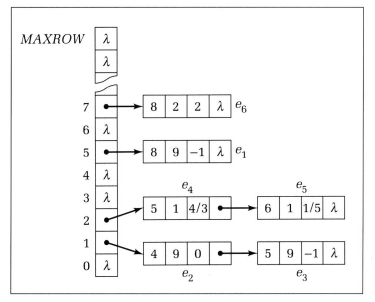

Figure 13.16.
Edge table characterizing the polygon.

With the edge table available, it is simple in the update process to identify those edges that must be added to the AEL. For the new current scan line at row y, all edges pointed to by *edge_table[y]* have been reached and are added to the AEL. The *x_int* value automatically contains the initial intersection value, and the other fields are already properly loaded. Therefore, only a few pointers must be adjusted to insert the new edge records. Before filling pixel runs, the AEL is resorted into ascending *x_int* values to maintain parity.

A skeleton of the overall algorithm is given next. It begins with an empty AEL and successively fills each scan line, starting at $y = 0$. It moves quickly through the main loop, drawing nothing until the first edges are added to the AET.

Code Fragment 13.7. Skeleton of the Polygon Fill Algorithm

```
ael := nil;                    {AEL initially empty}
for y := 0 to MaxRow do
begin
  add all edges in edge_table[y] to AEL;
  if ael <> nil then     {any edges to process yet?}
  begin
    sort AEL by x_int value;
    fill pixel values along y using AEL info;
    delete from AEL any records for which y_upper = y;
    update each x_int value by its recip_slope
  end
end;
```

13.3.5 Filling Several Polygons at Once

Most pictures consist of not a single polygon but several filled polygons. Each polygon has a *polypixel* specifying its vertices and a color. When polygons overlap, we also want to specify a **priority** for each, so that a polygon of higher priority will be drawn "on top of" all those of lower priority, thereby covering them. We assume that the application assigns in some fashion a different priority to each polygon.[1]

Before drawing the picture, each polygon is preprocessed and its edges (possibly shortened) are placed into a single edge table, as described. The *edge_info* data type used previously is enlarged to include the color and priority of the "parent" polygon to which the edge "belongs." (Alternatively, a field containing a pointer to the parent could be used.)

As before, the picture is scan converted line by line. At each new scan line the AEL is updated in precisely the same way as before. The real difference arises in identifying the runs of pixels that correspond to the same polygon, so that they can be filled with that polygon's color.

Figure 13.17 shows three overlapping polygons, *A*, *B*, and *C*, having priorities 6, 3, and 2, respectively, and the AEL loaded with data for painting in scan line *L*. There is one item on the AEL for each intersection of *L* with an edge, and they are sorted by the intersection *x*-values $x_1 \le x_2 \le x_3 \le \ldots \le x_8$. Each intersection points to a record containing the priority and color of its parent polygon. (Other AEL ingredients such as *y_upper* and *recip_slope* have been omitted to simplify the figure.) In addition, an array, *covers*[ ] of *boolean*, is maintained, one entry for each polygon. As the scanning progresses across line *L*, *covers*[ ] keeps track of which polygons cover the current pixel: For example, *covers*[*A*] will be *true* if the current *x*-value is inside polygon *A* and will be *false* otherwise. Variable *num_cover* records the number of polygons that cover the current pixel, and *vis_poly* points to the polygon of highest priority that covers the current pixel.

How does the filling method work for this example? Start scanning *L* at *x* = 0, with *num_cover* := 0 and all *covers*[ ] entries set to *false*. From the first entry in the AEL, determine the *x*-value at which *L* first encounters a polygon. Paint in the background color the single run up to this value of *x*. In the example, because line *L* enters polygon *B* at $x = x_1$, change *covers*[*B*] to *true*, *num_cover* to 1, and point *vis_poly* at *B*. We must now paint using *B*'s color for some run. How long is this run? Look further into the AEL and get the next intersection. *L* enters *A* at x_2, and so set *covers*[*A*] := *true* and *num_cover* := 2. Because *A* has higher priority, we must switch to its color; thus the run in *B*'s color ends here. This gray run is filled in. Look further into the AEL. The next intersection is with *B*, and because *covers*[*B*] = *true* we must be leaving *B*. Update *covers*[*B*] and *num_cover*. At x_4, *C* is entered, but its priority is lower than that of *vis_poly*, and so we just update *covers*[ ] and *num_cover* and continue. (What is *num_cover* now?) On to x_5, at which we see that *A* is being exited. Only here is any drawing done: The run of white pixels for *A* is drawn from x_2 to x_5. Hand simulate the remainder of scan line *L* to see how the algorithm operates.

In general, the algorithm looks ahead in the AEL through the sequence of intersections, just updating *covers*[ ] and *num_cover*. When a polygon of priority higher than that of *vis_poly* is entered, the current pixel run is colored, and *vis_poly* is set to the new winner. When the polygon currently visible is exited, *cover*[ ] is scanned to find the highest-priority polygon still covering the current pixel; the current run is filled (in which color?); and the *num_cover*, *covers*[ ], and so forth are adjusted.

---

[1]In some cases a polygon's priority is determined automatically. If the polygons are projections of polygons lying in 3D space, for instance, their priority will be set by their relative distance from the viewer's eye—see Chapter 17.

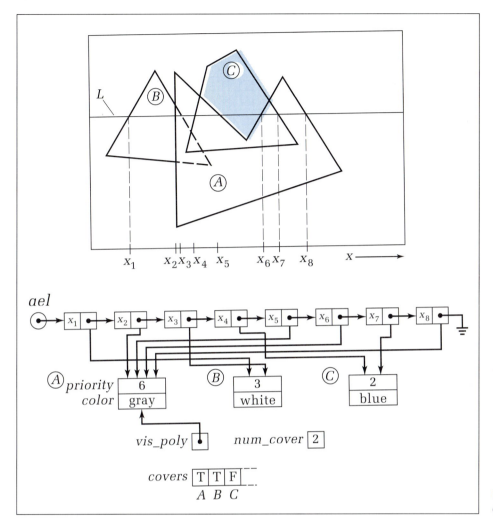

Figure 13.17.
Coloring several polygons.

Drill Exercises

13.13. Filling Several Polygons. The following three triangles, listed in order of decreasing priority, are to be scan converted into the frame buffer: A, $(4, 2)$, $(19, 2)$, $(11, 11)$, is white; B, $(22, 4)$, $(5, 12)$, $(16, 3)$, is blue; and C, $(8, 5)$, 8, $13)$, $(24, 5)$, is red. Use the preceding algorithm to determine the sequence of pixel colors at scan line $y = 10$. Repeat for $y = 7$.

13.14. Special Cases. Discuss whether the algorithm behaves properly on a scan line on which two edges from different polygons cross exactly through a pixel center.

13.3.6 Filling with Solid Colors and with Tiling Patterns

We have supposed so far that regions are to be filled with a solid color. But in some situations we may want to fill a region with a pattern, as shown in Figure 13.18. The pattern is often called a **tiling pattern**, and the process of filling the region is called **tiling**. It is similar to laying rectangular tiles of linoleum, all having the same decoration, side by side to cover a floor, with the condition that the boundary tiles may have to be cut and shaped to fit the contour of the region.

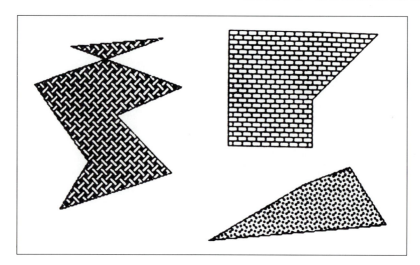

Figure 13.18.
Regions filled with tiling
patterns.

The application usually stores the pattern of colors in some array. The pattern might be stored in variable *pattern*[ ] having the type *tile*:

Code Fragment 13.8. Example Data Type for a Tiling Pattern

const *Tile_Size* = 16;
type *tile* = **array**[1..*Tile_Size*, 1..*Tile_Size*] **of** *color*;

Tile_Size is usually a power of two: 16-by-16 tiling patterns are quite common. An 8-by-8 example is shown in Figure 13.19.

It is simple to extend the preceding region-filling algorithms to paint in tiles rather than in a solid color. Because each algorithm eventually uses *SetPixel*(*x*, *y*, *value*) to draw each pixel inside a region, we simply choose *value* from the proper position within the tiling pattern. A simple approach for a 16-by-16 pattern is to use

SetPixel(*x*, *y*, *pattern*[*x* **mod** 16 + 1, *y* **mod** 16 + 1]).

The color drawn at (*x*, *y*) is the pattern value at (*x* **mod** 16 + 1, *y* **mod** 16 + 1), so that the pattern is effectively replicated or tesselated over the whole region.

Drill Exercise

13.15.   Using a Tiling Pattern. Sketch the patterns created by each of the following 4-by-4 tiling patterns:

Invent three other 4-by-4 tiling patterns that create interesting patterns.

```
1 1 1 1     0 1 0 1     1 0 0 0
0 1 1 0     1 0 1 0     1 1 0 0
0 1 1 0     0 1 0 1     1 1 1 0
1 1 1 1     1 0 1 0     1 1 1 1
```

Many other filling algorithms have been devised (see the exercises for two such examples). Some work only on polygons having certain geometric properties; others are fine-tuned to special polygon types; and several are described in Rogers (1985).

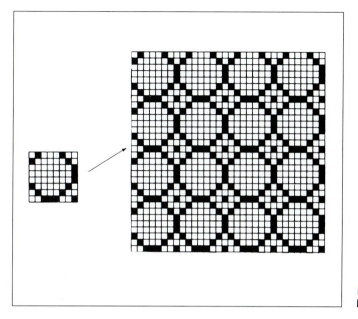

Figure 13.19.
Example of an array of type tile.

13.4 The Aliasing Problem: Antialiasing Techniques

The notion of the "jaggies" was brought up several times in earlier discussions. Jaggies are a form of **aliasing**, which is an inherent property of raster displays. They occur because of the discrete nature of pixels; that is, pixels occur on a display in a fixed rectangular array of points.

As an example, a black rectangle is shown in Figure 13.20, along with the way it would appear on a raster display having a certain resolution.[2] The rectangle could represent, for instance, a straight-line segment having a certain line width. In the figure a pixel will be drawn black if its center is covered by the rectangle. Because the rectangle is tilted at a slope of one-quarter, its edges appear as successively higher "runs" of four pixels.

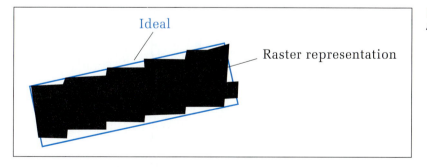

Figure 13.20.
Aliasing of a rectangle.

[2]For clarity, pixels are shown as square blocks, whereas on an actual display they appear as small "blobs" of light, perhaps blurred somewhat by the motion of the electron beam.

Origin of the Term *Aliasing*

The term *aliasing* comes from sampling theory in signal processing. The underlying notion is illustrated in Figure 13.21. Suppose we attempt to determine the nature of the (black) sinusoidal waveform by measuring or "sampling" it at uniformly spaced instants of time. After taking a large number of such samples, we discard the waveform and retain only the samples, from which we must obtain information about the sinusoid. If we sample it very densely—many times in each period—the samples together will precisely characterize it, and so we can determine its frequency, amplitude, and the like. But if the samples are taken at too low a rate, as shown by the dots, they will not be able to capture fully the character of the sine wave. What is worse, they could just as well have come from the more slowly varying (blue) sine wave, the "alias" of the black one. Both sine waves yield the same samples, and sampling the black curve too slowly makes it appear to be its alias.[3]

Aliasing also arises in graphics from the effects of sampling. Samples are taken spatially—at different points, rather than temporally—at different times. In Figure 13.20 a pixel is set to black based on the presence or absence of the rectangle at one point: the pixel's center. In effect, the rectangle is sampled at this one point, and no information is obtained about the rectangle's presence in other portions of the pixel. We are not "looking densely enough" within the pixel region, and thus we should test more points there, to see which ones the rectangle is covering.

13.4.1 Antialiasing Techniques

How can one reduce the aliasing produced by insufficient sampling? A higher-resolution display helps, because the jags are then smaller in size relative to the rectangle. But both current display technology and price limit how much one can increase the resolution. We must therefore look for other ways to deal with aliasing.

Antialiasing techniques involve one form or another of "blurring" to "smooth" the image. In the case of a black rectangle against a white background,

Figure 13.21.
Aliasing due to undersampling a signal.

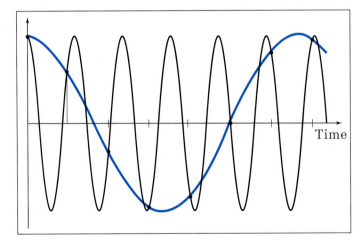

[3]The sampling theorem (Oppenheim and Willsky 1983) asserts that to capture the undulations of a waveform in equally spaced samples, it must be sampled at a rate at least twice the highest frequency of any component sinusoid in the signal.

the sharp transition from black to white is softened by using a mix of gray pixels near the rectangle's border. When these gracefully varying shades are looked at from afar, the eye tends to blend them together and thus to see a smoother edge.

There are three commonly used approaches to antialiasing: prefiltering, supersampling, and postfiltering.

Antialiasing Using Prefiltering: Pitteway–Watkinson

Prefiltering techniques compute the shades of gray based on how much of a pixel's area is covered by each object.

Consider scan converting a white polygon in a black background, as in Figure 13.22a. Suppose the intensity ranges from 0 for black to 1 for white. The polygon is situated in a square grid, where the center of each square corresponds to the center of a pixel on the display. A pixel that is half-covered by the polygon should be given the intensity 1/2; one that is one-third covered should be given the intensity 1/3; and so forth. If the frame buffer has 4 bits per pixel so that black is represented by 0 and white by 15, a pixel that is one-quarter covered by the polygon should be given the value of (1/4)15, which rounds up to 4. Figure 13.22b shows the pixel value that results from calculating the fraction of the area of each pixel covered by the polygon in Figure 13.22a. (What would the array of pixel values be if "pixel-center sampling" were used, that is, 15 when the rectangle covers the center of the pixel, and 0 otherwise?)

Not surprisingly, the geometric computations needed to determine the overlap area for each pixel can be very time-consuming! (Try to do it by hand in Figure 13.22a.) To make the computation as efficient as possible, a modification of Bresenham's line algorithm was developed by Pitteway and Watkinson (1980). As each edge of the polygon is scan converted, not only are the pixels that best approximate the edge determined, but in addition, the amount that each boundary pixel is overlapped by the polygon is found. This amount is then used to set the intensity of the edge pixel. The interior of the polygon is then filled with white in the usual fashion. In the spirit of Bresenham's algorithm, the computations are both incremental and based on integer arithmetic, which makes them very efficient.

The algorithm is best revealed through an example, and Figure 13.23 shows an edge having a slope of 4/10. The inside of the polygon lies below the edge. The pixels identified by the standard Bresenham algorithm are shown dotted,

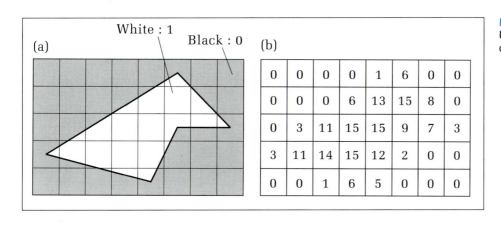

Figure 13.22.
Using the fraction of pixel area covered by the object.

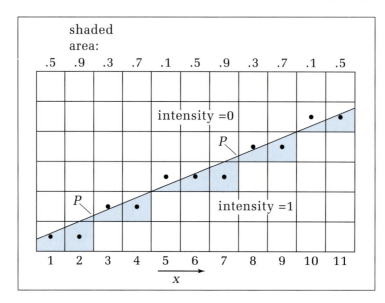

Figure 13.23.
Example of scan conversion
with antialiasing.

and the cross-hatched region for each of these pixels indicates the area inside the polygon. The numerical amount of this area is shown for each pixel: .5, .9, .3, and so forth. The first pixel is assumed to be 50 percent covered.

One can see by purely geometric reasoning (for the case in which the slope m lies between 0 and 1) that as we move pixel by pixel to the right, the shaded area either increases by $m = .4$ if the y-value stays the same, or decreases by $1 - m = .6$ if the y-value increments. (This is true only if we include in the area calculations of the pixels at $x = 2$ and $x = 7$ the small triangular areas labeled p, belonging to the next higher pixels.) Hence it is simple to update this area incrementally as part of the Bresenham algorithm. Suppose the frame buffer supports the maximum intensity value $MaxLevel$. For an edge of slope m we find the closest integer, $inc1 := MaxLevel * m$, and either increment the intensity of each Bresenham pixel by $inc1$ or decrement it by $inc2 := MaxLevel - inc1$. The main loop of Code Fragment 13.2 needs only slight adjustments: If $e < 0$, then in addition to updating the error $e := e + e\_noinc$, we update intensity: $col\_val := col\_val + inc1$. Similarly, when $e \geq 0$, the error is updated by e_inc, and intensity is updated by $-inc2$. In their original paper Pitteway and Watkinson improved efficiency further by adjusting matters so that col_val itself could replace e as the test variable!

Drill Exercises

13.16.   Checking Incremental Area. Show that the area of an edge pixel covered by a polygon either increases by m or decreases by $1 - m$ as one moves along the edge pixel by pixel.

13.17.   The Pitteway–Watkinson Algorithm in Other Quadrants. Our discussion restricted the slope of the polygon's edge to lie between 0 and 1. Extend the method to edges of arbitrary slope.

13.18.   Antialiasing a Polygon. For a frame buffer that holds values from 0 to 15, apply the antialiasing scan conversion we described to each edge of the white polygon with vertices (1, 3), (6, 7), (15, 4), (11, 15), and (1, 8). Assume a black background. Then fill the polygon with white using a boundary-fill algorithm. Is there any chance of a hole's appearing in the polygon's edge that would cause the fill routine to fail? How could this be fixed?

We see that prefiltering operates on the detailed geometric shape of the object(s) being scan converted and computes an average intensity for each pixel based on the objects found lying within each pixel's area. It is approximately the same as sampling the shape of the object very densely within a pixel region. For shapes other than polygons, it can be an expensive technique computationally, and so we shall seek alternative approaches to antialiasing.

Supersampling

The computational burden observed with prefiltering arises from densely sampling the scene within each pixel region. So we try to improve efficiency by sampling less densely, but still more than one sample per pixel. This is called **supersampling**: taking more intensity samples of the scene than are displayed. Several samples are averaged together to compute each display pixel value.

Figure 13.24 shows an example of double sampling: The object is sampled twice as densely in both x and y as it is displayed. The squares indicate display pixels, each of which is to be given a final intensity value. Think of this array as being laid on top of the scene, in this case a bar lying diagonally across the window. The scene is "looked at" through each pixel window. The x's denote spots at which the scene is sampled, and here four times as many samples are taken as there are display pixels. Each final display pixel can be formed as the average of the nine "neighbor" samples: the center one and the eight surrounding ones. Some samples are reused in several pixel calculations (which ones?). Display pixel at A is based on six samples within the bar and three samples of background. Its intensity is the sum of two-thirds the bar's intensity and one-third the background. The pixel at B is based on all nine samples within the bar: Its intensity is that of the bar.

Figure 13.25a shows a scene displayed at a resolution of 256-by-256 pixels. The jaggies are readily apparent. Figure 13.25b shows the benefits of double sampling. The same scene was sampled (using ray tracing—see Chapter 18) at a resolution of 512-by-512 samples, and each of the 256-by-256 display pixels is an average of nine neighbors, as in Figure 13.24. The jaggies have been softened

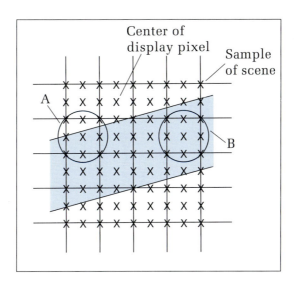

Figure 13.24.
Antialiasing using supersampling.

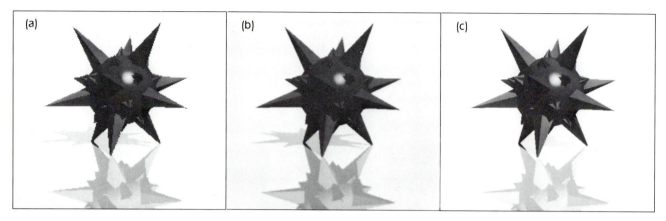

(a)   (b)   (c)

Figure 13.25.
Examples of antialiasing by supersampling. (Courtesy of Brett Diamond)

considerably. Figure 13.25c shows the improvement attainable if the user has a (more expensive) 512-by-512 pixel display, which shows the unaveraged 512-by-512 samples.

In general, supersampling computes N_s scene samples in both x and y for each display pixel, averaging some number of neighbor samples to form each display pixel value. Other ratios of scene samples to display samples are also used. Figure 13.26 shows the case of quadruple supersampling, for which $N_s = 4$. Each dot indicates where in the scene a sample is computed, the blue dots showing the locations of the centers of the display pixels. Each pixel might be formed here as the average of the 5-by-5 block of samples about its center, or perhaps even a 6-by-6 block might be used. (Why would a 3-by-3 block never be used here?)

One can also go to the other extreme and use no oversampling, $N_s = 1$. The scene is sampled at the "corner" of each display pixel, as suggested in Figure 13.27. The intensity of each display pixel is set to the average of the four samples taken at its corners. This is not true supersampling, because the density of samples is the same as the density of pixels displayed, but some softening of the jaggies is still observed.

Figure 13.26.
Quadruple supersampling.

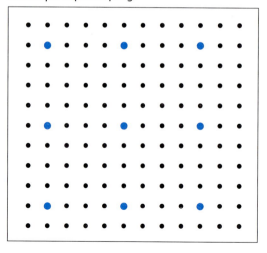

Figure 13.27.
Antialiasing by corner sampling.

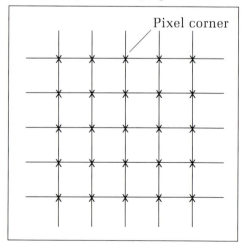

Pixel corner

Drill Exercise

13.19.   Corner Sampling. For a raster having R rows and C columns, how many samples of the scene must be computed? That is, how many corners are there? Compare this with "center-of-pixel" sampling and with double sampling.

Antialiasing Using Postfiltering

In the double-sampling method, nine neighboring samples are simply averaged to compute each display pixel's intensity. This gives all of the neighbors equal importance. This form of "blurring" or "filtering" might be improved by giving the center sample more "weight" and the eight neighbors less weight. Or it may help to include more neighbors in the averaging computation.

   Postfiltering computes each display pixel as a "weighted average" of an appropriate set of neighboring samples of the scene. Figure 13.28 shows the situation for double sampling. Each value represents the intensity of a scene sample, the ones in blue indicating the centers of the various display pixels. The square **mask** or **window function** of weights is laid over each blue square in turn. Then each window weight is multiplied by its corresponding sample, and the nine products are summed to form the display pixel intensity. For example, when the mask shown is laid over the sample of intensity 30, the weighted average is found to be

$$\tfrac{1}{2}(30) + \tfrac{1}{16}(28 + 16 + 4 + 42 + 17 + 53 + 60 + 62) = 32.625$$

which rounds to intensity 33. This mask gives eight times as much weight to the center as to the other eight neighbors. The weights always sum to 1.

   Note that supersampling as we described it is just a special case of postfiltering, in which all the weights have value $\tfrac{1}{9}$. Sampling and filter theory (Gonzalez and Wintz 1987, Oppenheim and Willsky 1983) provide analytical methods for determining how different classes of window functions perform as postfilters. Sometimes larger masks, 5-by-5 or even 7-by-7, are used. These "look farther" into the neighborhood of the center sample and can provide additional smoothing. Figure 13.29 shows some examples of masks that are often used in practice (Crow 1981). The fraction next to each mask gives the common factor that scales each mask element so that they sum to unity. In the first mask the center is weighted four times as heavily as the 4-connected neighbors are, and the corners have no weight at all. The third example is a 5-by-5 mask that gives

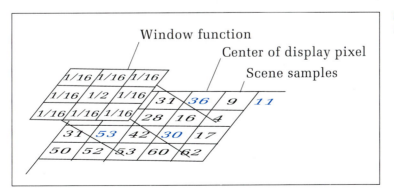

Figure 13.28.
Postfiltering a graphics image.

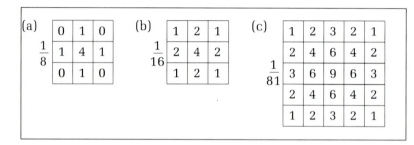

Figure 13.29.
Examples of window functions.

weight to the second ring of neighbors around each sample. Examples (b) and (c) are approximations to the "Bartlett window": The weights grow linearly from the edges toward the center.

Postfiltering can be performed for any value of oversampling N_s. If $N_s = 4$ is used, as in Figure 13.26, a 5-by-5, 7-by-7, or even 9-by-9 mask is appropriate (Crow 1981). If $N_s = 1$, as in the case of corner sampling, one might use a 3-by-3 mask that weights the center pixel most heavily. This blurring may or may not pay off, depending on the scene being rendered.

Drill Exercises

13.20.   Other Windows. Based on the patterns of the Bartlett windows in Figure 13.29b and c, what are the elements of a 7-by-7 Bartlett window? What is the common scaling factor?

13.21.   Hand Simulation of Postfiltering. Consider a square portion of a coordinate system extending in x from 0 to 16 and in y from 0 to 16. A white (intensity 15) triangle lies in the scene against a black (intensity 0) background. The corners of the triangle are at (1.6, 4.8), (12.4, 1.4), and (7.4, 11.2). Samples of the scene are computed at every point (i, j) where both i and j are integers. Suppose $N_s = 2$ so that there are only one-quarter as many display pixels as computed samples and that the display pixels are centered at (m, n) where both m and n are *odd* integers. Compute the postfiltered image using the mask of Figure 13.29b. Sketch it in pencil on a suitable grid, matching as best you can the lightness of each pixel to the computed intensity. Discuss the amount and quality of antialiasing that you achieve.

13.5 Use of the Color Lookup Table

As discussed in Chapter 2, many raster displays incorporate a color lookup table (LUT) that can be controlled by the application, thus offering some interesting extra degrees of freedom for the programmer. We shall explore some of them here.

For concreteness, consider the display shown in Figure 13.30, in which the frame buffer has four bit planes, and each of the 16 entries in the lookup table is six bits wide. As each pixel value is scanned, its value i is used as an index into the i-th entry in the LUT, and the 6-bit values found there are sent to the DACs (digital-to-analog converters).

Each of the three DACs is controlled by a 2-bit value. The usual mapping from binary values to beam intensities for a DAC is assumed:

$00 \rightarrow 0$ (off)
$01 \rightarrow 1/3$ (dim)
$10 \rightarrow 2/3$ (medium)
$11 \rightarrow 1$ (bright)

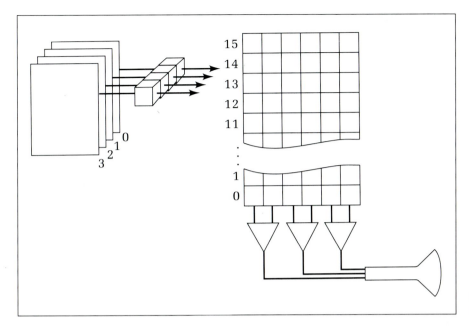

Figure 13.30.
Using the lookup table.

Because there are four possible values for each of the R, G, and B beam intensities, the palette consists of 64 colors. Suppose, for instance, that entry 5 (0101 in binary) in the LUT has been loaded with 11 01 10. When a pixel in the frame buffer contains 0101, it is displayed with the color having components

11 → bright red
01 → dim green
10 → medium blue

As we shall discuss in Chapter 16, these components combine to form a pinkish color. Normally the 16 entries are loaded with bit values so that 16 different desired colors are displayed. But the lookup table can also be loaded to produce other effects. We illustrate with two examples.

13.5.1 Text Overlays: Reserving One Bit Plane

It is possible to scan convert different pictures into the various bit planes of the frame buffer. For instance, text can be drawn into bit plane 3 and another picture into the remaining ones. We want to make the text appear and disappear rapidly on command by clever control of the LUT contents. When a text bit is on, it dominates, or "overlays," the other image, as if the text has been drawn over the image. When it is turned off, the other image can be seen intact. It does not have to be redrawn; the parts that were obscured instantly reappear.

How is this done? Pixel values in bit plane 3 control the first (most significant) bit of the index into the LUT. When this bit is 1, the index into the LUT has the form $1XXX$ (where X is either 0 or 1). To make the text dominate, we load all LUT entries having indices of this form (the top eight entries) with whatever color we want for the text, say 11 11 11 for white text. For those pixels not "covered" by a text character, the first bit is 0, and so we load LUT entries with indices of the form $0XXX$ (the bottom eight entries) with whatever colors we wish for the other 3-bit image. Now where there is text, it will dominate, and where there is no text, the other image will automatically be seen.

A possible loading of the table when we want to see white text is

Address	R G B		
1111	11 11 11	white	
1010	11 11 11		{text dominates}
1001	11 11 11		
. . .	. . .		
. . .	. . .		
1000	11 11 11	white	
0111	10 10 10	gray	
0110	10 00 10	magenta	
0101	00 10 10	yellow	{text invisible}
0100	10 10 00	cyan	
0011	00 00 10	blue	
0010	00 10 00	green	
0001	10 00 00	red	
0000	00 00 00	black	

To turn the text off, we simply alter some entries in the LUT: Copy into entries 1000..1111 the colors that are in 0000..0111. This makes it irrelevant whether the first bit is a 0 or a 1. The LUT contents can be changed very rapidly, as such a small number of values are involved.

13.5.2 Simple Animation by Table Cycling

Because the LUT can be altered so quickly, we can create simple animations by the proper "cycling" of its values. A succession of images, one for each bit plane, is written into the frame buffer. Then the contents of the LUT are cycled so that one bit plane after another is on and the others are invisible.

This is done in much the same way as for the text overlay plane: To make the image in bit plane 0—bright blue (00 00 11) against a white (11 11 11) background, for instance—load each entry having index of the form $XXX1$ with 00 00 11, and the other entries with 11 11 11. For a 4-bit plane frame buffer, we can cycle through four images in the animation.

If the various images in the sequence do not overlap spatially—as in the case of the bouncing-ball animation suggested in Figure 13.31—a much larger number of "frames" in the animation can be created: up to 2^n instead of n for an n-bit/pixel frame buffer! For each of the ball images, the value shown in the figure is written into those pixels "covered" by the ball. All pixels in the "floor" are given value 14, and all remaining pixels are given value 15.

Before the animation begins, the value 10 00 00 is loaded into entry 14 to make the floor red, and 11 11 11 is loaded into all other LUT entries so that the rest of the picture is white. All the balls are shown in the background color.

Now to make ball 4 visible, the ball color—say green 00 11 00—is loaded into entry 4 of the LUT. To "switch" to the next ball, load 11 11 11 into entry 4 and 00 11 00 into entry 5, and so forth. By the rapid changing of one entry to white and another to green every few tenths of a second, the ball appears to move cyclically through its paces.

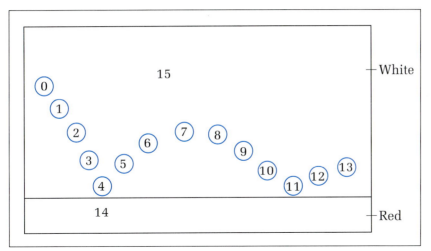

Figure 13.31.
Animating a bouncing ball.

Drill Exercises

13.22.   How Flexible Is This Method? Assuming the configuration of Figure 13.30:

a. Show how to load the LUT when the four images overlap spatially so that they appear as a medium green color against a yellow background.

b. If no image overlaps any other, in how many colors can each image be displayed against a white background?

c. If the images do overlap spatially, can they be composed of more than one color? Explain.

13.23.   What About This One? How many different non-overlapping balls can be drawn if each involves two colors? Explain. Can the different balls have different sizes and shapes? Can two be visible at once?

13.6   Drawing in Exclusive-Or Mode

Some routines write blindly into the frame buffer using *SetPixel*( ). Others (such as most region-fill routines) require the use of *GetPixel*( ), which first sees what is in the frame buffer and then alters it as required. This is called a **read–modify–write cycle** and has three steps:

1. Use *GetPixel*(*i*, *j*) to determine the current value of the pixel at (*i*, *j*).

2. Use this information to decide what the new value at (*i*, *j*) should be.

3. Write this value into (*i*, *j*) using *SetPixel*( ).

Often a function, *Combo*(*p*, *q* : *color*) : *color*, is defined that combines two colors in some fashion to produce a new color. In such a case the read–modify–write cycle can be summarized as

SetPixel(*i*, *j*, *Combo*(*v*, *Getpixel*(*i*, *j*)))

Several versions of *Combo*( ), are discussed in Section 13.9, but one example warrants special attention, in which *Combo*( ) forms the **exclusive-or** (or

xor) of its arguments. For binary values v and p the value (v *xor* p) is 1 only if v and p are different, as dictated by the truth table:

v	p	v *xor* p
0	0	0
0	1	1
1	0	1
1	1	0

If the frame buffer holds b bits/pixel, the *xor* of the b-bit words v and p will be performed *bitwise*, on pairs of corresponding bits in v and p. For example, with $b = 8$, (11010010) *xor* (01001001) = (10011011). The following exercise explores what colors can result when two "colors" are *xor*-ed.

Drill Exercises

13.24.   Drawing Multiple Colors in *xor* Mode. For a 3-bit-plane frame buffer, assign eight different colors to the eight possible pixel values, and describe what color is observed as the drawing color 110 is *xor*-ed with each of the possible pixel values.

Replacing p with (v *xor* p) is called writing v "in *xor* mode," and many graphics toolboxes provide this mode automatically. A routine such as *set_drawing_mode(xor)* initiates drawing in *xor* mode, after which *SetPixel(i, j, col)* by itself produces the same effect as does *SetPixel(i, j, col xor GetPixel(i, j))*.

Why is *xor* writing so useful? Its essential property is that if the same value is written twice, the original image will be restored: p *xor* v *xor* $v = p$. (Show that this is so.) We shall examine next how this can be used to good effect in raster graphics.

13.6.1 Rubber Banding

As discussed in Chapter 6, drawing "rubber band" lines provides a helpful echo to an interactive user. The "stretchable" line drawn from a pivot point to the current cursor position allows the user to preview a line before committing to it. A rubber band line must be continually erased and redrawn at a slightly different position. One way of erasing it is simply to redraw the old line in the background color, but this also erases any parts of the drawing that lie in the path of the line. But by using *xor* drawing, this problem is avoided. The line is simply drawn a second time in the same position, which makes the line disappear and automatically restores the original drawing.

Because of the *xor* property, the process of maintaining a rubber band echo quite straightforward. The pivot point *pivot* is established first: The user points at the desired spot for the pivot and clicks a button. A variable, *latest_pt*, that tracks the current mouse position, is initialized to the *pivot* value as well. Then a loop is entered, as suggested by the following pseudocode:

latest_pt := *pivot*;
set_drawing_mode(XOR);
repeat
   locate_mouse(mouse_point);
   if *mouse_point* <> *latest_pt* **then**
   begin
     line(pivot, latest_pt); {erase old line by redrawing it}
     latest_pt = mouse_point; {update *latest_pt*}
     line(pivot, latest_pt) {draw new line}
   end
until *mouse_click*;

Each time the locator is moved, the old rubber band line is erased, and the new one is drawn to the latest point. (When the user terminates the loop, what variable contains the final locator position?)

One phenomenon observed when drawing in *xor* mode is that the rubber band line does not have a uniform color. Instead, various segments of it have colors determined by the colors in the image that are covered by the rubber band. For a bilevel display, a black rubber band will have various white segments along its length. This is usually not too annoying and in fact can be useful, because any objects "under" the line are still visible. When it is unacceptable, more powerful techniques can be used, as described next.

13.7 Storing Images in Offscreen Memory

Because a raster image is just an array of numbers, it can easily be copied from the frame buffer to another area within system memory and then be copied back at a later time. When this can be done quickly, we obtain a powerful tool for manipulating images. When an image is copied to a region of memory other than the frame buffer, it is said to be in **offscreen memory** and is not displayed.

For simplicity, only rectangular images called **bitmaps** are stored offscreen. They might more properly be called *pixelmaps* because each pixel value can consist of many bits, but bitmap is conventionally used. Because bitmaps are rectangular, their shape is described by two numbers, *nrows* and *ncols*, the number of rows and columns in the image, respectively. The rest of the data in a bitmap are just a list of pixel values (of type *color*). The list normally traverses row by row from the top left-hand corner to the bottom right-hand corner.

Figure 13.32 shows the two forms of memory. The frame buffer is treated as the familiar array of pixels of type **array** [0..*MaxColumn*, 0..*MaxRow*] **of** *color*. Values stored in this array are displayed as pixels in a particular color. The pixels are "addressed" as usual by a (column, row) coordinate pair, as in *GetPixel*(23, 146). Offscreen memory, on the other hand, is shown as an amorphous collection of memory cells in which several bitmaps are stored. Bitmaps are often stored dynamically: Memory is allocated to them as needed from the "heap" maintained by the operating system, and this memory is released back to the system when the image is no longer needed. Each bitmap is identified by a

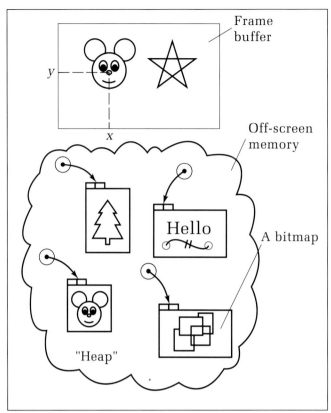

Figure 13.32.
Conceptual model of offscreen memory.

pointer (containing the address in memory at which the data begin). It is shown as a rectangle topped by the two fields containing *nrows* and *ncols*.

The following utilities allow us to copy bitmaps between on- and offscreen memory. The *bitmap* type here uses a large one-dimensional array to capture the pixel values. Because this can waste memory, one would probably develop more efficient (and system-dependent) ways to store bitmaps (see the exercises). These utilities are generalized in Section 13.8 using the powerful BitBLT operation.

Code Fragment 13.9. Utilities to Control Offscreen Memory

```
const MaxSize = 1024: {max number of pixels in a bitmap}
type
    map_ptr = ^bitmap;
    bitmap = record
                nrows, ncols : integer; {size of bitmap}
                pix: array[1..MaxSize] of color
             end;
    pixrect = record                    {rectangle on screen}
                l : col; t : row; {upper left corner}
                r : col, b : row; {lower right corner}
             end;
procedure Show(x : col; y : row; p : map_ptr);
{copy bitmap p^ to screen beginning at (x, y)}
function Store(box : pixrect) : map_ptr;
{copy region of frame buffer to offscreen memory}
```

As Figure 13.33 suggests, *Show*( ) copies the bitmap pointed to by *p* onto the screen, so that its upper left corner lies at (*x*, *y*). The new image "paints over" whatever was on that part of the screen before the operation. *Store(box)* allocates sufficient offscreen memory to contain the bitmap based on the portion of the screen image defined by *box*. It then writes the pixel data into this memory and returns a pointer to the bitmap. The image on the screen is not affected.

These routines can be used together to copy an image from one place on the screen to another. *Show(x, y, Store(rect1))* copies the portion of the displayed image residing in rectangle *rect1* to the new position having upper left-hand corner (*x*, *y*). An intermediate bitmap is formed in the process, and the application should release this memory after the copy is complete (see the exercises).

It may be much quicker simply to copy each pixel in the "source" rectangle to its corresponding place in the "destination." If the source and destination rectangles overlap, the order in which pixels are copied can be important. The normal order of copying is in scan line order, left to right on each line, top to bottom in scan lines. Figure 13.34 shows a case in which the source window is to be copied to a destination window lying slightly below and to its right. If copying is done left to right, the *xxxx* line will overwrite a part of the source that hasn't yet been read, thereby corrupting what is there. To avoid this, the source data must be copied from right to left (or bottom to top) (see the exercises).

13.7.1 Treating Text in Raster Displays

Offscreen memory can be useful when manipulating text on a raster display. First recall that three types of text characters are commonly found in graphics: hardware text, vector text, and bitmap text. **Hardware text** characters that are

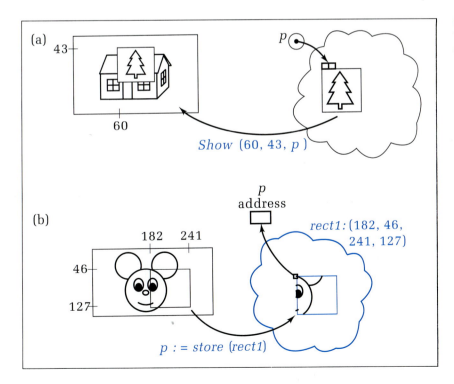

Figure 13.33.
The *Show*( ) and *Store*( ) operations.

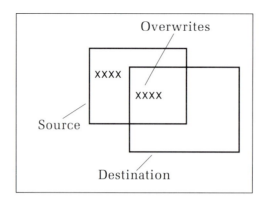

Figure 13.34.
Proper order of copying when source and destination overlap.

built into most graphics terminals are drawn quickly but are often available in only one size and with restricted positions. **Vector text** offers very high quality character shapes, each defined as a set of polylines (see Figure 2.21). (Some character sets are also based on more complex curves such as splines [Knuth 1979] and see Chapter 14.) Vector text has the advantage that each character can be scaled, rotated, and shifted with great precision. It can be drawn on a raster display just as can any other set of polylines. If the characters are described as polygons, their interiors can be filled in a choice of patterns and colors.

Raster displays also offer **bitmap text** for producing text. Character shapes are defined as patterns of pixels in bitmaps, as shown in Figure 13.35. These bitmaps provide "pictures" of characters defined inside some cell size, such as 12 rows of 8 columns each, typically by making some pixels 0 and the rest 1. A large cell size allows more freedom in creating the shape of each character, and more pleasing fonts can be fashioned. But large cell sizes consume more memory and require higher-resolution displays to show characters of a particular size.

When a workstation is initialized, a variety of fonts is usually loaded from disk into offscreen memory so that they will be readily available. Each character bitmap can have a separate pointer, perhaps using an array of pointers, as in *ch* : **array** ['A' . . 'z'] **of** *map_ptr*. To draw the uppercase A at position (37, 139), one then simply displays the proper bitmap, as in *Show*(37, 139, 'A'). The number of character sizes and fonts is limited only by the available offscreen memory. To draw a string of characters, *Show*( ) copies the bitmap of each character shape into the frame buffer at the proper spot, and the character picture appears, as shown in in Figure 13.36. Note that this method allows text to be drawn using

Figure 13.35.
Characters defined as bitmaps.

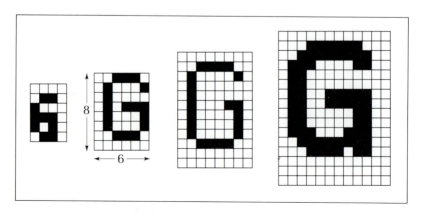

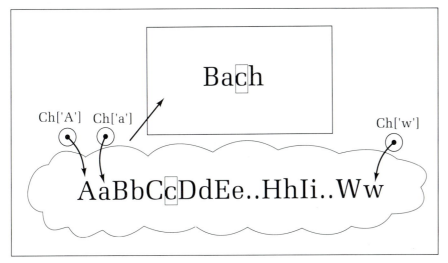

Figure 13.36.
Drawing text by copying character pictures.

proportional spacing. With **proportional spacing**, different characters in the font can have different widths (an "i" is usually the narrowest, a "w" the widest). This produces more aesthetically pleasing text.

The following code fragment shows how a string of text might be drawn, starting at (x, y) and using bitmaps for each character. The upper left corner of each successive bitmap is determined by accessing the width of the previous character.

Code Fragment 13.10. Drawing a String of Text Using Stored Character Bitmaps

```
var ch : array ['A' . . 'z'] of map_ptr; {pointers to bitmaps}
procedure DrawString(str : string; x : col; y : row);
var
  i : integer;
begin
  for i := 1 to length(str) do
  begin
    Show(x, y, ch[str[i]]);      {draw bitmap for i-th character}
    x := x + ch[str[i]]^.ncols {advance drawing point}
  end
end;
```

Transforming Characters Stored As Bitmaps

Although characters defined as bitmaps can be positioned precisely, they cannot be arbitrarily scaled or rotated. It is easy, however, to enlarge a character by some integer multiple, using "pixel replication." An example of pixel doubling is shown in Figure 13.37: Each pixel in the smaller character produces a 2-by-2 array of pixels, and so the character is enlarged by a factor of 2 in both directions. It is more difficult to enlarge a character by a noninteger factor or to reduce the size of a character, even by a simple factor of two (see the exercises). In these cases the character must often be entirely refashioned (Bigelow 1985). It thus is often simpler to load additional character sets into offscreen memory that contains different sizes of the characters.

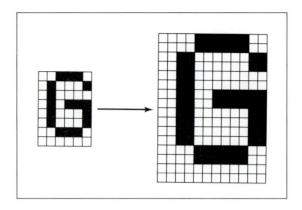

Figure 13.37.
Pixel doubling to scale a character.

A similar problem arises when one wants to rotate a bitmapped-defined character shape. It is easy to flip a character upside down (rotate by 180°) or even to reverse it by reflection (how?), but rotations by arbitrary angles again require refashioning each character shape. However, the special case of a rotation by 90° turns out to be relatively simple, as we shall find later.

Drill Exercise

13.25. Designing Characters. Design the most pleasing looking characters, a, A, r, R, ?, and 3, inside cells of r rows and c columns. Do this for each of the following cell sizes (r, c): (6, 4), (10, 8), (14, 12), assuming the display pixels are square (see Bigelow 1985).

A cell size of (5, 3) contains 15 pixels and so permits 2^{15} different pixel patterns. Can all of the printable ASCII characters be drawn in such a cell so that they are distinguishable (and recognizable)?

13.26. Scaling Down Characters. One way to reduce the size of a character defined in a cell is to cut in half the cell size in both dimensions. Then each pixel in the reduced cell must "mimic" what was a 2-by-2 array of pixels in the original cell. Develop an algorithm that produces a (6, 5) pixel pattern for a (12, 10) cell (12 rows and 10 columns). One approach will set each new pixel to 1 if two or more pixels in the 2-by-2 array are 1. Is this a good rule?

13.7.2 More Examples of Using *Show*( ) and *Store*( )

Some other tasks described here are made easy by the use of offscreen memory and the utilities *Show*( ) and *Store*( ). Each is enhanced by rapid transfer between the frame buffer and offscreen memory. When altering the visible image, the usual goal is to update the screen image during the "retrace interval" before a new scan begins (see Figure 2.6). Then the update appears instantaneous.

Window Scrolling

In applications such as word processors, the screen frequently fills with text, line by line. To make room for a new line of text at the bottom, all of the text above must be scrolled up one line (discarding the top line of text, of course), as suggested in Figure 13.38. To do this, the rectangle containing all but the top line is moved up one line by copying it, thereby overwriting what was previously there. Then a blank line is copied into the position of the last row.

Maintaining Multiple Windows

Many applications today use several overlapping windows to give the user glimpses into different parts of a file, or different processes. Figure 13.39 shows

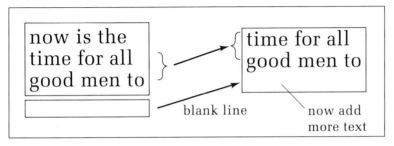

Figure 13.38.
Scrolling in a window.

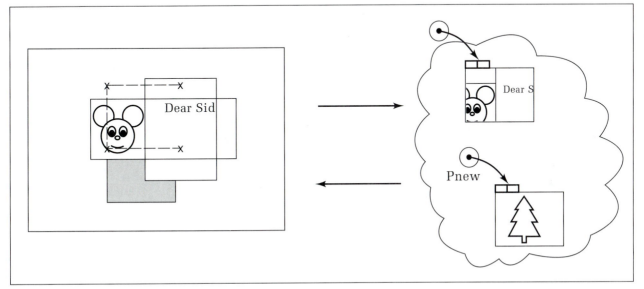

Figure 13.39.
Adding a window.

a display with several windows. Portions of one window overlap and obscure portions of another. Consider first the process of drawing another window at the position indicated. The region that is about to be obscured by the new window is copied to offscreen memory using *Store( )* in order to preserve it. Then the new window is "opened" at the designated spot. Whatever appears in this window is copied from offscreen memory by a *Show( )*. A "background" pattern can be copied to the screen if the window is initially empty. Later if this window must disappear, its contents are first *Store( )*-ed, and then the original rectangle is *Show( )*-n to restore the image.

This scheme works well when the image in an obscured window is "frozen" while the window is covered. Things become considerably more complicated, on the other hand, when the image in each window changes at will. The problem is how to handle the parts of images in a window that change while they are obscured. When the underlying window is later uncovered, its image must be up-to-date. Several schemes are discussed in the literature (O'Reilly 1988, Pike 1983). Often (as with *X*-windows) it is the application's responsibility to keep track of what happens in these windows and to regenerate the image when the window is uncovered each time.

Cursor Management

Offscreen memory is also useful for maintaining the cursor in interactive applications. It provides an alternative to using *xor* mode drawing as we described above. When the cursor is moved over the display (perhaps by a mouse), it obscures the portions of the image it overlaps. These obscured portions must reappear intact as the cursor moves on. Figure 13.40 shows how this can be done by copying bitmaps. The arrow shape of the cursor is placed in a bitmap (Figure 13.40a) and stored offscreen, as in Figure 13.40b. Suppose the cursor is originally placed at A over some text. Before drawing it there, the block of text that is about to be obscured is copied to offscreen memory to preserve it. When the cursor is moved to new position B, a sequence of three steps is taken:

● The previous image is restored from offscreen memory to A.

● A new rectangle is moved to offscreen memory from B.

● The cursor image is copied to B.

One problem with cursor management using *Show*( ) is that the background (white) areas in the cursor bitmap (Figure 13.40a) do not appear to be transparent. Rather, they are copied into the destination and so blot out the picture underneath. This effect is shown in Figure 13.41b, along with the more desirable transparent background in Figure 13.41c. When this blotting-out effect cannot be tolerated, the more powerful BitBLT operation should be used.

Figure 13.40.
Managing the cursor using offscreen memory.

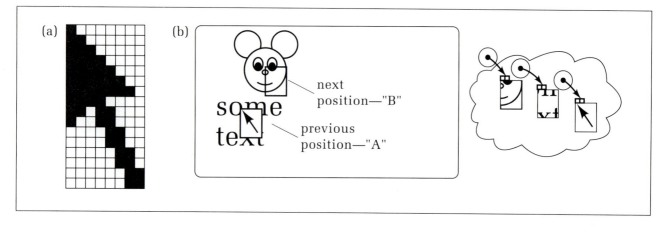

Figure 13.41.
Background of cursor is not transparent.

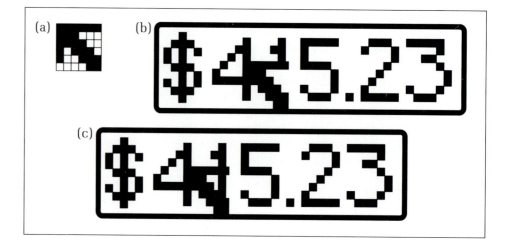

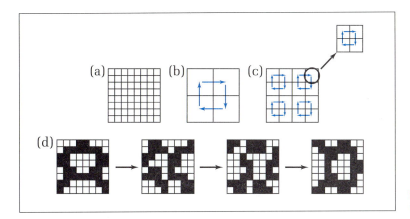

Figure 13.42.
Rotating a bitmap by 90°.

Ninety-Degree Rotations

As we mentioned, it is not difficult to rotate certain bitmaps through a 90° angle. For a square bitmap whose number of rows and columns is a power of 2, the rotation can be carried out by a clever sequence of bitmap copies, as suggested in Figure 13.42. An 8-by-8 bitmap (Figure 13.42a) is to be rotated clockwise by 90°. First, each of its 4-by-4 quadrants is simply shifted to its neighboring quadrant in a clockwise direction (Figure 13.42b). In the next step, each of the 2-by-2 quadrants of each of the larger quadrants is similarly shifted (Figure 13.42c). Finally, each of these smaller quadrants is similarly shifted: Individual pixels are copied into their neighboring spots. An example is shown in Figure 13.42d. This method has been called **parallel recursive subdivision**.

Drill Exercises

13.27. Simulating a Rotation. Carry out (by hand) a rotation through −90° of an example 8-by-8 bitmap, drawing each of the intermediate stages. In general, for a bitmap with 2^n rows and 2^n columns, how many bitmap copies must be performed?

13.8 The BitBLT Operation

Show( ) and *Store*( ) can be integrated into a single function with some added capabilities that vastly increase their power and applicability. The operation has become known as **BitBLT** (pronounced "bitblit"), which stands for Bit boundary BLock Transfer. It is also frequently called a **raster op** (Ingalls 1978, Newman and Sproull 1979). Just as bitmaps are sometimes called **pixelmaps** when more than one bit per pixel is involved, BitBLTs are sometimes called **pixelBLTs**. But we again shall follow tradition and use BitBLT uniformly.

A BitBLT is sometimes performed in software, but it has become such a fundamental and pervasive operation that several graphics processors and specially designed VLSI chips have been crafted to perform BitBLTs at very high speeds (in the order of 100 million pixels/second). A few parameters are written to the BitBLT chip, which then takes over and interacts directly with the system bus to move the data (National Semiconductor 1987). The BitBLT processor is a low-level device because it deals with individual addresses and bits of machine words and can manipulate them very rapidly. The programmer develops higher-level routines that interact with the processor, commanding it to perform a complex BitBLT operation.

In this section we shall examine the BitBLT operation and see the wealth of duties it performs.

Definition of the BitBLT Operation

There are several versions of the BitBLT that differ in various details. In its simplest form, BitBLT copies a source rectangle of pixels to a destination rectangle of the same height and width. Unlike *Store*( ) and *Show* ( ), which treat on- and off-screen memory differently, the source or the destination (or even both) may reside in either on- or off-screen memory. The BitBLT processor keeps track of the two rectangles in a simple manner: It stores the x- and y-coordinates of the upper left corner of each rectangle and also records their height and width (in pixels). It is therefore simplest to use the mental model of memory as a large 2D "sheet," as depicted in Figure 13.43. The processor makes all necessary conversions between an (x, y) pair and the corresponding address in memory (see the exercises). Two BitBLTs are shown, one that "blits" an on-screen source to an offscreen destination and one that is about to blit in the other direction.

Instead of just copying each source pixel to the corresponding destination pixel, the BitBLT does its copying using a read–modify–write cycle, just as with *xor* drawing. The destination pixel that it writes is a logical combination of the source pixel (*src*) and the current destination pixel (*dst*), as in $dst := dst\ op\ src$, in which *op* is some logical operator such as *and* or *xor*. Thus each "new" destination pixel is computed by applying *op* to the "old" destination pixel and the source pixel.

Assume, for simplicity, that there is one bit/pixel. Pixel values are treated as logical ones and zeros. There are 16 possible logical functions of the two variables *src* and *dst*, and BitBLT allows the programmer to choose any one of these for the combination operator. Some of the most important ones are listed next, and some are shown in Figure 13.44. The association of white or black with 0

Figure 13.43.
Alternative model of on- and offscreen memory.

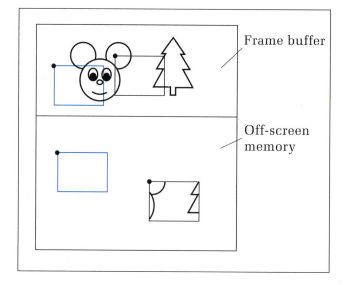

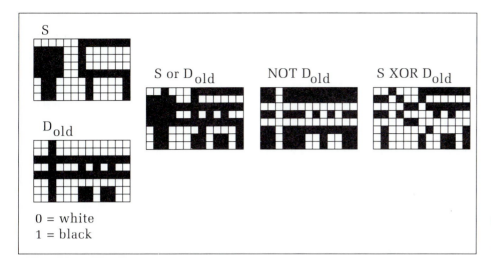

Figure 13.44.
Some logical combinations of source and destination.

and 1 can be made either way. Earlier we said that 0 implies black and 1 implies white, as when turning a pixel on in a CRT display makes it glow. Here it is convenient to reverse that and to think of printing on a piece of white paper: 0 implies white (no ink), and 1 implies black (with ink).

- *dst* := *src*: The current destination is ignored, and the source is painted in. This is equivalent to painting the source "over" the destination, obscuring whatever was previously there.

- *dst* := 0: All zeros are painted in, thereby clearing the region to the background color—white.

- *dst* := **not** *dst*: The current destination is inverted; white and black are interchanged.

- *dst* := *src* **or** *dst*: The pixel is 1 if either of the source or destination pixels is 1. This has the effect of "painting" the source "under" the destination, that is, putting the black ink of the source beneath the black paint of the destination. Any 0 pixels in the source obscured by 1 pixels in the destination become invisible. This is precisely the effect desired when managing a cursor that has some black background, as in Figure 13.41. Using the **or** mode thus circumvents the "blotting" effect that accompanies *Show* ( ).

- *dst* := *src* **xor** *dst*: The source is *xor*-ed with the current destination. A pixel appears black where the source and old destination are different, which can be useful for comparing two images to see at which pixels they differ.

Drill Exercises

13.28. **The Address of (x, y).** Suppose the computer word is 16 bits long and that the one bit/pixel frame buffer is 512-by-512 pixels in size. Suppose further that its upper left corner corresponds to address 32768. Thus the pixel at $(0, 0)$ is determined by the zero-th bit of the word at 32768, and the pixel at $(9, 0)$ corresponds to the ninth bit of this same word. Each row of 512 pixels consumes 32 words of memory, and so the leftmost pixel of the i-th row is the zero-th bit of the word having address $32768 + i \times 32$, for $i = 0, 1, \ldots$. Where is the bit located that determines $(x, y) = (35,118)$?

Clipping Within BitBLT

A BitBLT processor also usually provides for a clipping rectangle. Before each pixel in the destination is drawn, its coordinates are compared with the boundaries of the clipping rectangle, and the pixel will be drawn only if it lies within the boundaries. This can be done rapidly in hardware within the processor. The clipping rectangle effectively limits the region of the destination in which drawing can take place.

Using a Halftone Pattern

Other enhancements to BitBLT are popular too. In some versions the source is first "masked" using a **halftone pattern** to create the "masked source," *masked_src*, which is then combined with the destination as before: *dst := dst op masked_src*. The ingredients are as follows:

- The halftone mask is stored in a bitmap of some size, such as 16-by-16 pixels. If the mask is smaller than the source, it will be replicated (tiled) until it attains the size of the source. Figure 13.45a shows an example source and halftone mask.

- The (tiled) halftone mask is combined pixel by pixel with the source pattern according to the **halftone mode**. The use of the mode gives the programmer control of the "image" that is combined with the destination. This mode can take four values, with the following effect:

src: The masked source is simply the source itself; the halftone pattern is ignored.

mask: Ignore the source and use the halftone pattern itself.

black: All pixels are set to 1 (black); ignore both source and halftone (see Figure 13.45b).

and: The source and halftone mask are logically *and*-ed pixel by pixel: Each pixel is 1 only if both the source and halftone pixels are 1 (see Figure 13.45c).

Figure 13.45.
Using the halftone mask.

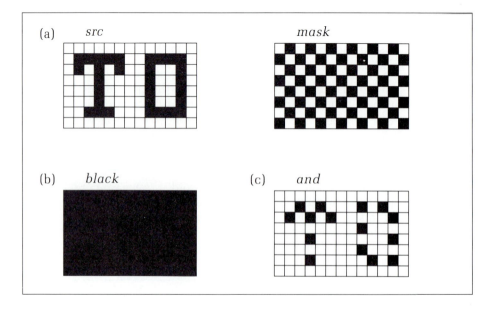

(a)   *src*   *mask*

(b)   *black*   (c)   *and*

All of the applications (scrolling, writing text, pop-up windows, and the like) that used *Show*( ) and *Store*( ) can be accomplished easily with the BitBLT. Some additional uses of it are

- *Boldfacing*: Text characters can easily be drawn in boldface by drawing the character twice, the second version being slightly displaced to the right and **or**-ed with the first version.

- *Drawing thick horizontal or vertical lines*: A thick horizontal or vertical straight line is drawn as a long and narrow filled rectangle. Thick lines are therefore rapidly drawn by blit-ing a rectangle to the appropriate position in the destination.

- *Magnification*: Consider the problem of enlarging an icon or character (Figure 13.46a) by means of pixel replication. Suppose you want to enlarge it by a factor of 2 in the *x*-direction and 3 in the *y*-direction. This can be done efficiently using BitBLT, as shown in Figure 13.46 (also see the exercises).

    1. "Spread by 1 in *x*." Copy each column of the source to the destination in turn, but position them farther apart, so that a blank column appears between each (see Figure 13.46b).

    2. "Smear" the result: **or** it with itself shifted one position to the right, thereby filling in the blank columns (see Figure 13.46c).

    3. Similarly spread by 2 in *y* (see Figure 13.46d).

    4. Finally, smear the result in *y* (see Figure 13.46e).

13.9 Creating More Shades of Gray: Halftoning and Dithering

Often a display supports an inadequate number of shades of gray or colors for a particular set of images. For example, bilevel displays produce only black and white, and many low-cost terminals permit only four or eight colors. How can one produce gradations of shade or color on such terminals?

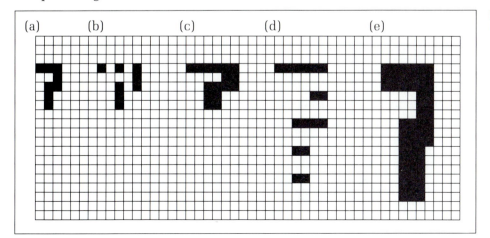

Figure 13.46.
Magnification using BitBLTs.

(a) (b) (c) (d) (e)

One method is "halftoning," which trades spatial resolution for intensity or color resolution. Newspapers are bilevel, printed using blobs of only black ink. But look carefully at a photo in a newspaper and you will see different shades of gray. These shades of gray are mimicked by varying the size of the blobs. The eye combines the blobs, thereby perceiving something like an average darkness over small regions. Closely spaced, large blobs of ink therefore appear much darker than do small blobs. Because the image is made up of distinct blobs, it exhibits less spatial resolution than it would if composed of solid lines and shapes.

In graphics and image processing, digital halftoning, or "patterning," uses arrays of small dots instead of variable-sized blobs, and again spatial resolution is exchanged for intensity resolution. Consider an original image given by a 16-by-16 array of pixels whose intensity values range from 0 to 4. Once again we adopt the printing analogy and associate level 0 with white (no ink) and 4 with black. This image exhibits five intensity levels. We wish to put this image on a bilevel display that shows only two intensity levels, with 0 for white and 1 for black. To do this we associate each original pixel with a 2-by-2 block of bilevel pixels, some black and some white, according to the correspondence shown in Figure 13.47. Depending on the number of black elements, the effective average blackness has values 0, 1/4, 2/4, 3/4, and 4/4. The original 16-by-16 image can be viewed on a bilevel display as a 32-by-32 pixel array. Viewing this from a distance, the eye manufactures various shades of gray out of the black and white patterns.

The positions of the black elements in the cell in Figure 13.47 were chosen to be as "irregular" as possible so as to avoid streaks or other artifacts in the image. If, instead, either of the patterns

$$\begin{pmatrix} 1 & 1 \\ 0 & 0 \end{pmatrix} \text{ or } \begin{pmatrix} 1 & 0 \\ 1 & 0 \end{pmatrix} \tag{13.15}$$

were used, the image might exhibit horizontal or vertical stripes in certain patterns.

Figure 13.48 shows an example of an image viewed on a bilevel display when 2-by-2 patterning is used. The five effective gray levels are clearly visible.

Larger cell sizes can be used to create a larger number of gray levels. Figure 13.49 shows a pattern using a 3-by-3 cell, which achieves ten gray levels. In general, an n-by-n cell of zeros and ones can produce $n^2 + 1$ gray levels (why?). Patterning is most applicable when the original image is of lower resolution than is the display device to be used.

13.9.1 Ordered Dither

In some situations we don't want to increase the number of pixels displayed: The number of bilevel pixels is required to be the same as the number of "gray-scale" pixels in the original image. We must then replace each original pixel intensity value with either 1 or 0. How do we decide when to use a 0 and when a 1?

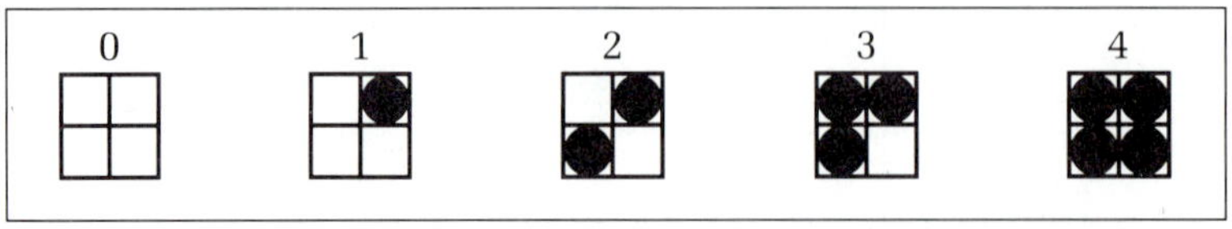

Figure 13.47.
2-by-2 patterns.

Figure 13.48.
Example of using 2-by-2 patterning. (Courtesy of Brett Diamond.)

One easy way to choose the pixel value is by **thresholding**. We define for each pixel a threshold value; for the pixel at (x, y) the value $t(x, y)$ is somehow specified. Suppose the original value in row y and column x is $p(x, y)$. We replace it by 0 or 1 according to the following rule:

if $p[x, y] < t[x, y]$ **then** *SetPixel*$(x, y, 0)$
                 else *SetPixel*$(x, y, 1)$;

The same threshold value could be used for every pixel, but that would create severe "contouring" in the image, with "islands" of black and white. (An example is given later.) Instead, an array of different thresholds is constructed by choosing a **dither pattern** and tiling the image with it. For example, suppose the pixels in the original image have values in 0..3. Choose the following 2-by-2 dither pattern:

$$\begin{pmatrix} 0 & 2 \\ 3 & 1 \end{pmatrix} \tag{13.16}$$

This pattern is laid down on the original image in a repeating checkerboard fashion, as shown in Figure 13.50a. The threshold value for each pixel value, $p(x, y)$, is simply the element of the dither pattern that falls on the pixel position. If the pattern is placed in a 2-by-2 matrix, D: **array** $[0..1, 0..1]$ **of** *integer*, the tiling process will be equivalent to defining the threshold array $t[x, y]$ according to

$t[x, y] := D[x \bmod 2, y \bmod 2]$

The array $t[,]$ need never actually be built: Each value is easily found as needed by indexing into $D[,]$ in this fashion.

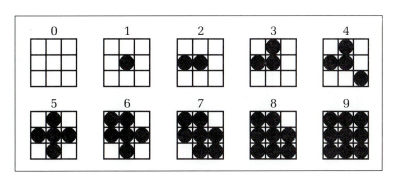

Figure 13.49.
3-by-3 patterns.

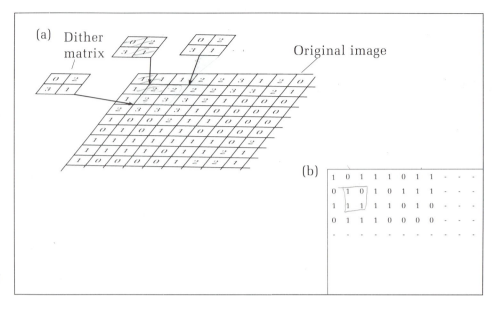

Figure 13.50.
The image tiled with the dither pattern.

Figure 13.50b shows the resulting bilevel image. The effect is like adding a random noise to the original image to "roughen" it and then thresholding. Note that for regions in the image that have a constant intensity, dithering yields the same effect as does halftoning: The proper fraction of final pixels is black, giving the proper average intensity. Figure 13.51 shows three versions of a computer-generated image. Part (a) shows the original 256-by-256 image with 256 gray levels. Part (b) shows simple thresholding: All pixel values less than 128 are set to 0, and those above are set to 1. Part (c) shows the original after 2-by-2 dithering. All pixel values are 0 or 1, but even so the original pattern is still well reproduced.

Larger dither patterns that produce more levels are also possible. Matrices of size 4-by-4, 8-by-8, and so on can be generated from the 2-by-2 matrix $D[,]$, using a recursive relation (see the exercises).

Note that various patterns of dots visible in Figure 13.51 could be considered objectionable, and many alternative dithering techniques attempt to overcome these artifacts. A good survey is presented along with some recent results in Knuth 1987. We also examine the application of dithering to colored images in Chapter 16.

Figure 13.51.
Example of 2-by-2 dithering.

(a)

(b)

(c)

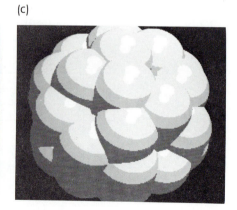

Drill Exercise

13.29. Larger Dither Matrices. Jarvis developed a recursion relation for generating dither matrices of sizes 2^n-by-2^n (Jarvis et al. 1976). If D_2 represents the 2-by-2 matrix $D[,]$, we can generate D_4, D_8, and so on by placing four submatrices into the pattern:

$$D_n = \begin{pmatrix} 4D_{n/2} & 4D_{n/2} + 2U_{n/2} \\ 4D_{n/2} + 3U_{n/2} & 4D_{n/2} + U_{n/2} \end{pmatrix} \quad (13.17)$$

(for $n \geq 4$) in which matrix U_n is an n-by-n matrix of all ones. Find the 4-by-4 dither matrix D_n by using the preceding recursive relation. *Answer:* The first row turns out to be 0 8 2 10.

13.10 Summary

The ability of a raster device to display regions solidly filled with a pattern of colors gives it a special importance in graphics. Raster devices build their images in an orderly array of small dots, each dot having a controllable color. Patterns of dots are integrated by the eye into recognizable objects, such as lines, text characters, and polygons. The raster's spatially discrete nature gives it great power but also offers challenges to the programmer.

This chapter discussed a variety of algorithms that manage image generation on a raster display. We examined methods for drawing straight lines and circles, as well as techniques for filling different types of regions with various patterns and colors.

A notion that pervades much of graphics is that of coherence. Pixel patterns for meaningful images are rarely "noiselike," having no structure. Instead, they tend to have a certain persistence: If a group of neighboring pixels has some property (say, being red), this same property is quite likely enjoyed by other nearby pixels. To speed up certain algorithms, we exploit this type of coherence wherever possible, sometimes at the expense of additional data structures and significant amounts of storage.

The jaggies plague raster images: The raster's discrete nature makes lines jump from scan line to scan line in a way that can be very distracting, particularly in animations. Thus antialiasing attempts to smooth over these irregularities, sometimes at the expense of some blurring of detail. We discussed several methods for softening the effects of aliasing.

Compared with a frame buffer, color lookup tables contain only a small number of bits, and so it is easy to change all of their values in a small fraction of a second. This ability can be exploited to make rapid changes in the displayed image, even providing a simple animation capability. The programmer can also use the LUT to manipulate individual bit planes of the frame buffer, so that text "overlays" can be created to provide convenient interaction with the user.

Because a frame buffer is just another form of memory, one can move images back and forth between the frame buffer and system memory. This opens the door to a host of techniques for manipulating images, such as windowing, scrolling, and cursor control. Because there are so many pixels in a frame buffer, one must be able to move large amounts of data very quickly. Thus some of the important data-copying processes are often carried out in hardware. The most noteworthy is the BitBLT, which goes beyond mere copying and can form complex logical combinations between a source image and the current displayed image. We described the BitBLT, as well as various applications to which it is well suited.

Finally, we addressed the problem of displaying "gray-scale" images on a bilevel display. An approximation of an original gray-scale image can be displayed by judiciously choosing the patterns of closely packed pixels: The eye is tricked into seeing the "average" intensity of lightness or darkness. Done properly, this can preserve much of the detail of the original image, although the result tends to look "noisy" or somewhat blurred.

Programming Exercises

13.30. A Complete Bresenham Algorithm. Develop a Bresenham algorithm that works with all cases of lines. Try to make the routine as efficient as possible.

13.31. Bresenham's Algorithm in Assembly Language. Implement a complete Bresenham's algorithm in machine language for an available host/graphics display. Make the code for the innermost loops as efficient as possible. Test the speed of the machine-language version against that of the Pascal version. Also test whether special code for horizontal and vertical lines improves the algorithm's speed.

13.32. Drawing in Patterns. Extend Bresenham's line algorithm to draw lines using a pattern of 16 bits. Arrange it so that if a polyline is drawn, the pattern will continue uninterrupted from one line segment to the next.

13.33. Ensuring That Endpoints Are On. Extend the pattern-drawing routine in the preceding exercise so that when drawing a polyline, the pixel at each vertex is always on. Otherwise, the pixel pattern will adhere as closely as possible to the given pattern.

13.34. Run-Based Region Fill. Implement the region-fill algorithm that scans for runs of pixels and fills them, in the case of a 4-connected, boundary-defined region. Test the routine on several example regions. Show how to adjust the routine for 8-connected and for interior-defined regions.

13.35. Implementing Edge Shortening. Design a routine that traverses a polygon and tests for a local extreme at each vertex, as described in Section 13.3. The routine shortens the lower edge appropriately to avoid the parity problem in filling the polygon.

13.36. Table-Fill Algorithm. The table-fill algorithm provides very fast filling of a certain class of polygons. Each edge of the polygon is first scan converted (perhaps using Bresenham's algorithm) to generate the (x, y) pairs that occur along its edges. As each pair (x, y) is formed, it is tested against two arrays, $min[y]$ and $max[y]$, that contain for each y-value the minimum and maximum x-values encountered so far. If $x < min[y]$, then $min[y]$ is updated to

contain the new x-value, and similarly for $max[y]$. The polygon is then filled by drawing in the run of pixels from $min[y]$ to $max[y]$ for each scan line y. No sorting is required, and so this algorithm is fast.

What are the geometric conditions on a polygon that guarantee it will be filled correctly? Give several examples of polygons for which the method works and several for which it fails.

13.37. Scan Converting Several Polygons. Implement the algorithm discussed in Section 13.3 for painting several polygons of different priorities. Take care to handle all special cases properly. Test the routine on a variety of sample polygon scenes.

13.38. Fence-Fill Algorithm. The fence-fill method for polygonal regions uses the notion of "complementing" or "reversing" certain pixels in the picture. For a bilevel display, a pixel of 1 (white) is set to 0 (black), and vice versa. The essential property of complementing is that doing it twice restores the original value.

Erect a vertical "fence"—perhaps through some vertex of the polygon to be filled. Set all pixels to 0. Now for each edge of the polygon do the following: On each scan line through the edge, complement all pixels from the edge to the fence. Pixels along a scan line that lie outside the polygon are complemented an even number of times and so are 0. Those that lie inside are complemented an odd number of times and so are 1 (filled). This is independent of where the fence lies.

Draw example polygons on paper and use the fence-fill method to fill the polygons by hand. Show that the method works for multiple polygons and for polygons with holes. What will happen if the method is used on a single line rather than on a polygon having a true inside and outside?

13.39. Reverse Mode Drawing. Drawing a pattern in "reverse mode" can also be used to erase a line and restore the original pixel values. A b-bit frame buffer has $N = 2^b$ possible pixel values, ranging from 0 to $2^b - 1$. Drawing a pixel in reverse mode means replacing the current pixel value d with the value $f(d) = N - d$. Note that this drawing function is an "involution": Drawing twice restores the original, because $f(f(d)) = N - f(d) = N - (N - d) = d$. Describe how this technique operates for rubber band drawing, and what colors are seen along the rubber band line as it crosses pixels of various colors. Is it the same as drawing in *xor* mode? For a single bit-plane, ($b = 1$), what is the difference between reverse mode and *xor* drawing?

13.40.   Implementing *Show*( ) and *Store*( ). Obtain or develop on your system the utilities to reserve offscreen memory for a bitmap and to copy bitmaps between the frame buffer and offscreen memory.

13.41.   Copying Portions of an Image. Implement two forms of the routine *Copy_block*(*x* : *col*; *y* : *row*; *rect1* : *pixrect*) which copies the region of display memory described by *rect1* to the rectangle with upper left-hand corner (*x*, *y*) (recall Section 13.7). The first form uses *Show*(*x*, *y*, *Store*(*rect1*)) and forms an intermediate bitmap. Be sure to release the bitmap storage after performing the copy. The second form copies individual pixels directly. When the two rectangles overlap, it chooses the correct order of pixel copying to avoid destroying image data.

13.42.   The 16 Logical Combinations That Are Used in the BitBLT. For a sample source, *src*, and a destination pattern, *dst*, draw the resulting image that uses *dst* := *src op dst* for each of the 16 binary logical operators *op*.

13.43.   Magnifying Characters. Write out pseudocode that uses BitBLTs to magnify bitmaps, as described, showing each of the steps necessary to magnify a 4-row-by-5-column bitmap by 3 in the horizontal direction and by 7 in the vertical direction. Count the number of BitBLTs required. More generally, how many BitBLTs are required to enlarge a source that is R rows by C columns by X in the *x*-direction and Y in the *y*-direction?

Chapter 14

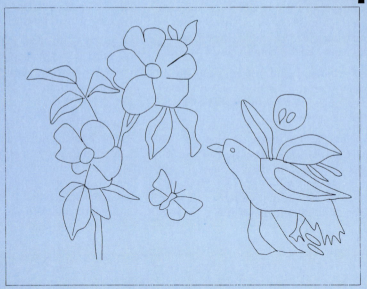

Curve and Surface Design for CAD

I could never make out what those damned dots meant.

Lord Randolph Churchill

You appear in splendid shape today, m'dear.

anonymous

Goals of the Chapter

- To develop a set of tools for designing curves and surfaces
- To examine some basic techniques of computer-aided geometric design
- To formulate Bezier and B-spline curves mathematically
- To develop methods for defining and drawing surface patches

14.1 Introduction

In this chapter we develop powerful tools for generating and representing smooth curves and surfaces. Like the curves of Chapter 4 and the surfaces of Chapter 9, these shapes are represented by parametric functions, such as $\mathbf{p}(t) = (x(t), y(t))$ for a 2D curve, or $\mathbf{p}(u, v) = X(u, v)\mathbf{i} + Y(u, v)\mathbf{j} + Z(u, v)\mathbf{k}$ for a surface. Given the component functions $x(t)$, $X(u,v)$, and so on, it is easy to draw the corresponding curve or surface using the techniques presented in those chapters. The issue before us is to determine the proper forms for these functions.

Whereas the curves and surfaces considered up to now have been based on relatively simple mathematical formulas—such as $\mathbf{p}(t) = (A\ \cos(2\pi t),\ B\ \sin(2\pi t))$ for an ellipse—here we want to develop tools that allow a designer to specify various shapes based on data. Assume, for example, that the curve of Figure 14.1a is sketched on a piece of paper and taped to a data tablet. It might be a part of an emerging design for a car fender, a turbine blade, or even the casing of an electric drill. Suppose we want to capture the shape of this curve in a form that permits it to be reproduced at will, adjusted in shape if desired, sent to a machine for automatic cutting or molding, or whatever. There is most likely no simple formula that matches it exactly. Can it be represented "accurately" with a small set of isolated points, $\mathbf{p}_1, \mathbf{p}_2, \ldots$?

One way to capture the shape is to use the tablet as a *Locator* and to sample the curve at a set of 30 or 40 closely spaced points. Maybe then some mathematical function can be found and adjusted to pass through these points in order to match the curve almost everywhere.

Another way is suggested in Figure 14.1b. We *Locate* a small set of so-called **control points,** as shown in color, and let the computer use an algorithm to build its own curve (shown dashed in color) based on these points. Because the orig-

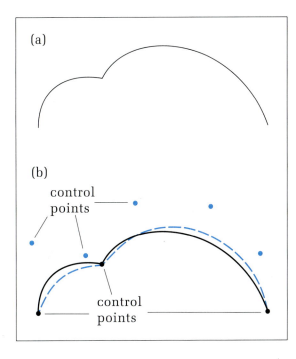

Figure 14.1.
A curve design scenario.

inal curve and the computer-based one probably will not agree very well on the first try, we shall move some of the control points and let the computer generate a new curve based on the new set. This process iterates until the computer-based curve matches the original satisfactorily. Now the curve is captured by the small set of control points and can be regenerated on demand.

This scenario of iterative curve design is a staple in the field of computer-aided geometric design (CAGD) and is often used when designing an item to be manufactured. In this chapter we shall build up a set of techniques for curve and surface design. Choosing from the many approaches one might take (see, for instance, Bartels et al. 1987, Farin 1988, Faux and Pratt 1979), the emphasis is placed on interactive curve design using Bezier and B-spline curves. These families of curves have become very popular in CAD applications. Our presentation will necessarily be brief, but we shall provide enough detail to enable you to write programs to perform interactive curve and surface design and to create drawings of the objects so designed.

For simplicity we begin with planar curves, $\mathbf{p}(t) = (x(t), y(t))$, and then see that the techniques extend easily to 3D curves, $\mathbf{p}(t) = (x(t), y(t), z(t))$, as well. In Section 14.7 we develop similar tools for designing surfaces.

14.2   Building a Curve Out of Control Points

We shall describe here a method that defines a curve, $\mathbf{p}(t)$, based on a set of points. It is based on the simple and elegant de Casteljau algorithm (Fari 1988) and leads easily to Bezier curves, which are fundamental to computer-aided geometric design (CAGD). Bezier curves were developed by P. de Casteljau in 1959 and independently by P. Bezier around 1962. They were formulated as ingredients in CAD systems at two automobile companies, Citroën and Rénault, to help design shapes for car bodies.

14.2.1 The de Casteljau Algorithm

The de Casteljau algorithm uses a sequence of points to construct for each value of t of interest a well-defined value for the point $\mathbf{p}(t)$. Thus it provides a way to generate a curve from a set of points. Changing the points changes the curve. The construction is based on a sequence of familiar "in-betweening" or linear interpolation steps that are easy to implement. Because in-betweening is such a well-behaved procedure, it is possible to deduce many valuable properties of the curves that it generates.

A Parabola Based on Three Points

Start with three points, $\mathbf{p}_0$, $\mathbf{p}_1$, and $\mathbf{p}_2$, as shown in Figure 14.2a. Choose some value of t between 0 and 1, and locate the point $\mathbf{p}_0^1$ that is fraction t of the way along the line from $\mathbf{p}_0$ to $\mathbf{p}_1$. Similarly, locate $\mathbf{p}_1^1$ fraction t between the endpoints $\mathbf{p}_1$ and $\mathbf{p}_2$ (using the same t). This is standard "in-betweening" (recall Chapter 7), and so we know that the new points can be expressed as

$$\mathbf{p}_0^1(t) = (1 - t)\mathbf{p}_0 + t\mathbf{p}_1$$
$$\mathbf{p}_1^1(t) = (1 - t)\mathbf{p}_1 + t\mathbf{p}_2$$

(14.1)

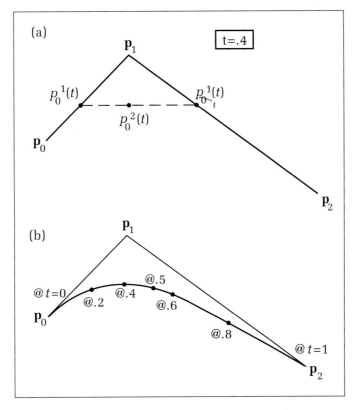

Figure 14.2.
The de Casteljau algorithm for three points.

Now repeat the linear interpolation step on these points (again using the same t): Find the point, $\mathbf{p}_0{}^2(t)$, that lies the same fraction of the way between them:

$$\mathbf{p}_0{}^2(t) = (1 - t)\mathbf{p}_0{}^1 + t\mathbf{p}_1{}^1 \qquad (14.2)$$

as shown. If this process is carried out for each t between 0 and 1, the curve $\mathbf{p}(t) = \mathbf{p}_0{}^2(t)$ will be generated, as shown in Figure 14.2b. (Note that for $t = .5$, we are simply finding the "midpoint between midpoints" for the three given points.)

What shape does the curve have? By direct substitution of Equation 14.1 into Equation 14.2, we obtain

$$\mathbf{p}(t) = (1 - t)^2\mathbf{p}_0 + 2t(1 - t)\mathbf{p}_1 + t^2\mathbf{p}_2 \qquad (14.3)$$

Because this is quadratic in t, the curve is a parabola. It will still be a parabola even if t is allowed to vary from $-\infty$ to ∞.

We thus have a well-defined process, once given three points, for generating a curve. This may seem pedestrian, but the method generalizes immediately to repeated linear interpolation for $(L + 1)$ points.

Drill Exercises

14.1. Generate the Curve by Hand. Using the de Casteljau method with the points $(0, 0)$, $(2, 4)$, and $(6, 1)$, locate $\mathbf{p}(t)$ on graph paper for the t-values 0, .2, .4, .6, .8, and 1.

14.2. Quadratic Curves Must Be Planar. Justify the assertion that there is a unique quadratic curve that passes through a set of three (distinct) points. Remembering that three (noncollinear) points determine a plane, show that the quadratic they determine never leaves this plane. Thus a parabola can never deviate from a plane. For extra benefit, show that a cubic curve can be nonplanar.

The Casteljau Algorithm for (L + 1) Points

This process generalizes gracefully to the case in which $(L + 1)$ points $\mathbf{p}_0$, $\mathbf{p}_1$, $\ldots$, $\mathbf{p}_L$ are given. For a given value of t, we successively build up the r-th "generation" of in-betweens, $\mathbf{p}_i^r(t)$, from the previous $(r - 1)$-st generation, according to

$$\mathbf{p}_i^r(t) = (1 - t)\mathbf{p}_i^{r-1}(t) + t\mathbf{p}_{i+1}^{r-1}(t) \tag{14.4}$$

for each generation, $r = 1, \ldots, L$, and for $i = 0, \ldots, L - r$. The process starts by using $\mathbf{p}_i$ for $\mathbf{p}_i^0$.

The "final" generation, $\mathbf{p}_0^n(t)$, is called the **Bezier curve** for the points $\mathbf{p}_0$, $\mathbf{p}_1, \ldots, \mathbf{p}_L$. The points themselves are called **control points** or **Bezier points**, and the polygon formed by these points is called the **control polygon** or **Bezier polygon.**[1]

Figure 14.3 shows the Bezier curve based on four control points, along with the various contributors to the final point at $t = .5$. Evidently this is a cubic polynomial (see the following reminder on polynomials), as is explored in the exercises.

> **Reminder of Definition: An L-th-Degree Polynomial**
>
> Recall that an L-th-degree polynomial in t is a function given by
>
> $$a_0 + a_1t + a_2t^2 + \cdots + a_Lt^L \tag{14.5}$$
>
> where the list $a_0, a_1, \ldots, a_L$ is its *coefficients*, each of which is associated with one of the powers of t. For this to be L-th degree, we insist that $a_L \neq 0$. The *degree* is the highest power to which t is raised. The *order* is the number of coefficients in the polynomial ($L + 1$ here) and is always one greater than the degree.

Drill Exercises

14.3.   Show That the Four-Point Bezier Curve Is Cubic. By direct substitution similar to Equation 14.3, show that a Bezier curve based on four points is cubic in t. Find its parametric formula.

14.4.   Bezier Polygons Can Be Nonsimple. The control points (0, 0), (0, 1), (1, 0), and (1, 1) lead to a control polygon that intersects itself. Draw it on graph paper and find the resulting Bezier curve for several values of t. Sketch it.

Figure 14.3.
The Bezier curve based on four points.

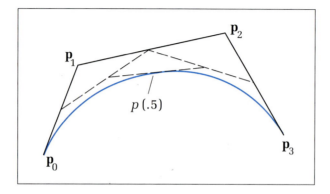

[1] Strictly speaking, the control polygon is a "control polyline" unless the first and last control points are connected. It has become common to use the term *polygon* in this context, however.

14.2.2 The Bernstein Form for Bezier Curves

The preceding approach develops a Bezier curve algorithmically but does not explicitly state its functional form. But there is also a "formula" for the Bezier curve that is easy to remember and is useful for analytical purposes. It generalizes the quadratic expression of Equation 14.3 and the cubic form in Exercise 14.3, in which we see that each term in the sum involves a product, $(1 - t)$, raised to some power, and t raised to another power (What is the sum of the two powers in each case?).

The Bezier curve, $\mathbf{p}(t)$, based on the $(L + 1)$ points $\mathbf{p}_0, \mathbf{p}_1, \ldots, \mathbf{p}_L$, is given by

$$\mathbf{p}(t) = \sum_{k=0}^{L} \mathbf{p}_k B_k{}^L(t) \qquad (14.6)$$

where the functions $B_k^L(t)$ are known as *Bernstein polynomials*. The k-th Bernstein polynomial is defined as

$$B_k{}^L(t) = \binom{L}{k}(1 - t)^{L-k}t^k \qquad (14.7)$$

where $\binom{L}{k}$ is the binomial coefficient function, the number of ways of choosing k items from a collection of L items. It is given by

$$\binom{L}{k} = \frac{L!}{k!(L - k)!} \text{ for } L \geq k \qquad (14.8)$$

and 0 otherwise. The Bernstein polynomials are easily remembered as the terms one gets when the expression $((1 - t) + t)^L$ is expanded out (as in Equation 14.3), that is, by multiplying out $((1 - t) + t)((1 - t) + t)\ldots((1 - t) + t)$ and collecting terms in $(1 - t)$ and t. Hence their sum is always 1 for any value of t (see the exercises). Each of the Bernstein polynomials is seen to be of degree L.[2]

Figure 14.4 shows the four Bernstein polynomials of degree 3 for t between 0 and 1. In the context of Equation 14.6 they are often called *blending functions*,

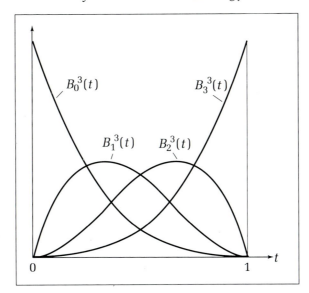

$B_0{}^3(t)$ $B_3{}^3(t)$

$B_1{}^3(t)$ $B_2{}^3(t)$

0   1 t

Figure 14.4.
The Bernstein polynomials of degree 3.

---

[2]Readers familiar with probability theory will also notice a strong resemblance between Equation 14.6 and an average over the binomial probability distribution.

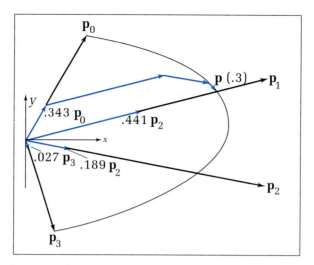

Figure 14.5.
Blending four vectors with
Bernstein polynomials.

because the vector $\mathbf{p}(t)$ is a "blend" of the four vectors $\mathbf{p}_0, \mathbf{p}_1, \ldots, \mathbf{p}_L$. For any given value of t, each Bernstein polynomial has some well-defined value that scales, or "weights," its corresponding vector. This is shown in Figure 14.5 for $t = .3$, in which the four polynomials have weights .343, .441, .189, and .027, respectively. The four weighted vectors are added using the parallelogram rule to form the vector $\mathbf{p}(.3)$. As t varies, the relative weights change, and so the blend of the four vectors also moves around the plane. Where is the blend at $t = 0$? At $t = 1$?

Drill Exercises

14.5. Building Intuition About Bezier Curves. Using Equation 14.6, compute the position of $\mathbf{p}(t)$ at the times $t = .2, .5, .9$, when the four control points are $(2, 3)$, $(6, 6)$, $(8, 1)$, and $(4, -3)$.

14.6. Recursion Relation for the Bernstein Polynomials. Show that the n-th-order Bernstein polynomial can always be formed from $(n - 1)$-th-order versions:

$$B_i^n(t) = (1 - t)B_i^{n-1}(t) + tB_{i-1}^{n-1}(t) \qquad (14.9)$$

where $B_0^0(t) = 1$, and where $B_j^n(t) = 0$ when j is not in the range $0, \ldots, n$. Hint: $\binom{n}{i} = \binom{n-1}{i} + \binom{n-1}{i-1}$.

14.7. Derive the Bernstein Form for Bezier Curves. Using induction with the de Casteljau algorithm, derive Equation 14.6 for the Bezier curve based on $(L + 1)$ points.

14.8. The Bernstein Polynomials Sum to 1. Use the fact that the Bernstein polynomials are the terms in $((1 - t) + t)^L$ to show that

$$\sum_{k=0}^{L} B_k^L(t) = 1 \qquad (14.10)$$

for any value of t.

14.3 Properties of Bezier Curves

Bezier curves have some important properties that make them well suited for CAGD. Exploring these properties and their proofs provides a great deal of insight into Bezier curves. These properties are later found to apply to B-splines as well.

Endpoint Interpolation

The Bezier curve $\mathbf{p}(t)$ based on control points $\mathbf{p}_0, \mathbf{p}_1, \ldots, \mathbf{p}_L$ does not generally pass through, or **interpolate,** all of the control points. But it always interpolates the first and last ones. This is a very useful property, because the designer thereby knows precisely where the Bezier curve will begin and end: at the first and last control points, respectively.

This property is apparent from the de Casteljau algorithm. For example, $\mathbf{p}(0)$ uses in-betweening where one moves 0 distance away from the first endpoint at each stage of the algorithm. Thus there is never deviation from $\mathbf{p}_0$.

The property may also be seen in Equation 14.6. The first and last Bernstein polynomials are $B_0{}^L(t) = (1 - t)^L$ and $B_L{}^L(t) = t^L$. Thus $B_0{}^L(t)$ has values 1 and 0 at $t = 0$ and 1, respectively. Similarly, $B_L{}^L(t)$ has values 0 and 1 at the two endpoints. See Figure 14.4 for an example. All the intermediate polynomials have terms in both t and $(1 - t)$, and consequently they disappear at both endpoints.

Affine Invariance

It is often important to subject a Bezier curve to an affine transformation in order to scale it, orient it, or position it for subsequent use. Suppose we wish to transform point $\mathbf{p}(t)$ on the Bezier curve of Equation 14.6 to the new point $\mathbf{p}'(t)$, using transformation matrix N and offset vector $\mathbf{tr}$ (recall Chapter 11). Thus

$$\mathbf{p}'(t) = \mathbf{p}(t)N + \mathbf{tr} = \sum_{k=0}^{L} \mathbf{p}_k B_k{}^L(t)N + \mathbf{tr} \qquad (14.11)$$

Must we transform every point in the curve separately? No, we just have to transform the control points and then use the same Bernstein form to re-create the transformed Bezier curve! This is what it means for a Bezier curve to be **affine invariant**. It is analogous to the property that affine transformations preserve straight lines, so that only their endpoints need be transformed to find the new line.

There are two simple ways to show that Bezier curves are affine invariant: (1) The de Castejau method reveals it geometrically, because in-betweening is preserved under an affine transformation, and the Bezier curve is determined by a sequence of in-betweenings. (2) The Bernstein form is used to show it analytically. Consider the curve

$$\sum_{k=0}^{L} (\mathbf{p}_k N + \mathbf{tr})B_k{}^L(t) \qquad (14.12)$$

formed by transforming each vector $\mathbf{p}_k$. To show that this is identical to $\mathbf{p}'$ in Equation 14.11, use linearity to write it as

$$\mathbf{p}'(t) = \sum_{k=0}^{L} \mathbf{p}_k N\, B_k{}^L(t) + \sum_{k=0}^{L} \mathbf{tr}B_k{}^L(t) \qquad (14.13)$$

But according to Equation 14.10, the second sum is just $\mathbf{tr}$ itself, which completes the proof.

Invariance Under Affine Parameter Transformations

The preceding Bezier curves are defined on the parametric interval $t\epsilon[0, 1]$, but it is sometimes convenient to let this be a different interval. Suppose we wish to define the Bezier curve (on the control points $\mathbf{p}_0, \mathbf{p}_1, \ldots, \mathbf{p}_L$ once again) as a parameter u varies over the interval from a to b. This is easily done by replacing each previous occurrence of t with

$$\frac{u - a}{b - a}$$

so that the Bezier curve now has the representation

$$\mathbf{p}'\,(u) = \sum_{k=0}^{L} \mathbf{p}_k B_k{}^{L}\!\left(\frac{u - a}{b - a}\right) \tag{14.14}$$

Notice that as u varies from a to b, the argument of each Bernstein polynomial varies from 0 to 1, as desired. Because the mapping from t to u given by $t = (u - a)/(b - a)$ is simply a translation followed by a scaling, it is clearly affine. The Bezier curve is invariant to this mapping in the sense that the same path is swept out by $\mathbf{p}'(\mathbf{u})$ for $u\epsilon[a, b]$ as is swept out by $\mathbf{p}(\mathbf{t})$ for $t\epsilon[0, 1]$.

Convex Hull Property

Another property that designers often rely on is that a Bezier curve, $\mathbf{p}(t)$, never wanders outside its convex hull.

Recall from Chapter 7 that the convex hull of the control points is the smallest convex set that contains them all. It is also the set of all convex combinations of the control points:

$$\sum_{k=0}^{L} \alpha_k \mathbf{p}_k \tag{14.15}$$

where each $\alpha_k \geq 0$ and they sum to 1.

But $\mathbf{p}(t)$ of Equation 14.6 is a convex combination of its control points for every t, as no Bernstein polynomial is ever negative, and we know that they sum to 1. Thus every point on the Bezier curve lies within the convex hull of the control points.

The convex hull property also follows immediately from the fact that each point on the curve is the result of in-betweening two points that are themselves in-betweens, and the in-betweening of two points forms a convex combination of them. Figure 14.6 illustrates how the designer can use the convex hull property. Even though the eight control points form a rather jagged control polygon, the designer knows the Bezier curve must flow smoothly between the two endpoints, never extending outside the convex hull.

Figure 14.6.
Using the convex hull property.

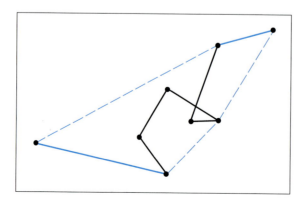

Linear Precision

Can a Bezier curve be a simple straight line? The convex hull property shows that it can: Placing all of the control points in a straight line collapses their convex hull to a line. The Bezier curve is "trapped" inside this hull and so must also be a straight line. The property of achieving a straight portion to a curve by properly positioning the control points is called **linear precision.**

Variation Diminishing Property

Roughly speaking, Bezier curves can't "wiggle" more than their control polygon. More precisely, no straight line (or, in three dimensions, no plane) can have more intersections with a Bezier curve than it has with the curve's control polygon. Figure 14.7 shows a Bezier curve based on the control polygon P. Line L cuts through P five times but through the Bezier curve only three times. No line can be found that cuts the curve more often than it cuts P. This can be proved in general for Bezier curves (see, for instance, Farin 1988). It is a useful property for curve designers as they lay down a control polygon: They may be confident that the resulting Bezier curve will not undulate wildly or exhibit extra bends and curves. (Some curve design techniques, such as certain interpolation schemes, can produce wild and unruly fluctuations; see Acton 1970.)

Derivatives of Bezier Curves

Because a curve can exhibit corners and other abrupt changes when its derivatives with respect to t have discontinuities, we must investigate the first, second, and so on derivatives of $\mathbf{p}(t)$ in Equation 14.6 with respect to t.

The first derivative, $\mathbf{p}'(t) = d\mathbf{p}(t)/dt$, is the **velocity** vector to the curve $\mathbf{p}(t)$ at t. Derivatives are taken componentwise: The velocity of a two-dimensional vector, $\mathbf{p}(t) = (x(t), y(t))$, is simply $\mathbf{p}'(t) = (x'(t), y'(t))$. For a three-dimensional curve, the velocity has three components, each a derivative. As suggested in Figure 14.8, the velocity shows the direction of travel a particle would take if it were suddenly released from traveling along the curve. A straight line through $\mathbf{p}(t)$ parallel to $\mathbf{p}'(t)$ is called the **tangent line** to the curve at that point. Notice the corner in the curve of Figure 14.8 at $t = t_4$, where there is an abrupt change in the direction of the velocity vector. The curve is continuous here, but its first derivative is not.

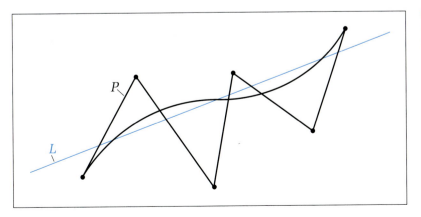

Figure 14.7.
The variation diminishing property of Bezier curves.

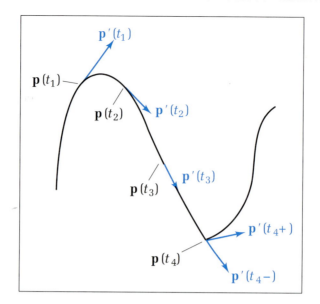

Figure 14.8.

The velocity at different points on a curve.

We are also interested in higher-order derivatives of parametric curves. The second derivative, $\mathbf{p}''(t)$, is simply the derivative of the velocity (it is sometimes called **acceleration**). In general, the k-th derivative is the derivative of the $(k-1)$-st derivative. For the k-th derivative to exist at a point, all lower-order derivatives must exist and be continuous there. It is handy to have some nomenclature for these ideas.

> **Terminology: Continuously Differentiable Curves**
>
> We wish to have a concise way to say that all derivatives of a curve, $\mathbf{p}(t)$, up through the k-th do in fact exist and are continuous at all points inside a given t-interval $[a, b]$. To express this, we say
>
> $$\mathbf{p}(\ ) \text{ is in } C^k[a, b] \qquad (14.16)$$
>
> $C^k[a, b]$ is sometimes called the "family of all curves that are continuously differentiable over the interval $[a, b]$."
>
> As an example, the curve in Figure 14.8 will not be in $C^1[a, b]$ if t_4 lies inside $[a, b]$. Note that a function in $C^k[a, b]$ is necessarily in $C^{k-1}[a, b]$. A function in $C^k[a, b]$ may or may not also be in $C^{k+1}[a, b]$.

For a Bezier curve we show below that the first derivative is

$$\mathbf{p}'(t) = L \sum_{k=0}^{L-1} \Delta \mathbf{p}_k B_k^{L-1}(t) \qquad (14.17)$$

where

$$\Delta \mathbf{p}_k = \mathbf{p}_{k+1} - \mathbf{p}_k \qquad (14.18)$$

Thus the velocity is another Bezier curve, built on the control vectors $\Delta \mathbf{p}_k$. We simply "difference" the original control points in pairs to form the control vectors of the velocity. Note from the form $B_k^{L-1}(t)$ that taking the derivative lowers the order of the curve by 1: For instance, the derivative of a cubic Bezier curve is a quadratic Bezier curve.

Figure 14.9a shows an example of a cubic Bezier curve, and Figure 14.9b shows its velocity vector. For instance, $\mathbf{p}'(1/3)$ is obtained by applying the de Casteljau algorithm at $t = 1/3$ to the three control vectors $\Delta\mathbf{p}_0$, $\Delta\mathbf{p}_1$, and $\Delta\mathbf{p}_2$. The velocity curve is a parabola here (why?).

Because taking the derivative of a Bezier curve simply requires building a Bezier curve on the first differences of its control points, the second derivative must be a Bezier curve formed by "differencing the differences." Thus from Equation 14.17,

$$\mathbf{p}''(t) = L(L - 1) \sum_{k=0}^{L-2} \Delta^2\mathbf{p}_k B_k^{L-2}(t) \qquad (14.19)$$

where

$$\Delta^2\mathbf{p}_k = \Delta\mathbf{p}_{k+1} - \Delta\mathbf{p}_k \qquad (14.20)$$

are the second differences of the control points. All higher-order derivatives are found in a similar fashion.

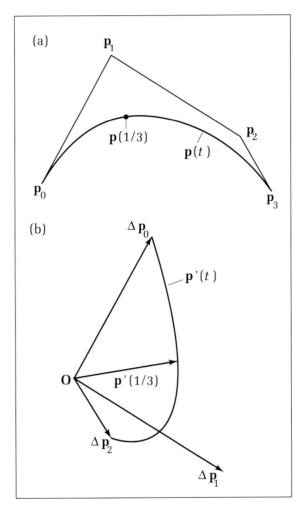

Figure 14.9.
A Bezier curve and its first derivative.

Drill Exercises

14.9.   Draw the Velocity. Plot four points on graph paper, sketch the Bezier curve, and carefully sketch its velocity and acceleration vectors as functions of t.

14.10.   Higher-Order Derivatives of Bezier Curves. Express the second difference, $\Delta^2 \mathbf{p}_k$, in terms of the original control points. Find a general form for the r-th differences

of the control points, and form an expression for the r-th derivative of a Bezier curve.

14.11.   How Differentiable are L-th-Order Bezier Curves? Is a Bezier curve based on L control points in $C^L[0, 1]$? If so, prove it. If not, what is the highest order of derivative that is continuous for such a curve?

Derivation of the First Derivative

By means of linearity, the derivative operates directly on the term $t^k(1-t)^{L-k}$ inside the k-th Bernstein polynomial, producing by the chain rule the difference of two terms: $kt^{k-1}(1-t)^{L-k} - (L-k)t^k(1-t)^{L-k-1}$. Note that the first of these has value 0 for $k=0$ and that the second is 0 for $k=L$. So we write the derivative as the difference of two sums:

$$\mathbf{p}'(t) = \sum_{k=1}^{L} \mathbf{p}_k \binom{L}{k} k t^{k-1}(1-t)^{L-k} - \sum_{k=0}^{L-1} \mathbf{p}_k \binom{L}{k}(L-k)t^k(1-t)^{L-1-k} \quad (14.21)$$

leaving off the terms that have value 0. The second sum is easily seen (why?) to be

$$-L\sum_{k=0}^{L-1} \mathbf{p}_k B_k^{L-1}(t) \quad (14.22)$$

By direct manipulation, the first sum is

$$L\sum_{k=1}^{L} \mathbf{p}_k \binom{L-1}{k-1} t^{k-1}(1-t)^{(L-1)-(k-1)} \quad (14.23)$$

in which we recognize $B_{k-1}^{L-1}(t)$, and so by a shift in the index the first sum becomes

$$L\sum_{k=0}^{L-1} \mathbf{p}_{k+1} B_k^{L-1}(t) \quad (14.24)$$

Putting these sums together, we obtain Equation 14.17.

A Matrix Form for the Bezier Curve

Some formulations of Bezier curves (e.g., Faux and Pratt 1979, Foley and Van Dam 1983) express them in terms of matrices, which can offer advantages when they are manipulated within a computer (for instance, if matrix multiplier hardware is available).

To this end it is convenient to define two arrays of now-familiar quantities: the Bernstein polynomial array $\mathbf{B}^L(t)$ and the control point array $\mathbf{P}$, defined as

$$\mathbf{B}^L(t) = (B_0^L(t), B_1^L(t), \ldots, B_L^L(t))$$

$$\mathbf{P} = (\mathbf{p}_0, \mathbf{p}_1, \ldots, \mathbf{p}_L) \quad (14.25)$$

Equation 14.6 expresses $\mathbf{p}(t)$ as a sum of products, which we can interpret formally as a dot product between these two arrays:

$$\mathbf{p}(t) = \mathbf{B}^L(t) \cdot \mathbf{P} \tag{14.26}$$

or, as shown in Appendix 2, as the product of a row array with a column array: $\mathbf{p}(t) = \mathbf{B}^L(t)\mathbf{P}^T$, where T denotes the transposition.

Because each Bernstein polynomial in turn is a polynomial of the form of Equation 14.5, it too can be written as a dot product. For instance,

$$B_2{}^3(t) = 3(1 - t)t^2 = (t^0, t^1, t^2, t^3) \cdot (0, 0, 3, -3) \tag{14.27}$$

Each polynomial, $B_k{}^L(t)$, requires a different array of coefficients. What is it for $B_0{}^3(t)$? An array of the powers of t such as (t^0, t^1, t^2, t^3) is often called the **power basis**. So the Bernstein array $\mathbf{B}^L(t)$ can be expressed by placing the various coefficient arrays for the different $B_k{}^L(t)$ terms side by side into a matrix $\mathbf{Bez}^L$. For the $L = 3$ case we get

$$\mathbf{B}^3(t) = (t^0, t^1, t^2, t^3)\mathbf{Bez}^3 \tag{14.28}$$

where

$$\mathbf{Bez}^3 = \begin{pmatrix} 1 & 0 & 0 & 0 \\ -3 & 3 & 0 & 0 \\ 3 & -6 & 3 & 0 \\ -1 & 3 & -3 & 1 \end{pmatrix} \tag{14.29}$$

Putting these ingredients together for the general L-th-order case, the Bezier curve may be expressed as

$$\mathbf{p}(t) = \mathbf{Pow}^L(t)\mathbf{Bez}^L\mathbf{P}^T \tag{14.30}$$

where $\mathbf{Pow}^L(t)$ represents the power basis $(1, t, t^2, \ldots, t^L)$ and where the matrix $\mathbf{Bez}^L$ may be shown (see the exercises) to have ij-th term:

$$m_{ij} = (-1)^{j-i}\binom{n}{i}\binom{i}{j} \tag{14.31}$$

Note that when you want to fashion curves from points using polynomials other than Bernstein polynomials, you obtain the same expression as in Equation 14.30, but some other matrix replaces $\mathbf{Bez}^L$ (see examples and details in Faux and Pratt 1979, Foley and Van Dam 1983). This uniformity makes the process of changing from one type of curve generation to another much more understandable.

Drill Exercises

14.12.   The Quadratic and Quartic Cases. Find the matrix $\mathbf{Bez}^L$ for the cases $L = 2$ and $L = 4$.

14.13.   Derive the Terms in $\mathbf{Bez}^L$. Show that the ij-th term of this matrix is properly reported in Equation 14.31.

Creating and Drawing Bezier Curves

Suppose we wish to build an application that draws the resulting Bezier curve from a sequence of control points. How might it be organized? The Bezier curve,

$\mathbf{p}(t)$, of Equation 14.6 (or Equation 14.30) will be drawn by an approximating polyline. The function $\mathbf{p}(t)$ is sampled at closely spaced values of t—say at $t_i = i/N$ for $i = 0, 1, \ldots, N$—and the points, $\mathbf{p}(t_i)$, are connected with straight lines. The only issue is the evaluation of $\mathbf{p}(t)$ at each desired value of t, which we suppose is performed in the following procedure:

Code Fragment 14.1. Creating Bezier Curves

procedure *Bezier* (*poly* : *polypoint*; *t* : *real*; **var** *spot* : *point*);
{compute position $\mathbf{p}(t)$ of Bezier curve due to control polygon *poly*}

This routine uses the control polygon stored in *poly* to evaluate Equation 14.30 for the given value of t, storing the resulting point in *spot*. Notice that the degree of the Bernstein polynomials is stored in *poly^.num*. Implementing this routine is left as a (valuable) exercise. A great deal of insight is gained by experimenting with a Bezier curve design application, to see the effect of using different control polygons.

14.3.1 The Problem of Local Control

It might appear that Bezier curves provide the ultimate tool for designing curves. An endless variety of smooth curves can be fashioned by placing control points judiciously in the plane, or even in three-dimensional space. The user observes the curve generated by the first choice of control points and then "edits" some of the points to generate a more desirable shape. This iteration continues until the entire curve satisfies the goals of the design.

The central problem in using Bezier curves is that of local control of the curve shape. As suggested in Figure 14.10a, certain parts of the Bezier curve

Figure 14.10.
Editing portions of a curve.

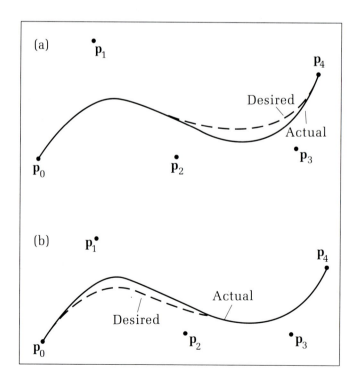

may look correct, whereas others do not seem quite right. The five control points give rise to the solid Bezier curve, which coincides with the desired (dashed) curve near $t = 0$ but deviates from it for t near 1. The user would most likely move $\mathbf{p}_2$ and $\mathbf{p}_3$ up somewhat to force the Bezier curve closer to the desired curve. But, as shown in Figure 14.10b, this also affects the shape of the first half of the curve, forcing it away somewhat from the desired version.

The problem is that any change to any control point alters the entire curve, because of the nature of Bernstein polynomials: As shown in Figure 14.4, each one is "active" (meaning nonzero) over the entire interval [0, 1]. The interval over which a function is nonzero is often called its **support.** Because every Bernstein polynomial is active at every t of interest, and the curve is a combination of the control points "blended" by these functions, it follows that each control point has an effect on the curve at all t-values between 0 and 1. Therefore, adjusting any control point affects the shape of the curve everywhere, with no local control.

Contrast that with the more favorable situation illustrated in Figure 14.11, in which a different set of blending functions, (to be defined), $R_0(t), R_1(t), \ldots,$ $R_5(t)$, is employed. Each blending function has a support that is only a part of the interval [0, 1]. For instance, the support of $R_0(t)$ is [0, .25] and that of $R_3(t)$ is [.25, 1.0]. In fact, at any value of t no more than three of the blending functions are active.

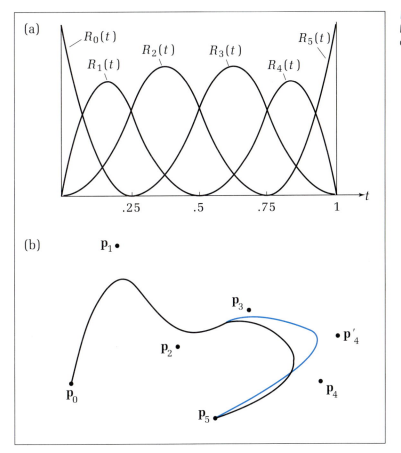

Figure 14.11.
Blending functions having concentrated support.

Consider building a curve, $\mathbf{v}(t)$, as a blend of six control points, $\mathbf{p}_0$, $\mathbf{p}_1$, . . . , $\mathbf{p}_5$, using these blending functions. The curve is given by

$$\mathbf{v(t)} = \sum_{k=0}^{5} \mathbf{p}_k R_k(t) \tag{14.32}$$

Figure 14.11b shows the curve for an example set of control points. (The curve interpolates the first and last control points. Why?) At each t the position $\mathbf{v}(t)$ depends on no more than three of the control points. In particular, for all t in [.75, 1.0] only the points $\mathbf{p}_3$, $\mathbf{p}_4$, and $\mathbf{p}_5$ control the shape of the curve. If the single control point $\mathbf{p}_4$ is moved to $\mathbf{p}'_4$, only a portion of the curve will change, shown as the colored part. Thus this set of blending functions gives some local control to the control points.

We therefore want to find classes of blending functions that share the attractive properties of the Bernstein polynomials yet have concentrated support in order to give the designer local control of the curve shape. We shall see that B-splines satisfy all of these requirements.

14.4 Piecewise Polynomials and Splines

The blending function we seek is built up as a collection of polynomials defined on adjacent intervals that are "pieced" together to form a continuous curve. Such curves are called **piecewise polynomials**.

The example shape, $g(t)$, shown in Figure 14.12 helps establish some nomenclature. We see that $g(t)$ consists of three polynomial **segments**, $a(t)$, $b(t)$, and $c(t)$, defined as

$$
\begin{aligned}
a(t) &= \tfrac{1}{2}t^2 \\
b(t) &= \tfrac{3}{4} - \left(t - \tfrac{3}{2}\right)^2 \\
c(t) &= \tfrac{1}{2}(3 - t)^2
\end{aligned}
\tag{14.33}
$$

The support of $g(t)$ is [0, 3]; $a(t)$ is defined on the **span** [0, 1], $b(t)$ on the span [1, 2], and $c(t)$ on the span [2, 3]. The points at which a pair of the individual segments meet are called **joints**, and the values of t at which this happens are called **knots**. There are four knots in this example: 0, 1, 2, and 3.

Is $g(t)$ continuous everywhere over its support? Because it is built from polynomials, it is certainly continuous inside each span, and so we need only check that the segments meet properly at the joints. This is easily checked: $a(1) = b(1) = \tfrac{1}{2}$, and $b(2) = c(2) = \tfrac{1}{2}$. Going further, the derivative of $g(t)$ is continuous everywhere, and so $g(t)$ is in $C^1[0, 3]$. To show this, note that its derivative is necessarily continuous inside each span (why?), and so check its continuity only at the knots. Direct calculation shows that $a'(1) = b'(1) = 1$, and $b'(2) = c'(2) = -1$. Thus as we move from one polynomial piece to the next, the slope does not jump abruptly. The second derivative is not continuous, however, but does jump abruptly between two values (which ones?) at the knots.

Figure 14.12.
Ingredients of a piecewise polynomial.

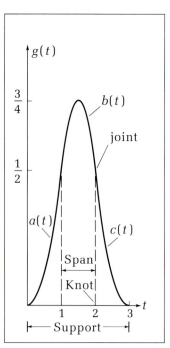

The shape $g(t)$ here is an example of a **spline function,** a piecewise polynomial function that enjoys "enough" orders of continuity. Specifically, we have

> ### Definition of a Spline Function
>
> An M-th-degree spline is a piecewise polynomial of degree M that has continuity of derivatives of order $M - 1$ at each knot.

Evidently $g(t)$ is a quadratic spline: It is a piecewise polynomial of degree 2 and has a continuous first derivative everywhere.

Drill Exercise

14.14. Are Bernstein Polynomials Splines? Show that the Bernstein polynomials $B_k^L(t)$ are indeed splines. How many polynomials are pieced together to form each one? Where are the knots? What degree is the spline? Is it sufficiently continuously differentiable?

14.4.1 Using Splines As Blending Functions

Consider building a curve, $\mathbf{p}(t)$, based on the control polygon $\mathbf{P} : \mathbf{p}_0, \mathbf{p}_1, \ldots, \mathbf{p}_4$ shown in Figure 14.13a. The curve is the familiar weighted sum:

$$\mathbf{p}(t) = \sum_{k=0}^{4} \mathbf{p}_k g_k(t) \tag{14.34}$$

For the blending functions $g_k(t)$ we use *shifted* versions of the spline $g(t)$:

$$g_k(t) = g(t - k) \text{ for } k = 0, \ldots, 4 \tag{14.35}$$

so that successive blending functions begin at successive knots but otherwise have identical shapes (Figure 14.13b).

The curve warrants careful examination: Many of the concepts that follow are embedded in it. At $t = 0$ all functions are zero, and so $\mathbf{p}(0) = 0$. At $t = 1$ $g_0(t)$

Figure 14.13.
Building a curve out of versions of g(t).

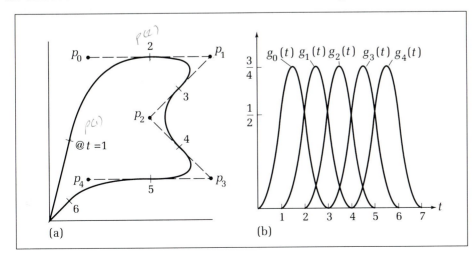

(a)

(b)

has reached value 1/2, and so $\mathbf{p}(1) = .5\mathbf{p}_0$, as shown. As t increases beyond 1, $g_1(t)$ begins to grow, and so the curve depends on a mixture of $\mathbf{p}_0$ and $\mathbf{p}_1$. In fact, at $t = 2$, both blending functions have weight 1/2, and so $\mathbf{p}(2)$ is located at the midpoint between $\mathbf{p}_0$ and $\mathbf{p}_1$. As t increases further, the various blending functions rise and fall, and the major influence on the curve is "passed on" from point to point. At each knot, the curve attains the midpoint between the two currently "active" control points. (Where is it halfway between two knots?) Finally, as t approaches 7, only $g_4(t)$ is active, and the curve moves back toward the origin.

How Good a Design Tool Do We Have?

The form in Equation 14.34 is easily extended to use more than five control points. Suppose we let k vary from 0 to L and let the designer place $L + 1$ control points to guide the curve. What are some of the properties of curves based on the $L + 1$ blending functions $g_k(t) = g(t - k)$:

$$\mathbf{p}(t) = \sum_{k=0}^{L} \mathbf{p}_k g(t - k) \tag{14.36}$$

as t varies from 0 to $L + 3$? In particular, does this family of curves meet our needs for designing curves?

One desirable property, that each curve is guaranteed to be in C^1, follows, as each blending function, $g(t - k)$, is in C^1. Furthermore, the designer can maintain some local control of the curve shape, because each function has support over an interval of only length 3. But one problem is the behavior of the curve near the ends of the t-interval $[0, L + 3]$. Not only does the curve not interpolate the first and last control point, it plummets to the origin! Near the endpoints, fewer than three of the blending functions are active (nonzero). For instance, only after t reaches 2 do three blending functions contribute, and so until then there is too little blending.

The designer can work around this by restricting the t-interval used for generating the curve. That is, for t-values in the interval $[2, L + 1]$ three blending functions are active, and so the curve is guided by three neighboring control points. The curve in Figure 14.13a is in fact controlled by some triplet of points for each t between 2 and 5. Furthermore, the designer knows that the curve starts at the midpoint between $\mathbf{p}_0$ and $\mathbf{p}_1$ at $t = 2$ and ends at the midpoint between $\mathbf{p}_{L-1}$ and $\mathbf{p}_L$. So the curve is generated only for this range of t.

This approach works adequately, but we shall develop in Section 14.4.2 a more general technique that changes the spacings between knots. This forces the curve to interpolate the first and last control points as desired and provides better control of the shape of the curve.

Drill Exercise

14.15.   Develop Intuition About Curve Shapes Based on Quadratic Splines. Draw 12 control points in some complex pattern, and sketch the curve generated using the preceding quadratic spline functions. This is made simple by noting that the curve must pass through the midpoint of almost every edge of the control polygon (which ones?). What interval of t should be used when drawing the curve? Mark the position of the curve at each knot value, labeling the corresponding value of t.

Closed (Periodic) Curves Based on Splines

One often wants to create curves that are "closed" in the sense that they form loops, as shown in Figure 14.14a. This can be accomplished using the form of Equation 14.36. Consider the five control points, $\mathbf{p}_0, \ldots, \mathbf{p}_4$, shown in Figure 14.14b (joined into a truly closed control polygon here for emphasis). Starting at $t = 2$, the curve lies midway between $\mathbf{p}_0$ and $\mathbf{p}_1$, and it meanders in a predictable fashion until $t = 5$, when it is midway between $\mathbf{p}_3$ and $\mathbf{p}_4$. Now to close it we add two more control points, $\mathbf{p}_5$ and $\mathbf{p}_6$, which duplicate two of the existing points: $\mathbf{p}_5 = \mathbf{p}_0$ and $\mathbf{p}_6 = \mathbf{p}_1$. Thus as t increases to 6, the curve is midway between $\mathbf{p}_4$ and $\mathbf{p}_5 = \mathbf{p}_0$, and as t increases to 7, the curve closes on itself. Thus making a closed curve based on this quadratic spline blending function simply requires duplicating the first two control points.

Drill Exercise

14.16. Building Closed Curves with No Extra Control Points. Show that a slight variation on Equation 14.36:

$$\mathbf{p}(t) = \sum_{k=0}^{L} \mathbf{p}_k g((t - k) \bmod (L + 1)) \qquad (14.37)$$

creates a closed curve based on $L + 1$ (distinct) control points as t varies from 0 to $L + 1$. No duplicate control points are required. The modulo function effectively "folds" the blending functions into the interval $[0, L + 1]$, making them active in different parts of the interval. To see how this works, sketch for $L = 4$ the five functions $g((t - k) \bmod (L + 1))$ for $k = 0, 1, 2, 3, 4$ as t varies from 0 to 5.

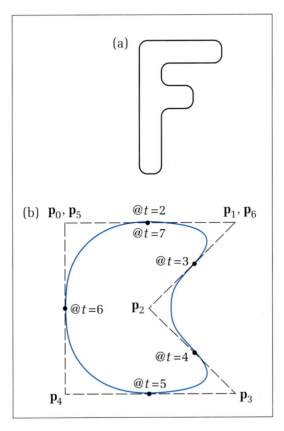

(a)

(b) $\mathbf{p}_0, \mathbf{p}_5$ @$t = 2$ $\mathbf{p}_1, \mathbf{p}_6$

@$t = 7$

@$t = 3$

@$t = 6$ $\mathbf{p}_2$

@$t = 4$

@$t = 5$

$\mathbf{p}_4$ $\mathbf{p}_3$

Figure 14.14.
Closed curves based on splines.

14.4.2 Generalizing the Blending Functions

In the preceding example all of the blending functions have the same shape—
they are just translations of one another. In addition, the knots are equispaced at
integer values. We want to retain the form of Equations 14.32 and 14.34 for the
curves to be generated, but also to introduce greater freedom for the designer.

We first generalize the set of knots from a sequence of integers to some
chosen sequence of real numbers, $t_0, t_1, \ldots$ We call the sequence the **knot
vector T:**

$$\text{knot vector}: \mathbf{T} = (t_0, t_1, t_2 \ldots) \tag{14.38}$$

where the knots must be nondecreasing: $t_i \leq t_{i+1}$. Some of the knots might have
the same value but are still given distinct names. The number of knots involved
in **T** is discussed later. As before, we associate one blending function with each
control point but now allow the blending functions to have different shapes.
Suppose there are $(L + 1)$ control points, $\mathbf{p}_0, \mathbf{p}_1, \ldots, \mathbf{p}_L$. To each control point,
$\mathbf{p}_k$, we associate some blending function, $R_k(t)$. The curve is then given by

$$\mathbf{p}(t) = \sum_{k=0}^{L} \mathbf{p}_k R_k(t) \tag{14.39}$$

Notice that both the Bezier curves and the quadratic spline curves fit into this
framework.

14.4.3 Spline Curves and Basis Functions

To keep manageable the family of possible blending function shapes, we insist
that each $R_k(t)$ be a continuous (no jumps) piecewise polynomial. So $R_k(t)$ is
described within each span $[t_i, t_{i+1}]$ by some polynomial, and it is continuous at
each knot. Because each $R_k(t)$ is a piecewise polynomial, the whole curve $\mathbf{p}(t)$ is
a sum of piecewise polynomials, weighted by the control points. For instance,
in some span the curve might be given by

$$\mathbf{p}(t) = \mathbf{p}_0(3t^2 - 4t + 2) + \mathbf{p}_1(8t^2 - 7.3t - 5.99) + \ldots \tag{14.40}$$

In an adjacent span it is given by a different sum of polynomials, but we know
that all segments meet to make the curve continuous. Such a curve is known as a
spline curve (Farin 1988).[3]

The question can now be posed: Given a knot vector, is there some family of
blending functions that can be used to generate every possible spline curve that
can be defined on that knot vector? Such a family is called a **basis** for the
splines, meaning that any spline curve whatsoever can be matched by the sum
in Equation 14.39 by choosing the proper control polygon.

The answer is that there are many such families, but there is one basis in
particular whose blending functions have the smallest support and therefore
offer the greatest local control. These are the *B-splines,* the B derived from the
word *basis*.

---

[3]Note the difference between a *spline function* as defined in Section 14.4 and a *spline curve*. A
spline function is simply a piecewise polynomial having a certain level of smoothness. A spline
curve is a blend of vectors using piecewise polynomial blending functions. A spline curve must be
continuous at knots but might have discontinuous derivatives at its knots.

14.4.4 The B-Spline Basis Functions

We wish to define the B-spline blending functions, $R_k(t)$, in a way that lends some intuition to them and, in addition, leads to a straightforward computer implementation. Although the literature offers many different approaches to formulating B-splines, there is a single formula that defines all the B-spline functions of any order. It is a recursive relation that is easy to implement in a program and is numerically well behaved. (Some other methods are more computationally efficient—see the exercises.)

Each B-spline function is based on polynomials of a certain order, m. If $m = 3$, the polynomials will be of order 3 and thus of degree 2, and so they will be quadratic B-splines. If the order is $m = 4$, the underlying polynomials will be of degree 3, or cubic. These are the two most important cases, although the formulation allows us to construct B-splines of any order.

It is useful to expose the order of a B-spline function in the notation, and so instead of saying simply $R_k(t)$, we denote the k-th B-spline blending function of order m by $N_{k,m}(t)$. Hence for B-spline curves Equation 14.39 becomes

$$\mathbf{p}(t) = \sum_{k=0}^{L} \mathbf{p}_k N_{k,m}(t) \tag{14.41}$$

Summarizing the ingredients to this point, we have

- a knot vector $\mathbf{T} = (t_0, t_1, t_2 \ldots)$
- $(L + 1)$ control points $\mathbf{p}_k$
- the order m of the B-spline functions

The fundamental formula for the B-spline function $N_{k,m}(t)$ is

$$N_{k,m}(t) = \left(\frac{t - t_k}{t_{k+m-1} - t_k}\right) N_{k,m-1}(t) + \left(\frac{t_{k+m} - t}{t_{k+m} - t_{k+1}}\right) N_{k+1,m-1}(t) \tag{14.42}$$

for $k = 0, 1, \ldots, L$. This is a recursive definition, specifying how to construct the m-th-order function from two B-spline functions of order $(m - 1)$. To get things started, the first-order function must be defined. It is simply the constant function 1 within its span:

$$N_{k,1}(t) = \begin{cases} 1 & \text{if } t_k < t \le t_{k+1} \\ 0 & \text{otherwise} \end{cases} \tag{14.43}$$

Example 14.1
What shape does $N_{0,2}(t)$, which is the first ($k = 0$) B-spline function of order $m = 2$, have when the knots are equispaced: $\mathbf{T} = (t_0 = 0, t_1 = 1, t_2 = 2, \ldots)$? With these parameters Equation 14.42 becomes

$$N_{0,2}(t) = \frac{t}{1} N_{0,1}(t) + \frac{2 - t}{1} N_{1,1}(t) \tag{14.44}$$

We see that a linear "up ramp" (given by the term t) multiplies $N_{0,1}(t)$ and that a linear "down ramp" $(2 - t)$ multiplies $N_{1,1}(t)$, as shown in Figure 14.15a. When these are summed, the result is a triangular pulse (Figure 14.15b). So $N_{0,2}(t) = t$ for $0 \le t \le 1$; it is $2 - t$ for $1 \le t \le 2$; and it is 0 otherwise.

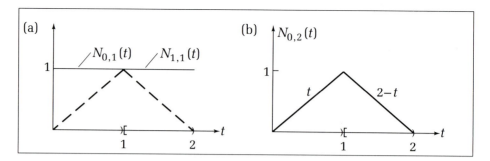

Figure 14.15.
Construction of linear B-splines.

The construction of other linear B-splines follows similarly. For instance, $N_{1,2}(t)$ is a triangular pulse beginning at $t = 1$ and ending at $t = 3$. It is just a shifted version of the first. More generally, <mark>every linear spline is a shifted version of the zeroth one when equispaced knots are used: $N_{i,2}(t) = N_{0,2}(t - i)$.</mark>

Note that a curve built on linear B-splines is the control polyline itself. (Is this also true if the knots are not equispaced?) Because linear splines offer nothing beyond simple straight lines, they are normally not used for curve design. But they arise, of course, in the process of constructing higher-order B-splines.

Example 14.2

Suppose we wish to determine the shape of the quadratic ($m = 3$) B-spline functions $N_{i,3}(t)$ based on the same equispaced knots. We need build only $N_{0,3}(t)$, as the others are simple translations of this one. Equation 14.42 shows that $N_{0,3}(t)$ is the sum:

$$N_{0,3}(t) = \frac{t}{2}N_{0,2}(t) + \frac{3 - t}{2}N_{1,2}(t) \tag{14.45}$$

The first term is an up ramp times the first triangular pulse, and the second is a down ramp times the second pulse. As shown in Figure 14.16a, a ramp times a triangular pulse produces two parabolas that meet at a corner. But when the two

Figure 14.16.
The first quadratic B-spline shape.

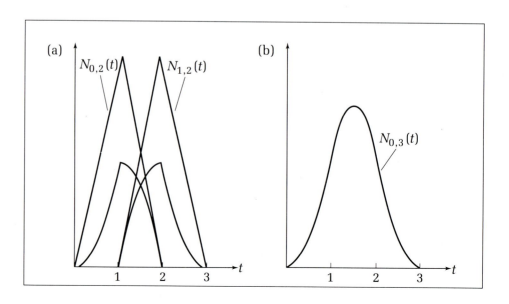

terms in Equation 14.45 are summed, the corners vanish and the resulting pulse shape, $N_{0,3}(t)$ (Figure 14.16b), has a continuous derivative.

Equation 14.45 can be used to determine the algebraic form of the quadratic spline for each segment. The middle segment involves the sum of two quadratics, and the result is

$$N_{0,3}(t) = \begin{cases} \frac{1}{2}t^2 & \text{for } 0 \le t \le 1 \\ \frac{3}{4} - \left(t - \frac{3}{2}\right)^2 & \text{for } 1 \le t \le 2 \\ \frac{1}{2}(3 - t)^2 & \text{for } 2 \le t \le 3 \\ 0 & \text{otherwise} \end{cases} \tag{14.46}$$

Note that it depends on the four knots 0, 1, 2, and 3 and that its support is the interval $[0, 3]$.

Compare $N_{0,3}(t)$ with $g(t)$ of Equation 14.33; they are precisely the same. This is because $g(t)$ was (secretly) chosen to be a B-spline function. Its first derivative has already been checked and found to be continuous. Its second derivative is not. Thus quadratic B-splines (at least on equispaced knots) are in fact splines.

The other quadratic spline shapes, $N_{k,3}(t)$, are obtained easily when the knots are equispaced. Because the first-order splines are simple translations of one another, and all the ramp terms in Equation 14.42 involve only differences among knot values, the quadratic B-splines must be simple translations of one another also. In fact, this is true for any order B-spline on equally spaced knots:

$$\text{if knot } t_k = k \text{ then } N_{k,m}(t) = N_{0,m}(t - k) \tag{14.47}$$

This form can be substituted directly into Equation 14.41 when the knots are equispaced.

Example 14.3

The cubic B-spline is perhaps the most frequently used. $N_{0,4}(t)$ is shown in Figure 14.17a. Its form is found in the same fashion as before (see the exercises). $N_{0,4}(t)$ is symmetrical about $t = 2$ and can be written compactly as

$$N_{0,4}(t) = \begin{cases} u(1 - t) & \text{for } 0 \le t \le 1 \\ v(2 - t) & \text{for } 1 \le t \le 2 \\ v(t - 2) & \text{for } 2 \le t \le 3 \\ u(t - 3) & \text{for } 3 \le t \le 4 \\ 0 & \text{otherwise} \end{cases} \tag{14.48}$$

[handwritten note: note: not $u * (1-t)$ but a function! $u(1-t)$]

where the two segments $u(\ )$ and $v(\ )$ are shown in Figure 14.17b and are given by

$$u(t) = \frac{1}{6}(1 - t)^3$$

$$v(t) = \frac{1}{6}(3t^3 - 6t^2 + 4) \tag{14.49}$$

Direct calculation of derivatives shows that the first and second derivatives of the cubic spline are everywhere continuous.

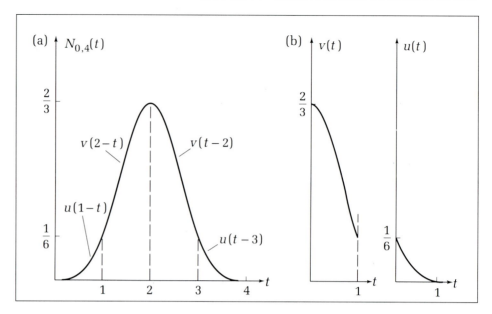

Figure 14.17.
The cubic B-spline on equispaced knots.

Based on the reasoning here, one can show (see the exercises) that in general the function $N_{k,m}(t)$ begins at t_k and ends at t_{k+m}: Its support is $[t_k, t_{k+m}]$. It is also never negative.

One must always be alert to a potential division by zero: One or both denominators in Equation 14.42 might become zero for certain choices of knot values. But whenever this happens, the corresponding lower-order function, $N_{k,m-1}(t)$ or $N_{k+1,m-1}(t)$, is also always zero. So we can adopt the rule that any term having a zero denominator is evaluated as 0.

Drill Exercises

14.17.   Potential Division by Zero. Show that when two knots have the same value, a denominator term in Equation 14.42 has value 0. Show that in this case the term in which this zero denominator appears is always 0 also.

14.18.   B-Spline Support. Show that in general $N_{k,m}(t)$ is nonzero outside the interval $[t_k, t_{k+m}]$, and so the support of an m-th order B-spline is m spans in the knot vector. Also show that this function is nonnegative for all t.

14.19.   Computation of the Cubic B-Spline. Verify the formulas in Equation 14.48 for the cubic B-spline based on equispaced knots. Also calculate the first and second derivatives for the cubic B-spline, and show that they are continuous everywhere.

It is easy to implement the recursive formulation of the function $N_{k,m}(t)$ in program code and therefore to compute its value at any t for any given knot vector. Note that the following code fragment is a direct translation of Equation 14.42:

Code Fragment 14.2. B-Spline Blending Functions

```
function N(k, m : integer; t : real) : real;
    {returns k-th B-spline of order m at t.}
    {uses global knot vector: knot : array[0 .. numknots] of real}
var
    denom1, denom2, sum : real;
```

```
begin
    if m = 1 then        {first order, evaluate directly}
        if (t < knot[k]) or (t >= knot[k + 1]) then
                N:= 0.0
        else N:= 1.0
    else begin       {m exceeds 1 . . use recursion}
        denom1:= knot[k + m − 1] − knot[k];
        if denom1 <> 0.0 then
                sum:= (t − knot[k])*N(k, m − 1, t) / denom1
        else sum:= 0.0;
        denom2:= knot[k + m] − knot[k + 1];
        if denom2 <> 0.0 then
                sum:= sum + (knot[k + m] − t)*N(k + 1, m − 1, t) / denom2;
        N:= sum
    end {else}
end;
```

Drill Exercises

14.20.   Hand Simulation. Hand-simulate the preceding algorithm to calculate the value of $N_{3,2}(2.6)$ for the case of equispaced knots: $t_i = i$.

14.21.   Periodic B-Spline Curves. Show that the curve based on $L + 1$ control points and m-th-order B-splines closes on itself and is therefore periodic in t.

$$\mathbf{p}(t) = \sum_{k=0}^{L} \mathbf{p}_k N_{0,m}((t − k) \bmod(L + 1))   \quad (14.50)$$

14.4.5 Using Multiple Knots in the Knot Vector

To this point we have used only B-splines based on equispaced knots. By varying the spacing between knots, the curve designer acquires much greater control of the shape of the final curve.

A central question is what happens to the shapes of the blending functions when two knots are set very close to one another. Figure 14.18 shows the situation when the knot vector is $\mathbf{T} = (0, 1, 2, 3, 3 + \epsilon, 4 + \epsilon, \dots)$, where ϵ is a small positive number. Now the "piece" of each piecewise polynomial lying in the interval $[3, 3 + \epsilon]$ has become "squeezed" into a very narrow span. The blending functions will clearly no longer be translations of one another. If ϵ is set to zero, this span will vanish altogether, and a **multiple knot** will occur at $t = 3$. This knot is said to have a "multiplicity of 2." Figure 14.19 shows the resulting

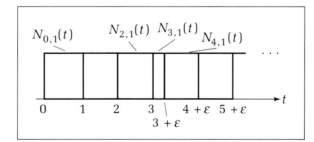

Figure 14.18.
Moving knots close together.

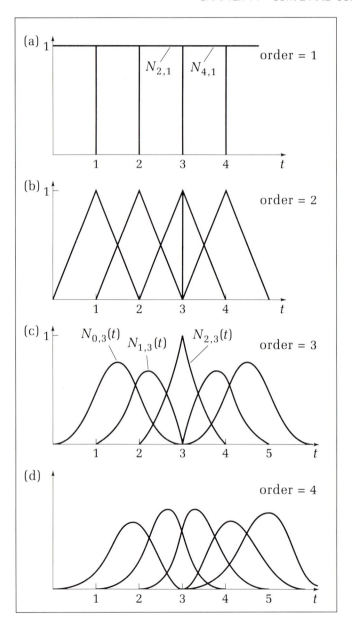

Figure 14.19.
B-spline shapes near a knot of
multiplicity 2.

blending functions. Now two of the linear B-spline shapes are discontinuous (Figure 14.19b), and the quadratic shapes have a discontinuous derivative at $t = 3$ (Figure 14.19c). In general, a C^i curve is reduced to a C^{i-1} curve at the multiple knot value. The cubic B-spline (Figure 14.19d) are C^1 everywhere, but not C^2 at $t = 3$. But notice in Figure 14.19c that if quadratic B-splines are used, the curve will interpolate control point $\mathbf{p}_2$ because the blending function $N_{2,3}(t)$ reaches value 1 at $t = 3$ and all the other blending functions are zero there. In general, when t approaches a knot of multiplicity greater than one, there is a stronger attraction to the governing control point (which one?).

Going further, quadratic splines become discontinuous near a knot of multiplicity 3. Cubic splines exhibit a discontinuous derivative near a knot of multiplicity 3, but they also interpolate one of the control points. By adjusting the multiplicity of each knot, the designer can therefore change the shape of the curve.

Neither Equation 14.42 nor Code Fragment 14.2 need be altered when the knot vector contains multiple knots. As we mentioned, some of the denominators in Equation 14.42 become zero, but the code automatically handles this situation, and no adjustments need be made.

14.4.6 Open B-Spline Curves: Standard Knot Vector

One special choice of knot vector has become a standard for curve design. With this arrangement, the curve interpolates the first and last control points, thus better enabling the designer to predict where the computed curve will lie.

The **standard knot vector** for a B-spline of order m begins and ends with a knot of multiplicity m and uses unit spacing for the remaining knots. We start with an example and then see how it arises. Suppose there are eight control points and we want to use cubic ($m = 4$) B-splines. The standard knot vector turns out to be

$$\mathbf{T} = (0, 0, 0, 0, 1, 2, 3, 4, 5, 5, 5, 5)$$

The eight blending functions, $N_{0,4}(t), \ldots, N_{7,4}(t)$, are defined on these knots using Equation 14.42 and are shown in Figure 14.20a. $N_{0,4}(t)$ and $N_{7,4}(t)$ are discontinuous and have a support of only one unit span. Only $N_{3,4}(t)$ and $N_{4,4}(t)$ have the usual span of four units. Their shapes are given by Equation 14.48. The remaining blending functions have two or three unit spans, and their shapes become more distorted as they approach the first and last knots. The specific polynomial functions that comprise the blending functions are requested in the exercises.

Notice that, taken together, this set of functions always insures interpolation of the first and last control points. For example, at $t = 0$, all blending functions are zero except for $N_{0,4}(t)$, which equals one. It is also not hard to show that the initial direction of the B-spline curve at $t = 0$ is along the first segment of the control polygon, and similarly for the final direction (see the exercises).

Figure 14.20 shows an example of a curve based on eight control points. Clearly the first and last points are interpolated and the curve directions at these points are as promised. Note that a B-spline curve can cross itself when the control polygon does.

The standard knot vector for $(L + 1)$ control points and order-m B-splines is described as follows (comments about the corresponding blending functions appear in parentheses):

1. There are $L + m + 1$ knots all together, denoted as $t_0, \ldots, t_{L+m}$.

2. The first m knots, $t_0, \ldots, t_{m-1}$, all share the value 0. (The first m blending functions start at $t = 0$.)

3. Knots $t_m, \ldots, t_L$ increase in increments of 1, from value 1 through value $L - m + 1$. (The final blending function, $N_{L,m}(t)$, begins at $t_L = L - m + 1$ and has a support of width 1.)

4. The final m knots, $t_{L+1}, \ldots, t_{L+m}$, all equal $L - m + 2$.

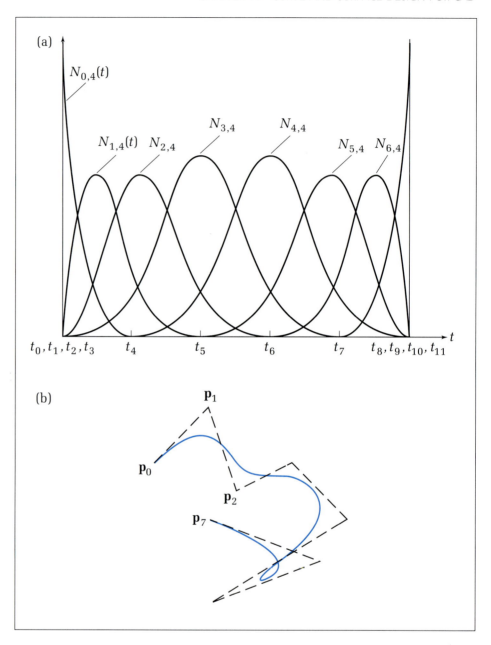

Figure 14.20.
Eight cubic B-spline blending
functions.

From these rules, it is easy to compose a procedure that generates the standard knot vector for given values of m and L, as shown by the following code fragment:

Code Fragment 14.3. Building Standard Knot Vectors

---

procedure *Build_Knots*(*m, L* : *integer;*
                    var *knot* : **array**[0 . . *numknots*] **of** *real*);
{***build the standard knot vector for $L + 1$ control points
 ***and B-splines of order m}
var *i* : *integer;*

begin
    if $(L < (m - 1))$ **or** $(m + L > numknots)$ **then** *Report_Error*
    else begin
        for $i := 0$ **to** $L + m$ **do**
            if $i < m$ **then** $knot[i] := 0.0$
            else if $i <= L$ **then** $knot[i] := i - m + 1$ {i is at least m here}
            else $knot[i] := L - m + 2$ {i exceeds L here}
    end {**else**}
end; {*Build_Knots*}

Note the error condition based on the values of m and L. For a given m there must be a sufficient number of control points so that there will be "room" for at least one span of width 1. This leads to the following constraint:

> **The order m cannot exceed the number of control points $(L + 1)$.**

Drill Exercises

14.22. Standard Knots for Quadratic B-Spline Curves. Show that the standard knot vector for an order $m = 3$ B-spline curve based on eight control points is

$$\mathbf{T} = (0, 0, 0, 1, 2, 3, 4, 5, 6, 6, 6)$$

14.23. Knot Vectors As Order m Is Increased. What is the standard knot vector when seven control points are used for B-splines of order (a) $m = 3$, (b) $m = 4$, (c) $m = 5$, (d) $m = 6$, and (e) $m = 7$?

14.24. Quadratic B-Splines on Standard Knot Vectors. Using Equation 14.42, find explicit expressions for the piecewise polynomials that describe the quadratic B-spline blending functions when defined on the standard knot vector.

14.25. Cubic B-Splines. Find analytically the first four cubic B-splines defined on a standard knot vector. Find also their derivatives at $t = 0$ and show that the initial direction of the B-spline curve is along the first segment of the control polygon.

Bezier Curves Are B-Spline Curves

Bezier curves were introduced earlier through two approaches: the de Casteljau algorithm and the Bernstein polynomials. We can now state a third approach: Bezier curves are also a special case of B-splines, because the B-spline blending functions defined on the standard knot vector are in fact Bernstein polynomials when $m = L + 1$! That is, $N_{k,L+1}(t) = B_L^k(t)$, for $k = 0, \ldots, L$.

To see this, recall from Exercise 14.23 what happens to the standard knot vector as the order m is increased up to $L + 1$: The first m knots have value 0; the last m have value 1; and t varies only over $[0, 1]$. For example, if $L = 5$ and $m = 6$, we obtain $\mathbf{T} = (0, 0, 0, 0, 0, 0, 1, 1, 1, 1, 1, 1)$. Thus each piecewise polynomial has only a single span, and each is a polynomial of order $m = L + 1$. This is precisely how the Bernstein polynomials behave. In fact, one can derive the Bernstein polynomials directly from Equation 14.42.

Drill Exercise

14.26. Deriving the Bernstein Polynomials. Show that when $m = L + 1 = 4$ the B-spline functions of Equation 14.42 are the Bernstein polynomials.

Recall that the prime motivation for going beyond Bezier curves to B-spline curves was the desire to obtain local control of the curve's shape. When the order of the B-spline polynomials is increased by 1, the support of each B-spline blending function extends one span further, reducing the amount of local control. When m reaches the bound of $L + 1$, the Bezier case is obtained, and local control is at a minimum. Figure 14.21 shows how B-spline curves become more "taut," thereby permitting less local control, as their order increases. There are eight control points, and so the order $m = 8$ curve is the Bezier curve. All of these curves were generated using Fragment 14.2. (What is the $M = 2$ curve?)

14.5 Useful Properties of B-Spline Curves for Design

It is useful to summarize the principal properties of B-splines and the curves they generate. We shall also see that many of the desirable properties attributed to Bezier curves carry over intact to B-spline curves.

1. The m-th-order B-spline functions are piecewise polynomials of order m. They are splines because they are in C^{m-2}. They exhibit $(m - 2)$ orders of continuous derivatives at every point in their support. They form a basis for any spline of the same order defined on the same knots; i.e., any spline can be represented as a linear combination of B-splines. Of all spline bases, the B-splines are the most concentrated, having the shortest supports.

2. The B-spline blending function, $N_{k,m}(t)$, begins at t_k and ends at t_{k+m}. Its support is $[t_k, t_{k+m}]$. The support of the family of functions, $N_{k,m}(t)$, for $k = 0, \ldots, L$ is the interval $[t_0, t_{m+L}]$.

3. A closed B-spline curve based on $L + 1$ control points may be obtained using Equation 14.50 (assuming evenly spaced knots in the definition of $N_{0,m}(.)$).

Figure 14.21.
Curves based on splines of
different orders.

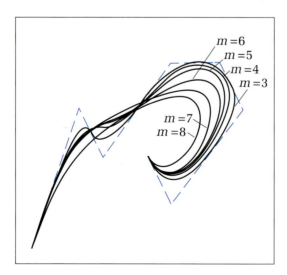

4. If the standard knot vector is used, the B-spline curve will interpolate the first and last control points. Its initial and final directions are along the first and last edges of the control polygon,
respectively.

5. Each B-spline function, $N_{k,m}(t)$, is nonnegative for every t, and
the family of such functions sums to 1:

$$\sum_{k=0}^{L} N_{k,m}(t) = 1 \qquad\qquad (14.51)$$

for every $t\epsilon[t_0, t_{m+L}]$. This can be proved by induction from Equation 14.42.

6. Curves based on B-splines are affine invariant. To transform a
B-spline curve, simply transform each control point, and generate the new curve based on the transformed control points. To
show this, apply the same proof (Equation 14.13) as for Bezier
curves, and use the preceding property 5.

7. According to property 5, a B-spline curve is a convex combination of its control points and so lies in their convex hull. A stronger statement is possible: At any t only m B-spline functions are
"active" (nonzero). Thus at each t the curve must lie in the convex hull of at most m consecutive active control points. Figure
14.22 shows a quadratic B-spline curve based on the standard
knot vector. At most three control points are active at each t, and
so the relevant convex hulls are triangles. As t increases, $\mathbf{p}(t)$
progressively passes out of each convex hull and into the next as
each new blending function becomes active in turn. At which
t-value does the curve enter and exit the shaded convex hull?

Convex hulls based on m control points are typically smaller
regions than the hull based on all the control points. The curve is

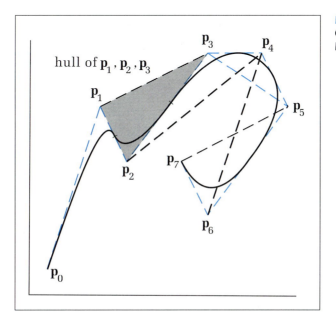

Figure 14.22.
Convex hulls for the quadratic
B-spline curve.

therefore "trapped" in a smaller region than is the case for a Bezier curve. The narrow support of the B-splines not only gives local control to the designer but also provides more insight into the nature of the curve.

8.   B-spline curves exhibit linear precision: If m consecutive control points are colinear, their convex hull will be a straight line, and the curve will be trapped inside it.

9.   B-spline curves are variation diminishing: A B-spline curve does not pass through any plane more times than does its control polygon (Farin 1988).

Drill Exercise

14.27.   Sketching the Convex Hull Property. Draw several example control polygons of eight points. Consider quadratic B-splines based on the standard knot vector. Draw the successive convex hulls, and determine the values of t for which the curve enters and exits each hull. Sketch the resulting B-spline curve, labeling various t-values along it. Be sure it also passes through the midpoints of each inner edge of the control polygon.

Using Multiple Control Points

The designer can usefully alter the shape of a B-spline curve by placing several control points at the same spot, producing a **multiple control point,** which attracts the curve more strongly to itself.

Figure 14.23 shows an example that uses cubic B-spline curves. The curve based on control points A, B, C, D, E, F, and G exhibits the usual behavior for cubic splines. When a double point is used at D, so that the control polygon is A, B, C, D, D, E, F, G, the curve is pulled more strongly toward D. When a triple point is placed at D, making the control polygon A, B, C, D, D, D, E, F, G, the curve must actually interpolate the point!

The interpolation effect is easily explained from Figure 14.20a. Note that at t-values such as t_5 and t_6, exactly three B-spline functions are nonzero and that

Figure 14.23.
Curve control using multiple control points.

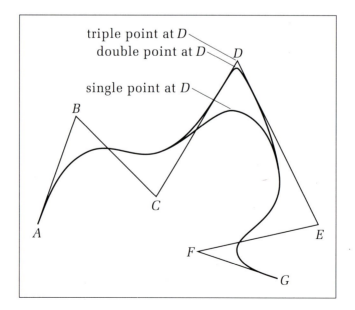

they sum to one. If they are all weighted by the same control point, the weighted sum will be the control point itself.

More generally, recall that a cubic B-spline is always trapped within some convex hull based on four consecutive control points. When a triple point is used at **D**, the convex hulls that surround **D** consist of edges of the control polygon, and so the curve is trapped "in" this edge for one span of the polynomials.

Notice that the use of multiple control points is not the same as the use of multiple knots, although their effects are similar. It is usually easier for a designer to increase the multiplicity of a control point than that of a knot, because control points are plainly visible and can be pointed to.

Many other curve design techniques are available. In particular, the class of *rational splines* has proved to be very effective in generating curves, including the conic sections. (See Farin 1988, or Faux and Pratt 1979, for example, for discussions of these splines.)

Drill Exercise

14.28. Multiple Control Points with Quadratic B-splines. Explain the effect of a double control point on a quadratic B-spline curve. Sketch an interesting control polygon having no multiple control points; show the sequence of convex hulls that trap the curve; and sketch the curve. Then increase the multiplicity of one of the control points and repeat.

14.6 Interpolation of Control Points with B-Splines

A curve based on B-spline blending functions does not automatically interpolate all of its control points. However, a preprocessing step can be carried out on the given control points so that the B-spline curve will in fact interpolate all of the control points. During preprocessing, a new set of control points is carefully fashioned out of the given set. This new set has the property that when a B-spline curve is formed from it, the curve passes through all of the points in the original set.

The idea is developed through a specific example, interpolating a set of six data points, $y_0, \ldots, y_5$, at equispaced values of t with cubic B-splines, as shown in Figure 14.24a. Equispaced knots are used, so that, for example, $N_{0,4}(t)$ begins at $t = 0$ and "bulges up" at $t = 2$. Thus we attempt to interpolate y_0 at $t = 2$, y_1 at $t = 3$, and so forth.

As shown in the figure, however, the sum

$$y(t) = \sum_{i=0}^{5} y_i N_{i,4}(t) \tag{14.52}$$

does not pass through the points. Because the B-spline functions overlap, the various terms in the sum interact in such a way that $y(t)$ falls short of the data values.

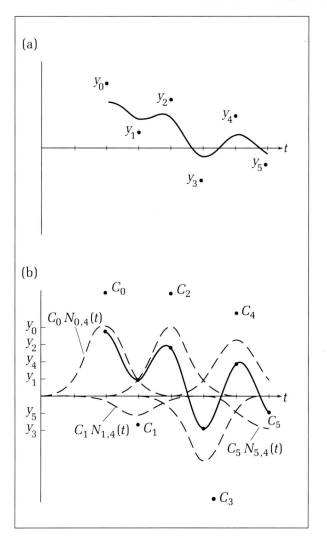

Figure 14.24.
Attempt to interpolate six points
with cubic B-splines.

To correct this, a different set of values, $c_0, \ldots, c_5$, is used instead of the y_i, so that the curve based on them:

$$p(t) = \sum_{i=0}^{5} c_i N_{i,4}(t) \qquad (14.53)$$

does indeed interpolate the y_i's, as shown in Figure 14.24b. We must find just the right set of c_i values to accomplish this. It is done by solving a set of linear equations. The conditions for interpolating the six points are $p(2) = y_0$, $p(3) = y_1$, $p(4) = y_2, \ldots, p(7) = y_5$. Because at integer values of t the only values taken on by the B-splines functions are 0, $1/6$, and $4/6$, these six conditions have the form

$$\begin{aligned} 4c_0 + c_1 &= 6y_0 \\ c_0 + 4c_1 + c_2 &= 6y_1 \\ c_1 + 4c_2 + c_3 &= 6y_2 \\ \ldots &= \ldots \\ c_4 + 4c_5 &= 6y_5 \end{aligned} \qquad (14.54)$$

or in matrix form (also see Appendix 2):

$$\begin{pmatrix} 4 & 1 & 0 & 0 & 0 & 0 \\ 1 & 4 & 1 & 0 & 0 & 0 \\ 0 & 1 & 4 & 1 & 0 & 0 \\ 0 & 0 & 1 & 4 & 1 & 0 \\ 0 & 0 & 0 & 1 & 4 & 1 \\ 0 & 0 & 0 & 0 & 1 & 4 \end{pmatrix} \begin{pmatrix} c_0 \\ c_1 \\ c_2 \\ c_3 \\ c_4 \\ c_5 \end{pmatrix} = 6 \begin{pmatrix} y_0 \\ y_1 \\ y_2 \\ y_3 \\ y_4 \\ y_5 \end{pmatrix} \qquad (14.55)$$

Solving for the New Control Points

Notice that the matrix is **tridiagonal**: Its nonzero terms are confined to three diagonals, which makes the set of equations rather easy to solve. We first perform a **forward elimination** pass through the set of equations to eliminate the lower strip of ones. First divide the top equation through by 4 so that its leading term is 1. Then, beginning with the second equation, subtract from each equation in turn the right amount of the equation directly above it to eliminate the 1, and then scale the equation so a 1 appears in the diagonal term. This converts the set of equations into the "upper triangular" form (having all zeros below the major diagonal):

$$\begin{pmatrix} 1 & g_0 & 0 & 0 & 0 & 0 \\ 0 & 1 & g_1 & 0 & 0 & 0 \\ 0 & 0 & 1 & g_2 & 0 & 0 \\ 0 & 0 & 0 & 1 & g_3 & 0 \\ 0 & 0 & 0 & 0 & 1 & g_4 \\ 0 & 0 & 0 & 0 & 0 & 1 \end{pmatrix} \begin{pmatrix} c_0 \\ c_1 \\ c_2 \\ c_3 \\ c_4 \\ c_5 \end{pmatrix} = 6 \begin{pmatrix} d_0 \\ d_1 \\ d_2 \\ d_3 \\ d_4 \\ d_5 \end{pmatrix} \qquad (14.56)$$

where the g_i and d_i terms are easily computed. The code to do this based on the arrays $d[]$ and $g[]$ looks like:

Code Fragment 14.4. The Forward Elimination Step

```
g[0] := 0.25;
d[0] := 6.0 * y[0] * g[0];
for i := 1 to L do
begin
    g[i] := 1.0 / (4.0 − g[i − 1]);
    d[i] := (6.0 * y[i] − d[i − 1]) * g[i]
end;
```

where L is 5 in the current example.

To finish solving for the c_i terms, note that the matrix in Equation 14.56 has a single term in the bottom row, and so we know immediately that $c_L = d_L$. Now work back up through the rows using the previously found c_{i+1} to obtain the next c_i, a process called **backward substitution**:

Code Fragment 14.5. The Backward Substitution Step

```
c[L] := d[L]:
for i := (L − 1) downto 0 do c[i] := d[i] − g[i] * c[i + 1]
```

Example 14.4

Consider the data values $y_0, \ldots, y_5 = 4, 1, 3, -2, 2, -1$, as are used in Figure 14.24. Direct application of the forward elimination and backward substitution calculations yields:

i	$y[i]$	$g[i]$	$d[i]$	$c[i]$
0	4	0.250	6.0	6.427
1	1	0.267	0.0	-1.707
2	3	0.268	4.82	6.400
3	-2	0.268	-4.51	-5.893
4	2	0.268	4.42	5.171
5	-1	0.268	-2.79	-2.793

Using these c_i values yields the curve shown in Figure 14.24b.

These ideas extend immediately to any number of data points, $y_0, y_1, \ldots, y_L$, simply by choosing the proper L. A procedure, $Adjust(y : data; \mathbf{var}\ c : data)$, can be developed to produce the array $c[]$ given the array $y[]$ (see the exercises). Here *data* would be a record type containing the number of data values and the array of real values itself.

To interpolate points $\mathbf{p}_i = (x_i, y_i)$ the preceding process is performed once for the x-components and once for the y-components. That is, $Adjust(x, new\_x)$ is called, followed by $Adjust(y, new\_y)$ to produce the two new arrays $new\_x[]$ and $new\_y[]$. Then the interpolating curve is given by

$$\mathbf{p}(t) = \sum_{i=0}^{L} \mathbf{w}_i \mathbf{N}_{i,4}(t) \tag{14.57}$$

where $\mathbf{w}_i = (new\_x[i], new\_y[i])$. An example is shown in Figure 14.25. Three-dimensional data points may be interpolated in the same manner.

Note that the amount of computation required to interpolate $L + 1$ data points in this way is proportional to $L + 1$, rather than growing at a faster-than-

Figure 14.25.

Example of two-dimensional interpolation with B-splines. (Courtesy of Tuan Le Ngoc)

linear rate, as is the case with other kinds of numerical algorithms. Therefore, very large sets of points can be easily handled.

There are many variations of this method, some of which give the user greater control over the shape of the curve. For example, one can vary the separation between knots (here taken to be the same) in the knot vector or add extra "ghost" points to the given data in order to control the curve's behavior at its endpoints. One can generate closed curves that interpolate the given data points. One can interpolate using quadratic B-splines (see the exercises) or higher-order splines. The reader interested in the various generalizations should consult one of the many sources on B-splines, such as Bartels et al. (1988), or Farin (1988).

Drill Exercises

14.29. Interpolation Using Quadratic B-Splines. Follow a parallel development to the preceding to interpolate an array of data points using quadratic B-splines defined on equispaced knots. Derive the form of the matrix that relates the original and the new control points, and follow through the forward elimination and backward substitution processes.

14.30.   On the Efficient Computation of B-Splines. When drawing a B-spline curve, many points have to be formed, and so values $N_{k,m}(t)$ must be computed at a large number of t-values. Using the recursive form of Code Fragment 14.2 at each t makes many redundant calls to lower-order B-spline functions. It is much more efficient, therefore, to compute values of each $N_{k,m}(t)$ once and store them in arrays, such as the array $N[k, i]$, which holds $N_{k,m}(t)$ evaluated at $t_i = i \Delta t$, where Δt is the fixed difference between the t-values desired. Samples of each $N[k, i]$ need only be formed over the support of the corresponding B-spline function. Furthermore, only a few different shapes, $N[k, i]$, are needed, as many are just translations of one another and have the same shape. If there are 55 control points, how many different cubic B-spline functions will be needed?

Once stored, each point on the curve can be fashioned by accessing the proper samples of the functions: $\mathbf{p}(t_i)$ is formed as the vector sum of the terms $P[k]N[n, j]$, where $P[k]$ is a control point, and proper values of n and j are selected. Determine, for the case of cubic splines, the proper values of n and j to be used, for each k and t_i. Note that when j is outside a certain region, it is known that the function $N[k, j]$ is certainly 0, and so the array is not accessed.

14.7 Designing Bezier and B-Spline Surfaces

Bezier and B-spline blending functions can be used to describe and draw surfaces as well as curves. Recall from Chapter 9 that a surface is conveniently represented parametrically as a vector function of two parameters, say u and v. The general form is $\mathbf{p}(u, v) = (X(u, v), Y(u, v), Z(u, v))$, or equivalently,

$$\mathbf{p}(u, v) = X(u, v)\mathbf{i} + Y(u, v)\mathbf{j} + Z(u, v)\mathbf{k} \qquad (14.58)$$

As u and v vary over some range of values, the functions $X(u, v)$, $Y(u, v)$, and $Z(u, v)$ change value, causing the position of $\mathbf{p}(u, v)$ to move around in three-dimensional space. The circular cylinder of Equation 9.11 provides a good example of this.

The surfaces of primary interest here are defined by blending together a set of control points rather than explicit mathematical functions. For example, the bilinear patch of Equation 9.14:

$$\mathbf{p}(u, v) = (1 - v)((1 - u)\mathbf{p}_{00} + u\mathbf{p}_{10}) + v((1 - u)\mathbf{p}_{01} + u\mathbf{p}_{11}) \qquad (14.59)$$

blends the four corners, $\mathbf{p}_{ij}$, of the patch by means of functions that are linear in both u and v. Recall that this is a "ruled" surface because both its u-contours and v-contours are straight lines. (As defined in Chapter 9, a u-contour is the curve swept out by letting v vary while u is fixed at some value, say u_1.)

14.7.1 Bezier Surface Patches

Consider the Bezier curve of Equation 14.6 written as a function of parameter v, where the $(L+1)$ control points depend in some fashion on parameter u:

$$\mathbf{p}(u,\ v) = \sum_{k=0}^{L} \mathbf{p}_k(u)B_k^L(v) \qquad (14.60)$$

That is, each u-contour is a standard Bezier curve, but at different u-values the control points are at different positions. As u varies, each $\mathbf{p}_k(u)$ "sweeps" out a specific curve. The surface can be viewed as the sweep of a Bezier curve through space. Visualize a control polygon moving through space, changing its shape as it moves. At each position the polygon creates a Bezier curve, and the surface is the trail left behind by this undulating Bezier curve.

Figure 14.26 shows a perspective projection of a surface built by linearly interpolating between two Bezier curves, based on the two control polygons P_0 and P_1. Each "control curve," $\mathbf{p}_k(u)$, linearly interpolates between two control points, $\mathbf{p}_k{}^0$ and $\mathbf{p}_k{}^1$, as u varies between 0 and 1:

$$\mathbf{p}_k(u) = (1-u)\mathbf{p}_k{}^0 + u\mathbf{p}_k{}^1 \text{ for } k = 0,\ 1,\ 2,\ 3 \qquad (14.61)$$

This is a ruled surface because each v-contour is a straight line. It generalizes the bilinear surface by allowing an arbitrary Bezier shape in one set of contours. Various u- and v-contours are drawn to show the general shape of the surface.

Drill Exercise

14.31.   When Is It a Cylinder or Other Simpler Creature? Would this surface be a cylinder (recall Chapter 9) if one control polygon were simply a translation of the other? What must one of the control polygons be to make this surface a cone? What shape must the control polygons have to reduce this to a bilinear surface?

Figure 14.26.
An in-betweening surface based on Bezier curves.

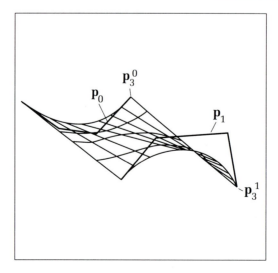

For greater design freedom, we move beyond linear interpolation and let the control curves $\mathbf{p}_k(u)$ themselves be Bezier curves, each based on its own $(M + 1)$ control points:

$$\mathbf{p}_k(u) = \sum_{i=0}^{M} \mathbf{p}_{i,k} B_i{}^M(u) \tag{14.62}$$

Putting this together with Equation 14.60, we obtain the **tensor product** form for the **Bezier patch**:

$$\mathbf{p}(u, v) = \sum_{i=0}^{M} \sum_{k=0}^{L} \mathbf{p}_{i,k} \, B_i{}^M(u) B_k{}^L(v) \tag{14.63}$$

An example is shown in Figure 14.27 based on three sets of four control points. The three control polygons that together form the **control polyhedron** of the patch are shown, along with various u- and v-contours of the patch itself.

In general, the control polyhedron is a network of $(M + 1)(L + 1)$ vertices. To create a patch, the designer carefully specifies the positions of these vertices and then applies Equation 14.63 to draw contours or otherwise to define the shape of the surface.

Drill Exercise

14.32. Regaining the In-Betweening Form. What is the nature of the control polyhedron used in Equation 14.63 that produces linear interpolation between two control polygons, as in Equation 14.61?

Patching Together Bezier Patches

The designer might want to model a complex shape out of several Bezier surface patches and have the patches meet smoothly at their common boundaries.

Figure 14.28 shows two control polyhedra, one in black, one in color, that define two Bezier patches. Equation 14.63 is used for both patches, and both u and v vary over 0 to 1 to generate each patch. Only the control polyhedra differ.

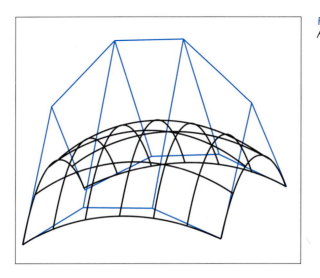

Figure 14.27.
An example of a Bezier patch.

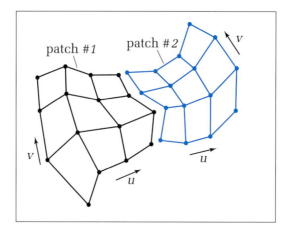

Figure 14.28.
Two Bezier patches meeting
continuously.

What conditions must the designer impose on the two control polyhedra so that
the two patches will meet "seamlessly"?

The two patches will meet at all points along a common boundary if their
control polyhedra coincide at the boundary. This is so because the shape of the
"boundary" Bezier curve depends only on the control polygon lying at the
boundary of the control polyhedron—see what happens when $u = 0$ in Equation 14.63. So the designer chooses these boundary control polygons for the two
patches to be identical.

How might tangent continuity be achieved? This will also achieve a continuous normal vector (recall Chapter 9) to the surface at the join between the
two patches. One sufficient condition (Faux and Pratt 1979, p. 214) is illustrated
in Figure 14.29: Each pair of polyhedron edges that meet at the boundary, such
as E and E^1, must be collinear. This can be awkward for a designer to satisfy.
Other slightly different conditions are discussed in Faux and Pratt (1979) as
well. Figure 14.30 shows the famous and lovely teapot (Crow 1987) designed by
Martin Newell from Bezier patches.

14.7.2 B-Spline Patches

B-spline functions can be used in the tensor product form in place of Bernstein
polynomials to achieve greater local control in surface design:

$$\mathbf{p}(u,\,v) = \sum_{i=0}^{M} \sum_{k=0}^{L} \mathbf{p}_{i,k} N_{i,m}(u) N_{k,m}(v) \qquad (14.64)$$

Figure 14.29.
Achieving tangent continuity
across the boundary.

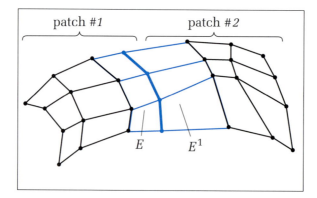

Figure 14.30.
The renowned teapot, based on Bezier patches (Courtesy of Jay Greco.)

Usually the standard knot vector is chosen for both B-spline forms, so that the corners of the polyhedron are properly interpolated. Closed surfaces (in u or v or both) will be formed if control points are duplicated or if a periodic form like that in Equation 14.50 is used. The control polyhedron consists of $(L + 1)(M + 1)$ control points, and u and v each vary from 0 to the maximum knot value in their respective knot vectors. Cubic B-splines are again the popular choice, and because there is no limit on the number of control points (this number does not affect the order of the polynomials as it does for Bezier curves), one can fashion extremely complex surface shapes. As before, the designer must choose the knot polyhedron to create a surface having the desired shape.

Many other techniques have been developed for defining surfaces and operating on them. Several books discuss such approaches, notably Bartels et al. 1988, Coons 1967, Farin 1988, Faux and Pratt 1979, and Mortenson 1985.

14.8 Summary

This chapter discussed how to generate smoothly varying curves by means of a set of control points. A designer can specify a small set of points that acts as data to control the shape of a curve as they are blended numerically. Out of a small set of control points an infinite set of points emerges, one for each value of the parameter t. But the points are, of course, related, being constrained to satisfy a family of geometric properties.

Bezier curves were defined first because of their simplicity. They arise from the iterative de Casteljau process of in-betweening, which lends a great deal of intuition to their properties. They were shown to have an assortment of desirable properties that make their shape predictable, thereby guiding the designer when laying down control points.

Bezier curves are useful in many design situations, but they suffer from lack of control, because the Bernstein polynomials on which they are based have support over the entire parametric interval. Another complication is that as the number of control points is increased in an attempt to introduce more variation in a curve, the order of the underlying polynomials also increases, which tends to "quench" the intended variation and can make the curves less stable numerically.

We therefore examined a richer class of blending functions based on splines, which are piecewise polynomials that piece together in such a way that various orders of derivatives are everywhere continuous. A particular family of basis functions, the B-splines, can generate any spline and are the most concentrated of such shapes. They therefore offer the designer the greatest amount of local control, and they also exhibit the same desirable properties seen in Bezier functions. When the order of the B-spline polynomials is increased to the number of control points being used, the B-splines become identical to Bernstein polynomials.

We also considered surface design using Bezier and B-spline functions. One may think of generating a Bezier patch by sweeping a Bezier curve of changing shape through space. Each point on the moving Bezier curve is moving along a trajectory that is itself a Bezier curve. Bezier patches may be pieced together if certain conditions on the control polyhedra are met. B-spline surfaces were also discussed and shown to offer more flexibility to the designer. Because the order of the polynomials involved does not increase as the number of control points increases, very complex surface shapes can be fashioned.

This chapter only touched on the fundamentals of curve and surface design. Many variations of these techniques have been developed, and large computer-aided design packages often include a broad assortment of methods. The designer can choose from among these and iteratively fine-tune the shapes they produce until the design goals are met. Some shapes, such as the wing of an airplane or the hull of a sailboat, are fashioned from a complex mixture of principles, aesthetics, intuition, and experience.

Programming Exercises

14.33.   Creating and Drawing Bezier Curves. Write and exercise a program that takes as input a control polygon stored as a *polypoint* record, evaluates the resulting Bezier curve, $\mathbf{p}(t)$, at a closely spaced set of t-values between 0 and 1, and draws the polyline they define.

14.34.   Efficient Computation of B-Splines. Based on the discussion of Exercise 14.30, write a routine that generates and stores, for given values of m and Δt, the necessary values of $N[.\,,\,.]$. Write a separate routine that accesses these arrays and draws B-spline curves for a given set of control points.

14.35.   Plotting B-Spline Curves. Write a program that accepts control points $\mathbf{p}_k$, for $k = 0, 1, \ldots, L$, and draws the resulting B-spline curve based on Equation 14.41. Experiment with different orders of B-splines and different configurations of control points. Attempt to predict the course of the curve before it is drawn.

14.36.   Plotting Closed B-Spline Curves. Extend the program in the preceding exercise so that it also draws closed B-splines based on the control points.

14.37.   Approximating a Circle with Closed B-Splines. Experiment with four and eight control points that lie on a circle to see how closely a closed cubic B-spline curve based on these points approximates a circle. Develop a reasonable numerical measure of the error between the curve and the circle, and try different configurations to determine the best curve.

14.38.   Transforming B-Spline Curves. Write a program that accepts a list of control points and auxiliary information that describes a B-spline curve, along with data describing an affine transformation. The program then transforms each control point and draws the B-spline curve based on the transformed control points.

14.39. Implementing *Adjust( )*. Use the two code fragments for forward elimination and back substitution to write and test the routine *Adjust( )* that generates new control points $c[\ ]$ based on original data points $y[\ ]$ so that a B-spline curve interpolates the $y[\ ]$ values.

14.40. Generating Closed Curves That Interpolate. Adjust the interpolation algorithm so that a given set of data points, p_i, for $i = 0, 1, \ldots, L$ is interpolated, and the curve also connects p_L with p_0.

14.41. Building a Curve Editor. Design and exercise a program that allows a user to enter and edit lists of control points and generates the B-spline curve for each on request. The program should allow for filing curve descriptions between design sessions.

Chapter 15

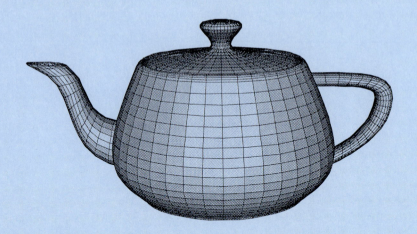

Adding Faces for
Visual Realism

*I never forget a face, but in your case
I'll make an exception.*

Groucho Marx

Goals of the Chapter

- To give solidity to wireframe models
- To define and draw polygon meshes
- To model solid objects as polyhedra
- To build tools that draw these models
- To study a simple hidden surface technique
- To study methods for realistically shading objects

15.1 Introduction: Polygon Mesh Models[†]

In Chapter 10 we used wireframe models to represent solid objects. A wireframe model approximates the surface shape of an object by specifying a set of points in space (the vertex list) and by connecting various pairs of them to form edges (the edge list). The object is "drawn" by drawing each edge in the edge list. Wireframe models look skeletal and hollow, only suggesting the actual shape of an object rather than truly showing it. Because we can see right through the models, it is difficult to tell which edges are closer and which are farther away. The stereo views crafted in Chapter 12 reduce this ambiguity, as does removing edges that should be obscured by closer parts of the solid (see Chapter 17), but we need a simple way to make a solid object look solid, and to color in its surfaces.

This is accomplished by altering the model of the object from a wireframe to a polygonal mesh. A **polygonal mesh** (or simply a **mesh**) approximates the surface shape of an object by specifying a set of points in space (forming a vertex list, as before), but now collections of these points are identified as the vertices of various polygonal **faces.** The faces are identified in a **face list.** Polygons are particularly simple objects to deal with, and we already have quite an arsenal of tools, both analytical and algorithmic, for describing and manipulating them.

An example mesh that describes a prism is shown in Figure 15.1. Each of the six vertices is numbered as shown and is specified in the usual vertex list. A suitable face list is given in Table 15.1.

Table 15.1 Face List for the Prism

Face number	Vertices
1	1 3 2
2	6 2 3 4
3	1 5 4 3
4	4 5 6
5	1 2 6 5

The list for each face begins with any one of its vertices and then proceeds around the face until a complete circuit has been made. A convenient convention is to list the vertices of each face in a particular order: counterclockwise as

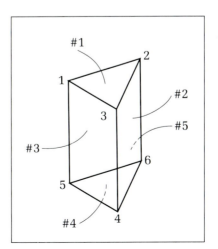

Figure 15.1.
An example mesh for a prism.

†This chapter may be read after Chapter 13.

seen from outside the object. An algorithm can then use this convention to distinguish an inside from an outside surface of a face.

The mesh for the prism has several properties:

- It is a connected mesh; that is, every face shares at least one edge with some other face. Therefore, it is possible to traverse from any face to any other by moving across the appropriate set of edges.

- Every edge in the prism is shared by exactly two faces. This much stronger property makes the object closed, with a definite inside and outside. The prism is in fact a polyhedron:

Definition

A *polyhedron* is a connected mesh of simple polygons such that every edge is shared by exactly two faces.

- Each of the prism's faces is a simple polygon, none of whose edges intersect except at their endpoints.

- Each face of the prism is also a planar polygon; that is, all of its vertices lie in a plane. (Recall the test for planarity in Chapter 7.)

- The prism is a convex polyhedron. As mentioned in Chapter 7, a set of points, I (in this case the interior of the object), is convex if for any two points in I the line joining them lies entirely within I.

Objects to be modeled with polygonal meshes may have some or all of these properties, whose importance varies according to what we want to do with the model. If we are using the model to represent a physical object made of some material, perhaps to determine its mass or center of gravity, we may insist that it be a true polyhedron. Much greater freedom is available if we just want to draw the object, because a face can still be colored red even if it represents an infinitessimally thick part of some surface and no physical object is intended. In some contexts, properties such as connectedness or convexity are important, but in others they are not. For now, there are no particular restrictions on the ingredients of a mesh.[1]

Figure 15.2 shows other examples of objects that are represented by meshes. PYR is a pyramid with a triangular base. Is it a polyhedron? It has four triangular faces that we can list as $(1, 3, 4)$, $(2, 3, 1)$, $(1, 4, 2)$, and $(3, 2, 4)$. The faces need not be equilateral triangles, but if they are, then PYR is a tetrahedron, one of the platonic solids (recall Figure 10.9). Each platonic solid is a regular polyhedron, and they are the only ones possible. Their vertex and face lists are given in Appendix 8.

DONUT shows a solid object with a hole. Is it a polyhedron? STRANGE shows a nonsense object. Can it be described by a polygonal mesh? And BARN suggests a situation that often arises in graphics. Faces that represent windows

---

[1]The obvious constraints are imposed, of course; that is, a face list should refer only to vertices that are defined in the vertex list.

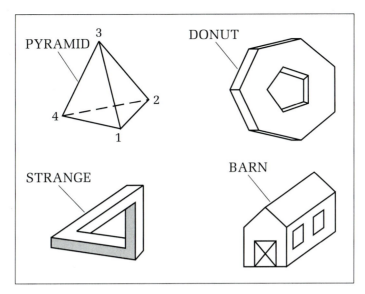

Figure 15.2.
Examples of solids to be
described by meshes.

and doors have been added to the mesh model as "texture." That is, the side of
the barn shown is a rectangle with no holes in it, and the two square windows
are additional faces that happen to lie in the plane of the side. Notice that this is
not a connected mesh, but it can still be displayed on a graphics device.

Drill Exercises

15.1.   Is This Mesh Connected? Is the mesh defined by the
list of faces—(4, 1, 3), (4, 7, 2, 1), (2, 7, 5), (3, 4, 8, 7, 9)—
connected? Try to sketch the object, choosing arbitrary
positions for the nine vertices. What algorithm might be
used to test a face list for connectedness?

15.2.   A Face List for the Barn. Construct a face list for the
basic barn of Figure 10.2, using the vertex labeling shown

there. Follow the conventional ordering of vertices for a
face: counterclockwise when viewed from the outside.

15.3.   Build Meshes. For the DONUT, STRANGE, and
BARN objects in Figure 15.2, assign numbers to each vertex
and then write a face list similar to Table 15.1.

Figure 15.3 shows examples of other objects that can be characterized by
polygonal meshes. These are surfaces rather than solids, however, and are best
thought of as infinitessimally thick "shells." BOX is an open box whose lid has
been raised. In a graphics context we might want to color the outside of BOX's
six faces blue and their insides green. In addition, we will obtain a shell if we
remove a face of a solid. Likewise, if we delete a face from the face list of the
preceding prism or from PYR, only a shell will remain.

Figure 15.3 also shows the surfaces STRUCT and FACE, suggesting the
complexity of some meshes. An important aspect of these examples is that the
polygonal faces are being used to approximate a smooth underlying surface.
Indeed, the mesh may be all that is available, perhaps from digitizing points on a
person's face. If each face of the mesh is drawn as a shaded polygon, the picture
will look artificial, as seen in FACE. Later we shall examine tools that attempt to
draw the underlying surface based only on the mesh model.

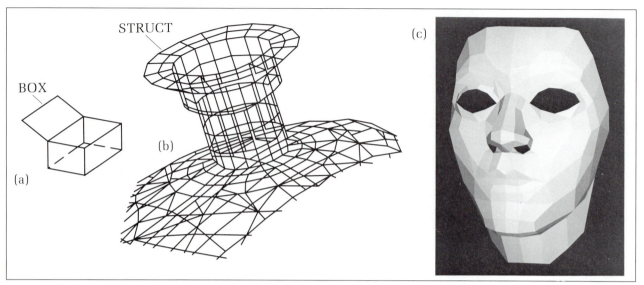

Figure 15.3.

Examples of surfaces to be described by meshes. (Part c is courtesy of the University of Utah.)

Many geometric modeling software packages construct a model for some object—a solid or a surface—that tries to capture the true shape of the object in a polygonal mesh. The problem of composing the lists can be complex. As an example, consider creating an algorithm that can generate the vertex and face lists for a mesh that approximates the shape of an engine block, a prosthetic limb, or a building. This area in fact is a subject of much ongoing research (Mantyla 1988, Mortenson 1985). By using a sufficient number of faces, a mesh can approximate the "underlying surface" to any degree of accuracy desired. This property of completeness makes polygon meshes a versatile tool for modeling.

Notice that for all polygonal meshes, the vertex list contains *locational* or geometric information, and the face list contains *connectivity* or topological information. The vertex list tells where each corner lies, and the face list tells which vertices are connected in a face. By contrast, in wireframe models it is the edge list that contains the connectivity information.

Building Wireframe Models from Polygonal Meshes

Wireframes can be drawn very rapidly on a graphics display. For that reason we may want to preview a scene or animation by drawing wireframe pictures of the objects instead of coloring every face in each mesh model.

A wireframe model of an object is easily built from its polygon mesh. The vertex list for the wireframe is the same as that for the mesh, and the edge list is built by scanning the face list and finding every edge. For example, the pyramid PYR of Figure 15.2 contains the faces $(1, 3, 4)$, $(2, 3, 1)$, $(1, 4, 2)$, and $(3, 2, 4)$. The edges are simply read off: $(1, 3)$, $(3, 4)$, $(4, 1)$, $(2, 3)$, and so forth. Each edge that is shared by two faces appears twice during the scan, but these duplicates are easily culled from the list (see the programming exercises).

By contrast, a polygonal mesh cannot always be constructed from a wireframe model. Figure 15.4 shows the classic example. From an edge list alone there is no way to tell where the faces are: Even a wireframe model for a cube could be a closed box or an open one. There is more information, therefore, in a polygon mesh representation than in an edge list.

Figure 15.4.
An ambiguous object.

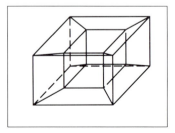

15.1.1 Data Structures for a Polygon Mesh

What is a good way to structure the data for a polygonal mesh? We have already discussed vertex lists. Now we shall build a face list as a linked list of records of type *face*. Figure 15.5 and the following code fragment show how type *face* might be organized.

Code Fragment 15.1. Suggested Data Type for Face Lists

```
face_ptr = ^face;
face = record
          vert : vertexlist_ptr;
          face_plane : plane;
          nature : attributes;
          next : face_ptr
       end;
```

As shown in the figure, the *vert* field points to the list of specific vertices that belong in the face. Each element in this list points to some vertex in the vertex list (or contains its index if the vertices are stored in an array), and the vertices are listed in the counterclockwise order discussed earlier. A linked list is convenient here because the number of vertices varies from face to face.

The *face_plane* field stores a description of the plane in which the face lies, assuming that it is a planar polygon. We shall see later that this plane information is used to determine how light reflects off the face. A data type for planes was introduced in Chapter 7 (also see Appendix 3). It contains the vector $\mathbf{n}$ and the position d of the plane's point normal form, $\mathbf{n} \cdot \mathbf{p} = d$. The values of $\mathbf{n}$ and d are easily computed for each face in the mesh (see Section 7.8.2).

Usually a color is associated with each face, as well as some surface characteristics that describe how light reflects off the surface, such as glossy, dull matte, smooth, or possibly clay, pewter, or zinc. So a field, *nature*, of type *attributes* is included, in which *attributes* might itself be a complex list of surface

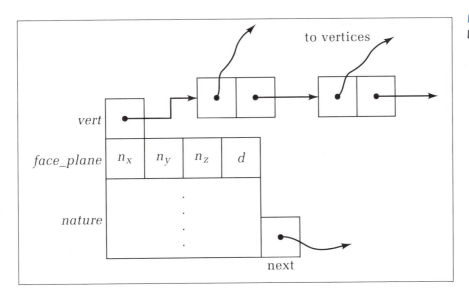

Figure 15.5.
Data type for faces in a mesh.

properties. We shall defer the details of *attributes* until later. Note that when both the inside surface and the outside surface are of interest, separate data can be kept for both.

15.1.2 Building Some Polygon Meshes

In Chapter 10 we examined some ways to generate wireframe models of various classes of objects, such as patches, surfaces of revolution, and prisms. Here we shall extend those ideas to creating face lists for the same kinds of objects.

The Prism

Figure 15.6 shows ARROW, an example prism based on a polygonal base having seven vertices. What is its face list? In regard to connectedness, we can "unfold" the prism, as shown, to expose its nine faces, as seen from the outside. There are seven "side" rectangular faces plus the top and bottom caps. Face 3, for instance, is defined by vertices 3, 10, 11, and 4.

Suppose more generally that the prism's base is a polygon with N vertices. We number the vertices of the top cap $1, \ldots, N$ and those of the bottom cap $N + 1, \ldots, 2N$, so that an edge joins vertices i and $i + N$, as in the example. Then if we number the side faces $1, \ldots, N$ the j-th of these faces will have vertices $j, j + N$, $j + N + 1$, and $j + 1$. (What adjustments must be made when $j = N$?)

The vertex list for the j-th side face (for $j = 1, \ldots, N$) can be built as suggested by the following pseudocode fragment. A new face record, pointed to by *new_face*, is allocated to hold the face, and then a list of the four vertices shared by this face is built.

This is done by creating a record for each of them, loading the proper index value of its vertex, and using the routine *AddVert( )* to add the new node to the list. Because the sequence of vertex numbers that must be taken from the vertex list is rather irregular, an array of appropriate values is loaded, taking into account that the last side face involves a "wrap-around" to the first face. When the vertex list for this face is complete, it is scanned to obtain geometric information in order to compute the point normal form for the plane in which the face lies. Finally, the new face record is inserted into the face list for the prism.

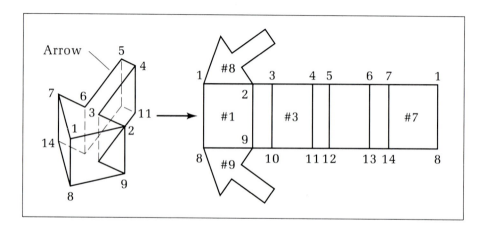

Figure 15.6.
An example prism.

Code Fragment 15.2. Building the j-th Side Face of the Prism

```
var
  j, jp1, k : integer;
  v : array[1. .4] of integer;
    .
    .
    .

  new (new_face); {build new side face of prism}
  if j < N then jp1 := j + 1 else jp1 := 1; {wrap-around for last face}
  v[1] := j; v[2] := j + N; v[3] := N + jp1; v[4] := jp1; {index of vertex}
  for k := 1 to 4 do
  begin
    new(new_vert);
    new_vert^.which_vertex := v[k];
    < add new_vert to list using vert field >
  end;
  <scan this list to compute normal vector and d of plane>
  <enter attributes of face>
  <add new_face to face list>
```

Finally two more faces, one for each polygon cap, are added to the face list (see the programming exercises).

Patches and Mathematical Surfaces

A variety of surfaces was described in Chapter 9, including patches, surfaces of revolution, mathematical surfaces, and superquadrics. Drawing their wireframes was discussed in Chapter 10. Each of these is defined parametrically as the vector function, $\mathbf{p}(u, v)$, of the two parameters, u and v. To draw them as wireframes, we selected a set of u-values, $u_1, u_2, \ldots$ and v-values, $v_1, v_2, \ldots$ and fashioned each surface point $\mathbf{p}_{i,j} = \mathbf{p}(u_i, v_j)$ into a vertex in the vertex list.

The same vertex list can be used here. Figure 15.7 shows a portion of such a surface with a vertex defined at each intersection of a u-contour and a v-contour.

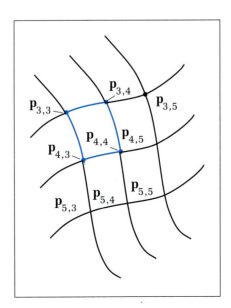

Figure 15.7.
Building faces for a parametric surface.

For instance, the face shown colored has vertices $\mathbf{p}_{3,3}$, $\mathbf{p}_{4,3}$, $\mathbf{p}_{4,4}$, and $\mathbf{p}_{3,4}$. Each face has four vertices, which can be inserted into a face list in much the same way as we did for the prism. Each straight edge of a face may only approximate the (generally curved) contour segment of the true surface between the corresponding pair of vertices, but when the contours are closely spaced, this does not present a problem. Also, the four corners of a face might not be coplanar. The Newell method (see Section 7.8.2) for finding the normal to a plane may still be used in this case. It returns an approximation to the desired normal. Some modelers form only triangular faces using various triangulation algorithms (Brodlie 1980). Triangles have the advantages of being both convex and planar. Note that we could build a face list of triangular faces by subdividing each face into two triangles. For example, for the face colored in Figure 15.7, we would form two triangles by adding an edge from $\mathbf{p}_{3,4}$ to $\mathbf{p}_{4,3}$.

Drill Exercise

15.4. Modeling Stacked Blocks. Appendix D discusses another class of solids based on stacks of blocks. Choose a configuration of four blocks, and write the face and vertex lists for it by hand. When two blocks abut so that each has a face that lies in the same plane and shares an edge with the other, combine these faces into a single face. Show the resulting face list.

15.2   Preparing a Mesh Model for Viewing

How is a polygon mesh model drawn? We first establish the desired view of the scene by using a synthetic camera, as discussed in Chapter 12. With this particular view in mind, we then scan the model and do some geometric preprocessing:

- *Remove back faces.* A **back face** is one that is "turned away from the eye" of the camera. When the model represents a solid object that has opaque faces, these back faces are not visible, and so they can be skipped in the drawing process. Skipping back faces gives pictures of a mesh much greater realism and, of course, speeds up the rendering process.

- *Clip the faces.* Each face can be clipped against the view volume. Some faces are thereby completely eliminated, some are left unscathed, and others have their vertices altered.

These steps are discussed later and can be done in either order. Removing back faces is very simple and so is often done first. Then the remaining "front" faces can be clipped. On the other hand, clipping is fairly involved and so is sometimes skipped. This should present no problem when one is confident that the entire mesh lies inside the intended view volume.

The two preprocessing steps result in a new visible face list for the particular view seen by the camera. (The original face list of the model should not be tampered with, as we may need it later for other views.) This list might well be called the *potentially visible face list*, as there is no guarantee that all faces on it will be completely visible.

Figure 15.8 shows views of objects in which only the front faces have been drawn. (For simplicity these are line drawings; just the edges of each face on the visible face list have been drawn.) BARN1 is a clipped version of Figure 12.11. Because all front faces should in fact be drawn in their entirety here, the picture is correct. Notice how much easier it is to interpret than Figure 12.11 is. BARN2 and DODECA have also been drawn correctly, and they look solid and opaque. But BLOCK has a front face that is partially obscured by another front face. This gives rise to some extra "false lines" in the drawing.

The first three objects in the figure are drawn properly because each of their faces is either totally visible or totally invisible; one face never partially covers another. This is generally true of convex polyhedra.

Fact: Every face of a convex polyhedron is either wholly visible or wholly invisible.

Therefore, for convex polyhedra, eliminating the back faces means completely removing any hidden surfaces! On the other hand, drawing all front faces of objects that are not convex can lead to incorrect results. For now we must just accept this possibility and concentrate on shading issues. More reliable hidden-surface elimination techniques are developed in Chapter 17.

To render the drawing, we scan the visible face list and color in each face in turn, using a shading model that dictates how the light interacts with the surface in question. We shall describe various shading models that achieve different degrees of visual realism in section 15.3.

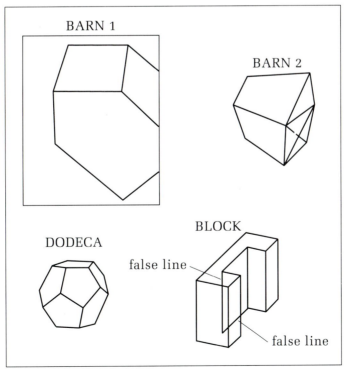

Figure 15.8.
Objects with back faces removed.

15.2.1 Preprocessing I: Removing Back Faces

How are back faces distinguished from front faces? Happily we need only test the sign of a single dot product! Figure 15.9 shows how to test a face, F, on some mesh object, when the camera's eye is at position vector $\mathbf{e}$. Face F has the outward normal $\mathbf{n}_F$. Choose any point, $\mathbf{q}$, on the face. Suppose θ is the angle between $\mathbf{n}_F$ and a line from $\mathbf{q}$ to the eye, represented by vector $\mathbf{e} - \mathbf{q}$. F is a back face if θ is larger than 90 degrees. Recall from Chapter 7 that $\theta > 90°$ only when the dot product $\mathbf{n}_F \cdot (\mathbf{e} - \mathbf{q})$ is negative. If the dot product is zero, the face lies parallel to the line of sight and is again invisible.

To carry out this test, we must know the three quantities $\mathbf{q}$, $\mathbf{n}_F$, and $\mathbf{e}$. Of these, $\mathbf{q}$ and $\mathbf{n}_F$ are easy: $\mathbf{q}$ is the position of any one of the vertices in the vertex list for face F. If **var** $F : face\_ptr$ points to face F, the first vertex in its vertex list will be $F\hat{}.vert\hat{}$ (see Code Fragment 15.1). In addition, $\mathbf{n}_F$ is obtained directly as $F\hat{}.face\_plane.normal$. To specify $\mathbf{e}$ we must take into account the arbitrary position and orientation of the synthetic camera, summarized by the vectors $\mathbf{u}$, $\mathbf{v}$, $\mathbf{n}$, and the view reference point $\mathbf{r}$ (see Figure 15.9 and Equation 12.6). Because $\mathbf{e}$ is usually specified in viewing coordinates $\mathbf{e} = (e_u, e_v, e_n)$, we must convert it into world coordinates. The discussion following Equation 12.6 shows that in world coordinates, it is given by $(e_x, e_y, e_z) = \mathbf{e}M + \mathbf{r}$.

The following function, $BackFace(\ )$, implements this test. It will return $true$ if the face is a back face. The conversion of the eye position from viewing into world coordinates is assumed to be carried out in an appropriate procedure, $ViewToWorld(e : point3D; \textbf{var}\ eye : point3D)$.

Code Fragment 15.3. Testing for a Back Face

```
function BackFace(q, e : point3D; nf : vector3D) : boolean;
{true if face with outward normal nf and vertex q is a back face}
var eye : point3D; {eye in world coordinates}
begin
   ViewToWorld(e, eye); {convert into world coordinates}
   if(nf.dx * (eye.x − q.x)
       + nf.dy * (eye.y − q.y) + nf.dz * (eye.z − q.z)) <= 0.0
   then BackFace := true else BackFace := false
end;
```

Figure 15.9.
Testing for a back face.

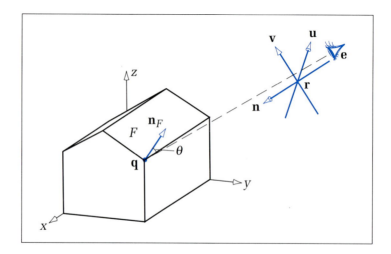

The construction of the visible face list, F_{vis}, therefore begins with a scan through each face in the model's face list, F_{mod}. For each front face found in F_{mod} a copy is made of its record (of type *face*) and added to F_{vis}. Any back faces are ignored. It is wise during this process to build a new vertex list, V_{vis}, adding all vertices that belong to a front face (but never adding the same vertex twice). This removes from further consideration those vertices belonging only to back faces. More important, all subsequent processing for this view of the object can take place in the copy of the vertex list—the original list of the model is never corrupted. The moral applies here too: Be sure to keep modeling and viewing separate! The exercises request an implementation of this process.

Drill Exercises

15.5. Building F_{vis} for a View of the Barn. The camera position is described by $\mathbf{r} = (.5, .5, .5)$, $\mathbf{norm} = (-1, 4, -2)$, $\mathbf{up} = (0, 0, 1)$, and $\mathbf{e} = (0, 0, -5)$. Construct the visible face list, F_{vis}, for this view of the basic barn. Refer to the wireframe rendering of this view shown in Figure 12.7 and defend your result.

15.6. Convex Objects. Prove that each of the faces in a convex polyhedron is either wholly visible or wholly invisible.

15.7. Back Faces for the Arrow Prism. Consider different orientations of the ARROW prism of Figure 15.6 relative to the eye. Describe the class of orientations for which the elimination of back faces results in perfect hidden line removal. Repeat for the DONUT in Figure 15.2.

15.2.2 Preprocessing II: Clipping Faces

Whereas detecting back faces was easily performed in world coordinates using the original vertex list of the model, clipping against the view volume is most easily carried out in viewing coordinates. In Chapter 12 we described one overall matrix transformation that maps a point, $\mathbf{p}$, in world coordinates into a convenient final form for clipping and viewing.

Consider a vertex, $\mathbf{p} = (p_x, p_y, p_z)$, of the mesh. According to Equation 12.37, we first convert it into the homogeneous coordinate form by appending a 1 and then multiply it by the matrix:

$$\hat{M}_{all} = \hat{A}_{WV}\hat{M}_S\hat{M}_P \qquad (15.1)$$

$\hat{A}_{WV}$ (see Equation 12.12) converts a point from world coordinates into the viewing coordinates of the camera; $\hat{M}_S$ (of Equation 12.24) accounts for a shear when the eye does not lie on the **n**-axis; and $\hat{M}_P$ (of Equation 12.22) performs the perspective transformation that warps the view volume into a parallelepiped. (The normalization transformation of Equation 12.40 could also be included here, but it is more convenient not to for the rendering approach presented in Section 15.4.2.) Call the result of this transformation $\hat{g} = (g_u, g_v, g_n, g_w)$:

$$\hat{g} = \hat{p}\hat{M}_{all} \qquad (15.2)$$

This is the form of the vertices to be used in the clipping algorithm.

Suppose we have removed back faces as described and have built the "visible face list," F_{vis}, and the "visible vertex list," V_{vis}. To set things up for clipping and drawing, we store additional information for each vertex in V_{vis}. Each vertex, $\mathbf{p}$, in V_{vis} is transformed into a 4-tuple, $\hat{g}$, according to Equation 15.2, and stored along with its corresponding $\mathbf{p}$. As we shall see, the original vertex positions in world coordinates must be retained to make proper shading calculations. So to reserve space for $\hat{g}$, each record in V_{vis} uses the following datatype:

Code Fragment 15.4. Suggested Data Type for the Visible Vertex List

```
type
    VisVertPrt = ^VisVert;
    VisVert = record
                    model_pt : point3D;
                    view_pt : point4D;
                    next : VisVertPtr
              end;
```

This version assumes that V_{vis} is constructed as a linked list. Alternatively, we could use arrays.

Examples of Clipping Faces

Suppose for the moment that we wish to produce a line drawing of the model. For this we need only clip each edge of each face in F_{vis} against the view volume, as defined by the front and back planes and the window (W_l, W_t, W_r, W_b). The clipping method of Code Fragment 12.3 can be used intact for each edge. New endpoints, $\hat{g}$ and $\hat{h}$, are found by the clipper for each surviving edge. Then because $\hat{M}_{\text{all}}$ maps points with the proper perspective foreshortening, the endpoints are projected into the window as (g_u/g_w, g_v/g_w) and as (h_u/h_w, h_v/h_w) (why?). So we simply use *Line*( ) to draw the surviving portion of each edge.

On the other hand, suppose that we wish to fill polygons with colors. The primitive object is now a polygon rather than an edge, and we must preserve its identity as a polygon for later filling. To do this, a polygon-clipping algorithm such as the Sutherland–Hodgman clipper (see Appendix 6) must be used. This method traverses each face polygon and clips each successive edge against the view volume. Edge clipping is done here in four-dimensional space, just as in Code Fragment 12.3. The result of clipping a face against the planes of the view volume is a vertex sequence that describes the clipped polygon. For instance, in Figure 15.10, face G originally had vertex sequence 3 4 6 7, but after clipping against plane P of the view volume, only the part with vertex sequence b 4 6 e remains. Two new vertices, b and e, have been created. The data for face G in F_{vis} must be adjusted to reflect this, with appropriate changes being made to V_{vis} also.

The result of clipping may also be more than one polygon, as in the case of face F in Figure 15.10. Originally face F had vertex sequence 1 5 4 3 2. After clipping against P, the new vertex sequence is a b 4 c d 1, as shown. This describes the two faces with vertices b 4 c and d 1 a, along with an "extraneous edge" from d to c. The vertex sequence a b 4 c d 1 is scanned to identify the extraneous edge (how?) and to form the two polygons, which are put on the face list.

With the clipping completed (if it is done at all), the vertices are next converted from homogeneous into ordinary coordinates by the usual division operation. If no hidden surfaces are to be removed, the faces will simply be displayed by a polygon fill algorithm based on the x- and y- components of the vertices in the vertex list.

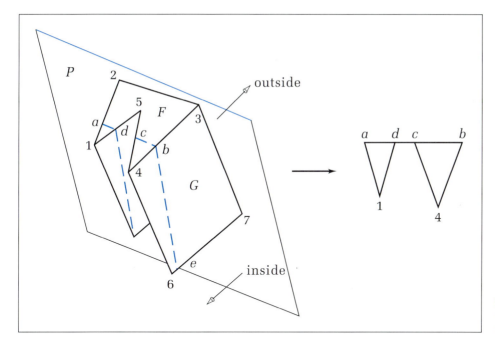

Figure 15.10.
Clipping faces against the view
volume.

15.3 Shading Models for Faces

Having fashioned the preprocessed lists, F_{vis} and V_{vis}, that describe the view of
the model, we turn to filling in each face with a suitable color or set of colors. A
pointer, F, moves through F_{vis}, and a routine such as *ColorFace(F : face_ptr)*
colors the face pointed to by F. (Keep in mind that "color" includes simple
shades of gray as a special case. In this chapter we focus on determining the
proper shade of gray for each pixel. Chapter 16 deals with more general colors.)
The implementation of *ColorFace( )* that computes the proper color depends on
the choice of shading model, and we shall examine several different models
here.

15.3.1 Types of Shading Models

Various types of face drawing are available, with the choice depending on the
degree of visual realism desired. Typically the computational cost increases
with the degree of realism. The main types of drawing are as follows:

- *Line drawing.* The edges of each front face are drawn. This generates the
  familiar wireframe drawings, except that the extra information present
  in a face list has been exploited to identify the back faces.

- *Filled wireframes.* Each face is filled uniformly with a single shade or
  color using a simple polygon fill algorithm. Only the colors of each face
  (or possibly the color of its inside and outside surfaces) need be stored in
  the face list. Filling wireframes can give objects a solid and opaque
  appearance, but they tend to look flat and artificial. If two adjacent faces
  have the same color, the boundary between them will be invisible.
  (What would a cube look like in this case?)

- *Flat shading.* Each face is filled with a single shade or color, but the shade is determined by a **shading model.** A *shading model* combines information about various sources of light in the environment with data about the roughness and color of the face's surface to approximate how the actual light reflects from the surface of the face. With flat shading the shading model is applied to only one point on each face, and the shade determined there is used to fill the entire face.

- *Smooth shading.* The color or shade varies at different points on the face. The shading model is applied to several points within the face, and the different shades found at these points are blended to yield the shade at each point within the face. To reduce computation time, the shading model is sometimes applied at only a few points on each face, and interpolation is used to approximate the shade at other points on the face.

- *Mesh smoothing.* When the shading model is applied to some points on two neighboring faces, and interpolation is used to find the shade for points in between, we may receive an important bonus: The facetlike nature of the model with its individual polygonal faces is deemphasized in the picture. That is, the technique effectively smooths out the sharp edges between the faces and produces a drawing that looks more like the underlying surface being modeled by the polygonal mesh!

- *Ray tracing.* Ray tracing of polygonal meshes is an extension of smooth shading. The shading model is applied to the object at a very dense set of points. As we shall see, each pixel on the display corresponds to a "direction of looking" into the scene. A ray is cast from the eye in that direction, and the shading model is applied to the first surface point that this ray encounters. This is done for every pixel in the image. Ray tracing can be applied in this way to polygonal mesh models, but it is even more effective on models with complex smooth surfaces, such as spheres, cones, and cylinders. Scenes rendered using ray tracing often exhibit stunning realism. Indeed, ray tracing is a fascinating subject in itself and is discussed further in Chapter 18.

15.3.2 Introduction to Shading Models

Imagine a collection of polyhedra built from different materials and having different colors. The objects are bathed in light from some light source. A camera is situated in the scene. From its point of view some faces are in shadow, and others reflect light from the source. Some faces are seen straight on, and others are seen at a grazing angle. Furthermore, some faces might be shinier than others and might show highlights.

When the polyhedra being drawn are supposed to represent physical objects (real or imagined) and a realistic rendering is desired, the appropriate shade of color of each face must be computed according to the nature of the light reflected from the surface. Different points on a given face may reflect different amounts of light, and so the various pixels that "see" the face must be set to different colors or intensities. Simple uniform fill algorithms cannot be used in such cases, resulting in a much greater computational burden in rendering a scene.

The mechanism of light reflection from an actual surface is very complicated, as it depends on many factors. Some of these are geometric, such as the relative directions of the light source, the observer's eye, and the normal to the surface. Others are related to the nature, roughness, and color of the surface.

A shading model dictates how light is scattered or reflected from a surface. We shall examine some simple shading models here, focusing on achromatic light. **Achromatic** light has brightness but no color; it is only a shade of gray. Hence it is described by a single value: intensity. We shall see how to calculate the intensity of the light reaching the synthetic camera from each portion of the object. In Chapter 16 the algorithms are extended to include colored light and colored objects. The computations are almost identical to those here, except that separate intensities of red, green, and blue components are calculated.

A shading model frequently used in graphics supposes that two types of light sources illuminate the objects in a scene: *point* light sources and **ambient** light. These light sources "shine" on the various surfaces of the objects, and the incident light interacts with the surface in three different ways: (1) Some is absorbed by the surface and is converted to heat; (2) some is reflected from the surface; and (3) some is transmitted into the interior of the object, as in the case of a piece of glass. If all incident light is absorbed, the object will appear black and is known as a **black body.** If all is transmitted, the object will be visible only through the effects of refraction, which we shall discuss in Chapter 18.

Here we focus on the part of the light that is reflected from the surface. Some fraction of this reflected light travels in just the right direction to reach the eye, causing the object to be seen. The fraction that travels to the eye is highly dependent on the geometry of the situation. We assume that there are two types of reflection of incident light: diffuse reradiation and specular reflection.

- **Diffuse reradiation,** or **scattering,** occurs when some of the incident light slightly penetrates the surface and is reemitted uniformly in all directions. Scattered light interacts strongly with the surface, and so its color is usually affected by the nature of the surface material (as we shall consider in Chapter 16).

- **Specular reflections** are more mirrorlike and are highly directional: Incident light does not penetrate the object but instead is reflected directly from its outer surface. This gives rise to highlights and makes the surface look shiny. Specularly reflected light has the same color as the incident light.

Most surfaces produce some combination of the two types of reflection, depending on surface characteristics such as roughness and material. We say that the total light reflected from the surface in a certain direction is the sum of the diffuse component and the specular component. For each surface point of interest we compute the size of each component that reaches the eye. Algorithms are developed next to accomplish this.

Geometric Ingredients for Finding Reflected Light

Figure 15.11 indicates the three directions that are used in computing the diffuse and specular components of light reaching the eye from a point, **p**, on a surface:

1. The normal vector, **n**, to the surface at **p**.
2. The vector **v** from **p** to the viewer's eye.
3. The vector **s** from **p** to the light source.

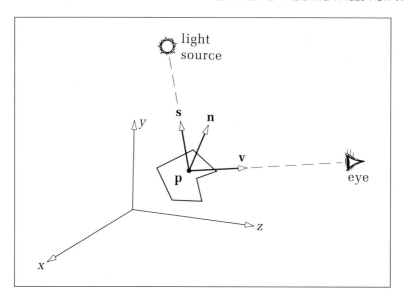

Figure 15.11.
Important directions in
computing reflected light.

The angles between the various vectors related to these three directions form the
basis for computing light intensities. Note that the figure shows the surface in
world coordinates. Computations involving the angles between vectors are normally performed in world coordinates, because some transformations such as
the perspective transformation do not preserve angles.

Computing the Diffuse Component: Lambert's Law

Suppose that light falls from a point source onto a **facet** (a small piece of a
surface), S. A fraction of it is reradiated diffusely in all directions. Some fraction
of the reradiated part reaches the eye, with intensity of, say, I_d. How does I_d
depend on the directions **n**, **v**, and **s**?

Because the scattering is uniform in all directions, the orientation of the
facet relative to the eye is not significant (assuming, of course, the facet is not
pointed away from the eye). Therefore, I_d is independent of the angle between **n**
and **v**. On the other hand, the amount of light that illuminates facet S does
depend on the orientation of S relative to the point source: It is proportional to
the area of S that it sees, or the area subtended.

Figure 15.12a shows in cross section a point source illuminating facet S
when **n** is aligned with **s**. In Figure 15.12b the facet is turned partially away from
the light source through angle θ. The area subtended is now only $\cos(\theta)$ as much
as before, so that the brightness of S is reduced by this same factor. This relationship between brightness and surface orientation is often called *Lambert's
law*. Notice that for θ near 0, the dependence of brightness on angle is rather
slight, because the cosine changes slowly there. As θ approaches 90°, however,
the brightness falls rapidly to 0.

We know from Chapter 7 that the cosine of the angle between **s** and **n** is
proportional to the dot product between their normalized versions, that is, to
$\mathbf{u}_s \cdot \mathbf{u}_n$. We can therefore summarize the strength of the diffuse component
reaching the eye from facet S by

$$I_d = I_s r_d \, (\mathbf{u}_s \cdot \mathbf{u}_n) \qquad\qquad (15.3)$$

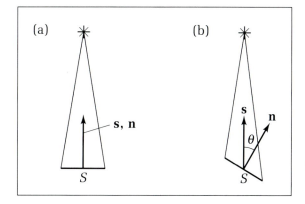

Figure 15.12.
The brightness depends on the
area subtended.

In this equation, I_s is the intensity of the light source, and r_d is the **diffuse** *reflection coefficient.* In reality, however, the mechanism behind diffuse reflection is much more complex than this simple model. The reflection coefficient r_d depends on the wavelength (color) of the incident light, the angle θ, and various physical properties of the surface. But for simplicity and to reduce computation time, these effects are usually suppressed when rendering images. A "reasonable" value for r_d is chosen for each surface, sometimes by trial and error according to the realism observed in the resulting image.

In some shading models the effect of distance is also included, although it is somewhat controversial. The light intensity falling on facet S in Figure 15.12 from the point source is known to fall off as the inverse square of the distance between S and the source. But experiments have shown that using this law directly yields pictures with exaggerated depth effects. (What is more, it is sometimes convenient to model light sources "at infinity," whereby the use of this law quenches all of the light!) The problem is thought to be in the model: We model light sources as point sources for simplicity, but most scenes are actually illuminated by additional reflections from the surroundings, which are difficult to model. (These effects are lumped together into an ambient light component.) It is not surprising, therefore, that strict adherence to a physical law based on an unrealistic model can lead to unrealistic results.

The realism of most pictures is not enhanced by the introduction of a distance term. Some approaches force the intensity to be inversely proportional to the distance between the eye and the object, but this is not based on physical principles. It is interesting to experiment with such effects, but we don't include a distance term in the following development.

Specular Reflection

Real objects do not scatter light uniformly in all directions, and so a specular component is added to the shading model. Specular reflection causes highlights, which can add significantly to the realism of a picture of objects that are somewhat shiny. Figure 15.13a shows incident light on a facet from direction **s** that is scattered in a variety of directions, but most strongly in the "reflection direction," **r**, the direction in which all the light would travel if the surface were a pure mirror. From Chapter 7 we know that this direction is

$$\mathbf{r} = -\mathbf{s} + 2(\mathbf{s} \cdot \mathbf{u}_n)\mathbf{u}_n \tag{15.4}$$

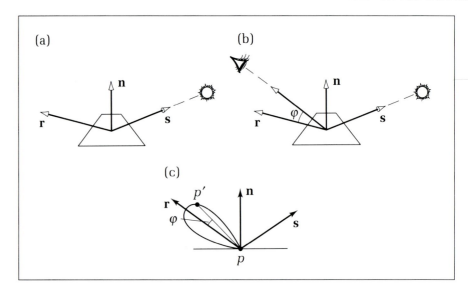

Figure 15.13.
Specular reflection from a shiny
surface.

For surfaces that are shiny but not true mirrors, the amount of light reflected falls off as the angle φ between **r** and **v** increases (see Figure 15.13b). Figure 15.13c suggests in cross section a way of envisioning this: A beam pattern is shown about **r**, the length of the line from p to p' measuring the relative strength of the reflection at an angle φ away from **r**. The actual amount of falloff is a complicated function of φ, but it can be approximated by the Phong model (Phong 1975). In this model the amount of light varies as some power f of the cosine of φ, that is, according to $(\cos(\phi))^f$, in which f is chosen experimentally and usually varies from 1 to 200.

Figure 15.14 shows how this intensity function varies with φ for different values of f. As f increases, the reflection becomes more mirrorlike and is more highly concentrated along the direction **r**. A perfect mirror could be modeled using $f = \infty$, but pure reflections are usually handled in a different manner, as described in Chapter 18.

Using the equivalence $\cos(\phi) = \mathbf{u}_r \cdot \mathbf{u}_v$, the contribution I_{sp} due to specular reflection is modeled by

$$I_{sp} = I_s r_s (\mathbf{u}_r \cdot \mathbf{u}_v)^f \tag{15.5}$$

where the new term r_s is the **specular reflection coefficient**. Like most other coefficients in the shading model, it is usually determined experimentally.

Figure 15.14.
Falloff of specular light with
angle.

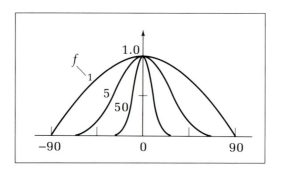

Drill Exercises

15.8. Drawing Beam Patterns. Draw beam patterns similar to that in Figure 15.13c for the cases $f = 1$, $f = 10$, and $f = 100$.

15.9. Efficient Approximation to cos(φ). Often an approximation to the specular term is used in order to reduce computation. Instead of using the cosine of the angle between $\mathbf{r}$ and $\mathbf{v}$, one finds a vector halfway between $\mathbf{s}$ and $\mathbf{v}$, that is, $\mathbf{b} = \mathbf{s} + \mathbf{v}$, and approximates $\mathbf{u}_r \cdot \mathbf{u}_v$ by $\mathbf{u}_b \cdot \mathbf{u}_n$. By examining the geometry of the situation, determine how accurate this approximation is.

15.3.3 The Role of Ambient Light

The diffuse and specular components of reflected light are found by simplifying the "rules" by which physical light reflects from physical surfaces. The dependence of these components on the relative positions of the eye, model, and light sources greatly improves the realism of a picture over renderings that simply fill a wireframe with a shade.

But our desire for simple reflection rules leaves us with far from perfect renderings of a scene. As an example, shadows are seen to be unrealistically deep and harsh. To soften these shadows, we can add a third light component called ambient light.

Shadows

Diffuse and specular reflections arrive from those points on a face that are bathed in illumination from the point light source. A point on the object, such as B in Figure 15.15, cannot "see" the light source because some face lies between the point and the source. In that case the point is in shadow. Sometimes an entire face, such as face A, is in shadow, as when it is turned away from the source. The calculation of the geometry of shadows is closely related to the hidden-surface removal problem—computing which parts of faces hide other parts—and so its development will be deferred until Chapter 17.

With only diffuse and specular reflections, any parts of a surface that are shadowed from the point source receive no light and so are drawn black! But this is not our everyday experience. The scenes we observe around us always seem to be bathed in some soft nondirectional light. This light arrives by multiple reflections from various objects in the surroundings and from extended sources (as opposed to point sources) that populate the environment, such as light coming through a window, fluorescent lamps, and the like. But it would be very expensive computationally to model this kind of light precisely.

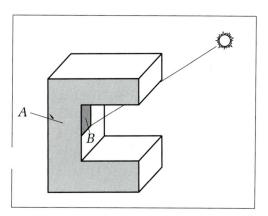

Figure 15.15.
Parts of an object lying in shadow.

Ambient Sources and Ambient Reflections

To overcome the problem of totally dark shadows, we imagine that a uniform "background glow" called **ambient light** exists in the environment. This ambient light source is not situated at any particular place, and it spreads in all directions uniformly. The source is assigned an intensity, I_a. Each face in the model is assigned a value for its **ambient reflection coefficient**, r_a (often this is the same as the diffuse reflection coefficient, r_d), and the term $I_a r_a$ is simply added to whatever diffuse and specular light is reaching the eye from each point **p** on that face. I_a and r_a are usually arrived at experimentally, by trying various values and seeing what looks best. Too little ambient light makes shadows appear too deep and harsh; too much makes the picture look washed out and bland.

15.3.4 Computing the Final Pixel Values

We can now sum the three light contributions—diffuse, specular, and ambient—to form the total amount of light I that reaches the eye from point **p**:

$$I = I_a r_a + I_s [r_d (\mathbf{u}_s \cdot \mathbf{u}_n) + r_s (\mathbf{u}_r \cdot \mathbf{u}_v)^f] \qquad (15.6)$$

I depends on the various source intensities and reflection coefficients, as well as on the relative positions of the point **p**, the eye, and the point light source. If several point light sources are present, there will be a diffuse and specular term for each (but still only one ambient term). The parts that change from source to source are I_s, $\mathbf{u}_s$, and $\mathbf{u}_r$.

To gain some insight into the variation of I with the position of **p**, consider again Figure 15.11. I is computed for different points **p** on the facet shown. The ambient component shows no variation over the facet; **n** is the same for all **p** on the facet, but the directions of both **s** and **v** depend on **p**. If the light source is fairly far away (the typical case), **s** will change only slightly as **p** changes, so that the diffuse component that varies as $\mathbf{u}_s \cdot \mathbf{u}_n$ will change only slightly for different points **p**. This is especially true when **s** and **n** are nearly aligned, as the value of cos( ) changes slowly for small angles. For remote light sources, the variation in the reflection direction, **r**, also is slight as **p** varies. On the other hand, if the light source is close to the facet, there can be substantial changes in **s** and **r** as **p** varies. Then $\mathbf{u}_r \cdot \mathbf{u}_v$ can change significantly over the facet, and the bright highlight can be confined to a small portion of the facet. This effect is increased when the eye is also close to the facet—causing large changes in the direction of **v**—and when the exponent f is very large.

Drill Exercise

15.10.   Effect of the Eye Distance. Consider how much the various light contributions change as **p** varies over a facet when the eye is far away from the facet and when the eye is near the facet.

Mapping I to Pixel Values

Each intensity value I is calculated using real (floating-point) values, such as .3547 or 23.178. But pixel values in a frame buffer must be integers. Suppose that the frame buffer supports b bits/pixel. Then the pixel values range from 0 to $M - 1$, where $M = 2^b$. How do we map values of I into the range 0 to $M - 1$? This depends on whether or not we have a color lookup table (LUT).

The raster displays used to view achromatic (gray-scale) images might be built to produce either shades of gray or full-color images. A monochrome display usually maps pixel values, v, directly into intensity values, so that $v = 0$ is seen as fully dark (black) and $v = M - 1$ as the brightest level attainable. Values of v between 0 and $M - 1$ normally map to intensity levels so that the perceived brightness is proportional to v.

Sometimes we may want to display an achromatic image even when a full-color display is available. Achromatic images are easier and faster to compute, and therefore we may want to preview the scene in grays while debugging an application, before rendering the scene in full color. We may also want to create and store an image for subsequent display on a monochrome monitor.

Color displays often have LUTs. Each of the $M = 2^b$ entries in the LUT is loaded with a value to produce a gray level proportional to its index value. Gray levels are produced by setting the red, green, and blue components to equal intensities. For example, suppose that $b = 4$ and each of the 16 entries in the LUT holds 12 bits, 4 bits for each of the DACs (recall Chapter 2). Set entry 0 to 0000 0000 0000 for black, entry 8 to 1000 1000 1000 for medium gray, entry 15 to 1111 1111 1111 for white, and so on.

Drill Exercise

15.11. Other LUT Sizes. Provide suitable contents for a LUT to produce gray levels when there are $M = 8$ entries and when each entry holds $N = 12$ bits. Repeat for $M = 8$ and $N = 15$ and for $M = 8$ and $N = 6$. What will happen if there is no LUT, if each of the eight pixel values is hard-wired to produce one of eight particular colors?

If we can produce M intensity values between 0 and $M - 1$, how do we map each I value into its appropriate pixel value? The mapping depends on the range of the I values that is computed as the whole scene is rendered, something we don't know in advance. We can't map each I as it is computed. Rather, we must first compute them all for a given scene, then determine the proper mapping, and finally map I to the proper integer for each pixel.

The simplest approach is to store the value of I for each pixel as it is computed. For an image consisting of R rows and C columns, this requires storing RC real values. If insufficient memory is available to place these values in an array, an external file can be used. This has the advantage of preserving the image in a neutral, device-independent form for later use. A reasonable file format simply gives the number of rows and columns and then lists the RC values, as in the following code fragment:

Code Fragment 15.5. Suggested File Format for Intensity Values

```
256 348
3.145 3.145 3.253 2.335 2.445 1.567
3.147 3.067 3.000 2.562 2.122 2.056
    .
    .
    .
```

The collection of I values stored in this way might be called the **intensity population**. The file is easily scanned to find the minimum and maximum values of I present in the population (see the programming exercises). Call these values I_{min} and I_{max}, respectively. We now need to define a suitable mapping

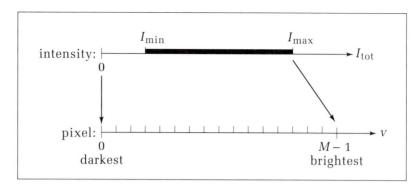

Figure 15.16.
Mapping intensities to pixel
values.

between the range $I_{min}...I_{max}$ and $0...M - 1$, as suggested in Figure 15.16. The simplest approach makes v proportional to I:

$$v = round\left(\frac{(M - 1)I}{I_{max}}\right) \tag{15.7}$$

where *round* denotes a function that rounds a value to the nearest integer. (How might *round* be implemented in Pascal?) I is first mapped linearly from the interval $[0, I_{max}]$ to $[0, M - 1]$ and then rounded. The rounding operation is sometimes called **quantization**: Values that lie in a continuum of real numbers are "quantized" to the nearest value in a finite set of values. It is a common operation when digitizing an image (Gonzalez and Wintz 1987). Quantization destroys information because it maps a whole range of I values into the same resultant value. (For $M = 8$ and $I_{max} = 13$, what range is mapped into $v = 2$?) If M is small, this can produce some *contouring* or *banding in* an image, as the following example demonstrates.

Figure 15.17.
Bands appearing on a face.

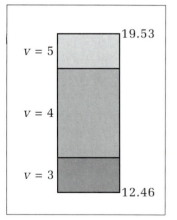

Example
Consider a rectangular face, F, reflecting light from some source. Suppose that intensity I varies linearly from value 12.46 at the bottom edge of F to 19.53 at the top edge. If $I_{max} = 28$ and the display supports $M = 8$ levels, what levels will the image reveal?

Solution
The mapping converts a real value in $0...28$ into the appropriate integer in $0...7$, and so we have $v = round(I/4)$. Thus $v = 0$ for $I\epsilon[0, 2)$, where $I\epsilon[0, 2)$ denotes all I that satisfy $0 \le I < 2$, $v = 1$ for $I\epsilon[2, 6)$, and so forth. For face F the relevant ranges are $v = 3$ for $I\epsilon[10, 14)$, $v = 4$ for $I\epsilon[14, 18)$, and $v = 5$ for $I\epsilon[18, 22)$. The linear increase in intensity over F from 12.46 to 19.53 indicates that the intensity reaches value 14 at a point 22 percent of the way from the bottom to the top and reaches 18 at a point 78 percent of the way. The quantization causes F to be drawn with three bands of gray, as shown in Figure 15.17.

Drill Exercise

15.12. Alternative Mappings. How will an image be changed if we spread out the I-values by mapping I_{max} to $M - 1$ and I_{min} into 0? This is done with the mapping $v = round((I - I_{min}) \times (M - 1)/(I_{max} - I_{min}))$. If I_{min} represents a darkish gray, how will it be displayed? Is this always desirable? Ever desirable?

Alternatively, consider the nonlinear mappings $v = round((M - 1) \times (I/I_{max})^2)$ and $v = round((M - 1) \log(1 + (I/I_{max}))/\log(2))$ that divide up the range of intensities unevenly and emphasize either one extreme or the other. Sketch a v-versus-I plot for these mappings, and discuss their advantages when displaying gray-scale images.

By examining the intensity population of I values, one can sometimes fine-tune the mapping from I to v. For instance, if very few pixels have values near I_{max}, it may not matter if they are accurately displayed. (This of course depends on how these brightest pixels are situated spatially in the image!) One can choose some smaller value, say I_{big}, and change all pixels with I values larger than I_{big} to I_{big}. This effectively reduces the former I_{max} to I_{big}. When the smaller range $[0, I_{big}]$ is mapped to $[0, M-1]$, the error made by each rounding step will be slightly smaller, and so there will be a better "spread" of intensity values. Some experimentation is usually required when fine-tuning an image in this manner.

15.4 Rendering the Polygon Mesh

We now have the tools to determine how bright any particular point on a face is, once given the synthetic camera and light source positions. We shall now look at techniques to fill each face of a mesh with a single shade or a family of shades in order to render it realistically. Different approaches yield different levels of realism. Keep in mind that we shall not attempt a complete removal of hidden surfaces here (see Chapter 17). Back face removal is an important first step in achieving realism, but pictures of solids usually exibit some bizarre elements unless all hidden surfaces are removed.

15.4.1 Flat Shading of Polygon Meshes

Because I is a fairly expensive quantity to calculate, it is best to compute it as infrequently as possible. Pictures of adequate realism may be obtained for some applications by calculating I at just one place on the face and then filling the whole face with the intensity found from this single sample. This is called **flat shading** or **uniform filling** of each face.

An algorithm to perform flat shading on a polygon mesh model is simple. The visible face list is formed as discussed in Section 15.2. Then for each face, F, on the list,

1. Choose a point, **p** on F.

2. Find the normal to F.

3. Compute I at **p** using Equation 15.6.

4. Fill the projected polygon with shade I.

The simplest choice for **p** is any vertex of F. For slightly better results, one can alternatively choose **p** to be some center point of the face, perhaps based on a convex combination (recall Chapter 7) of the vertices of F, such as their average.

Note the distinction between flat shading and the filled wireframe model defined in Section 15.3.1: With flat shading the intensity depends on both a shading model and the scene geometry, whereas the filled wireframe approach simply looks up in a table the intensity or color of each face and fills the face accordingly. With flat shading one can distinguish the different faces of a cube even if they have the same nominal color, because they have different normal vectors and hence reflect light differently.

Flat shading of polygon meshes is simple and fast, but the resulting pictures are not usually realistic, as can be seen in Figure 15.18. (This object is modeled in Appendix 4). Note that for this choice of view, no front face obscures any part of another, so that additional hidden-surface removal is unnecessary. Highlights are rendered poorly with flat shading. If there happens to be a large specular component at **p**, the brightness will not be concentrated at **p** but will be drawn uniformly over the entire face. For this reason, there is little incentive for including the specular reflection component in the computation of I, and it might as well be omitted.

15.4.2 What Does a Pixel See?

A mesh model can be made to look more realistic by computing I at more points on each face. We expect that as more samples of the light are taken, the rendering will become more accurate. The ultimate sampling density is to compute the light that reaches the eye "through" *every* pixel. This is the approach taken in ray tracing. We set up the tools needed to discuss any density of sampling and then consider ways to achieve realism without necessarily sampling the light through every pixel.

Recall from Code Fragment 13.1 that the pixel in column i and row j can be set to the intensity *shade* by using the routine *SetPixel*($i, j, shade$), where i is of type *col* = *0..MaxColumn* and j is of type *row* = *0..MaxRow*. This routine can be used to make shaded pictures, by computing the intensity of the light reaching the eye through pixel (i, j). But what does the eye see through pixel (i, j)?

We know how to project any point in a scene onto the viewplane, but we still need a relation between a point on the viewplane and a particular pixel. Then we can say what part of the viewplane is "covered" by a given pixel. But we also must turn the question around and in some sense undo a projection, asking what points in the scene are associated with a given pixel. We can't determine a 3D point from its projection, but given a point on the viewplane, we can find the direction of the ray that emanates from the eye and passes through that point. This is useful when drawing mesh models, and it is the basis of ray tracing.

Figure 15.18.
A polygon mesh rendered with flat shading.

To Which Point in the Window Does a Pixel Correspond?

Figure 15.19 shows the window W lying in the viewplane, covered with a rectangular grid of points. Each point shown corresponds to the center of a pixel. For simplicity, only a 6-by-8 array of pixels is shown, much smaller than one would actually use. The center of the pixel at column 4 and row 2 lies at (u_4, v_2). The eye sees a portion of the scene through this pixel. Our goal is to use the shading model to compute how much light passes down the pyramid shown, from the scene to the eye.

We want to find the center point (u_i, v_j) of the pixel (i, j). Window W has corners (W_l, W_t) and (W_r, W_b), as usual. By inspection, $u_0 = W_l$ and u increases by $\Delta u = (W_r - W_l)/MaxColumn$ from pixel to pixel. A similar form holds for v (noting that rows are counted from top to bottom in the display). Thus we obtain

$$u_i = W_l + i\,\Delta u$$
$$v_j = W_t - j\,\Delta v \qquad (15.8)$$

where

$$\Delta u = (W_r - W_l)/MaxColumn$$
$$\Delta v = (W_t - W_b)/MaxRow \qquad (15.9)$$

Notice that if pixel centers are separated from their neighbors by the same amount horizontally and vertically, the image will have a displayed aspect ratio of

$$\text{image aspect ratio} = \frac{MaxRow}{MaxColumn} \qquad (15.10)$$

Normally the user chooses the window, W, to have this same aspect ratio so that the image will be an undistorted version of the scene observed through the window.

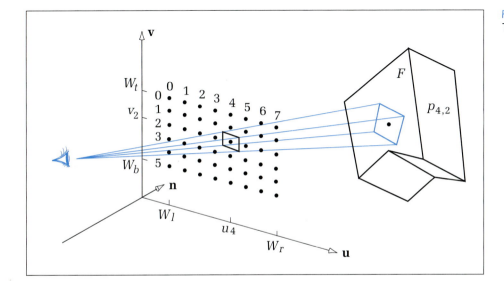

Figure 15.19.
The light seen through a pixel.

Drill Exercises

15.13.   Strange Displays. In some raster displays, the pixel centers are not separated by the same amounts horizontally and vertically. If they are 20 percent closer vertically than horizontally, what aspect ratio should the window, W, have to compensate for this, so that the final image of a sphere is a circle for instance?

15.14.   Positioning a Small Image. Equation 15.8 causes the upper left corner of the window to correspond to the upper left corner of the actual display. Suppose we want to draw a 350-by-480 pixel image on a 512-by-512 display and want the upper leftmost pixel of the image to appear at row 30 and column 20 of the display. What arguments are used in *SetPixel*( ) to write the image pixel (i, j)?

What Is the Looking Direction Through a Pixel Center?

Equation 15.8 relates points within the camera to pixels on a physical display. Given this correspondence, what direction is the eye looking in when it looks through a given pixel?

Figure 15.19 shows the point, $\mathbf{p}_{4,2}$, on face F that corresponds to the pixel center, (u_4, v_2). The point is found by determining where a ray from the eye through (u_4, v_2) intersects the face. We call this the ray "belonging to pixel (4, 2)" or "(4, 2)'s ray." In general, what is (i, j)'s ray? Suppose we set up the ray so that it passes through the eye at $t = 0$ and through the pixel center on the viewplane at $t = 1$. In viewing coordinates, the eye lies at $\mathbf{e} = (e_u, e_v, e_n)$, and the pixel center is at $(u_i, v_j, 0)$. So in viewing coordinates the ray lies at time t at $\mathbf{e}(1 - t) + (u_i, v_j, 0)t$ (why?). Because face F is described in world coordinates, we must describe the ray in world coordinates as well. We saw in Chapter 12 how to represent in world coordinates a point, (u, v, n), given in viewing coordinates: Simply multiply (u, v, n) by matrix M of Equation 12.6 and add the view reference point, $\mathbf{r}$. When this is done to the ray and some terms are rearranged, we obtain for (i, j)'s ray:

$$\mathbf{p}_{i,j}(t) = \mathbf{eye} + \mathbf{dir}_{i,j}t \qquad (15.11)$$

where $\mathbf{eye} = \mathbf{e}M + \mathbf{r}$ is the location of the eye in world coordinates, and the ray has direction

$$\mathbf{dir}_{i,j} = ((u_i, v_j, 0) - \mathbf{e})M \qquad (15.12)$$

(It is valuable to work through the manipulations to obtain this result. Why doesn't the direction of the ray depend on the position of the camera?) Note that for the usual case in which the eye lies on the **n**-axis ($(e_u, e_v, e_n) = (0, 0, -E)$), the direction of the ray simplifies nicely to $(u_i, v_j, E)M$.

This is a valuable result. It establishes a direct correspondence between a display pixel and the direction the eye is looking in through the center of that pixel. It is useful to implement a routine, *RayPoint*($i : col; j : row; t : real;$ **var** *spot* : *point3D*), that computes the point *spot* through which the ray from the eye through the center of pixel (i, j) passes at time t (see the exercises). This is used frequently in Chapter 18.

What Point on a Face Does the Eye See?

Finally, where does the ray belonging to pixel (i, j) intersect face F? We first find where it intersects the plane in which face F lies. Use reasoning identical to that in Section 8.1.1. Data for the plane $\mathbf{n} \cdot \mathbf{p} = D$ in which F lies are available from the face list for F. Substitute Equation 15.11 into the plane equation and solve for the hit time t_{hit}. This produces

$$t_{\text{hit}} = \frac{D - \mathbf{n} \cdot \mathbf{eye}}{\mathbf{n} \cdot \mathbf{dir}_{i,j}} \qquad (15.13)$$

Use this hit time in Equation 15.11 to obtain the point of intersection, $\mathbf{p}_{i,j}(t_{\text{hit}})$, of the ray with the plane of F. This point lies in the plane of F but may not lie within F itself. If necessary, a parity test (see Section 13.3.4) can be used to see whether the point actually lies within F.

Applying the Shading Rule to Every Point

We bring together the preceding ingredients and show a pseudocode fragment that makes a shaded picture of face F. Each display pixel is tested to see where its ray intersects the plane of face F. Call the point of intersection *spot*. If *spot* lies within face F, the intensity, I, of Equation 15.6 will be found at *spot* through a routine, *Intensity*(*spot* : *point3D*), and the pixel will be set to this intensity.

> *Code Fragment 15.6. Drawing the Image*

```
for j := 0 to MaxRow do
for i := 0 to MaxColumn do begin
   <find spot where (i, j)'s ray hits plane of F>;
   if <spot lies in face F> then shade := Intensity(spot);
   SetPixel(i, j, shade)
end;
```

But this approach is costly, for two reasons: (1) Every pixel is tested to see whether its ray intersects the plane of F within F, and (2) the shading rule is applied to every such pixel. We shall now examine some ways to reduce computation time.

15.4.3 A Scan-Line Approach to Shading Faces

Filling faces with shades is similar to filling polygons with a fixed color. In Chapter 13 we found that filling runs of pixels at one time increased the efficiency of a fill algorithm, and so here we seek a run-based rendering algorithm for face F.

Consider filling a run of pixels along the j-th scan line, as suggested in Figure 15.20. According to Equation 15.8, scan line j passes across the viewplane at $v_j = W_t - j\Delta v$. The run begins at $u = u_a$ and ends at $u = u_b$. If we can find the values of u_a and u_b, it will be simple to determine which pixels $i_a, \ldots, i_b$ are involved in the run. Just invert Equation 15.8:

$$i_a = round\left(\frac{u_a - W_l}{\Delta u}\right) \qquad (15.14)$$

and similarly for i_b.

To find u_a and u_b we project the edges of face F onto the viewplane to build polygon P. Projecting a vertex, $\mathbf{p}$, of F is simple because the 4-tuple, (g_u, g_v, g_n, g_w), of Equation 15.2 has already been saved in the augmented vertex list for the mesh model (see Code Fragment 15.4). The projected vertex, $(u*, v*)$, is found

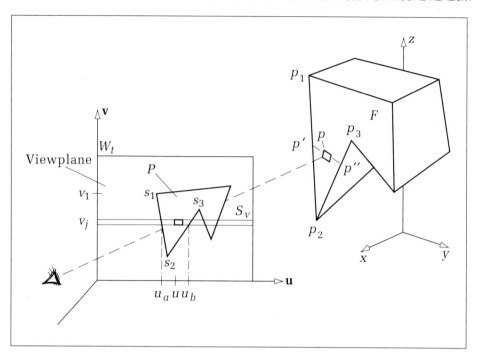

by converting back into ordinary coordinates (and ignoring the pseudo-depth):

$$(u*, v*) = (g_u/g_w, g_v/g_w) \tag{15.15}$$

Once the projected vertices, such as s_1 and s_2 in Figure 15.20 are known, it is simple (how?) to find u_a and u_b, and hence the first and last pixels of the run.

We scan the face list for face F, project its vertices, and build an edge list essentially identical to that in Section 13.3.4. The scan-line routine of Code Fragment 13.6 can then be used with little change. For each new scan line the active edge list (AEL) is scanned for pairs $i1$ and $i2$ of the edge intersections, and runs are filled between each pair. The main change is that the code **for** $x := x1$ **to** $x2$ **do** *SetPixel(x, y, value)*; must be altered to the following:

Code Fragment 15.7. Shading Runs Along a Face

```
for i := i1 to i2 do
begin
    <find spot where (i, j)'s ray hits plane of F>;
    shade := Intensity(spot);
    SetPixel(i, j, shade)
end;
```

Because we know that *spot* lies in face F, we needn't perform that arduous test anymore! Only pixels that are covered by face F are processed, and much faster.

Figure 15.21 shows the model rendered using this technique. A light source behind the camera (and close to it) illuminates the scene, and a vivid highlight is

Figure 15.21.
The shaded model. (Courtesy of Brett Diamond.)

seen in some of the faces. At those places where the specular reflection is dim, we see that there is still some variation in the diffuse component at different points on a face.

Drill Exercise

15.15. Interpolating Intensity Values. A further increase in efficiency is possible if we don't evaluate *Intensity*(*spot*) at every pixel along a run, but only at its first and last pixels. The pixels in between are found by linear interpolation. If the values at i_1 and i_2 are I_1 and I_2, respectively, we can render the run using $I(i) = I_1 + (I_2 - I_1)(i - i_1)/(i_2 - i_1)$. Discuss how much realism is lost by this approach, specifically how the highlights are rendered.

15.4.4 An Aside on How the Eye Sees

In the shaded pictures presented so far, we can see abrupt changes in shading between various pairs of adjacent faces. These changes in brightness are experienced by the eye to be greater than they really are, and this has ramifications in rendering various models. The eye tends to emphasize abrupt changes in brightness because of an interesting physiological phenomenon known as **lateral inhibition**.

Figure 15.22 suggests how this works. When looking at a surface that exhibits an abrupt change in brightness, some cells in the retina of the eye receive less light and some receive more light. Those that receive less light obviously respond less strongly than do those that receive more light. But cells will exaggerate this difference if they are situated (laterally) next to cells receiving a different amount of light. Those receiving dim light will respond even less if they are next to cells receiving bright light; they are inhibited by their neighbors. And those bathed in bright light will respond more vigorously than usual if they are next to cells receiving dim light. Figure 15.22b compares true brightness with perceived brightness at different positions on the retina. This effect holds not only for abrupt shifts in intensity but also for discontinuities in the rate of change (derivative) of intensity. In both cases the eye sees extra bands of light along a discontinuity. These bands are named **Mach bands**, after Ernst Mach, who discovered the effect in 1865 (Ratliff 1965).

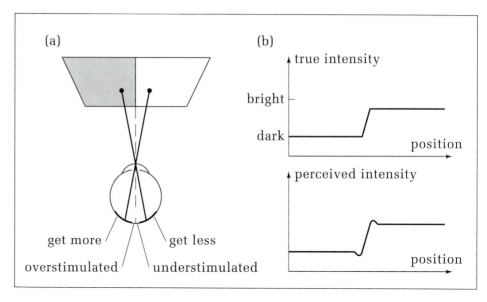

Figure 15.22.
Lateral inhibition within the eye.

15.4.5 Drawing a Smooth Surface Beneath a Mesh Model

So far we have rendered a polygonal mesh model on a face-by-face basis, which is appropriate for such objects as the stack of blocks in Figure 15.21. For such models we want to discern the edges between the flat faces, which can be done by means of Mach banding.

But mesh models are also used as a convenient approximation to a smooth underlying surface, as we discussed earlier. Call the surface we wish to approximate S. The modeler (a human designer or a CAD software package) fashions a polygonal mesh model, M, that approximates S to the degree desired. This may require using a large number of small facetlike faces positioned to conform closely to S. Figure 15.23 shows in cross section an example surface, S, and the approximating mesh model, M.

When a shading model is applied separately to each face of M, Mach banding tends to overemphasize the discontinuities in the directions of the faces. We would like to see an approximation to the smooth surface S, but our rendering scheme is too faithful to the model M. So a different rendering approach is sought that might deemphasize the facetlike nature of the model. That is, it should smooth out the facets in some fashion so that the picture of M looks like S.

The key to this is the construction of appropriate normal vectors at strategic points of M. Figure 15.23 shows two normal vectors, $\mathbf{N}_1$ and $\mathbf{N}_2$, at two points on S. $\mathbf{N}_1$ is closely matched by the normal $\mathbf{N}_a$ to the corresponding face of the model, but neither $\mathbf{N}_a$ nor $\mathbf{N}_b$ provides a good approximation to normal vector $\mathbf{N}_2$ near vertex $\mathbf{v}_2$ of M. We can, however, form an approximation to $\mathbf{N}_2$ by averaging $\mathbf{N}_a$ and $\mathbf{N}_b$.

$$\mathbf{N}_2' = \frac{\mathbf{N}_a + \mathbf{N}_b}{2} \tag{15.16}$$

has a direction that is between those of $\mathbf{N}_a$ and $\mathbf{N}_b$, and it may provide an acceptable approximation to the true normal to S at that point.

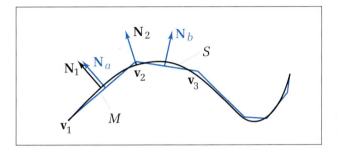

Figure 15.23.
A smooth surface and an
approximating mesh model.

We shall consider two approaches to rendering the surface S approximated by the model M. Both methods form nearly normal vectors to S by averaging face normals at the vertices of M, and both apply these normals to the shading model of Equation 15.6. Both also reduce the required amount of computation by interpolating rather than recalculating various values. They differ in the quantities that are interpolated.

Intensity Interpolation

Gouraud shading (Gouraud 1971) constructs an approximate normal vector to S situated at each vertex of mesh model M. It then uses this normal in Equation 15.6 to compute I that "comes from" the vertex. Light intensities at other points on each face are found by interpolation.

Figure 15.24 shows the method applied to a model of a gearshift knob. The graphics screen displaying a projected view of the gearshift is shown in Figure 15.24a, featuring the scan line at v. Suppose we want to fill in the run of pixels that is covered by the projection of face 8. We first find the light intensities I_a and I_b at the two ends of the run from u_a to u_b. Then we linearly interpolate between I_a and I_b to find the intensity at u:

$$I(u) = I_a + (I_b - I_a)\frac{u - u_a}{u_b - u_a} \qquad (15.17)$$

To increase efficiency we can compute $I(u + 1)$ incrementally by simply adding a constant to $I(u)$ (see the exercises). Therefore, the span on face 8 can be filled very rapidly once I_a and I_b are known.

Drill Exercises

15.16.   Incremental Calculation of $I(u + 1)$. Show how $I(u + 1)$ in Equation 15.17 can be computed by adding a constant term to $I(u)$.

15.17.   Retaining Corners in Gouraud Shading. In some cases we may want to show specific creases and edges in the model. Discuss how this can be controlled by the choice of the vertex normals that are calculated. For instance, to retain the edge between faces 7 and 8 in Figure 15.24 when rendering face 8, what face normals should be averaged when computing $\mathbf{n}_A$ and $\mathbf{n}_B$? Other tricks and issues can be found in the references (Rogers 1985).

How are the intensities I_a and I_b calculated? The gearshift knob is shown in Figure 15.24b with various normal vectors labeled $\mathbf{n}_8$, $\mathbf{n}_9$, $\mathbf{n}_6$, and so on. These face normals are used to compute the vertex normals such as $\mathbf{n}_A$ and $\mathbf{n}_B$ shown emanating at the model's vertices. The directions of the vertex normals are cal-

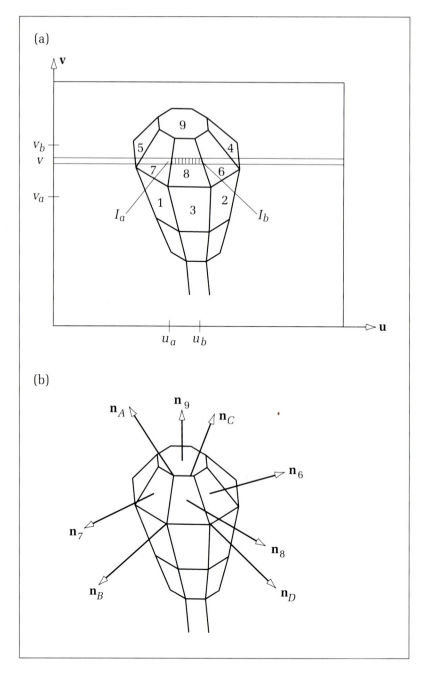

Figure 15.24.
Derivation of the Gouraud
shading method.

culated by averaging (or simply summing, as the average and the sum have the
same direction) the face normals of the adjacent faces. For instance,

$$\mathbf{n}_A = \mathbf{n}_9 + \mathbf{n}_7 + \mathbf{n}_8 \qquad (15.18)$$

Similarly, $\mathbf{n}_B$ is an average of four face normals. The vertex normal $\mathbf{n}_A$ is used in
Equation 15.6 to compute the light intensity I_A at the point from which $\mathbf{n}_A$
emanates, and similarly for I_B. Then the intensity I_a we need in Equation 15.17
for the span of pixels along scan line v is found from I_A and I_B by linear inter-

polation in the v-direction between v_A and v_B.

For each (front) face, then, the process is as follows:

1. Find the vertex normals of each vertex by summing the normals of the surrounding faces.

2. Find the light intensity I at each of the vertices.

3. For each scan line find the intensity at the start and end of each span on the face by interpolation in v.

4. For each pixel in the span find the intensity by interpolation in u.

Figure 15.25 shows a surface of revolution—a chess piece—rendered with both flat shading and Gouraud shading. The individual faces are clearly visible in the flat-shaded image, whereas the polygon mesh has essentially been eliminated in the Gouraud version. Because the silhouette of the model has not been smoothed, the polygons are still visible there.

Because intensities are formed by interpolating rather than computing I at every pixel, Gouraud shading tends to picture highlights only poorly. Therefore, when Gouraud shading is used, one normally suppresses the specular component of intensity in Equation 15.6. Highlights are better reproduced using the second technique, discussed next.

15.4.6 Normal Vector Interpolation

Greater realism can be achieved—particularly with regard to highlights on shiny objects—by a better approximation of the normal vector to surface S at each pixel. This type of shading is called **Phong shading**, after its inventor Phong Bui-tuong (Phong 1975).

In this technique the vertex normals for each face are formed in the same way as for Gouraud shading. The normals $\mathbf{n}_A$ and $\mathbf{n}_B$ of Figure 15.24a are employed again. But instead of using them to calculate directly the intensities I_A and I_B at scan line v, we use them to find the *interpolated normal vector* at the start and end of the run along v. For instance, the normal at the start of the run is found as

$$\mathbf{n}_S = \mathbf{n}_A + (\mathbf{n}_B - \mathbf{n}_A)\frac{v - v_a}{v_b - v_a} \qquad (15.19)$$

Similarly, the normal $\mathbf{n}_E$ at the end of the span is formed by interpolating between $\mathbf{n}_C$ and $\mathbf{n}_D$ (see Figure 15.24b). The normal to surface S along the span is then approximated using one last interpolation, in u between $\mathbf{n}_S$ and $\mathbf{n}_E$.

Thus with Phong shading, a much greater effort is made to approximate the normal vector for the smooth underlying surface S. This approximating normal is found by interpolation for every relevant pixel, and then the normal is used in Equation 15.6 to calculate the diffuse and specular components. Because the direction of the normal vector is more accurate and varies smoothly from point to point, the production of specular highlights is much more faithful. This also makes the result much more realistic.

Figure 15.26 shows the same chess piece shaded using this method. The specular highlights are clearly visible, and the overall effect is greatly improved over that using Gouraud shading.

Figure 15.25.
An example of Gouraud shading (courtesy of Weimer and Bishop 1986).

15.5 Summary

Wireframe models that are adequate for many line drawings of objects do not provide the proper description for rendering solids. Consequently, we developed a polygon mesh model that describes each polygonal face of an object. Meshes provide a powerful data structure for describing a broad class of objects. They model many shapes exactly and also offer an excellent approximate shape description for many objects that have smoothly varying surfaces. A variety of CAD software packages is available that build mesh models for objects, and we examined some techniques for building simple ones.

We studied in some detail techniques for viewing mesh models. Once a synthetic camera is defined looking into the scene composed of meshes, each mesh can be preprocessed, if desired, to eliminate back faces and to clip the remaining faces to the view volume. Once this is done, the model is described by a vertex list and a visible face list.

Figure 15.26.
The Phong shaded chess piece. (Courtesy of Weimer and Bishop 1986.)

Each visible face can be filled with various intensities and colors, according to an adopted shading model. A shading model describes how light reflects off a surface depending on its characteristics and its orientation to light sources and to the eye of the camera. Diffuse and specular reflections are the components most commonly modeled in graphics, and an ambient component is included to prevent shadows from being drawn too deep and harsh. The various source levels and reflection coefficients that appear in the calculations of these light contributions are often determined experimentally, owing to the great complexity of physical reflection phenomena.

We discussed the relationship between a pixel on the display and a point on the viewplane that permits finding the ray "belonging" to each pixel, that is, the ray that passes from the eye through the center of the pixel. This allows us to ask what the eye sees through a particular pixel, which we used in a scan-line algorithm for shading faces of a mesh. To avoid having to test whether a ray penetrates the plane of a face inside or outside the face itself, we first projected the face onto the viewplane and filled the polygon, as in Chapter 13. But instead of filling each pixel with the same color, we determined the proper shade using the shading model.

When a mesh model is supposed to approximate an underlying smooth surface, one can apply Gouraud or Phong shading techniques to draw a smoothly varying surface, even though the model is faceted. This is done by averaging normal vectors to adjacent faces in order to approximate what the normal to the underlying surface might be and then by using this approximate normal vector in the shading model. If light intensities are found along the edges by using this approach and then interpolated elsewhere (Gouraud shading), the surfaces that are drawn will indeed be smooth—except along silhouettes—but the highlights will not be realistic. Instead, greater realism is achieved at the cost of greater computation time, by approximating the normal to the underlying surface at more closely spaced points and then recomputing the shading model at each point (Phong shading).

Programming Exercises

15.18. Building an Edge List from a Face List and Culling Duplicate Edges. Develop a routine that creates an edge list from the face list of a polygon mesh. Before each new edge is added to the list, the list should be checked to see whether the edge is already there. How can this be done efficiently?

15.19. Computing *face_plane* Information. Write a routine that computes the values **n** and d for the plane of a face. The routine uses the cross product of two edges of the face (found from the vertex list) to find the outward-pointing normal vector. It normalizes the vector and then uses any vertex in the face to find d.

15.20. The Platonic Solids. Based on information given in Appendix 8, write a routine that builds a vertex list and a face list for each of the platonic solids.

15.21. Building the Mesh for the Prism. Consider the prism of height H based on a polygon with vertices $v_1, \ldots, v_N$. The base of the prism lies in the x, y-plane, and its axis is parallel to the z-axis in a right-handed coordinate sys-

tem. Write a routine that constructs the vertex list (stored in an array) and the face list (stored in a linked list) for this prism. The routine also computes plane information for each face and includes it in the list.

15.22. Convert from Viewing Coordinates into World Coordinates. Write the procedure *ViewToWorld(e : point3D;* **var** *eye : point3D)* used in *BackFace( )* of Code Fragment 15.3 that converts point e in viewing coordinates to eye in world coordinates.

15.23. Removing Back Faces. Use the routine *Back-Face( )* of Code Fragment 15.3 to build the procedure *FrontFaces(F : face_ptr;* **var** *Fvis : face_ptr)* which creates a list, *Fvis*, of front faces of the object in *F*.

15.24. Computing *I_tot*. Design and implement the routine *Total(p, n, v, s : vector3D) : real* which computes *I* of Equation 15.6. Decide on a good strategy for storing the various constants (such as k and r_d) that must be available to the routine.

15.25.   Filing and Scanning Image Values. Write a routine that builds a file of I values as they are computed, using the format of Code Fragment 15.5. The user is prompted for the name of the file; the file is created; and then as each value I is found, it is appended to the file. Write another routine that scans an image file and returns the maximum and minimum intensity values stored there.

15.26.   Flat Shading of a Mesh Model. Write a routine that uses flat shading of each face to render a mesh model. Equation 15.6 is used at one point on each visible face, and the projected polygon is filled with the computed intensity. Render at least one of the "stacked cube" models described in Appendix 4.

15.27.   The Ray Through the *ij*-th Pixel. Write the routine *RayPoint(i : col; j : row; t : real;* **var** *spot : point3D)* which returns the point *spot* through which the ray from the eye through the center of the *ij*-th display pixel passes at time *t*. What information must be globally available to this routine?

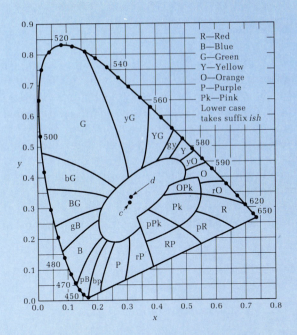

Chapter 16

Color Theory: Coloring Faces

Colors and textures will become important to you.

Found in fortune cookie, Amherst, Mass.

Goals of the Chapter

- To study the nature of color and its numerical description
- To examine some standards for color representation
- To study how colored light reflects off colored surfaces
- To define and use various color spaces

16.1 | Introduction

So far our shading models have dealt only with the intensity of light reaching the eye from points on an object. This is useful for output devices that can display only shades of gray or for early debugging of programs. But we experience the world in a rich variety of colors, and much information is derived from the colors of things. Computer-generated pictures should be able to provide this extra dimension as well, and so we need tools to describe and control color in applications.

The subject of color is extremely complex, depending on subtle interactions between the physics of light radiation and the eye–brain system (see Feynman 1963 for a superb discussion). From the point of view of writing computer graphics applications, we must be able to answer several questions:

- How are colors described accurately in numerical terms?

- How do these descriptions relate to everyday ways of describing color?

- How does one compare colors?

- What range of colors can a CRT display or a printed page reveal?

- How do we describe numerically the color of light reflecting off a surface, when it is bathed by a light source of a certain color?

- How can color lookup tables be loaded to produce the colors required?

Light itself is an electromagnetic phenomenon, like television waves, infrared radiation, and x-rays. By light, we mean those waves that lie in a narrow band of wavelengths in the so-called visible spectrum. Figure 16.1 shows the location of the visible spectrum (for humans) within the entire electromagnetic spectrum, along with the spectra of some other common phenomena. The frequency of vibration f increases to the right, whereas wavelength λ increases to the left.[1] The eye responds to light with wavelengths between approximately 400 and 700 nm (nanometers).

Figure 16.1.
Electromagnetic spectrum.

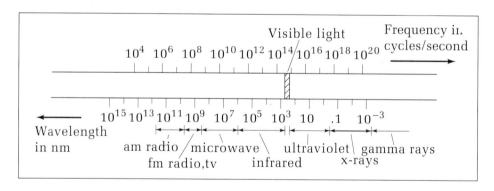

[1]The wavelength of a wave is the distance it travels during one cycle of its vibration. Wavelength and frequency are inversely related by $\lambda = v/f$, where v is the speed of light in the medium of interest. In air (or a vacuum) $v = 300,000$ km/sec; in glass it is about 65 percent as fast.

An Aside on the Eye

The retina of the eye is its light-sensitive membrane. It lines the posterior portion of the eye's wall and contains two kinds of receptor cells, cones and rods.

The **cones** are the color-sensitive cells, each of which responds to a particular color, red, green, or blue. According to the tri-stimulus theory, the color we see is the result of our cones' relative responses to red, green, and blue light. Each eye has 6 to 7 million cones, concentrated in a small portion of the retina called the **fovea**. Each cone has its own nerve cell, thereby allowing the eye to discern tiny details. To see an object in detail, the eye looks directly at it in order to bring the image onto the fovea.

By contrast, the **rods** cannot distinguish colors, nor can they see fine detail. Seventy-five million to 150 million rods are crowded onto the retina surrounding the fovea. Moreover, many rods are attached to a single nerve cell, preventing the discrimination of fine detail (Gonzalez and Wintz 1987). What do rods do then? They are very sensitive to low levels of light and can see things in dim light that the cones miss. At night, for instance, it is best to look slightly away from an object so that the image falls outside the fovea. Detail and color are lost, but at least the general form of an object (a predator?) is visible. Indeed, this sensitivity of our peripheral vision to dim light was probably instrumental in our evolution.

Some light sources, such as lasers, emit light of essentially a single wavelength, or "pure spectral" light. We perceive 400 nm light as violet and 620 nm light as red, with the other pure colors lying in between these extremes. Figure 16.2 shows some example **spectral densities** $S(\lambda)$ (power per unit wavelength) for pure lights and the common names given to their perceived colors.

The light from most sources does not consist of only one wavelength; instead, it contains power of various amounts over a continuous set of wavelengths, and their spectral densities (or "spectra") cover a band of wavelengths. The total power of the light in any band of wavelengths is found as the *area* under the density curve over that band. Figure 16.3 shows several example spectra for lights. The label for each indicates the color that we perceive when we look at such light. Note that white light contains approximately equal amounts of all frequencies, whereas reds tend to have more power concentrated at the longer wavelengths. Gray light also exhibits a "flat" spectral density, but

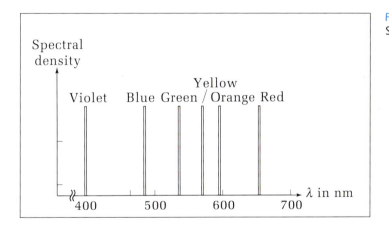

Figure 16.2.
Spectra for some pure colors.

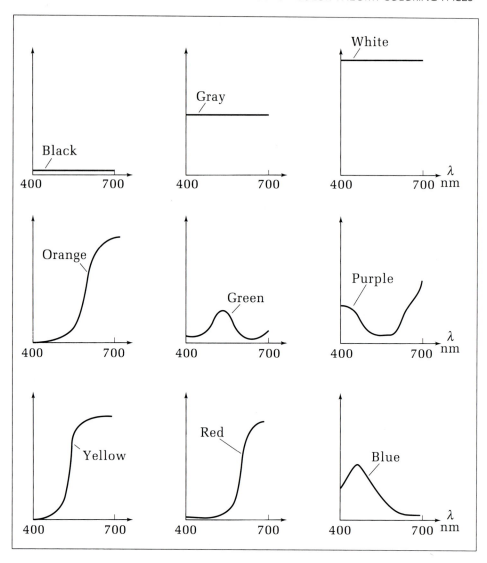

Figure 16.3.
Example spectra for light and their perceived colors.

at a lower intensity. These example spectra highlight one of the difficulties of trying to describe color numerically; that is, an enormous variety of spectral density functions is perceived by the eye as having the same color. For example, a given color sample can be "matched" by many different spectral density shapes, in that the colors of the sample and any of the spectral densities are indistinguishable when placed side by side.

16.2 Color Description

Suppose that we want to describe a color precisely over the telephone, perhaps to a dye manufacturer or a production manager in a publishing company. It isn't enough to say "a bright robin's egg blue"; we must make sure that the listener receives a precise characterization of the color we have in mind. If we knew the spectral density curve of the color, as in Figure 16.3, we could try to describe its level at a dozen or so wavelengths, but that is clearly awkward and seems too specific, as many different spectral shapes produce the same color. Ideally, we would be able to recite a few numbers, such as "the target color is 3.24, 1.6, 85, and 1.117," and we would be assured that exactly the same color could be reproduced from this description.

How many numbers are required, and what do they mean? Remarkably, the answer is three numbers, for color perception is three dimensional. But we still must agree on what "coding" scheme is to be used to map colors into numbers, and vice versa. We shall examine several conventions in the following sections and then discuss the ideas behind the current international standard.

16.2.1 Dominant Wavelength

One simple way to describe a color capitalizes on the variety of spectra that produce the same (perceived) color. It specifies a spectrum having the very simple shape shown in Figure 16.4, by stating three numbers: dominant wavelength, saturation, and luminance. The spectrum consists of a "spike" located at a dominant wavelength—620 nm in the example. The location of the **dominant wavelength** specifies the *hue* of the color, in this case red. In addition, a certain amount of white light is present, represented by the rectangular "pedestal" that "desaturates" the red light, making it appear pink.

The total power in the light, known as its **luminance**, is given by the area under the entire spectrum: $L = (D - A)B + AW$. (What is W?) The **saturation** (or **purity**) of the light is defined as the percentage of luminance that resides in the dominant component (Billmeyer and Saltzman 1981):

$$\text{purity} = \frac{(D - A)B}{L} \times 100\% \tag{16.1}$$

If $D = A$, the purity is 0, and white light is observed without any trace of red. If $A = 0$, no white light is present, and a pure red light is seen. Pastel colors contain a large amount of white and are said to be **unsaturated**. When two colors differ only in hue, the eye can distinguish about 128 different hues. When two colors differ only in saturation, the eye can distinguish about 20 different saturations, depending on the hue.

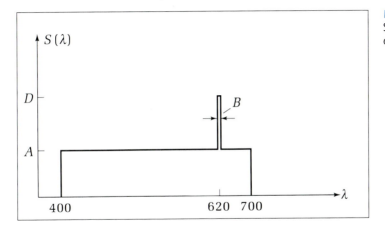

Figure 16.4.
Spectrum of a color using a dominant wavelength.

The notions of saturation, luminance, and dominant wavelength are useful for describing colors, but when presented with a sample color, it is not clear how to measure their values. We shall thus consider some more effective ways to describe color. To get started, we need a way of testing when two colors are the "same." This leads to the area of *color matching*, which is the basis for specifying all colors.

16.2.2 Color Matching

Colors are often described by comparing them with a set of standard color samples and finding the closest match. Many such standard sets have been devised and are widely used in the dyeing and printing industry (Munsell 1941). One can also try to produce a sample color by matching it to the proper combination of some test lights, as shown in Figure 16.5. The sample color with spectral density $S(\lambda)$ is projected onto one part of a screen, and the other part is bathed in the superposition of three test lights, with spectral densities $A(\lambda)$, $B(\lambda)$, and $C(\lambda)$. The observer adjusts the intensities (a, b, and c) of the test lights until the test color $T(\lambda) = aA(\lambda) + bB(\lambda) + cC(\lambda)$ is indistinguishable from the sample color, even though the two spectra, $S(\lambda)$ and $T(\lambda)$, may be quite different. The temptation is then to say that the sample color consists of a "sum" of the "amounts" a, b, and c of the three test colors. In what sense is this meaningful?

There is a remarkable "algebra" of color superposition (Feynman 1963). Suppose that two spectral shapes, $S(\lambda)$ and $P(\lambda)$, have the same (perceived) color, a fact that we denote as $S = P$. Now add a third color, N, to both of these, by superposing light with spectrum $N(\lambda)$ on both. It is an experimental fact that these two new colors will also be indistinguishable!

Along with the symbol $=$, which means that two colors are indistinguishable, we define the meaning of $+$ for colors so that $S + N$ denotes the color observed when the spectra $S(\lambda)$ and $N(\lambda)$ are added. This experimental fact can then be written as

$$\text{if } (S = P) \text{ then } (N + S = N + P) \tag{16.2}$$

Figure 16.5.
Color matching using
superposition of test lights.

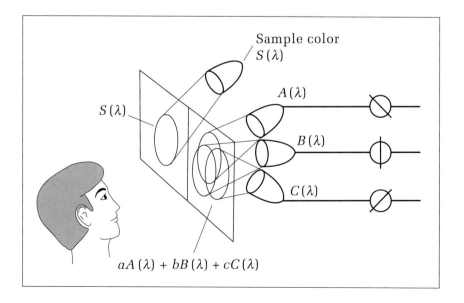

Sample color
$S(\lambda)$

$A(\lambda)$

$S(\lambda)$

$B(\lambda)$

$C(\lambda)$

$aA(\lambda) + bB(\lambda) + cC(\lambda)$

The same goes for *scaling* colors, or scaling their spectral densities or over-all brightness: If $S = P$, then $aS = aP$ for any scalar a. And it is meaningful to write *linear combinations* of two colors, A and B, as in $T = aA + bB$, where a and b are scalars (recall Chapter 7). Thus there is an experimentally verified *vector algebra* of colors, in which we treat colors as vectors, add them, scale them, decompose them into their components, and so forth.

As we mentioned, another remarkable fact of human color perception is that it is three dimensional.[2] Any color, C, can be constructed as the superposition of just three primary colors, say R, G, and B:

$$C = rR + gG + bB \tag{16.3}$$

where r, g, and b are scalars dictating the amounts of each of the primaries contained in C. The symbols R, G, and B are suggestive of red, green, and blue, which are often used as the primaries in a discussion. (The reason for stressing red, green, and blue stems from the sensitivity of our cones to these three colors). But Equation 16.3 works with any choice of primaries, as long as one of them is not just a combination of the other two.

Given a set of three primary colors, R, G, and B, any other color, $C = rR + gG + bB$, can be represented in three-dimensional space by the point (r, g, b). For instance, if R, G, and B correspond to some versions of what we normally call red, green, and blue, $(0, 1, 0)$ will represent a pure "green" of unit brightness, and $(.2, .3, .5)$ will represent a yellow. If we double each component, we will obtain a color that is twice as bright but appears as the same "color." We shall restrict our attention to "unit brightness" colors, for which $r + g + b = 1$. This means that given a colored light for testing, we first normalize its unit brightness and then find its components, r, g, and b. This forces all triples (r, g, b) to lie in the $r + g + b = 1$ plane. Removing variations in brightness allows us to specify colors with only two numbers, say (r, g), as we can always determine b through $b = 1 - r - g$.

The *pure-spectral-color curve* is shown in Figure 16.6, in which some judicious choices of the spectral densities R, G, and B have been made for the three primaries. Each point on this curve represents a pure color of unit brightness that has a single spike in its spectral density at some wavelength, λ. In dominant wavelength terms it is 100 percent saturated and has dominant wavelength λ. As the parameter λ varies over the wavelengths of interest (400 to 670 nm), the relative amounts of R, G, and B must vary to generate the color. Thus r, g, and b are functions of λ. This generates a curve, $\mathbf{p}(\lambda) = (r(\lambda), g(\lambda), b(\lambda))$, having parameter λ, which meanders around the $r + g + b = 1$ plane as λ varies.

Notice in the figure that for λ near 400 nm, the b component (the amount of blue) of $\mathbf{p}(\lambda)$ is large and the others are small, whereas around $\lambda = 670$ the r component (the amount of red) dominates. The primaries R, G, and B need not themselves be pure spectral colors, but if we happened to choose B to be the pure spectral blue at $\lambda = 420$ nm, we would know that $\mathbf{p}(420) = (0, 0, 1)$ (why?).

But there is a rub: For a given set of choices of R, G, and B, some of the scalars r, g, and b may have to be *negative*, to make Equation 16.3 correct! Note, for instance, that $r < 0$ for λ near 520. What is the physical meaning of the minus

[2]Another way of saying this is that any four colors are always linearly related; that is, any one of them can be represented as a combination of the other three.

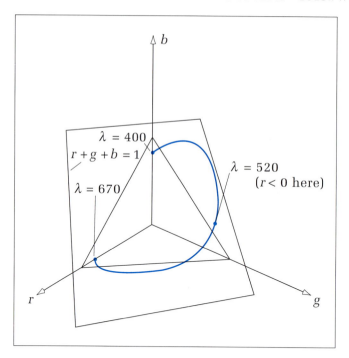

Figure 16.6.
A typical pure-spectral-color
curve using three primaries.

sign in a color such as $C = .7R + .5G - .2B$? One cannot remove light that isn't there. But this contradiction will disappear if we rewrite the equation as $C + .2B = .7R + .5G$. Whereas C alone cannot be constructed as the superpositions of positive amounts of the primaries, the color $C + .2B$ can be matched by positive amounts of R and G. This is in fact what happens with any visible primaries such as red, green, and blue light. Many colors can be fabricated (using positive coefficients r, g, and b), but some cannot, and one primary must be "put on the other side of the equation." Roughly speaking, the problem is that when two colors are added, the result is a less saturated color, and so it is impossible to form a highly saturated color by superposing two others. This is particularly obvious for any of the pure spectral colors, which are themselves saturated.

16.3 The CIE Standard

How can colors be specified precisely in a way that everyone agrees on? Because color perception is three dimensional, we need only agree on three primaries and describe any color desired by the right 3-tuple, as in (r, g, b). What primaries are to be used? Unfortunately, all physically realizable primaries require using negative coefficients for at least some visible colors.

To circumvent this awkwardness, a standard was devised in 1931 by the International Commission on Illumination (Commission Internationale de l'Éclairage, or CIE). The CIE defined three special "supersaturated" primaries, X, Y, and Z. They don't correspond to real colors, but they do have the property that all real colors can be represented as *positive* combinations of them.

How were the X, Y, and Z primaries determined? They were defined by means of an affine transformation applied to a selection of three primaries like

R, G, and B. The transformation was chosen to map the $r + g + b = 1$ plane into another plane, $x + y + z = 1$ (to maintain unit brightness), so that the pure spectral color curve $\mathbf{s}(\lambda) = (x(\lambda), y(\lambda), z(\lambda))$ would reside entirely within the positive octant of three-dimensional space, as suggested in Figure 16.7. Thus all spectral colors can be represented using the positive coefficients x, y, and z in this new space. (The specific nature of the original primaries used, and the details of deriving the transformation, can be found in various references, for example, Billmeyer and Saltzman 1981, Conrac Corporation 1985. However, you need not know this in order to understand and use the CIE standard.)

16.3.1 Constructing the CIE Chart

The spectral color curve $\mathbf{s}(\lambda)$ lies in three-dimensional space, but because it lies on the $x + y + z = 1$ plane, it is easy to represent its shape in a two-dimensional chart that can be printed on a page for reference. Only x and y are needed to specify a (unit intensity) color, because given (x, y) we can find z trivially (how?).

$z = 1 - x - y$

Thus the standard *CIE Chromaticity Diagram* is the curve $\mathbf{s}'(\lambda) = (x(\lambda), y(\lambda))$, shown in Figure 16.8. (Think of viewing the 3D curve of Figure 16.7 in an orthographic projection looking along the z-axis.) The diagram displays the horseshoe-shaped locus of all pure spectral colors, labeled according to wavelength. Inside the horseshoe lie all other visible colors. Points outside the horseshoe region do not correspond to visible light.

Various regions are labeled in the figure with names that people commonly use to describe the colors found there: For example, points near $(.6, .3)$ are perceived as red. Unfortunately, equal distances between points in the chart do not correspond to equal differences in perceived color. For instance, small changes in position in the G region cause only slight changes in perceived color. On the other hand, rather small changes in position near the B or Y regions cause large changes in perceived color.

The CIE Chromaticity Diagram defines certain special points. Point c at $(x, y) = (.310, .316)$ is a white color known as 'Illuminant C,' which is taken to be

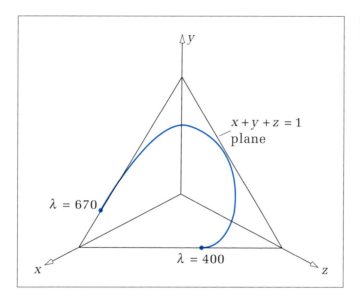

Figure 16.7.
Building the CIE standard.

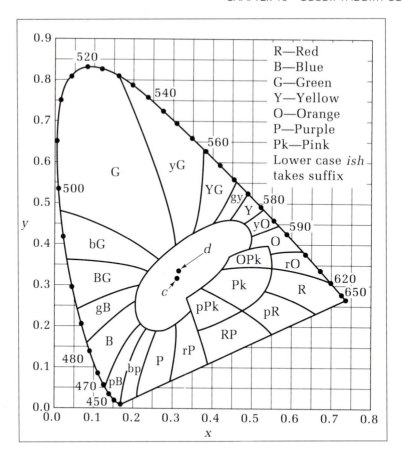

Figure 16.8.
The CIE Chromaticity Diagram.

the "fully unsaturated" color. It is often used as the reference color "white" in aligning some graphics monitors. Illuminant C has the color of an overcast sky at midday. Point d at (.313, .329) is the color that an ideal black-body radiator emits when raised to the white-hot temperature of 6504 K. It is a little "greener" than Illuminant C. Many other colors, such as those emitted by a tungsten filament light bulb, moonlight, red-hot steel at certain temperatures, and so on have been carefully measured (Conrac Corporation 1985, Rogers 1985).

The great value of the CIE Chromaticity Diagram is that it provides a worldwide standard for describing any color. Instruments have been devised that can generate the color represented by (x, y, z) inside the horseshoe, and so by careful matching one can measure the "value" for any color desired. (Instruments also exist that automatically measure (x, y, z) for a given color sample.) The chart also permits important calculations to be performed on colors, as we shall see next.

16.3.2 Using the CIE Chromaticity Diagram

The CIE chromaticity diagram has many uses. Several of them stem from the ease with which we can interpret straight lines on the chart, as suggested in Figure 16.9. Consider line l between the two colors a and b. All points on l are convex combinations (recall Chapter 7) of a and b, having the form $(\alpha)a + (1 - \alpha)b$ for $0 \leq \alpha \leq 1$. Each point is a legitimate color (its x, y, and z components sum

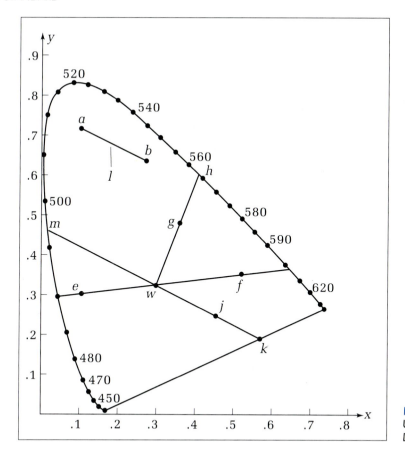

Figure 16.9.
Uses for the CIE Chromaticity Diagram.

to 1—why?), so we can assert that any color on the straight line (and only these) can be generated by shining various amounts of colors *a* and *b* onto a screen.

When two colors are added and their sum turns out to be white, we say that the colors are **complementary** (with respect to the choice of white). Thus *e* (blue-green) and *f* (orange-pink) are seen to be complementary colors with respect to *w*, because proper amounts of them added together form white, *w*. Some familiar pairs of complementary colors, to be discussed further, are listed in Table 16.1:

Table 16.1 Complementary Colors

red	cyan
green	magenta
blue	yellow

The diagram can also be used to measure the dominant wavelength and purity of a given color such as *g* in the figure. Accordingly, *g* must be the linear combination of some pure spectral color (found on the edge of the horseshoe) and a standard white, *w*. To find which spectral color is involved, just draw a line from *w* through *g* (to *h* here) and measure the wavelength—in this case 564 nm, a yellowish green. Similarly, the saturation or purity is just the ratio of distances gw/hw. The color at j has no dominant wavelength, because extending line wj hits k on the so-called purple line, which does not correspond to a single pure spectral color. (Colors along this line are combinations of red and violet.) In such a case the dominant wavelength is specified by finding the complement of j at m and using its wavelength with a c suffix, 498_c.

16.3.3 Color Gamuts

The CIE diagram is especially useful in defining *color gamuts*, the range of colors that can be produced on a device. For instance, a CRT monitor can produce combinations of only the basic red, green, and blue primaries that its three phosphor types can generate (recall Chapter 2). Plate 3 shows the locations of phosphor colors r, g, and b for a typical color CRT monitor. Table 16.2 shows these positions (see Stone et al. 1988):

Table 16.2. **CIE Coordinates for Typical CRT Monitor Primaries**

Primary	x	y
red	.628	.330
green	.285	.590
blue	.1507	.060

The three points define the triangular region shown. Any color within this triangle is a convex combination of the three primaries and can be displayed.[3] Colors outside this triangle are not in the gamut of the display and thus cannot be displayed. White falls within the gamut, reflecting the well-known fact that appropriate amounts of red plus green plus blue yield white.

Also shown is the gamut for a color printing process. (Because of the mechanism by which color is placed on paper, colors are not directly additive, and so the gamut is not a simple triangle.) It is somewhat smaller than the gamut for a CRT monitor, and so some colors that can be reproduced on this monitor cannot be displayed by a printer. On the other hand, some points that the printer gamut can reach lie outside the monitor gamut. Therefore, some colors can be printed but not observed on the CRT monitor.

Note that for any choice of three primaries, even the pure spectral colors on the horseshoe edge, a triangular gamut can never encompass all visible colors, because the horseshoe "bulges" outside any triangle whose vertices are within it. Red, green, and blue are natural choices for primaries, as they lie far apart in the CIE chart and therefore produce a gamut that "covers" a large part of the chart's area. If yellow, cyan, and magenta were used as primaries, for instance, the gamut would be much smaller. (Could white still be produced?)

Drill Exercise

16.1.   Why Red, Green, and Blue? Provide physical and philosophical arguments why the cones in our eyes have peak sensitivities to red, green, and blue lights. Why are these three colors situated at the three corners of the CIE chart, so that the gamut is about as large as possible?

---

[3]The National Television Standards Committee (NTSC) defines the following standard primaries in CIE coordinates: red = (.670, .330), green = (.210, .710), and blue = (.140, .080) (Rogers 1985).

16.4 Color Spaces

The CIE's specification of color is precise and standard, but it is not necessarily the most natural. In computer graphics particularly it is most natural to think of combining red, green, and blue to form the colors desired. Other people are more comfortable thinking in terms of hue, saturation, and lightness, and artists frequently refer to tints, shades, and tones to describe color. These all are exampels of **color models**, choices of three "descriptors" by means of which colors are described. If one can quantify the three descriptors, one can then describe a color by means of a 3-tuple of values, such as (tint, shade, tone) = (.125, 1.68, .045). This establishes a 3D coordinate system in which to describe color. The different choices of coordinates then give rise to different **color spaces**, and we need ways to convert color descriptions from one color space to another.

16.4.1 The RGB and CMY Color Spaces

The RGB (short for "red, green, blue") color model describes colors as positive combinations of three appropriately defined red, green, and blue primaries, as in Equation 16.3. If the scalars r, g, and b are confined to values between 0 and 1, all definable colors will lie in the cube shown in Figure 16.10. Unlike the CIE diagram, there is no normalization for the intensity of the color here: Points close to (0, 0, 0) are dark, and those farther out are lighter. For example, (1, 1, 1) corresponds to pure white. This color space is the most natural for computer graphics, in which a color specification such as (.3, .56, .9) can be directly translated into values stored in a color lookup table. Note that the corner marked magenta properly signifies that red light plus blue light produces magenta light, and similarly for yellow and cyan. Colors at diagonally opposite corners are complementary.

When normalized to unit intensity, all of the colors that can be defined here will of course lie in the CIE Chromaticity Diagram, once suitable positions of

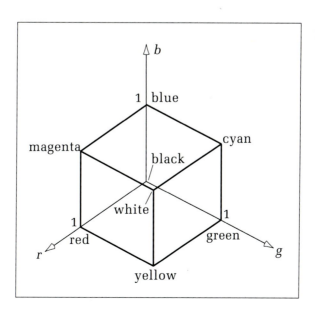

Figure 16.10.
The RGB color cube.

red, green, and blue have been provided. (What shape is the gamut?) It is not hard to convert a color specified in CIE coordinates (x, y, z) into (r, g, b) space, and vice versa. Because the R, G, B primaries are linear combinations of the $X, Y,$ and Z CIE primaries, a linear transformation suffices. The mapping depends on the definition of the primaries $R, G,$ and B and on the definition of white. For the primaries given in Table 16.2 and the white given by point d in Figure 16.8, the transformation is as follows (see Rogers 1985 for the details):

$$(r, g, b) = (x, y, z)\begin{pmatrix} 2.739 & -1.119 & .138 \\ -1.145 & 2.029 & -.333 \\ -.424 & .033 & 1.105 \end{pmatrix} \tag{16.4}$$

The conversion from RGB to XYZ of course uses the inverse of this matrix.

Drill Exercise

16.2.   Converting from RGB to CIE Space. Find the inverse of the preceding matrix to provide the transformation from RGB coordinates to CIE space. An important property of CIE space is that all colors can be expressed as positive linear combinations of the $X, Y,$ and Z primaries. What property does this impose on the inverse matrix? Does the inverse you calculate satisfy this condition?

Additive and Subtractive Color Systems

So far we have considered summing contributions of colored light to form new colors, an *additive* process. An **additive color system** expresses a color, D, as the sum of certain amounts of primaries, usually red, green, and blue: $D = (r, g, b)$. An additive system can use any three primaries, but because red, green, and blue are situated far apart in the CIE chart, they provide a large gamut.

Subtractive color systems are used when it is natural to think in terms of removing colors. When light is reflected (diffusely) from a surface or is transmitted through a partially transparent medium (as when photographic filters are used), certain colors are absorbed by the material and thus removed. This is a *subtractive* process.

A **subtractive color system** expresses a color, D, by means of a 3-tuple, just as an additive system does, but each of the three values specifies how much of a certain color (the complement of the corresponding primary) to *remove* from white in order to produce D. To clarify this, consider the most common subtractive system, the CMY system, which uses the subtractive primaries cyan, magenta, and yellow. If we say that $D = (c, m, y)_{CMY}$, we are saying that D is formed from white by subtracting amount c of the complement of cyan (i.e., red), amount m of the complement of magenta (green), and amount y of the complement of yellow (blue). Thus we immediately have the following relationship between the RGB and CMY systems:

$$(r, g, b)_{RGB} = (1, 1, 1) - (c, m, y)_{CMY} \tag{16.5}$$

That is, the amount of blue b in a color is reduced by increasing y, as y specifies the amount of yellow's complement to remove from white.

Figure 16.11 illustrates this. The three glass slides are described in the CMY system by $(.4, .5, .2)_{CMY}$, and so they contain amounts .4 of cyan, .5 of magenta, and .2 of yellow respectively. When white light—given by $(1, 1, 1)_{RGB}$ in the RGB additive system—penetrates the cyan-colored slide, 40 percent of the red component is absorbed, and a "cyanish" light containing $(.6, 1, 1)_{RGB}$ emerges.

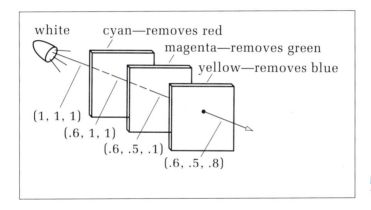

Figure 16.11.
The subtractive process.

When this light penetrates the magenta slide, 50 percent of the green light is removed, and the color $(.6, .5, 1)_{RGB}$ emerges. (What color is it now?) Finally, this light penetrates the yellow slide, and 20 percent of the blue component is absorbed, and the color $(.6, .5, .8)_{RGB}$ emerges.

A similar description applies to light scattering from a colored surface. In a three-color printing process, for instance, cyan, magenta, and yellow pigments are suspended in a colorless paint. Each subtracts a portion of the complement component of its incident light. For example, if magenta particles are mixed into a colorless paint, the particles will subtract the green portion of the white light and reflect only the red and blue components. The subtractive system is used for color hard-copy devices to fashion colors by mixing the three CMY primaries.

Plate 5 shows the additive and subtractive primaries and their interaction. In part a, red, green, and blue beams of light shine on a white surface. Where the two beams overlap, their lights combine to form a new color. For instance, red and green add to form yellow light. Where all three overlap, white light is formed.

Plate 5, part b shows a different situation. Each circle is formed by laying down ink in the color shown. Be sure to view it in white light. One disk appears yellow because its pigment subtracts the complement (blue) from the incident white light. When the yellow and cyan pigments are blended, one sees green, as both the blue and the red components have been removed. The center is black because all the components have been removed.

The HLS Color Model

A more intuitive color model uses coordinates hue (H), lightness (L), and saturation (S) to describe colors, because these are qualities that the human eye easily recognizes and can distinguish. The model arises from a distortion of the RGB cube into a double cone, as shown in Figure 16.12. By looking along the diagonal from (1, 1, 1) to (0, 0, 0) of the RGB cube, the six principal hues (R, G, B, and their three complements) are seen to lie on the vertices of a hexagon. Thus hue can be associated with an angle between 0 and 360 degrees, and convention puts 0 degrees at red. Lightness varies from 0, when all the RGB components are 0, to 1, when they all are 1. This corresponds nicely to the distance along the diagonal of the RGB cube from black to white. Saturation, which is roughly the distance a color lies away from the diagonal of the RGB cube, is mapped into radial distance from the lightness axis of the HLS cones.

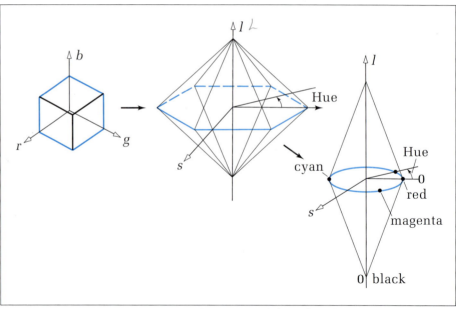

Figure 16.12.
Warping the RGB system to the HLS system.

One color space is based on a distortion of the other, leading us to seek an algorithm that maps from one to the other. The distortion is quite complex, and so we don't insist on an exact geometric transformation. The principal algorithm converting from RGB into HLS coordinates follows. Note that it pays the most attention to the largest and smallest of the R, G, and B components, but it provides a useful conversion and is invertible (see the exercises). Some examples follow the code fragment.

Code Fragment 16.1. Conversion from the RGB into the HLS Color System

```
procedure RGB_to_HLS(r, g, b : real; var h, l, s : real);
{convert (r, g, b), each in [0, 1], to h, l, s}
var
   mx, mn, rc, gc, bc : real;
begin
   mx := max(r, g, b);
   mn := min (r, g, b);
   l := (mx + mn) / 2.0; {lightness}
   {compute the saturation}
   if mx = mn then s := 0.0; {color is gray}
   else begin {color is chromatic}
      if l <= 0.5 then s := (mx − mn) / (mx + mn)
                  else s := (mx − mn) / (2 − mx + mn);
      rc := (mx − r) / (mx − mn); {compute hue}
      gc := (mx − g) / (mx − mn);
      bc := (mx − b) / (mx − mn);
      if r = mx then h := bc − gc;
      else if g = mx then h := 2 + rc − bc
      else if b = mx then h := 4 + gc − rc;
      h := h * 60;
      if h < 0.0 then h := h + 360
   end {color is chromatic}
end;
```

Worked Examples of the Conversion

1. Find H, L, S for a pure green: $(r, g, b) = (0, 1, 0)$. From the preceding algorithm we see that $mx = 1$ and $mn = 0$, and so lightness $L = .5$. Based on this L, we get a saturation of $S = 1.0$, which is reasonable, as this is a pure color. Finally, $rc = bc = 1$ and g is the largest, and so $h = 2$, yielding $H = 120°$, as is expected. Thus $(r, g, b) = (0, 1, 0)$ implies that $(H, L, S) = (120°, .5, 1.0)$.

2. Find H, L, S for a shade of gray: $(r, g, b) = (.4, .4, .4)$. Here $mx = .4$ and $mn = .4$, and so $L = .4$. Because $mx = mn$, the light is achromatic, with saturation $S = 0$. In this case the hue is not defined.

Drill Exercises

✓ **16.3.   Perform Some Conversions.** Find (H, L, S) for each of the following cases, and explain why the result is reasonable.
$(r, g, b) = (.2, .8, .1)$
$(r, g, b) = (0, 0, .8)$
$(r, g, b) = (1, 1, 1)$
$(r, g, b) = (0, .7, .7)$

16.4.   HLS to RGB Conversion. Work out an algorithm, $HLS\_to\_RGB(\ )$, that converts from HLS into RGB coordinates. It should provide an inverse transformation to the RBG to HLS conversion that we discussed, in that it recovers the original R, G, B values when applied to the H, L, S values obtained using the preceding algorithm.

16.5.   The HSV Color Model. Another color model, the hue (H), saturation (S), and value (V) system, is also based on a warped version of the RGB cube but is a single cone rather than a double one, as suggested in Figure 16.13. Hue is again mapped to angle (with the hexagon distorted into a circle, as in the HLS system, and the saturation having the same interpretation as with the HLS system). The light's intensity is captured in the value V, which varies from 0 to 1, as shown. Develop an algorithm that converts from RGB into HSV coordinates.

16.4.2 The Color of Reflected Light

In Chapter 15 we described a shading model for the intensity (gray level) of light reaching the eye from each point on an object. This culminated in Equation 15.6:

$$I_{tot} = I_a r_a + I_s[r_d(\mathbf{u_s} \cdot \mathbf{u_n}) + r_s(\mathbf{u_r} \cdot \mathbf{u_v})^f] \qquad (16.6)$$

giving values for the ambient, diffuse, and specular components of light intensity. The reflection coefficients, r_a, r_d, and r_s, report the fraction of incident light

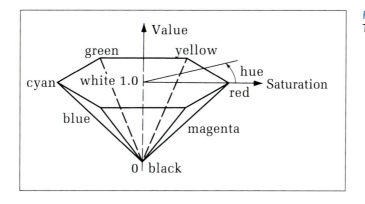

Figure 16.13.
The HSV color model.

that bounces or scatters back from the surface. Now we extend this to the case of colored light and colored surfaces.

Surprisingly, specular reflection is the simplest to deal with. Because it is mirrorlike, the color of the specular component is the same as that of the light source. For instance, the specular highlight seen on a glossy red apple when illuminated by a yellow light is not red but yellow. Thus there is no interaction between the color of the surface and the color of the light source.

On the other hand, the ambient and diffuse components do depend on the color of the surface. When a surface is bathed in white light, the light scattered back because of the ambient or diffuse reflection has the color of the surface itself. We say that a surface is red if it appears red when bathed in white light. But when a surface is bathed in colored light, the calculation of the color of the reflected light is more complicated.

Physically a surface has a **reflectance function,** $R(\lambda)$, which reports the fraction of the light at wavelength λ that is reflected. (This reflectance function typically depends on several other variables as well, but we are ignoring those details here.) So if the surface is bathed in light having spectral density $S(\lambda)$, then the reflected light will have spectral density $S(\lambda)R(\lambda)$. There are methods to convert this spectrum into equivalent CIE variables, (x, y, z), but this would be too costly to do in a graphics application.

Instead—as an approximation to the truth—we exploit the three-dimensional nature of perception and define three **diffuse reflection coefficients,** r_{dR}, r_{dG}, and r_{dB}, for the red, green, and blue primaries. This is akin to "sampling" the reflectance function, $R(\lambda)$, at only three key wavelengths. Each of the three coefficients reports the fraction of the light of its color that is reflected from the surface.

Similarly, each source of light, I_a and I_s, is modeled as the sum of red, green, and blue intensities:

$$I_a = I_{aR} + I_{aG} + I_{aB}$$
$$I_s = I_{sR} + I_{sG} + I_{sB}$$

$$(16.7)$$

and the received light is computed separately for each of the primaries using Equation 16.6. For instance, the red component of the light reaching the eye from a point is

$$I_R = I_{aR}r_{dR} + I_{sR}[r_{dR}(\mathbf{u}_s \cdot \mathbf{u}_n) + r_s(\mathbf{u}_r \cdot \mathbf{u}_v)^f]$$

$$(16.8)$$

with similar expressions for the green and blue components, I_G and I_B. This model uses the same reflection coefficient for both the ambient and the diffuse light components. Also note that the same specular reflection coefficient, r_s, is used for each light component, as the specular component is the same color as the source is.

Although this model only approximates the physical truth, it is efficient computationally and can lead to very realistic pictures. (Note that the vectors **s**, **n**, and so on are the same for the red, green, and blue components, and so the dot product terms need be calculated only once and can be reused in the three expressions.) The question of how to choose the various reflection coefficients then arises. Many studies have been conducted on the reflection of light from different materials such as copper, marble, or pewter (see Cook and Torrance 1981, Rogers 1985). Various approaches and tables have been devised to guide the choice of the coefficients, but often they are chosen merely by judicious guessing and experimentation. When a greater level of realism is required, one usually must explore more fully the nature of electromagnetic waves and their interaction with surfaces. Algorithms that attempt to capture the physics in this way have proved successful but generally require a great deal more computation for each pixel (Potmesil and Chakravarhy 1982).

16.5 Programming the Color Lookup Table

We must translate computed pixel values from the 3-tuples of floating-point numbers into a discrete set of programmed colors that is supported by the display. As we know, most color displays use a lookup table (LUT) that can be loaded under program control to specify a set of colors. We thus seek a good strategy for choosing the colors to load into the LUT and for assigning the proper LUT index to each pixel, given its color 3-tuple.

Note that for a composed image the strategy is simple. A **composed image** is one created by an artist using a graphics editor or paint system. The artist can try various colors for each bar graph, company logo, or cartoon figure to see how they look, refining the palette of colors interactively until the best set has been found. At this point the colors are already stored in the LUT, and each object is easily associated with the appropriate index into the LUT.

For **computed images** such as those produced by our shading models, however, the mapping from 3-tuples to final colors is more difficult to determine. If the scene is very simple, perhaps consisting of a red brick and a blue ball bathed in white light, it will be known ahead of time that various intensities of one particular red and one blue will be required. In this case a selection of different intensities of these few hues can be loaded into the LUT and indexed as needed. But unfortunately, most scenes contain many hues and saturations, each occurring with many intensities, and the LUT does not have enough room to hold all the colors in the image.

In Chapter 15 we took the approach of filing all the pixel intensities as they were computed. This allows a routine to scan through them to determine the population of intensities present in the image, so that they can be mapped appropriately into allowable pixel values. The same approach can be used for color images. Each pixel is represented by a 3-tuple (r, g, b) of floating-point values. As the image is computed, its pixel values are stored in a file containing the 3-tuples of pixel values. Call it the **3-tuple file.** A suitable device-independent format for this file might store the number of rows and columns and then list all of the pixel 3-tuples, as in the following code fragment:

Code Fragment 16.2. Example Format for the 3-tuple Image File

```
640 480
0.342 1.456 0.894
2.367 1.678 6.333
3.011 2.576 0.067
```

Comments and other pertinent information could also be stored, so that the circumstances of the image (objects in the scene, date of creation, light sources, and the like) can be retrieved.

The remaining steps in creating the image are as follows:

- Scan the 3-tuple file to determine the color population.

- Set up the mapping from 3-tuples to LUT values.

- Build the LUT-based image file.

- Send the file to a device.

In the first step a small routine scans the 3-tuple file for the range of pixel 3-tuples residing in the image. In particular it looks for the extreme values for each of the three color components: r_{min} and r_{max} for the r component, g_{min} and g_{max} for the green, and so forth. These values define a parallelepiped in RGB-space, as suggested by Figure 16.14. The entire color population resides within this block.

The color block represents a continuum of color values, whereas the LUT can hold only a collection of discrete color values. Suppose, as in Chapter 15, we assume that there are b bits per pixel in the frame buffer, so that the LUT has $M = 2^b$ entries. Our strategy is to choose M specific points within the color block as "color representatives." Digital versions of each are loaded into the M entries in the LUT. Then the 3-tuple pixel file is scanned once again, and each 3-tuple is approximated by the "closest" color representative in the LUT. A new LUT-based image file is created, with a format such as the following:

Code Fragment 16.3. Example File Format for the LUT-Based Image File

640 480	% number of rows and columns
256	% number of LUT entries
3b2 3c4 56e 57f 662 66a	
4b4 545 cbd cbe cbf dba	% 256 LUT color values in hex
34a 35b 56c 456 12c 3da	
.	
.	
34 35 56 8c 23 12 a4 a5	
23 25 26 2d 26 28 b5 b7	% entries for each pixel in hex
78 87 8e 92 1d b2 8d 72	
.	
.	

As the comments suggest, the number of rows and columns is given first, followed by the number of LUT entries. Then each LUT entry is given (in this case as a triple of hexadecimal digits, as discussed in Exercise 16.9), followed by a single index value (also in hex) for each pixel.

The final step is scanning the LUT-based file to (1) load the LUT and (2) write final pixel values into the frame buffer of the target display device.

Drill Exercise

16.6.   How Big Are the Files? How many bytes are required to store the image data for the 3-tuple file and the LUT-based file? Assume that for the 3-tuple file each real value is stored in six bytes, and for the LUT-based file each LUT entry is stored in three bytes and each LUT index in two bytes. What can be concluded about the relative sizes of the two file formats? Which format is more device independent?

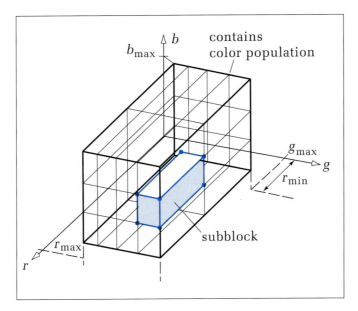

Figure 16.14.
All colors lie in a color block.

Subdividing the Color Block

To set up the mapping to LUT values, we must choose the M color representatives that will be stored in the LUT. The simplest approach is to subdivide the color block into a number of non-overlapping subblocks and to choose as the representative of each subblock a color value near its center. This is essentially a three-dimensional version of the (one-dimensional) quantization process we used in Chapter 15 for gray-scale images.

How should the color block be subdivided? Here we describe only the simplest approach: The block is subdivided by "slicing" it along each of the three axes, as shown in Figure 16.14. This allows the red, green, and blue components of the color representatives to be chosen independently. For instance, if $M =$ 256, the red range $r_{min}, \ldots, r_{max}$ might be divided into 8 slices, the green into 8, and the blue into 4, creating exactly 256 subblocks. Alternatively, we might break both the red and blue into 6 slices and the green into 7 slices, to produce a total of 252 subregions. The four remaining entries in the LUT would not be used or could be used for the color of a border or some text annotation.

An equally important consideration is where to locate the color representatives, which are digital values that must "fit" in the LUT entries. For instance, suppose there are four bits in each entry for the green value, permitting green intensities from 0 to 15 (0000 to 1111 in binary). If we decide on six slices for green, which six values between 0 and 15 should we select? Note that the actual green brightness that corresponds to level 15 can be set independently on most raster displays by adjusting a control knob in its front panel. For such terminals, only the relative intensities must be encoded. An example will help clarify how the various ingredients interact.

Example

Consider a typical case in which the LUT has $M = 256$ entries, each of which contains 4 bits for each of the red, green, and blue intensities. The 3-tuple image file is scanned, and it is found that r_{min}, g_{min}, and b_{min} all are very close to 0 but that $r_{max} = 4.0$, $g_{max} = 7.0$, and $b_{max} = 3.0$. How can we map 3-tuples into LUT values?

We decide to use 7 representatives for green and 6 each for red and blue. We also choose, for simplicity, to space the representative values as equally as possible over the 16 possible LUT values. For the red and blue colors, the 6 values 0, 3, 6, 9, 12, 15 do a fine job. For green, we can't achieve an equal spacing, but 0, 3, 5, 8, 11, 13, 15 provides a reasonable approximation.

Now how are these values stored in LUT entries? The array $r[\ ]$: **array**$[0 . . 5]$ **of** *integer* is created to store the 6 red values, and similarly for the arrays $g[\ ]$ and $b[\ ]$. For instance, $r[\ ]$ holds the 6 values 0, 3, 6, 9, 12, and 15. As shown next, three embedded loops cycle through all combinations of the values stored in these arrays, and for each combination a single 12-bit number is created and stored in the $LUT[\ ]$ array:

Code Fragment 16.4. Loading the LUT

```
for i := 0 to 5 do
  for j := 0 to 6 do
    for k := 0 to 5 do
      LUT[42 * i + 6 * j + k] := 256 * r[i] + 16 * g[j] + b[k];
```

Multiplying by 256 shifts the red value $r[i]$ over by 8 bits so that the red level appears in the top 4 most significant bits of the LUT. For instance, when i, j, and k are 3, 2, and 5, respectively, the index into the LUT is 143, and the value composed from $r[3] = 9$, $g[2] = 5$, and $b[5] = 15$ is 2399, which in hexadecimal is $95f$, as desired.

Now when the 3-tuple pixel list, (r_i, g_i, b_i), for the image file is rescanned, each r_i is compared with the 6 red representatives, and the nearest one is identified: Find j_r such that r_i is closest to $r[j\_r]$. For instance, if $r_i = 8.23$, the closest value will be 9, and so $j\_r = 3$. Do the same to identify index values j_g and j_b. Then compute the index value into the LUT itself as $j := 42 * j\_r + 6 * j\_g + j\_b$.

Drill Exercise

16.7. Trying Out Some Values. For the example, show the first 20 entries of the LUT. Does this seem like an orderly arrangement? What is stored in $LUT[29]$? What about $LUT[231]$?

This uniform quantization approach works adequately, particularly if the number of bits per pixel is large and the LUT offers a large palette. But for displays that support only a small number of colors, more sophisticated approaches may be necessary. Heckbert (1982) surveyed several approaches and introduced others, determining both how rapidly they operate and the quality of the final images they produce. In some methods the image file is scanned to determine statistical information about the colors that appear. Those colors that appear in only a few pixels are usually not important and can be replaced by other nearby colors. If a large number of pixels contain colors that are "close" to one another, this subset of colors should be quantized further. (Further discussions of this complex subject can be found in Heckbert 1982, Kopec 1985, Meyer and Greenberg 1980.)

16.6 Summary

The eye–brain system perceives colors in a complex way. The color of a light may be specified precisely according to its spectral density function, but this is an inconvenient format for communicating color information, and in addition the same perceived color can arise from myriad different spectral densities. In fact, our perception of color is three dimensional, and so we seek methods for describing color through a 3-tuple of numbers.

The CIE standard provides a precise approach to specifying colors. Any color, S, of unit brightness is described by two numbers, (x, y). The notion is that S is created by adding the proper amounts of three special primary lights, X, Y, and Z, as defined by the standard. Specifically, $S = xX + yY + (1 - x - y)Z$. The special primaries—which are supersaturated and cannot actually be seen—are chosen so that any pure spectral color (based on a single wavelength of light) can be formed using positive amounts of x and y. The CIE Chromaticity Diagram provides a useful worldwide standard for describing colors and calculating the ingredients of a given color. It is also used to display the gamut of colors that can be formed by adding together various amounts of available primaries.

Some methods convert the colors described in one color system into those of another system, so that one can convert from CIE coordinates into more familiar RGB coordinates. Other color spaces are commonly used as well, such as hue, saturation, and lightness.

For computer graphics we must calculate the color of objects when they are bathed in lights of various colors. Computing the true color pixel by pixel is very complicated, but simple approximations can be made that provide rather realistic images.

When computing colored images, it is wise to file all of the pixel 3-tuples as they are calculated and then to scan this file to determine the color population of the image. In this way one can set up judicious mappings between color 3-tuples and entries into a LUT.

Programming Exercises

16.8. Image File Formats and Filters. Design a "neutral" (device-independent) file format for storing pixel data for a color image. The number of rows and columns in the image is given, followed by each pixel represented as a 3-tuple of floating-point values. Include comment fields (denoted perhaps as any line beginning with #) to permit data such as the author, date of creation, and name of scene to be included in the file. Write a "filter" program that reads an image file and determines the minimum and maximum values for each of the red, green, and blue pixel components.

16.9. Representing LUT Values. Suppose the LUT supports 4 bits for each of the red, green, and blue intensities. Four bits of information can be expressed using a single hexadecimal (base 16) digit that ranges from $0, \ldots, f$: 0011 is given by 3, 1001 by 9, 1101 by d, and so forth (Hill and Peterson 1984). Thus the 12 bits for each LUT entry fit nicely into 3 hexadecimal digits (e.g., $5fa$) having values from $0, \ldots, f$. Write a routine, $Hex\_String(r, g, b : integer;$ **var** $st : string)$, that converts a triple (r, g, b) of integer values lying between 0 and 15 into the corresponding string of 3 hexadecimal digits.

Chapter 17

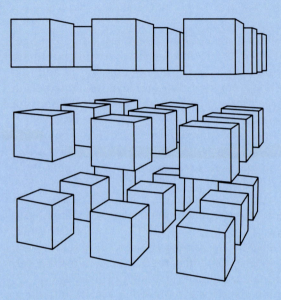

Hidden Surface Elimination

Why hidest thou thy face from me?

Psalms 88:14

Behind a frowning providence he hides a shining face.

William Cowper, "Light Shining Out of Darkness," 1779

Goals of the Chapter

- To add greater realism to pictures by eliminating hidden lines and surfaces on solid objects
- To survey several hidden surface removal techniques
- To develop in detail some fundamental hidden surface removal methods

17.1 Introduction

Most of the solid objects we wish to draw are opaque, so that only their "front" surfaces and edges should be seen. Any surface or edge that is *occluded*, or covered by a closer surface, thus should not be drawn. In Chapter 15 the only attention we paid to occluded faces was to discard "back" faces. To draw a mesh model we simply clipped each front face to the view volume, projected it, and drew it. We produced both line drawings and shaded images in this way. For a line drawing we drew the edges of the face, whereas for a shaded image we filled each face using a shading algorithm. But if hidden surfaces or edges are not removed, the resulting picture rarely will look right. In a line drawing the object looks transparent, and its interpretation is ambiguous, as shown in Figure 15.4.

Two closely related problems are *hidden line removal* (*HLR*) and *hidden surface removal* (*HSR*). The first applies to line drawings, in which the edges of each face are drawn. The second applies to shaded images in which the faces are filled in with colors. Figure 17.1 shows an HLR example in action: two "edge" renditions of a simple mesh model. In the first picture all the edges are shown, whereas in the second only the visible portion of each edge has been drawn. Some edges, such as E_1, have not been drawn at all, whereas others, such as E_2, have been drawn only in part: E_2 is effectively clipped at the point where it intersects edge E_3.

In Figure 17.2, the same object is drawn with its faces filled in with various shades. In Figure 17.2a the faces are simply painted in a haphazard order "on top of" any previously drawn faces. Clearly, this mindless approach makes many mistakes. In Figure 17.2b true HSR methods have been used so that only the visible part of each face is colored, and the image is correct.

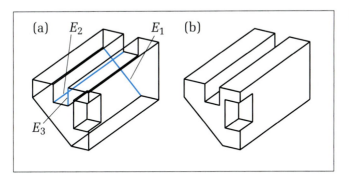

Figure 17.1.
Hiding occluded edges.

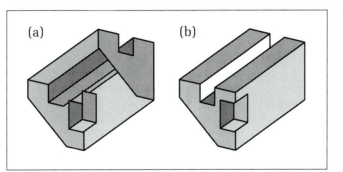

Figure 17.2.
Drawing faces in different orders.

In this chapter we examine various HLR and HSR algorithms, lumping them together under the name *hidden surface removal* owing to their similarity. The goal of these algorithms is to identify efficiently which parts of one surface or edge are occluded by some other surface. The answer to this lies in the complex interaction between the positions of the viewer and the various objects in the scene.

17.1.1 Dealing with Shadows

There is a strong resemblance between HSR methods and the treatment of shadows. Recall from Chapter 15 that a point is in shadow if it can't be "seen" by the point light source, if some surface lies between the source and the point. Then the diffuse and specular components are absent, and only the ambient component is visible. Once the visible part of a face has been determined, the HSR algorithm can be applied again from the point of view of the light source to see what parts of the visible surface are also visible to the light source. Figure 17.3 shows light from a point source falling on an open book, but a suspended triangle causes part of the book to be in shadow. Points in shadow are visible to the eye but not to the light source, whereas points bathed in light are visible to both the eye and the light source. We shall refer at various points to the shadowing problem in connection with specific HSR methods.

17.1.2 Object Space Versus Image Space Approaches

Algorithms to remove hidden lines or surfaces take different forms depending on the dichotomy (Sutherland et al., 1974):

- *Object space.* Compute, to the precision of the machine, the coordinates of each visible edge of each face. Algorithms of this type are implemented in the physical coordinate system in which the objects are

Figure 17.3.
Drawing shadows in shaded pictures.

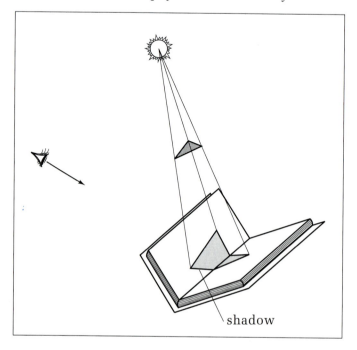

shadow

described. This kind of precision is useful for engineering drawings. Using an object space approach, a picture can be enlarged many times, and the results will still be satisfactory.

- *Image space.* For each display pixel, determine which element of which face is the closest to the viewer, and draw the pixel in the appropriate shade. Image space algorithms are implemented in the screen coordinate system only to the precision of the display. If the results are enlarged, some imperfections will become noticeable, such as two edges not meeting properly.

Because of their prevalence in graphics, we shall discuss the HSR methods in a common framework of mesh models with opaque surfaces. (Extensions of these ideas to performing HSR on parametrically defined surfaces can be found in Blinn et al. 1980, Lane and Carpenter 1979.) A different approach—ray tracing—is discussed in Chapter 18. Ray tracing automatically performs HSR, but only with a great deal of computation.

HSR algorithms should operate as rapidly as possible. We are interested in how the computation time depends on the complexity of the objects in a scene, as well as the number of such objects. If we informally denote the number of elements—edges or faces—in a scene by n, we might expect that an object space HSR algorithm would take time proportional to n^2, as every element must be tested against every other element to see which of them obscures which. We would say that such an algorithm "grows as n^2" with the scene complexity.

On the other hand, an image space algorithm might well grow in a different way. If there are N pixels in the display, we might expect such an algorithm to grow as nN, since for each of N pixels we must test each of n scene elements. In practice, N is much larger than n.

One goes to great lengths to use *coherence* when developing an HSR algorithm, in order to reduce the number of tests that must be made. The purpose is to reduce the growth of computations from n^2 or nN to a more manageable growth, such as $n \log(n)$, $N \log(n)$, or even n. An extensive study in Sutherland et al. 1974 provides useful estimates of many popular HSR algorithms.

17.1.3 Description of the Polygon Mesh Data

To set the stage, we suppose that the mesh data are preprocessed as described in Chapter 15. A particular synthetic camera and view volume are established, and for that view the back-facing faces of the model are identified and deleted from the face list (see Section 15.2.1).

Each of the vertices that belongs to a front face is then subjected to the viewing, perspective, and normalization transformations summarized by matrix $\hat{M}_{tot}$ in Equation 12.41. Recall that the viewing transformation $\hat{A}_{WV}$ expresses a world point (x, y, z) in the viewing coordinates (u, v, n) of the synthetic camera. $\hat{M}_S$ will adjust points as needed if the eye lies off the n-axis, and $\hat{M}_P$ will transform the object into a warped version that can then be viewed using an orthographic projection. $\hat{M}_P$ also converts the depth of a point from the eye into a "pseudodepth." Finally, $\hat{N}$ causes an enhanced window-to-viewport mapping: The window in the viewplane is mapped to the viewport in NDC, and the pseudodepth is mapped into the interval 0 to 1. Thus points transformed by $\hat{M}_{tot}$ lie in a special three-dimensional NDC space. We continue to denote their components as (x, y, z) for convenience, but it should be remembered that these are not world coordinate points. Because the x-, y-, and z-axes are distorted versions of the camera's u-, v-, and n-axes, the x, y, z system is left-handed, with the z-axis receding from the viewer.

Including the perspective transformation $\hat{M}_P$ in this mapping provides an important benefit for HSR algorithms. To draw a point (x, y, z), we need only project it orthographically: just draw it at (x, y). Therefore the overlap between two faces as seen by the eye can be found by testing the x- and y-coordinates alone! By the same token, if two points (x, y, z_1) and (x, y, z_2) have the same x- and y-components so that one might occlude the other, we need only test the sizes of z_1 and z_2 to see which point is closer.

Once the vertices have been transformed, the edges of each face are clipped to the (prewarped) view volume in homogeneous coordinates. (The clipping can be omitted if it is certain the model lies entirely within the view volume.) If the clipping is done, some faces may become subdivided into two or more faces, as described in Section 15.2.2, in which case the additional faces are added to the face list.

When this preprocessing is complete, the geometry of the particular view of the model is captured in a vertex list and a face list. These can be implemented either as arrays or as linked lists. We choose arrays here as this simplifies the discussion.

The Vertex List

The vertex list resides in the array $vert$: **array** [1 . . *MAXNUMVERTS*] **of** *point3D*. Because of the preprocessing of the vertices, we are assured that

- $vert[i].x$ and $vert[i].y$ lie within the borders (V_l, V_t, V_r, V_b) of the viewport in NDC.

- The projection of 3D point $vert[i]$ is simply $(vert[i].x, vert[i].y)$.

- $vert[i].z$ is the pseudodepth of the i-th vertex; it lies between 0 and 1.

The Face List

The face list resides in the array $face$: **array**[1 . . *MAXNUMFACES*] **of** *face_info*, where type *face_info* is similar to the type *face* used in Code Fragment 15.1. It includes extra information about the face to improve the speed of HSR algorithms. The type is defined as follows:

Code Fragment 17.1. Data Type of Faces

```
cuboid = record
              l, t, r, b, near, far : real
          end;
face_info = record
              num_verts : 0 . . MAX_VERTS_IN_FACE;
              verts : array [1 . . MAX_VERTS_IN_FACE]
                  of 0 . . MAXNUMVERTS;
              face_plane : plane;
              nature : attributes;
              extent : cuboid
          end;
```

Consider the information stored in the following fields:

1. The *verts* field lists the *num_verts* indices of the vertices that reside in the face. (See Table 15.1 for an example.)

2. The *face_plane* field stores $\mathbf{n}$ and D used in the point normal form $\mathbf{n} \cdot \mathbf{p} = D$ to describe the plane in which the face lies. Because this information is used to determine when one face is closer than another, we need the version of $\mathbf{n}$ and D for the plane expressed in three-dimensional NDC coordinates, after the mapping owing to matrix $\hat{M}_{\text{tot}}$. The effect of an affine transformation on a plane is discussed in Chapter 11.

3. As described in Chapter 15, the surface attributes of the face are stored in the *nature* field.

4. The new field *extent* describes the extent of its face. The *extent* (or *bounding box*) is a rectangular parallelepiped—having six walls aligned with the coordinate axes—that fits snugly about the polygon. It is easily found by scanning the vertices of the face to identify the largest and smallest x-, y-, and z-coordinates.

Figure 17.4 shows an example. Face P has extent $E = (E_l, E_t, E_r, E_b, E_{\text{near}}, E_{\text{far}})$. No point on P lies closer to the eye than E_{near} does or farther than E_{far} does. Extents are widely used in HSR routines because they allow very fast tests of a face's approximate position.

Example

The information for face 3 of the prism of Figure 15.1 might look like the following:

num_verts :   4
verts :   4 3 1 5
nature :   red shiny smooth brass . . .
face_plane : .948 .316 0
extent :   .3 .8 .75 .4 .3 .9

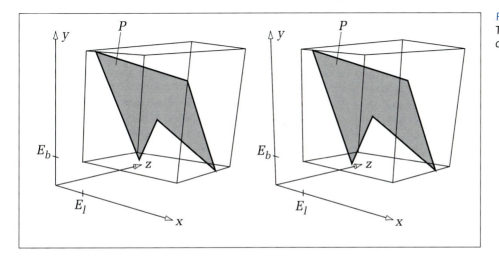

Figure 17.4.
The extent of a face in three dimensions.

17.2 Elementary Hidden Surface Elimination for Shaded Surfaces

The first class of HSR techniques we shall examine applies to rendering views on raster displays, when the faces of the object are filled with a color or colors. They fall into the "image space" category.

The job is easy if only a single face must be drawn. The x- and y-components of the vertices of the face are converted into screen coordinates, and the edges of the face are stored in an edge list (EL). Then for each scan line the appropriate "runs" of pixels inside the face are set to the face's color.

However, when there are several faces to draw, the situation is much more complex. We have to determine which face is the closest in a region of the screen and therefore occludes all other faces there. The answer to this can change from pixel to pixel along a scan line.

We shall study some HSR approaches that have the following general shape:

Code Fragment 17.2. A Class of HSR Algorithms: Pseudocode

For each pixel:
  determine the closest face that "covers" that pixel;
  set the pixel to the color of the closest face.

(The notion of a face covering a pixel is discussed in Section 15.4.2.) HSR algorithms in this class are distinguished mainly by the way the closest face is determined and by the order in which the ingredients of the problem are processed.

17.2.1 The Heedless Painter's Algorithm

The first attempt is very simple and introduces several key ideas, but it often produces erroneous images, some as bad as that in Figure 17.2a! Each face of the object is filled in turn *in its entirety*. This is a form of the *Painter's algorithm*: As each face is painted into the frame buffer, its color paints over whatever was drawn there before, just as a painter covers old layers of paint with new ones. Thus the color shown at each pixel is the most recently drawn color, and if two faces overlap in x and y, then the last one drawn will obscure the first one, whether or not it is in fact closer. (One could bend a familiar acronym and call this a LIFO organization: "last in, first observed.")

To give this method at least a chance of drawing the scene properly, we use the *extent.far* field in the face array to determine which face has the most remote vertex, the second most remote, and so forth. That is, the face list is sorted using *extent.far* as the sort key, and then the faces are painted into the frame buffer, beginning with the farthest one, until finally the closest one is painted. A skeleton version therefore looks like the following:

Code Fragment 17.3. Heedless Painter's Algorithm

Sort the faces by their extent.far value;
Paint entire faces in order from the farthest to the closest;

Note the presence of a sort routine in this algorithm. Sorting is an integral part of every HSR algorithm in one form or another, as objects that are presented to the algorithm must be ordered in some way. (A variety of sort routines is readily found in texts on data structures and algorithms, such as Kruse 1984. Code for Quicksort is given in Appendix 3.)

When does the Heedless Painter's algorithm work? Figure 17.5 shows various situations, involving two faces, A and B. Each situation is shown using two orthographic views of NDC in concert. The view that is actually drawn looks onto the x, y-plane from a point having negative z. The other looks onto the x, z-plane from some point having positive y (so depth increases in the upward direction). In Figure 17.5a the x-extents X_A and X_B of A and B overlap, as do the y-extents Y_A and Y_B, and so we suspect that one face partially occludes the other.

Figure 17.5.
Depth ordering of faces.

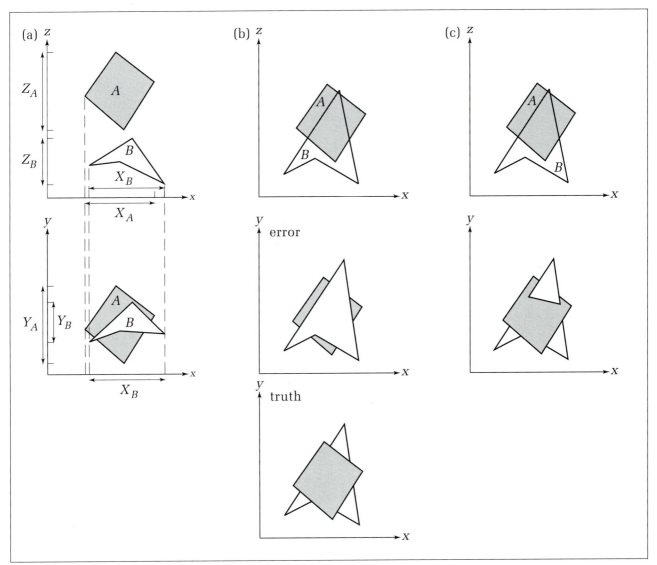

Drill Exercise

17.1   Occlusion? Show that one face need not occlude another even when both their *x*- and *y*-extents overlap.

In the case shown, one face does occlude the other. But because their *z*-extents happen not to overlap, the Heedless Painter's algorithm works well. Face *A* is drawn first, and then face *B*. There is no way, therefore, that *A* can partially obscure *B*.

In Figure 17.5b the faces have been shifted slightly, and the situation is quite different. Face *A* is the more remote according to the farthest-vertex criterion, and so it would be painted first, producing the result marked *error*. But in fact, because of its "tilt," *A* is closer where it overlaps *B*, and so it should obscure *B*, thereby producing the result marked *truth*. (It is helpful to cut out some test faces from stiff paper and experiment with various orientations.) The situation in Figure 17.5c is even more complex: *B* interpenetrates with *A*. Here the Heedless Painter's algorithm would mindlessly paint *B* over *A*.

The Heedless Painter's algorithm therefore fails to distinguish correctly the portions of one face that overlap another. We cannot simply paint entire faces over one another based on a single criterion such as maximum depth. We shall fix the Painter's algorithm later by performing additional tests on the faces involved, but the algorithm then becomes much more complicated.

First we shall look at a few other HSR approaches. Each works properly but has some deficiencies. Together they provide a great deal of insight into ways to attack the HSR problem.

Drill Exercise

17.2.   When Does the Heedless Painter's Algorithm Work? What is the class of meshes for which this algo- rithm works for any view of the object? For objects not in this class, what condition causes the algorithm to fail?

17.2.2 The Depth Buffer Approach

The depth buffer (or *z*-buffer) algorithm is one of the simplest and most easily implemented HSR methods. Its principal limitation is the amount of memory that it requires. The idea is to dedicate some system memory to create a depth buffer, as shown in Figure 17.6. The depth buffer is similar to the frame buffer, in that it reserves a certain number of bits for every pixel. For example, the value $d[i, j]$ stored for the i, j-th pixel is a **depth** or *z*-component, of the depth of the closest face (found so far) that covers that pixel.

The depth buffer algorithm is simple and fast and requires no sorting! The faces are scan converted one after the other, as described in Chapter 13. But before each pixel is given the color of the current face, a test is made: The depth of the face at that pixel is computed and compared with the depth stored in the buffer. If the face is closer, its color will be written into the frame buffer, and its depth value will be placed in the depth buffer. Otherwise nothing will be done.

In pseudocode this looks like the following:

Code Fragment 17.4. Depth Buffer Algorithm

___

for *each face F* **do**
  for *each row i covered by face F* **do**
    for *each column j covered by face F* **do**
    begin
      find depth z of face F at the (x, y) corresponding to [i, j];
      if $z < d[i, j]$ **then**
      begin
        $p[i, j] :=$ <color of face at (x, y)>;
        $d[i, j] := z$
      end
    end;

The array $d[,]$ is initially loaded with value 1.0: the greatest pseudodepth value possible. The frame buffer $p[,]$ is initially loaded with the background color. Note that this algorithm works for objects of any shape (even curved surfaces, as described in Chapters 9 and 14), because it finds the closest surface based on a point-by-point test.

To test whether a row or pixel is covered by a face, it is most efficient to build an edge table for each face, as described in Chapter 13. Similarly, for each new row the active edge list is updated to facilitate scanning runs of pixels for the face in that row.

How is the depth $z(x, y)$ calculated for a face? The description of the plane of the face is readily available in the *face_plane* field of the face list, and so the plane equation $n_x x + n_y y + n_z z = D$ is known. Given x and y, it is therefore easy to find $z(x, y)$, as follows:[1]

$$z(x, y) = \frac{D - n_x x - n_y y}{n_z} \qquad (17.1)$$

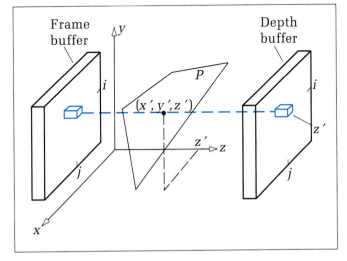

Figure 17.6.
Conceptual view of the depth buffer.

___

[1] If $n_x = 0$, then the face is being viewed "on edge" and is invisible.

As with so many scan-line calculations, this one is best performed incrementally, as discussed in the exercises.

Drill Exercise

17.3.   Incremental Calculation of Depth. Suppose that two adjacent pixels on a scan line, y, are at x_0 and $x_0 + dx$. Express $z(x_0 + dx, y)$ in terms of $z(x_0, y)$ using Equation 17.1. Show that if $z(x, y)$ is computed at the beginning of each run, each successive depth will be found by a single addition. Show how to find the depth $z(x_{start}, y_s)$ for the first pixel in the run (or runs) in each scan line, based on the depth at the start of the run on the previous scan line (at $y = y_s - dy$). Given that the left side of a face is determined by the edge from (x_a, y_a) to (x_b, y_b), show how to compute incrementally the depths at the start of each run.

One disadvantage of the depth buffer algorithm is that many pixels in the frame buffer are reread and rewritten many times before the final color is written. For those systems in which communication with the frame buffer or the depth buffer is slow, the many executions of *set_pixel( )*—or depth management routines such as *Get_Depth( )* and *Set_Depth( )*—slow down the process significantly. By contrast, alternative approaches do extra calculations within the host to determine the final pixel values before any are written.

Memory Requirements for the Depth Buffer Method

How much storage does the depth buffer method need? Suppose the frame buffer has R rows and C columns and provides b bits per pixel. For each pixel we need additional memory to store a depth between 0 and 1.

How much memory is needed to store depths? Suppose that 8 bits are used to represent each depth value. Then the range in depths between 0 and 1 is effectively partitioned into 256 "bins," and two depths closer than 1/256 cannot always be distinguished. This might cause the incorrect face to be drawn when two faces are very near each other in depth, such as when one face penetrates another. In some applications such errors are unacceptable, and so 10, 16, or even 20 bits must be used for the depth buffer.

If we have determined that a d bit number provides sufficient accuracy for storing depths, then $R \times C \times d$ additional bits of storage will be needed to retain the $R \times C$ depths. Where might this memory be located? In some systems the main memory can be used, by declaring an R-by-C array of *integer,* if an integer word on the machine provides enough accuracy. In other cases the frame buffer itself is used to store the depths. Some frame buffers can be programmed, in that some of the bit planes can be disconnected from the color lookup table, so that they are not viewed directly. In these cases we can use d of the b available bits to hold the depth information. This leaves only $b - d$ bits per pixel for distinguishing the colors that are displayed. Thus, for a given amount of frame buffer memory, fidelity in the hidden surface elimination process must be traded for color resolution.

Reducing the Size of the Depth Buffer

If there is not enough memory to implement a full depth buffer, one can generate the picture in pieces. A depth buffer is established for only a fraction of the scan lines, and the algorithm is repeated for each fraction. For instance, in a 512-by-512 display, one can allocate memory for a depth buffer of only 64 scan lines and do the algorithm eight times. Each time the entire face list is scanned, depths are computed for faces covering the scan lines involved, and comparisons are made with the reigning depths so far. Having to scan the face list eight times, of course, makes the algorithm operate more slowly.

This fragmentation of the frame buffer into subregions can be taken to an extreme when the depth buffer corresponds in size to only one scan line. Call this a *monoline* depth buffer algorithm. It appears to require more computation, as each face is "brought in fresh" to the process many times, once for each scan line (see the exercises). Extents are used to determine quickly those faces covered by a given scan line.

Note the ordering of steps performed by this monoline buffer approach: For each scan line it loops as **for** *each face* **do for** *each pixel* **do**. By reversing the looping order to **for** *each pixel* **do for** *each face* **do**, we obtain quite a different HSR method, one that needs no depth buffer at all and that can exploit certain forms of coherence in the scene. We shall develop this method next.

17.3   A Scan-Line HSR Method

Section 13.3.5 described an algorithm for filling a number of polygons at the same time. Runs of pixels are filled along a scan line with the color of the polygon that covers the run. If more than one polygon covers a pixel, the one with highest "priority" (a user-assigned quantity) will determine the color to be used. To do this efficiently, the algorithm creates and manages various lists in order to capitalize on the tremendous amount of coherence along a scan line. That is, if one pixel is covered by some polygons, it is highly likely that its neighboring pixels will also be covered by them.

The polygon fill algorithm needs only a little adjustment to become an efficient HSR algorithm. The main change is that the priority of a face is not preassigned but is based on the depth of each face that covers the current pixel, with closer faces having higher priority.

The example in Figure 17.7 shows how the fill algorithm is adapted to perform HSR. As in Figure 13.17, the projections of three overlapping 3D planar faces, A, B, and C, are seen. The active edge list (AEL) shows the x-values at which an edge of some face intersects the scan line. The AEL holds these intersections in sorted order. Each node in the AEL points to the face responsible for the intersection: *num_covers* reports the number of faces that cover a given pixel, and the array *covers*[ ] contains *true* for the faces that cover.

At the start of the scan in x across the line, all elements of *covers*[ ] are initialized to *false*, and *num_covers* is set to 0. No face covers the pixels between $x = 0$ to $x = x_1$, and so the background color is applied. At x_1, face B is reached, and so *covers*[B] is set to *true*, and *num_covers* is set to 1. The depth of each covering face at the current pixel is maintained in a new *depth* field in the face nodes. This field is initialized according to Equation 17.1 as each face is "entered" during the scan across the line. At each successive x-value, the depth need only be incremented by a constant. This constant is stored in *depth_inc*.

In moving from $x = x_1$ to x_2, face B is the only covering face, and so each of its pixels can be filled using the applicable shading rule (recall Chapter 15).

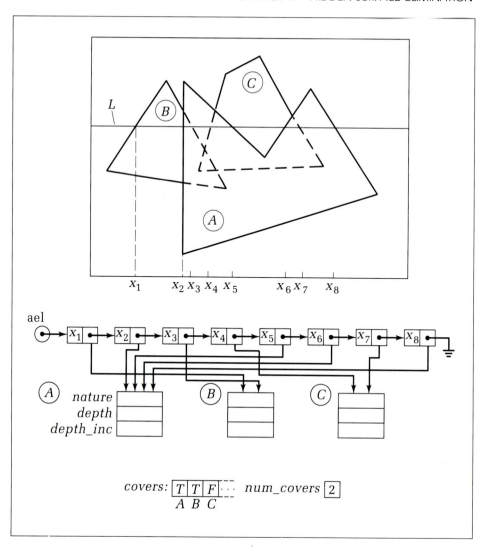

Figure 17.7.
A scan-line example and the
active edge list.

Depending on the shading rule, the entire run from x_1 to x_2 might be filled at once.

At x_2, face A is entered, and so its depth is determined; *num_covers* becomes 2; and *covers*[A] is set to *true*. By "looking ahead" in the AEL, the routine knows that from x_2 to x_3 there are only two faces covering the pixels, and so the closer face at each pixel is found by a simple depth comparison. If face A starts out being closer than face B, there is no guarantee that it will remain so; that is, the faces may interpenetrate. This can be checked by finding the two depths at x_3 (adding the right multiples of *depth_inc* to each *depth*). If the depth ordering is maintained over the run to x_3, the run can be filled as if there were only one covering face. At x_3, face B no longer covers, and so the pixel color is easy to determine (how?). At x_4, face C begins to cover, and so the relative depths of faces A and C must be resolved.

In general, at each successive pixel across the scan line the depth of each covering face is incremented. At each edge crossing, *covers*[ ] will be set to *true* for a face if it is being entered or to *false* if it is being exited, and *num_covers* will be adjusted accordingly. Whenever more than one face covers a pixel, the closest one is identified, and the face shade or color is computed. Because edges are crossed relatively infrequently, the scan-line coherence is being exploited.

When scan line L has been traversed, the current scan line is incremented; all *covers*[   ] elements are reinitialized to *false*; and the AEL is updated so that it faithfully represents the edge crossings that are encountered along the new scan line. Updating the AEL is the same as for the polygon fill, using an edge table for efficiency.

Figure 17.8 shows a view of the triple block (see Appendix 4) rendered using this scan-line algorithm, with simple filled wireframe shading (recall Chapter 15). The results show that the HSR algorithm works properly here.

Shadowing can be dealt with in a reasonably efficient manner as well. When the closest face has been identified, either at a pixel or within a run, a test can be performed to see whether it is in shadow. This of course increases the amount of computation, but only the single visible face needs to be considered at each pixel.

Drill Exercises

17.4. Objects That Don't Interpenetrate. Often one knows some properties of the objects being rendered, and this knowledge can allow a simpler HSR algorithm to be used. What simplifications in the scan line algorithm become available if it is known that no two faces ever interpenetrate?

17.5. Testing Depth Over a Run. Show how the algorithm, knowing the depths of all covering faces at the beginning of a run, can "look ahead" to the end of a run and determine with a simple calculation the depths of the covering faces there. If it detects a reversal in the depth ordering of faces, can it find the pixel at which the ordering reverses? How?

Figure 17.8.
Example rendering using the scan-line algorithm.

17.4   Area Subdivision Approaches

A rather different approach to HSR can be constructed that capitalizes on area coherence for a scene. Scan-line coherence as we have used it is the notion that many neighboring pixels along a scan line share the same property of being covered or not covered by a face: There is coherence along x for a given y. **Area coherence**, on the other hand, is the notion that many pixels that are neighbors in either x or y share the same property. Hence there is symmetry between the x and y directions here.

Area subdivision methods are based on partitioning a picture into subregions and testing each subregion for visible surfaces. Whereas the scan-line method asks depth questions at each pixel, or at most along runs, area subdivision methods use a "divide-and-conquer" approach. They ask when a subregion is "simple" enough to be drawn in its entirety without further depth testing. If it is simple in this way, it will be drawn immediately; otherwise it will be subdivided into a collection of smaller subregions, and the tests will be repeated for each subregion. If the size of a subregion reduces to some predetermined minimum (often that of a single pixel), the subdivision will terminate, and explicit depth tests will be performed to resolve the closest surface. The region is then drawn with the proper color.

There are several variations of area subdivision algorithms, which have generally become known as *Warnock algorithms* after John Warnock, who first developed the area subdivision approach (Warnock 1969). They differ mainly in the definition of simple and in the way a region is partitioned.

17.4.1 Quadrant Subdivision

We shall focus on a **quadrant subdivision** method that is particularly easy to implement. Other approaches are considered in the exercises.

Figure 17.9 shows an example that uses a quadrant subdivision of a rectangular region. Figure 17.9a shows in region R the projections of two 3D faces, with no clue given as to which face is closer. Figure 17.9b shows the true arrangement that must finally be drawn: The faces are seen to interpenetrate.

To start, suppose we decide that a region is simple enough to draw immediately if at most one face is "involved" with the region. Face F is involved with region R if any part of F overlaps any part of R. When only a single face is involved, the HSR problem is automatically solved, and the region is rendered easily. If no faces are involved, just the background color will be drawn.

Because two faces are involved with region R in Figure 17.9, R must be subdivided. We choose to subdivide regions into four quadrants, labeled as in a map: northwest (NW), northeast (NE), southwest (SW), and southeast (SE), as in Figure 17.9c.

In the example both the NW and SW quadrants are involved with only a single face, and so the portions of the relevant faces are drawn. (Suppose for convenience that at the outset we have flooded the entire screen with the background color.) On the other hand, both the NE and SE quadrants have two involved faces and must be subdivided, yielding Figure 17.9d. All but two of the new subregions can now be rendered. The subdivision process continues with these two remaining subregions.

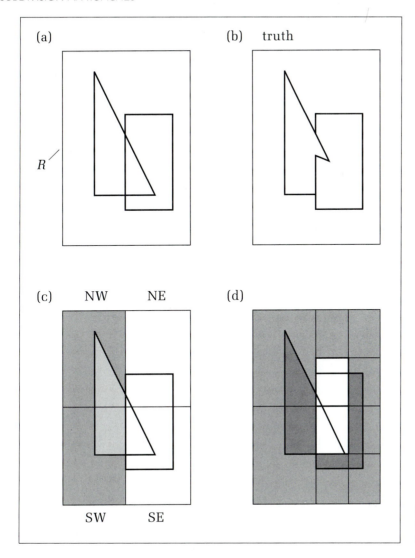

Figure 17.9.
Quadrant subdivision of a region.

To facilitate our study of Warnock algorithms, we shall put aside for a moment the details of how to decide whether a region is simple enough to be drawn directly. We "hide" the specifics in the following routine:

procedure *EasyRegion* (*region* : *rect*;   {region to be tested}
                    var *easy* : *boolean*; {is it simple?}
                    var *faces* : *face_ptr*); {face involved}

This routine does some analysis of *region*. If the region is simple enough to be rendered without further depth testing of faces, *EasyRegion*( ) will set *easy* to *true* and will point *faces* to the face that is to be drawn in the region. If the region is not simple, *or if it is too hard to tell whether it is simple*, *easy* will be set to *false*.

Regions can become extremely small in the subdivision process. How do we decide that a region is small enough that further subdivision is unwarranted? Regions are defined in the viewport in NDC, and so we could decide on some arbitrary minimum size, such as one-thousandth the width of the viewport. But because our principal interest is in rendering pictures on a raster display, we adopt an "image space" approach that closely relates regions in NDC to pixels. Accordingly, we think of the viewport as "tiled" with pixels (see Figure 15.19) and associate the NDC coordinates with pixels, as in Equation 15.8.

When a region has been subdivided so finely that it contains only one pixel center, we don't subdivide it further, even if it is not simple (a common occurrence). Instead, the surface to draw is determined by testing the depths of all involved faces and finding the closest. The pixel is then set to the color of that face. If a region is so small that it contains no pixel center at all, it is ignored.

The following simple recursive procedure *DrawRegion*(*region* : *rect*) embodies an entire Warnock algorithm. It uses *RegionSize*( ) to test how many pixel centers lie within *region*. If none is present, nothing will be done. If only one pixel center is present, the depths of all involved faces will be computed at the pixel center, and the pixel will be set to the color of the closest face. If more than one pixel is present, *EasyRegion*( ) will test whether the region is simple, and if so, it will be drawn. Otherwise four subregions are constructed, and the routine calls itself for each subregion.

Code Fragment 17.5. Skeleton for the Warnock Algorithm

```
procedure DrawRegion(region : rect);
var
  NW, NE, SW, SE : rect;
    size : integer;
    easy : boolean;
    faces : face_ptr;
{define the required utility functions here}
begin
  size := RegionSize(region); {0, 1, or many}
  if size >1 then
  begin
    EasyRegion(region, easy, faces);
    if easy then DrawFaces(faces) {region is simple}
    else begin
      BuildRegions(region, NW, NE, SW, SE); {subdivide}
      DrawRegion(NW); {test subregions}
      DrawRegion(NE):
      DrawRegion(SW);
      DrawRegion(SE)
    end {else}
  end
  else if size = 1 then DrawClosestFace
end;
```

Various utility routines must be defined inside this procedure. Leaving the details to the exercises, we have

- *RegionSize(region : rect) : integer*; This function uses the correspondence between NDC coordinates and the pixels, as in Equation 15.8. It returns 0, 1, or 2 depending on whether 0, 1, or more than 1 pixel centers lie within *region*. (If more than one pixel lies in the region, should the routine count the exact number? Why?)

- *DrawClosestFace*: When the region consists of a single pixel, this procedure tests the depth of each involved face and identifies the closest. It then sets the pixel to the color of that face (possibly using a shading rule, as in Chapter 15). In addition, shadows can be dealt with, by testing for the visibility of each light source from this point.

- *DrawFaces(faces : face_ptr)*: This is used when the region is simple. If *faces* = **nil** no face is involved, and so it does nothing. Otherwise the single face to be drawn is scan converted into the region.

- *BuildRegions( )*: This procedure builds the four regions NW, NE, SW, and SE by splitting *region* horizontally and vertically. For example, the right edge of the NW quadrant is found by

$$NW.r := 0.5 * (region.l + region.r)$$

Note that after a subdivision, subsequent testing of the "child" subregions needs to consider only those faces that were found to be involved with the "parent" region. Any faces that are disjoint from the parent region are surely disjoint from the subregions. We shall discuss later how to eliminate from further consideration those faces known to be disjoint from a region.

The meat of the Warnock algorithms lies in the geometric analysis performed by *EasyRegion( )*. The more clever it is, the faster the HSR algorithm will operate. What tests might be required in this function? There are various ways that a face *F* can be involved or not involved with a rectangular region, *R*, as suggested in Figure 17.10.

- *Extent-disjoint*. Face *F* is extent-disjoint from region *R* if the extent of *F* has no overlap with *R* (Figure 17.10a). If *F* is extent-disjoint from *R*, then *F* must lie entirely outside *R*. This is the simplest of the geometric situations to detect.

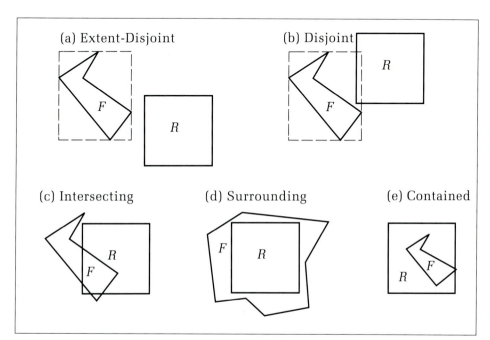

(a) Extent-Disjoint   (b) Disjoint

(c) Intersecting   (d) Surrounding   (e) Contained

Figure 17.10.
Varieties of involvement of a face and a region.

● *Disjoint.* Face *F* may not overlap *R*, even though its extent does (Figure 17.10b). To test for this, clip each of the edges of *F* against region *R*. If all edges of *F* are clipped out, they must lie entirely outside *R*, and thus *F* is disjoint from *R*. This is a more complex test than the extent-disjoint test, and so it is performed only when the extent-disjoint test fails.

● *Intersecting.* At least one edge of *F* intersects a boundary of *R* (Figure 17.10c). We shall see later how to combine the test for intersecting with that for disjoint. Note that there can be an intersection even if no vertex of *F* actually lies inside *R*. (How?)

● *Surrounding.* Region *R* is completely surrounded by *F* (Figure 17.10d). After many subdivisions, the subregions of *R* are very small, and so this often happens.

● *Contained.* *F* is totally contained within region *R* (Figure 17.10e). This situation obtains if, and only if, all vertices of *F* lie inside *R*.

Face *F* is seen to be involved with *R* if it is intersecting, surrounding, or contained. Our earlier criterion for simplicity was therefore

Definition 1

R is simple if at most one face is intersecting, surrounding, or contained.

Within procedure *EasyRegion*( ) we test each face in turn against the current subregion *R*. If some face is found to be involved, *faces* will be set to point to it. If a second one is also found to be involved, the routine will terminate, with *easy* set to *false*. If all faces are tested without finding two involved ones, *easy* will be set to *true*, and the face pointed at by *face* (if any) will be scan converted.

Reducing the Number of Faces Requiring Testing

So far we have been testing every face in the scene against each subregion. Therefore, when the scene consists of many faces that occupy only small areas, it is a relief to be able to reduce the number of faces that must be tested at each step. To do this, *EasyRegion*( ) reads faces from an input list of faces and produces an output face list:

procedure *EasyRegion*(*region* : *rect*;   {region to be tested}
                        in_faces : *face_ptr*;   {candidate faces}
                   var *easy* : *boolean*; {is it simple?}
                   var *faces* : *face_ptr*); {all faces involved}

The list *in_faces* contains faces that might be involved with *region*. *EasyRegion*( ) uses the *faces* pointer to build a list of any faces it determines are involved with *region*. If the region is found to be simple, this list will be used just as before: It will be empty if no faces are involved or will contain the single involved face. If the region is not simple, it will contain the smaller list of involved faces that is passed to recursive calls of *DrawRegion*. The parameter list for this routine is extended to **procedure** *DrawRegion*(*region* : *rect*; *face* : *face_ptr*).

With this enhancement, *EasyRegion*( ) operates as follows. It is initialized to *false*, and *faces* is set to **nil**. Each face in *in_faces* is tested for involvement with the region. (Because this list is tested by four instances of *DrawRegion*, it must be preserved until all four scans are complete.) The involvement is determined by a function, *Involved*(*f* : *face_ptr*) : *boolean*, that will return *true* if face *f* is involved with the region and *false* otherwise. A copy of a pointer to each involved face is pushed onto *faces*, and a count is kept of the number of pushes. When *in_faces* has been traversed, the count is examined, and if it is 0 or 1, *easy* will be set to *true*. Note that this version of *EasyRegion*( ) must test every face on its input list, regardless of involvement: It does not terminate as soon as two involved faces are identified (see the exercises).

Drill Exercises

17.6.   Disposing of Many Lists. Many lists of faces are created during the operation of *DrawRegion*( ). Determine how to dispose of lists that are no longer needed for further processing.

17.7.   Hand Simulation of Warnock Algorithm. For a situation in which an isosceles right triangle fits snugly into a square region, hand simulate the operation of *DrawRegion*( ), showing the creation of various face lists. Carry out the simulation until all necessary subregions of one-sixteenth of the original area have been tested.

17.8.   Estimating Relative Efficiencies. It has been asserted that computation time can be saved by creating the face lists *in_faces* and *faces*, because fewer faces are tested for involvement in each subregion. But this gain is offset by the need to test every face in the input list, rather than stopping after two involved faces have been found. For the preceding hand simulation exercise, estimate the number of involvement checks required with and without the maintenance of these face lists.

The Structure of Involved(f : ptr)

The central ingredient of *EasyRegion*( ) is the function *Involved*(*f*). It performs the serious geometric tests on face *f*: whether or not *f* intersects, surrounds, or is contained in region *R*. How can this be done efficiently?

It first does the simplest test: Is face *f* extent-disjoint from *R*? If not, its best bet is to traverse around the vertices of polygon *f*, testing each vertex and edge against the region. It is easy to test whether a vertex lies within *R* (how?) and whether an edge intersects one of the horizontal or vertical edges of R (how?)

In its traversal of *f* as soon as a vertex is found to be inside *R*, or an edge is found to intersect *R*, the testing terminates, and *Involved*( ) returns *true*. On the other hand, if all vertices are outside and no edges intersect, then the face is either disjoint or it is a **surrounder** of *R*. To distinguish these two situations, test whether a vertex of *R* lies inside the face. This can be done using a parity-type test, as discussed in Section 13.3.4.

17.4.2 Other Definitions for the Simplicity of a Region

So far we have considered only one definition of *simple* for a region: A region is simple if zero or one face is involved. Other criteria can be used, however, that trade speed for simplicity.

Simple Means Empty

The most primitive definition of *simple* is that the region is empty, that exactly zero faces are involved. Many more subregions are found to be not simple with this criterion, of course, and so many more subdivisions are performed. In fact, for each pixel covered by any face, the subdivisions must proceed down to the single pixel level, as this is the only way to stop the subdivisions! In effect it gives many "false alarms." It asserts that a region is too complex to answer the hidden surface question, when in fact the region is simple according to the previous definition. An advantage of this approach is that it needs no scan conversion; the only drawing tool (after flooding with the background color) is *SetPixel( )*.

Using Surrounders

Another widely used definition of *simple* requires somewhat more complex testing, but it is very good at identifying simple regions and so necessitates far fewer subdivisions. This definition does not insist that at most one face be involved in a region. Instead, many faces may be involved as long as one **dominates.** For example, face *F* will dominate region *R* if it is a surrounder that is everywhere closer than are all other involved faces. A situation for which this meaning of simple saves many subdivisions is shown in Figure 17.11. Region *A* is simple after only these two levels of subdivision, even though more than one face is involved, because the single surrounding face is closest and masks off the others. If the first definition of simple were used, this region would be subdivided to the pixel level, as the more remote house has a face that overlaps the visible face entirely within *A*. (*Question*: Under which of the definitions of simple is region *B* simple?)

How is a surrounder tested to see whether it is everywhere closest within a subregion, *R*? Its depth need be tested only at the four corners of *R* and compared with the depths of the planes of all other involved faces at those corners. If the surrounder is closest at all four corners, no other involved face can possibly occlude it.

As the face list *in_faces* is scanned, we flag all surrounders before placing them in the *faces* list. When all faces have been tested, we test the depths of the surrounders, to see whether one surrounder is closer than all the others. (It needn't be—why?) If so, we test this winner against the planes of all the remaining faces in *faces*. If there is a "winning" surrounder, region *R* will be filled with its color and no further subdivisions will be performed. Otherwise, *faces* is passed recursively, as before. Note that when the surrounders have been flagged in *faces*, they need not be retested after the next subdivision, as they will certainly still be surrounders.

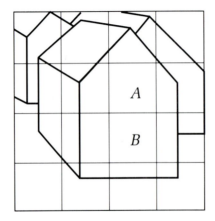

Figure 17.11.
A surrounding face lies closest.

When using this definition of simple, there is a clear trade-off between the complexity of testing each face and the need for additional cycles of subdivision. Much more testing must be done on each region, in the hope that many fewer regions will have to be tested (because fewer subdivisions will be performed).

Drill Exercises

17.9.   Another Meaning of Simple. The first definition of simple required that at most one face be involved in a region. But if several nonoverlapping faces are involved, no depth calculations need be performed to solve the HSR problem. In this case, *EasyRegion( )* can point *faces* at a list of the faces involved in the region, and each can be scan converted in turn. Discuss the complexity of this approach. In particular, how does one test whether a collection of faces known to be involved with the region does or does not overlap? Is this definition of simple likely to be worth the effort to implement it?

17.10.   Dealing with Shadows in the Warnock Method. Determine how to add shadows to a region that has been found to be simple. Alter the definition of simple to insist that the entire region be in or out of shadow. How would this be incorporated into the main algorithm?

17.11.   Alternative Subdivision Approaches. When edges of faces run diagonally across the display (as in Figure 17.9), many levels of subdivision may have to be per-

formed, because the borders of the regions never "line up" with the edges. Figure 17.12 suggests a different way to subdivide, at a vertex, A, of a prominent face in the scene. The two edges, E_1 and E_2, are extended to the borders of the region, thus defining four subregions, $R_1, \ldots, R_4$. The triangle is now disjoint from three of these new regions, vastly simplifying them. The same tests as before are applied to each subregion; simple regions are rendered; and nonsimple ones are subdivided further.

Discuss the changes required in the quadrant subdivision method in order to implement this approach. Sketch a scene with several polygonal faces, and show how the subdivisions would be carried out to determine the visible surfaces.

17.12.   Incorporating Antialiasing. How can one incorporate antialiasing (recall Chapter 13) while performing HSR using area subdivision? Consider subdividing below the pixel level and then averaging. Discuss how this is to be done and how effective the technique is.

17.5 On Hidden Line Removal Methods

Several of the methods we discussed require that the display device be able to "paint over" an element—a point or line—and therefore cover what was drawn previously. This is easy to do on raster devices, but on some devices it is awk-

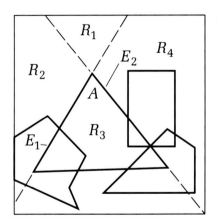

Figure 17.12.
Subdividing a region along an edge.

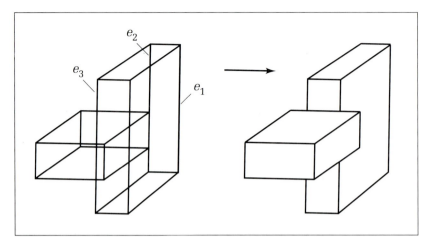

Figure 17.13.
Performing hidden line removal.

ward, if not impossible. That is, once a pen plotter has drawn a line, it cannot be "undrawn." Also, some raster devices such as photorecorders do not permit rewriting lines, as overwriting tends to blend colors rather than paint over them.

In this section we turn to approaches in which each element is drawn only after a complete test of its visibility has been performed, so that no "painting over" is attempted. We focus on drawing the visible edges of a mesh object.

A direct approach clips each edge of the object against all faces that occlude it. As shown in Figure 17.13, some edges are not affected (e_1); some are entirely removed from the scene (e_2); some are clipped at one end; and others are broken into several pieces (e_3).

Must every edge be tested against every face? No. For a closed, solid object, we know two important facts: (1) If a back face obscures an edge, surely some front face must also obscure it (why?), and (2) every edge "belongs" to two faces. The first fact implies that we need to clip edges only against front faces, that back faces can be deleted at the start just as they were in the preceding algorithms. The second fact implies that any edge that belongs to two back faces must be invisible and so need not be considered further.

Drill Exercise

17.13.   Hand Simulation of the HLR. For the object in Figure 17.13, label each front face and each edge that belongs to at least one front face. List the front faces that occlude each back face. Show what happens to each edge as it is clipped against all of the front faces.

A face can split an edge into many segments. (Show a situation in which a face with eight edges breaks an edge into five pieces.) The algorithm must keep track of all the "surviving" pieces, and each survivor must be tested against the remaining faces in the face list. An edge stack is a natural repository for edges that require further testing. The model is first processed to identify all of its potentially visible edges, which are pushed onto the edge stack. A cycle then begins where an edge is popped from the stack and processed. It is clipped against every (front) face, and if it survives, it is drawn. If a clip breaks it into pieces, one of the survivors will be tested against the remaining faces, and the other pieces will be pushed back onto the stack. If at any point the whole edge is clipped out, the cycle will start again by popping the next edge. The cycles continue until the stack is empty.

Data Type for Edges

The following information should be stored with each edge in order to promote efficiency.

- The indices of its first and second vertices define an edge.

- The edge's extent, the parallelepiped that just encloses it, will prove useful, as always.

- When an edge is split and part of it is put back on the stack, it has already been processed against some of the faces. Therefore, when it is later popped, we need test it against only the remaining faces in the list. To facilitate this, the pointer *next_face* points to the next face in the face list against which to test the edge. Figure 17.14 shows an example in which edge E extending from vertex 3 to vertex 8 is tested against face *faces^* and split into four visible parts. Six new vertices are created and added to the vertex list. Each of the four survivors should next be tested against face *faces^.next*. All but the first survivor are pushed onto the edge stack, with their *next_face* field set to *faces^.next*.

- As we mentioned, each edge in a solid object belongs to two faces. Because neither of these faces can possibly obscure the edge, they needn't be included in the test. Pointers to them are stored with the edge to allow them to be skipped.

Putting these together, a reasonable structure for edges on the stack is as follows:

Code Fragment 17.6. Data Type for the Edge List

```
type
    e_ptr = ^edge_data;
    edge_data = record
                    first, second : 1. . MAXNUMVERTS;
                    face1, face2 : face_ptr;          {endpoint indices}
                    extent : cuboid;                   {its two faces}
                    next_face : face_ptr;              {3D extent of edge}
                    next : e_ptr;                      {next face for testing}
                end;                                   {pointer to next edge}
```

We now build the initial edge stack. Suppose that a linked list of front faces has been created, pointed to by *faces*. The initial edge stack is formed from this face list by removing any duplicate edges from each pair of adjacent vertices and filling in the preceding information. There are several interesting elements in this preprocessing. For instance, to what should *face2* point if an edge has one front face and one back face? (See the exercises.)

Note that there might be some benefit when preprocessing the faces in putting "prominent" faces near the front of the face list. In this way the edges are tested first against those faces that are most likely to eliminate them. That is, the faces most likely to hide many edges are those that are large and close to the viewpoint.

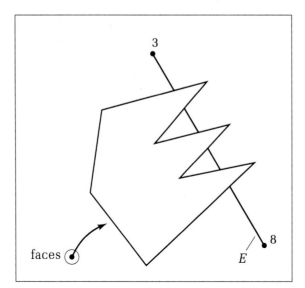

Figure 17.14.
Effect of splitting an edge into visible pieces.

Drill Exercise

17.14.   Situation for Sorting the Face List. For what kind of scene is it particularly advantageous to presort the face list? Does it consist of many faces or just a few? What about faces that contain many sides? Draw some examples for which it would, and some for which it would not, be worth presorting.

It is convenient to isolate the geometric testing of an edge against a face in a routine such as

function *EdgeTest(E : e_ptr; Face : face_ptr) : e_ptr;*

which tests the edge pointed to by *E* against face *Face* and returns a pointer to a list of surviving edge pieces. Each survivor is of type *edge_data*, and *EdgeTest( )* loads the data fields of each with appropriate values. *EdgeTest( )* will return **nil** if there are no survivors.

These ideas lead to the following skeleton of the algorithm:

Code Fragment 17.7. Skeleton of the HLR Algorithm

```
var
    E, E_surv : e_ptr; {current edge and survivors}
    this_face : face_ptr;
    invis : boolean;
begin
    <Remove backfaces from face list>;
    <build edge stack of all potentially visible edges>;
    while stack(edge_stack) not empty do
    begin
        E : = pop(edge_stack);          {get next edge}
        invis : = false;                {edge may be visible}
        this_face : = E^.next_face;      {test remaining faces}
        while (this_face <> nil) and (not invis) do
            if (this_face <> E^.face1) and (this_face <> E^.face2) then
```

```
        begin
            E : = EdgeTest(E, this_face);  {get pieces of E}
            if (E = nil) then invis := true {E is invisible}
            else begin
                E_surv : = E^.next;
                if E_surv <> nil then
                <push rest of E_surv list onto edge stack>
            end; {else}
            this_face := this_face^.next      {try next face}
        end; {while if}
        if not invis then <draw projection of edge E>
    end {while stack not empty}
end;
```

Drill Exercise

17.15. **Hand Simulation.** For the object in Figure 17.13, hand simulate the preceding algorithm. Draw an appropriate face and edge list, and show the state of all pointers when edge e_3 has just been clipped against the closest face to the eye.

17.5.1 The Geometric Testing in *EdgeTest( )*

The main work of this HLR algorithm lies in the function *EdgeTest(E, F)*. The easiest tests should be performed first, in the hope of deciding about E as quickly as possible. If one test is inconclusive, the next test should be performed. Although many variations are possible, the following tests appear to form a reasonable sequence:

- *Extent testing.* The extent in x of edge E is tested against that of face F. If there is no overlap, F cannot obscure E. If there is an overlap, the extents in y are then tested, and E will again survive if there is no overlap. These are very fast tests.

- *Edge on the near side.* If both endpoints of E are closer to the viewpoint than is the plane of face F, the edge cannot be occluded by F and therefore survives. Because F is a front face, a point will lie closer than does the plane of F if it lies on the side pointed to by the outward normal $\mathbf{n}$ of F (stored in the face list). Recall from Section 7.4.6 that a point, q, will lie on the "outside" of the plane, $\mathbf{n} \cdot \mathbf{p} = d$, if, and only if, the quantity $s = \mathbf{n} \cdot \mathbf{q} - d$ is positive. Therefore, form the quantities s_1 and s_2 for the two endpoints of E and test their signs. If both are positive E survives.

- *Edge penetrates plane.* If the quantities s_1 and s_2 differ in sign, the edge must pierce the plane of the face. It is convenient to split the edge into two pieces here, one on the near side and one on the far side of the face plane. The near one is a clear survivor and so goes on the survivor list to be returned by *Edgetest( )*. The fate of the far one is still unknown. Similarly if both s_1 and s_2 are negative then all of E lies on the far side, and further testing is required.

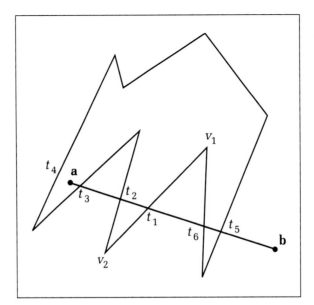

Figure 17.15.
Finding the intersection of E
and the edges of F.

To find where edge E with endpoints **a** and **b** penetrates the plane, write the usual parametric form, $\mathbf{a}(1 - t) + \mathbf{b}t$, and substitute it into the plane equation for the face. Solve for the hit time t_{hit}, as in Equation 7.38. Use t_{hit} in the parametric form to compute the piercing point of E.

● Only an edge that lies wholly on the far side of the plane of *face[i]* will reach this testing stage. The face may or may not occlude the edge. If the edge was split in the previous step, it is wise to retest the x and y-extents of the remaining piece, in the hopes that there is now no overlap. Assuming that the extents do overlap, there is little choice but to compute the intersections of the edge (call it E still) with each of the edges of F. Again use a parametric form for E—with t varying between 0 at endpoint **a**, to 1 at endpoint **b** (see Figure 17.15)—and calculate each time, t_j, for the intersection of E with some edge of the face. This provides a list of t-values. For the case shown in Figure 17.15, the list is t_1, t_2, t_3, t_5, t_6 (because the calculations begin with the edge between vertices v_1 and v_2). Sort the t-values and analyze this list to determine where the portions that lie outside the face are situated (see the exercises). Finally, place these outside portions on the survivor list to be returned by *Edge-Test( )*.

Figure 17.16 shows a complicated scene drawn using an algorithm based on the preceding steps. Other scenes are easily modeled using the block builder tool in Appendix 4.

Drill Exercise

17.16.   Analyzing the *t*-value List. Testing edge E for intersections with the sides of face F yields a list of t-values, as discussed. Suppose the list is .6, .4, .1, -.3, -.8, 1.4. What intervals in t correspond to pieces of E lying outside the face? Devise a general method for analyzing such a list and building the desired t-intervals.

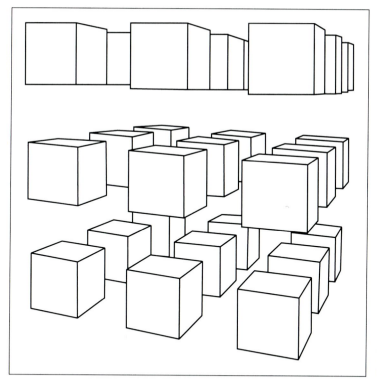

Figure 17.16.
A complex line drawing with hidden lines removed.

17.6 Summary

Removing hidden surfaces and lines is a fundamental problem in computer graphics, and several techniques to do this have been developed. HSR algorithms tend to be complex, with long execution times, and a great deal of effort has been devoted to increasing their efficiency.

We examined various HSR approaches for the important class of objects modeled as polygonal meshes. To make it easier to detect hidden lines and surfaces, the model data are preprocessed for the desired camera position. This preprocessing means removing back faces, clipping to the view volume, and transforming the perspective. The warping produced by the perspective transformation is particularly helpful, as it converts each point (x, y, z) into a point (x', y', z') such that the projection is simply (x', y') and z' measures the distance from the eye. This makes it simple to detect when one point occludes another: They must have the same x'- and y'-components, and the first point must have a smaller z'-component.

We considered a variety of HSR algorithms, noting that each tends to make a different trade-off among speed, storage space, and simplicity. Some of the algorithms differ only in the order in which they process data, as in **for** *each pixel* **do for** *each face* **do** . . versus **for** *each face* **do for** *each pixel* **do**. . . Because the occlusion of one element by another involves the relative size of their z'-components, HSR algorithms require some kind of sorting. But because sorting can be expensive, methods such as the depth buffer algorithm use vast amounts of memory to reduce the sorting burden.

We explored a scan-line HRS method that figures out for each pixel which face is the closest and draws it directly. It can fill in a whole run of pixels at a time by using scan-line coherence, as the same face tends to be the closest over a portion of each scan line.

The area subdivision approach carries this idea to two dimensions, by seeking regions over which a single face is easily identified as being the closest. If the region contains faces that still need depth sorting, the algorithm simply will subdivide it into smaller regions, hoping to find a simpler answer in each one.

We also looked at some HLR methods that test the visibility of each edge against all of the front faces in the model. Because the geometric testing of an edge against a face can be complicated, a series of tests of increasing complexity is performed until an answer is found. An edge that lies partly behind a face can be fractured into several pieces, each of which must be processed in turn. To organize this process, we used the familiar technique of saving on a stack "things yet to be done."

There are many other HSR/HLR methods. Some explore additional ways to improve efficiency at the expense of simplicity (e.g., see Foley and Van Dam 1983, Rogers 1985). Others work with different kinds of objects, such as parametric surfaces (Blinn et al. 1980) or mathematical functions (Butland 1979, Rogers 1985).

Programming Exercises

17.17. Finding Extents. Write the routine **procedure** *Find Extent*(**var** *F* : *face_data*); which builds the six values for the *extent* field in face *F*.

17.18. Implementation of the Heedless Painter's Algorithm. Write the routine *Heedless_Painter*( ) which executes the algorithm. Test it on some of the mesh models given in Appendix 4.

17.19. Partitioning the Picture. Consider partitioning a 512-by-512 pixel frame buffer into 16 subregions, each having 128-by-128 pixels. A depth buffer large enough to store depths for all pixels in each subregion is allocated, and the depth buffer algorithm is executed for each subregion. Extents for each face are used to eliminate faces that do not cover a subregion. Implement this algorithm and test it on several scenes.

17.20. Algorithm for a Monoline Depth Buffer. Implement and test a depth buffer algorithm in which the depth buffer *d*[ ] corresponds to a single scan line of pixels and so is a simple array. For each row the depth buffer elements are reinitialized to 1. Then each face, *F*, that covers this scan line (use extents to determine this) is scanned pixel by pixel, and the depth buffer and frame buffer are updated. Estimate how much more computation is required for this approach than when one depth buffer covers the entire display.

17.21. Implementing the Utility Routines for the Warnock Algorithm. Write the four routines that are used in the Warnock procedure. Decide how the routines should share information, so that, for instance, *EasyRegion*( ) can pass to *Draw_Face* a pointer to the face to be drawn, or **nil** if only the background is visible.

17.22. Developing *Involved*( ). Design and write the routine *Inside*(*v* : *point*; *R* : *rect*) : *boolean* which will return *true* if, and only if, point *v* lies inside rectangular region *R*. Also implement *Intersects*(*first*, *last* : *point*; *R* : *rect*) : *boolean* which will return *true* if, and only if, the edge from *first* to *last* intersects *R*. Finally, build a function that tests whether a point lies inside a face. Using these tools, build the function *Involved*( ) which is central to *EasyRegion*( ) of the Warnock algorithm.

17.23. Using Other Subdivision Methods. Implement a Warnock algorithm that subdivides along two edges of the largest face that has a vertex in a region.

17.24. Constructing the Edge Stack. The HLR removal algorithm of Section 17.5 uses an initial edge stack that is constructed as the front faces of the polygon mesh are scanned. Devise an algorithm that constructs the initial stack from a face list, taking care to avoid putting on the same edge twice. The routine should fill each of the fields in the structure *edge_data*. Decide how to deal with edges that belong to one back face.

Chapter 18

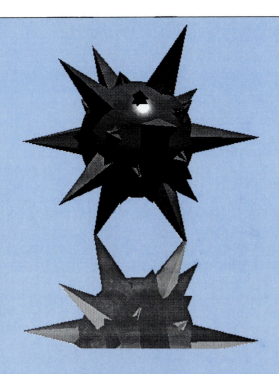

Introduction to Ray Tracing

Goals of the Chapter

- To develop the fundamental ideas used in ray tracing.
- To set up the mathematics and algorithms to perform ray tracing.
- To build scenes of spheres, cones, cylinders, and convex polyhedra.
- To create highly realistic images, including transparency and refraction of light.

18.1   Introduction

In Chapter 15 we described methods for rendering scenes composed of polygon meshes, including shading models that represent—at least approximately—how light reflects from the surface of a polygon. In addition, the Gouraud and Phong interpolation schemes were applied to suppress the "faceted" nature of the mesh model. Pictures formed in this way show a smooth surface, even though the model consists of discrete faces.

Ray tracing (sometimes called *ray casting*) provides a related but even more powerful approach for rendering scenes. For each pixel in the image the question is asked: What does the eye "see" through this pixel? One can think of a ray of light arriving at the eye through the pixel center from some point in the scene. The color of the ray—which of course depends on what the ray has encountered en route to the eye—is computed and displayed for that pixel.

In actuality, the process is reversed. A ray is cast from the eye through the pixel center and out into the scene. Its path is traced to see what object it hits first and at what point. (This process automatically solves the hidden surface problem, as the first surface hit by the ray is the closest object to the eye; more remote surfaces are never reached.) Armed with a description of light sources in the scene, the same shading model as before is then applied to the point first hit, and the ambient, diffuse, and specular components of light are computed. The resulting color is then filed for subsequent processing or is displayed using *SetPixel*( ).

Because the path of a ray is traced through the scene, interesting visual effects such as shadowing, reflection, and refraction are easy to incorporate, producing images of dazzling realism that are difficult to create by any other method.

Another feature of ray tracing is its ability to work comfortably with a richer class of geometric objects than polygon meshes. Solid objects are constructed out of various geometric primitives such as spheres, cones, and cylinders. These shapes are represented exactly through mathematical expressions; they are not approximated as a faceted body. They can also be subjected to transformations to alter their shape and orientation before they are added to the scene, further enhancing the modeling of complex scenes.

In this chapter we shall describe the algorithmic artillery needed to produce high-quality ray-traced images of complex scenes. Our development will be incremental to enable us to produce simple images with little programming after only a few sections. Additional tools are developed as needed to build up a repertoire of techniques.

18.2   Setting Up the Geometry of Ray Tracing

In order to trace rays, we need a convenient parametric representation for the ray that passes through the center of the i, j-th pixel. This was discussed in Chapter 15. For easy reference, we gather together the required ingredients of the synthetic camera from Chapters 12 and 15:

1. The view reference point (VRP), located at **r** in world coordinates, is the origin of the synthetic camera (see Figure 12.2).

2. Matrix M_C (called M in Equation 12.6) captures the orientation of the camera and allows any point (a, b, c) in viewing coordinates to be converted into world coordinates (x, y, z) by[1]

$$(x; y, z) = (a, b, c)M_C + \mathbf{r} \qquad (18.1)$$

3. The eye (see Figure 12.6) lies at $\mathbf{e} = (e_u, e_v, e_n)$ in viewing coordinates. It is simpler and conventional in ray tracing to have the eye rest on the n-axis, and so $\mathbf{e} = (0, 0, -E)$, which we hereafter assume. E is called the *eye distance*. Using Equation 18.1, we see that the eye has position **eye** given in world coordinates by

$$\mathbf{eye} = (0, 0, -E)M_C + \mathbf{r} \qquad (18.2)$$

4. As shown in Figure 15.19, the window in the viewplane has corners (W_l, W_t) and (W_r, W_b). It is covered with a rectangular array of points, each corresponding to the center of a pixel on the display. The rows are numbered from 0 to *MAXROW*, and the columns from 0 to *MAXCOLUMN*. The i, j-th pixel has the following viewing coordinates:

$$\begin{aligned} u_i &= W_l + i\,\Delta u \\ v_j &= W_t - j\,\Delta v \end{aligned} \qquad (18.3)$$

where $\Delta u = (W_r - W_l)/MAXCOLUMN$ and $\Delta v = (W_t - W_b)/MAXROW$.

5. The parametric representation of the ray that emanates from the eye at $t = 0$ and passes through point $(u_i, v_j, 0)$ on the viewplane at $t = 1$ was developed in Chapter 15. Combining Equations 15.11 and 15.12 with the simplified eye position, we obtain

$$\mathbf{p}_{i,j}(t) = \mathbf{eye} + (u_i, v_j, E)M_C t \qquad (18.4)$$

Note an important property of each ray in this family: As t increases from 0, the ray point moves farther and farther from the eye. If the ray strikes two objects in its path, the object lying closer to the eye will be the one hit first having the lower value of t. Therefore, depth sorting the objects corresponds to sorting the hit times at which they are intersected by the ray. Also, any objects that are hit at a negative t must lie behind the eye and so are ignored.

Drill Exercises

18.1. Work Out the Details. Show that Equation 18.4 accurately describes the ray in question. Where is the ray at $t = 0$? At $t = 1$?

18.2. In Homogeneous Coordinates. Find the expression of the ray of Equation 18.4 in homogeneous coordinates.

18.3. For the General Eye Position. Find the expression for the ray of Equation 18.4 for the general eye position $\mathbf{e} = (e_u, e_v, e_n)$.

18.4. Numerical Calculation of a Ray. Recalling the definitions of the relevant quantities from Chapter 12, find the expression for the ray that passes through point $(1, 2, 0)$ on the viewplane when $\mathbf{r} = (3, 3, 5)$, **norm** $= (-1, -4, -2)$, **up** $= (0, 0, 1)$, and $E = 8$.

18.5. Numerical Calculation of a Ray—Revisited. Find the expression for the ray $\mathbf{p}_{i,j}(t)$ using **u**, **v**, and **n** of the preceding exercise when $(W_l, W_t, W_r, W_b) = (-3, 2, 3, -2)$,

---

[1]If one wishes to work instead in homogeneous coordinates, the transformation from viewing into world coordinates is given by the inverse of matrix $\hat{A}_{WV}$ of Equation 12.12. The elements of this inverse matrix are easily found. (What are they?)

  Homogeneous coordinates are not sufficiently useful here to present both ordinary and homogeneous coordinate forms at each step of the development, and so we shall give only the ordinary form.

$MAXCOL = 30$, and $MAXROW = 20$. Note that along a scan line, one ray can be found incrementally from the previous one by means of a single (vector) addition: Express $\mathbf{p}_{(i+1),j}(t)$ in terms of $\mathbf{p}_{i,j}(t)$.

18.6.   Ray Tracing Using a Parallel Projection. What expression is appropriate for the ray through the i, j-th pixel if a parallel projection is used?

18.3   Overview of the Ray-Tracing Process

Before delving into the details, we shall look at the basic steps of ray tracing. A ray-tracing application has a simple skeletal form:

Code Fragment 18.1. Pseudocode Skeleton of a Ray Tracer

```
<define the objects and light sources in the scene>
<set up the camera>
for j := 0 to MAXROW do
for i := 0 to MAXCOLUMN do {cast i, j-th ray}
begin
    <build the parameters of the i, j-th ray>
    <find all intersections of the ray with objects in the scene>
    <identify the intersection that lies closest to the eye>
    <find the color of light returning to the eye along the ray from the point of
        intersection>
    <save the pixel color in array element A[i, j], or draw it with SetPixel(i, j,
        color)>
end; {for i, j-th ray}
```

Some of this should be familiar. From Chapter 12 we know how to set up the camera, which establishes the values for **eye** and matrix M_C. The process of building the i, j-th ray is a matter of simply evaluating the vector $(u_j, v_j, E)M_C$ in Equation 18.4. Also familiar from Chapter 16 is storing the array $A[.,.]$ of computed color values for later postprocessing, in order to determine the proper values to load into the look up table.

The scene to be ray traced is inhabited by various geometric objects and light sources. A typical scene may contain spheres, cones, boxes, cylinders, and the like, each having a specified shape, size, and position. Figure 18.1 shows an example of a winter scene based on some of these. Two light sources, L_1 and L_2, are also shown. The tree consists of a cylinder, three cones, and some sphere ornaments. The snowman consists mainly of spheres. (What are the ingredients of his hat?) Notice that the objects in the scene can interpenetrate, but as far as a picture is concerned, we are interested only in the outermost surfaces.

Descriptions of all the objects are stored in an **object list,** suggested in the figure by the linked list of descriptive records pointed to by the pointer *objects.* As each ray is cast, the object list is scanned. Each object is tested to see whether the ray intersects the object and, if so, at what hit time. The ray shown in the figure hits four spheres (which ones?) and one cone. All the other objects are missed. The object with the smallest hit time (S_5 in the example) is identified.

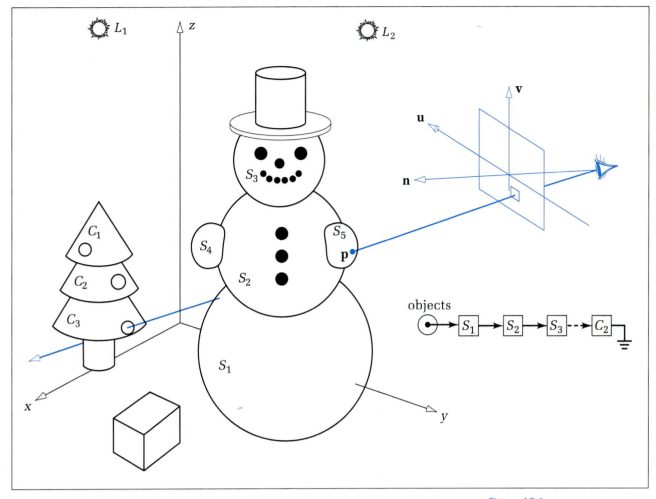

Figure 18.1.
Ray tracing a scene.

The hit spot, $\mathbf{p}_h$, is then easily found from the ray itself by evaluating the ray of Equation 18.4 at the hit time, t_h:

$$\mathbf{p}_h = \mathbf{eye} + (u_i, v_j, E)M_C t_h \qquad (18.5)$$

In order to find the diffuse and specular components of reflected light at $\mathbf{p}_h$, the normal, $\mathbf{u}_n$, to the surface must be found there. Once computed, the various light components are combined to provide a final color or intensity value for each pixel.

Storing Pixel Values

As in Chapter 15, it is usually advantageous to store all pixel values for later postprocessing and archiving. A 2D array, $A[.\ ,\ .]$, is created, and the value computed for the i, j-th pixel is stored in $A[i, j]$. What types of values might be stored in $A[i, j]$? Because one of the great strengths of ray tracing is the high realism of the images created, most ray-tracing images are rendered in full color, in which case the value is the familiar red, green, and blue 3-tuple described in Chapter 16. If, instead, a gray-scale image is to be generated, the value can be a single intensity. And in some cases, particularly during debugging, we may want to know only which of the objects in the scene is hit first by each ray. In that case, no light calculations are performed; we need not even determine the hit spot. Instead, each object is assigned an identifying integer as its *id*. The 27 objects of the winter scene might have ids 1 through 27, for instance. An id of 0 can be used when the ray misses every object. A **signature image** that displays only ids can be drawn by assigning a distinguishing color to each integer.

Thus pixel values can be of any of the following types:

Code Fragment 18.2. Types for Pixel Values in an Image

---

type
  signature = **array** [0..*MAXCOLUMN*, 0..*MAXROW*] **of** *integer*;
  grayscale = **array** [0..*MAXCOLUMN*, 0..*MAXROW*] **of** *real*;
   fullcolor = **array** [0..*MAXCOLUMN*, 0..*MAXROW*] **of** *color-triple*;

where *color_triple* is a record having three real fields, *red, green,* and *blue.*

18.4   Scene Building: Objects As Instances

In order to build the object list, we need an organized approach to defining the objects in the scene. That is, we must provide each object's size, orientation, and position. A unified approach is to think of each object as an instance of some generic primitive.

A **generic sphere,** for example, is a sphere of unit radius centered at the origin and is defined by the inside–outside function (see Chapter 9):

$$\text{generic sphere: } f(x, y, z) = x^2 + y^2 + z^2 + 1 \tag{18.6}$$

A variety of spheres and "spheroidal" objects can be created in the scene as instances of the generic sphere. Each is formed by subjecting the generic sphere to an affine transformation that scales it to the right size, orients it, and translates it into the desired position. Plate 4 shows an interesting scene consisting of spheres that have only been scaled and positioned. The use of a general affine transformation can create a large class of shapes. Differential scaling or shearing can be used on a sphere to create *ellipsoids.* For example, the transformation

$$\begin{pmatrix} 1 & 0 & 0 \\ 0 & 2 & 0 \\ 0 & 0 & .5 \end{pmatrix} \begin{pmatrix} 1 & 0 & 0 \\ 0 & .866 & .5 \\ 0 & -.5 & .866 \end{pmatrix} \tag{18.7}$$

scales the generic sphere into a smooth ellipsoidal "tablet" and then rotates it about the *x*-axis (sketch it). It can now be positioned as desired using a translation. Figure 18.2 shows a scene composed of spheres and ellipsoids. Each of the sphere instances is formed by simply translating the generic sphere into the desired position. On the other hand, the crosspieces are ellipsoids formed by differential scaling of the generic sphere into a long and thin needlelike shape. For example, one of the pieces uses the scaling matrix:

$$\begin{pmatrix} 3 & 0 & 0 \\ 0 & 1/4 & 0 \\ 0 & 0 & 1/4 \end{pmatrix} \tag{18.8}$$

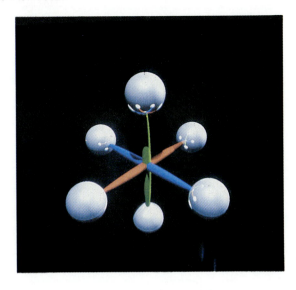

Figure 18.2.
A jack composed of ellipsoids.
(Courtesy of Andreas Meyer.)

Drill Exercises

18.7. Modeling the Jack. Assume a convenient coordinate system for the jack of Figure 18.2, and give the transformation matrix and offset vector for each of the instances in the scene.

18.8. Build an Ellipsoid. Find a transformation that converts a generic sphere into the ellipsoid:

$$\left(\frac{x-5}{2}\right)^2 + y^2 + (3z - 6)^2 = 1 \qquad (18.9)$$

Sketch this object. Then build the transformation that rotates this ellipsoid first through 20° about the x-axis and then through 45° about the y-axis. Sketch the final ellipsoid.

18.4.1 Some Other Generic Primitives

Many different geometrical shapes can be used for generic primitives. Figure 18.3 shows six particularly simple and useful ones, including the sphere just described.

1. *Plane.* The generic plane is taken to be the plane $z = 0$. It extends infinitely far in x and y.

2. *Square.* It is often useful to work with a portion of a plane, and the square is the part of the generic plane for which $|x| \leq 1$ and $|y| \leq 1$.

3. *Cube.* The eight vertices of the unit cube are given by $(\pm1, \pm1, \pm1)$, taking all eight combinations of $+$ and $-$. Its faces are portions of the six planes $x = \pm1$, $y = \pm1$, and $z = \pm1$. We shall see later that the cube is actually a special case of a much larger class of primitives, the convex polyhedra.

4. *Cylinder.* The generator (see Chapter 9) of a right circular cylinder is a circle of unit radius lying in the x, y-plane, whose directrix extends from $(0, 0, -1)$ to $(0, 0, 1)$. Thus its "wall" is given by $x^2 + y^2 = 1$, with z extending from -1 to 1; its "cap" is the unit circle at $z = 1$; and its "base" is the unit circle at $z = -1$.

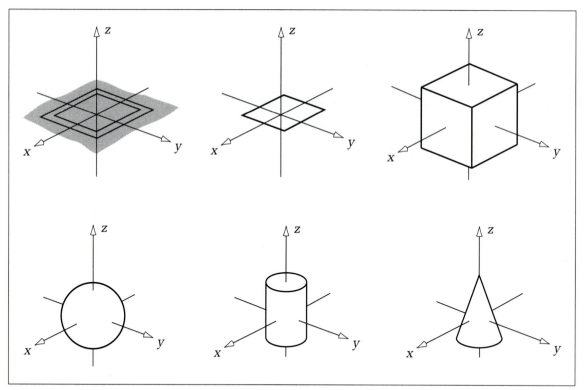

Figure 18.3.
Some common generic
primitives.

5. *Cone.* The apex of the cone lies at $(0, 0, 1)$, and its base is the unit
    circle $x^2 + y^2 = 1$ displaced to $z = -1$. The wall of the cone is
    given by $x^2 + y^2 = (1 - z)^2/4$, for $1 > z > -1$.

Notice that all the primitives (except the plane) lie snugly inside the unit
cube. This can prove convenient in some settings, for the unit cube can act
as the "bounding box" or "extent" for each of these primitives. The shapes
of these primitives (and their extents) can be changed by applying different
affine transformations. Methods for ray tracing each type will be discussed
later.

Drill Exercises

18.9.   Transforming the Generic Plane. Find the transformation that converts the generic plane into the plane
through $(1, 2, 1)$ with outer normal vector $(2, -1, 3)$. Sketch
the plane.

18.10.   Transforming the Generic Cylinder. Determine
the defining equation of the cylinder obtained by transforming the generic cylinder by (a) scaling in x, y, z by 1,
.5, and -1, respectively, (b) rotating about the y-axis
through 30°, and finally (c) translating it through $(2, 5, -3)$.
Sketch the resulting cylinder.

18.4.2 Data Types for Objects

A suitable data type must be fashioned to hold instances, in order to describe
each object in the object list. The following provides the basics; other information fields will be added as the need arises. (See Appendix 3 for the complete
data type.) We also define a convenient type for a ray, representing both its
starting position and direction as vectors.

Code Fragment 18.3. Suggested Data Type for a Ray and Object Instances, Version 1

```
ray = record
     start, dir : vector3D
         end;
generic_type = (sphere, cone, cylinder, cube, plane, square, polyh);
obj_ptr = ˆinstance;
instance = record
                kind : generic_type; {which kind}
                transf : affine3D; {instance transformation}
                nature : . . . ; {surface properties}
                next : obj_ptr;
                {other fields to be added}
            end;
```

The generic type *polyh* is for the convex polyhedron, to be discussed later. The *kind* field tells which type of generic object an instance is, and *transf* stores the 3D affine transformation that places it in the scene at the proper size. The *nature* field can be of type *attributes* (as in Code Fragment 15.1): it captures certain surface properties of the object, such as its reflection coefficients, color, and roughness. Or it might simply store the identifying integer for the object when we want to form only a signature image. As always, *next* makes it easy to construct a linked list.

18.4.3 Creating the Object List: Instantiating Objects

An object in the scene is created by **instantiating** it, or allocating a new record to hold its data and the filling the proper fields in the record to complete the object description. The following fragment suggests how this can be done. Data for the objects in the scene are read from a **scene description file** (See an example in Appendix 4. Also see the programmming exercises). Three actions are performed for each object: A new instance record is created; the data for the instance are read from the file into the appropriate fields; and the new record is pushed onto the object list.

Code Fragment 18.4. Pseudocode: Building the Object List

```
var objects, p : obj_ptr;
begin
    objects := nil; {initialize object list}
    <open the scene_file>
    for < each object listed in file> do
    begin
        new(p); {allocate space for instance}
        with pˆ do begin
            read(scene_file, kind);
            read(scene_file, transf);
            read(scene_file, nature);
            next := objects; {push it onto object list}
            objects := p
        end
    end
end;
```

18.5 Intersection of a Ray with an Object

The fundamental task in ray tracing is determining where a ray intersects an object. It is usually also the most costly step computationally. Consider a general ray given by

$$\mathbf{r}(t) = \mathbf{s} + \mathbf{c}t \qquad (18.10)$$

where $\mathbf{s}$ and $\mathbf{c}$ are arbitrary vectors. (Why should $\mathbf{c}$ not be the zero vector?)

We want to find where this ray intersects a given object. For simplicity, we first choose a specific kind of object, a generic sphere that has been subjected to an affine transformation, T, as in Figure 18.4, to form the ellipsoidal instance S. T consists of a 3-by-3 matrix, M, and an offset vector, $\mathbf{d}$, so that every point $\mathbf{q}'$ on the generic sphere has been transformed into the point $\mathbf{q}$ given by

$$\mathbf{q} = \mathbf{q}'M + \mathbf{d} \qquad (18.11)$$

As always, M scales, rotates, and shears the generic sphere, and $\mathbf{d}$ moves it into the desired postion. Figure 18.4 shows S being intersected by the ray at point $\mathbf{p}$, which we must compute.

A generic sphere is a simple object, but the transformed sphere S could be very awkward to deal with (see Exercise 11.49). How do we find the intersection of the ray and S? An excellent trick is used: Instead of transforming the sphere and intersecting it with the original ray, we inverse transform the ray and intersect it with the generic sphere.

We know from Chapter 11 that an affine transformation converts one ray into another ray. Specifically, apply the inverse transform T^{-1} to the ray of Equation 18.10 by subtracting $\mathbf{d}$ and then multiplying by M^{-1}:

$$(\mathbf{s} + \mathbf{c}t - \mathbf{d})M^{-1} \qquad (18.12)$$

Figure 18.4.
Intersecting a ray and an ellipsoid.

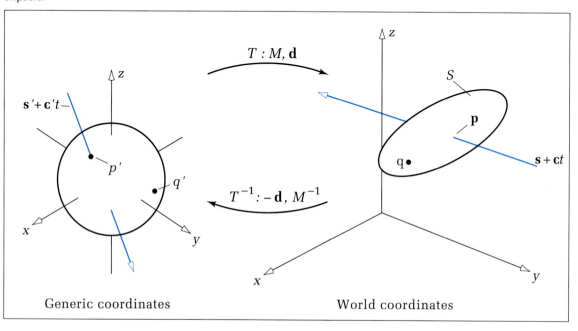

T : M, \mathbf{d}

T^{-1} : -\mathbf{d}, M^{-1}

Generic coordinates

World coordinates

By linearity this is the sum of two vectors, $\mathbf{s}' + \mathbf{c}'t$, one of which is scaled by t. So it is surely a ray. Its ingredients are

$$\mathbf{s}' = (\mathbf{s} - \mathbf{d})M^{-1}$$
$$\mathbf{c}' = \mathbf{c}M^{-1}$$

$$(18.13)$$

The principal fact in regard to ray tracing is that if the original ray, $\mathbf{r}(t)$, passes through point $\mathbf{p}$ at time t_0, we can be assured that the transformed ray, $\mathbf{r}'(t)$, passes through point $\mathbf{p}'$ at the same time, t_0. So the hit time of the transformed ray with the generic sphere is identical to the hit time of the original ray with the ellipsoid.

Intersecting a Ray with the Generic Sphere

Where then does the ray $\mathbf{s}' + \mathbf{c}'t$ intersect the generic sphere? In Chapter 8 we described a 2D experiment that closely resembles ray tracing. There, a ray was intersected with a circle of radius R centered on the plane at $\mathbf{h}$. To solve for the intersection time, the ray was substituted into the equation of the circle, yielding a quadratic equation (Equation 8.11) for the hit time.

The same reasoning is applied here. In fact, because all calculations are in terms of dot products, they have the same form whether the vectors involved are two dimensional or three dimensional, and so the formulas of Chapter 8 may be applied directly. For the generic circle—radius 1, center at $(0, 0, 0)$—Equations 8.12 through 8.14 show the hit time to be

$$t_h = -\frac{B}{A} \pm \frac{\sqrt{B^2 - AC}}{A}$$

$$(18.14)$$

where the quantities A, B, and C are

$$A = |\mathbf{c}'|^2$$
$$B = \mathbf{s}' \cdot \mathbf{c}'$$
$$C = |\mathbf{s}'|^2 - 1$$

$$(18.15)$$

As in the 2D case, if the discriminant $B^2 - AC$ is negative, there can be no solutions, and the ray must miss the sphere. If the discriminant is zero, the ray will graze the sphere at one point, and the hit time will be $-B/A$. If the discriminant is positive, there will be two hit times, t_1, found by subtracting the square root in Equation 18.14, and t_2, found by adding it.

Example

Suppose sphere S is centered at $(2, 4, 9)$ and has radius 4. Find where the ray $(10, 20, 5) + (-8, -12, 4)t$ intersects it.

Method 1:
The sphere is a generic sphere that has been scaled uniformly by 4 and then translated through $(2, 4, 9)$. Inverse transforming the ray:

$$((10, 20, 5) + (-8, -12, 4)t - (2, 4, 9)) \begin{pmatrix} .25 & 0 & 0 \\ 0 & .25 & 0 \\ 0 & 0 & .25 \end{pmatrix}$$

$$(18.16)$$

$$= (2, 4, -1) + (-2, -3, 1)t$$

From Equation 18.15, we find $(A, B, C) = (14, -17, 20)$ so that the discriminant is 9. Hence there are two intersections. From Equation 18.14, we obtain the hit times 1 and 10/7. The hit spot is found by using a time of 1 in the ray representation, yielding $(2, 8, 9)$. (Check that this point lies on the sphere.)

Method 2:
Apply Equations 8.11 through 8.14 directly, using 3D vectors. The ingredients of Equation 8.12 are $(A, B, C) = (224, -272, 320)$, and so $B^2 - AC = 2304$. Using these in Equation 8.14 yields the same hit times as in Method 1.

Drill Exercise

18.11.   Find the Intersection Points. Find the times and points of intersection of the ray $(3, 5, 8) + (-4, -2, -6)t$ with the sphere of radius 5 centered at $(1, 2, 1)$. Do this in two ways: first, by the direct use of Equations 8.11 through 8.14 and, second, by inverse transforming the ray and intersecting it with the generic sphere. *Answer:* $t = .41751$ or $t = 1.58248$, and the two intersections occur at $(1.33, 4.165, 5.495)$ and $(-3.33, 1.835, -1.495)$.

We incorporate these equations into the routine *Ray_Sphere* (*ThisRay* : *ray*; **var** *hit* : *boolean*; **var** *t_hit* : *real*); which determines whether the ray *ThisRay* given by $\mathbf{a} + \mathbf{b}t$ (in generic coordinates), hits the generic sphere and at what time. The boolean variable *hit* reports whether there is a legitimate intersection, and if so, the proper hit time will be returned in *t_hit*.

Because the eye can be situated anywhere in the scene, even inside an object, we first decide what a legitimate intersection is. Matters are simplified by saying that the intersection must take place "in front of " the start point, $\mathbf{a}$, of the ray (usually the eye position itself in generic coordinates). This means that the intersection time must be greater than 0.

Figure 18.5 distinguishes the various cases. In case I, $\mathbf{a}$ is outside the sphere and $\mathbf{b}$ is pointed so that there are two intersections. Here both t_1 and t_2 are positive, and so the hit time is the lesser: t_1. In case II the start point is on or inside the sphere itself (a rather common occurrence, as we shall see later), and $\mathbf{b}$ is aimed so that there is another intersection. Here $t_1 \leq 0$, and so we take t_2 as the hit time. In case III, $\mathbf{a}$ is on or outside the sphere and $\mathbf{b}$ is aimed so that there are no intersections in front of $\mathbf{a}$. Neither t_1 nor t_2 is positive. In summary, *hit* will be *true* if there is at least one positive intersection time, in which case it will be the smallest such positive value.

Figure 18.5.
Determining a legitimate intersection.

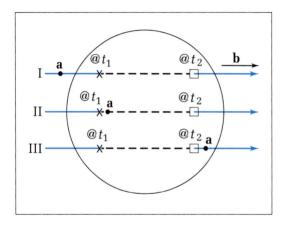

The following procedure, *Ray_Sphere*( ), implements these ideas and closely parallels Code Fragment 18.3:

Code Fragment 18.5. Intersecting a Ray and the Generic Sphere

```
procedure Ray_Sphere (ThisRay : ray; var hit : boolean; var t_hit : real);
var AA, BB, CC, discrim, disc_root : real;
begin
  hit := false;
  with ThisRay do begin
    AA := Dot3D (dir, dir);
    if AA = 0 then ReportError {ray is sick}
    else begin
      BB := Dot3D(start, dir);
      CC := Dot3D(start, start) −1.0;
      discrim := BB ∗ BB − AA ∗ CC;
      if discrim >= 0.0 then {there is an intersection}
      begin
        disc_root := sqrt(discrim);
        if −BB > disc_root then {smaller solution is pos.}
        begin
          hit := true;
          t_hit := (−BB − disc_root)/AA
        end
        else if −BB > −disc_root then {larger is pos.}
        begin
          hit := true;
          t_hit := (−BB + disc_root)/AA
        end
      end
    end {else}
  end {with}
end;
```

An Aside on Computational Complexity

How costly is it to intersect a ray with a sphere? Calculating a dot product for vectors requires three multiplications. Therefore, to compute A, B, and C, nine multiplies are required. Two more must be done to form the discriminant, at which point we can determine whether or not the ray hits the sphere. (How many adds and/or subtracts are required?) If there is an intersection, an additional square root and a divide will be needed to find t_h.

18.5.1 Putting Together the Ingredients

We can clarify these concepts by bringing them together into a simple ray-tracing application. We flesh out parts of Code Fragment 18.1 in order to compute the signature of the scene, that is, to identify which object each ray hits first.

To do this, we specify the basic routine, *RaytraceID*( ), which scans the object list and returns the id of the first object encountered by a given ray.

RaytraceID( ) works with the parameters, **s** and **c**, of an arbitrary ray, **s** + **c***t*, and applies the ray to each object on the list.

Each object has its own affine transformation, and the inverse of this transformation must be applied to **s** + **c***t* to obtain the generic coordinate version **a** + **b***t*. To avoid computing this inverse for every ray, we compute it once and store it in the additional field, *itransf* : *affine3D*, in the instance record of the object (see the *instance* type in Appendix 3).

The ray is transformed in *TransformRay(itransf* : *affine3D*; *RayIn* : *ray*; **var** *RayOut* : *ray*)—see the exercises. *RaytraceID( )* then performs the proper intersection test—different for each generic primitive—to determine the hit time. If the object is a sphere, for instance, *Ray_Sphere( )* as defined will be applied. When the list has been scanned, *RaytraceID( )* sets *id* to the identification of the first object hit by the ray or to 0 if no object is hit. *RaytraceID( )* takes the following form:

Code Fragment 18.6. The RaytraceID( ) *Routine*

```
var head : obj_ptr; {global pointer to object list}
procedure RaytraceID(SceneRay : ray; var id : integer);
<definitions of the 6 procedures Ray_Sphere( ), Ray_Plane( ), etc.>
var
   obj : obj_ptr;
   GenRay : ray;
   hit : boolean;
   t_hit, t_this : real;
begin
   obj := head;    {first object in list}
   id := 0;        {nothing hit yet}
   t_hit := 100000000.0; {bigger than any actual hit time}
   while obj <> nil do with obj ^ do
   begin
      TransformRay(itransf, SceneRay, GenRay); {from world to generic}
      case kind of
         cube : Ray_Cube(GenRay, hit, t_this);
         cone : Ray_Cone(GenRay, hit, t_this);
         <other intersection routines>
         polyh : Ray_Polyh(GenRay, hit, t_this);
      end; {case}
      if hit then if t_this < t_hit then {closest hit so far?}
      begin
         t_hit := t_this; {smallest positive hit time so far}
         id := nature {closest object so far}
      end; {if hit}
      obj := next
   end {with, while}
end;
```

Intersection routines such as *Ray_Cone( )* and *Ray_Polyh( )* have yet to be defined, but their roles here should be clear.

With these tools in place, the overall ray-tracing program takes a rather simple shape:

Code Fragment 18.7. Pseudocode: Ray Tracer to Build the Signature

```
var
  A : signature;
  i, j : integer;
  eye : vector3D;
  ThisRay : ray;
begin
  <read scene description and build object list>
  <set up the camera>
  ThisRay.start := eye;
  for j := 0 to MAXROW do {do j-th scan line}
  for i := 0 to MAXCOLUMN do
  begin
    <build direction ThisRay.dir of the i, j-th ray>
    RaytraceID(ThisRay, A[i, j])
  end;
  <draw picture>
end;
```

At this point tools are available to implement a signature ray tracer for instances of the sphere. A method for doing this in text mode is suggested in the exercises.

Figure 18.6 shows a signature of a version of the winter scene using a distinctive color for each object. Note that it clearly shows where the various objects are, which ones lie in front of others, and so forth.

Figure 18.6.
A signature of the winter scene.

Drill Exercises

18.12.   Building the Direction of the *i*, *j*-th Ray. Spell out the steps for computing the variable *dir* for the direction of the *i*, *j*-th ray.

18.13.   Incremental Calculation of Each Ray. Because ray tracing is very repetitive, any trick that avoids repeating the same calculation is welcome. Along a scan line each successive ray may be found by a simple addition to the previous ray (see Equations 18.3 and 18.4). Most parts of the ray parameters do not change at all with *i*. These parts and the increments, properly transformed by each object's instance transformation, can be stored directly in additional fields in the object record, and accessed by each ray as needed. Show what quantities should be computed and stored in this way, and estimate the savings in computation time.

18.6   Intersecting Rays with Other Primitives

The process of finding the intersection of a ray with other kinds of primitives follows the same pattern as for the sphere. The ray is first transformed into the generic coordinates of the object in question; thus we need only figure out how to intersect a ray, $\mathbf{a} + \mathbf{b}t$, with each generic object.

18.6.1 Intersecting with a Plane

A scene often includes a "floor" on which the various objects rest. This floor might be colored uniformly; it might have a checkerboard pattern on it; or it might be "painted" with some digital image.

The generic plane is given by $z = 0$, and the ray $\mathbf{a} + \mathbf{b}t$ strikes it when its z-component $a_z + b_z t = 0$, hence at

$$t_h = -a_z/b_z \tag{18.17}$$

If $b_z = 0$, the ray is moving parallel to the plane, and there is no intersection (unless, of course, a_z is also 0, in which case the ray hits the plane end-on and cannot be seen anyway). *Ray_Plane*( ) is easily implemented—see the programming exercises.

18.6.2 Intersecting with a Square

The generic square is a piece of the generic plane, and so we first find where the ray hits the generic plane and then test whether this hit spot lies within the square, that is, whether neither its x-nor its y-coordinates exceed 1 in size.

Code Fragment 18.8. Intersecting a Ray and the Generic Square

```
procedure Ray_Square(TheRay : ray; var hit : boolean; var t_hit : real);
begin
   with TheRay do begin
      hit := false;
      if dir.dz <> 0.0 then {not parallel to plane}
      begin
         t_hit := −start.dz/dir.dz;
         if t_hit > 0.0 then {test that ray hits in front of eye}
```

```
        if (abs(start.dx + dir.dx * t_hit) <= 1.0) and
           (abs(start.dy + dir.dy * t_hit) <= 1.0) then hit := true
      end {if}
   end {with}
end;
```

18.6.3 Intersecting with a Cylinder

First determine whether the ray strikes the infinitely long wall of the cylinder given by $x^2 + y^2 = 1$. Substitute $\mathbf{a} + \mathbf{b}t$ into this equation to obtain the quadratic equation $At^2 + 2Bt + C = 0$, where

$$A = b_x^2 + b_y^2$$
$$B = a_x b_x + a_y b_y \qquad\qquad (18.18)$$
$$C = a_x^2 + a_y^2 - 1$$

If $A = 0$, the ray is moving parallel to the axis of the cylinder (why?), and there is no intersection with the wall. (The case in which it happens to be passing "down through" the cylinder is detected in a subsequent test.) If $A \neq 0$ but $B^2 - AC < 0$, the ray passes by the cylinder wall. If this discriminant is not negative, the ray does strike the wall, and the hit time can be found by solving the quadratic equation.

The ray might hit the wall but not the finite portion of it on the cylinder. Find the z-component of the hit spot: $a_z + b_z t_h$. The ray will hit the cylinder if this value lies between -1 and 1. This must be tested for *both* hits of the ray with the wall (why?).

We must also see whether the ray pierces the cap or the base of the cylinder. For the cap, intersect the ray with the plane $z = 1$. (What adjustments are needed in Equation 18.17 for this?) The hit spot lies within the cap if $(a_x + b_x t_h)^2 + (a_y + b_y t_h)^2 < 1$ (why?). Do the same for the base.

When these cases have been tested, there can be at most two remaining intersection times (why?). Find the smallest of all the positive hit times found in the preceding tests. An implementation of these details in the routine *Ray_Cylinder*( ) is left as an exercise.

18.6.4 Intersecting with a Cone

The intersection with a cone parallels that with a cylinder. First determine whether the ray strikes the infinite wall of the cone given by $x^2 + y^2 = (1 - z)^2/4$. Again a quadratic equation is formed, with

$$A = b_x^2 + b_y^2 - \frac{1}{4}b_z^2$$
$$B = a_x b_x + a_y b_y + b_z(1 - a_z)/4 \qquad\qquad (18.19)$$
$$C = a_x^2 + a_y^2 - \frac{1}{4}(1 - a_z)^2$$

Again see whether any solutions for the hit time exist and, if so, whether the hit spot lies between 1 and -1 in z. To see whether the ray pierces the base of the cone, intersect it with the plane $z = -1$, and check whether the hit spot lies within the base: $(a_x + b_x t_h)^2 + (a_y + b_y t_h)^2 < 1$. If there are two hit times, find the smaller positive one, if any. An implementation of *Ray_Cone( )* is left as an exercise.

Drill Exercises

18.14. How Many Ways Can a Ray Intersect a Cylinder? Sketch all possible intersections between a ray and a cylinder: wall and cap, cap and base, and so on.

18.15. On Computational Complexity. How many adds/subtracts and multiplies/divides are required to intersect a ray with a square, cylinder, and cone?

18.6.5 Intersecting with a Cube (or any Convex Polyhedron)

Boxes abound in graphics, and therefore we define the generic cube as a separate geometric primitive and see how to intersect one with a ray. But in fact the cube is just one member of the infinite family of **convex polyhedra**, and precisely the same method is used to intersect a ray with any of them. (In fact one can delete the separate generic type *cube* and the separate routine *Ray_Cube( )* if desired.)

Intersecting a ray with a cube harkens back to Section 7.4.7, in which a line is clipped against a convex window. Recall that each edge of the window defines a half-space, and a point is inside the window if, and only if, it lies on the "inside" of every half-space. The Cyrus–Beck clipping algorithm tests a line against each of the window's half-spaces in turn and successively "chops" away at the interval in the parameter t on which the line lies within the window. The piece (if any) of the t-interval that remains after all the half-spaces have been tested defines the portion of the line that lies within the window.

The thinking is the same for ray tracing a generic cube. The cube is a convex 3D shape, defined as the set of all points that simultaneously lie on the "inside" half-space of its six bounding planes. Figure 18.7 shows an example in which the planes, P_i, are numbered according to the following table:

Table 18.1 The Six Planes Defining the Generic Cube

Plane	Equation
1	$y = -1$
2	$y = 1$
3	$x = 1$
4	$x = -1$
5	$z = 1$
6	$z = -1$

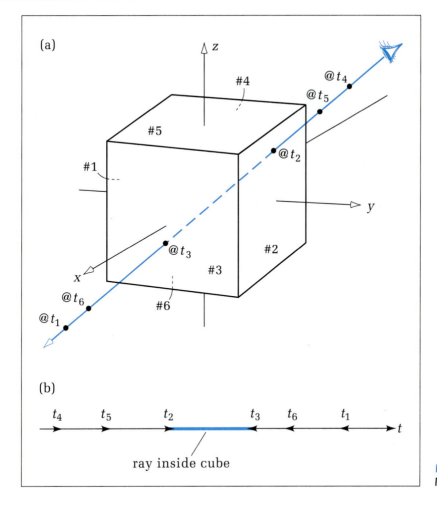

Figure 18.7.
Ray piercing the generic cube.

Each plane, P_i, either is parallel to the ray $\mathbf{a} + \mathbf{b}t$ or is pierced by it at some hit time. If P_i and the ray are parallel, the ray will lie either wholly on the inside or wholly on the outside half-space of P_i. If they are not parallel, the ray will hit the plane and either pass into ("enters") the inside half-space or pass out of ("exits") the inside half-space at the hit time.

In the figure the ray hits plane P_i at hit time t_i, as shown, either entering or exiting its inside half-space. Figure 18.7b locates the six hit times along a time line. Each arrow points to the (infinite) interval of t-values for which the ray lies in the inside half-space of the corresponding plane. The colored segment from t_2 to t_3 shows the interval in which the ray is inside the cube. Therefore, the ray first hits the cube at t_2.

Before describing the intersection method, we observe that it applies equally well to a much richer class of objects, the convex polyhedra.

Extension to General Convex Polyhedra

Convex polyhedra form a large and interesting class of solids, including the platonic solids such as the tetrahedron and dodecahedron (see Appendix 8), as well as an infinite number of other solids. They are formed by a "diamond-cutting'' process: slicing a plane through a piece of material, discarding the portion that lies in the outside half-space, and chopping off half-spaces until the desired shape is obtained. A tetrahedron is formed by chopping with four planes, and a dodecahedron with 12.

Thus any convex polyhedron is defined by a list of planes, each of which defines a half-space. It is convenient but not essential to define a "generic" version for each convex polyhedron. If desired, one might choose a convenient orientation and then scale the object to fit snugly inside the generic sphere—as in Appendix 8—or inside the generic cube. Whatever version is adopted, one simply sets up the proper affine transformation to position each instance of the convex polyhedron in the scene.

Drill Exercises

18.16.   The Planes of a Tetrahedron. Using Appendix 8 as a guide, show the ingredients of the list of planes for the regular tetrahedron.

18.17.   The Musical Note. The prism shape shown in Figure 18.8 is the union of a cylinder and two convex polyhedra. It is one unit thick. Show the data fields for each instance in the object list.

The Intersection Algorithm

Consider an arbitrary plane given by (recall Equation 7.36)

$$\mathbf{n} \cdot \mathbf{p} = D \tag{18.20}$$

where $\mathbf{n}$ is the outward-pointing normal and $\mathbf{p} = (x, y, z)$. As in Equation 7.39, we apply the ray $\mathbf{a} + \mathbf{b}t$ to form the two quantities:

$$\begin{aligned} numer &= D - \mathbf{n} \cdot \mathbf{a} \\ denom &= \mathbf{n} \cdot \mathbf{b} \end{aligned} \tag{18.21}$$

If $denom \neq 0$, Equation 7.38 will give the hit time as

$$t_h = \frac{numer}{denom} \tag{18.22}$$

As discussed in Section 7.4.7, the ray can interact with the plane in one of four ways, as summarized in the following table:

Figure 18.8.
A musical wedge.

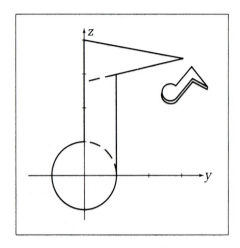

Table 18.2 Interaction of a Ray and a Plane

pass to inside	$denom < 0$
pass to outside	$denom > 0$
wholly inside	$denom = 0, numer > 0$
wholly outside	$denom = 0, numer < 0$

Follow the Cyrus–Beck clipping alogrithm and chop away at an interval (t_{in}, t_{out}) with each of the planes in the cube. This interval is initially $(-\infty, \infty)$, and after each chop it reports the interval within which the ray is on the inside half-space of every plane tested so far. Thus we know the ray might still be inside the cube for t-values in this interval. As each plane is tested, t_{in} may increase (the ray may have to go farther to enter the new half-space), or t_{out} may decrease (the ray may exit earlier). If the ray is wholly in the inside half-space, there will be no change in the t-interval. If the ray lies wholly outside some plane, terminate the test by setting t_{in} larger than t_{out}. We know the ray will intersect the cube if t_{in} is still smaller than t_{out} when all planes have been tested. Just as with the sphere (recall Figure 18.5), the hit time is then taken as the smallest positive intersection time, if any occurs.

Suppose the planes are defined in an appropriate linked list pointed to by *plane_list*. (This requires adding a pointer field *next* to the *instance* type.) Then in pseudocode the intersection algorithm takes the following form:

Code Fragment 18.9. Pseudocode: Ray_Polyh( ) *Test for Intersections with a Convex Polyhedron*

```
hit := false;
<initialize t_in to <-infinity>, t_out to <infinity>>;
p := plane_list; {head of list of planes}
while (p <> nil) and (t_in < t_out) do
begin
   <compute numer and denom for i-th plane>
   if denom = 0 then {ray is parallel}
   begin
      if numer < 0 then t_in := t_out + 1 {ray outside - stop}
   end
   else begin {ray not parallel}
      t_hit := numer / denom;
      if denom > 0 then t_out := min(t_out, t_hit) {ray exits}
      else t_in := max(t_in, t_hit) {ray enters}
   end; {else}
   p := p^.next {test next plane}
end; {while}
if t_in < t_out then {ray intersects}
   if t_in > 0.0 then
   begin
      hit := true;
      t_hit := t_in
   end
   else if t_out > 0.0 then
   begin
      hit := true;
      t_hit := t_out
   end;
```

Drill Exercises

18.18.   Hand Calculation of Pierce Times for the Generic Cube. For the ray $(4, 5, 6) + (-8, -8, -10)t$, find the six pierce times, plot them as in Figure 18.7b, and determine the t-interval for which the ray is inside the cube. Repeat for the ray $(4, 5, 6) + (-12, -8, -10)t$. Does this ray intersect the cube?

18.19.   Intersection with a Tetrahedron. Find the t-interval for which the ray $(0, 0, 0) + (1, 2, 3)t$ is inside the tetrahedron with vertices $(1, 0, 0)$, $(-1, 0, -1)$, $(-1, 0, 1)$, and $(0, 1, 0)$.

18.20.   On Computational Complexity. How many multiplications/divisions are required to test each plane of a convex polyhedron? Sometimes t_in exceeds t_out after only a few planes have been tested. What is a good rule of thumb for the average number of plane tests that are made for an N-plane polyhedron when a randomly chosen ray is tested? Compare this complexity with that for determining a ray–sphere intersection.

18.21.   Stellations of Convex Polyhedra. An additional class of solids offering simple ray tracing are the various stellations of the convex polyhedra. Examine first the 2D versions shown in Exercise 4.22. Consider the pentagon of Figure 4.29a to be the set of all points that are simultaneously on the inside half-spaces of all five sides. The first stellation of the pentagon is the pentagram. This is the set of all points simultaneously on the inside half-spaces of at least four of the sides (i.e., inside all of them or all but one). Note that adjacent side walls extend up to form a new vertex. What is the nature of Figure 4.29c?

In three dimensions, stellate in the same way a convex polyhedron such as a dodecahedron (see Appendix 8). If the polyhedron has n faces, a point will be in its first stellation if it is on the inside half-space of at least $n - 1$ of the polyhedron's bounding planes. (More generally, a point is in the k-th stellation if it lies on the inside of at least $n - k$ planes.) An example is shown in Figure 13.48 (courtesy of Brett Diamond, who suggested the technique). What are the first stellations of a cube, a tetrahedron, and an octahedron? Try to sketch the first stellation of an icosahedron. How many vertices, edges, and faces does it have?

Adjust the algorithm above so that it finds for any given ray the interval (t_in, t_out) over which the ray lies inside the stellation of the convex polyhedron. (Also see the programming exercises.)

18.6.6 Adding More Primitives

One can go beyond the generic primitives considered here to include other kinds of shapes. Recall the inside–outside function $f(x, y, z)$ for a surface, discussed in Section 9.2. A point (x, y, z) will be outside the object if $f(x, y, z) > 0$ and will lie on it if $f(x, y, z) = 0$. Thus to find where a ray, $\mathbf{a} + \mathbf{b}t$, intersects the surface, we find the hit time by solving the following equation:

$$f(a_x + b_xt, a_y + b_yt, a_z + b_zt) = 0 \tag{18.23}$$

Thus intersecting a ray is equivalent to solving an equation. For the sphere, cone, and cylinder, this leads to a simple quadratic equation. This is true also for any of the quadric surfaces of Section 9.8, because their inside–outside functions are quadratic (see Equation 9.26).

A classic example with a more awkward solution is the *torus,* which has an inside–outside function (see Table 9.2):

$$f(x, y, z) = (\sqrt{x^2 + y^2} - d)^2 + z^2 - 1 \tag{18.24}$$

When the ray components are substituted here, a *quartic* (fourth-order) equation in t_h results. Closed-form solutions may be found in any mathematical handbook.

The left-hand side of Equation 18.23 can be viewed as a function $d(.)$ of t. Figure 18.9 shows some typical variations of $d(t)$ with t. If the ray starts outside the object, $d(t)$ will be positive. As the ray approaches the surface, $d(t)$ decreases, reaching 0 if the ray intersects the surface (at t_1 in the figure). There is then a period of t during which the ray is inside the object and $d(t) < 0$. When the ray emerges again, $d(t)$ passes through 0 and begins to increase forever. If instead the ray misses the object (colored curve), $d(t)$ may decrease for a while, but it will never reach 0.

For quadrics such as the sphere, $d(t)$ has a parabolic shape, and for the torus, a quartic shape. For other surfaces there is little recourse but to seek a numerical solution to Equation 18.23, that is, to search numerically for the roots of $d(t) = 0$. Consider the superellipsoid of Table 9.2, for instance. The application of Equation 18.23 leads to

$$d(t) = ((a_x + b_x t)^{n_2} + (a_y + b_y t)^{n_2})^{n_1} + (a_z + b_z t)^{n_1} - 1 \qquad (18.25)$$

for constants n_1 and n_2. To find the smallest positive value of t that yields 0, we evaluate $d(t)$ at a sequence of t-values, searching for one that makes $d(t)$ very small. Techniques such as Newton's method (Acton 1970, Conte and deBoor 1980) provide clever ways to construct the next test value of t based on the trials so far, but in general these numerical techniques require many iterations. This of course slows down the ray-tracing process dramatically.

Techniques have been developed for ray tracing a variety of other objects. Notable among these are fractal surfaces, surfaces of revolution, and prismlike cylinders (Kajiya 1983). The search for efficient algorithms to ray trace ever-larger collections of shapes is an ongoing subject of research in graphics.

Drill Exercises

18.22.   Intersections with a Torus. Determine from a mathematical handbook how to find the solutions to a quartic equation, and set up the steps necessary to find the intersection(s) of a ray, $\mathbf{a} + \mathbf{b}t$, with the torus in Equation 18.24.

18.23.   Ray Tracing the Saddle—Hyperbolic Paraboloid. Set up the steps to find the intersections of the ray $\mathbf{a} + \mathbf{b}t$ with the hyperbolic paraboloid of Table 9.1.

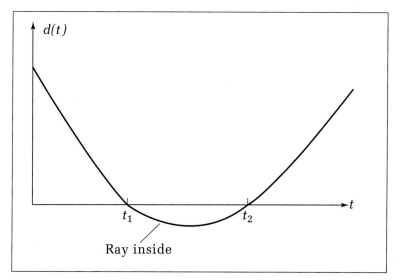

Figure 18.9.
For a ray and an object, $d(t)$ versus t.

18.7 Previewing Scenes for Ray Tracing

Ray tracing a scene can consume a great deal of time, and so it is reassuring to know that the camera has been set up properly; the instances have been placed as intended in the scene; and so forth. With only a little programming effort, one can preview where the objects reside in the scene and then watch the details fill in as the actual ray tracing proceeds. This is easily done by drawing a wireframe approximation for each object in the scene.

We associate with each generic primitive a "suggestive" wireframe model. For the cube it is natural to use its eight vertices and 12 edges. For the cone we are most likely to use its apex along with some vertices selected around its circular base and to join them as appropriate with edges. For a square or plane we would use a set of grid lines. Because the wireframe model must provide only a rough idea of how the object looks in the scene, it need not be a precise representation of the generic object. (What wireframe might one use for a cylinder? A sphere?)

For each kind of object in type *generic_type* (see Code Fragment 18.3) we therefore create a record of type *wireframe* (see Code Fragment 10.1) and store appropriate vertex and edge arrays. The following data type provides a convenient array to hold all the resulting wireframes:

Code Fragment 18.10. Data Type for Arrays of Generic Wireframes

type *generic_wireframes* = **array**[*generic_type*] **of** *wireframe*;

For instance, if variable *frames* is of this type, we can access the vertex list for the cone wireframe using *frames*[*cone*].*vert*.

For each instance in the object list we apply the affine transformation of the instance to the vertices of the appropriate generic wireframe. Thus if the object is a generic cylinder transformed by matrix M and offset d, the i-th vertex, w_i, of the cylinder wireframe found in *frames*[*cylinder*].*vert* will be transformed into $w_iM + \mathbf{d}$ (as in Equation 18.11) to place it in the scene.

To draw the wireframe, it must be projected onto the viewplane, as in Chapter 12. To project this i-th vertex, we first express it in viewing coordinates, which is done by inverting Equation 18.1: Subtract the position vector for the view reference point $\mathbf{r}$ and multiply by the inverse of matrix M_C of Equation 12.6. The corresponding vertex in viewing coordinates is then

$$(p_u, p_v, p_n) = (\mathbf{w}_iM + \mathbf{d} - \mathbf{r})M_C^{-1} \qquad (18.26)$$

(This can be written more compactly in homogeneous coordinates if desired. How?) Finally, this vertex is easily projected onto the viewplane, as in Equation 12.17. The vertex appears at

$$\left(\frac{p_u}{1 + p_n/E}, \frac{p_v}{1 + p_n/E} \right) \qquad (18.27)$$

The pixel associated with this point is found using the same kind of conversion as in Equation 15.14. Then each edge of the wireframe is drawn (scan converted) between the appropriate projected vertices, so that the user sees a wireframe version of each object in the scene in its proper position and orientation.

Figure 18.10 shows an example preview of the winter scene, demonstrating that the various instances are in their proper positions. Because the cap and base of a cylinder are approximated by hexagons in the wireframe, the cylinder wireframe consists of 12 vertices and 18 edges. Similarly, the base of the cone is approximated by a hexagon. (How many vertices and edges are therefore involved?) The sphere wireframe is based on six meridians and five hexagonal parallels.

18.8 Using Extents

Because ray tracing is so repetitive, performing the same function for a very large number of rays, we welcome any technique that reduces the number of rays or the number of objects that must be scrutinized. Extents or bounding boxes can be used to gain significant performance advantages.

As in the hidden surface removal algorithms of Chapter 17, an extent approximates the actual shape of an object by means of a simpler shape that is easier to test, in an attempt to eliminate quickly any need for a more precise test. In ray tracing we surround an object by a simpler object, which allows a faster ray intersection test. If this test shows that the ray cannot possibly hit the object, that object will be "trivially" rejected, thereby saving more elaborate computation.

In a typical scene, each object "covers" only a small fraction of the image area, and so most rays miss it. For each instance in the scene, we set up a rectangle on the viewplane that completely covers the projection of the instance. This rectangle is called the object's **projection extent**. Figure 18.11 shows the projection extent for an instance of a cylinder. It is the box that just fits around

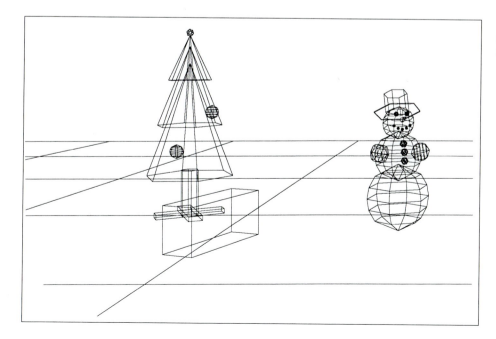

Figure 18.10.
A wireframe preview of the scene.

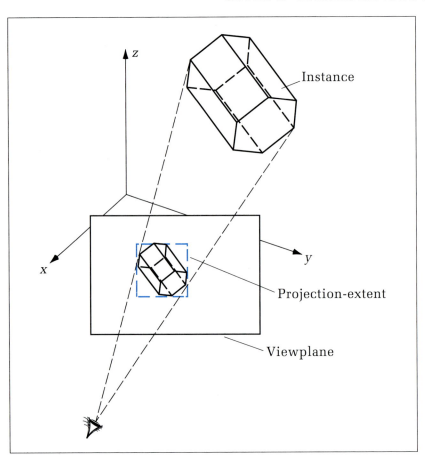

Figure 18.11.
The projection extent for a
cyclinder.

all of the projected vertices of the instance wireframe. If a ray penetrates the viewplane at a point outside this box, it cannot possibly intersect the object, and we need not test it further with this object.

The projection extent for each object in the scene is computed once before the ray tracing begins, and it is stored in additional fields of the instance record in the object list. Then for each ray the extent for each object is accessed, and only those objects whose projection extents encompass the ray are tested further. This can save a great deal of computation time (see the exercises).

Drill Exercise

18.24.　How Much Time Is Saved Using Extents? Suppose for a typical scene that the projection extent of each object covers on the average only 5 percent of the image. If it costs e units of time to test the projection extent and $30e$ units to test thoroughly for an intersection, what will be the relative time required for ray tracing with and without using extents? *Answer:* Without extents it takes 12 times as long. Generalize to the case in which fraction f of the image is covered by a projection extent and thorough testing is r times more expensive than extent testing is.

Computing Extents

A projection extent is a rectangle of type *rect*; call it $Ext = (Ext_l, Ext_t, Ext_r, Ext_b)$. Each element reports how far the projection of the object's wireframe extends on the viewplane. If the i-th vertex of the wireframe projects to (u_i, v_i) we will have

$Ext_l = min(u_1, u_2, \ldots)$, $Ext_t = max(v_1, v_2, \ldots)$, and so forth. The projection extent is easily formed at the same time that each preview wireframe is drawn, by comparing each (u_i, v_i) as it is computed with the currently reigning extremes (see the exercises).

The record structure for the type *instance* has been growing as new concepts have been introduced, so for reference we show its latest form.

> *Code Fragment 18.11. Refined Data Type for Instances—Extents and Planes Added*

```
type
    instance = record
                    kind : generic_type;    {which kind}
                    transf : affine3D;       {instance transform}
                    itransf : affine3D;      {inverse transform}
                    nature : attributes;     {id, or surface properties}
                    extent : rect;           {projection extent}
                    planes : plane_list;     {planes if kind = convex_poly}
                    next : obj_ptr;
                    .
                    . {others still to be added}
                    .

            end;
```

Recall that *planes* is a pointer to a linked list of planes, used when the *kind* of object is a convex polyhedron. For other kinds of instances, *planes* := **nil**. The other new field here is *extent*, to hold the projection extent.

To test whether the *i, j*-th ray lies in the projection extent during ray tracing, we fashion the function *RayInExtent*(*u, v* : *real*; *Ext* : *extent*) : *boolean*. It tests whether the point (*u, v*) at which the ray passes through the viewplane (see Equation 18.3) lies within the rectangular *Ext* (how?). The extent test is inserted in the routine *RaytraceID*( ) of Code Fragment 18.6. Directly following the **begin** after the line **while** *obj* < > **nil do with** . . we insert **if** *RayInExtent*(*u, v, Ext*) **then begin**. The corresponding **end** appears just before *obj* := *next*. In this way, if the ray does not lie in the extent, the ray will be neither transformed nor tested against the object.

Drill Exercises

18.25.   The Tightness of Extents. One measure of the tightness of an extent is the ratio of two areas:

$$\text{efficiency} = \frac{\text{area of object's projection}}{\text{area of extent}} \times 100\% \quad (18.28)$$

This tells what percentage of the rays "accepted" by the extent test do in fact intersect the object. For long, skinny objects whose projections are tilted at about 45°, this efficiency can be very small, whereas for other objects it can be nearly 100 percent. Draw various cases and roughly estimate the efficiency of each extent.

18.26.   Union Extents for Further Time Savings. In some scenes large areas of an image show only background and contain no objects at all. To save additional time during ray tracing, we can form the **union extent**, the smallest rectan-gle that encloses all of the individual extents of the objects in the scene. Each ray is first tested against this extent. If it lies outside, it will be set immediately to the background color. Otherwise the object list will be scanned as always. Show how to form the union extent.

18.27.   Lists for Clustered Objects. Another refinement saves significant computation time when it is applicable. When groups of objects appear in more or less isolated "clusters" in the scene, each cluster of objects can be placed in a separate object list—call it a **cluster list**. A union extent is computed for each cluster. The object list becomes a list of cluster lists. During ray tracing, each ray is tested against the union extent of each cluster list, and only if it passes this test will the ray be tested against the objects in the cluster. Show how to organize the data types and ray-tracing algorithm in order to implement this approach.

18.28.   Finding Extents for Convex Polyhedra. A convex polyhedron is defined not by vertices but by planes. The vertices can be computed from the plane information

(how?), but this is quite complicated. What is a more reasonable approach to defining a projection extent for such an object? *Hint:* Surround the polyhedron by some simple shape.

18.9   Drawing Shaded Pictures of Scenes

We wish to produce realistic ray-traced pictures by applying the shading model developed in Chapter 15. To do this, we must determine the nature of the light that is reflected toward the eye from the hit point, the point at which each ray first hits an object. This in turn requires that we compute both the position of the hit point and the normal vector to the surface at the hit point.

Figure 18.12 shows the i, j-th ray intersecting a spheroid at hit point $\mathbf{p}_h$, which is found from Equation 18.5 once the hit time, t_h, has been computed. A light source is located at $\mathbf{L}$. We wish to compute the amount of light that travels back from $\mathbf{p}_h$ to the eye. The principal vectors of interest—first encountered in Figure 15.11—are shown as $\mathbf{s}$, $\mathbf{v}$, and $\mathbf{n}$. Here $\mathbf{s}$ points to the light source and is therefore given by $\mathbf{s} = \mathbf{L} - \mathbf{p}_h$; $\mathbf{v}$ points to the viewer and so is just the negative of

Figure 18.12.
Applying the shading model.

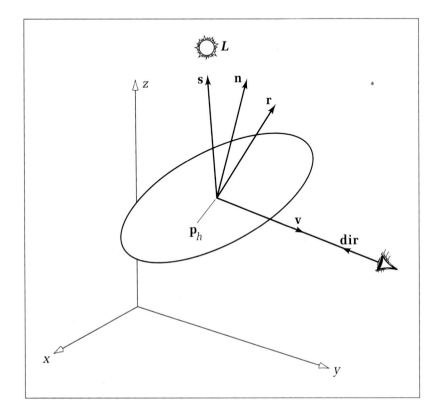

the ray's direction **dir**; and **n** is the normal to the surface at $\mathbf{p}_h$ discussed next. From Equation 15.6 the (monochromatic) light intensity observed by the eye is

$$I = I_{\text{amb}} + I_{\text{diff}} + I_{\text{spec}} \tag{18.29}$$

consisting of the ambient, diffuse, and specular components given by

$$
\begin{aligned}
I_{\text{amb}} &= I_a r_a \\
I_{\text{diff}} &= I_s r_d (\mathbf{u_s} \cdot \mathbf{u_n}) \\
I_{\text{spec}} &= I_s r_s (\mathbf{u_r} \cdot \mathbf{u_v})^f
\end{aligned}
\tag{18.30}
$$

Here $\mathbf{u_s}$ is the normalized version of **s**, and similarly for $\mathbf{u_v}$ and $\mathbf{u_n}$, and $\mathbf{u_r}$ is the (normalized) reflection direction needed to find the specular component (see Figure 15.13). It is given by Equation 15.4. The various reflection coefficients, r_a, r_d, and r_s, are stored in the *nature* field of each instance in the object list.

If several light sources are present in the scene, there will be an I_{diff} and an I_{spec} contribution from each, which are summed to form I. Recall that the ambient term is an approximation that lumps together diverse contributions from multiple reflections off neighboring bodies and the environment. We shall see next that while ray tracing we in fact trace some rays individually through multiple reflections when an object is shiny enough. The ambient term still helps approximate the effect of all the less prominent rays circulating about the scene, which are too numerous to trace individually.

18.9.1 Finding the Normal at the Hit Spot

How is the normal vector, **n**, at the hit spot determined? It is most easily found first in generic coordinates and then transformed into world coordinates. In Section 11.10 we showed that if one object is transformed into another using matrix M and offset **d**, the normal vector **n** will be transformed into the normal vector **n′** given by

$$\mathbf{n'} = \mathbf{n}M^{-T} \tag{18.31}$$

where M^{-T} denotes the transpose of the inverse of M (also see Appendix 2). Because vectors are position independent, the offset **d** has no effect on the normal vector. Thus the desired normal is found by computing the normal vector to the surface of the generic object at the hit spot and then postmultiplying it by M^{-T}.

During the ray intersection process in generic coordinates we solve for the hit time, t_h, from which it is simple to find the hit spot, (x, y, z). What is the direction of the normal vector there? The calculation depends on which kind of generic primitive is involved. Consider each:

- *Sphere.* The normal points out radially from the center of the sphere to the hit spot and so has value (x, y, z). Its value, of course, depends on the actual point of contact.

- *Plane and square.* The generic plane and square lie in the x, y-plane and hence have normal $\mathbf{n} = (0, 0, 1)$.

- *Cylinder.* If (x, y, z) lies on the wall of the cylinder, the normal will point out radially from the axis and so will be simply $(x, y, 0)$. On the other hand, if (x, y, z) lies on the cap, the normal will be $(0, 0, 1)$, and if on the base, it will be $(0, 0, -1)$.

- *Cone.* If (x, y, z) lies on the wall of the cone, we can apply Equation 9.16 to the inside–outside function to obtain $(2x, 2y, (1 - z)/2)$ for the normal vector. If (x, y, z) lies on the base, the normal will be $(0, 0, -1)$.

- *Convex polyhedron (including the cube).* The direction of the normal is simply the outward normal to the plane that is hit first by the ray. This value is stored in the list of planes accompanying the object (pointed to by *planes* in Code Fragment 18.11).

It is simplest to compute the normal vector directly inside the routines *Ray_Cube( )*, *Ray_Cylinder( )*, and so forth (see Code Fragment 18.6), and so we extend their argument list to pass back this normal. *Ray_Cylinder( )*, for example, becomes

Code Fragment 18.12. Ray_Cylinder( ) Revisited

---

procedure *Ray_Cylinder* (*GenRay* : *ray*; **var** *hit* : *boolean*; **var** *t_hit* : *real*; **var** *norm* : *vector3D*);

The value of *norm* is most conveniently stored in an additional field in the instance record. It might be argued that this is wasteful computationally because the normal is not used unless this object happens to be the first one hit by the ray. But the calculation of *norm* is very simple and costs little to perform. Otherwise, we would have to keep track of the surface first hit (i.e., was it the wall or cap of a cylinder?) for later use if in fact this object were found to be the first one hit.

Drill Exercise

18.29. Incorporating the Normal Calculation. Show what calculations must be included in *Ray_Cube( )*, *Ray_Cylinder( )*, and so forth to find the normal at the hit spot.

18.9.2 Computing the Light Intensity for Each Pixel

For simplicity, we shall discuss the ray-tracing application first for monochromatic (gray-scale) images, adding color later. The calculation of the real-valued light intensity, I, of Equation 18.29 is carried out in a new procedure, *Shade( )*, having the following interface:

procedure *Shade* (*SceneRay* : *ray*; {ray in world coords}
 obj : *obj-ptr*; {object hit by ray}
 t_hit : *real*; {hit time}
 var *inten* : *real*); {resulting intensity}

In order to find I, *Shade( )* computes four vectors, of which $\mathbf{u_v}$ is found by normalizing the negative of the ray direction. To form $\mathbf{u_s}$, the hit spot, $\mathbf{p}_h$, is found, and $\mathbf{L} - \mathbf{p}_h$ is normalized. The normal direction (in generic coordinates) at the hit spot is accessed from the instance record, multiplied by the appropriate M^{-T}, and then normalized. Then, $\mathbf{u_r}$ is computed from $\mathbf{u_n}$ and $\mathbf{u_s}$. The surface data, r_a, r_d, r_s, and f, are accessed from the *nature* field of the object.

The overall ray-tracing program has the same shape as in Code Fragment 18.7, except that $\mathbf{A}[,]$ is now set to be of type *grayscale* (see Code Fragment 18.2) and *RaytraceID( )* is replaced with another version, *Raytrace (SceneRay : ray;* **var** *inten : real)* which returns the intensity value *inten* in *A[i, j]*. *Raytrace( )* is almost identical to *RaytraceID( )* except at the end. If the condition $t\_this < t\_hit$ is satisfied, it will perform $t\_hit := t\_this$ to save the best hit time so far, *which* $:= obj$, so that *which* (initialized to **nil**) will point to the closest object found so far, and it will store back in the instance record the normal *norm* computed at the hit spot. Then instead of storing an integer, *id*, in its final argument, it will perform the following:

Code Fragment 18.13. Using Shade( ) *in* Raytrace( )

---

if *which* = **nil then** *inten := background*
else *Shade(SceneRay, which, t_hit, inten)*;

Thus if no object is hit by the ray, *inten* will be set to the desired background intensity, but if some object is hit, *inten* will be computed as described.

18.9.3 Adding Patterns to the Square

The square (or its infinite cousin the plane) is often used to provide a kind of background surface to a picture, a "floor" on which other objects are seen to rest. To add visual interest, we want a pattern such as a checkerboard to appear "painted" on the surface. This can be done by making the reflection coefficients of the object depend on position within the square.

Figure 18.13 shows the generic square covered with a checkerboard pattern. Values of Δx and Δy are chosen to set the dimensions of the dark and light squares. For instance, if $\Delta x = .1$ and $\Delta y = .2$, the pattern will contain 20 rows of ten columns each of such squares.

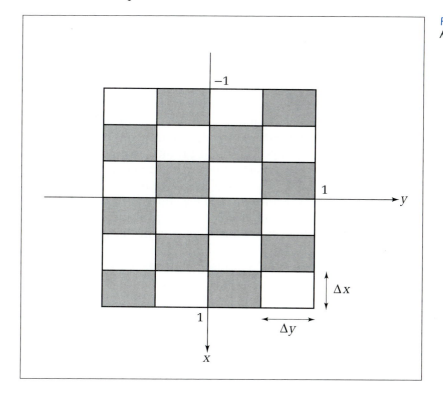

Figure 18.13.
Adding a pattern to the square.

To make the pattern visible, we need to make the reflection coefficients jump alternately between two values as x and y vary. The function $jump(x, y)$ given by

$$jump(x, y) = (\lfloor x/\Delta x \rfloor + \lfloor y/\Delta y \rfloor)\bmod 2 \qquad (18.32)$$

(where $\lfloor x \rfloor$ denotes the largest integer less than or equal to x) jumps between 0 and 1 as x and y move from square to square. Thus when the ray first hits the square, we find the hit point (x, y) in generic coordinates and set each reflection coefficient to the value $dark + lighter * jump(x, y)$, in which $dark$ and $lighter$ are appropriately chosen values. When (x, y) is such that $jump(x, y)$ is 0, the reflection coefficient is the low value $dark$, and little light is reflected, producing a dark square. When $jump(x, y) = 1$, the reflection coefficient is $dark + lighter$, and the square reflects more light.

Drill Exercise

18.30.   On the Checkerboard Pattern. Show that the function $jump(x, y)$ behaves as promised, jumping between 0 and 1 on alternating squares. Can this same function be used on the infinite plane object? Explain. How can this patterning be implemented in code in the procedure $Shade(\ )$?

Instead of using a procedurally defined pattern function such as a checkerboard, we may instead want to paint onto the square a "data-defined" pattern based on a precomputed image. Suppose an image array is stored as intensity values in the two-dimensional array $B[.\,,.]$. The value $B[j, k]$ is made to correspond to the (j, k)-th "square" of the checkboard by means of the function

$$value(x, y) = B[\lfloor x/\Delta x \rfloor, \lfloor y/Deltay \rfloor] \qquad (18.33)$$

That is, for all (x, y) lying in the j, k-th square, $value(x, y)$ takes on the value $B[j, k]$. The reflection coefficients can be set directly to $value(x, y)$ or perhaps to $K_1 value(x, y) + K_2$ for some suitably chosen values of K_1 and K_2.

It is quite easy to map patterns onto flat surfaces such as the square. We can also experiment with "texture mapping" onto more complex curved surfaces. We want to associate with each generic primitive a function, say $refl(x, y, z)$, that produces the value of a reflection coefficient to be used when the ray hits the object at (x, y, z). For a complicated surface shape, it can be become quite challenging to achieve a specific effect (Foley and Van Dam 1983, Rogers 1985), but simple experimentation can produce rather pleasing results.

Figure 18.14 shows a ray-traced version of the winter scene rendered in shades of gray on a planar background. Specular highlights can be seen on several of the objects, and the diffuse reflections show their promised intensity variations with angle.

Note that some features in the figure have not yet been discussed. Objects cast shadows. The white background is mirrorlike and shows a reflected image of the scene. The block of "ice" is actually transparent and refracts the light passing through it. Each of these techniques requires the generation and tracing of additional rays, an approach discussed in the next section.

Figure 18.14.
Monochromatic ray-traced scene. (Courtesy of Brett Diamond).

18.10 Spawning Additional Rays for Greater Realism

The techniques we have discussed have by no means explored all of the power of ray tracing. We can produce dramatically more realistic images by incorporating such effects as shadowing, mirrorlike reflections, and refraction through transparent objects.

18.10.1 Determining Points in Shadow

The light intensities we have calculated up to now have assumed that the point of intersection, $\mathbf{p}_h$, of the ray with the closest object is bathed in light from the light source. But other objects often lie between $\mathbf{p}_h$ and the light source. In that case $\mathbf{p}_h$ is in shadow with respect to that light source, and both the diffuse and specular contributions are eliminated. This leaves only the ambient light component.

Figure 18.15 shows various shadowing situations. Because point $\mathbf{p}$ is able to "see" source L_1, it is not in shadow. But it is in the shadow of the cube with respect to light source L_2. In addition, the sphere "self-shadows" $\mathbf{p}$ with respect to source L_3.

We need a function, *InShadow( )*, that determines whether any part of an object lies on the line segment between $\mathbf{p}_h$ and the light source at $\mathbf{L}$. *InShadow (NewRay : ray) : boolean* detects the presence of any intermediate objects by "spawning" a new **secondary ray**, $\mathbf{p}_h + (L - \mathbf{p}_h)t$, from $\mathbf{p}_h$ in the direction of the light source. The ray emanates from $\mathbf{p}_h$ at $t = 0$ and reaches $\mathbf{L}$ at $t = 1$. The object list is scanned, and each object is tested for an intersection with this ray. If any intersection is found that lies between $t = 0$ and $t = 1$, the routine will terminate and return *true*. If no object lies in this path, it will return *false*.

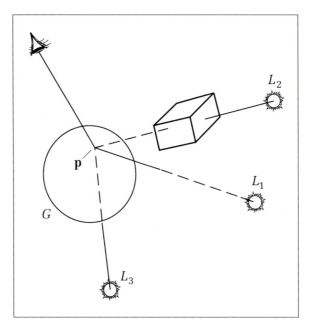

Figure 18.15.
Various cases of shadowing the
point of intersection.

     InShadow( ) is similar to *RaytraceID*( ) of Code Fragment 18.6. It is a little simpler, however, because it is not looking for the smallest hit time, but instead for any hit with a hit time lying between 0 and 1. (What changes in the logical flow of *RaytraceID*( ) are required?)

Drill Exercise

18.31.   The Self-shadowing Issue. There is the possibility of "self-shadowing" a hit spot on an object by the object itself. In Figure 18.15 the sphere does not self-shadow **p** as far as source L_1 is concerned, but it does self-shadow with respect to L_3.

    The hit spot $\mathbf{p}_h$ lies of course on the object that is hit, and so an intersection always occurs at $t = 0$ when this object is tested against the secondary ray. But in fact self-shadowing will occur only if there is another intersection at some $t > 0$. What, if anything, must *InShadow*( ) do to determine whether self-shadowing is actually occurring? (*Hint*: Recall how routines like *Ray_Sphere*( ) operate.

18.10.2 Extents for Secondary Rays

Note that *InShadow*( ) cannot use a projection-extent test to eliminate objects rapidly. Projection extents require a fixed eye and a viewplane, both of which are missing when a secondary ray is spawned. During ray tracing, secondary rays can emanate from any point and be aimed in any direction. Therefore, any extent that is used must be a 3D extent.

    Because the direction of the ray is arbitrary, a sphere seems like a good candidate for an extent shape. But it is actually more efficient computationally (see the exercises) to surround each object in the scene with an "extent box" that fits it snugly. When a secondary ray is cast, we test whether it intersects the object's extent box. If not, it cannot possibly intersect the object inside. On the other hand, if the extent box is intersected, we will have to test the object further.

    How is an extent box formed for each instance? It is very efficient computationally to orient the extent box so that its faces are aligned with the various coordinate axes of the scene. (Other boxes might fit more tightly around the object, but they would be harder to find, and much more computation would be required to determine whether a ray intersects them.) When aligned this way, two of the components of the outward-pointing normal **n** of each face are zero. For instance, the "top" face of the box has normal **n** = (0, 0, 1). Therefore, no multiplications are required to find the dot products in *numer* and *denom* of Code Fragment 18.9!

With the orientation of the extent box fixed, we need only find the positions of its six faces. An easy way to determine these for each instance is to use the vertices of its wireframe. All the vertices of the generic wireframe are mapped to world coordinates using the transformation of the instance. If the instance is an ellipsoid, for example, the wireframe vertices of the generic sphere will form an ellipsoidal "cloud" of points. The cloud of vertices is scanned to find the largest and smallest values of x, y, and z, and these six values completely determine the extent box. For instance, the "top" face has plane equation given by $z = z_{max}$. It is convenient to store the six values x_{min}, x_{max}, y_{min}, . . . in additional fields of the instance record.

To test for an intersection between a ray $\mathbf{a} + \mathbf{b}t$ and an instance, we follow the lines of Code Fragment 18.9 and form the six values of *numer* and *denom* (of Equation 18.21) required. The "top" face, for example, uses *numer* = $z_{max} - a_z$ and *denom* = b_z. (What are the other five forms for these quantities?) No multiplications are required, and the code can be made very "tight" and efficient. This code results in a routine we call *RayInBox*(*ThisRay* : *ray*; *obj* : *obj_ptr*) : **boolean**. It returns *true* if and only if *ThisRay* intersects the extent box of the instance *obj* (see the exercises).

Drill Exercises

18.32.   An Example Box Extent. An instance is formed by scaling the generic cone by 3 in the x-direction and by 2 in the y-direction, and then translating it through (4, 1, 6). Find a box extent.

18.33.   Using Sphere Extents. As an alternative to box extents, one can find a sphere that snugly fits about each instance, and test for an intersection between the ray and this sphere. For each instance the vertices defined by its wireframe are first mapped into scene coordinates. Then a suitable center for the sphere is found by computing the centroid (the sum of the vertices divided by the number of them). The radius of the sphere is found as the maximum of the distances from this center to any vertex. The center and radius are stored back in the instance record for later use during actual ray tracing.

How many multiplications are required to determine whether a ray $\mathbf{a} + \mathbf{b}t$ intersects this sphere? If a floating-point accelerator is available that can perform multiplications as rapidly as it performs additions, are there any advantages to using sphere extents over box extents? Which type of extent will tend to fit more snugly "on the average" about instances?

18.34.   Finding the Sphere Extent for an Instance. Suppose an instance wireframe has vertices $\mathbf{v}_1, \mathbf{v}_2, \ldots, \mathbf{v}_n$ in world coordinates. Find the center **c** and radius R of a sphere that tightly encloses every $\mathbf{v}_i$, using the centroid. Is there a better choice for **c** that will in general lead to a smaller sphere?

18.11 Reflections and Transparency

One of the great strengths of the ray-tracing method is the ease with which it can handle both the reflection and the refraction of light. This allows one to build scenes of exquisite realism, containing mirrors, fish bowls, lenses, and the like.

There can be multiple reflections in which light bounces off several shiny surfaces before reaching the eye, or elaborate combinations of refraction and reflection. Each of these processes requires the spawning and tracing of additional rays.

Figure 18.16 shows a ray emanating from the eye and hitting a surface at point $\mathbf{p}_h = \mathbf{eye} + \mathbf{dir}\, t_h$. (*Note*: A three-dimensional situation is depicted, even though it seems to be two dimensional. Because of the nature of light reflection and refraction, all vectors shown lie in the same plane.) When the surface is mirrorlike or transparent, or even both, the light I reaching the eye may have five components:

$$I = I_{\text{amb}} + I_{\text{diff}} + I_{\text{spec}} + I_{\text{refl}} + I_{\text{refr}} \qquad (18.35)$$

The first three are familiar from Equation 18.29 and consist, respectively, of the ambient, diffuse, and specular contributions. The diffuse and specular parts come from light sources in the environment that are visible at $\mathbf{p}_h$, such as L.

I_{refl} is the **reflected light** component, arising from the light, I_R, that is incident at $\mathbf{p}_h$ along direction $-\mathbf{b}$. This direction is such that the angles of incidence and reflection are equal, and so $\mathbf{b}$ is given according to Equation 15.4 by

$$\mathbf{b} = \mathbf{dir} - 2(\mathbf{dir} \cdot \mathbf{u_n})\mathbf{u_n} \qquad (18.36)$$

where $\mathbf{u}_n$ is the unit normal to the surface at $\mathbf{p}_h$.

Similarly, I_{refr} is the **refracted light** component, from the light, I_T, that is transmitted through the transparent material to $\mathbf{p}_h$ along direction $-\mathbf{d}$. A portion of this light passes through the surface and in so doing is "bent," continuing its travel along $-\mathbf{dir}$. The refraction direction, $\mathbf{d}$, depends on several factors, and its details are developed next.

Just as I is a sum of various light contributions, I_R and I_T each arise from their own five components: ambient, diffuse, and so on. As the figure shows, I_R is the light that would be seen by an eye at $\mathbf{p}_h$ along a ray from $\mathbf{p}'$ to $\mathbf{p}_h$. To determine I_R, we do in fact spawn a secondary ray from $\mathbf{p}_h$ in the direction $\mathbf{b}$, find the first object it hits, and repeat the same computation of light components as in Equation 18.35. This may in turn require spawning additional secondaries.

Figure 18.16.
Including reflected and refracted light.

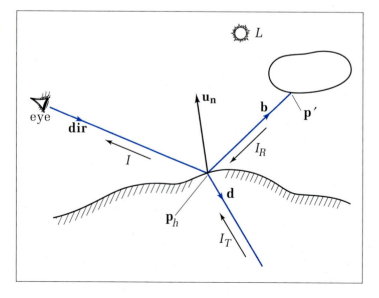

Similarly, I_T is found by casting a ray in direction $\mathbf{d}$ and seeing what surface is hit first, then computing the light contributions there, and so forth.

Figure 18.17a shows how the number of contributions of light grows at each contact point. I is the sum of three components, the reflected component R_1, the transmitted component T_1 from the refraction, and the "local" component L_1. The local component is simply the sum of the usual ambient, diffuse, and specular reflections at $\mathbf{p}_h$. (Local components depend only on actual light sources; they are *not* computed based on casting secondary rays. Recall that the role of the ambient term is to approximate the effect of diffuse and specular reflections off other surfaces.) R_1 is in turn the sum of R_3, T_3, and the local L_3. And T_3 is itself a sum of three other contributions (which ones?). Each contribution is the sum of three others, possibly ad infinitum. This suggests a recursive approach to computing each light intensity.

Figure 18.17b organizes the various light components into a "tree" of light contributions, with the transmitted components arriving on the left branches, and the reflected components arriving on the right branches (Whitted 1980). At each node a local component must also be added, but for simplicity it is not shown.

We isolate the light-computing algorithm in a single recursive function, *Shade*( ), a refinement of the earlier procedure *Shade*( ). As illustrated in Figure 18.18, it computes the amount of light that an eye at point *get_pt* on the object

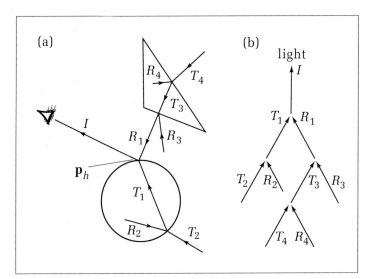

Figure 18.17.
The tree of light.

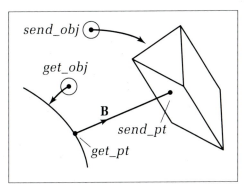

Figure 18.18.
The parameters for *Shade*( ).

pointed to by *get_obj* would see coming from the point *send_pt* on the object pointed to by *send_obj*. It has the following interface:

Code Fragment 18.14. Interface for the Function Shade( )

function Shade*get_pt* : *vector3D*; *get_obj* : *obj_ptr*;
          send_pt : *vector3D*; *send_obj* : *obj_ptr*) : *real*;

Shade( ) fits into the overall ray-tracing program as follows:

Code Fragment 18.15. Skeleton of the Ray-Tracing Program

```
var
  A : grayscale;
  TheRay : ray;
  hit_pt : vector3D;
  hit_obj : obj_ptr;
begin
  <set up scene, camera, preview, and extents>
  for i := 0 to MAXROW do
  for j := 0 to MAXCOL do
  begin
    <build ij–th ray: TheRay>
    {find first object hit}
    Raytrace_1(TheRay, hit_pt, hit_obj);
    A[i, j] := Shade(eye, nil, hit_pt, hit_obj)
  end; {for i, j}
  <draw picture>
end
```

Raytrace_1(*TheRay* : *ray*; **var** *hit_pt* : *vector3D*; **var** *hit_obj* : *obj_ptr*) is very similar to the earlier *Raytrace*( ). The suffix 1 indicates that it is designed for primary rays and hence uses projection extents. It casts the *i, j*-th ray and returns the hit spot *hit_pt*. It also returns a pointer *hit_obj* to this first hit object. Once *Raytrace_1*( ) has found where the ray hits, *Shade*( ) takes over and finds the light that returns to the eye. (The pointer to the eye is set to **nil**, since the eye is not an actual object in the scene.) *Shade*( ) places the final light intensity in the usual image array for postprocessing and display.

Operation of Shade( )

How does *Shade*( ) operate? Reduced to its most elementary form, it performs
$$Shade(A, . , P, .) := Local + refl * Shade(P, . , L, .) +$$
$$refr * Shade(P, . , T, .);$$

To determine the light arriving at *A* from *P*, it computes the local light emanating from *P* and then casts two secondary rays from *P*, one in the reflection direction finding hit spot *L* and one in the refraction direction finding hit spot *T*. *Shade*(*P*, . , *L*, .) finds the amount of light arriving at *P* from *L* and scales it by a suitable reflection coefficient *refl*. *Shade*(*P*, . , *T*, .) finds the light arriving at *P* from *T* and scales it by a refraction coefficient *refr*. Both *refl* and *refr* depend on the angle of incidence (Halliday and Resnick 1970), but they are usually treated as constants for convenience when ray tracing. The sum of the three components is the final value returned.

In some cases one or more of these three components is suppressed. If the ray from *A* to *P* is traveling inside a transparent object (as is the case for the component labeled T_1 in Figure 18.17), one usually assumes that the local light emanating from *P* is negligibly small. Furthermore, many objects are not "shiny enough" to warrant the spawning of a reflected ray, or "transparent enough" to warrant the spawning of a refracted ray. Two values, *nature.shiny* and *nature.transparent*, are stored in the instance record of each object to specify when these rays should be spawned.

When a reflected or refracted ray is spawned, its direction must be computed. The direction of the reflected ray is found using Equation 18.36. Note, however, that when the ray is traveling inside a transparent object, the inner normal—the negative of the outer normal—must be used. The direction of the refracted ray must be computed based on the angle of incidence of the ray and the optical properties of the transparent medium. This is discussed fully in Section 18.11.1.

To simplify the internal logic of *Shade*( ) we restrict the class of allowable scenes slightly such that no two transparent objects in the scene may interpenetrate, or both occupy the same space. (The removal of this restriction is discussed in the exercises.) This makes it easier to discern which medium the ray is passing through: It is either passing through a single transparent object or it is outside every object. We call the medium in which the scene is immersed air. Thus, at each intersection with a transparent object the ray is either passing from air into the object, or from the object into air. *Shade*( ) can easily determine whether the ray is inside or outside the object pointed to by *send_obj*. If the pointers *get_obj* and *send_obj* are equal, the ray is inside (the object pointed to by) *send_obj*; otherwise, it is passing through air. (Why?) This is strictly true only for convex objects (why?), but all of our generic objects are in fact convex.

We flesh out the process of computing the light that reaches a point in the following pseudocode version of *Shade*( ). If it is desired to suppress the refraction component until it has been discussed more completely, simply delete the portion beginning "**if** *nature.transparent* >*.1* **then**. . . ."

Code Fragment 18.16. Pseudocode for the Shade( ) *Routine*

```
function Shade(get_pt : vector3D; get_obj : obj_ptr;
              send_pt : vector3D; send_obj : obj_ptr) : real;
  {find light arriving at get_pt on object get_obj
  along ray from send_pt on object send_obj.}
var
  light, refl, refr : real;
  ray_in_air : boolean;
  next_obj : obj_ptr;
  next_pt, refl_dir, refr_dir, source_spot : vector3D;
  ReflectedRay, RefractedRay : ray;
begin
  if send_obj = nil then Shade := background
  else with send_obj^ do
  begin
    if send_obj <> get_obj then ray_in_air := true
    else ray_in_air := false;
    if ray_in_air then
```

```
begin {if ray_in_air}
    light := <ambient at send_pt>;
    for <each light source at source_spot> do
    if not InShadow(send_pt, source_spot) then
    light := light + <diffuse> + <specular>
end {if ray_in_air}
else light := 0.0; {if ray is inside object}
if nature.shiny > 0.1 then {add reflected light}
begin
    <get refl_dir, using ray_in_air to tell proper normal>;
    <build ReflectedRay := send_pt + refl_dir * t>
    {find first hit:}
    Raytrace_2(ReflectedRay, next_pt, next_obj);
    if next_obj <> nil then light := light +
        refl * Shade(send_pt, send_obj, next_pt, next_obj)
end; {if shiny}
if nature.transparent > 0.1 then {add refracted light}
begin
    <get refr_dir using proper value of medium>;
    if not total_reflection then
    begin
        <build RefractedRay := send_pt + refr_dir * t>
        {find first hit}
        Raytrace_2(RefractedRay, next_pt, next_obj);
        if next_obj <> nil then light := light +
            refl * Shade(send_pt, send_obj, next_pt, next_obj)
    end
    end; {if transparent}
    Shade := light
end {else}
end; {shade}
```

Each light source has a position, *source_spot*, stored in some globally accessible list, and if visible, the diffuse and specular contributions it produces will be summed. *Raytrace_2( )* differs slightly from *Raytrace_1( )*, by using box extents rather than projection extents. This is necessary because all the rays traced within *Shade( )* are secondary rays. The variables *nature.shiny* and *nature.transparent* are part of the object description and are compared with the threshold values (.1 here is only an illustrative example) to test whether the surface is "shiny enough" or "transparent enough" to warrant casting further secondary rays.

If the object is shiny enough, the direction of the reflected ray, *refl_dir*, will be computed, and a ray will be cast in that direction to find the "next" object from which light might be coming. If something is found there, its light contribution will be scaled by *refl* and added to the total so far.

A similar sequence of steps is carried out for the refracted light component. For refracted light there is the additional test to see whether a phenomenon known as *total reflection* occurs, as we shall explain. If it does occur, there will be no contribution from refracted light at this surface.

18.11.1 The Refraction of Light

When a ray of light strikes a transparent object, a portion of the ray penetrates the object, as shown in Figure 18.19. The ray will change direction from $\mathbf{b}$ to $\mathbf{d}$ if the speed of light is different in medium 1 and medium 2 ($\mathbf{d}$ still lies in the same plane as $\mathbf{b}$ and $\mathbf{u_n}$). If the angle of incidence of the ray is θ_1, Snell's law states that the angle of refraction θ_2 will be (Halliday and Resnick 1970, Rogers 1985)

$$\frac{\sin(\theta_2)}{c_2} = \frac{\sin(\theta_1)}{c_1} \qquad (18.37)$$

where c_1 is the speed of light in medium 1 and c_2 is the speed of light in medium 2, as shown in the figure. Only the ratio of c_1 to c_2 is important. It is called the **index of refraction**, n_{21}, of medium 2 with respect to medium 1:

$$n_{21} = \frac{c_1}{c_2} \qquad (18.38)$$

Let medium 1 in Figure 18.19 be air, and let medium 2 be some form of glass. Suppose that light travels 1.7 times faster in air than in this glass. The index of refraction of this kind of glass with respect to air is then $n_{21} = 1.7$. Some typical indices of refraction (with respect to air) are 2.42 for diamonds, 1.33 for water, and between 1.52 and 1.89 for various kinds of glass.

The speed of light in a material generally varies with the wavelength of the light. For instance, the index of refraction (with respect to air) of fused quartz varies from 1.470 at $\lambda = 400$ nm (red) to 1.46 at $\lambda = 520$ nm (green), to 1.455 at $\lambda = 680$ nm (blue) (Halliday and Resnik 1970). This variation produces the familiar effect of splitting a beam of white light into its "rainbow" of spectral colors when the beam is passed through a glass prism.

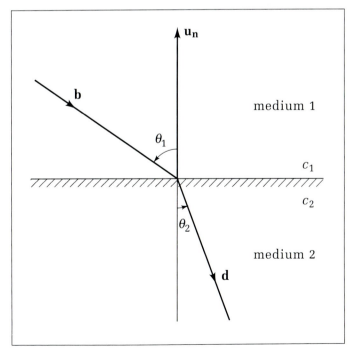

Figure 18.19.
The refraction of light in a transparent medium.

Drill Exercises

18.35.   On the Effects of Refraction. Figure 18.20a shows an eye at height H looking from air into a pool of water. A fish at horizontal distance L is located at depth D. Where does the eye see the fish if light travels twice as fast in air as in water?

18.36.   Making a Rainbow. Figure 18.20b shows a beam of white light entering a prism having an internal angle of 60 degrees. The prism is made of fused quartz. Calculate and sketch the paths of the red, green, and blue components of light as they pass through and emerge from the prism. If the white beam passes instead through a slab of fused quartz having parallel walls, will a rainbow be seen as the light emerges?

Consider Snell's law when light travels more rapidly in medium 1 than in medium 2. The former could be air, for instance, and the latter glass. From

$$\sin(\theta_2) = \frac{c_2}{c_1} \sin(\theta_1) \tag{18.39}$$

we see that $\sin(\theta_2)$ is smaller than $\sin(\theta_1)$, and so θ_2 is smaller than θ_1: Rays of light are bent more toward the normal direction when light enters a medium with a lower speed of light. The reverse is true when light enters a medium with a higher speed of light. In fact there is a **critical angle** beyond which all light is reflected back at the surface. This is called **total reflection**, and it occurs when θ_1 increases to the point that the right-hand side of Equation 18.39 increases beyond 1, so that no solution is possible for θ_2. From Equation 18.39 the critical angle is θ_1 such that

$$\frac{c_2}{c_1} \sin(\theta_1) = 1 \tag{18.40}$$

One must look almost straight down into a pond to see what is under the surface: Light cannot escape from the pond except at small angles from the normal.

For ray-tracing purposes, we must find the direction, **d**, in Figure 18.19 given the unit surface normal, $\mathbf{u_n}$, and the ray direction, **b**. This is done in a coordinate-free form using only dot products, so that it applies to any directions for **b** and $\mathbf{u_n}$. The result is a linear combination of two vectors:

$$\mathbf{d} = \delta \mathbf{c} + (1 - \delta)(-\mathbf{u_n}) \tag{18.41}$$

where:

$$\delta = \frac{1}{\sqrt{\frac{c_1^2}{c_2^2}|\mathbf{c}|^2 - |\mathbf{c} + \mathbf{u_n}|^2}} \tag{18.42}$$

and

$$\mathbf{c} = \frac{\mathbf{b}}{|\mathbf{b} \cdot \mathbf{u_n}|} \tag{18.43}$$

(Check that **d** has the correct value when there is no change in the light speeds between media 1 and 2. Hint: show that $\delta = 1$.)

There will be total reflection if the quantity in the square root within δ becomes negative, in which case **d** becomes irrelevant. The exercises request an implementation of the routine *Refract( )* that computes **d** given **b**, $\mathbf{u_n}$, and the index of refraction.

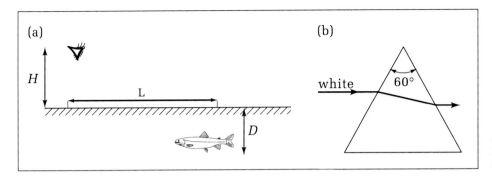

Figure 18.20.
Some experiments with refraction.

Aside: Deriving the Refraction Direction

The derivation of direction **d** is simplified by defining two intermediate vectors, **c** and **a** (see Figure 18.21). Define **c** as an elongated version of **b** according to Equation 18.43, so that the projection of **c** onto $\mathbf{u_n}$ has unit length. (Check that $\mathbf{c} \cdot \mathbf{u_n} = 1$.) Therefore **c** is resolved into the components $-\mathbf{u_n}$ and $\mathbf{a} = \mathbf{c} + \mathbf{u_n}$ shown in the figure.

Because of refraction the vector **d** has an altered component, $\delta\mathbf{a}$, in the **a** direction, for some value of δ to be determined by Snell's law. Once found, the direction of the refracted ray is simply obtained as $\mathbf{d} = \delta\mathbf{a} - \mathbf{u_n}$.

In terms of the vectors defined so far, then, simple trigonometry yields $\sin(\theta_1) = |\mathbf{a}|/|\mathbf{c}|$ and $\sin(\theta_2) = \delta|\mathbf{a}|/|\mathbf{d}|$. Relating these through Snell's law and simplifying, we find $|\mathbf{d}| = c_1\delta|\mathbf{c}|/c_2$. From Figure 18.21 we can relate $|\mathbf{d}|$ to δ in another way: $|\mathbf{d}|^2 = 1 + \delta^2|\mathbf{a}|^2$. These are easily combined to obtain δ, as in Equation 18.42.

Notice that for rays moving from a slower to a faster medium ($c_1 < c_2$), there is a possibility of total reflection. This will occur if the term in the square root of δ becomes negative, which is equivalent to $1 < c_2|\mathbf{a}|/c_1|\mathbf{c}|$. But as we have seen, $|\mathbf{a}|/|\mathbf{c}|$ is simply $\sin(\theta_1)$, and so this condition is the same as Equation 18.40.

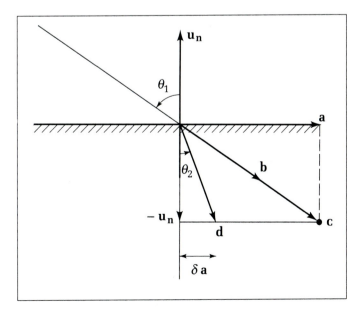

Figure 18.21.
Derivation of the refracted ray.

Because the derivation uses only dot products, it is equally applicable to a 2D situation, as in Figure 18.19. (See the exercises for an interesting 2D demonstration program of refraction.) This makes it easy to check that the direction **d** satisfies Snell's law.

Drill Exercise

18.37.   Show That Snell's Law Holds. View Figure 18.19 in a 2D coordinate system in which $\mathbf{u_n}$ is along the second coordinate and hence is given by (0, 1). Further, let $\mathbf{b} = (b_x, -b_y)$, where both b_x and b_y are positive, so that **b** is moving down and to the right, as in the figure. Use these equations to find **c**, δ, and **d**. Then express $\sin(\theta_1)$ and $\sin(\theta_2)$ in terms of the appropriate vector lengths. Show that their ratio satisfies Snell's law of Equation 18.37.

Dealing with Refraction in *Shade( )*

When including refraction in the model, we must keep track of the medium through which a ray is passing. In particular, the speed of light in the medium must be known, so that we can find the ratio $(c_1/c_2)^2$ at the interface between two objects. We therefore store this information in each object's instance record. Let the field *medium* hold the square of the index of refraction of the relevant medium with respect to air:

$$\text{medium} = \frac{c_{\text{air}}^2}{c^2} \tag{18.44}$$

where c_{air} is the speed of light in air. Then use the value $medium_2/medium_1$ to obtain c_1^2/c_2^2 when finding δ of Equation 18.42.

Routine *Shade( )* must determine which object the ray is passing through so it can access the correct value of medium. Following from the assumption that no two transparent objects interpenetrate, a ray is either traveling inside a single transparent object or it is traveling through "air" (for which *medium* = 1.0). As described earlier, *Shade( )* checks for the equality of two object pointers to determine whether a ray is inside an object or in air.

Figure 18.22 clarifies this with an example. The primary ray strikes object *hit_obj* at *hit_pt*. This hit is found in Code Fragment 18.15 using *Raytrace_1(TheRay, hit_pt, hit_obj)* (where *TheRay* is given by *eye* + *dir* * *t*). Then *Shade(eye, nil, hit_pt, hit_obj)* is used to find the light reaching the eye.

Now suppose that *Shade( )* finds that object *hit_obj* is "transparent enough." It proceeds to find the refracted light arriving at *hit_pt*. Because *hit_obj* is different from **nil**, the ray must pass from air into *hit_obj* at *hit_pt*, so *medium* is accessed in the nature field of *hit_obj* to determine the index of refraction. Based on this, *Shade( )* finds the direction of refraction. If there is total reflection, *Shade( )* ignores any refracted component and only the reflected ray is traced. Otherwise it calls *Raytrace_2(Refracted, next_pt, next_obj)* (see Code Fragment 18.16) to find the first intersection of the refracted ray. *Shade(hit_pt, hit_obj, next_pt, next_obj)* is then used to find the light arriving at *hit_pt* back along the refracted ray from *next_pt*. As shown in the figure, *hit_obj* is the same as *next_obj*, so the ray is passing inside the object. Because the ray is inside the object, the ambient, diffuse, and specular components emanating from *next_pt* are most likely assumed to be absent, and only the reflected and refracted components must be found. The reflected direction at *next_pt* is found using the inner normal since the ray is inside *next_obj*.

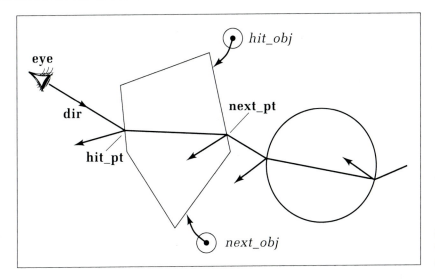

Figure 18.22.
Refraction traced through several objects.

The refracted component arriving at *next_pt* must be coming from air into *next_obj*, so *Shade*( ) uses 1.0/*medium* in its calculation of the refracted direction.

This process continues at each new interface. It is revealing to trace the course of *Shade*( ) for the example in Figure 18.22, keeping track of each argument at each step.

Preventing Endless Reflections

If the geometry is just right (just wrong?), the tree of light can extend forever, owing to cyclical internal reflections, or perhaps to a ray bouncing forever back and forth between two objects. Some provision must be made to inhibit endless invocations of *Shade*( ). This can be done by passing to *Shade*( ) a parameter, *depth*, that reports the current recursion depth. As *Shade*( ) is invoked, it checks *depth* against some user-defined *MaxDepth*. If this depth has been exceeded, *Shade*( ) will terminate and return 0. Otherwise it will increment *depth* and continue as usual. Just before exiting, it will decrement its *depth* to keep it up to date.

18.11.2 Full-Color Ray-Traced Images

Only gray-scale images have been fashioned with the ray-tracing techniques discussed so far. The extension to color follows much the same lines as in Section 16.5. Instead of collecting one light intensity with *Shade*( ) at each object's boundary, three light intensities are collected simultaneously. This is easily done by having *Shade*( ) return a pointer to a record of type *color_triple* containing three real values:

Code Fragment 18.17. Record for Holding Color Values

```
color_ptr = ^color_triple;
color_triple = record
          red, green, blue : real
     end;
```

Then in Code Fragment 18.16

*light := light + refl * Shade(send_pt, send_obj, next_pt, next_obj);*

becomes three statements, the first of which is

light^.red := light^.red +
*refl.red * Shade(send_pt, send_obj, next_pt, next_obj)^.red;*

followed by one each for the green and blue components. Each reflection and refraction coefficient is now a triple of coefficients, one for each color.

The usual practice is to model transparent objects so that their index of refraction does not depend on wavelength. In this case the same rays are used to trace the three color components. To do otherwise would require tracing separate rays for each of the color components, as they would refract in somewhat different directions. This would be very expensive computationally and would still provide only an approximation, because it should be done for a large number of colors, not just the three primaries.

Figure 18.23 shows the winter scene of Figure 18.14 in full color. Figure 18.24 shows another ray-traced scene with a checkerboard background scene containing both shiny and transparent objects. The reflection of one object in another is visible, and the distortions produced when light is refracted through a transparent object are also apparent. Also see Plate 4.

Figure 18.23.
The winter scene in full color.
(Courtesy of Brett Diamond.)

Figure 18.24.
Examples of shiny and transparent spheres. (Courtesy of Russell Turner.)

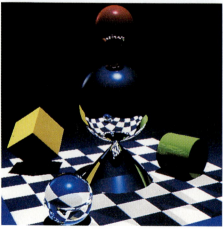

Drill Exercises

18.38.   Light Transmission Through Colored Glass. Discuss how to include the effect of refracted light that passes through an orange glass sphere.

18.39.   Ray Tracing Interpenetrating Transparent Objects. Matters are complicated when the scene contains interpenetrating transparent objects. A decision has to be made as to what value is assigned to *medium* in the region shared by two transparent objects. Usually the modeler gives them the same index of refraction. But if not (as when a diamond lies in a glassful of water), the objects should be assigned priorities so as to specify which index of refraction is to be used. Specify how a priority can be set up with the instance record of each transparent object.

The logic of *Shade*( ) becomes more complex in order to handle this situation also. Suppose we know that the only way two objects can interpenetrate is for one of them to enclose the other totally, as when one glass marble is imbedded inside another. In this case the ray follows a first-in, first-out pattern as it enters first the outer object, then enters the inner, then leaves the inner object, and finally leaves the outer. Can a stack be used to keep track of which object the ray is passing through? How is the stack "shared" by the various calls to *Shade*( )?

Consider the more general case where two transparent objects partially interpenetrate. That is, consider what must be done if the objects in the winter scene are transparent. What extra logic must be contained within *Shade*( ) to handle this situation?

18.12 Compound Objects: Boolean Operations on Objects

We can significantly enlarge the class of objects in a scene by building compound objects out of simpler ones using set operations.[1] Set operations are applied here to generic primitives in order to form such shapes as lenses, hollow fishbowls, and plates with holes. This approach of modeling compound objects hierarchically through set operations on simpler ones is known as **constructive solid geometry** (CSG) (Ballard and Brown 1982, Mortenson 1985). One of the great strengths of ray tracing is the ease with which it collaborates with CSG models.

Figure 18.25 shows two compound objects built from spheres. Figure 18.25a is a lens shape constructed as the **intersection** of two spheres. That is, a point is in the lens if, and only if, it lies in both spheres. Symbolically "L is the intersection of the spheres S_1 and S_2" is written as

$$L = S_1 \cap S_2 \qquad (18.45)$$

A bowl is shown in Figure 18.25b, constructed using the **difference** operation. A point is in the difference of sets A and B, denoted $A - B$, if it is in A and not in B. Differencing is analogous to removing material, to "cutting" or "carving." The bowl is specified by

$$B = (S_1 - S_2) - C \qquad (18.46)$$

The solid globe, S_1, is "hollowed out" by removing all the points in the inner sphere, S_2. This forms a hollow spherical shell. Then the top is opened by removing all points in the cone, C.

---

[1]The set operations of union, intersection, and difference are also studied in Appendix 6 in the context of clipping polygons.

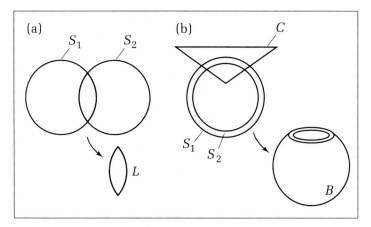

Figure 18.25.
A lens and a fishbowl.

A point is in the **union** of two sets A and B, denoted $A \cup B$, if it is in A or in B or in both. We have already encountered unions of two objects when they interpenetrate. Forming the union of two objects is analogous to "gluing" them together. Figure 18.26 shows a rocket constructed as the union of two cones and two cylinders:

$$R = C_1 \cup C_2 \cup C_3 \cup C_4 \tag{18.47}$$

Cone C_1 rests on cylinder C_2. Cone C_3 is partially embedded in C_2 and rests on the fatter cylinder C_4.

Drill Exercise

18.40.   Decomposing Compound Shapes. Give an equation that expresses each of the objects shown in Figure 18.27 in terms of set operations on spheres, cones, cylinders, and rectangular parallelepipeds.

Figure 18.26.
A union of four primitives.

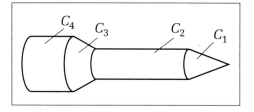

Figure 18.27.
Various shapes made from primitives.

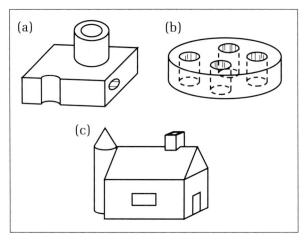

18.12.1 Ray Tracing Compound Objects

How can we ray trace objects that are boolean combinations of simpler objects? First consider the preceding examples. Figure 18.28 shows a ray entering and exiting the spheres S_1 and S_2 at the times indicated. It is therefore inside lens L from t_3 to t_2, and the hit time is t_3. This reasoning closely parallels the thinking for rays in a convex polyhedron. If the lens is opaque, the familiar shading rules will be applied to find what color the lens is at that spot. If it is mirrorlike or transparent, the secondary rays having the proper direction are found and are traced.

The situation is similar for the bowl in Figure 18.28b. Ray 1 first strikes the bowl at t_1, the smallest of the times for which it is in S_1 but not in either S_2 or C. Ray 2, on the other hand, first hits the bowl at t_5. Again this is the smallest time for which the ray is in S_1 but in neither the other sphere nor the cone. It cannot see the "opening" of the bowl because it is in C for its entire travel through that region.

We organize these ideas to ray trace any compound object (Roth 1982). Consider two objects, A and B, and a ray. Build a list of times at which the ray enters and exits from A, ordered so that the times are increasing. Because the object is solid, the enter and exit times alternate. Build a similar list of enter and exit times for B. Two such lists are shown in Figure 18.29. The interval between each enter and the next exit time is shown darkened: The ray is inside the object throughout each darkened interval. Call the set of t-values for which the ray is inside the object its **inside set**. An inside set is defined by an ordered inside list that contains the alternating enter and exit times of the ray $(t_1, t_2, \ldots)$, where t_1 is an enter time, t_2 is an exit time, and so forth.

When is the ray inside a compound object built out of A and B? The four new objects we can build are $A \cup B$, $A \cap B$, $A - B$, and $B - A$. Consider $A \cup B$. The ray is inside the union of the objects if it is in either of the objects. Thus the inside set for $A \cup B$ is simply the union of the individual inside sets. The same thinking applies to the other three objects. The inside set for $A \cap B$ is the intersection of the individual inside sets; the inside set for $A - B$ is composed of the difference of the inside set for A and that for B, and similarly for $B - A$ (just reverse the roles of A and B). In general, if we denote by $T(A)$ and $T(B)$ the inside sets of two objects, A and B, then

$$T(A \; op \; B) = T(A) \; op \; T(B) \qquad (18.48)$$

where op is $\cup$, $\cap$, or $-$. Therefore, finding inside sets for compound objects is equivalent to performing boolean operations on lists of intervals.

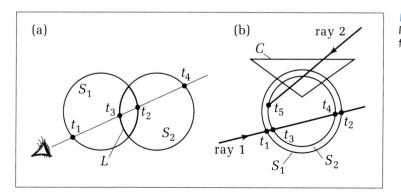

Figure 18.28.
Ray tracing the lens and
fishbowl.

(a)

(b)   ray 2

C

ray 1

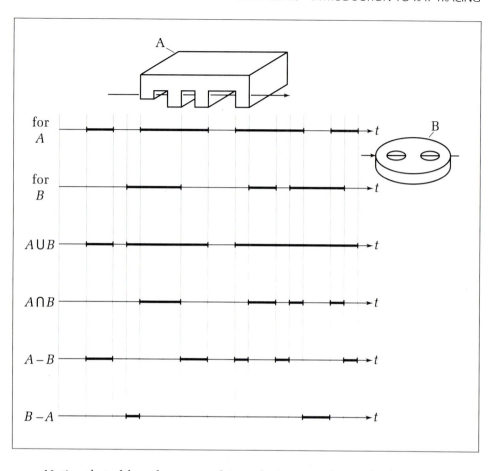

Figure 18.29.
Lists of *t*-values for a ray with
two objects.

Notice that although we are ultimately interested in only the first item in the inside list—the first hit time—entire inside lists must be retained during the list building because the ultimate "first" hit time may reside deep within one of the intermediate lists.

Drill Exercise

18.41.   Why Does Ray Tracing Handle Unions Automatically? Explain why ray tracing the union of two objects (whether or not they interpenetrate) is equivalent to ray tracing their union.

Example

Consider the following two inside lists:

A_list: 1.2   1.5   2.1   2.5   3.1   3.8
B_list: 0.6   1.1   1.8   2.6   3.4   4.0

We apply the preceding rules to build four new inside lists (check them):

$$A \cup B = .6,\ 1.1,\ 1.2,\ 1.5,\ 1.8,\ 2.6,\ 3.1,\ 4.0$$

$$A \cap B = 2.1,\ 2.5,\ 3.4,\ 3.8$$

$$A - B = 1.2,\ 1.5,\ 3.1,\ 3.4$$

$$B - A = .6,\ 1.1,\ 1.8,\ 2.1,\ 2.5,\ 2.6,\ 3.8,\ 4.0$$

(18.49)

To construct new inside lists, we build a routine, **function** *Combine(L1, L2 :*
t_list; op : operation) : t_list, that takes as arguments two lists of *t*-values and an
operation, *op*, of **type** *operation*=(*union, inter, diff*) and returns a new list of
t-values based on the preceding four combining methods. Type *t_list* is simply a
pointer to a record of type **record** *t : real; next : t_list* **end**;. The implementation
of this routine is left as an exercise.

   The ray-tracing process for a compound object boils down to ray tracing its
component objects, building inside lists for each, and finally combining them.
The first element of the combined list yields the point of the compound object
first hit by the ray. The usual shading is then done, including the casting of
secondary rays if the surface is shiny or transparent.

Data Structure for Compound CSG Objects

What data structure should be used for compound objects to facilitate ray tracing them? Note the resemblance between these hierarchical objects and those
described in Section 11.8. A tree structure can be used to show that some parts
are combinations of others, as suggested in Figure 18.30. Each internal node
(circle) represents an operator, and each leaf (square) is a primitive object. An
algebraic expression for this object is

$$(B_1 \cup B_2 \cup C_2 \cup ((S_1 - S_2) - B_3)) - C_1$$

Several others are possible.

   As there are two kinds of items in the tree, it is natural to use a variant
record type that can represent either a compound or a simple object. The *item*
field determines which of these is being represented. If *item = compound*, the
record contains the combining operation *union, intersection,* or *difference*, as
well as pointers to the two objects (themselves either simple or compound) that
are being combined. On the other hand, if *item = simple*, the rest of the record

Figure 18.30.
A compound object and its CSG
tree.

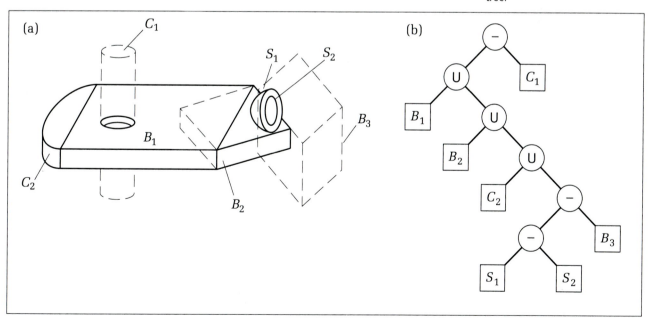

contains the now-familiar description of one of the generic primitives. The data type might take the following form:

Code Fragment 18.18. A Simple Data Type for Compound Objects

```
operation = (union, intersection, difference);
obj_ptr : ^object; {pointers used to build tree}
object = record
                trans, itrans : affine3D; {to orient object}
                extent : rect; {proj. extent of object}
                box_extent : cuboid;
                next : obj_ptr; {to next object on list}
                case item : (simple, compound) of
                        compound : (op : operation; {union, inter, or diff}
                                        left, right : obj_ptr); {children}
                        simple : (kind : generic_type;
                                nature : attribute;
                                planes : planeptr); {for convex polyh}
        end {case}
    end;
```

Note that both simple and compound objects have affine transformations and extents. The transformations have been moved from their former position connected with a generic object to allow an entire compound object to be scaled, oriented, and positioned, affording much greater modeling power and flexibility. And having extents (both a projection extent and a box extent) associated with an entire subtree assists in rapidly eliminating a whole compound object from further ray intersections. In some cases it is not too hard to compute reasonable extents for compound objects—see the exercises—and so this route can be exploited. When the extent is not readily available, it can be ignored, whereupon the subtree is thoroughly tested for intersections. Note also that the *next* field is still present in this record, which allows a scene to be described by an object list, just as before. Now, however, each object can be compound.

Figure 18.31 reveals this structure for a compound object, featuring the various transformations involved. T_2, for instance, operates on its entire subtree—the intersection of a cone and a tetrahedron—perhaps shearing and orienting it before combining it with the (warped) sphere.

Drill Exercises

18.42.   Lists of Lists? What are the implications of using the *next* field inside a compound object, so that each subtree within a compound object can itself be a list of objects? Is this a useful modeling device?

18.43.   The Whole Scene As One Object. Discuss the pros and cons of modeling an entire scene as *one* compound object, rather than using a list of simpler (possibly compound objects).

18.44.   Projection Extents for Compound Objects. Examine how one might compute a projection extent for the union, intersection, or difference of two objects. For instance, if the projection extents of both objects A and B are known, what will be the smallest rectangle one can use for the projection extent of $A–B$? Draw several example situations and show the extents that might be used. Try to formulate appropriate algorithms to construct such extents.

18.45.   Box Extents. Given the box extents for two objects, what is a reasonable method for building a box extent for the union of the objects? Repeat for the intersection and difference operations. Can one obtain tighter extents by more elaborate processing of the compound objects? Is it likely to be worth the effort?

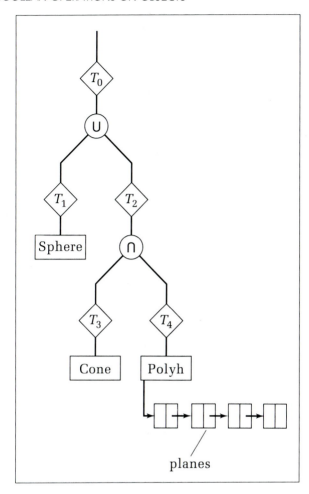

Figure 18.31.
Including transformations in
compound objects.

These ideas must be pulled together to fashion a ray tracer for compound objects. Consider a routine that "probes" an object with a ray, $\mathbf{R} = \mathbf{a} + \mathbf{b}t$, in order to build an inside list of intersections. Its interface might look like

function *Probe*(R : *ray*; *obj* : *obj_ptr*) : *t_list*;

Along the same lines as *Raytrace*( ), the routine *Probe*( ) first transforms the ray into the local coordinate system of the object pointed to by *obj*. The inverse transformation *invtrans* is used to do this, just as it did to transform a ray into the coordinate system of a generic primitive.

If the object is simple, the ray-tracing techniques described throughout the chapter will be applied. A routine, *Build_List*, is used to form an inside list for the ray and the generic object. This list will be empty if the ray misses the object or will consist of one entrance and one exit time if the ray intersects the generic object.[2]

If, on the other hand, *obj*[2] is compound, the left subtree will be probed (calling *Probe*( ) recursively) to form a list, then the right subtree will be probed,

[2]For nonconvex objects such as the torus, there may be two enter and two exit times.

and finally the two inside lists will be combined. The following code fragment shows how this can be done.

Code Fragment 18.19. Pseudocode: Ray Tracing a Compound Object

```
function Probe(R : ray; obj : obj_ptr) : t_list;
{build the inside list for ray a + bt and compound object obj}
var
  p : obj_ptr;
  NewRay : ray;
  list : t_list;
<function Build_List defined here.. use extents if available>
begin {Probe}
  if obj = nil then Probe := nil
  else with obj^ do
  begin
    TransformRay(itransf, R, NewRay);
    if item = simple then Probe := Build_List
    else Probe := Combine(Probe(NewRay, left), Probe(NewRay, right), op)
  end {else}
end; {Probe}
```

Notice that the various transformations in the tree are compounded in the proper fashion as the ray penetrates deeper into the tree, until the ray is expressed in the coordinate system of the generic primitive itself.

When the final inside list for the object has been formed, the first t-value gives the time of the first hit, and the object is shaded or further explored. Figure 18.32 shows an example of a compound object that has been ray traced using these techniques.

Drill Exercise

18.46.   Adjusting *Ray_Sphere*( ). How must the ray intersection routines *Ray_Sphere*( ), *Ray_Cone*( ), and so on be altered to work for primitives within compound objects?

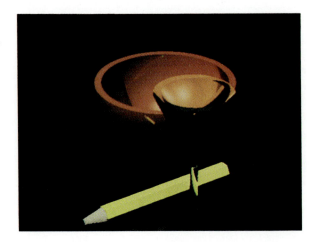

Figure 18.32.
Example of ray-traced compound objects. (Courtesy of Lars Cederman.)

18.13 Summary

Ray tracing offers a conceptually simple and uniform approach to creating dazzlingly realistic images. A large collection of relevant rays of light is traced through a scene composed of various objects, and each is analyzed to find how much light it returns to the observer's eye. This mechanism makes possible many visual effects. In addition to modeling how light scatters from faces through an ambient, diffuse, and specular component, it is straightforward with ray tracing to include the effects of reflections from mirrorlike surfaces, or refractions through transparent objects.

The heart of a ray-tracing application is the set of routines that finds the intersections between rays and objects. A huge number of rays is cast to create a high-resolution image, and many of these rays spawn several secondary rays, so that much of the computation time is spent in finding intersections. Because each ray is tested against each object in the scene, the time required for ray tracing grows nearly linearly with the complexity of the scene. The judicious use of extents can quickly relieve a large number of objects from requiring a more complete intersection test, vastly speeding up the ray-tracing process.

Some object shapes are easy to ray trace, because finding their intersection with a ray is equivalent to solving a linear or quadratic equation. Typical among these are planes, spheres, cylinders, and cones. The scene designer starts with generic versions of each of these and transforms them into their desired sizes, orientations, and positions, using an affine transformation. This can change spheres into ellipsoids, cubes into parallelepipeds, and so forth, thereby greatly enlarging the class of objects that appears in the scene. It is also simple to model and ray trace any convex polyhedron, because its interior is merely the intersection of a number of half-spaces.

Ray tracing offers one of the most powerful approaches to computer-synthesized images today. Although the enormous amount of computation involved makes it one of the slower methods for image generation, the resulting images offer a degree of realism that is hard to match with any other technique.

Programming Exercises

18.47. Transforming the Ray. Write the routine *TransformRay*(tran : affine3D; Ray1 : ray; **var** Ray2 : ray) that applies the affine transformation *tran* to the ray *Ray1* to create the ray *Ray2*. Use the routine *Transform3D*( ) of Chapter 11. Keep in mind that only the position portion, **s**, of the ray undergoes the translation part of *tran*.

18.48. Displaying Signature Images in Text Mode. The signature of a scene is formed by storing in $A[i, j]$ an integer that identifies which object is hit first by the *i*, *j*-th ray. Instead of associating a color with each id and displaying $A[,]$ on a graphics terminal, one can associate a character with each id and display the signature on a text terminal! Write a program that uses *RaytraceID*( ) and displays signatures in this way.

18.49. Finding Changes in the Surface First Hit. One can process the array $A[i, j]$ and look for changes in the surface that is hit first by rays. A dot (or a character on a text display) is drawn at pixel (i, j) if the id of the surface is different there from the pixel to the left or above, that is, if $A[i, j] <> A[i - 1, j]$ or $A[i, j] <> A[i, j - 1]$. This produces "outlines" of the various objects. Extend the program in the previous exercise to do this.

18.50. Building *Ray_Plane*( ). Write the routine discussed in Section 18.6.1 that determines the hit time of a given ray and the generic plane.

18.51. Building *Ray_Cylinder*( ). Implement the routine discussed in Section 18.6.3 that determines whether a ray intersects the generic cylinder and, if so, at what time. Be sure to consider all situations.

18.52. Building *Ray_Cone*( ). Implement the routine discussed in Section 18.6.4 that determines whether a ray intersects the generic cone and, if so, at what time. Be sure to consider all situations.

18.53. Ray Tracing Stellations. Stellations of convex polyhedra are discussed in Exercise 18.21. Write a routine that determines the hit time between a given ray and the first stellation of a convex polyhedron.

18.54. Building Wireframes for Previewing. Implement a routine that constructs a wireframe model for each of the six generic primitives in type *generic_type* of Code Fragment 18.3. It returns an array, **array** [*generic_type*] **of** *wireframe*, for subsequent use when previewing scenes and building extents.

18.55. Building Projection Extents for Instances. Write and test a routine that computes the projection extent for each object on the object list.

18.56. Implementing *InShadow*( ). Write and test the function *InShadow*( ) discussed in Section 18.10, which will return *true* if any object lies between the given point and light source. Deal with any self-shadowing of the point.

18.57. Implementation of *Shade*( ). Flesh out the details of the recursive routine *Shade*( ) of Section 18.11, and compute several arrays, *A*[. , .], to test the full ray tracer.

18.58. Project: Scene Description Files. Devise a file format that can be used conveniently to describe a scene. The file should be able to be read by humans so that it can be prepared using a text editor, and it should be easy to interpret. Each object in the scene is described by its kind, its affine transformation, and its surface attributes. See Appendix 4 for an example format. How would a convex polyhedron be specified?

Write a small interpreter that can read a file in your chosen format and build the camera and object list. Exercise it on some scenes.

18.59. Project: The Monochromatic Ray Tracer. Use the implementation of *Shade*( ) worked out in a previous exercise to write the ray-tracing program described in Section 18.11 that produces monochromatic images of a scene.

18.60. The Interactive Ray Sprayer. Instead of devoting the time required to ray trace all the pixels on a screen, one might want to build the image in only certain portions. This is particularly useful during debugging. Write a routine that allows the user to specify (with a *Locctor*) a rectangular region on the screen. Then only those pixels lying within the rectangle will be ray traced. Allow the user to do this repeatedly, so that a succession of "interesting" regions of the image can be filled in.

18.61. Forming *RayInBox*( ). Implement the routine *RayInBox* of Section 18.10.

18.62. The Reflected and Refracted Directions. Write the procedures *Reflect*(. .) and *Refract*(. .) which compute the direction vector for the reflected ray and the refracted ray given the direction of the incoming ray, the surface normal direction, and the speed of light in the two media.

18.63. Program for Demonstrating Refraction in Two Dimensions. Because the formula for the refracted direction, **d**, in Equation 18.41 uses only dot products, it is equally correct for two-dimensional as for three-dimensional vectors. Write and exercise a program that generates pictures such as that in Figure 18.19. The user gives the index of refraction and the angle of incidence, and the program draws the incident and refracted rays.

18.64. Implementing *Combine*( ). Write and exercise the function discussed in Section 18.12.1:

function *Combine*(*L1*, *L2* : *t_list*; *op* : *operation*) : *t_list*;

which combines the two linked lists of sorted *t*-values, *L1* and *L2*, to form a new list of *t*-values.

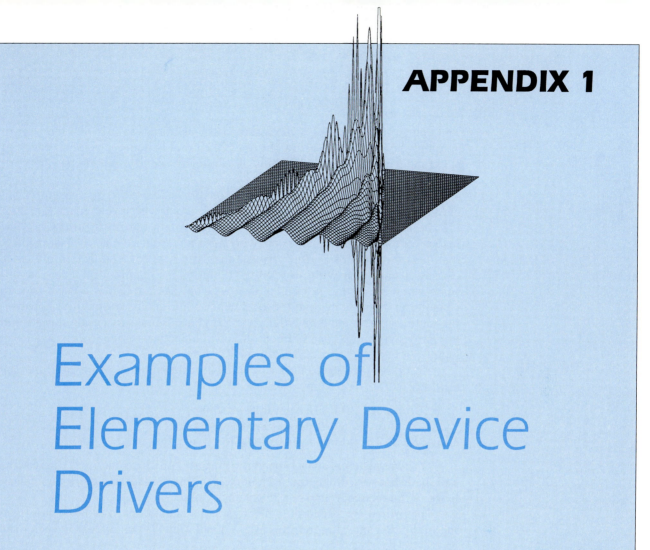

APPENDIX 1

Examples of Elementary Device Drivers

A1.1 Building Device Drivers

The first step in graphics is often the most frustrating: simply making a given graphics device display a straight line. Once this is done, it is much easier to experiment with other capabilities of the device, such as changing line attributes or displaying text.

This appendix attempts to facilitate the first step by offering the equivalent of *LineNDC()* for a variety of example devices, along with mechanisms for entering and exiting graphics mode. Devices tend to fall into different classes, (for instance, IBM personal computers with certain graphics cards, or laser printers that can interpret PostScript). Drivers are given here for a collection of device classes currently in wide use within the graphics community. There is still some variation among devices within a given class, and it is always wise to consult the device's manual (or local experts) for details. Hopefully, however, the routines presented here will at least provide guidance in getting started, and in many cases can be used directly to fashion a simple driver for the device at hand.

We present for each class of device an implementation of the three key routines:

Enter_Graphics;   {initialize graphics mode}
Exit_Graphics;   {return to text mode}
LineNDC();   {draw a line in NDC}

The two principal aspects of controlling a graphics device are (1) converting NDC to device coordinates and (2) sending the proper sequences of characters or bytes to the device to make it behave as desired.

The principles of coordinate conversions are summarized next, culminating in the two mapping routines *MapX()* and *MapY()* that appear in each driver.

A1.1.1 Proper Coordinate Conversions

Each graphics device has its own built-in coordinate system, and one of the goals of *LineNDC()* is to hide such details from higher-level drawing routines. *LineNDC()* converts NDC coordinates to device coordinates. As discussed in Chapter 2, we can choose to make *LineNDC()* either map all of NDC to the *largest square* within the display area or map a particular rectangular portion of NDC to the *entire* display area. Both choices will be considered.

We suppose, unless stated otherwise, that for each graphics device x ranges from 0 to some *Maxx* and y ranges from 0 to some *Maxy*, with (0,0) situated in the upper-left-hand corner, so that x increases to the right and y increases downward. We also suppose that the aspect ratio $R = Maxy/Maxx$ of the device is less than unity. Then there are two mappings of particular interest.

Using the Largest Square

Here all of NDC is mapped to the largest square on the display (see Figure 2.14): (0,0) in NDC maps to $((Maxx - Maxy)/2, Maxy)$ in device coordinates, and (1,1) maps to $((Maxx + Maxy)/2, 0)$ in device coordinates. This leads to the routine of Code Fragment 2.3, which implements

$$dx = trunc\left(Maxy * x + \frac{Maxx - Maxy}{2}\right)$$

$$dy = trunc(Maxy * (1 - y)) \qquad \text{(A1.1)}$$

converting the NDC position (x,y) to the device coordinate pair (dx,dy). *trunc* truncates the real value to the next lower integer. A *round* operation, if available, can replace *trunc*.

Using the Entire Display

Here the proper rectangular portion of NDC having aspect ratio R is mapped to the whole display space (similar to Equation 2.8). The whole display area can now be used, but the calling program must be aware of the device's aspect ratio and should not send any value of y that exceeds R. (0,0) in NDC maps to $(0,Maxy)$ in device coordinates, and $(1,R)$ in NDC maps to $(Maxx,0)$ in device coordinates. The mapping is then

$$dx = trunc(Maxx * x)$$

$$dy = trunc(Maxy - Maxx * y) \qquad \text{(A1.2)}$$

Both of these mappings produce dx as a function of x and dy as a function of y. Whichever mapping is chosen, it is convenient to implement the two resulting functions as

function MapX(x : real) : integer;
function MapY(y : real) : integer;

These functions will appear in each version of *LineNDC()* to be presented.

A1.1.2 Sending Control Sequences to the Device

How are devices controlled? In some cases, routines such as *Enter_Graphics* simply make low-level calls to routines that are available in a particular package. For instance, the Turbo Pascal[1] environment for the IBM-PC supports routines such as *initgraph()* and *line()* that control a built-in graphics card that, in turn, controls what is displayed on the screen. The version of *LineNDC()* to be given for the Turbo Pascal environment calls *line()* directly.

In other cases, the graphics device is a true peripheral device such as a plotter or laser printer, connected to the host through some communications link. In these cases, routines such as *LineNDC()* encode coordinate data and other information into special character sequences and send them to the device using a form of *writeln()* such as *writeln([dev], [sequence])*. Here *[dev]* denotes an external device or file, and *[sequence]* is the relevant sequence of characters. For example, if the graphics device is a plotter connected to the printer (the *lis*) port of an IBM-PC running Turbo Pascal, then the appropriate statement is *writeln(lis, [sequence])*.

Sometimes the device is not even connected to the host or is not currently available. Then it is appropriate for the graphics application to write *[sequence]* to a file, to be sent later to the device when it becomes available. The following code fragment shows a typical way to do this:

var *filepointer : text*; {pointer to text file}

---

[1]Turbo Pascal is a trademark of the Borland International Corp.

begin
  assign(filepointer, 'plotter.dat'); {create the file}
  rewrite(filepointer);   {prepare it for writing}
  .
  .
  .
  writeln(filepointer,[sequence]);
  .
  .
  .
  close(filepointer); {close up the file}

In the drivers to be presented, we use the simpler form of *writeln( )*.

Control sequences for peripheral devices often contain various special characters, such as the escape character *esc*, which represents a particular pattern of bits. For instance, a ReGIS-class device enters its graphics mode when it receives the three characters *esc*Pp.

Table A1.1 shows the ASCII[2] encoding of characters that is used by almost every device.

The ASCII representation for a character is found by adding its row number to the number at the top of its column. For example, the representation for the character A is 65. 65 written in binary form is 1000001. Similarly, *esc* is 27, which is equivalent to the binary code 0011011.

Table A1.1 The ASCII Code

	0	16	32	48	64	80	96	112
0	null	dle	sp	0	@	P	'	p
1	soh	dc1	!	1	A	Q	a	q
2	stx	dc2	"	2	B	R	b	r
3	etx	dc3	#	3	C	S	c	s
4	eot	dc4	$	4	D	T	d	t
5	enq	nak	%	5	E	U	e	u
6	ack	syn	&	6	F	V	f	v
7	bel	etb	'	7	G	W	g	w
8	bs	can	(	8	H	X	h	x
9	ht	em	)	9	I	Y	i	y
10	lf	sub	*	:	J	Z	j	z
11	vt	esc	+	;	K	[	k	{
12	ff	fs	,	<	L	\	l		
13	cr	gs	–	=	M	]	m	}
14	so	rs	.	>	N	^	n	~
15	si	us	/	?	O	_	o	del

[2]American Standard Code for Information Interchange.

A1.2 IBM-PC with Turbo Pascal

Several graphics cards are available for the IBM-PC and its many compatible variations. A given graphics card can also be placed in a variety of graphics modes. Turbo Pascal supports a range of these cards and modes, most of which are listed in the following table. (Here *MaxColor* describes the number of different colors that each mode can display.)

Name	Driver	Mode	MaxX	MaxY	MaxColor
cga lo	1	0	319	199	3
cga hi	1	2	639	199	1
ega lo	3	0	639	199	1
ega med	3	1	639	349	15
ega64 lo	4	0	639	199	15
ega64 hi	4	1	639	349	3
hercules	7	0	719	347	1
ATT lo	8	0	319	199	3
ATT med	8	2	639	199	1
ATT hi	8	3	639	399	1
vga lo	9	0	639	199	15
vga med	9	1	639	349	15
vga hi	9	2	639	479	15
PC3270	10	0	719	349	1

```
procedure Enter_Graphics(driver, mode : integer);
{assumes the proper driver file (e.g., EGAVGA.BGI) resides}
{in the current directory}
begin
    initgraph(driver,mode,'') {turbo routine}
end;
{ ------------------------------------------------------------------------}
procedure Exit_Graphics;
begin
    TextMode(c80) {turbo routine}
end;
{ ------------------------------------------------------------------------}
procedure lineNDC(p1, p2 : point);
{version for turbo Pascal on IBM-PC}
begin {calls Turbo routine line ()}
    line(MapX(p1.x), MapY(p1.y), MapX(p2.x), MapY(p2.y))
end;
```

A1.3 Macintosh Graphics

The various Pascal compilers for the Macintosh, such as Macintosh Pascal,[3] Turbo Pascal[4] and Lightspeed Pascal,[5] all use the powerful QuickDraw routines that are stored in read-only memory within the Macintosh. The procedures *Enter_Graphics* and *Exit_Graphics* are not needed if default settings are used. The built-in routines *MoveTo( )* and *LineTo( )* may be freely used in the active drawing window. (For Turbo Pascal begin with the statement "*uses Quick-draw.*" For Lightspeed Pascal include the line "*ShowDrawing*" to reveal the drawing window.) The upper left corner of this window has coordinates (0, 0) by default. The coordinates of its lower right corner depend on how large the default window is. Typical values are *Maxx* = 511 and *Maxy* = 341.

procedure *lineNDC(p1, p2 : point)*;
begin
   MoveTo(MapX(p1.x), MapY(p1.y));
   LineTo(MapX(p2.x), MapY(p2.y))
end;

A1.4 PostScript

PostScript[6] is a page description language that can be used to drive many graphics devices in use today. It is particularly effective for laser printers, many of which contain a microprocessor-based interpreter that can receive and translate PostScript commands into patterns of ink. See *Adobe Systems' PostScript Language Reference Manual* (Addison-Wesley Publishing Co., Reading, MA, 1985) for more information.

The default coordinate system places (0, 0) at the lower left corner of the page, with x increasing to the right and y increasing upward. One unit in this default space corresponds to $1/72$th of an inch (close to the size of the standard "point" in the printing industry, which is $1/72.27$th of an inch). *Maxx* and *Maxy* depend on the size and orientation of the page ("portrait" or "landscape"), and the desired margin.

Example: Suppose that the printer is to draw on standard 8½ by 11 inch paper in the usual portrait orientation, so that the 11-inch side is vertical. Further, suppose that we wish to map all of NDC into the largest possible square, centered on the page with a left and a right margin of ¼ inch, or *Xoffset* = $72/4$ = 18 units. This leaves 8 horizontal inches, or *Xwidth* = 8 × 72 = 576 units for drawing. The vertical center of the page is 5½ inches up from the bottom, so y = 0 must lie 4 inches below that, at *Yoffset* = 72 × (5.5 − 4) = 108 units. Thus the mapping from NDC to device units used in *MapX()* and *MapY()* is

$$dx = trunc(Xwidth * x + Xoffset)$$
$$dy = trunc(Xwidth * y + Yoffset)$$

(A1.3)

PostScript uses a "postfix" notation in which parameters precede the function. Hence to draw a line from the current position to the display position (124, 67), the string "124 67 lineto" would be sent to the PostScript device.

[3]By Think Technologies, Inc., and Apple Computer, Inc.
[4]By Borland International, Inc.
[5]By Symantec Corporation.
[6]PostScript is a trademark of Adobe Systems, Inc.

```
procedure Enter_Graphics;
{initialize the device and select font and font size}
begin
    writeln;
    writeln('%!PS-Adobe-1.0'); {not required by all printers}
    writeln('/Times-Roman findfont 12 scalefont setfont');
    {or you might use: '/Helvetica findfont 10 scalefont setfont'}
    writeln('0 0 moveto')
end;

{---------------------------------------------------------------------}
procedure Exit_Graphics;
{used to print and eject a complete page}
begin
    writeln('stroke');
    writeln('showpage')
end;
{---------------------------------------------------------------------}
procedure lineNDC(p1, p2 : point);
begin
    writeln(MapX(p1.x):4,' ',MapY(p1.y):4,' moveto');
    writeln(MapX(p2.x):4,' ',MapY(p2.y):4,' lineto');
end;
```

A1.5 ReGIS Devices

Several graphics devices manufactured by Digital Equipment Corporation, including the VT125, VT242, and VT340, support the ReGIS (Remote Graphics Instruction Set) protocol. ReGIS devices are controlled by character strings. For instance, to draw a line from device coordinates (23,149) to (214,465), one sends the string 'P[23,149]V[214,465]', where 'P' is the "position" indicator and 'V' is the "vector" indicator. For the VT240 $Maxx = 799$ and $Maxy = 479$.

```
procedure Enter_Graphics;
begin
    writeln(chr(27),'Pp') {esc, then upper- and lowercase p's}
end;
{---------------------------------------------------------------------}
procedure Exit_Graphics;
begin
    writeln(chr(27),'\')
end;
{---------------------------------------------------------------------}
procedure lineNDC(p1, p2 : point);
begin
    write('P[', MapX(p1.x):4,',', MapY(p1.y):4, '];');
    write('V[', MapX(p2.x):4, ',', MapY(p2.y):4, '];')
end;
```

A1.6 Tektronix 4000 Series Encoding

In the early days of graphics, Tektronix adopted an interesting encoding scheme that is used in many Tektronix plotters and display terminals. The device enters graphics mode when it receives the control character *gs* (29 in ASCII), and exits graphics mode upon receipt of *us* (31 in ASCII). For instance:

procedure *Enter_Graphics*;
begin
    write(*chr*(29)) {the *gs* character}
end;

Once in graphics mode, the device receives each (*x,y*) pair by means of four consecutive characters. (An abbreviated encoding format is also available, which we ignore here.) Receipt of a pair (*x,y*) causes the "beam" or "pen" to move to that pair. The beam or pen moves visibly—drawing the line—unless the pair directly follows a *gs* character, in which case it moves invisibly. Thus, to effect a *moveto*(), we resend *gs*, causing the device to reenter graphics mode.

Encoding Coordinates

The *x* and *y* values in a coordinate pair (*x,y*) range from 0 to 1,023. (On some devices, such as the Tektronix 4014, only values less than 780 are displayed, although those up to 1,023 are acceptable.) Values ranging from 0 to 1,023 can be represented by a 10-bit binary number.

Each 10-bit quantity is transmitted in two characters, called the **Hi** and **Low bytes,** each of which contains 5 data bits preceded by two "prefix bits." The prefix bits specify the meaning of the data bits. Bytes are transmitted in the order Hi *y*, Low *y*, Hi *x*, Low *x*. For example, the binary equivalent for the *y* coordinate value 205 is 0011001101. The 5 most significant bits 00110 go into the Hi *y* byte, and the other 5 bits 01101 go into the Low *y* byte. The accompanying table shows how the prefix bits determine the meaning of the data bits. (MSB = most significant bit; LSB = least significant bit.)

Hi and Low Bytes for *x,y* Coordinates

Type of Byte	Prefix	Data Bits
Hi *y*	01	5 MSBs for *y*
Low *y*	11	5 LSBs for *y*
Hi *x*	01	5 MSBs for *x*
Low *x*	10	5 LSBs for *x*

Example Encoding of an (x,y) Coordinate Pair

The following example shows how to cause a *lineto*() the *x,y* position (324,41).

- The *x* coordinate 324 is represented by the binary number 0101000100.

- The *y* coordinate 41 is represented by the binary number 0000101001.

Each binary number is divided into two 5-bit values, and the appropriate 2-bit prefixes are added. These are then transmitted as

Hi y	Low y	Hi x	Low x
0100001	1101001	0101010	1000100

These data are sent as the four separate characters !i*D, with no spaces between them.

The following code implements this encoding. (0,0) lies at the lower left hand corner, so $MapY()$ should be adjusted to produce $dy = trunc(Maxy * y)$ in Equation 1.1 and $dy = trunc(Maxx * y)$ in Equation 1.2.

```
procedure lineNDC(p1, p2 : point);
{------------------------------------------------------------------------}
procedure Tek_Encode(x,y : integer);
begin
   if (x > 1023) or (y > 1023) then ReportError {out of range}
   else begin
      write(lis, 32 + (y div 32)); {prefix + 5 MSBs of y}
      write(lis, 96 + (y mod 32)); {prefix + 5 LSBs of y}
      write(lis, 32 + (x div 32)); {prefix + 5 MSBs of x}
      write(lis, 64 + (x mod 32)) {prefix + 5 LSBs of x}
   end
end;
{------------------------------------------------------------------------}
begin {lineNDC}
   write(chr(29)); {gs: reenter graphics mode}
   Tek_Encode(MapX(p1.x), MapY(p1.y));
   Tek_Encode(MapX(p2.x), MapY(p2.y))
end; {lineNDC}
```

A1.7 HPGL (Hewlett-Packard Graphics Language)

Many devices from several manufacturers obey the HPGL protocol, including the LVP-16, HP7470A, HP7580, and HP7220 graphics plotters. Most HPGL instructions consist of two-letter mnemonics followed by numeric parameters.

```
const
   Maxx = 10000; {for HP7470A}
   Maxy = 7200;
{------------------------------------------------------------------------}
procedure Enter_Graphics;
{initialize plotter; set communications parameters}
begin
   write(chr(27),'.Y;'); {put plotter on-line}
   {send other "handshake" characters as required}
   write('IN;'); {initialize plotter}
   write('SP1;'); {select pen 1}
   writeln('PA;') {set plot mode to absolute}
end;
{------------------------------------------------------------------------}
```

```
procedure Exit_Graphics;
{turn plotter off}
begin
   writeln(chr(27),'.Z;')
end;
{--------------------------------------------------------------------------}
procedure lineNDC(p1, p2 : point);
begin
   writeln('PU ',MapX(p1.x),',',MapY(p1.y),';');
   writeln('PD ',MapX(p2.x),',',MapY(p2.y),';')
end;
```

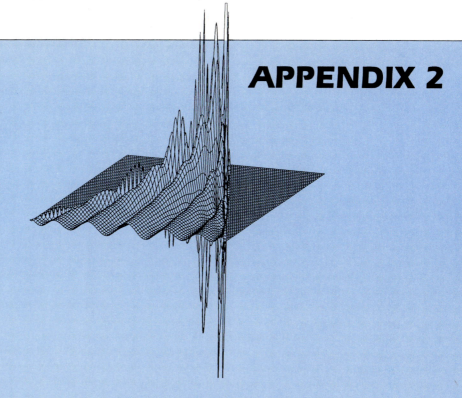

APPENDIX 2

Review of Matrix Algebra

A2.1 Some Key Definitions

In this appendix, we review some fundamental concepts of matrices and ways to manipulate them, with emphasis on the ways they are used in graphics. More general treatments are available in many books (for instance, Birkhoff and MacLane 1965, Faux and Pratt 1979).

A **matrix** is a rectangular array of elements. The elements are most commonly numbers. A matrix with m rows and n columns is said to be an $m \times n$ matrix. As an example,

$$A = \begin{bmatrix} 3 & 2 & -5 \\ -1 & 8 & 0 \\ 6 & 3 & 9 \\ 1 & 21 & 2 \end{bmatrix} \tag{A2.1}$$

is a 4×3 matrix of integers and

$$B = [1.34, -6.275, 0.0, 81.6] \tag{A2.2}$$

is a 1×4 matrix, also called a "4-tuple" or a **vector** (see Chapter 7). In common parlance, a $1 \times n$ matrix is a **row vector,** and an $n \times 1$ matrix is a **column vector.**

The individual elements of a matrix are conventionally given lowercase symbols and are distinguished by subscripts: The ijth element of matrix B is denoted as b_{ij}. This is the element in the ith row and jth column, so for matrix A above, $a_{32} = 3$.

A matrix is **square** if it has the same number of rows as columns. In graphics we frequently work with 2×2, 3×3, and 4×4 matrices (see Chapter 11). Two common square matrices are the **zero matrix** and the **identity matrix.** All of the elements of the zero matrix are zero. All are zero for the identity matrix too, except those along the **main diagonal** (those elements a_{ij} for which $i = j$), which have value 1. The 3×3 identity matrix is therefore given by

$$I = \begin{bmatrix} 1 & 0 & 0 \\ 0 & 1 & 0 \\ 0 & 0 & 1 \end{bmatrix} \tag{A2.3}$$

A2.1.1 Manipulations with Matrices

A matrix B of numbers may be **scaled** by a number s. Each element of B is multiplied by s. The resulting matrix is denoted sB. For the preceding example matrix, for instance,

$$6A = \begin{bmatrix} 18 & 12 & -30 \\ -6 & 48 & 0 \\ 36 & 18 & 54 \\ 6 & 126 & 12 \end{bmatrix} \tag{A2.4}$$

Two matrices C and D having the same number of rows and columns are said to have the same **shape.** They may be added together. The ijth element of the sum $E = C + D$ is simply the sum of the corresponding elements: $e_{ij} = c_{ij} + d_{ij}$. Thus:

$$
\begin{bmatrix} 3 & 2 & -5 \\ -1 & 8 & 0 \\ 6 & 3 & 9 \\ 1 & 21 & 2 \end{bmatrix} + \begin{bmatrix} 0 & 5 & -1 \\ 9 & 8 & -3 \\ 2 & 6 & 18 \\ 4 & 2 & 7 \end{bmatrix} = \begin{bmatrix} 3 & 7 & -6 \\ 8 & 16 & -3 \\ 8 & 9 & 27 \\ 5 & 23 & 9 \end{bmatrix} \tag{A2.5}
$$

Since matrices can be scaled and added, it is meaningful to define **linear combinations** of matrices (of the same shape), such as $2A - 4B$. The following facts about three matrices A, B, and C of the same shape result directly from these definitions:

$$A + B = B + A \tag{A2.6}$$
$$A + (B + C) = (A + B) + C$$
$$(f + g)(A + B) = fA + fB + gA + gB \tag{A2.7}$$

The **transpose** of a matrix M, denoted M^T, is formed by interchanging the rows and columns of M: the ijth element of M^T is the jith element of M. Thus the transpose of A in Equation A2.1 is

$$
A^T = \begin{bmatrix} 3 & -1 & 6 & 1 \\ 2 & 8 & 3 & 21 \\ -5 & 0 & 9 & 2 \end{bmatrix} \tag{A2.8}
$$

The transpose of a row vector is a column vector. A matrix is **symmetric** if it is identical to its own transpose. Only square matrices can be symmetric. Thus an $n \times n$ matrix M is symmetric if $m_{ij} = m_{ji}$ for i and j between 1 and n.

A2.1.2 Multiplying Two Matrices

The transformations discussed in Chapter 11 involve multiplying a vector by a matrix and multiplying two matrices together. The first is a special case of the second.

The product AB of two matrices A and B is defined only if the matrices **conform**: if the number of columns of the first matrix, A, equals the number of rows of the second one, B. Thus if A is 3×5 and B is 5×2, then AB is defined but BA is not. Each term of the product $C = AB$ of A with B is simply the dot product (recall Chapter 7) of some row of A with some column of B. Specifically, the ijth element c_{ij} of the product is the dot product of the ith row of A with the jth column of B. Thus the product of an $n \times m$ matrix with an $m \times r$ matrix is an $n \times r$ matrix. For example:

$$
\begin{bmatrix} 2 & 0 & 6 & -3 \\ 8 & 1 & -4 & 0 \\ 0 & 5 & 7 & 1 \end{bmatrix} \begin{bmatrix} 6 & 2 \\ -1 & 1 \\ 3 & 1 \\ -5 & 8 \end{bmatrix} = \begin{bmatrix} 45 & -14 \\ 35 & 13 \\ 11 & 20 \end{bmatrix} \tag{A2.9}
$$

Here, for instance, $c_{12} = -14$, since $(2, 0, 6, -3) \cdot (2, 1, 1, 8) = -14$. A routine to multiply square matrices is given in Appendix 3. It is easily extended to find the product of any two matrices that conform.

We list some useful properties of matrix multiplication. Assume that matrices A, B, and C conform properly. Then

$$\begin{aligned}
(AB)C &= A(BC) \\
A(B + C) &= AB + AC \\
(A + B)C &= AC + BC \\
A(sB) &= sAB
\end{aligned} \tag{A2.10}$$

where s is a number.

When forming a product of two matrices A and B, the order in which they are taken makes a difference. For the expression AB, we say "A **premultiplies** B" or "A is **postmultiplied** by B." If A and B are both square matrices of the same size they conform both ways, so AB and BA are both well defined (why?), but the two products may contain different elements. If $AB = BA$ for two matrices, we say that they **commute.** (Do two symmetric matrices always commute?)

Multiplying a Vector by a Matrix

A special case of matrix multiplication occurs when one of the matrices is a row vector or column vector. In graphics we often see a row vector $\mathbf{v}$ being postmultiplied by a matrix, M, in the form $\mathbf{v}M$. For example, let $\mathbf{v} = (3, -1, 7)$ and

$$M = \begin{bmatrix} 2 & 0 & 6 \\ 8 & 1 & -4 \\ 0 & 5 & 7 \end{bmatrix} \tag{A2.11}$$

Then $\mathbf{v}$ conforms with M, and we can form

$$\mathbf{v}M = (3, -1, 7) \begin{bmatrix} 2 & 0 & 6 \\ 8 & 1 & -4 \\ 0 & 5 & 7 \end{bmatrix} = (-2, 34, 71) \tag{A2.12}$$

By the same rules as those given previously, each component of $\mathbf{v}M$ is the dot product of $\mathbf{c}$ and the appropriate column of M. One can also postmultiply a matrix by a column vector $\mathbf{w}$, as in

$$M\mathbf{w} = \begin{bmatrix} 2 & 0 & 6 \\ 8 & 1 & -4 \\ 0 & 5 & 7 \end{bmatrix} \begin{bmatrix} 2 \\ 5 \\ -3 \end{bmatrix} = \begin{bmatrix} -14 \\ 33 \\ 4 \end{bmatrix} \tag{A2.13}$$

The Dot and Cross Products Revisited

It is useful in some analytical derivations (see, for example, Section 11.10) to write the dot product $\mathbf{a} \cdot \mathbf{b}$ of two n-tuples as a vector times a matrix. Simply view vector $\mathbf{b}$ as a row matrix, and transpose it to form the $n \times 1$ column matrix $\mathbf{b}^T$. Then

$$\mathbf{a} \cdot \mathbf{b} = \mathbf{a}\mathbf{b}^T \tag{A2.14}$$

By the same reasoning, $\mathbf{a} \cdot \mathbf{b} = \mathbf{b}\mathbf{a}^T$.

Similarly, the cross product of two 3-tuples $\mathbf{a} \times \mathbf{b}$ may be written as the product

$$\mathbf{a} \times \mathbf{b} = (a_1, a_2, a_3) \begin{bmatrix} 0 & -b_3 & b_2 \\ b_3 & 0 & -b_1 \\ -b_2 & b_1 & 0 \end{bmatrix} \qquad \text{(A2.15)}$$

This form also proves useful when deriving various results.

A2.1.3 Partitioning a Matrix

It is sometimes convenient to subdivide a matrix into blocks of elements and to give names to the various blocks. For example,

$$M = \begin{bmatrix} 2 & 0 & 6 \\ 8 & 1 & -4 \\ 3 & 2 & 7 \end{bmatrix} = \left[\begin{array}{c|c} M_1 & M_2 \\ \hline M_3 & M_4 \end{array} \right]$$

where the blocks are identified as:

$$M_1 = \begin{bmatrix} 2 & 0 \\ 8 & 1 \end{bmatrix}, \ M_2 = \begin{bmatrix} 6 \\ -4 \end{bmatrix}, \ M_3 = \begin{bmatrix} 3 & 2 \end{bmatrix}$$

and M_4 consists of the single element 7. This is called a **partition** of M into the four blocks shown. Note that when one block is positioned above another, the two blocks must have the same number of columns. Similarly, when two blocks lie side by side, they must have the same number of rows. Two matrices that have been partitioned in the same way (corresponding blocks have the same shape) may be added by performing these operations on the blocks. To transpose a partitioned matrix, transpose each block individually and then transpose the arrangement of blocks. For instance:

$$\left[\begin{array}{c|c} M_1 & M_2 \\ \hline M_3 & M_4 \end{array} \right]^T = \left[\begin{array}{c|c} M_1{}^T & M_3{}^T \\ \hline M_2{}^T & M_4{}^T \end{array} \right]$$

A2.1.4 The Determinant of a Matrix

Every square matrix M has a number associated with it called its **determinant** and denoted by $|M|$. As discussed in Chapters 7 and 11, the determinant describes the volume of certain geometric shapes and provides information concerning the effect that a linear transformation has on areas and volumes of objects.

For a 2×2 matrix M, the determinant is simply the difference of two products:

$$|M| = \begin{vmatrix} m_{11} & m_{12} \\ m_{21} & m_{22} \end{vmatrix} = m_{11}m_{22} - m_{12}m_{21} \qquad \text{(A2.16)}$$

If M is a 3×3 matrix its determinant has the form

$$|M| = \begin{vmatrix} m_{11} & m_{12} & m_{13} \\ m_{21} & m_{22} & m_{23} \\ m_{31} & m_{32} & m_{33} \end{vmatrix} = m_{11} \begin{vmatrix} m_{22} & m_{23} \\ m_{32} & m_{33} \end{vmatrix} - m_{12} \begin{vmatrix} m_{21} & m_{23} \\ m_{31} & m_{33} \end{vmatrix} + m_{13} \begin{vmatrix} m_{21} & m_{22} \\ m_{31} & m_{32} \end{vmatrix}$$

$$\text{(A2.17)}$$

For example:

$$\begin{vmatrix} 2 & 0 & 6 \\ 8 & 1 & -4 \\ 0 & 5 & 7 \end{vmatrix} = 294 \qquad \text{(A2.18)}$$

Note that $|M|$ here is the sum of three terms: $m_{11}M_{11} + m_{12}M_{12} + m_{13}M_{13}$, so it has the form of a dot product: $|M| = (m_{11}, m_{12}, m_{13}) \cdot (M_{11}, M_{12}, M_{13})$. What are the M_{ij} terms? M_{ij} is called the cofactor of element m_{ij} for matrix M. We see cofactors emerging again when finding the inverse of a matrix, so it is convenient to define them formally.

Definition

Each element m_{ij} of a square matrix M has a corresponding **cofactor** M_{ij}. M_{ij} is $(-1)^{i+j}$ times the determinant of the matrix formed by deleting the ith row and the jth column from M.

Note that as one moves along a row or column, the value of $(-1)^{i+j}$ alternates between 1 and -1. One can visualize a checkerboard pattern of 1's and -1's distributed over the matrix.

The general rule for finding the determinant $|M|$ of any $n \times n$ matrix M is: Pick any row of M, find the cofactor of each element in the row, and take the dot product of the row and the n-tuple of cofactors. Alternatively, pick a column of M and do the same thing. (Does this rule hold for a 2×2 matrix as well?)

Some useful properties of determinants are as follows:

- $|M| = |M^T|$.

- If two rows (or two columns) of M are identical, $|M| = 0$.

- If M and B are both $n \times n$, then $|MB| = |M||B|$.

- If B is formed from M by interchanging two rows (or columns) of M, then $|B| = -|M|$.

- If B is formed from M by multiplying one row (or column) of M by a constant k, then $|B| = k|M|$.

- If B is formed from M by adding a multiple of one row (or column) of M to another, then $|B| = |M|$.

A2.1.5 The Inverse of a Matrix

An $n \times n$ matrix M is said to be **nonsingular** whenever $|M| \neq 0$. In this case, M has an **inverse,** denoted M^{-1}, that has the property

$$MM^{-1} = M^{-1}M = I \qquad \text{(A2.19)}$$

where I is the $n \times n$ identity matrix.

It is simple to specify the elements of M^{-1} in terms of cofactors of M:

Rule for Finding the Inverse of M: Denote the inverse of M by A. Then A has $ijth$ element

$$a_{ij} = \frac{M_{ji}}{|M|} \tag{A2.20}$$

That is, find the cofactor of the term m_{ji} and divide it by the determinant of the whole matrix. Carefully note the subscripts here: The cofactor of m_{ji} is used when determining a_{ij}. An equivalent procedure is as follows:

1. Build an intermediate matrix C of cofactors: $c_{ij} = M_{ij}$;

2. Find $|M|$ as the dot product of any row of C with the corresponding row of M;

3. Transpose C to get C^T;

4. Scale each element of C^T by $1/|M|$ to form M^{-1}.

Example

Find the inverse of

$$M = \begin{bmatrix} 2 & 0 & 6 \\ 8 & 1 & -4 \\ 0 & 5 & 7 \end{bmatrix} \tag{A2.21}$$

Solution

Build the matrix C of cofactors of M:

$$\begin{bmatrix} 27 & -56 & 40 \\ 30 & 14 & -10 \\ -6 & 56 & 2 \end{bmatrix}$$

Find $|M|$ as $(2,0,6) \cdot (27,-56,40) = 294$. Transpose C and scale each element by $1/|M|$ to obtain

$$M^{-1} = \frac{1}{294} \begin{bmatrix} 27 & 30 & -6 \\ -56 & 14 & 56 \\ 40 & -10 & 2 \end{bmatrix} \tag{A2.22}$$

Check this by multiplying out MM^{-1} and $M^{-1}M$.

The inverse is often used to solve a **set of linear equations:**

$$(x_1, x_2, \ldots, x_n)M = (b_1, b_2, \ldots, b_n) \tag{A2.23}$$

where an $n \times n$ matrix M is given, along with the row vector **b,** and it is necessary to find the row vector **x** that causes all n of the equations to be satisfied simultaneously. If M is nonsingular, the solution may be found as

$$\mathbf{x} = \mathbf{b}M^{-1} \tag{A2.24}$$

Note: Although the use of row vectors is more natural in graphics when composing several affine transformations (see Chapter 11), in certain fields it is more common to use column vectors and to write this same set of equations as

$$N \begin{bmatrix} x_1 \\ x_2 \\ \vdots \\ x_n \end{bmatrix} = \begin{bmatrix} b_1 \\ b_2 \\ \vdots \\ b_n \end{bmatrix} \tag{A2.25}$$

It is not difficult to show that this is the same set of equations as the previous ones, when $N = M^T$.

Orthogonal Matrices

For some transformations such as rotations (see Chapter 11), the associated matrix has an inverse that is particularly easy to find. A matrix M is called **orthogonal** if simply transposing it produces its inverse: $M^T = M^{-1}$. Therefore $MM^T = I$. For example, the matrix in Equation 11.65 is orthogonal. If M is orthogonal, $MM^T = I$ implies that each of its rows is a unit length vector and that the rows are mutually orthogonal. The same is true for its columns (why?). For instance, if M is 3×3, partition it into three rows as follows:

$$M = \begin{bmatrix} \mathbf{a} \\ -- \\ \mathbf{b} \\ -- \\ \mathbf{c} \end{bmatrix} \tag{A2.26}$$

Then the 3-tuples $\mathbf{a}$, $\mathbf{b}$, and $\mathbf{c}$ are each of unit length, and $\mathbf{a} \cdot \mathbf{b} = \mathbf{a} \cdot \mathbf{c} = \mathbf{b} \cdot \mathbf{c} = 0$.

Exercises

2.1. Multiplying by I. Show that the product of any matrix A and the (conforming) identity matrix yields A again.

2.2. Extending the Matrix Multiply Routine. Adjust the routine **procedure** *MatMult*() of Appendix 3 so that it can form the product of any two conforming matrices.

2.3. Practice with Multiplication. Form all possible products (e.g., *AB, BA, AC*) of the following matrices when it is meaningful to do so:

$$A = \begin{bmatrix} 2 & 0 & 6 & 8 \\ 8 & 1 & -4 & 0 \\ 0 & 5 & 7 & 2 \end{bmatrix}$$

$$B = \begin{bmatrix} 2 & 0 \\ 8 & 1 \\ 0 & 5 \end{bmatrix}$$

$$C = \begin{bmatrix} 2 & 0 & 6 \\ 8 & 1 & -4 \\ 0 & 5 & 7 \end{bmatrix}$$

$$D = \begin{bmatrix} 1 & 0 & 6 \\ 5 & 6 & -2 \\ -3 & 1 & 3 \end{bmatrix}$$

In particular, note whether $CD = DC$.

2.4. Nulling Out. The product of two nonzero matrices can be the zero matrix. Find a 2×2 matrix A such that $AB = 0$ where

$$B = \begin{bmatrix} 2 & -2 \\ -1 & 2 \end{bmatrix}$$

2.5. Solving Sets of Linear Equations. Show that Equation A2.24 and Equation A2.25 represent the same set of equations whenever $N = M^T$.

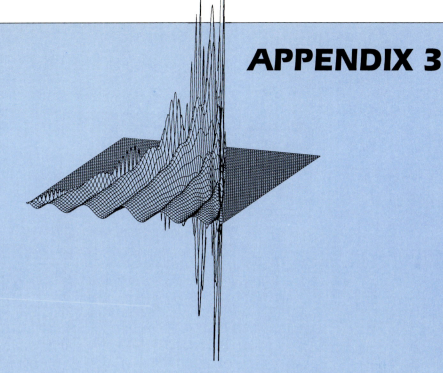

APPENDIX 3

Summary of Pascal Data Types

A3.1   Pascal Data Types

In this appendix, we gather together the important data types and declarations used throughout the text. We also include a listing of several important functions and procedures used in the text.

{Important Constants}
const

PI	= 3.141592654;
TWOPI	= 6.283185308;
PHI	= 1.618033989; {the golden ratio}
DEG_PER_RAD	= 57.2957795 ; {radians to degrees}
RAD_PER_DEG	= 0.01745329 ; {degrees to radians}

{The following constants are device or application dependent}

MAXNUM	= 100	; {used for various array lengths}
MAXNUMVERTS	= 100	; {max number of vertices in a model}
MAXNUMEDGES	= 150	; {max number of edges in a model}
MAX_VERTS_IN_FACE	= 10	; {max number of vertices in a face}
NUMBUTTONS	= 4	; {number of available input buttons}
MAXCOLUMN	= 639	; {largest column in raster}
MAXROW	= 479	; {largest row in raster}
MAXSIZE	= 1024	; {max number of pixels in a bitmap}
MAXCOLOR	= 255	; {largest color index in raster display}
TILE_SIZE	= 16	; {length of tiling pattern row}

{TYPE Declarations}
type
```
    button = 1.. NUMBUTTONS;
    col    = 0..MAXCOLUMN;
    row    = 0..MAXROW;
    color  = 0..MAXCOLOR;
    pixel  = record
                  x : col;
                  y : row
             end;
    map_ptr = ^bitmap;
    bitmap = record
                  nrows, ncols : integer; {bitmap size}
                  pix : array[1..MAXSIZE] of color
             end;
    pixrect = record {rectangle on screen}
                  l : col; t : row; {upper left}
                  r : col; b : row {lower right}
             end;
    color_triple = record
                       red, green, blue : real
                  end;
    signature = array[0..MAXCOLUMN, 0..MAXROW] of integer;
    grayscale = array[0..MAXCOLUMN, 0..MAXROW] of real;
    fullcolor = array[0..MAXCOLUMN, 0..MAXROW] of color_triple;
    tile = array[1..TILE_SIZE, 1..TILE_SIZE] of color;
```

```
point = record
          x, y : real
        end;
point3D = record
            x, y, z : real
          end;
point4D = record
            x, y, z, w : real
          end;
vector = record
           dx, dy : real
         end;
vector3D = record
             dx, dy, dz : real
           end;
rect = record
         l, t, r, b : real
       end;
line = record
         norm : vector;
         d : real;
       end;
ray = record
        start, dir : vector3D
      end;
line_list = record
              num : 0..MAXNUMEDGES;
              edge : array[1..MAXNUMEDGES] of line
            end;
spot = record
         id : integer;
         kind : (intersection, vertex);
         x, y : real ; {location}
         visited : boolean
       end;
plane = record
          normal : vector3D; {outward pointing normal}
          d : real              {position of face}
        end;
range = record
          min, max : real
        end;
matrix3 = array[1..3, 1..3] of real;
affine = record
           mat : array[1..2, 1..2] of real;
           tr : vector
         end;
affine3D = record
             mat : array[1..3, 1..3] of real;
             tr : vector3D
           end;
```

```
wireframe = record
                numverts : 0..MAXNUMVERTS;
                vert : array[1..MAXNUMVERTS] of point3D;
                numedge : 0..MAXNUMEDGES;
                edge : array[1..MAXNUMEDGES] of
                        array[1..2] of 0..MAXNUMVERTS
           end;
VertexPointer = ^VertexNode;
VertexNode = record
                x, y, z : real;
                next : VertexPointer
             end;
face_ptr = ^face;
face = record
          vert : VertexPointer;
          face_plane : plane;
          nature : attributes;
          next : face_ptr
       end;
cuboid = record
                l, t, r, b, near, far : real
         end;
face_info = record
                num_verts : 0..MAX_VERTS_IN_FACE;
                verts : array[1..MAX_VERTS_IN_FACE] of 0..MAXNUMVERTS;
                nature : attributes; {surface info, etc.}
                face_plane : plane; {plane of face}
                extent : cuboid {bounding box of face}
            end;
edge_ptr = ^edge_info;
edge_info = record
                y_upper : row;       {y at upper endpoint}
                x_int : real;        {x-value of intersection}
                recip_slope : real; {1/m}
                next : edge_ptr      {to next one}
            end;
e_ptr = ^edge_data;
edge_data = record
                face : face_ptr;   {face owning the edge}
                y_upper : row;     {y at upper endpoint}
                x_int : real;      {x-value of intersection}
                inv_slope : real; {reciprocal of slope}
                depth : real;      {of point on face}
                next : e_ptr {to next one}
            end;
sequence = record
                num : 0..MAXNUM;
                values : array[1..MAXNUM] of real
           end;
polypoint = record
                num : 0..MAXNUM;
```

```
                    pt : array[1..MAXNUM] of point
                 end;
   polypoint3D = record
                        NumVerts : 0..MAXNUM;
                        pt : array[1..MAXNUM] of point3D
                     end;
   polypixel = record
                   num : 0..MAXNUMVERTS;
                   pt : array[1..MAXNUMVERTS] of pixel
                end;
   generic_type = (sphere, cone, cylinder, cube, square, plane, polyh);
   generic_wireframes = array[generic_type] of wireframe;
   object_ptr = ^object;
   object = record
               center : point;
               Info : {. . . . other data};
               next : object_ptr
            end;
   obj_ptr = ^instance;
   instance = record
                  kind     : generic_type; {which kind}
                  transf   : affine3D;      {instance transform}
                  itransf  : affine3D;      {inverse transform}
                  nature   : attributes;    {id, or surface properties}
                  p_extent : rect;          {projection extent}
                  planes   : plane_list;    {planes if kind = convex_poly}
                  normal   : vector3D;      {normal to surface at hit spot}
                  extent   : cuboid;        {for box extent}
                  next     : obj_ptr
               end;
   polyptr = ^polylink; {for polyline editor}
   vertptr = ^vert;
   polylink = record
                  start : vertptr;
                  next : polyptr
              end;
   vert = record
              vertex : point;
              next : vertptr
          end;
   menu_ptr = ^menu_item;
   menu_item = record
                   id : integer; {the item's ID}
                   box : rect; {the item's bounding box}
                   next : menu_ptr; {point to next item in list}
                   case kind : (text,icon) of
                      text : (word : string; {item's text string}
                               height,width : real; {character size}
                               corner : point); {where to draw it}
                      icon : (poly : polylink) {where to find polylines}
                end;
```

```
edge = record
          first, second : integer
       end;
edgearray = record
               NumEdges : 0..MAXNUM;
               ed : array[1..MAXNUM] of edge
            end;
VisVertPtr = ^VisVert;
VisVert = record
             model_pt : point3D;
             view_pt : point4D;
             next : VisVertPtr
          end;
EdgePointer = ^EdgeNode;
EdgeNode = record
              first, second : VertexPointer;
              next : EdgePointer
           end;
axis = (x, y, z);
norm_transf = record
                 window, viewport : rect;
                 tran : affine
              end;
```

A3.2 Some Utility Functions in Pascal

A variety of utility routines are given here in Pascal to assist in program development. These include several vector routines, procedures to multiply two matrices, Quicksort, and some random number generators.

```
procedure ReportError;
{This is a catchall routine for a variety of
error-reporting routines. Insert appropriate message.}
begin
   writeln('Error has occurred in <. . . . .>')
end;
{------------------------------------------------------------------------}
procedure Extremes(s : sequence; var min, max : real);
   {find largest and smallest values in a sequence}
var i : integer;
begin
   with s do begin
     if num = 0 then ReportError {no data}
     else begin
       min := values[1]; max := min;
       if num > 1 then for i := 2 to num do
       begin {test other values}
         if values[i] < min then min := values[i];
         if values[i] > max then max := values[i]
       end {for}
     end {else}
```

```pascal
      end {with}
   end;
{-----------------------------------------------------------------------}
   procedure set_pt(var pt : point3D; x, y, z : real);
      {set pt fields to x, y, z}
   begin
      pt.x := x; pt.y := y; pt.z := z
   end;
{-----------------------------------------------------------------------}
   procedure SetRect(left, top, right, bot : real; var wind : rect);
   {set boundary of rectangle}
   begin
      wind.l := left; wind.t := top;
      wind.r := right; wind.b := bot
   end;
{----------------------VECTOR ROUTINES----------------------}
   function Length(v : vector) : real;
      {find norm of vector v}
   begin
      Length := sqrt(v.dx * v.dx + v.dy * v.dy)
   end;
{-----------------------------------------------------------------------}
   procedure Scale(v : vector; r : real; var ans : vector);
   {scale vector v by r to build vector ans}
   begin
      ans.dx := r * v.dx;
      ans.dy := r * v.dy
   end;
{-----------------------------------------------------------------------}
   procedure Normalize(v : vector; var ans : vector);
   {normalizes vector v to produce vector ans}
   {uses Length()}
   var len, r : real;
   begin
      len := Length(v);
      if len = 0.0 then writeln('zero vector in Normalize()')
      else begin
         ans.dx := v.dx / len;
         ans.dy := v.dy / len
      end
   end;
{-----------------------------------------------------------------------}
   function Dot(a, b : vector) : real;
   begin
      Dot := a.dx * b.dx + a.dy * b.dy
   end;
{-----------------------------------------------------------------------}
   function Dot3D(a, b : vector3D) : real;
   begin
      Dot3D := a.dx * b.dx + a.dy * b.dy + a.dz * b.dz
   end;
{-----------------------------------------------------------------------}
```

```
procedure Cross(a, b : vector3D; var c : vector3D);
{build cross product c = a × b}
begin
  c.dx := a.dy * b.dz − a.dz * b.dy;
  c.dy := a.dz * b.dx − a.dx * b.dz;
  c.dz := a.dx * b.dy − a.dy * b.dx
end;
{ ----------------MATRIX MULTIPLICATION ---------------- }

type
  matrix = array[1..N, 1..N] of real;
  {set N to the desired value}
procedure MatMult(A, B : matrix; var C : matrix);
{multiply N by N matrices A and B to form C : C = A * B.}
var
  i, j, k : integer;
  sum : real;
begin
  for i := 1 to N do
  for j := 1 to N do
  begin
    sum := 0.0;
    for k := 1 to N do sum := sum + A[i, k] * B[k, j];
    C[i, j] := sum
  end
end;
```

A3.2.1 Sorting an Array of Values

Qsort() uses the Quicksort algorithm to sort an array of values. *arr* is of type *arr* = **array**[MIN..MAX] **of** *values*, where *values* is set to one the types *integer*, *real*, or *char*. Example: To sort the array M : **array**[1..num] **of** *real*, use **type** *values* = *real* and call *Qsort(M,1,num)*.

```
procedure Qsort(var L : arr; lo, hi : integer);
var
  i, j : integer;
  mid, tmp : values;
begin
  i := lo; j := hi;
  mid := L[(lo + hi) div 2] ; {choose pivot}
  repeat
    while L[i] < mid do i := i + 1;
    while mid < L[j] do j := j − 1;
    if i <= j then
    begin {swap ith and jth}
      tmp := L[i]; L[i] := L[j]; L[j] := tmp;
      i := i + 1; j := j − 1
    end;
  until i > j;
  if lo < j then Qsort(L, lo, j); {sort left half}
  if i < hi then Qsort(L, i,hi) {sort right half}
end;
```

A3.2.2 Random Number Generators

Each time *GetRand* is called, a new random value between 0 and 1 is returned, apparently unrelated to all previous values. In actuality, the sequence of values generated by *GetRand* is "pseudorandom" rather than strictly random, as each value in the sequence depends in a perfectly deterministic way on two previously computed values, the 5th and 17th most recent values (Marsaglia 1983). (It is no coincidence that these are two Fibonacci numbers!) This generator passes stringent statistical tests, producing uncorrelated random values that take on any value between 0 and 1 with equal probability. Extraordinarily long sequences of values are generated before the sequence repeats, and no noticeable patterns have been observed in the sequences.

Before *GetRand* is called the first time, the user sets the global "seed" variable *the_seed* to any integer value desired and then calls *InitRand* once to establish the necessary 17-tuple of values. Thereafter the "random sequence" is completely determined (but, of course, appears random). The same sequence can be generated by calling *InitRand* again with the same seed. A different sequence results if a different seed is used.

Sometimes it is desired to generate integer random values in the range $0..(vmax - 1)$. To accomplish this use $trunc(vmax * GetRand)$.

```
{------global quantities for random number generator------}
const MODULUS = 32767;
var
  the_seed : integer;
  ranlist : array[1..17] of integer;   {global list}
  i_ran, j_ran : integer;              {global indices}
{-------------------------------------------------------------------------}
procedure InitRand;
{loads random values into global array ranlist[]}
var
  i : integer;
  all_even : boolean;
begin
  all_even := true;
  repeat {try until one or more values are odd}
    for i := 1 to 17 do {load array}
    begin
      the_seed := (the_seed * 2743 + 5923) mod MODULUS;
      {adjust if value "overflowed" capacity of an integer:}
      if the_seed < 0 then the_seed := the_seed + MODULUS;
      if odd(the_seed) then all_even := false;
      ranlist[i] := the_seed
    end
  until not all_even;
  i_ran := 17; j_ran :=5;
end;
{-------------------------------------------------------------------------}
function GetRand : real;
{generate a random number in the range 0.0 to 1.0}
{use global ranlist, i_ran, and j_ran}
var t, randnum : integer;
```

```
begin
  randnum := (ranlist[i_ran] + ranlist[j_ran]) mod MODULUS;
  if randnum < 0 then randnum := randnum + MODULUS;
  ranlist[i_ran] := randnum;
  i_ran := i_ran − 1; if i_ran = 0 then i_ran := 17;
  j_ran := j_ran − 1; if j_ran = 0 then j_ran := 17;
  Getrand := randnum / MODULUS
end; {GetRand}
```

Gaussian Random Number Generator

Gauss returns an approximately normally distributed (i.e., gaussian) random value with a mean of 0 and a standard deviation of 1. It adds together 12 independent, uniformly distributed random values using the routine *GetRand*. (Call *InitRand* only once before using *Gauss*, not before each call to *Gauss*.) To produce a gaussian random number with mean M and standard deviation S, simply scale *Gauss* by S and then add M.

```
function Gauss : real;
{return a gaussian random number with mean 0 and std. dev. 1}
var
  i : integer;
  v : real;
begin
  v := 0.0;
  for i := 1 to 12 do v := v + GetRand;
  Gauss := v − 6.0 {set mean to 0}
end;
```

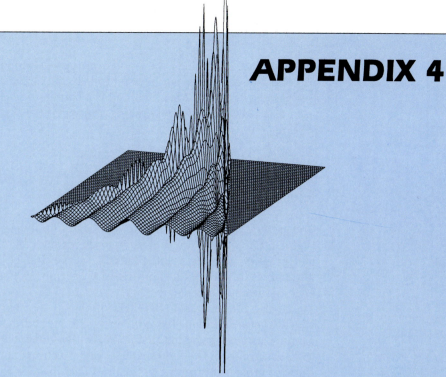

Example Solids

This appendix provides data and routines to model several kinds of solid objects. These models can be used to test the various algorithms and methods discussed in the text. Also included is a complete scene description that can be used as a test case for a ray-tracing application.

A4.1   Some Example Polyhedral Objects

The use of vertex and face lists to render solid polyhedral objects is discussed in Chapter 15. Given a point of view of the camera, each visible face is projected and filled with some color. (Back faces can first be removed if desired.) If a wireframe drawing is desired instead, Section 15.1 describes how to form an edge list from a face list.

Figure A4.1 suggests the class of objects that we model in this section. A specific vertex and face list is given for the "wondrous widgit" of Figure A4.1a. (Similar lists are provided in Appendix 8 for the five Platonic solids.) The other three examples in the figure consist of collections of distorted cubes. A procedural approach to forming vertex and face lists for them will be given.

4.1.1 The Wondrous Widgit

The "wondrous widgit" pictured in Figure A4.1a has the 26 vertices and 15 faces listed in the accompanying tables. This object is also shown in Figures 17.1 and 17.2.

Figure A4.1.
Example of solid objects.

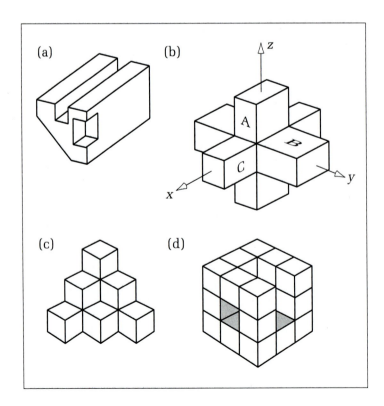

Vertex List for the Widgit

Vertex	x	y	z	Vertex	x	y	z
1	0	15	0	14	22	13	14
2	22	15	0	15	0	0	6
3	22	15	5	16	22	0	6
4	0	15	5	17	0	0	0
5	0	13	5	18	22	0	0
6	22	15	5	19	0	9	3
7	22	13	9	20	0	5	3
8	0	13	9	21	0	5	0
9	0	16	9	22	5	5	0
10	22	16	9	23	5	9	0
11	22	16	14	24	5	9	3
12	0	16	14	25	5	5	3
13	0	13	14	26	0	9	0

Face List for the Widgit

Face	Vertices
1	17, 21, 20, 19, 26, 1, 4, 5, 8, 9, 12, 13, 15
2	12, 9, 10, 11
3	8, 5, 6, 7
4	4, 1, 2, 3
5	9, 8, 7, 10
6	4, 3, 6, 5
7	2, 18, 16, 14, 11, 10, 7, 6, 3
8	12, 11, 14, 13
9	1, 26, 23, 22, 21, 17, 18, 2
10	17, 15, 16, 18
11	13, 14, 16, 15
12	26, 19, 24, 23
13	19, 20, 25, 24
14	20, 21, 22, 25
15	23, 24, 25, 22

A4.1.2 The Jack of Blocks

Figure A4.1b shows three interpenetrating blocks, which together resemble a crude stick-like "jack." (See Figure 18.2 for a less crude jack-like object.) This jack makes a simple test object for hidden line and surface removal algorithms. (Also see Figure 17.8).

The jack is conveniently represented as three scaled cubes. Begin with a "generic" cube having edges of length 2. The cube is centered at the origin and has its edges aligned with the coordinate axes. (This cube is one of the Platonic solids: see also Appendix 8.) To form Block A, scale this cube by some factor ϕ in the z-direction. (A pleasing choice is to set ϕ to the golden ratio.) Similarly scale the cube by ϕ in the y-direction to form Block B, and scale it by ϕ in the x-direction to form Block C.

A routine is needed that allows the user to build vertex and face lists containing the blocks in this jack. The procedure $Add\_Box()$, given subsequently, provides this capability. It can be used to create much more general objects than just the jack: an arbitrary collection of blocks (all of whose edges are aligned with the coordinate axes). For each block in the object, the user specifies the position of the center (cx, cy, cz) and three scaling factors (sx, sy, sz) that size the block in the x, y, and z directions, respectively. As each block is specified, its vertices and faces are added to the overall vertex and face lists. (Elementary arrays $vert[]$ and $face[]$ are used for the vertex and face lists here for simplicity.) The indices V and F keep track of the total number of vertices and faces in the object so far. They would both be initialized to 0.

Code Fragment A4.1 Adding the Next Box to the Model

```
var {the vertex and face lists}
   vert : array[1..MAXNUMVERTS] of point3D;
   face : array[1..MAXNUMFACES] of array[1..4] of integer;
   V, F : integer; {global indices into lists}
{-----------------------------------------------------------------------}
procedure Add_Box(cx, cy, cz, sx, sy, sz : real);
   {create data for a cube scaled by (sx,sy,sz) with its center at (cx,cy,cz). Add
   vertices to the vertex list starting with index V, and faces to the face list
   starting with index F.}
var
   left, right, top, bot, near, far : real;
   Vstart : integer;
{-----------------------------------------------------------------------}
procedure Add_Vert(xx, yy, zz : real);
{include index in vertex list and add new vertex (xx,yy,zz)}
begin
   V := V + 1; {increment index into vertex list}
   vert[V].x ;= xx; vert[V].y := yy; vert[V].z := zz
end;
{-----------------------------------------------------------------------}
procedure Add_Face(a, b, c, d : integer);
{include index in face list and add new rectangular face}
begin
   F := F + 1; {increment the index into the face list}
   face[F,1] := a + Vstart; face[F,2] := b + Vstart;
   face[F,3] := c + Vstart; face[F,4] := d + Vstart
end;
{-----------------------------------------------------------------------}
begin {Add_Box}
   left  := cx − sx; right := cx + sx;
   bot   := cy − sy; top   := cy + sy;
   near := cz − sz; far    := cz + sz;
   {add eight vertices to list}
```

Vstart := *V*; {"base" index of vertices in this box:
                used in *Add_Face*()}
Add_vert(*right*, *bot*, *near*); *Add_vert*(*left*, *bot*, *near*);
Add_vert(*left*, *bot*, *far*); *Add_vert*(*right*, *bot*, *far*);
Add_vert(*right*, *top*, *near*); *Add_vert*(*left*, *top*, *near*);
Add_vert(*left*, *top*, *far*); *Add_vert*(*right*, *top*, *far*);
{add six faces to list}
Add_Face(2, 6, 7, 3); *Add_face*(1, 5, 6, 2);
Add_face(1, 4, 8, 5); *Add_face*(3, 7, 8, 4);
Add_face(5, 8, 7, 6); *Add_face*(1, 2, 3, 4)
end; {*Add_Box*}

4.1.3 Models Based on Stacked Sugar Cubes

The *Add_Box*() procedure can be used to create a large class of interesting shapes. For instance, several "sugar cubes" can be stacked in various patterns, as in Figures A4.1c and A4.1d.

Some interesting approaches are as follows:

1.   All boxes are cubes of the same size and are touching. For this case, make $(sx, sy, sz) = (1, 1, 1)$, and place the cubes at various positions in a square grid laid out on the *xy*-plane. To specify the pile of 11 cubes shown in Figure A4.1c, for instance, the user would make 11 calls to *Add_Box*(), as in

     F := 0; *V* := 0;
     Add_Box(1,1,1,1,1,1); {3 cubes at $(x,y)=(1,1)$}
     Add_Box(1,1,3,1,1,1);
     Add_Box(1,1,5,1,1,1);
     Add_Box(1,3,1,1,1,1); {2 cubes at $(x,y)=(1,3)$}
     Add_Box(1,3,3,1,1,1);
     Add_Box(1,5,1,1,1,1); {1 cube at $(x,y)=(1,5)$}
     <etc>

2.   A single box of the appropriate height is placed in each spot within the grid, as in

     F := 0; *V* := 0;
     Add_Box(1,1,3,1,1,3);
     Add_Box(1,3,2,1,1,2);
     Add_Box(1,5,1,1,1,1);
     <etc>

     The same solid results from each of these approaches, but the two models have quite different face lists (what are they?).

3.   The boxes can be separated, as in the example of Figure 17.16. Use the same center positions for each as previously, but reduce the scale factors by a small amount. Models formed in this way are useful for testing hidden line and surface algorithms.

     In each of these cases, it is simple to distort the objects in a variety of ways by altering the scale factors.

A4.2 The Lid of the Teapot

Chapter 14 discusses modeling "free-form" surfaces by piecing together Bezier and *B*-spline patches.

Figure A4.2a shows a view of the lid of Martin Newell's famous teapot (Crow 1987), fashioned from eight cubic Bezier patches. (The entire teapot is pictured in Figure 14.30 and at the start of Chapter 15.) The form of each patch is given by Equation 14.63, with $M = L = 3$. Each patch is characterized by 16 control points $\mathbf{p}_{i,k}$.

In Newell's design, the lid enjoys a fourfold symmetry: Figure A4.2b shows the quarter of the lid defined by just two of the patches. So we need only list the vertices for these two patches; the others can be determined from them as described below.

The indices of the vertices for the two patches are listed in the accompanying table. Each row of four control points forms a control "polygon," and the four control polygons together form the control polyhedron. Note that in the first patch, two of the control polygons degenerate to a single point on the *z*-axis. (The axis of the lid is aligned with the *z*-axis.) The first degeneracy causes the surface to close at the topmost point of the lid, and the second causes the surface to "pinch" in to form a narrowing of the handle.

Vertex Indices for Two of the Patches of the Lid

Patch 1				Patch 2			
1	1	1	1	7	8	9	10
2	3	4	5	11	12	13	14
6	6	6	6	15	16	17	18
7	8	9	10	19	20	21	22

Figure A4.2.
Lid of the teapot. (Courtesy of Jay Greco.)

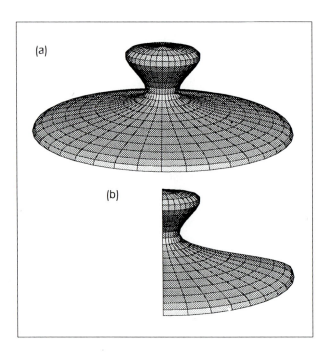

(a)

(b)

Control Vertices for the Two Patches

Vertex	x	y	z
1	0	0	3.15
2	0.8	0	3.15
3	0.8	−0.45	3.15
4	0.45	−0.8	3.15
5	0	−0.8	3.15
6	0	0	2.85
7	0.2	0	2.7
8	0.2	−0.112	2.7
9	0.112	−0.2	2.7
10	0	−0.2	2.7
11	0.4	0	2.55
12	0.4	−0.224	2.55
13	0.224	−0.4	2.55
14	0	−0.4	2.55
15	1.3	0	2.55
16	1.3	−0.728	2.55
17	0.728	−1.3	2.55
18	0	−1.3	2.55
19	1.3	0	2.4
20	1.3	−0.728	2.4
21	0.728	−1.3	2.4
22	0	−1.3	2.4

How are the vertices for the remaining six patches formed? Simply alter the x and y coordinates in every vertex in the table of control vertices leaving the x-coordinate unchanged.

1. To form patches 3 and 4, negate both the x and y coordinates of every vertex.

2. To form patches 5 and 6, interchange the x and y coordinates of every vertex.

3. To form patches 7 and 8, first negate each x-coordinate, and then interchange the x and y coordinates.

For instance, patch 7 uses vertices with the following values:

0	0	3.15
0	−0.8	3.15
−0.45	−0.8	3.15
−0.8	−0.45	3.15

etc.

A4.3 The Model of a Scene for Ray Tracing

Figure A4.3 shows an image formed by ray tracing the scene described in this section. (Also see Figure 2.29.) The scene description (courtesy of Brett Diamond) may be placed in a "scene file" as discussed in Chapter 18, and read into a ray-tracing application for testing and debugging purposes. A procedure recognizes each keyword in turn, reads the appropriate parameters, and takes the proper action. For instance, *translate 0 3 1.1* concatenates a translation by (0.0,3.0,1.1) to the instance transformation of the object being described.

Most of the ingredients of the scene description are self-explanatory. All characters from a # to the end of the line are comments and are ignored. The keyword *'set'* sets the current attributes for all objects that follow to those indicated. To save space, we condense some of the data into notes to the reader, such as <*repeat first black line, but use translate 0 −1.5 0.10001*>. These are not part of the file proper, but a note to copy the five instructions that describe a square, substituting different translation parameters. Many variations in the format of the scene description are possible, of course.

viewref 4 2 3
viewnorm −4 −2 −3
viewup 0 0 1
eyedist 50
window 4.5 6 # height and width
screen 480 640 # rows and cols
light 1 2 3 1 # location and brightness
ambient 0.075
the board
cube
  scale 8 8 0.1
  diffuse 1
  color 1 1 1
the first black line

Figure A4.3
The Tic-Tac-Toe board scene.
(Courtesy of Brett Diamond)

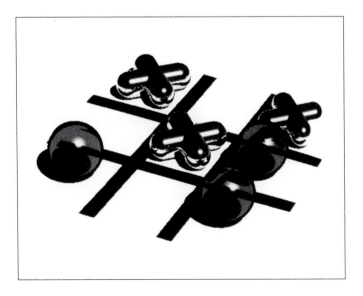

```
square
  noshadow
  scale 5 0.3 1
  color 0 0 0
  translate 0 1.5 0.10001
### the other lines ###
<repeat first black line, but use translate 0 −1.5 0.10001>
<repeat first black line, but use translate 1.5 0 0.10001>
<repeat first black line, but use translate −1.5 0 0.10001>
### the OH's ###
set
  specular 1
  refract 1 1.212
  color 1 0 0
sphere
  translate 0 3 1.1
sphere
  translate 3 −3 1.1
sphere
  translate 3 3 1.1
### the first EX ###
set
  specular 1
  reflect .8
  diffuse .50
  color 0 0 1
cylinder
  scale .5 .5 1
  rotate x 90
  rotate z 45
  translate 0 0.6 0
cylinder
  scale .5 .5 1
  rotate x 90
  rotate z −45
  translate 0 0.6 0
sphere
  scale .5 .5 .5
  translate .707 .707 .6
sphere
  scale .5 .5 .5
  translate .707 −.707 .6
sphere
  scale .5 .5 .5
  translate −.707 .707 .6
sphere
  scale .5 .5 .5
  translate −.707 −.707 .6
### the other two EX's ###
<repeat the first EX, but append a translate −3 −3 0 in each.>
<repeat the first EX, but append a translate −3 3 0 in each.>
```

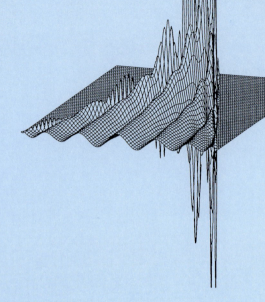

On Spherical Coordinates

APPENDIX 5

708

A5.1 Spherical Coordinates

It is a simple matter to convert back and forth from spherical coordinates to Cartesian coordinates. Figure A5.1 shows how a point U is defined in spherical coordinates. R is the radial distance of U from the origin. ϕ is the angle that U makes with the z-axis, known as the "colatitude" of point U. θ is the "azimuth" of U: the angle between the xz-plane and the plane through U and the z-axis. ϕ and θ are restricted to the intervals $0 \leq \phi \leq \pi$ and $0 \leq \theta < 2\pi$, respectively.

Using simple trigonometry, it is straightforward to work out the relationships between these quantities and the Cartesian coordinates (u_x, u_y, u_z) for U. They are

$$u_x = R \sin(\phi) \cos(\theta)$$

$$u_y = R \sin(\phi) \sin(\theta) \tag{A5.1}$$

$$u_z = R \cos(\phi) \tag{A5.2}$$

One can also invert these relations to express (R, ϕ, θ) in terms of (u_x, u_y, u_z):

$$R = \sqrt{u_x^2 + u_y^2 + u_z^2}$$

$$\phi = \cos^{-1}\left(\frac{u_z}{R}\right) \tag{A5.3}$$

$$\theta = \arctan(u_y, u_x).$$

The function arctan(,) is the two-argument form of the arctangent as defined in Equation A5.4. It can distinguish between the case where both u_x and u_y are

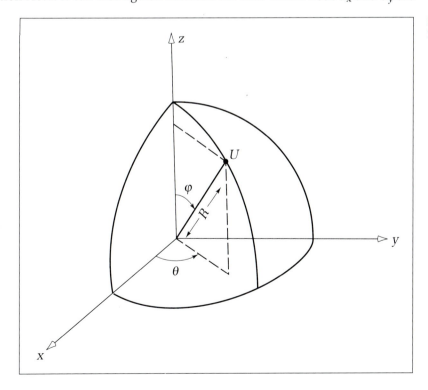

Figure A5.1.
Spherical coordinates.

positive and the case where both of them are negative, unlike the usual form
arctan (u_y/u_x), which always produces angles between $-\pi/2$ and $\pi/2$.

The arctan (,) is defined as

$$
\text{arctan}(y, \, x) = \begin{cases} \tan^{-1}(y/x) & \text{if } x > 0 \\ \pi + \tan^{-1}(y/x) & \text{if } x < 0 \\ \pi/2 & \text{if } x = 0 \quad \text{and} \quad y > 0 \\ -\pi/2 & \text{if } x = 0 \quad \text{and} \quad y < 0 \end{cases}
\tag{A5.4}
$$

Example

Suppose that point U is at distance 2 from the origin, is $60°$ up from the xy-plane,
and is along the negative x-axis. Hence U is in the xz-plane. Then U is expressed
in spherical coordinates as $(2, 30°, 180°)$. Using Equation A5.1 to compute U in
Cartesian coordinates, we obtain $U = (-1, 0, 1.732)$.

A5.1.1 Direction Cosines

The direction of point U in the preceding example is given in terms of two
angles, the azimuth and the colatitude. Directions are often specified in an alternative useful way through direction cosines. The direction cosines of a line
through the origin are the cosines of the three angles it makes with the x-, y-, and
z-axes, respectively.

Recall from Chapter 7 that the cosine of the angle between two unit vectors
is given by their dot product. Using the given point U, form the position vector
(u_x, u_y, u_z). From the preceding discussion we see that its length is R, so it must
be normalized to the unit length vector $\mathbf{m} = (u_x/R, u_y/R, u_z/R)$. Then the cosine
of the angle it makes with the x-axis is given by $\mathbf{m} \cdot \mathbf{i} = u_x/R$, which is simply the
first component of $\mathbf{m}$. Similarly, the second and third components of $\mathbf{m}$ are the
second and third direction cosines, respectively. Calling the angles made with
the x-, y-, and z-axes by α, β, and γ, respectively, the three direction cosines for
the line from 0 to U are therefore

$$
\cos(\alpha) = \frac{u_x}{R}
$$

$$
\cos(\beta) = \frac{u_y}{R}
\tag{A5.5}
$$

$$
\cos(\gamma) = \frac{u_z}{R}
\tag{A5.6}
$$

Clearly, angle γ is the same as the colatitude used in the spherical coordinate
representation of U. Note that the three direction cosines are related, since the
sum of their squares is always 1.

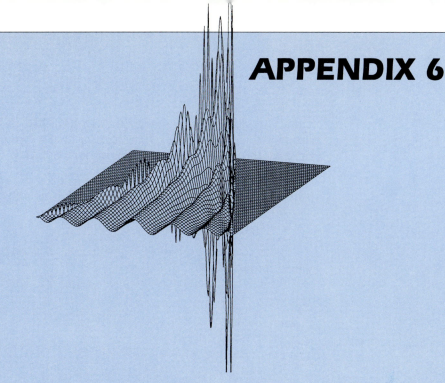

APPENDIX 6

Advanced Clipping Algorithms

A6.1   The Cyrus–Beck Clipping Algorithm

The Cyrus–Beck clipping algorithm is described in Chapter 7. It clips a line segment L with endpoints P_1 and P_2 against a convex polygonal window W. Here we build an implementation of the method in Pascal with the following interface:

procedure *CB_Clip*(**var** *P1*, *P2*:*point*; {endpoints of segment}
     window : *line_list*; {edge list of window}
     var *vis* : *boolean*); {is any of *L* visible?}

If any of line L lies within the window, *vis* is set to *true* and P_1, P_2 are set to the endpoints of the clipped line.

Window W is an array of edges of the following **type:**

type
     line = **record**
               norm : *vector*;
               D : *real*
        end;
     line_list = **record**
               num : 0..*MAXNUMEDGES*;
               edge : **array**[1 .. *MAXNUMEDGES*] *of line*
        end;

so each edge is stored as an infinite line in point normal form. (If a window is initially described instead as a list of vertices, it is worthwhile to preprocess it into a *line_list*, since the clipper is called so many times in a drawing.)

L is represented parametrically as $P(t) = P_1 + \mathbf{c}t$ for t varying from 0 to 1, where $\mathbf{c} = P_2 - P_1$ is the "direction" of L. As described in Chapter 7, each edge E of the window takes a turn at chopping off a piece of L, and after each chop the interval (t_{in}, t_{out}) specifies what portion of L still remains visible. If a chop eliminates this interval (an "early out"), the chopper returns *true* and the clipper terminates with *vis* = *false*. If there is anything left of segment L to draw after all edges have performed their chops, the final values of t_{in} and t_{out} are substituted into the parametric form of the segment: $P_1 + \mathbf{c}t$ to obtain the endpoints of the clipped line, and *vis* is set to *true*.

The implementation of the chopper is a direct implementation of the tests given in Chapter 7. **Function** *Chop*(*numer*, *denom* : *real*): *boolean* takes two parameters:

$$numer = D - \mathbf{n} \cdot P_1 \tag{A6.1}$$

$$denom = \mathbf{n} \cdot \mathbf{c} \tag{A6.2}$$

which are formed using D and $\mathbf{n}$ of edge E, and P_1 and $\mathbf{c}$ of the line segment. Two dot products (four multiplications) are required to construct these values.

Chop( ) finds the intersection time $r := numer / denom$ of L and E and determines whether the segment is "entering" or "exiting" the window (according to the sign of *denom*.) It then adjusts either t_{in} or t_{out} accordingly. If *denom* = 0, L is parallel to E, and the sign of *numer* specifies whether L is wholly inside or wholly outside the half-space. *Chop*( ) returns *true* if the entire segment has been annihilated by the chop.

If *gone* is *false* when *CB_Clip*( ) finishes, t_{in} and t_{out} are substituted into the parametric form of the segment to form the endpoints of the clipped line.

The final form of the Cyrus–Beck clipping algorithm is shown in Code Fragment A6.1. It is obtained from a straightforward fleshing out of the skeleton of the algorithm given in Chapter 7.

Code Fragment A6.1. Skeleton of the Cyrus–Beck Clipper

```
procedure CB_Clip(var P1, P2 : point;
                      window : line_list;
         var vis : boolean);
{clip segment from P₁ to P₂ against window}
{vis := true if any piece lies in window.}
{Visible piece has new endpoints P₁,P₂}
var
   t_in, t_out, numer, denom, D : real;
   F : point;
   c, norm, Pvec : vector;
   i : integer;
   gone: boolean;
{------------------------------------------------------------------------}
function Chop(numer, denom : real) : boolean;
var
   chopped : boolean;
   r : real;
begin
   chopped := false;
   if denom < 0 then {edge is entering}
   begin
      r := numer / denom;
      if r > t_out then chopped := true
      else if r > t_in then t_in := r; {chop at r}
   end
   else if denom > 0 then {edge is exiting}
   begin
      r : = numer / denom;
      if r < t_in then chopped := true
      else if r < t_out then t_out := r
   end
   else {denom = 0} if numer <= 0 then chopped := true;
   Chop := chopped
end;
{------------------------------------------------------------------------}
begin {CB_Clip}
   t_in := 0.0; t_out := 1.0; {initialize times}
   c.dx := P2.x − P1.x; {get direction of segment}
   c.dy := P2.y − P1.y;
   Pvec.dx : = P1.x; {construct vector from P1}
   Pvec.dy : = P1.y ;
   i := 1;
   gone := false; {some of segment L is still visible}
   with window do
```

```
  repeat
     denom := Dot(edge[i].norm,c);
     numer := edge[i].D − Dot(edge[i].norm, Pvec);
     i := i + 1;
     gone := Chop(numer,denom); {an early out?}
  until gone or (i > window.num);
  if not gone then
  begin
     F.x := P1.x; F.y := P1.y;
     if t_in > 1.0 then {need to change first endpoint}
     begin
        P1.x := F.x + c.dx * t_in;
        P1.y := F.y + c.dy * t_in
     end;
     if t_out < 1.0 then {need to change second endpoint}
     begin
        P2.x := F.x + c.dx * t_out;
        P2.y := F.y + c.dy * t_out
     end
  end;
  vis := not gone
end; {CB_Clip}
```

A6.2 Polygon Clipping

In most applications, polygons are defined by a sequence of vertices $p_i = (x_i, y_i)$, $i = 1,\ldots, N$ in world coordinates. A window is also defined, and the intent is to draw that part of the polygon that lies within the window.

With single lines, the clipping methods discussed in Chapter 3 suffices: Each line segment is clipped against each of the window boundaries in turn, and new endpoints are formed as needed. With polygons the situation is more complicated, because a polygon can be fragmented into several polygons in the clipping process, as suggested in Figure A6.1. The polygon may need to be filled with a color or pattern, which means that each of the clipped fragments must be associated with that color. Therefore a clipping algorithm must add edges ab, cd, and so on, and fashion a new set of polygons out of the old one. It is also important that an algorithm not introduce extraneous edges such as bc in the process, since the clipped polygon might be displayed in red against a blue background, and edge bc should not be visible.

The polygon to be clipped will be called the "subject" polygon, S. The window will be called the "clip" polygon, C, and in fact, it will cost almost nothing to generalize it from a simple rectangle to a more complex polygon, as we shall see.

The question, then, is how to clip polygon S, represented by a vertex list, against polygon C to generate a collection of vertex lists that properly represent the set of clipped polygons.

In the next two sections, we examine two well-known algorithms for polygon clipping.

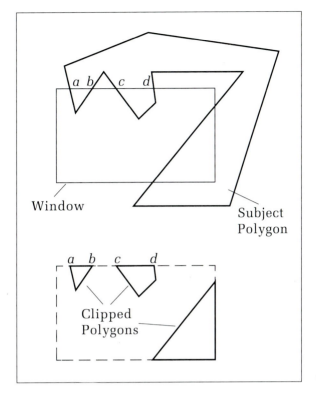

Clipping a polygon.

1. *The Sutherland–Hodgman clipping algorithm.* This method is quite simple and clips any subject polygon against a convex clip polygon. A rectangular window is a special case of a convex polygon. The algorithm can leave extraneous edges that must be removed later.

2. *The Weiler–Atherton clipping algorithm.* This approach is more complicated, but it is also more powerful. It will clip any subject polygon against any clip polygon. The polygons may even contain holes.

A6.3   Sutherland–Hodgman Clipping Algorithm

Because of all the different cases that can occur when a subject polygon S is clipped against a convex clip polygon C, we need a very organized method for keeping track of the clipping process. The Sutherland–Hodgman algorithm takes a divide-and-conquer approach: It breaks the difficult problem into a set of simpler ones. Specifically, it capitalizes on the fact that each edge of a convex polygon defines an "inside" and an "outside" half-space, as in the Cyrus–Beck algorithm. The method clips polygon S against the (infinite) line defined by each edge of polygon C in turn, leaving only the part that is inside C. Once all of the edges of C have been used as "clipedges," S will have been clipped against C as desired. Figure A6.2 shows the algorithm in action for a seven-sided subject

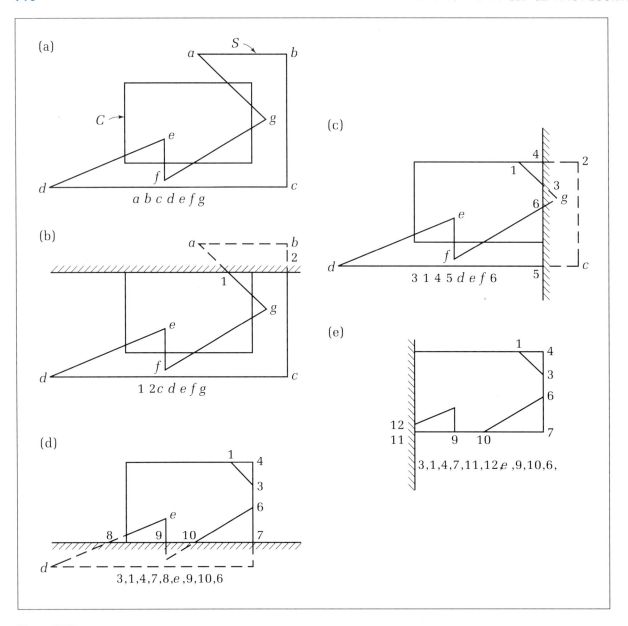

Figure A6.2.
Sutherland–Hodgman polygon clipping.

polygon S and a rectangular clip polygon C. We will describe each step in the process. S is characterized by the vertex list $a\,b\,c\,d\,e\,f\,g$. S is clipped against the top, right, bottom, and left edges of C in turn, and at each stage a new list of vertices is generated from the old. This list describes one or more polygons and is passed along as the subject polygon for clipping against the next edge of C.

The basic operation, then, is to clip the polygon(s) described by an input vertex list V against the current clip edge of C and produce an output vertex list. Traverse V, forming successive edges with pairs of adjacent vertices. Each such edge E has a first and a second endpoint we call s and p, respectively. There are four possible situations for endpoints s and p: s and p can both be inside, both can be outside, or they can be on opposite sides of the clip edge. In each case, certain points are output to the new vertex list, as shown in Figure A6.3.

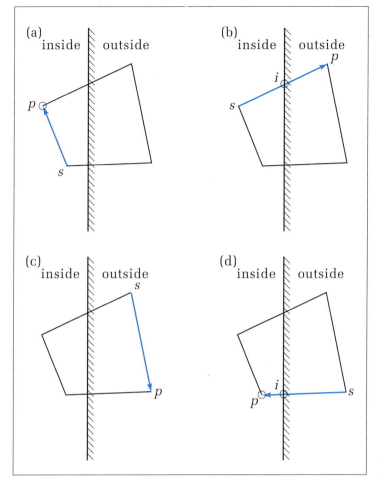

Figure A6.3.
Four cases for each edge of S.

a.   Both s and p are inside: p is output.

b. s is inside and p is outside. Find the intersection i and output it.

c.   Both s and p are outside. Nothing is output.

d. s is outside and p is inside. Find intersection i, and output i and then p.

Now follow the progress of the Sutherland–Hodgman algorithm in Figure A6.2. Consider clipping S against the top edge of C. The input vertex list for this phase is $a\,b\,c\,d\,e\,f\,g$. The first edge from the list is taken for convenience as that from g to a, the edge that "wraps around" from the end of the list to its first element. Thus point s is g and point p is a here. Edge g, a, meaning the edge from g to a, intersects the clip edge at a new point "1", which is output to the new list. (The output list from each stage in the algorithm is shown below the subsequent figure in Figure A6.2.) The next edge in the input list is a, b. Since both end-points are above the clipping edge, nothing is output. The third edge, b, c, generates two output points, 2 and c, and the fourth edge, c, d, outputs point d. This process continues until the last edge, f, g, is tested, producing g. The new vertex list for the next clipping stage is therefore *1 2 c d e f g*. It is illuminating to follow the example in Figure A6.2 carefully in its entirety to see how the algorithm works.

Notice that extraneous edges 3, 6 and 9, 10 are formed that connect the three polygon fragments formed in the clipping algorithm. Such edges can cause problems in some tools such as parity filling algorithms. It is possible but not trivial to remove these offending edges (Sutherland 1974).

A6.4 Weiler–Atherton Clipping Algorithm

The preceding algorithm exploits the convexity of the clipping polygon through the use of inside-outside half-spaces. This leads to a simple attack on the clipping problem. In some applications, such as hidden surface removal and rendering shadows (Chapter 17), however, one must clip one concave polygon against another. Clipping is more complex in such cases. The Weiler–Atherton approach clips any polygon against any other, even when they have holes. It also allows one to form the set theoretic **union, intersection,** and **difference** of two polygons.

We start with a simple example, shown in Figure A6.4. Here two concave polygons, SUBJ and CLIP, are represented by the vertex lists, (*a, b, c, d*) and (*A, B, C, D*), respectively. We adopt the convention here of listing vertices so that the interior of the polygon is to the right of each edge as we move cyclically from vertex to vertex through the list. For instance, the interior of SUBJ lies to the right of the edge from *c* to *d* and to the right of that from *d* to *a*. This is akin to listing vertices in "clockwise" order.

All of the intersections of the two polygons are identified and stored in a list (see later). For the example here, there are six such intersections. Now to clip

Figure A6.4.
Weiler–Atherton clipping.

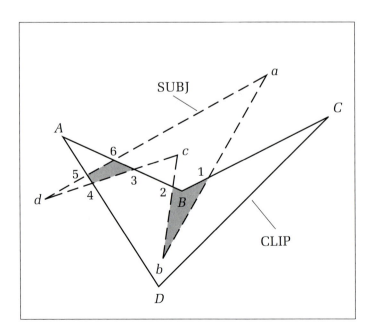

SUBJ against CLIP, traverse around SUBJ in the "forward direction" (i.e., so that its interior is to the right) until an "entering" intersection is found: one for which SUBJ is moving from the outside to the inside of CLIP. Here we first find 1, and it goes to an output list that records the clipped polygon(s).

The process is now simple to state in geometric terms: Traverse along SUBJ, moving segment by segment, until an intersection is encountered (2 in the example). The idea now is to turn away from following SUBJ and to follow CLIP instead. There are two ways to turn. Turn so that CLIP is traversed in its forward direction. This keeps the inside of both SUBJ and CLIP to the right. Upon finding an intersection, turn and follow along SUBJ in its forward direction, and so on. Each vertex or intersection encountered is put on the output list. Repeat the "turn and jump between polygons" process, traversing each polygon in its forward direction, until the first vertex is revisited. The output list at this point consists of (1, *b*, 2, *B*).

Now check for any other entering intersections of SUBJ. Number 3 is found and the process repeats, generating output list (3, 4, 5, 6). Further checks for entering intersections show that they have all been visited, so the clipping process terminates, yielding the two polygons (1, *b*, 2, *B*) and (3, 4, 5, 6).

An organized way to implement this "follow in the forward direction and jump" process is to build the two lists

SUBJ_LIST: *a*, 1, *b*, 2, *c*, 3, 4, *d*, 5, 6
CLIP_LIST: *A*, 6, 3, 2, *B*, 1, *C*, *D*, 4, 5

that traverse each polygon (so that its interior is to the right) and list both vertices and intersections in the order they are encountered. (What should be done if no intersections are detected between the two polygons?) Therefore traversing a polygon amounts to traversing a list, and jumping between polygons is effected by jumping between lists.

Notice that once the lists are available, there is very little geometry in the process—just a "point outside polygon" test to properly identify an entering vertex. The proper direction in which to traverse each polygon is embedded in the ordering of its list. For the preceding example, the progress of the algorithm is traced in Figure A6.5.

A more complex example involving polygons with holes is shown in Figure A6.6. The vertices that describe holes are also listed in order such that the interior of the polygon lies to the right of an edge. (For holes this is sometimes

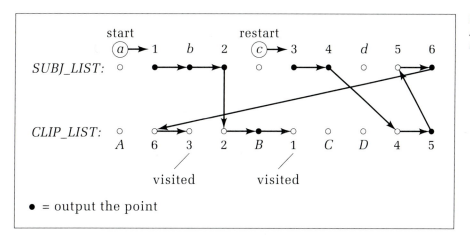

Figure A6.5.
Applying the Weiler–Atherton method.

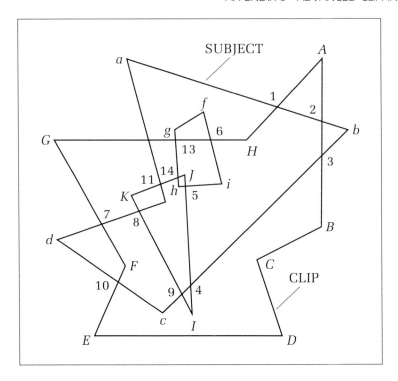

Figure A6.6.
Weiler–Atherton clipping:
polygons with holes.

called "counterclockwise order.") The same rule is used as earlier: Turn and follow the other polygon in its forward direction. Beginning with entering intersection 1, the polygon (1, 2, 3, 4, 5, *i*, 6, *H*) is formed. Then, starting with entering intersection 7, the polygon (7, 8, 9, *c*, 10, *F*) is created. What entering intersection should be used to generate the third polygon? It is a valuable exercise to build *SUBJ_LIST* and *CLIP_LIST* and to trace through the operation of the method for this example.

As with many algorithms that base decisions on intersections, we must examine the preceding method for cases where edges of CLIP and SUBJ are parallel and overlap over a finite segment. See the exercises.

Exercise

A6.1.　Dangling Edges in Weiler–Atherton Clipping. Consider the operation of the Weiler–Atherton algorithm in situations that could easily arise in practice:

- Some edges of SUBJ and CLIP are parallel and overlap over a finite segment,

- SUBJ or CLIP or both are nonsimple polygons

- Some edges of SUBJ and CLIP overlap only at their endpoints,

- CLIP and SUBJ are disjoint,

- SUBJ lies entirely within a hole of CLIP,

as well as other degenerate situations. How must the approach be modified to operate properly in each case?

A6.4.1 Boolean Operations of Polygons

If we view polygons as sets of points (the set of all points on the boundary or in the interior of the polygon), then the result of the previous clipping operation is the **intersection** of the two polygons, the set of all points that are in both CLIP and SUBJ. The polygons output by the algorithm consist of points that lie both within the original SUBJ and within the CLIP polygons.

Here we generalize from intersections to other set theoretic operations on polygons, often called "Boolean" operations. Such operations arise frequently in modeling [mortenson 1985] as well as in graphics (as in Chapter 18). In general, for any two sets of points A and B, the three set theoretic operations are

intersection: $A \cap B = \{\text{all points in both } A \text{ and } B\}$

union: $A \cup B = \{\text{all points in } A \text{ or in } B \text{ or both}\}$

difference: $A - B = \{\text{all points in } A \text{ but not } B\}$

with a similar definition for the set difference $B - A$. Examples of these sets are shown in Figure A6.7.

It is not hard to adjust the preceding clipping method to generate the other set operations on polygons A and B.

1. *Computing the union of A and B.* Traverse around A in the forward direction until an exiting intersection is found: one for which A is moving from the inside to the outside of B. Output the intersection and traverse along A until another intersection with B is found. Now turn to follow B in its forward direction. At each subsequent intersection, output the vertex and turn to follow the other polygon in its forward direction. Upon returning to the initial vertex, look for other exiting intersections that have not yet been visited.

2. *Computing the difference A–B(outside clipping).* Whereas finding the intersection of two polygons results in clipping one against the other, the difference operation "shields" one polygon from another. That is, the difference SUBJ − CLIP consists of the parts of SUBJ that lie *outside* CLIP. No parts of SUBJ are drawn that lie within the border of CLIP, so the region defined by CLIP is effectively protected, or shielded.

Traverse around A until an entering intersection into B is found. Turn to B, ɔllowing it in the reverse direction, (so that B's interior is to the left). Upon

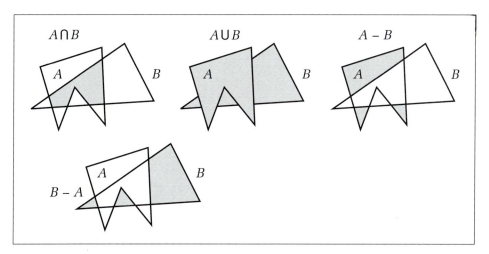

Figure A6.7.
Polygons formed by set theoretic operations on polygons.

reaching another intersection, jump to *A* again. At each intersection, jump to the other polygon, always traversing *A* in the forward direction and *B* in the reverse direction. Some examples of forming the union and difference of two polygons are shown in Figure A6.8. The three set operations generate the following polygons:

POLY_A ∪ *POLY_B:*
   4, 5, *g, h*   (a hole)
   8, *B, C, D,* 1, *b, c, d*
   2, 3, *i, j*   (a hole)
   6, *H, E, F,* 7, *f* (a hole)

POLY_A − *POLY_B:*
   4, 5, 6, *H, E, F,* 7, *e,* 8, *B, C, D,* 1, *a*
   2, 3, *k*

POLY_B − *POLY_A:*
   1, *b, c, d,* 8, 5, *g, h,* 4, *A,* 3, *i, j,* 2
   7, *f,* 6, *G*

Notice how the holes (*E, F, G, H*) and (*k, i, j*) in the polygons are properly handled, and that the algorithm generates holes as needed (holes are polygons listed in counterclockwise fashion).

Exercises

A6.2.   On the Symmetry of Union and Intersection. Using the preceding algorithms on some example polygon pairs, show that it doesn't matter which polygon is taken first, that is, that *A* ∩ *B* = *B* ∩ *A* and *A* ∪ *B* = *B* ∪ *A*.

A6.3.   List Manipulations for the Boolean Operations. The Weiler–Atherton method builds the lists *SUBJ_LIST*

and *CLIP_LIST* from the polygons and traverse these lists, jumping back and forth. Develop similar list-traversing methods for forming the union and difference of two polygons, and use them on some pencil-and-paper examples.

Figure A6.8.
Forming the union and
difference of two polygons.

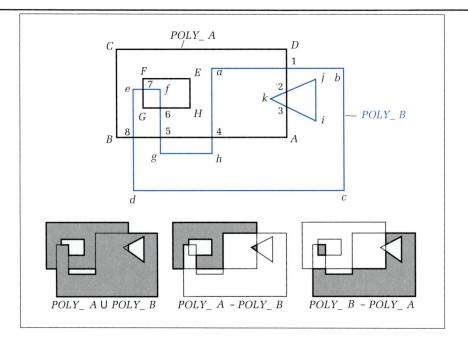

POLY_ A ∪ POLY_ B   POLY_ A − POLY_ B   POLY_ B − POLY_ A

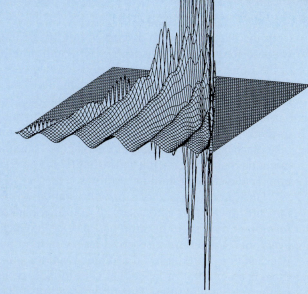

A Closer Look at Graphics Standards

A7.1 Introduction

Graphics standards were discussed briefly in Chapter 1, focusing on GKS. Here we describe some other aspects of GKS and provide a concise overview of some of the other graphics standards in use today.

The development of a graphics standard is a long and difficult process. A standard, particularly an international standard, must serve the needs of a wide variety of people or it will never gain acceptance. A committee is usually formed to begin developing a proposal, and many (often heated) discussions take place before any consensus is reached. Standards should capture ideas and methods that are of lasting value, but this is particularly difficult to do in such a rapidly developing field as graphics.

One important goal of a graphics standard is to provide a common language for both developers and users of graphics packages. Terms such as *polyline*, *locator*, and *segment* become part of that language and are then understood by everyone. A standard also provides a common perspective on what a graphics package does and doesn't do. When a vendor sells a GKS package, for instance, there is an explicit promise that certain tools reside within and that these tools conform to a set of rules. This understanding, of course, limits the extra features that a vendor can include, but it vastly simplifies the task of the user who wishes to compare GKS packages.

Standards also provide a uniform interface for programmers of applications. An application such as a polyline editor can be written simply with a GKS interface, and the programmer need not consider the idiosyncrasies of any particular computer or graphics device. This greatly simplifies the job of porting the application to different computers, operating systems, GKS packages, and devices. When the application is installed in a particular environment, it may have to be "tuned," requiring name changes and cosmetic adjustments. But the organization and logical flow of the application can remain intact from environment to environment. The installer can at least get the program up and running without having to disect every routine fully, and can then focus on those easily identifiable points within the application that request graphics input and output. This is particularly important when someone other than the original programmer is doing the installation.

A7.2 The CORE System

The CORE System was developed in 1975–77 by the ACM/SIGGRAPH Graphics Standards Planning Committee (Bergeron et al. 1978). It was further revised in 1979. It places a strong emphasis on vector CRT displays and line-drawing devices tied to a mainframe computer. Graphics workstations were not available at that time (even the mouse was hardly known), and raster devices were still emerging. Certain capabilities such as color and area fill were added as raster graphics became more important, but the full capability of raster devices was never exploited. From the beginning, the CORE included functionality to deal with 3D graphics and was well suited to applications that need rapid display of wireframe drawings. The CORE also developed the notion of logical input functions such as LOCATOR, PICK, and VALUATOR, which have been adopted in more recent standards. Several graphics packages based on the CORE proposal, such as Precision Visuals' DI-3000, are still widely used today.

A7.2.1 CORE Graphics Primitives

The CORE defines six types of graphics output primitives. Each is discussed in Chapter 2. For simple line drawing there are *line* () and *polyline* (), which take 2D or 3D points as arguments. The CORE (unlike GKS) supports the current position (CP), so that functions such as *moveto* () and *lineto* () are defined as well. Markers can be placed with *marker* () and *polymarker* (), and a closed polygon primitive is available that can be filled with some pattern. There is also the *text* () primitive that draws text characters starting at the CP.

These primitives can be given the usual attributes such as line width, style, fill pattern, and color. Text has a variety of attributes such as size, slant, and path direction, as discussed in Chapter 2.

A7.2.2 Viewing Functions

With its emphasis on 3D graphics, it is not surprising that the CORE supports functions to establish a synthetic camera (see Chapter 12) and to perform perspective or parallel projections. The user can establish both 2D and 3D windows and viewports, and clipping in 2D and 3D is provided. Viewports are defined within NDC to promote device independence.

A7.2.3 Input Devices

In the 1970s, the most widely used input devices were keyboards, light pens, thumbwheels, and tablets. Rather than develop functions to control each of these physical devices, the CORE developed the concept of logical input functions. As discussed in Chapter 2, these functions include the LOCATOR, STROKE, VALUATOR, BUTTON, KEYBOARD, and PICK. Specific physical input devices at each installation are assigned device numbers, and device drivers are used to associate commands such as *Locate* (..) with the appropriate control signals.

A7.2.4 CORE Segments

The CORE allows creation of segments. As discussed in Chapter 6, a segment is a group of graphics primitives that can be manipulated together as a unit. Segments are defined in NDC and can be thought of as 2D graphic "snapshots." Routines exist to open and close segments. Whatever primitives and attributes are defined between the opening and closing of a segment become part of that segment. Once a segment has been created, it cannot be edited; all of its primitives are frozen within the segment. In addition, CORE segments cannot refer to other segments, so no hierarchical structures can be created (unlike PHIGS structures; see below).

Routines are provided to set various **dynamic segment attributes** after a segment has been created. These include highlighting (such as blinking), visibility, detectability, and image transformations. Image transformations permit the primitives in a segment to be scaled, translated, and rotated before being displayed.

A7.2.5 Metafiles

The CORE also proposed a device-independent format for storing pictures in a **metafile**. For instance, a complex map or engineering drawing can be saved in a file and sent later to an ouput device such as a plotter. Each device requires a metafile translator to convert the device-independent information into its specific control strings. Metafiles are useful for archiving pictures and transferring them between sites.

A7.3   The Graphical Kernel System (GKS)

GKS was adopted as a general-purpose 2D system by ISO (the International Standards Organization) in 1984 and by ANSI (the American National Standards Institute) a year later. Like the CORE, it emphasizes interactive graphics and has only limited functions for raster graphics. A thorough treatment of GKS is available in Enderle et al. (1984).

A7.3.1 Logical Workstation

GKS introduced the concept of the logical workstation, an abstraction of a physical device. Logical workstations can be of various types. An OUTPUT workstation contains a single addressable display surface of fixed resolution and no input devices. An INPUT workstation supports input only, as in a tablet, and an OUTIN workstation supports both a single display surface and input devices. An application can "open" and work with several workstations at once. GKS maintains a workstation description table for each open workstation that describes its characteristics (e.g., whether it is raster or vector, what fonts are available, what properties the input device has), and the application can query this table at any point to test a certain feature.

GKS provides routines to assign attributes to workstations such as the boundary of a viewport. This flexibility allows pictures to be sent to different workstations simultaneously and displayed in different viewports. Input devices can also be associated with different logical input functions under the control of the application using special GKS routines.

A7.3.2 Graphics Primitives

GKS supports the output primitives and attributes discussed in Chapter 2. GKS does not support a CP. It was felt that cleaner code results when both endpoints of each line segment are passed to the line-drawing routine. Its basic line-drawing primitive is the polyline, which is also used to draw a single line segment. The GKS equivalent of the CORE's polygon is the fill area; in addition, GKS supports the cell array as an early attempt to provide some elementary raster support. The GPD described in Chapter 2 provides a mechanism to access special built-in features of some workstations, such as arc- and spline-drawing capabilities.

A7.3.3 Logical Input Devices

GKS offers essentially the same logical input devices as the CORE, with slightly different names (see Chapter 2). But GKS provides three **modes of interaction** by which an application can interact with a device. An input device is initialized in one of these modes:

1. REQUEST Mode: The application pauses and waits until the user positions the input device and triggers the input function. This is the mode discussed in connection with the *Locate*() function in Chapter 6.

2. SAMPLE Mode: The workstation immediately returns the most recent measurement made by the device (e.g., the most recent position of a valuator knob), with no triggering required of the user.

3. EVENT Mode: Relevant input data from a device are placed in an Event Report, which is added to an event queue. GKS allows the application to test the queue and to remove the reports in the order in which they occurred for subsequent processing.

A7.3.4 Segmentation in GKS

The GKS treatment of segments is very similar to that of the CORE. The primitives and attributes defined within a segment cannot be edited, and no hierarchical segments are possible, although segments can be inserted within other segments.

When a segment is created it is sent to all active workstations, which may store it and/or display it. En route, it can be subjected to a 2D affine **segment transformation** (see Chapter 11). GKS provides functions to build and adjust segment transformations. GKS segments have the same dynamic attributes as those defined by the CORE.

A7.3.5 GKS Metafiles

GKS provides almost the same metafile capability as the CORE. Pictures, the state of an application, and user data can be stored in a metafile for archiving and later use. The GKS metafile acts like another workstation, although no workstation transformation is available.

A7.3.6 3D Extensions to GKS: GKS-3D

GKS is inherently a 2D system, but extensions are being proposed to add to it a 3D capability similar to that of the CORE.

Programmers Hierarchical Interactive Graphics Standard (PHIGS)

PHIGS is a logical evolution of the CORE and GKS (see Brown and Heck 1985). PHIGS includes more powerful 3D graphics functions than can be found in the CORE proposal. In addition, a PHIGS user can interactively create and manipulate complex data structures that represent objects.

Many of the concepts from the CORE and GKS have been carried over into PHIGS. It has the same graphics primitives and logical devices as GKS and the same three input modes: REQUEST, SAMPLE, and EVENT. PHIGS also maintains the notion of the logical workstation.

The most marked enhancement provided by PHIGS is the **structure**. A structure is a list of **structure elements** that can be edited interactively by the user, much as a word processor can edit lines of text. There are several types of structure elements, including 3D graphics primitives and attributes, transformations, application data, and selections of the synthetic camera. An object is displayed by **executing** or traversing the structure that represents it. For instance, a rotated house consisting of a red and a green polyline would be displayed on a particular workstation by the command "*execute structure HOUSE*," where *structure HOUSE* might have the following general form:

Open structure HOUSE;
set color red;
set transformation M_house; {set the rotation matrix}
polyline 1;
set color green;
polyline 2;
close structure;

Here *M_house* is a matrix transformation (see Chapter 11) that performs the desired rotation on the two subsequent polylines indicated.

PHIGS maintains a **current transformation** (see Section 11.8) that is applied to all subsequent graphic primitives. Suppose that the current transformation is given by some matrix M just before HOUSE is executed. A copy of M is saved for later use, and then each element of HOUSE is executed in turn. When "*set transformation M_house*" is encountered, the current transformation is composed with *M_house*, and the polylines are transformed by the total current transformation. When HOUSE has been completely traversed, the current transformation is restored to M.

Structures are made hierarchical by allowing one structure to execute another. For instance, the "robot" of Figure 11.22 could be stored in a PHIGS structure as a list of elements such as the following:

Open structure ROBOT;
set transformation M_body;
execute structure BODY;
set transformation M_arm;
execute structure ARM;
set transformation M_hand;
execute structure HAND;
execute structure FINGER1;

execute structure FINGER2;
close structure;

The structure BODY would contain the primitives and attributes for drawing the robot body, and similarly for ARM and HAND. Each successive transformation within ROBOT is composed with the current transformation, so each part of the robot "inherits" the transformations of its "parents," as suggested by Figure 11.25. Note, however, that we don't want FINGER2 to inherit the transformation of FINGER2, so their individual transformations are placed inside their structures. FINGER1 would contain elements such as the following:

Open structure finger_1;
set transformation M_finger1;
execute structure FINGER;
close structure;

and FINGER2 would contain the following:

Open structure finger_2;
set transformation M_finger2;
execute structure FINGER;
close structure;

Note that FINGER1 and FINGER2 both refer to the same structure FINGER, since they consist of the same primitives. This allows structures to represent **directed acyclic graphs** (see footnote 4 in Section 11.8), rather than simple trees, with an attendant saving in both design effort and memory space.

PHIGS provides functions that allow one to represent and draw objects such as the robot from tables of data (the structures), rather than as procedures (as in Code Fragment 11.6.). In this way, applications can be developed in the absence of detailed information about the objects to be modeled and manipulated. This information becomes available when the application is run, by reading in data files that describe the objects, and by letting the user create and edit structures interactively.

A7.4.1 PHIGS+

Although PHIGS offers great power to the programmer and the user, it does not fully exploit raster concepts. The need for full raster support led in 1986 to a new effort, known as PHIGS+, to extend PHIGS to include such rendering capabilities as light sources, depth cuing, reflection models, and Gouraud shading (see Chapter 15). Another goal of PHIGS+ is to include support for handling more advanced primitives such as polygonal meshes (see Chapter 10) and parametric curves and surfaces (see Chapter 14). A complete description of the PHIGS+ proposal is given in Van Dam (1988).

A7.5 X WINDOWS

The goals of the X Window System are rather different from those of the standards efforts described in previous sections (Scheifler and Gettys 1986, Jones 1989). X is a windowing system that supports window management operations such as the creation and manipulation of several overlapping, resizable windows. It also supports functions for input devices such as a mouse, as well as simple 2D graphics operations.

Development of X began in 1984 at MIT. By 1986, X was in widespread use and was supported by a number of workstation vendors. It has since become an industry standard in raster-graphics workstations, due to its effectiveness in a network environment. X Windows is a public domain system; anyone is free to use it.

X is designed to operate transparently on a network that connects many dissimilar computers and workstations. A user can have several windows open on a workstation, with each one connected to a different application running on a different computer somewhere in the network. X provides a common interface for all such applications, so that the type of computer running the application and its location become effectively irrelevant to the programmer and the user.

A7.5.1 PHIGS, PHIGS+, and Extensions to X (PEX)

Begun in 1987, the PEX effort is aimed at defining an industry-standard 3D extension to the X Window System (Rost et al. 1989). Its purpose is to extend X in a graceful fashion so that it supports 3D graphics on a variety of workstations with widely different graphics capabilities. It must support PHIGS and PHIGS+ concepts efficiently, and mesh sufficiently well with X to gains wide acceptance by the X community.

A7.6   Other Standards

A7.6.1 Computer Graphics Interface (CGI)

The proposed CGI standard (originally known as *VDI* for *virtual device interface*) attempts to specify precisely which codes are to be sent from a host to graphics hardware to define each function the device can perform. If such a standard is implemented, graphics displays will be much more interchangeable, without the need for adjustments in the software that drives them. There will be a single **graphics device** for which applications are written, and device-independent software will no longer be necessary.

A7.6.2 Computer Graphics Metafile (CGM)

The proposed CGM standard (originally know as *VDM* for *virtual device metafile*) defines the way graphics images are stored in a device-independent fashion in peripheral storage devices for archiving and for transfer to other systems. CGM strives for maximum compatibility with the CORE and GKS metafiles.

A7.6.3 Initial Graphics Exchange System (IGES)

IGES, like CGM, focuses on the encoding and storage of graphic information in a form that can be transferred from one computer installaton to another for later reconstruction (CONRAC Corporation 1985). IGES, however, is designed primarily to serve the CAD/CAM community, so it contains several dozen basic graphic primitives such as surfaces of revolution and splines, as well as many different types of **finite elements.** It is designed to capture not only graphic objects but entire annotated drawings and engineering information on mechanical parts and assemblies.

A7.6.4 North American Presentation-Level Protocol Syntax (NAPLPS)

NAPLPS establishes a standard for the transmission of text and graphics to the large number of videotext and teletext teminals that are expected to be installed in schools, homes, and offices around the world (CONRAC Corporation 1985). Based on the assumption that communication links of limited data transmission capacity will be used, NAPLPS stresses the efficient encoding of graphic data. The "picture description instructions" defined within NAPLPS also exploit the assumption that there will be significant processing power in each receiving station for reconstructing images.

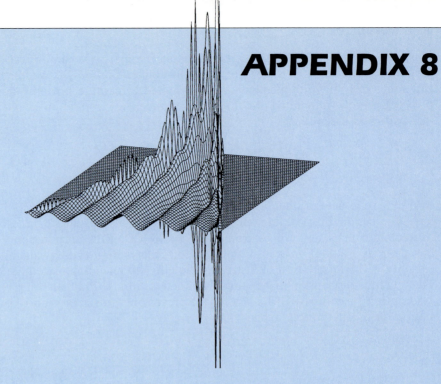

APPENDIX 8

The Platonic Solids

What immortal hand or eye
Could frame thy fearful symmetry?

William Blake, *Songs of Experience*

A8.1   The Platonic Solids

The Platonic solids are polyhedra that exhibit a sublime symmetry and an extraordinary array of interesting properties. They are frequently used as objects of study in computer graphics (See Chapter 10), and also appear in many solid modelling CAD applications.

In this appendix, we examine the properties of the Platonic solids and provide detailed information on their geometry and topology. With this information, both wireframe and shaded pictures of the Platonic solids can be drawn, and Platonic solids can easily be included in scenes and rendered using ray tracing (see Chapter 18).

All polyhedra are composed of faces, edges, and vertices. If V, F, and E denote the number of vertices, faces, and edges, respectively, then Euler's formula states that for any polyhedron

$$V + F = E + 2$$

The Platonic solids are listed in Figure A.8.1 and in the following table. Values of V, F, and E are given in the table for each solid, as is the **Schläfi symbol** (p,q), which states that each face is a p-gon and that q of them meet at each vertex.

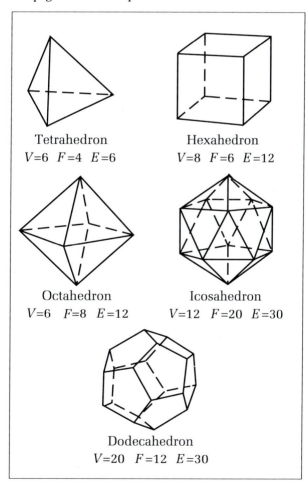

Figure A8.1.
The five Platonic solids.

Tetrahedron
$V=6$ $F=4$ $E=6$

Hexahedron
$V=8$ $F=6$ $E=12$

Octahedron
$V=6$ $F=8$ $E=12$

Icosahedron
$V=12$ $F=20$ $E=30$

Dodecahedron
$V=20$ $F=12$ $E=30$

Name	(p,q)	V	F	E
Tetrahedron	(3,3)	4	4	6
Hexahedron (cube)	(4,3)	8	6	12
Octahedron	(3,4)	6	8	12
Icosahedron	(3,5)	12	20	30
Dodecahedron	(5,3)	20	12	30

In addition to this topological information, the Platonic solids possess extraordinary geometric symmetry : All of the faces of a Platonic solid are identical, and each is a regular polygon. These constraints are so severe that there can only be five such solids (Coxeter 1961).

One of the remarkable properites of the Platonic solids is that they occur in pairs called **duals** of one another.

- The tetrahedron is its own dual.

- the cube and octahedron are duals.

- the icosahedron and dodecahedron are duals.

Dual solids are grouped together in Figure A8.2. Duals have the following topological symmetries:

- Duals have the same number, E, of edges.

- V for one is F for the other.

- If (p,q) is the Schläfi symbol for one, then it is (q,p) for the other.

In addition duals have exquisite geometric regularities. To each vertex of one solid there corresponds a face of the other, and vice versa, in the following sense: Place one solid inside its dual so that their centers coincide; then rotate and scale the inner one so that some of its vertices just touch the midpoints of the faces of the other, as in Figure A8.2. Every vertex of the inner solid exactly coincides with the midpoint of a face of the other. Furthermore, a line drawn from the center to each vertex (of the inner or outer solid) is normal to the corresponding face of the dual.

Using these properties, we can build up a complete description of one solid by referencing information about its dual. This is particularly helpful when trying to describe the icosahedron and dodecahedron numerically.

The following information given for each Platonic solid assumes that the solid has been centered at the origin, oriented in some natural manner, and scaled to some convenient size.

For each Platonic solid, we give the following information : [1]

1. Its vertex list.[2]

2. Its face list, giving the vertices for each face (listed in counterclockwise order when the solid is viewed from the outside). If a wireframe model is desired for a Platonic solid, its edge list is easily fashioned from its face list, as described in Exercise 15.18.

[1]See Blinn (1987) for a slightly different approach.
[2]All objects are represented here in the usual right-handed coordinate system used for modeling, as seen, for example, in Figure 10.2.

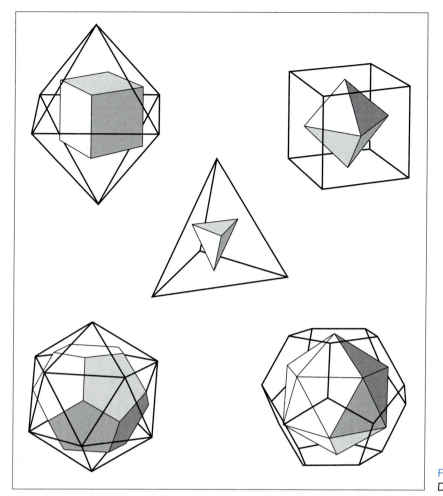

3. The coefficients n_x, n_y, n_z, and d of the equation $n_x x + n_y y + n_z z = d$ that describe the plane in which each face lies. This equation has the equivalent dot product form $\mathbf{n \cdot p} = d$ using $\mathbf{p} = (x,y,z)$ (recall Chapter 7). As it is homogeneous, the four coefficients may all be scaled by any convenient factor. We choose $\mathbf{n} = (n_x, n_y, n_z)$ to be the *outward* normal vector to each face but do not necessarily force it to have unit length. The **bounding plane** information provided by n_x, n_y, n_z, and d is particularly useful for modeling solids in preparation for ray tracing (see Chapter 18).

A8.1.1 Computing the Coefficients of the Plane Equation

Because of the symmetry of each Platonic solid, the normal vector to each face must be parallel to a line from the origin through the *center* of the face. Again, by symmetry, this normal direction is found simply by summing the coordinates of all the vertices of the face. For instance, if a face of the cube has vertices $\mathbf{P^1}$, $\mathbf{P^4}$, $\mathbf{P^6}$, and $\mathbf{P^7}$, then $\mathbf{n}$ for that face is the vector sum : $\mathbf{P^1} + \mathbf{P^4} + \mathbf{P^6} + \mathbf{P^7}$. Given $\mathbf{n}$ and any point, say $\mathbf{P^4}$, on the face, the value of d is simply $\mathbf{n \cdot P^4}$.

A8.1.2 The Cube

The basic cube chosen here is often called the **unit cube**. It is centered at the origin and has its edges aligned with the coordinate axes. Its vertices consist of all combinations of $(\pm 1, \pm 1, \pm 1)$. The vertices may be labeled in any order. We choose the following order:

Vertex List for the Cube

Vertex	x	y	z
1	1	1	1
2	−1	1	1
3	−1	−1	1
4	1	−1	1
5	1	1	−1
6	−1	1	−1
7	−1	−1	−1
8	1	−1	−1

Question: If we want this cube to fit exactly within a unit sphere, how must each coordinate of each vertex be scaled?

We further choose to label the edges and faces according to the model of Figure A8.3a. This model is formed by "unfolding" the cube and laying it out flat, so that each face is viewed from the outside. The vertex list for each face is easily read, and is given in the following table.

The face normals for the cube are aligned with the coordinate axes. The top face, for instance, has normal $(0,0,1)$. d is found by using one of the vertices of this face and forming its dot product with the normal, as in $(0,0,1) \cdot (1,1,1) = 1$. By symmetry d is the *same* for every face of a Platonic solid.

Face List and Bounding Planes for the Cube
Each normal vector has length $|\mathbf{n}| = 1$, and $d = 1$.

Face	Vertices	n_x	n_y	n_z
1	5, 8, 7, 6	0	0	−1
2	1, 2, 3, 4	0	0	1
3	4, 3, 7, 8	0	−1	0
4	5, 6, 2, 1	0	1	0
5	1, 4, 8, 5	1	0	0
6	6, 7, 3, 2	−1	0	0

A8.1.3 The Octahedron

The octahedron is the dual of the cube. We choose as the generic octahedron the version whose vertices are on the midpoints of the faces of the unit cube above. (Thus the octahedron fits exactly inside the cube.) By duality the vertices are simply the *face normals* of the cube (e.g., vertex k of the octahedron has coor-

(a) Cube

(b) Octahedron

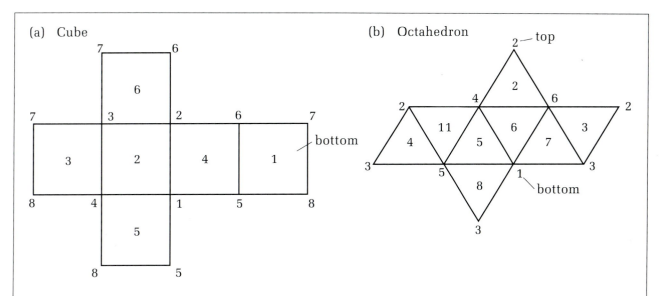

(c) Tetrahedron

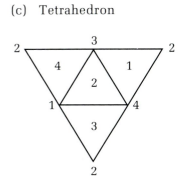

(d) Icosahedron

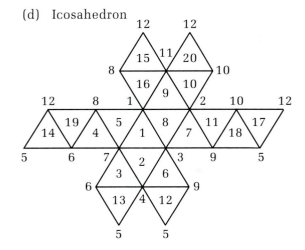

(e) Dodecahedron

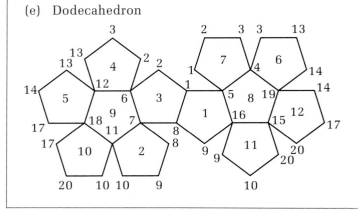

Figure A8.3.
Models defining the edges and faces.

dinates equal to those of face normal k of the cube). So, reading from the face list of the cube, we have the following:

Vertex List for the Octahedron

Vertex	x	y	z
1	0	0	−1
2	0	0	1
3	0	−1	0
4	0	1	0
5	1	0	0
6	−1	0	0

Similarly, we label the faces of the octahedron so that they correspond to the vertices of the cube. The normal to face k of the octahedron is therefore given by the coordinates of the kth vertex of the cube! (Alternatively, we can find the normal to the kth face by adding together the coordinates of its four vertices.) d is found by using any vertex of the octahedron that lies on the face, yielding $d = 1$.

Face List for the Octahedron
Each normal vector has length $|\mathbf{n}| = \sqrt{3}$, and $d = 1$.

Face	Vertices	n_x	n_y	n_z
1	2, 5, 4	1	1	1
2	2, 4, 6	−1	1	1
3	3, 2, 6	−1	−1	1
4	2, 3, 5	1	−1	1
5	1, 4, 5	1	1	−1
6	1, 6, 4	−1	1	−1
7	1, 3, 6	−1	−1	−1
8	1, 5, 3	1	−1	−1

A8.1.4 The Tetrahedron

There are many orientations for a centered tetrahedron that may seem generic. We choose the one oriented and sized to fit inside the unit cube, with the following vertex list:

Vertex	x	y	z
1	1	1	1
2	1	−1	−1
3	−1	−1	1
4	−1	1	−1

The normal vector to each face is easily found by summing appropriate vertices. We label the faces as shown in Figure A8.3c. Then each face normal $\mathbf{n}_i$ is simply the negative of vertex i. (Note from Figure A8.2 that the dual of a tetrahedron is another tetrahedron having a different orientation.)

Face List for the Tetrahedron
Each normal vector has length $|\mathbf{n}| = \sqrt{3}$, and $d = 1$.

Face	Vertices	n_x	n_y	n_z
1	2, 3, 4	-1	-1	-1
2	1, 4, 3	-1	1	1
3	1, 2, 4	1	1	-1
4	1, 3, 2	1	-1	1

A8.1.5 The Icosahedron

It is more challenging to build the lists for the last two Platonic solids, but a remarkable fact gets one started. Figure A8.4 shows that three mutually perpendicular **golden rectangles** (see Chapter 3) inscribe the icosahedron, and so a vertex list may be read from this picture. We choose to align each golden rectangle with a coordinate axis. For convenience, we size the rectangles so that the icosahedron fits inside the unit cube. Thus the sides of each golden rectangle are 1 and $1/\phi$ where $\phi = (1 + \sqrt{5})/2$. The symbol τ is often used for $1/\phi$. Because we know that $\phi = 1 + 1/\phi$, we know that $\tau = (\sqrt{5} - 1)/2$ and $\phi - \tau = 1$.

The 12 vertices of the generic icosahedron have the following values:

$$(0, \pm1, \pm\tau)$$
$$(\pm\tau, 0, \pm1)$$
$$(\pm1, \pm\tau, 0)$$

This leads to the following vertex list:

Vertex List for the Icosahedron, with $\tau = (\sqrt{5} - 1)/2$

Vertex	x	y	z
1	0	1	τ
2	0	1	$-\tau$
3	1	τ	0
4	1	$-\tau$	0
5	0	-1	$-\tau$
6	0	-1	τ
7	τ	0	1
8	$-\tau$	0	1
9	τ	0	-1
10	$-\tau$	0	-1
11	-1	τ	0
12	-1	$-\tau$	0

Question: What is the radial distance of each vertex from the origin?

The faces of the icosahedron are labeled using the model shown in Figure A8.3d. Since the normal to each face passes through the midpoint of the face, just sum the appropriate three vertices to compute the normal vector. In the following list, all coefficients have been scaled so that $d = 1$.

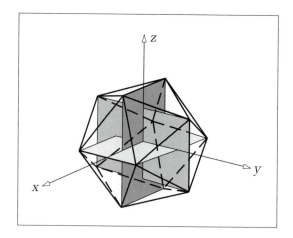

Figure A8.4.
Golden rectangles defining the dodecahedron and icosahedron.

Face List for the Icosahedron
Each normal vector has length $|\mathbf{n}| = \sqrt{3}\tau$, and $d = 1$.

Face	Vertices	n_x	n_y	n_z
1	1, 7, 3	τ	τ	τ
2	3, 7, 4	1	0	τ^2
3	4, 7, 6	τ	$-\tau$	τ
4	6, 7, 8	0	$-\tau^2$	1
5	1, 8, 7	0	τ^2	1
6	3, 4, 9	1	0	$-\tau^2$
7	3, 9, 2	τ	τ	$-\tau$
8	1, 3, 2	τ^2	1	0
9	1, 2, 11	$-\tau^2$	1	0
10	11, 2, 10	$-\tau$	τ	$-\tau$
11	2, 9, 10	0	τ^2	-1
12	4, 5, 9	τ	$-\tau$	$-\tau$
13	5, 4, 6	τ^2	-1	0
14	5, 6, 12	$-\tau^2$	-1	0
15	8, 11, 12	-1	0	τ^2
16	8, 1, 11	$-\tau$	τ	τ
17	5, 12, 10	$-\tau$	$-\tau$	$-\tau$
18	9, 5, 10	0	$-\tau^2$	-1
19	6, 8, 12	$-\tau$	$-\tau$	τ
20	12, 11, 10	-1	0	$-\tau^2$

A8.1.6 The Dodecahedron

The dodecahedron is the dual of the icosahedron, so we can make direct use of the lists for the previous icosahedron. The vertex list can be taken directly from the normal vectors of the bounding planes of the icosahedron. For instance, vertex 6 of the dodecahedron is $(1, 0, -\tau^2)$, found from face 6 of the icosahedron. Similarly, the normal to face 8 of the dodecahedron is $(-\tau, 0, 1)$, found from vertex 8 of the icosahedron. Figure A8.3e may also prove useful.

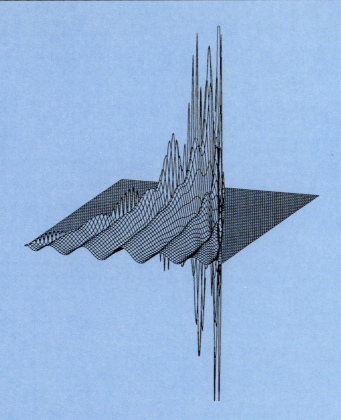

References

Abelson, H., and A. A. diSessa. 1981. *Turtle geometry*. Cambridge, Mass.: MIT Press.

Abi-Ezzi, S., and S. E. Kader. 1986. PHIGS in CAD. *Computers in Mechanical Engineering* (CIME) 5 (July): 28–36.

Acton, F. S. 1970. *Numerical methods that work*. New York: Harper & Row.

Ahuja, D. V., and S. A. Coons. 1968. Geometry for construction and display. *IBM System Journal* 3: 188–205.

Anderson, D. P. 1982. Hidden line elimination in projected grid Surfaces. *ACM Transactions on Graphics* 1 (October): 274–288.

Apostol, T. M. 1961. *Calculus*. New York: Blaisdell.

Asimov, I. 1972. *Asimov's biographical encyclopedia of science and technology*. Garden City, N.Y.: Doubleday.

Ayers, F. 1967. *Projective geometry*. New York: McGraw-Hill.

Ball, W. W. R., and H. S. M. Coxeter. 1974. *Mathematical recreations and essays*. Toronto: University of Toronto Press.

Ballard, D. H., and C. M. Brown. 1982. *Computer vision*. Englewood Cliffs, N.J.: Prentice-Hall.

Barnhill, R. E., and R. F. Riesenfeld. 1974. *Computer Aided Geometric Design*. New York: Academic Press.

Barnsley, M. F., and A. D. Sloan. 1988. "A Better Way to Compress Images," *Byte* (January): 215–223.

Barr, A. 1981. Superquadrics and angle-preserving transformations. *IEEE Computer Graphics* 1 (January): 11–25.

Bartels, R. H., J. C. Beatty, and B. A. Barsky. 1987. *An introduction to splines for use in computer graphics and geometric modeling*. Los Altos, Calif.: Morgan Kaufman Publishers, Inc.

Bergeron, R. D., P. R. Bono, and J. D. Foley. 1978. Graphics programming using the CORE system. *ACM Computing Surveys* 10: 389–443.

Berlekamp, E. R., J. H. Conway, and R. K. Guy. 1982. *Winning ways*. New York: Academic Press.

Bigelow, C. 1985. Font design for personal workstations. *Byte* (January): 255–270.

Billmeyer, F. W., and M. Saltzman. 1981. *Principles of color technology*. New York: Wiley.

Birch, T. W. 1964. *Maps—Topographical and statistical*. Oxford: Oxford University Press.

Birkhoff, G., and S. MacLane. 1967. *A survey of modern algebra*. New York: Macmillan.

Blinn, J. E. 1977. Models of light reflection for computer synthesized pictures. *Computer Graphics* 11: 192–198.

Blinn, J. E. 1987. Platonic solids. *IEEE Computer Graphics and Applications* (November): 62–66.

Blinn, J. E., L. Carpenter, J. Lane, and T. Whitted. 1980. Scan-line methods for displaying parametrically defined surfaces. *Communications of the ACM* 23 (January): 23–34.

Blinn, J. E., and M. E. Newell. 1978. Clipping using homogeneous coordinates. *Computer Graphics* 12 (August): 245–251.

Bishop, G., and D. M. Weimer. 1986. Fast phong shading. *SIGGRAPH 86, Computer Graphics* 20 (August): 103–106.

Bloomenthal, J. 1985. Modeling the mighty maples. *Computer Graphics* 19: 305–311.

Bresenham, J. E. 1965. Algorithm for computer control of digital plotter. *IBM Systems Journal* 4: 25–30.

Brodlie, K. W. 1980. *Mathematical methods in computer graphics and design.* New York: Academic Press.

Brown, M. D., and M. Heck. 1985. *Understanding PHIGS.* Template Corp., 9645 Scranton Rd., San Diego, Calif. 92121.

Butland, J. 1979. Surface drawing made simple. *Computer-aided Design* 11 (January): 19–22.

Carlbom, I., and J. Paciorek. 1978. Planar geometric projections and viewing transformations. *ACM Computing Surveys* 10 (December): 465–502.

Conrac Corporation. 1985. *Raster graphics handbook*, 2nd ed. New York: Van Nostrand Reinhold.

Conte, S. D., and C. deBoor. 1980. *Elementary numerical analysis.* New York: McGraw-Hill.

Cook, R. L., and K. E. Torrance. 1981. A reflectance model for computer graphics. *Computer Graphics* 15 (August): 307–316.

Coons, S. A. 1967. Surfaces for computer-aided design of space forms. Report MAC-TR-41, Project MAC, Massachusetts Institute of Technology, Cambridge, Mass.

Coxeter, H. M. S. 1961. *Introduction to geometry.* New York: Wiley.

Crow, F. C. 1981. A comparison of antialiasing techniques. *IEEE Computer Graphics and Applications* 1 (January): 40–49.

Crow, F. C. 1987. The origins of the teapot. *IEEE Computer Graphics and Applications* (January): 8–19.

Cundy, H. M., and A. P. Rollett. 1961. *Mathematical models.* Oxford: Oxford University Press.

Cyrus, M., and J. Beck. 1978. Generalized two- and three-dimensional clipping. *Computers and Graphics* 3: 23–28.

DeBoor, C. 1978. *Practical guide to splines.* New York: Springer-Verlag.

Demko, S., L. Hodges, B. Naylor 1985. Construction of fractal objects with iterated function systems SIGGRAPH 1985, *Computer Graphics* 19 (July): 271–278.

Dewdney, A. K. 1988. *The armchair universe, an exploration of computer worlds.* New York: Freeman.

Dodge, C. W. 1972. *Euclidean geometry and transformations.* Reading, Mass.: Addison-Wesley.

Enderle, G., K. Kansy, and G. Pfaff. 1984. *Computer graphics programming: GKS—The graphical kernel system.* New York: Springer-Verlag.

Ernst, B. 1976. *The magic mirror of M. C. Escher.* New York: Ballantine.

Farin, G. 1988. *Curves and surfaces for computer-aided geometric design.* Orlando, Fla.: Academic Press.

Faux, I. D., and M. J. Pratt. 1979. *Computational geometry for design and manufacture.* New York: Horwood/Wiley.

Feynman, R. 1963. Color vision, in *The Feynman lectures on physics*. Reading, Mass.: Addison-Wesley.

Finkbeiner, D. T. 1960. *Introduction to matrices and linear transformations*. San Francisco: Freeman.

Foley, J. D., and A. Van Dam. 1983. *Fundamentals of interactive computer graphics*. Reading, Mass.: Addison-Wesley.

Forrest, A. R. 1972. On coons and other methods for the representations of curved surfaces. *Computer Graphics and Image Processing* 1: 341–359.

Gardner, M. 1961. *Second Scientific American book of mathematical puzzles and diversions*. New York: Simon & Schuster.

Gardner, M. 1971. *New mathematical diversions from* Scientific American. New York: Simon & Schuster.

Gardner, M. 1975. Piet Hein's superellipse, in *Mathematical carnival*. New York: Knopf.

Gardner, M. 1978. White and brown music, fractal curves and one-over-*f* fluctuations. *Scientific American* (April): 16–32.

Giloi, W. F. 1978. *Interactive computer graphics*. Englewood Cliffs, N.J.: Prentice-Hall.

Gleick, J. 1987. *Chaos: Making a new science*. New York: Viking Penguin.

Goldman, R. N. 1985. Illicit expressions in vector algebra. *ACM Transactions on Graphics* 4 (July): 223–243.

Gonzalez, R. C., and P. Wintz. 1987. *Digital image processing*. Reading, Mass.: Addison-Wesley.

Gordon, W. J., and R. F. Riesenfeld. 1974. B-spline curves and surfaces, *Computer-aided geometric design,* edited by R. E. Barnhill and R. F. Riesenfeld. New York: Academic Press.

Gouraud, H. 1971. Continuous shading of curved surfaces. *IEEE Transactions on Computers* (June): 623–629.

Graphical Kernel System (GKS). 1984. Information-processing in computer graphics. *ACM Transactions in Graphics* (February):

Griffiths, J. G. 1983. Table-driven algorithms for generating space-filling curves. *Computer-aided Design* 17 (January): 37.

Halliday, D., and R. Resnick. 1970. *Fundamentals of physics*. New York: John Wiley.

Hausner, M. 1965. *A vector space approach to geometry*. Englewood Cliffs, N.J.: Prentice-Hall.

Hayes, B. 1984. On the ups and downs of hailstone numbers. *Scientific American* 250 (January): 10–13.

Heckbert, P. 1982. Color image quantization for frame buffer display. *Computer Graphics* 16: 297–307.

Hilbert, D., and S. Cohn-Vossen. 1952. *Geometry and the imagination*. New York: Chelsea.

Hill, F. S., Jr. 1978. Phi—A precious jewel. *IEEE Communications Society Magazine* (September): 35–37.

Hill, F. S., Jr. 1979a. An elliptic triptych. *IEEE Communications Magazine* (September): 34–40.

Hill, F. S., Jr. 1979b. What's new in ellipses. *IEEE Communications Magazine* (July): 23–27.

Hill, F. S., Jr. 1980a. Gentle inversions in a circle: Part I. *IEEE Communications Magazine* (May): 36–41.

Hill, F. S., Jr. 1980b. Upon further reflection. . . . *IEEE Communications Magazine* (September): 49–57.

Hofstadter, D. R. 1979. *Godel, Escher, Bach*. New York: Basic Books.

Hofstadter, D. R. 1985. *Metamagical themas*. New York: Basic Books.

Hopgood, F. R. A., D. A. Duce, J. R. Gallop, and D. C. Sutcliffe. 1983. *Introduction to the graphical kernel system* (*GKS*). New York: Academic Press.

Huntley, H. E. 1970. *The divine proportion: A study in mathematical beauty*. New York: Dover.

Ingalls, D. H. 1978. The Smalltalk-76 programming system design and implementation. Fifth ACM Symposium on Principles of Programming Languages (January).

Jacobs, H. R. 1970. *Mathematics, a human endeavor*. San Francisco: Freeman.

James, M. L. 1977. *Applied numerical methods for digital computation with FORTRAN and CSMP*, 2d ed. New York: Thomas Y. Crowell.

Jarvis, J. F., C. N. Judice, and W. H. Ninke. 1976. A survey of techniques for the display of continuous tone pictures on bilevel displays. *Computer Graphics and Image Processing* 5: 13–40.

Jones, O. 1989. *Introduction to the X window system*. Englewood Cliffs, N.J.: Prentice-Hall.

Kajiya, T. 1983. New techniques for ray tracing procedurally defined objects. *ACM Transactions on Graphics* 2 (July): 161–181.

Kenner, H. 1976. *Geodesic math and how to use it*. Berkeley and Los Angeles: University of California Press.

Kerlow, I. V., and J. Rosebush. 1986. *Computer graphics for designers and artists*. New York: Van Nostrand Reinhold.

Knuth, D. E. 1973a. *The art of computer programming*. Vol. 1: *Fundamental algorithms*. Reading, Mass.: Addison-Wesley.

Knuth, D. E. 1973b. *The art of computer programming*. Vol. 3: *Sorting and searching*. Reading, Mass.: Addison-Wesley.

Knuth, D. E. 1980. *The art of computer programming*. Vol. 2: *Seminumerical algorithms*. Reading, Mass.: Addison-Wesley.

Knuth, D. E. 1979. *Tex and Metafont*. Bedford, Mass.: Digital Press.

Knuth, D. E. 1987. Digital halftones by dot diffusion. *ACM Transactions on Graphics* 6(October): 245–273.

Kopec, T. E. 1985. Adaptive quantization of color images, Master's thesis, University of Massachusetts.

Kruse, R. L. 1984. *Data structures and program design*. Englewood Cliffs, N.J.: Prentice-Hall.

Kubert, B., J. Szabo, and S. Giulieri. 1968. The perspective representation of functions of two variables. *Journal of the ACM* 15 (April): 193–204.

Lane, J., and L. Carpenter. 1979. A generalized scan line algorithm for the computer display of parametrically defined surfaces. *Computer Graphics and Image Processing* 11: 290–297.

Leavitt, R. 1976. *Artist & Computer.* New York: Harmony.

Liang, Y. D., and B. Barsky. 1984. A new concept and method for line clipping. *ACM Transactions on Graphics* 3 (January): 1–22.

Loutrel, P. 1970. A solution to the "hidden-line" problem for computer-drawn polyhedra. *IEEE Transactions on Computers* C-19 (March): 205–213.

Mandelbrot, B. 1983. *The fractal geometry of nature.* New York: Freeman.

Mantyla, M. 1988. *An introduction to solid modelling.* Rockville, Md.: Computer Science Press.

Marsaglia, G. 1983. Random number generation, in *Encyclopedia of Computer Science,* edited by A. Ralston and E. D. Reilly, Jr. New York: Van Nostrand Reinhold Co.

Martin, G. E. 1982. *Transformation geometry, an introduction to symmetry.* New York: Springer-Verlag.

Maxwell, E. A. 1946. *Methods of plane projective geometry based on the use of homogeneous coordinates.* Cambridge, England: Cambridge University Press.

Maxwell, E. A. 1951. *General homogeneous coordinates in three dimensions.* Cambridge, England: Cambridge University Press.

McGregor, J., and A. Watt. 1986. *The art of graphics.* Reading, Mass.: Addison-Wesley.

McKay, L. 1984. *GKS primer.* Nova Graphics International, 1015 Bee Cave Woods, Austin, Tex. 78746.

Melzak, Z. A. 1976. *Mathematical ideas, modeling and applications.* New York: Wiley.

Meyer, G., and D. Greenberg. 1980. Perceptual color spaces for computer graphics. *Computer Graphics* 14: 254–261.

Modenov, P. S., and A. S. Parkhomenko. 1965. *Geometric transformations.* New York: Academic Press.

Mortenson, M. 1985. *Geometric modelling.* New York: Wiley.

Munsell, A. H. 1941. *A color notation*, 9th ed. Baltimore: Munsell Color Co.

National Semiconductor Corp. 1987. DP8500 Raster Graphics Processor Data Sheet.

Newman, W. M., and R. F. Sproull. 1979. *Principles of interactive computer graphics.* New York: McGraw-Hill.

Nicholl, T. M., D. T. Lee, and R. A. Nicholl. 1987. An efficient new algorithm for 2-D line clipping: Its development and analysis. *Computer Graphics* 21 (July): 253–262.

Ogilvy, C. S. 1969. *Excursions in geometry.* New York: Oxford University Press.

Oppenheim, A. V., and A. S. Willsky. 1983. *Signals and systems.* Englewood Cliffs, N.J.: Prentice-Hall.

O'Reilly, T., V. Quercia, and L. Lamb. 1988. *The X windows system user's guide*, Vol. 3. Newton, Mass.: O'Reilly and Assoc.

Peitgen, H. O., and P. H. Richter. *The beauty of fractals.* New York: Springer-Verlag.

Peitgen, H. O., and D. Saupe. 1988. *The science of fractal images.* New York: Springer-Verlag.

Penna, M., and R. Patterson. 1986. *Projective geometry and its applications to computer graphics.* Englewood Cliffs, N.J.: Prentice-Hall.

Phong, B-T. 1975. Illumination for computer generated images. *Communications of the ACM* 18: 311–317.

Pike, R. 1983. Graphics in overlapping bitmap layers. *Computer Graphics* (July): 331–356.

Pipes, L. A. 1985. *Applied mathematics for engineers and physicists.* New York: McGraw-Hill.

Pitteway, M. L. V., and D. J. Watkinson. 1980. Bresenham's algorithm with gray scale. *Communications of the ACM* 23: 625–626.

Potmesil, M., and I. Chakravarty. 1982. Synthetic image generation with a lens and aperture camera model. *ACM Transactions on Graphics* 1: 85–108.

Ratliff, F. 1965. *Mach bands: Quantitative studies on neural networks in the retina.* San Francisco: Holden-Day.

ReQuicha, A. A. G. 1980. Representations for rigid solids: Theory, methods, and systems. *Computing Surveys* 12 (December): 437–464.

Rogers, D. 1985. *Procedural elements for computer graphics.* New York: McGraw-Hill.

Rost, R. J., J. D. Friedberg, and P. Nishimoto. 1989. PEX: A network-transparent 3D graphics system, *IEEE Computer Graphics and Applications* 9 (July): 14–26.

Roth, Scott D. 1982. Ray casting for modelling solids. *Computer Graphics and Image Processing* 18: 109–144.

Scheifler, R. W., and J. Gettys. 1986. The X window system. *ACM Transactions on Graphics* (April): 79–109.

Semple, J. G., and G. T. Kneebone. 1952. *Algebraic projective geometry.* Oxford: Oxford University Press.

Sorenson, P. 1984. Fractals. *Byte* (September): 157.

Steinhaus, H. 1969. *Mathematical snapshots.* New York: Oxford University Press.

Stone, M. C., W. B. Cowan, and J. C. Beatty. 1988. Color gamut mapping and the printing of digital color images. *ACM Transactions on Graphics* 7: 249–292.

Sutherland, I. E., R. F. Sproull, and R. A. Schumacker. 1974. A characterization of ten hidden-surface algorithms. *ACM Computing Surveys* 6 (March): 1–55.

Thomas, G. B. 1953. *Calculus and analytic geometry.* Reading, Mass.: Addison-Wesley.

Torrance, K. E., and E. M. Sparrow. 1967. Theory of off-specular reflection from roughened surfaces. *Journal of the Optical Society of America* 57: 1105–1114.

Ulichney, R. 1987. *Digital halftoning.* Cambridge, Mass.: MIT Press.

Van Dam, A. 1988. PHIGS+ functional description, revision 3.0, *Computer Graphics* 22 (July): pp. 125–218.

Walker, J. 1985. On kaleidoscopes. *Scientific American* (September): 134–145.

Warnock, J. 1969. A hidden surface algorithm for computer generated half-tone pictures. University of Utah Computer Science Dept., TR-4-15, NTIS AD-753 671.

Weiler, K., and P. Atherton. 1977. Hidden surface removal using polygon area sorting. *Computer Graphics* 11(2): 214.

Whitted, T. 1980. An improved illumination method for shaded display. *Communications of the ACM* 23 (June): 343–349.

Williamson, H. 1972. Hidden-line plotting program. *Communications of the ACM* 15 (February): 100–103.

Wirth, N. 1976. *Algorithms + data structures = programs*. Englewood Cliffs, N.J.: Prentice-Hall.

Yates, R. C. 1946. *Curves*. Dept. of Mathematics, U.S. Military Academy, West Point, N.Y.

Index